THE PRESIDENCY
AND THE POLITICAL SYSTEM

Timothy Sherratt
Gordon College

THE PRESIDENCY
AND THE POLITICAL SYSTEM

Second Edition

Michael Nelson, editor
Vanderbilt University

A Division of Congressional Quarterly Inc.
1414 22nd Street N.W., Washington, D.C. 20037

Cover photo: Jake McGuire

Library of Congress Cataloging-in-Publication Data

The Presidency and the political system.

    Includes index.
    1. Presidents—United States. I. Nelson, Michael.
JK516.P639   1987   353.03′1   87-13454
ISBN 0-87187-438-5

To my beloved wife, Linda.

*She opens her mouth with wisdom
and the teaching of kindness is on
her tongue.*

Proverbs 31:26

CONTENTS

PREFACE

The presidency stands aloof and apart in American political culture. Columnists and commentators often portray the office as the "loneliest job in the world" and its occupants as "alone at the top." Historians commonly organize American political history into a succession of presidential administrations. Periods of great policy change are described by political scientists as eras of "presidential government." Only about half the citizenry—college students not excepted—know who their representatives or senators are, but almost everyone knows the president's name.

In truth the presidency is woven into the fabric of the larger political system. The power of the modern presidency is shaped by decisions that were made at the Constitutional Convention in 1787 and by two centuries of change in the system since that event. It is shaped as well by the skills and personalities of individual presidents, who are elected through the political system.

Each of the twenty chapters in this book treats some important aspect of the relationship between the presidency and the political system. The chapters are organized into five parts: Approaches to the Presidency, Elements of Presidential Power, Presidential Selection, Presidents and Politics, and Presidents and Government. Each part begins with a brief essay that introduces the authors and their topics.

While most of the contributors to this volume are established authorities on the presidency, others are young scholars who are well on their way to becoming established authorities. Each reports the results of important new research about or interpretations of the presidency. All have written their essays expressly for this book.

The most noteworthy addition to this second edition is the roster of new authors—Bert Rockman, John Aldrich, Bruce Miroff, Benjamin Ginsberg, Martin Shefter, John Burke, Mark Peterson, Sidney Milkis, Joseph Pika, Elizabeth Sanders, and Thomas Weko—and new topics, including the vice presidency, the institutional presidency, second-term presidencies, and the presidency in comparative perspective.

I do not agree with everything the authors have to say, nor will any reader. But together they have written a collection of essays whose readability is fully matched by its intellectual substance. Students may be assured of gaining the widest possible understanding of the presidency. Scholars will find the essays valuable in conducting their research. Journalists, government officials, and other citizens can read them with interest and profit.

A number of people—the twenty-three contributors first among them—have worked to bring this book to fruition. Susan Sullivan and Jean Woy, formerly of Congressional Quarterly, and Professor Erwin C. Hargrove of Vanderbilt University helped me to think through the themes and organization of the first edition, and Barbara de Boinville served as a capable and gracious editor. For this second edition, Joanne Daniels, Nola Healy Lynch, and Tracy White worked skillfully, tactfully, and enthusiastically in various and manifold ways to help produce an edition of the book that I hope will be even better received than its predecessor.

Michael Nelson

Part I

APPROACHES TO THE PRESIDENCY

First impressions are important in politics as in almost everything else. Americans' first impression of their political system is of the president, and it generally is favorable. Long before children have any real knowledge of what the government actually does, they already think of the president in terms of almost limitless power and benevolence. The president, as described by grade school children, "gives us freedom, . . . worries about all the problems of the states, . . . makes peace with every country but bad, . . . is in charge of the United States and has many wise men to tell him what is best." [1]

The first chapter in Part I, "Evaluating the Presidency," uncovers powerful traces of these childhood first impressions in the formed impressions of adults. Four groups in particular—journalists, bureaucrats, members of Congress, and members of the voting public—make up constituencies whose support presidents need if they are to function successfully during their terms of office. The attitudes of each group seem at first glance to be detrimental to presidential leadership. Reporters are cynical about the presidency, career civil servants are preoccupied with their own careers, representatives and senators are obsessed with pleasing the voters, and the voters themselves are wed to contradictory expectations of the presidency that no individual president can possibly satisfy. Closer inspection, however, reveals that these surface attitudes overlie more fundamental orientations that exalt strong presidential leadership.

As active participants in the political process, journalists, legislators, bureaucrats, and voters cannot be judged severely for a lack of detachment. Objective analysis of politics and government is the province of historians and political scientists. Yet what is true for these four groups turns out to be true for presidential scholars as well: visible confusion, but underlying awe with regard to the presidency. "Presidential scholarship in recent years has been marked by a bewildering succession of new models of the presidency, each the product of an admixture of empirical and normative assessments, each constructed in hasty overreaction to the most recent president," Chapter 1 concludes. But "underlying the scholars' confusion is an implicit appreciation that significant policy change, whatever its ideological direction, requires a strong president."

George Edwards, in his chapter, "Studying the Presidency," sheds light on the sources of scholarly confusion. All of the approaches that historians and political scientists traditionally have taken to the presidency are valuable, he argues, but each contains pitfalls that must be avoided if accurate understanding is to be attained. What Edwards calls the legal approach, for example, is particularly subject to an uncomfortable mix of empirical and normative concerns. The psychological approach tends to "stress the pathological aspects of a presidency"; conversely, the political power approach often "carries an implicit assumption that the president should be the principal decision maker in American politics." The goal for researchers, then, should be to select approaches that are appropriate to studying whatever aspects of the presidency interest them and to employ methods that are suitable to those approaches.

Still, for all Edwards's catholicity, "the rigor of the scientific method" is his watchword for studying the presidency. In "The Interpretable Presidency," Jeffrey Tulis judges this standard to be unhelpfully confining. Classical social science relies heavily on statistical analysis, he argues, but presidential scholarship is limited in this regard by "the fatal flaw of a small N (roughly forty presidents)." The alternative Tulis offers is drawn from the new "interpretive turn" in social science, which is marked by "more a search for meaning than for causes, more a concern for significance than for laws, more a quest for coherence than for certainty." For such analysis the presidency, as the nation's preeminent leadership position, is uniquely suited.

Approaches and methods aside, Bert Rockman urges in "The American Presidency in Comparative Perspective" that much can be learned about the presidency simply by studying it from a different vantage point. "What does the American presidency look like when viewed from the perspective of other types of political systems?" Rockman asks. He answers by reviewing the effects on leadership of such influences as "the varying characteristics of states, their political systems, governmental arrangements, and political cultures," the "kinds of situations" that affect leaders, and "leadership roles as these differ across systems as well as . . . differences in the styles of leaders within similar roles." One of Rockman's most provocative conclusions is that the obvious differences between the presidency and other national leadership posts, such as prime minister of Great Britain, often mask more important similarities.

Notes

1. Fred Greenstein, "The Benevolent Leader: Children's Images of Political Authority," *American Political Science Review* (December 1960): 934-944. See also Fred Greenstein, "The Benevolent Leader Revisited: Children's Images of Political Leaders in Three Democracies," *American Political Science Review* (December 1975).

1. EVALUATING THE PRESIDENCY

Michael Nelson

The November 1, 1948, issue of *Life* magazine is a collector's item because of a picture on page 37 that is captioned, "The next president travels by ferry over the broad waters of San Francisco bay." (The picture is of Thomas E. Dewey.) Of greater significance, however, is an article that begins on page 65, called "Historians Rate U.S. Presidents." It was written by Professor Arthur M. Schlesinger, Sr., who had called upon fifty-five fellow historians to grade each president as either "great," "near great," "average," "below average," or "failure," then tallied up the results. Abraham Lincoln, George Washington, Franklin D. Roosevelt, Woodrow Wilson, and Andrew Jackson scored as great presidents, Ulysses S. Grant and Warren G. Harding as failures, and the rest fell in between.

As interesting as the Schlesinger evaluations and their many imitators are, the important lessons may be more about the judges than their judgments, more about the office of the presidency than about individual presidents. What standards do scholars use to evaluate presidents? What image of the presidency do they measure the Lincolns and Hardings, or Carters and Reagans, against? What standards for evaluation do other important judges of the presidency use: journalists, citizens, members of Congress, bureaucrats?

Answering these questions can tell us a lot, not only about the presidency's evaluators, but also about the presidency itself.[1] Presidents, after all, want the "verdict of history" that scholars eventually render to be favorable. In the short run, they need to win the support of journalists, the mass public, and congressional and bureaucratic office-holders if they are to succeed. To do so, presidents must understand the standards of evaluation such groups apply to them.

Scholars: Strength amid Confusion

Schlesinger followed his 1948 survey of historians with another in 1962. The results were strikingly similar: the same pair of "failures" and, with the narrow exception of Jackson, the same set of "greats."

More important, so were the standards that historians in the late 1940s and early 1960s appeared to measure presidents against: strength and the desire to be strong. "Washington apart," Schlesinger wrote," none of [the great presidents] waited for the office to seek the man; they pursued it with all their might and main." Once in office, their greatness was established by the fact that "every one of [them] left the Executive branch stronger and more influential than he found it." When dealing with Congress, they knew "when to reason and to browbeat, to bargain and stand firm, . . . and when all else failed, they appealed over the heads of the lawmakers to the people." Nor did the great presidents shy away from confrontations with the Supreme Court. They were, to be sure, inattentive to administration of the bureaucracy, but this freed them, according to Schlesinger, for the more important tasks of "moral leadership." [2] A 1968 survey by Gary Maranell not only confirmed Schlesinger's conclusion that "strength" and "active-ness" were important criteria in the historians' model of the presidency, but also found that "idealism" and "flexibility" were not.[3]

The historians' model was very much like that of the other group of scholars who write and talk about the presidency, political scientists.[4] Their view in the 1950s and 1960s was summed up nicely in the title of an article by Thomas Cronin: "Superman: Our Textbook President." [5] After reviewing dozens of political science textbooks written in those two decades, Cronin found that political scientists characterized the presidency as both omnipotent and benevolent. This idea that strength and goodness go hand in hand shined through, for example, in James MacGregor Burns's assessment that "the stronger we make the Presidency, the more we strengthen democratic procedures." [6] It also animated the most influential book on the presidency of this period, *Presidential Power.* "A president's success" in maximizing power, wrote its author, Richard Neustadt, "serves objectives far beyond his own and his party's. . . . Presidential influence contributes to the energy of the government and to the viability of public policy. . . . What is good for the country is good for the president, and *vice versa.*" [7]

Underlying the political scientists' model was a quasi-religious awe of the presidency. Clinton Rossiter began his book *The American Presidency* by confessing his "feeling of veneration, if not exactly reverence, for the authority and dignity of the presidency." He described Lincoln as "the martyred Christ of democracy's passion play" and quoted favorably the "splendid judgment" of Englishman John Bright in 1861 that

> there is nothing more worthy of reverence and obedience, and nothing more sacred, than the authority of the freely chosen magistrate of a great and free people; and if there be on earth and

amongst men any right divine to govern, surely it rests with a ruler
so chosen and so appointed.[8]

Herman Finer was equally reverent, although in a polytheistic way.
Finer characterized the presidency not only as "the incarnation of the
American people in a sacrament resembling that in which the wafer
and the wine are seen to be the body and blood of Christ," but also as
"belong[ing] rightfully to the offspring of a titan and Minerva
husbanded by Mars." [9]

Thus, strength and the desire to be strong, power and virtue,
omnipotence and benevolence, all were tied in with each other in what
only half-facetiously might be called the "Savior" model of the
presidency. The model's underlying rationale was that the president is
the chief guardian of the national interest, not only in foreign policy because no one else can speak and act for the nation, but also in domestic
affairs because of the pluralistic structure of government and society.
Members of Congress cater to wealthy and influential interests within
their constituencies, it was argued, but the president can mobilize the
unorganized and inarticulate and speak for national majorities against
special interest groups.

Clearly, scholars' normative preference for presidential strength in
the 1950s and 1960s had more to it than their value judgments about
the proper distribution of power among the branches of government. It
was rooted in their liberal policy preferences as well. Democratic
historians outnumbered Republicans by two to one in the Schlesinger
samples, for example. One of the reasons they found the strength of the
presidents they chose as great so appealing was that, as Schlesinger put
it, each of these presidents "took the side of liberalism and the general
welfare against the status quo." [10] William Andrews observed a similar
partisan and ideological bias among his fellow political scientists, many
of whom had worked in liberal Democratic administrations. When it
comes to the presidency, he concluded, "the constitutional theory
follows the party flag." [11]

Presidential strength and ambition would benefit the nation,
argued scholars of the Savior school in this period. How, then, to
explain the nation's experience with Lyndon B. Johnson and Richard
M. Nixon? In foreign affairs the power of these presidents sustained a
large-scale war in Vietnam long after public opinion had turned
against it. The power of the president as "chief legislator," in Rossiter's
phrase, prompted such hasty passage of Great Society social welfare
programs that their flaws, which might have been discovered in
bargaining between the president and Congress, were not found until
later. Many of these flaws were in administrative design and implementation, the very area of activity the Savior model had encouraged

presidents to avoid. Finally, in 1972 and 1973, the abuses of presidential power, which have been grouped under the umbrella term "Watergate," occurred that forced Nixon's resignation in August 1974.

The flawed presidencies of Johnson and Nixon convinced scholars that presidential strength and the general welfare, far from being synonymous, were more likely to appear as opposites: Satan to the earlier model's Savior. Arthur M. Schlesinger, Jr., had helped to create the Savior model with his glowing biographies of Jackson, Roosevelt, and Kennedy and in eulogistic passages such as this one from *A Thousand Days:* "Thinking of the young Roosevelts, lost suddenly in middle age, and of the young Kennedys, so sure and purposeful, one perceived an historic contrast, a dynastic change, like the Plantagenets giving way to the Yorks." In 1973, he came back with a book berating the "imperial presidency." [12] Marcus Cunliffe called the office a "Frankenstein monster." [13] Nelson Polsby noted that the careers of most of the "great" presidents were tied up with total war.[14]

The new task for scholars, of course, was to explain why strength in the presidency was likely to be harmful to the nation rather than helpful, as previously had been thought. Their search carried them into two primary areas: the person and the office.

The expedition into personality as a source of presidential pathology was led by James David Barber. Barber identified a presidential personality type, the "active-negative," whose efforts to maximize power are born of a deep-seated and psychologically unhealthy need to dominate others.[15] When active-negatives encounter serious challenges to their power while in office, as all presidents eventually do, they react rigidly and aggressively. Such was the case with Johnson and Nixon. The nation survived their presidencies, but given the nature of modern weaponry, Barber argued, even one more active-negative could be too many.

Other scholars looked to the institution to explain why presidential strength was likely to be destructive. Cronin claimed that the "swelling of the presidency"—the sheer growth in the size of the White House staff—had turned it into "a powerful inner sanctum of government isolated from the traditional constitutional checks and balances." [16] George Reedy suggested that "the life of the White House is the life of a [royal] court" in which the president "is treated with all the reverence due a monarch." He added:

> There is built into the presidency a series of devices that tend to remove the occupant of the Oval Office from all of the forces which require most men to rub up against the hard facts of life on a daily basis. . . . No one interrupts presidential contemplation for anything less than a major catastrophe somewhere on the globe. No one

speaks to him unless spoken to first. No one ever invites him to "go soak your head" when his demands become petulant and unreasonable.[17]

Ironically, no sooner had the Satan model of a powerful but dangerous presidency taken hold among political scientists and historians than events again intruded: the unusually weak presidencies of Gerald R. Ford and Jimmy Carter. The response of presidential scholars was not unlike that of the people of ancient Israel to Samson when he transgressed and had his strength cut away: they beheld the new weakness and were distressed by it. The Samson model of the presidency—others have called it the "imperiled" or "tethered" presidency—came in startling contrast to those that had preceded it.[18] It ruefully portrayed a large and growing gap between what presidents can do and what they are expected to do.

The model traced to two sources the presidency's incapacity to deliver: its constitutional dependence on other political institutions for support and the recent decline in the ability or willingness of those institutions to provide it. According to Samson theorists, parties had grown too weak to help, Congress too decentralized to bargain with, the bureaucracy too fragmented and powerful to lead, and the media too adversarial to make its spotlight an asset for the president. Among the public, single-issue groups harshly critical of government were proliferating, while those parts of the population most inclined to support the president—the less educated, religiously fundamentalist, and strongly partisan—were dwindling in number. Thus, presidents "have to work harder to keep the same popularity." [19]

Yet even as the president's ability to meet demands for action supposedly was declining, the volume, intensity, and complexity of those demands were said to be increasing. Godfrey Hodgson argued that the American people expect too much of their president:

> He must simultaneously conduct the diplomacy of a superpower, put together separate coalitions to enact every piece of legislation required by a vast and complex society, manage the economy, command the armed forces, serve as a spiritual example and inspiration, respond to every emergency.[20]

With demands on the presidency so high, Samson theorists argued, no individual president could be expected to meet them. They cited the recent high turnover in the presidency as a sign of the weakness of the institution. Ronald Reagan's inauguration on January 20, 1981, made him the sixth president to be sworn into office in only twenty years.

But once in office, Reagan quickly refuted the Samson model just as the Johnson and Nixon administrations had the Savior model and

Ford and Carter had the Satan model. A political cartoon from the summer of 1981 depicts an angry professor storming out of a door marked "Political Science Department." Papers fly around the office in his wake, one a title page marked "The Limits of Power," another a newspaper with the headline "Stunning Tax, Budget Wins for Reagan." In the foreground a secretary explains to a startled student: "He just completed the definitive, 600-page work on why special-interest groups, weak parties, and a fragmented Congress make presidential leadership impossible."

Savior, Satan, Samson—the sheer velocity of the turnover in these models since the 1960s would seem to indicate that the best single-word description of how scholars evaluate the presidency is confusion. The sources of this confusion are not hard to trace. Although the models purport to describe the enduring institution of the presidency, they were created in response to specific presidents. Like a newspaper, a topical model becomes obsolete quickly. In addition, each of the three models combined, albeit unwittingly, an empirical question (Is the presidency strong or weak?) and a normative one (Is this condition of presidential strength or weakness good or bad for the American political system?). Both types of questions are worth asking, but not in the same breath. Thus in the Savior model, which prevailed from the Roosevelt through the Kennedy administrations, the answers were: the presidency is a strong office, and this is good for the system. The Satan model displaced it when scholars, overreacting to the lessons of Johnson and Nixon, decided that the strength of the presidency, although great, was pathological. Then, startled once again by the weak administrations of Ford and Carter, they went back to the drawing board and constructed the Samson model of the presidency (the office is weak, which is bad).[21]

Yet underlying this confusion has been a recurring, if sometimes implicit, celebration of presidential strength. The Savior model exulted in its presence; the Samson model mourned its apparent demise. The Satan school may be understood best as the scholarly equivalent of a lovers' quarrel with the presidency. (Even while warning of active-negative personality types, for example, Barber placed his hopes for the country in the election of "active-positives," presidents who would seek to dominate the system out of zest rather than zeal. And Schlesinger, Jr., in attacking the excessive power of the "imperial presidency," stopped short of endorsing any serious effort to limit the office constitutionally.) Finally, it is interesting to note a 1984 poll in which a substantial majority of political scientists in the Presidency Research Group not only rated Reagan a "good," "near-great," or "great" president, but gave as their main reason his "leadership qualities." [22]

In the 1980s and 1990s, strength as the standard for scholarly evaluation of presidents actually may be more solidly grounded than it was during the heyday of the Savior model in the 1950s and 1960s (despite the predictable short-term antipresidentialist reaction to the Iran-contra affair). As always, those who want action from the government—and liberal scholars like those who made up the Schlesinger surveys certainly do—will urge the president to lead. What is new is that conservatives have learned from the Reagan experience that a strong presidency can work to serve their interests too.

Journalists: Strength amid Cynicism

If confusion is the key word for understanding changing scholarly views of the presidency, the comparable shorthand description of journalistic standards of evaluation in recent years is cynicism. Underlying this surface attitude, however, is an implicit exaltation of presidential strength. Like presidential scholars, the White House press corps encourages a powerful presidency.

Historically, journalistic cynicism toward the presidency can be traced to Vietnam and Watergate.[23] White House reporters felt that a breach of trust occurred in the late 1960s and early 1970s: they had been lied to repeatedly by presidents and their aides and, by reporting those lies in their newspapers and news broadcasts in good faith, had been used. Stephen Hess describes "the residue of that era" among the Washington journalists he interviewed as "distrust of public institutions and politicians in general." [24] That distrust has carried over into such routine events as the presidential press secretary's daily briefing where, according to *Newsweek* editor Mel Elfin, "reporters vie with each other to see who can ask the toughest questions and never let Watergate happen to us again." [25]

A more deeply rooted and important source of cynicism among journalists, however, may be the "status frustration" of the White House press corps. This frustration has developed out of the growing imbalance between their social and professional status, which is exalted, and the nature of the job itself, which is degrading.

Of the high status of the White House press corps, little needs to be said. The White House correspondent, says Martin Tolchin of the *New York Times*, is "part of the whole social circle" of Supreme Court justices, cabinet secretaries, and prominent members of Congress.[26] Professionally, the presidency is among a handful of what Hess calls "high-prestige beats" in Washington; journalist Stewart Alsop listed it as first in the pecking order.[27] White House reporters usually are guaranteed prominent placement for their daily dispatches and tend to be high on the list of journalists who are invited to give paid lectures or write magazine articles or books. The presidential beat also is a gateway to better things in the profession. David Halberstam describes it as "an institutional ticket. The guy who gets to the White House goes on to some bigger job," such as editor, columnist, or television anchor.[28]

In stark contrast to these external indicators of success and prestige is the job itself, which has been well described as "the body watch." The body, of course, is the president's; the purpose of the watch is to find out all that he does in his waking hours, both officially and privately. That means staying near; as Elfin puts it, "the worst thing in the world that could happen to you is for the president of the United States to choke on a piece of meat, and for you not to be there." [29]

Staying near, however, is a goal that usually can be achieved only in the most technical sense. The White House press room is only yards away from the Oval Office, but the distance rarely is spanned. Reporters not only are forbidden to "roam the halls" of the White House and Executive Office Building in the time-honored *modus operandi* of their profession, but their free access even to the office of the press secretary is limited to his assistants' outer sanctums. Charged by their editors to "body-watch" the president, they usually are forced to rely on the secondhand reports of his press secretary, who comes out once a day to brief them, or on other presidential aides or visitors to the Oval Office, who may choose to speak to them or not. When reporters are allowed to see the president, it almost always is in a setting that is defined both physically and procedurally by the White House. Members of the White House press corps enjoy high status in part because they are so visible, but the irony is that "they are visible because of the large amount of time they spend waiting for something to happen—for the briefing to start, for the president to appear for a White House ceremony in the Rose Garden, for a visitor to arrive, for a statement or a transcript to be released." [30]

The frustration that journalists feel in a job whose main activities are stenographic is great. A briefing room full of White House reporters when the press secretary appears is not unlike a classroom full of junior high school students who have just been informed that a substitute teacher is on the way. In their daily dispatches to the public, where professional and editorial standards forbid overtly hostile displays, status frustration, joined to the hangover from Vietnam and Watergate, shows up in subtler form. As one study of the subject records,

> reporters now present news about the White House along with an item that casts doubt on the credibility of what has been said or on the reliability of the person who has said it. They indicate to their

viewers that a cynical approach is a realistic approach when analyzing the motives of the president and his advisers.[31]

Cynicism boils over into overtly negative coverage when a president's rectitude comes to be doubted. Nixon and Watergate, Ford and his early pardon of Nixon, Carter's reluctance to fire scandal-tainted budget director Bert Lance—in all cases, suspicion of presidential wrongdoing provided a seeming license for journalists to place a black hat on the president's head and white ones on their own. Not surprisingly, they took out after Reagan when it became known in late 1986 that his administration had broken or evaded laws by selling arms to Iran and diverting the proceeds to the contra rebels in Nicaragua.

Yet, on balance, presidents still receive highly favorable press coverage. In their study of how *Time* and the *New York Times* covered the presidency from 1953 to 1978, Michael Grossman and Martha Kumar found that about twice as many stories were favorable to the presidency as were unfavorable. This was true not only for the total period, but for its last five years. Their study of a decade of CBS evening news coverage showed a similar balance in favor of the presidency from 1974 to 1978, up markedly from the Vietnam and Watergate years of 1968 to 1973. If anything, this two-to-one ratio in favor of the presidency understates the true situation. Flattering pictures of presidents in *Time*, the *Times*, and CBS outnumbered unflattering ones by margins of 33-1, 34-1, and 6-1, respectively.[32] And local and regional media, which the authors did not study, tend to be more supportive than national organs.

Even more pertinent to our concern with journalists' standards for evaluating the presidency are the kinds of actions by presidents that generate the most favorable coverage. According to Grossman and Kumar, reporters respond enthusiastically to presidential actions that convey strength. They list five categories of such stories:

1. appearing decisive—military leadership;
2. appearing decisive—firing contrary subordinates;
3. being in command—the president as expert;
4. being in command—the president as effective intellectual; and
5. being recognized as a leader—foreign travel.[33]

In sum, when strong action—or the appearance of strong action—comes from the White House, journalists tend to applaud it.

Why do reporters who are cynical about the presidency continue to cover it favorably? One reason is occupational necessity. Most White House correspondents must file at least one story every day. Because of the severe limitations placed on reporters' ability to gather information independently, the president or the press secretary is in a good position to define the agenda they cover. "They have this huge built-in element of control over you," explains Austin Scott of the *Washington Post.* "You're locked into this little press room with only a telephone connecting you to the rest of the White House, and they have the option of taking your calls or not. All you get is staged events—press conferences, briefings, photo opportunities." [34] Dom Bonafede of the *National Journal* observed during the Ford years that "every day when [Press Secretary Ron] Nessen gets out there he determines, with his opening statement, what the news is going to be for that day." [35] Within a few months of taking office in 1981, the Reagan administration had refined the task of information management to an art, alternating techniques of secrecy and publicity to shape the flow and even the "spin" (the public relations term for meaning) of news. Thus, even when reporters tag on a cynical twist, it usually is to a story that the White House has concocted.

Editors demand more than a daily story from their White House correspondents, of course; they also expect an occasional exclusive to put them a leg up on the competition. These usually come about through leaks of information from members of the White House staff. Such leaks almost always are intended to make the president look good: the personal success of presidential assistants, after all, is tied very closely to the political success of the president. But according to Peter Lisagor of the *Chicago Daily News,* reporters really have little choice but to use what they get:

> The competition and competitive pressure is such that guys have to get a story. If they get something that someone else might not have— no matter how self-serving [for the White House] it may seem and no matter how hardnosed they may feel themselves to be—they may often go with the story.[36]

Considerations other than occupational necessity contribute to reporters' favorable portrayal of a powerful presidency. Their world view, or implicit conception of how the political system works, greatly affects how they perform their job. "Journalists define the center of government action as the executive," note David Paletz and Robert Entman, and "personalize the institution as one man." [37] A study by Elmer Cornwell of front-page newspaper headlines from 1885 to 1957 found "a long-term upward trend [in presidency-centered coverage] in absolute terms and relative to news about Congress"; Alan Balutis's extension of Cornwell's data through 1974 found both trends growing stronger.[38] The favorable or unfavorable nature of presidential coverage may be less important than the coverage itself. Simply by dwelling on the presidency, the media reinforces images of its strength and importance.[39] Finally, reporters tend to look at government through the lenses of electoral politics. They often describe relationships between the presidency and other policy-making institutions, especially Congress, in terms of victories and defeats for the president. This, too, reinforces the notion that strong presidents who dominate the system are good presidents.

Citizens: Strength amid Contradiction

The American presidency combines the roles of chief of government and chief of state. As chief of government, the president is called upon to act in the manner of the British prime minister, as a political leader of the partisan causes and coalition that elected him to the office. As chief of state, he is the equivalent of the British monarch: the ceremonial leader of the nation and the living symbol of its unity.

Because the presidency embodies both roles, the general public tends to evaluate it by standards that seem contradictory. According to Cronin, Americans want the president to be "gentle and decent but forceful and decisive," "inspirational but 'don't promise more than you can deliver,'" "open and caring but courageous and independent," a "common man who gives an uncommon performance," and a "national unifier-national divider." [40] George Edwards suggests several similar sets of contradictory public expectations about presidential style, including "leadership vs. responsiveness," "statesman vs. politician," and "empathy vs. uniqueness." [41]

The public's expectations of presidential policy making also seem to be contradictory. On the one hand, they expect the president to reduce unemployment, cut the cost of government, increase government efficiency, deal effectively with foreign policy, and strengthen national defense. In a survey taken shortly after Carter's election in 1976, 59 to 81 percent of the respondents, depending on the policy in question, said that they expected these accomplishments. The comparable figures following Reagan's 1980 election ranged from 69 to 89 percent.[42]

Yet the conventional wisdom among scholars is that the public also would prefer that Congress—the other, constitutionally coequal branch they elect—dominate the presidency in the policy-making process. After reviewing a wide variety of poll data from 1936 to 1973, Hazel Erskine concluded: "Whenever given a choice between congressional vs. presidential decision-making, the people tend to trust Congress over the chief executive. Whether the issue pertains to specific domestic or military matters, or to authority in general, seems immaterial." [43] Donald Devine agreed: "The American people believe ... that the Congress should be supreme." He cited as evidence the 61 to 17 percent margin by which they chose Congress in response to this 1958 Survey

Research Center question: "Some people say that the president is in the best position to see what the country needs. Other people think the president may have some good ideas about what the country needs but it is up to Congress to decide what ought to be done. How do you feel about it?" [44] A 1979 Gallup poll question that asked whether Congress or the president "ought to have major responsibility" in three policy areas found that Congress was preferred for energy and the economy and the president only for foreign policy. [45]

In apparent contradiction of their high expectations of presidential performance, then, Americans are "philosophical congressionalists." But in truth, all this means is that when pollsters ask abstract questions of a theoretical nature, the public tends to side with Congress against the president. (It is hard to imagine that such questions come up very often in ordinary discussions.) [46] When one looks at evidence about attitudes and feelings that bear more directly on political behavior, the balance shifts. The American public, like American scholars and journalists, wants and admires strength in the presidency.

One finds first that Americans are "operational presidentialists." Whatever they may say about proper institutional roles in theory, the presidents they like are the ones who take the lead and the Congresses they like are the ones that follow. Stephen Wayne provides evidence for the first half of this proposition in his report on a 1979 survey that asked people what qualities they admired most in their favorite president. "Strong" led the list by far; "forceful," "ability to get things done," and "decisive" ranked third, fifth, and seventh, respectively. "Concern for the average citizen," "honest," and "had confidence of people" were the only oft-mentioned qualities that were not clear synonyms for strength. [47] As for Congress, the only times that a majority of the respondents have rated its performance as either "excellent" or "pretty good" in more than two decades of Harris surveys were in 1964 and 1965, the two years in which Congress was most responsive to strong presidential leadership. [48]

Americans also can be described as "emotional presidentialists." Almost all of their political heroes from the past are presidents; [49] when candidates run for president, they promise to be like the best of their predecessors. (In contrast, members of Congress—the "only distinctly native American criminal class," in Mark Twain's jest—serve in political folklore as the butt of jokes. Congressional aspirants tend to "run *for* Congress by running *against* Congress.") [50] Heroic feelings about the presidency show up most dramatically when a president dies. Surveys taken shortly after President John F. Kennedy's assassination found Americans to be displaying symptoms of grief that otherwise appear only at the death of a close friend or relative. They "didn't feel like eating" (43 percent), were "nervous and tense" (68 percent), and felt "dazed and numb" (57 percent). [51] They also feared, for a short time at least, that the Republic was in danger.[52] Similar emotional outpourings seem to have accompanied the deaths in office of all presidents, whether by assassination or natural causes and whether they were popular or not. In Great Britain, it is the monarch's death that occasions such deep emotions, not the death of the prime minister, the chief of government.[53]

The public's emotional attachment to the presidency has implications of its own for strong leadership. The honeymoon that each new president enjoys with the people at the start of his term is, in a sense, an affirmation of faith in the office. New and reelected presidents invariably receive the early approval of millions of citizens who had voted against them, and most presidents are able to keep their public approval ratings at near-honeymoon levels for a year or more. As we will see, nothing is more helpful to presidential leadership of Congress than popularity with the voters.

Presidents also can trade on the public's emotional support for the office in foreign affairs. Citizens will "rally 'round the flag" in the form of their chief of state in all sorts of international circumstances.[54] According to a study by Jong Lee, wars and military crises head the list of support-inspiring events, followed by new foreign policy initiatives, peace efforts, and summit conferences.[55] Nixon's approval rating in the Gallup poll went up 12 percentage points after his October 1969 "Vietnamization" speech, Ford's jumped 11 points after he "rescued" the *Mayaguez,* and Carter added 12 points to his rating as a result of the Camp David summit that brought Israel and Egypt together. Reagan enjoyed a number of such boosts: from 45 to 53 percent after the Grenada invasion in 1983 and from 62 to 68 percent after the 1986 bombing of Libya, for example.

Rossiter sums up the symbolic and political importance of the presidency:

> No president can fail to realize that all his powers are invigorated, indeed are given a new dimension of authority, because he is the symbol of our sovereignty, continuity, and grandeur. When he asks a senator to lunch in order to enlist support for a pet project, . . . when he orders a general to cease caviling or else be removed from his command, the senator and . . . the general are well aware—especially if the scene is laid in the White House—that they are dealing with no ordinary head of government.[56]

The presidency evaluators to whom Rossiter refers, of course, are not outside of government but are fellow officeholders. Like scholars, journalists, and the general public, members of Congress and bureaucrats evaluate the presidency in ways that are superficially detrimental to presidential leadership, yet their underlying attitudes offer support for strong presidents.

Members of Congress:
Strength amid Constituency-Centeredness

Whether animated by a selfish urge to do well or a generous desire to do good, the modern member of Congress wants to be reelected.[57] As Richard Fenno explains, "For most members of Congress most of the time, [the] electoral goal is primary. It is the prerequisite for a congressional career and, hence, for the pursuit of other member goals." [58] From 1946 to 1986, an average 91.7 percent of all representatives sought reelection, as did 85 percent of all senators.[59]

To be reelected, of course, members must please their constituents, a task best accomplished by working in Congress to advance local interests as defined by local people. A 1977 Harris survey conducted for the House Commission on Administrative Review asked respondents whether they thought their representative should be primarily concerned with looking after the needs and interests of "his own district" or "the nation as a whole." They chose "own district" by a margin of 57 to 34 percent. About twice as many voters in a 1978 survey said that when a legislator sees a conflict between "what the voters think best" and "what he thinks best," he should obey the voters.[60]

Personal ambition and constituents' demands powerfully influence how members of Congress behave in office. Most channel their energy and resources into activities that translate readily into votes. This creates an anomaly: although Congress's main constitutional task is to legislate in the national interest, most of the activities that produce votes for members are nonlegislative, primarily "pork-barreling" and casework.[61] (Pork-barreling involves getting federal grant and project money for their home states and districts; casework is handling constituents' complaints about their personal experiences with the federal bureaucracy.) David Mayhew adds "advertising" to the list of leading congressional activities: newsletters or questionnaires mailed home, personal visits, and similar efforts "to create a favorable image but in messages having little or no issue content." [62]

What time is left for legislative activity generally is spent in two reelection-oriented ways. First, members propose laws pleasing to the voters. This takes little effort but enables them to gain publicity in local media and to answer almost any constituent's inquiry about policy or legislation with: "I introduced (or cosponsored) a bill on that very subject." At the same time, it commits them to none of the difficult, time-consuming, and largely invisible activities needed to get legislation over the hurdles of subcommittee, committee, and floor passage in each house.

Second, legislators work very hard on those few areas of lawmaking that are of particular interest to the local constituency. For example, a representative from a farm district can be certain that his effectiveness, not just his rhetoric, on agricultural issues will be monitored closely by opinion leaders back home. This explains why, for example, the Agriculture committees in both houses are dominated by farm-state members, the House Interior and Insular Affairs and Senate Environment and Public Works committees by westerners, and the House Merchant Marine and Fisheries Committee by coastal-state representatives.[63] Once on these committees, members often enter into mutually beneficial relationships with the interest groups and executive agencies in their policy "subgovernment." By supporting programs that interest groups favor, legislators may obtain campaign contributions and other electoral benefits. From agencies they may receive special consideration for their constituents and influence over the distribution of patronage and contracts in return for generous appropriations and loose statutory reins.

Not surprisingly, representatives and senators also evaluate the presidency by constituency-based criteria. For presidents who have an extensive legislative agenda, this can seem very discouraging. Their difficulty in moving bills through a constitutionally bicameral legislature is compounded by Congress's culture of constituency service, which distracts members away from serious legislative activity into the more electorally rewarding business of pork-barreling, casework, and advertising. Successful presidential leadership also requires that members direct their attention to national concerns. But congressional ambition is such that local issues, or the local effects of national issues, come first. Finally, most presidential initiatives call for legislative alteration of the status quo. Such proposals often conflict with the general satisfaction that each component of the various subgovernments, including the congressional committees and subcommittees, has in existing arrangements.

Nevertheless, in other, perhaps more important ways, Congress's constituency-centered culture enhances rather than inhibits presidential strength. These are the power to initiate, the power of popularity, and power in foreign policy.

Power to Initiate

During the past century, the public has placed ever greater demands for action on the federal government, most of which have required the passage of new legislation. To satisfy each of these demands, Congress as an institution has had to move through the long, tortuous, and largely subterranean process of developing programs and steering them past its own internal obstacles to action. Representatives and senators naturally have wanted to see this happen, but as noted earlier, the pursuit of reelection takes them mainly into nonlegislative areas of activity.

Again and again since 1932, members of Congress have found their way out of this dilemma by turning to the presidency. Not only did Congress give Franklin D. Roosevelt a virtual blank check to deal with the Great Depression as he saw fit—in the fabled first hundred days, it passed more than a dozen pieces of Roosevelt-spawned legislation—it also authorized actions that allowed the president to institutionalize his role as policy initiator. The Bureau of the Budget was transferred from the Treasury Department to a newly created Executive Office of the President and empowered to screen all departmental proposals for legislation before Congress could see them. In addition, the president was authorized to hire a personal political staff, largely for the purpose of developing and selling legislation to Congress.

In succeeding administrations, these trends continued. The Employment Act of 1946 called upon the president (with the aid of the new Council of Economic Advisers) to monitor the economy and recommend corrective legislation in times of economic distress. Similar congressional requests for presidential initiative were included in the Manpower Development and Training Act of 1962, the Housing and Urban Development Act of 1968, the National Environmental Policy Act of 1969, and several others. Remarkably, when Congress wanted to express its deep dissatisfaction with President Nixon's economic policies in 1971, it passed a law that forced on him the power to impose wage and price controls on the entire economy. Congress sometimes demands strength from the president even when the president does not want to give it.

Power of Popularity

The power to initiate legislation that members of Congress have ceded to the presidency in the interests of their own reelection is formidable in itself, but what of the power to secure legislative passage? Again, the constituency-centered culture of Congress can work to the advantage of presidential strength. The same congressional preoccupation with reelection that has led members to try to insulate their relationship with the voters from national political forces also has made them extremely sensitive to any national forces that might cost them votes. In particular, when legislators think that the president's support among voters is high, they are likely to follow his legislative leadership.

Perceptions of presidential popularity may grow out of a landslide election victory that is accompanied by unusually large gains for the president's party in Congress. (Gains of thirty to forty seats are large enough to seem unusual nowadays; until recently, they were quite ordinary.) Such gains invariably are attributed, accurately or not, to the president's coattails or to a mandate that he and Congress share. Either way, the election creates a heightened disposition among legislators of both congressional parties to support the president's legislative agenda: copartisans because they want to ride his bandwagon, electorally vulnerable members of the opposition party because they want to avoid being flattened by it. Such was the case following the landslide elections of Johnson in 1964, whose party gained thirty-seven seats in the House, and Reagan in 1980, when Republicans won thirty-three new seats in the House and took control of the Senate with a gain of twelve seats.

The obsession with reelection that governs legislators' reactions to election results causes them to respond in a similar manner to indices of presidential popularity during a president's term. Because reelection-oriented members of Congress "are hypersensitive to anticipated constituent reaction" to their actions, it is not surprising that the amount of support Congress gives to a president's legislative agenda is strongly related to his Gallup approval rating.[64] Each president, of course, enjoys a honeymoon period of high voter approval at the start of his term. Among recent reelected presidents, Eisenhower and Kennedy maintained their initial popularity throughout their terms, Johnson and Nixon kept theirs for the first two years, and Carter and Reagan held their ground in the polls for at least the first year. Even after their approval ratings declined, all but Johnson were able to revive their initial popularity, at least for short periods.[65] And Johnson and Reagan held on long enough to get their particularly dramatic legislative programs through Congress virtually intact, Johnson in 1964 and 1965 and Reagan in 1981.

As many scholars have pointed out, approval ratings are down in general; both the peaks and the valleys in presidential "fever charts" are lower than they used to be. But as with new-style election "landslides" of thirty to forty seats, hills now are as impressive to members of Congress as mountains once were. Reagan's highest first-term approval rating barely exceeded Kennedy's lowest, but members were more impressed by Reagan's popularity, which contrasted so favorably with his predecessors', than by Kennedy's, which seemed typical after Eisenhower.

Power in Foreign Policy

Congress's constituency-centered culture also encourages presidential strength in foreign policy. Historically, Congress has been assertive only on the minority of foreign policy issues that concern voters the most, especially unpopular wars and issues that have a clear domestic politics coloration: foreign trade, support for nations such as Israel and Greece that have vocal and well-organized ethnic lobbies in this country and hostility to nations such as South Africa, and the like. For a member of Congress to pursue an interest in foreign policy much further than that is to tempt electoral fate. Between 1970 and 1984, three consecutive Senate Foreign Relations Committee chairs were defeated in reelection bids by opponents who charged that they cared more about world politics than about local politics.

Bureaucrats: Strength amid Careerism

Career civil servants might appear to be the group whose favorable evaluations presidents need the least. In civics book theory, they are part of the president's executive chain of command and perform purely administrative, not policy-making functions. In practice, however, Congress and the courts, as well as the chief executive, have a rightful say over what bureaucrats do. And the nature of administration in modern society increasingly involves those who implement policy in the making of it.

Like members of Congress, career civil servants, who represent virtually 99 percent of the federal civilian work force, often are motivated by self-interest. "The prime commitments of civil servants," writes Erwin Hargrove, "are to their career, agency, and program. The markers of success are autonomy for their bureaus and expansion of budgets." [66] Such self-interested commitments make life difficult for the remaining few: the departmental secretaries, under secretaries, assistant secretaries, bureau chiefs, regional directors, and other "political executives" whom the president appoints to manage the bureaucracy in pursuit of his policies.

The stance of both presidents and their political executives toward the career bureaucrats, observes James Fesler, includes "an assumption that the bureaucracy is swollen, a doubt of careerists' competence, and an expectation of their unresponsiveness to the administration." [67] This view of the unresponsive bureaucrat seemed to be validated by Joel Aberbach and Bert Rockman's 1970 study of the political beliefs of high-ranking civil servants in several social service agencies. [68] Large majorities of the supergrade bureaucrats they interviewed disapproved of President Nixon's policies to reduce the social agencies' programs and budgets. This was especially true for the 47 percent who were Democrats, but the bulk of the 36 percent who were independents also opposed the president. These data seemed so supportive of the stereotype of the self-centered bureaucrat resisting the policies of the elected president that Nixon actually quoted the authors' conclusion in his memoirs: "Our findings ... pointedly portray a social service bureaucracy dominated by administrators hostile to many of the directions pursued by the Nixon administration in the realm of social policy." [69]

But far from proving Nixon's point, Aberbach and Rockman actually laid the groundwork for a later study that appears to have refuted it. In 1976, Richard Cole and David Caputo conducted a similar survey and discovered that most supergrade bureaucrats, including Democrats and especially independents, by then supported Nixon's policies. "We find the 'pull' of the presidency to be very strong," they concluded. [70]

What accounts for the apparent willingness of career bureaucrats to respond to strong presidential leadership? In part, it seems that the stereotype of bureaucratic self-interest has been overdrawn. As Fesler notes, most careerists feel obliged "to serve loyally the people's choice as president. Because senior careerists have served through several changes in administration, this is a well-internalized commitment." [71] Presumably, the stronger a president's leadership, the easier it is for loyal bureaucrats to follow.

A more important explanation may be the apparent harmony of self-interest between careerist bureaucrats and strong presidents. Cole and Caputo report that the Nixon administration played an unusually purposeful and active role in the job promotion process within the upper reaches of the civil service. Civil servants sympathetic to the administration's policies were favored. This group included Republicans, of course, but also many independents and some Democrats who recognized that the administration meant business and therefore adapted their views to further their own careers.

In sum, the civics books are not entirely wrong. Some bureaucrats follow the ethic of loyal service to the president because they believe in it. Others will follow when promotions are based on faithful obedience to the president. In either event the result is the same: "Senior bureaucrats, like Supreme Court justices, 'follow the election returns.'" [72]

Summary and Conclusion

Presidential scholarship in recent years has been marked by a bewildering succession of new models of the presidency, each the product of an admixture of empirical and normative assessments, each constructed in hasty overreaction to the most recent president. Journalists' coverage of the presidency has been tinged by a Vietnam- and Watergate-induced cynicism whose real source may be the status frustration of the modern White House press corps. Citizens pin all their hopes for chief of state-like symbolic leadership and chief of government-like political leadership on one office, the presidency. Members of Congress view the White House through constituency-colored lenses, judging it by the narrow standard of personal reelection ambitions. Tenured civil servants, whose working life is committed to the bureaucracy, also evaluate the presidency in terms of their own careers.

But in all cases, these evaluations turn out to be superficial. Underlying the scholars' confusion is an implicit appreciation that significant policy change, whatever its ideological direction, requires a strong president. The career needs and world view of journalists lead them to exalt presidential strength as well. Citizens apparently want to have the contradictions in their expectations resolved through presidential actions that are strong but appear to be unifying. Legislators and bureaucrats realize, albeit reluctantly at times, that their career interests can be served by strong presidential initiatives.

On the whole, the underlying admiration for and celebration of presidential strength by scholars, journalists, citizens, members of Congress, and career bureaucrats should be a source of comfort to presidents and to all who have fretted in recent years about a decline in the authority of the presidency. But two cautionary notes need to be sounded.

First, strength means different things to different people. Scholarly celebrants of a strong presidency traditionally have dismissed the president's administrative duties as distractions from the real tasks of moral and political leadership. Yet many bureaucrats will respond to strong presidential initiatives only when they seem likely to influence their own careers. Similarly, although the public tends to respond enthusiastically to strong presidential action of a unifying kind, journalists write most approvingly when a president defeats his political opponents.

Second, the urge that presidents may feel to impress audiences both present and future as a strong—and hence a "great"—president may lead them to behave in ways that disserve themselves, the government, and the nation. "For fear of being found out and downgraded," writes Nelson Polsby, "there is the temptation to hoard credit rather than share it . . . [and] to export responsibility away from the White House for the honest shortfalls of programs, thus transmitting to the government at large an expectation that loyalty upward will be rewarded with disloyalty down." The final and most dangerous temptation is "to offer false hopes and to proclaim spurious accomplishments to the public at large." [73]

The complete lesson for presidents who wish to exert strong leadership, then, is that they need not worry about threats from the rest of the political system. Their problems really begin only when the concern for appearing strong distracts them from the business of the presidency.

Notes

1. Some of the themes in this chapter are discussed in more detail in Erwin Hargrove and Michael Nelson, *Presidents, Politics, and Policy* (New York: Knopf, 1984).
2. Arthur Schlesinger, "Our Presidents: A Rating by 75 Historians," *New York Times Magazine,* July 29, 1962, 12ff.
3. Gary Maranell, "The Evaluation of Presidents: An Extension of the Schlesinger Polls," *Journal of American History* (June 1970): 104-113.
4. A study of how social scientists rated presidents from Franklin D. Roosevelt through Richard M. Nixon found economists' rankings to be similar to those of political scientists and historians. Malcolm B. Parsons, "The Presidential Rating Game," in *The Future of the American Presidency,* ed. Charles Dunn (Morristown, N.J.: General Learning Press, 1975), 66-91.
5. Thomas Cronin, "Superman: Our Textbook President," *Washington Monthly,* October 1970, 47-54.
6. James MacGregor Burns, *Presidential Government: The Crucible of Leadership* (Boston: Houghton Mifflin, 1965), 330.
7. Richard Neustadt, *Presidential Power: The Politics of Leadership* (New York: John Wiley & Sons, 1960). The theme of Neustadt's book is that although presidents can do little by direct command, they can and should wield great power through skillful bargaining and persuasion.
8. Clinton Rossiter, *The American Presidency* (New York: Harcourt, Brace & World, 1960), 15-16, 108.
9. Herman Finer, *The Presidency* (Chicago: University of Chicago Press, 1960), 111, 119.
10. Schlesinger, "Our Presidents," 40.
11. William Andrews, "The Presidency, Congress and Constitutional Theory," in *Perspectives on the Presidency,* ed. Aaron Wildavsky (Boston: Little, Brown, 1975), 38. For further evidence of partisan and ideological bias in scholarly assessments of the presidency, see Parsons, "Presidential Rating Game."
12. Arthur M. Schlesinger, Jr., *A Thousand Days* (Boston: Houghton Mifflin, 1965), 677; and Schlesinger, Jr., *The Imperial Presidency* (Boston: Houghton Mifflin, 1973).
13. Marcus Cunliffe, "A Defective Institution?" *Commentary* (February 1968): 28.
14. Nelson Polsby, "Against Presidential Greatness," *Commentary* (January 1977): 63.
15. James David Barber, *The Presidential Character* (Englewood Cliffs, N.J.: Prentice-Hall, 1972).

16. Thomas Cronin, *The State of the Presidency* (Boston: Little, Brown, 1975), 138.
17. George Reedy, *The Twilight of the Presidency* (New York: New American Library, 1970), chap. 1. See also Bruce Buchanan, *The Presidential Experience* (Englewood Cliffs, N.J.: Prentice-Hall, 1978); and Irving Janis, *Victims of GroupThink* (Boston: Houghton Mifflin, 1972).
18. Gerald Ford, "Imperiled, Not Imperial," *Time*, November 10, 1980, 30-31; and Thomas Franck, ed., *The Tethered Presidency* (New York: New York University Press, 1981).
19. Aaron Wildavsky, "The Past and Future Presidency," *Public Interest* (Fall 1975): 56-76.
20. Godfrey Hodgson, *All Things to All Men* (New York: Simon & Schuster, 1980), 239.
21. A fourth, Seraph, model of the presidency, as an institution that is and should be weak, never has dominated presidential scholarship. But it has its adherents. See, for example, Fred Greenstein, "Change and Continuity in the Modern Presidency," in *The New American Political System*, ed. Anthony King (Washington, D.C.: American Enterprise Institute for Public Policy Research, 1978); and Peter Woll and Rochelle Jones, "The Bureaucracy as a Check upon the President," *The Bureaucrat* (April 1974): 8-20.
22. Barber, *Presidential Character*, chap. 13; Schlesinger, Jr., *Imperial Presidency*, chap. 11; and Dom Bonafede, "Presidential Scholars Expect History to Treat the Reagan Presidency Kindly," *National Journal*, April 6, 1985, 743-747.
23. Pre-Vietnam and Watergate press attitudes are described in Tom Wicker, "News Management from the Small Town to the White House," *Washington Monthly*, January 1978, 19-26.
24. Stephen Hess, *The Washington Reporters* (Washington, D.C.: Brookings Institution, 1981), 78.
25. Michael Baruch Grossman and Martha Joynt Kumar, *Portraying the President: The White House and the News Media* (Baltimore: Johns Hopkins University Press, 1981), 131.
26. Ibid., 206-207.
27. Hess, *Washington Reporters*, 49; Stewart Alsop, *The Center* (New York: Popular Library, 1968), 161.
28. Grossman and Kumar, *Portraying the President*, 183.
29. Ibid., 43.
30. Ibid., 36.
31. Ibid., 301.
32. Ibid., chap. 10.
33. Ibid., 232-238.
34. David Paletz and Robert Entman, *Media Power Politics* (New York: Free Press, 1981), 57.
35. Grossman and Kumar, *Portraying the President*, 33.
36. Ibid., 182.
37. Paletz and Entman, *Media Power Politics*, 55.
38. Elmer Cornwell, "Presidential News: The Expanding Public Image," *Journalism Quarterly* (Summer 1959): 282; and Alan Balutis, "The Presidency and the Press: The Expanding Public Image," *Presidential Studies Quarterly* (Fall 1977).
39. Bruce Miroff, "Monopolizing the Public Space: The President as a Problem for Democratic Politics," in *Rethinking the Presidency*, ed. Thomas Cronin (Boston: Little, Brown, 1982), 218-232.
40. Thomas Cronin, "The Presidency and Its Paradoxes," in *The Presidency*

Reappraised, 2d ed., ed. Thomas Cronin and Rexford Tugwell (New York: Praeger, 1977), 69-85.

41. George C. Edwards III, *The Public Presidency* (New York: St. Martin's, 1983), 196-198.
42. "Early Expectations: Comparing Chief Executives," *Public Opinion* (February/March 1981): 39.
43. Hazel Erskine, "The Polls: Presidential Power," *Public Opinion Quarterly* (Fall 1973): 488.
44. Donald Devine, *The Political Culture of the United States* (Boston: Little, Brown, 1972), 158.
45. Thomas Cronin, "A Resurgent Congress and the Imperial Presidency," *Political Science Quarterly* (Summer 1980): 211.
46. Richard Fenno, Jr., *Home Style: House Members in Their Districts* (Boston: Little, Brown, 1978), 245. According to Fenno: "Most citizens find it hard or impossible to think about Congress as an institution. They answer questions about it; but they cannot conceptualize it as a collectivity."
47. Stephen Wayne, "Great Expectations: What People Want from Presidents," in *Rethinking the Presidency,* 192-195.
48. Roger Davidson and Walter Oleszek, *Congress and Its Members* (Washington, D.C.: CQ Press, 1981), 152.
49. Devine, *Political Culture,* 128.
50. Fenno, *Home Style,* 168.
51. Paul Sheatsley and Jacob Feldman, "The Assassination of President Kennedy: Public Reactions," *Public Opinion Quarterly* (Summer 1964): 197-202.
52. Ibid., 197.
53. Sebastian de Grazia, *The Political Community* (Chicago: University of Chicago Press, 1948), 112-115.
54. John Mueller, *War, Presidents, and Public Opinion* (New York: John Wiley & Sons, 1973), 69-74, 122-140.
55. Jong R. Lee, "Rally Round the Flag: Foreign Policy Events and Presidential Popularity," *Presidential Studies Quarterly* (Fall 1977): 255.
56. Rossiter, *American Presidency,* 16-17.
57. See Morris Fiorina, *Congress: Keystone of the Washington Establishment* (New Haven: Yale University Press, 1977), 41-49; and David Mayhew, *Congress: The Electoral Connection* (New Haven: Yale University Press, 1974).
58. Fenno, *Home Style,* 31.
59. Calculated from data presented in Gary C. Jacobson, *The Politics of Congressional Elections,* 2d ed. (Boston: Little, Brown, 1987), 50-51. In that same period, 91.2 percent of the representatives and 79.2 percent of the senators who ran were reelected.
60. Morris Fiorina, "Congressmen and their Constituents: 1958 and 1978," in *The United States Congress,* ed. Dennis Hale (Chestnut Hill, Mass.: Boston College, 1982), 39.
61. Fiorina, *Congress,* 41-49.
62. Mayhew, *Congress,* 49.
63. Kenneth A. Shepsle, *The Giant Jigsaw Puzzle: Democratic Committee Assignments in the Modern House* (Chicago: University of Chicago Press, 1978).
64. Roger Davidson, *The Role of the Congressman* (New York: Pegasus, 1968), 121. For evidence about the link between popularity and legislative leadership, see George C. Edwards III, *Presidential Influence in Congress* (San Francisco: W. H. Freeman, 1980), chap. 4; and Harvey G. Zeidenstein, "Presidential Popularity

and Presidential Support in Congress: Eisenhower to Carter," *Presidential Studies Quarterly* (Spring 1980): 224-233.

65. Edwards, *Public Presidency*, 219-220.
66. Erwin Hargrove, *The Missing Link* (Washington: Urban Institute, 1975), 114.
67. James Fesler, "Politics, Policy and Bureaucracy at the Top," *Annals* (March 1983): 32.
68. Joel Aberbach and Bert Rockman, "Clashing Beliefs within the Executive Branch: The Nixon Administration Bureaucracy," *American Political Science Review* (June 1976): 456-468.
69. Richard Nixon, *RN* (New York: Grossett & Dunlap, 1978), 768.
70. Richard Cole and David Caputo, "Presidential Control of the Senior Civil Service," *American Political Science Review* (June 1979): 399-412.
71. Fesler, "Politics, Policy and Bureaucracy," 34.
72. Francis Rourke, "Grappling with the Bureaucracy," in *Politics and the Oval Office*, ed. Arnold Meltsner (San Francisco: Institute for Contemporary Studies, 1981), 137.
73. Polsby, "Against Presidential Greatness."

2. STUDYING THE PRESIDENCY

George C. Edwards III

Although many people consider the presidency the most fascinating aspect of American politics, unfortunately it is not easy to research. This chapter is not a "how to study the presidency" essay, nor is it a bibliographic review of the vast literature on the chief executive. Rather it is an attempt to alert students to the implications, both positive and negative, of adopting particular research approaches and methodologies. Armed with this awareness, students of the presidency should be able to construct research designs that better suit their needs.

Approaches

There are many approaches to studying the presidency, ranging from those concerned with the constitutional authority of the office to those dealing with the personality dynamics of a particular president. By *approaches* we mean orientations that guide researchers to ask certain questions and employ certain concepts rather than others. In this section four of the principal approaches used by political scientists who study the presidency are examined. The legal, institutional, political, and psychological perspectives are neither mutually exclusive nor comprehensive. The goal here is not to create an ideal typology of scholarship on the presidency. Instead, it is to increase our sensitivity to the implications of different approaches for what is studied, how a subject is investigated, and what types of conclusions may be reached. Similarly, our focus is on approaches per se rather than the works of individual authors or a comprehensive review of the literature.[1]

Legal

The oldest approach to studying the presidency, what we shall term the legal perspective, concerns the president's formal powers. Legal researchers analyze the Constitution, laws, treaties, and legal precedents in order to understand the sources, scope, and use of the president's formal powers, including their legal limitations.[2] Because these have changed over time, the legal approach has a historical orientation. With its emphasis on the historical development of the office and the checks and balances in the Constitution, it also lends itself to discussion of the president's place in our system of government, both as it is and as scholars think it ought to be. Thus, there is often a clear prescriptive or normative element in these studies.

The range of issues involving presidential authority is great. Illustrations from the recent past include the right of the president to impound funds appropriated by Congress, the scope of the president's power to issue executive orders and proclamations, the president's authority to freeze federal hiring, the president's use of the pocket veto during brief congressional recesses, the constitutionality of the legislative veto, the role of the comptroller general in triggering budget reductions, and claims of executive privilege. Foreign policy issues also have reached the courts. These include Lyndon B. Johnson's and Richard M. Nixon's conduct of the Vietnam War without explicit congressional authorization, Jimmy Carter's termination of a defense treaty with Taiwan and his settlement of the Iranian assets and hostage issues, and, more generally, the president's use of executive agreements as substitutes for treaties.

Although the legal perspective has a deservedly honored place both in political science and in a nation that prides itself on the rule of law, it has its limitations. Most of what the president does cannot be explained through legal analysis. The Constitution, treaties, laws, and court decisions affect only a small portion of the president's behavior. Most of the president's relationships with the public, the Congress, the White House staff, and the bureaucracy do not fall easily within the purview of the legal perspective. Instead, this behavior can be described only in terms of informal or extraconstitutional powers. Similarly, since the legal perspective is heavily government-centered, topics such as the press's coverage of the presidency, the public's evaluation of the president, and other relationships that involve nongovernmental actors are largely ignored.

Equally significant, although it requires rigorous analysis, the legal perspective does not lend itself to explanation. Studies of the boundaries of appropriate behavior do not explain why actions occur within those boundaries or what their consequences are. Moreover, the heavy reliance on case studies by scholars employing this approach inevitably makes the basis of their generalizations somewhat tenuous. Thus, although studies that adopt the legal perspective make important contributions to our understanding of American politics, they do not answer most of the questions that entice researchers to study the presidency. For answers to these questions we must turn to alternative approaches.

Institutional

A second basic approach regards the presidency as an institution in which the president has certain roles and responsibilities and is involved in numerous structures and processes. Thus, the structure, functions, and operation of the presidency become the center of attention. These concerns are broad enough to include agencies such as the Office of Management and Budget (OMB) and units in the White House such as the legislative liaison operation. Scholars who follow this approach can move beyond formal authority and investigate such topics as the formulation, coordination, promotion, and implementation of the president's legislative program or the president's relationship with the media.[3] Like the legal perspective, the institutional approach often traces the persistence and adaptation of organizations and processes over time. This gives much of the literature a historical perspective and also lends itself to evaluations of the success of institutional arrangements.

Although at one time many institutional studies emphasized formal organizational structure and rules, such as organization charts of the White House or budgetary process procedures, in recent years the behavior of those involved in the operation of the presidency has drawn more attention. This has increased the value of institutional research. It is, after all, necessary to collect empirical data about what political actors are doing before we can discuss the significance of their behavior, much less examine analytical questions such as those pertaining to influence. By seeking to identify patterns of behavior and study interactions between the White House and Congress, OMB, or the media, institutional research not only tells us what happens but, more significantly, helps us understand why it happens. When scholars examine presidential efforts to influence the media, for example, they are looking at typical and potentially significant behavior that may explain patterns of media coverage of the White House.

The institutional approach has two principal limitations. First, description often is emphasized at the expense of explanation. We know a great deal more about how presidents have organized their White House staffs, for example, than about how these arrangements have affected the kinds of advice they received. In other words, more is known about the process than about its consequences. This in turn provides a tenuous basis for the prescriptive aspect of some institutional research. We cannot have confidence in recommendations about presidential advisory systems, for example, until we understand their effects.

The second limitation of some institutional studies is that they downplay or even ignore the significance of political skills, ideology, and personality in their emphasis on organizations and processes. Indeed, the implicit assumption that underlies the often extensive attention scholars devote to structures and processes is that they are very significant. Yet this assumption may not always be justified. It may be that the world view a president brings to the White House influences his decisions more than the way he organizes his advisers. Similarly, ideology, party, and constituency views may be more important than the White House legislative liaison operation in influencing congressional votes on the president's program.

Political Power

In the political power approach to the study of the presidency, researchers examine not institutions but the people within them and their relationships with each other.[4] These researchers view power as a function of personal politics rather than formal authority or position. They find the president operating in a pluralistic environment in which there are numerous actors with independent power bases and perspectives different from his. Thus, the president must marshal his resources to persuade others to do as he wishes.

The president's need to exercise influence in several arenas leads those who follow the power perspective to adopt an expansive view of presidential politics that includes both governmental actors, such as the Congress, bureaucracy, and White House staff, and those outside of government, such as the public, the press, and interest groups. The dependent variables in studying presidential interactions (what authors are trying to explain) are many and may include congressional or public support for the president, presidential decisions, press coverage of the White House, or bureaucratic policy implementation. Because this approach does not assume presidential success or the smooth functioning of the presidency, the influence of bureaucratic politics and other organizational factors in the executive branch is as important to investigate as behavior in more openly adversarial institutions such as Congress.

Although the power approach examines a number of questions left unexplored in other approaches, it also slights certain topics. The emphasis on relationships does not lead naturally to the investigation of the president's accountability, the limitations of his legal powers, or the day-to-day operation of the institution of the presidency.

Some commentators are bothered by the "top-down" orientation of the power approach, that is, its view of the presidency from the perspective of the president.[5] They feel that this carries an implicit assumption that the president should be the principal decision maker in American politics. These critics argue that such a premise is too

Machiavellian and that an evaluation of the goals and methods of presidents must be added to analyses of power. Others find exaggerated the depiction of the president's environment as basically confrontational, with political actors' conflicting interests creating centrifugal forces the president must try to overcome. Moreover, they claim that the heavy emphasis on power relationships may lead analysts to underestimate the importance of ideology or other influences on behavior.[6]

Psychological

Perhaps the most fascinating and popular studies of the presidency are those that approach the topic through psychological analysis. Some take the form of psychobiographies of presidents;[7] others are attempts to categorize presidents on the basis of selected personality dimensions.[8] They all are based on the premise that continuing personality needs may be displaced onto political objects and become unconscious motivations for presidential behavior. A psychological perspective forces us to ask why presidents behave as they do and leads us to look beyond external influences for answers. If individual presidents were not strongly affected by their personalities, they would neither be very important nor merit such attention.

Psychological analysis also has a broader application to the study of the presidency. Presidents and their staffs view the world through cognitive processes that affect their perceptions of why people and nations behave as they do, how power is distributed, how the economy functions, and what the appropriate roles of government, presidents, and advisers are. Cognitive processes also screen and organize an enormous volume of information about the complex and uncertain environment in which presidents function. Objective reality, intellectual abilities, and personal interests and experiences merge with psychological needs (such as those to manage inconsistency and maintain self-esteem) to influence the decisions and policies that emerge from the White House. Cognitive processes simplify decision making and lessen stress, especially on complex and controversial policies such as the war in Vietnam. Group dynamics also may influence decision making, limiting the serious appraisal of alternatives by group members. Efforts to sort out the effects of these psychological influences are still in their early stages, but there is little question that we cannot claim to understand presidential decision making until those efforts succeed.[9]

Although psychological studies can make us sensitive to important personality traits that influence presidential behavior, they are probably the most widely criticized writings on the presidency. A fundamental problem is that they often display a strong tendency toward reductionism, that is, they concentrate on personality to the exclusion of most other behavioral influences. As a result, they convey little information about the institution of the presidency or the relationships between psychological and institutional variables. Alternative explanations for behavior rarely are considered in psychological studies.

A related drawback is that psychological studies tend to stress the pathological aspects of a presidency. Scholars, like others, are drawn quite naturally to investigate problems. Their principal interest often becomes the relationship between the personality flaws of the president and what the author feels to be some of his most unfortunate actions in office. This reinforces the reductionist tendency because it usually is not difficult to find plausible parallels between psychological and decisional deficiencies.

Data are also a problem for psychological studies. It is difficult both to discern unconscious motivations or cognitive processes and to differentiate their effects from those of external influences. Often authors must rely upon biographical information of questionable validity about the behavior and environment of presidents, stretching back to their childhoods.

Summary

The legal, institutional, political power, and psychological approaches all have advantages and disadvantages for the researcher. Each concerns a different aspect of the presidency and concentrates on certain variables at the expense of others. Thus, those thinking of doing research on the presidency should carefully determine what it is they want to investigate before selecting an approach. Although the power and psychological approaches are stronger in their concern for explanation, the legal and institutional orientations are better at providing broad perspectives on the presidency. Selecting an approach is not the only decision one must make in building a research strategy, however. Appropriate methods must also be chosen.

Methods

Although political scientists have always been keenly interested in the American presidency, their progress in understanding it has been very slow. One reason for this is their reliance upon methods of analysis that are either irrelevant or inappropriate to the task of examining the basic relationships in which the presidency is involved. This section examines some of the advantages and limitations of methods used by scholars to study the presidency. Throughout, we should remember that methods are not ends in themselves but techniques for examining research questions generated by the approaches discussed earlier.

Traditional

Studies of the presidency usually describe events, behavior, and personalities. Many are written by journalists or former executive branch officials, who rely upon their personal experiences. Unfortunately, such anecdotal evidence is generally subjective, fragmentary, and impressionistic. The commentary and reflections of insiders, whether participants or participant observers, is limited by their own, often rather narrow, perspectives. For example, the memoirs of aides to Presidents Johnson and Nixon reveal very different perceptions of the president and his presidency. As Henry Kissinger writes about the Nixon White House staff:

> It is a truism that none of us really knew the inner man. More significant, each member of his entourage was acquainted with a slightly different Nixon subtly adjusted to the President's judgment of the aide or to his assessment of his interlocutor's background.[10]

Proximity to power actually may hinder rather than enhance an observer's perspective and breadth of view. The reflections of those who have served in government may be colored by the strong positions they advocated while in office or by a need to justify their decisions and behavior. Faulty memories further cloud such perceptions. Moreover, few insiders are trained to think in terms of analytical generalizations based on representative data and controls for alternative explanations. This is especially true of journalists.

Several examples illustrate the problem. One of the crucial moments in America's involvement in Vietnam came in July 1965, when President Johnson committed the United States to large-scale combat operations. In his memoirs Johnson goes to considerable lengths to show that he considered very carefully all the alternatives available at the time.[11] One of his aide's detailed account of the dialogue between Johnson and some of his advisers shows the president probing deeply for answers, challenging the premises and factual bases of options, and playing the devil's advocate.[12] Yet a presidency scholar has argued persuasively that this "debate" was really a charade, staged by the president to lend legitimacy to the decision he already had made.[13]

Even tapes of conversations in the Oval Office may be misleading. As Henry Kissinger explains regarding the Watergate tapes:

> Anyone familiar with Nixon's way of talking could have no doubt he was sitting on a time bomb. His random, elliptical, occasionally emotional manner of conversation was bound to shock, and mislead, the historian. . . . One of Nixon's favorite maneuvers . . . was to call a meeting for which everybody's view except one recalcitrant's was either known to him or prearranged by him. He would then initially

seem to accept the position with which he disagreed and permit himself to be persuaded to his real views by associates, some of whom had been rehearsed in their positions, leaving the potential holdout totally isolated.[14]

Although insiders' accounts have limitations, they often contain useful insights that may guide more rigorous research. They also provide invaluable records of the perceptions of participants in the events of the presidency. As long as the researcher understands the limitations of these works and does not accept them at face value, they can be of considerable use.

Not all studies of the presidency that use traditional methods are written by insiders. Many are written by scholars, based primarily on the observations of others.[15] As one might expect, a common criticism of the traditional literature on the presidency is that it appears to be the same presentation, repeated in slightly different versions. Although such studies may be useful syntheses of the conventional wisdom or present provocative insights about the presidency, they are more likely to suffer from the limitations of their data.

Quantitative

Research on the presidency, then, often has failed to meet all the standards of contemporary political science, including the careful definition of concepts, the rigorous specification and testing of propositions, and the use of empirical theory to develop hypotheses and explain findings. We generally have not concentrated on explanation of why things happen as they do. To explain we must examine relationships, and to generalize we must look at these relationships under many circumstances. Quantitative analysis can be an extremely useful tool in these endeavors.[16]

There have been three principal constraints on the use of quantitative analysis to study the presidency. The frequent failure to pose analytical questions already has been discussed. The second constraint has been the small number of presidents. Viewing the presidency as a set of relationships, however, helps to overcome this problem. Although the number of presidents may be small, many people are involved in relationships with them, including the entire public, members of Congress, the federal bureaucracy, and world leaders. Because there are so many people interacting with the president, we are no longer inhibited by the small universe of presidents.

The third constraint on the quantitative study of the presidency is lack of data. When we pose analytical questions, we naturally are led to search for information about the causes and consequences of presidential behavior. For example, we may ask what the president wants people to do. Among other things, the president wants support from the public, positive coverage from the media, votes for his programs from Congress, sound analysis from his advisers, and faithful policy implementation from the bureaucracy. Thus, we can look for data on these political actors, whose behavior is usually the dependent variable in our hypotheses, that is, what we are trying to explain.

The advantage of quantitative analysis of the presidency can be seen in the quantitative studies that already have been done. For example, one of the most important relationships of the presidency is that between the president and the public. Why are presidents as popular or unpopular as they are? We are just beginning to make some headway in the investigation of this question.[17] Related to these studies are those of the attitudes and beliefs of children toward the presidency and the president.[18] This research has come out of the subfield of political socialization. Substantial progress in understanding public support for the president would be impossible without the use of quantitative analysis and the techniques of survey research.

The other side of this relationship is the president's leadership of public opinion. We know that presidents devote considerable efforts to this task, but without quantitative analyses our understanding of the effects of presidential attempts to lead or manipulate public opinion will remain almost completely conjectural. Fortunately, a few scholars have begun to explore this area with quantitative techniques, including experimentation. Some have examined the public's response to presidential leadership,[19] while others have looked at the content or timing of what the president presents to the public.[20] The nature of media coverage[21] and its effect on public approval and expectations of the president[22] are other topics of research.

The study of presidential-congressional relations also has been advanced through the use of quantitative analysis. We have been able to test propositions about the extent of presidential coattails, the pull of the president's party affiliation, the influence of the president's public approval and electoral support, and the significance of presidential skills.[23] Many findings have been counterintuitive, and none would have been possible without the use of quantitative analysis.

Quantitative analysis may be applied to less developed areas of presidency research, such as presidential decision making. Who influences the president? How do external constraints and pressures, such as public opinion, the state of the economy, and international events, affect presidential decisions? What are the effects of a crisis on decision-making processes? How does the public's approval of the president affect the scheduling and conduct of press conferences? What are staff attitudes, communications, and influence patterns in domestic policy making? Quantitative analyses of presidential decision making explore these and other questions.[24]

Policy implementation is another area that invites quantitative analysis. Scholars generally have given the president's role as executor of the law limited attention, and most of what attention it has received has been of an anecdotal or case study nature. Identifying the variables that are critical to successful implementation, such as communications, resources, implementors' dispositions, bureaucratic structure, and follow-up mechanisms, is an important first step.[25] Measures of these variables as well as of implementation itself then can be developed. To understand presidential policy implementation, we should use quantitative methods to relate, systematically and empirically, possible causes with possible effects.

Although quantitative analysis can help to answer many fundamental questions about the presidency, it is important to remember that methods and models must be appropriate to the questions under investigation. If researchers ignore this seemingly obvious rule, their conclusions are likely to be inaccurate. Impressive, and therefore authoritative-looking, statistics only make matters worse. Time series analyses of "presidential popularity" are a good example of the use of inappropriate methods.[26] The conclusions many of these studies reach are unreliable and often uninterpretable.

The proper use of quantitative analysis, like any other type of analysis, is predicated upon a close affinity between the methods selected and the theoretical arguments that underlie the hypotheses being tested. A statement that something causes something else to happen is an assertion, not a theoretical argument. A theoretical argument requires an emphasis on explanation of why two variables are related.

Even at its best, quantitative analysis is not equally useful for studying all areas of the presidency. It is least useful when there is little change in the variables under study. If the subject of research is just one president, and the researcher is concerned not with the president's interactions with others but with how his personality, ideas, values, attitudes, and ideology have influenced his decisions, then quantitative analysis will be of little help. These independent variables are unlikely to change much during a president's term. Similarly, important elements in the president's environment, such as the federal system or the basic capitalist structure of the U.S. economy, vary little over time. It is therefore difficult to employ quantitative analysis to gauge their influence on the presidency.

Quantitative methods also are unlikely to be useful for the legal approach to studying the presidency. There are well-established techniques for interpreting the law, and scholars with this interest will continue to apply them.[27]

Normative questions and arguments have always occupied a substantial percentage of the presidency literature, and rightly so. Can quantitative analysis aid scholars in addressing these concerns? The answer is, partially. For example, to reach conclusions about whether the presidency is too powerful or not powerful enough (the central normative concern regarding the presidency) requires a three-part analysis. The first is an estimation of just how powerful the presidency is. The second step requires an analysis of the consequences of the power of the presidency. In other words, given the power of the presidency, what difference does it make? Is the power of the presidency relevant? Or is it important only when it interacts with other crucial variables such as crisis conditions or public support? To answer these and similar questions requires that we correlate levels of power with policy consequences.

Quantitative research will be much less useful in the third part of the analysis: Do we judge the consequences of presidential power to be good or bad? Our evaluation of these consequences will be determined, of course, by our values. Nevertheless, it is important to remember that quantitative analysis can be very useful in helping us to arrive at the point where our values dominate our conclusions.

Quantitative analysis can help us to test and refine theoretical relationships. The question remains, however, whether quantitative analysis is useful for developing theories themselves, basic conceptions of the relationships between variables.

Although quantitative studies cannot replace the sparks of creativity that lie behind conceptualizations, they may produce findings upon which syntheses may be built. Conversely, they may produce findings contrary to the conventional wisdom and thus prod scholars into challenging dominant viewpoints. To the extent that they make these contributions, they will be useful in theory building.

Case Studies

One of the most widely used methods for studying the presidency is the case study of an individual president, a presidential decision, or presidential involvement in a specific area of policy. The case study method offers the researcher several advantages. It is a manageable way to present a wide range of complex information about individual and collective behavior. Since scholars typically have found it difficult to generate quantitative data regarding the presidency, the narrative form often seems to be the only available choice.

Conversely, case studies are widely criticized on several grounds. First, they have been used more for descriptive than for analytical purposes, a failing not inherent in the nature of the case study. A more intractable problem is the idiosyncratic nature of case studies and the failure of different authors to reapply the same analytical frameworks. This makes the accumulation of knowledge difficult because scholars often, in effect, talk past each other. In the words of one scholar of case studies:

> The unique features of every case—personalities, external events and conditions and organizational arrangements—virtually ensure that studies conducted without the use of an explicit analytical framework will not produce findings that can easily be related to existing knowledge or provide a basis for future studies.[28]

Naturally, reaching generalizations about the presidency on the basis of unrelated case studies is a hazardous task. But case studies can be very useful in increasing our understanding of the presidency. For example, analyzing several case studies can serve as the basis for identifying chronic problems in decision making or in policy implementation.[29] These in turn may serve as the basis for recommendations to improve policy making. Case studies also may be used to test hypotheses or refute theories such as propositions about group dynamics drawn from social psychology.[30]

Some authors use case studies to illustrate the importance of certain aspects of the presidency that have received little scholarly attention, such as presidential influence over interest groups.[31] On a broader scale, Richard Neustadt used several case studies to help develop his influential model of presidential power.[32] Graham Allison used a case study of the Cuban missile crisis to illustrate three models of policy making.[33]

Writing a case study that has strong analytical content is difficult. It requires considerable skill, creativity, and rigor because it is very easy to slip into a descriptive rather than an analytical gear. Those who embark on preparing case studies are wise to remind themselves of the pitfalls.

Conclusion

Few topics in American politics are more interesting or more important to understand than the presidency. Studying the presidency is not a simple task, however. There are many reasons for this, including the small number of models to follow and the relative sparsity of previous research that applies the approaches and methods of modern political science. But the obstacles to studying the presidency also present researchers with an opportunity. Few questions about the presidency are settled; there is plenty of room for committed and creative researchers to make significant contributions to our understanding. The prospects for success will be enhanced if researchers realize the implications of the approaches and methods they employ and choose those that are best suited to shed light on the questions they wish to investigate.

In this task, researchers will do well to reject artificial distinctions among orientations toward studying the presidency. Some authors seek refuge in the nebulous world of "interpretation," arguing that by doing so they need not be "scientific." Although no one can dispute the importance of asking broad questions about the meaning and significance of the presidency, those who eschew the methods of social science are ill-equipped to answer such questions. The reason is plain: to accept an "interpretation" we would require the careful definition of concepts, systematic evidence, the rigorous specification and testing of propositions—including consideration of rival hypotheses—and the application of theory. In other words, there is no escape from the rigor of the scientific method. Moreover, there is no need to seek one. Virtually every question of meaning and significance is ultimately composed largely of empirical questions, as we saw in the example of how powerful the president should be.

In sum, students of the presidency are in a position to make major advances in our understanding of this crucial institution. Yet to do so will require that we remain mindful of the nature of the enterprise and not succumb to the temptation of ignoring the standards of the discipline. The issue is not whether one should adopt an exclusively legal, historical, or quantitative methodology. The appropriate data base and method of analysis depend on the question under study. The real issue is how to reach conclusions in which we can have confidence.

Notes

Portions of this essay are reprinted by permission of The University of Tennessee Press. From Edwards, George, C., III and Wayne, Stephen J.: *Studying the Presidency*. Copyright © 1983 by The University of Tennessee Press.

1. For a more extensive discussion of approaches to studying the presidency, see Stephen J. Wayne, "Approaches," in *Studying the Presidency*, eds. George C. Edwards III and Stephen J. Wayne (Knoxville: University of Tennessee Press, 1983), 17-49.
2. The classic work from the legal perspective is Edward S. Corwin, *The President: Office and Powers*, 4th rev. ed. (New York: New York University Press, 1957). An

excellent recent example is Louis Fisher, *Presidential Spending Power* (Princeton: Princeton University Press, 1975).

3. See, for example, Stephen J. Wayne, *The Legislative Presidency* (New York: Harper & Row, 1978); and Michael Baruch Grossman and Martha Joynt Kumar, *Portraying the President: The White House and the News Media* (Baltimore: Johns Hopkins University Press, 1981).

4. The political power approach is best represented in Richard E. Neustadt, *Presidential Power: The Politics of Leadership from FDR to Carter* (New York: John Wiley & Sons, 1980). Other recent examples include Fred I. Greenstein, *The Hidden-Hand Presidency* (New York: Basic Books, 1982); Bert A. Rockman, *The Leadership Question* (New York, Praeger, 1984); George C. Edwards III, *Presidential Influence in Congress* (San Francisco: W. H. Freeman, 1980); and George C. Edwards III, *The Public Presidency* (New York: St. Martin's, 1983).

5. Bruce Miroff, "Beyond Washington," *Society* 17 (July/August 1980): 66-72.

6. Peter W. Sperlich, "Bargaining and Overload: An Essay on Presidential Power," in *The Presidency,* ed. Aaron Wildavsky (Boston: Little, Brown, 1969), 168-192.

7. See, for example, Alexander L. George and Juliette L. George, *Woodrow Wilson and Colonel House: A Personality Study* (New York: Dover, 1964).

8. The most notable example is James David Barber, *The Presidential Character: Predicting Performance in the White House,* 3d ed. (Englewood Cliffs, N.J.: Prentice-Hall, 1985).

9. Some relevant studies include Alexander L. George, *Presidential Decisionmaking in Foreign Policy: The Effective Use of Information and Advice* (Boulder, Colo.: Westview Press, 1980); Bruce Buchanan, *The Presidential Experience: What the Office Does to the Man* (Englewood Cliffs, N.J.: Prentice-Hall, 1978); John D. Steinbruner, *The Cybernetic Theory of Decision* (Princeton: Princeton University Press, 1974); Irving L. Janis, *Groupthink,* 2d ed. (Boston: Houghton Mifflin, 1982); and Richard E. Neustadt and Ernest R. May, *Thinking in Time* (New York: Free Press, 1986).

10. Henry Kissinger, *Years of Upheaval* (Boston: Little, Brown, 1982), 1182.

11. Lyndon Baines Johnson, *The Vantage Point: Perspectives of the Presidency, 1963-1969* (New York: Popular Library, 1971), 144-153.

12. Jack Valenti, *A Very Human President* (New York: W. W. Norton, 1975), 317-319.

13. Larry Berman, *Planning a Tragedy: The Americanization of the War in Vietnam* (New York: W. W. Norton, 1982), 105-121.

14. Kissinger, *Years of Upheaval,* 111-112.

15. See, for example, Richard Tanner Johnson, *Managing the White House* (New York: Harper & Row, 1974).

16. For a more extensive discussion of quantitative analysis of the presidency, see George C. Edwards III, "Quantitative Analysis," in *Studying the Presidency,* 99-124.

17. Samuel Kernell, "Explaining Presidential Popularity," *American Political Science Review* 72 (June 1978): 506-522; Stephen J. Wayne, "Great Expectations: Contemporary Views of the President," in *Rethinking the Presidency,* ed. Thomas Cronin (Boston: Little, Brown, 1982); and Edwards, *The Public Presidency,* chap. 6.

18. Fred I. Greenstein, "The Benevolent Leader Revisited: Children's Images of Political Leaders in Three Democracies," *American Political Science Review* 69 (December 1975): 1371-1398; and Jack Dennis and Carol Webster, "Children's Images of the President and of Government in 1962 and 1974," *American Politics*

Quarterly 3 (October 1975): 386-405.

19. Lee Sigelman, "Gauging the Public Response to Presidential Leadership," *Presidential Studies Quarterly* 10 (Summer 1980): 427-433; Carey Rosen, "A Test of Presidential Leadership of Public Opinion: The Split-Ballot Technique," *Polity* 6 (Winter 1973): 282-290; Lee Sigelman and Carol K. Sigelman, "Presidential Leadership of Public Opinion: From 'Benevolent Leader' to Kiss of Death?" *Experimental Study of Politics* 7, no. 3 (1981): 1-22; Benjamin I. Page and Robert Y. Shapiro, "Presidential Leadership through Public Opinion," in *The Presidency and Public Policy Making*, ed. George C. Edwards III, Steven A. Shull, and Norman C. Thomas (Pittsburgh: University of Pittsburgh Press, 1986), 22-36; Dennis M. Simon and Charles W. Ostrom, Jr., "The President and Public Support: A Strategic Perspective," in *The Presidency and Public Policy Making*, 50-70; and Dan Thomas and Lee Sigelman, "Presidential Identification and Policy Leadership: Experimental Evidence on the Reagan Case," in *The Presidency and Public Policy Making*, 37-49.

20. Lawrence C. Miller and Lee Sigelman, "Is the Audience the Message? A Note on LBJ's Vietnam Statements," *Public Opinion Quarterly* 42 (Spring 1978): 71-80; John H. Kessel, "The Parameters of Presidential Politics," *Social Science Quarterly* 55 (June 1974): 8-24; Kessell, "The Seasons of Presidential Politics," *Social Science Quarterly* 58 (December 1977): 418-435; and Lyn Ragsdale, "The Politics of Presidential Speechmaking, 1949-1980," *American Political Science Review* 78 (December 1984): 971-984.

21. Grossman and Kumar, *Portraying the President*, chap. 10.

22. David L. Paletz and Richard I. Vinegar, "Presidents on Television: The Effects of Instant Analysis," *Public Opinion Quarterly* 41 (Winter 1977-78): 488-497; Dwight F. Davis, Lynda L. Kaid, and Donald L. Singleton, "Information Effects of Political Commentary," *Experimental Study of Politics* 6 (June 1978): 45-68, and "Instant Analysis of Televised Political Addresses: The Speaker versus the Commentatory," in *Communication Yearbook I*, ed. Brent D. Ruben (New Brunswick, N.J.: Transaction Books, 1977), 453-464; and Thomas A. Kazee, "Television Exposure and Attitude Change: The Impact of Political Interest," *Public Opinion Quarterly* 45 (Winter 1981): 507-518.

23. Edwards, *Presidential Influence in Congress*, chaps. 3-7; and Edwards, *The Public Presidency*, 83-93.

24. Richard L. Cole and Stephen J. Wayne, "Predicting Presidential Decisions on Enrolled Bills: A Computer Simulation," *Simulation and Games* 11 (September 1980): 313-325; Lee Sigelman and Dixie Mercer McNeil, "White House Decision-Making under Stress: A Case Analysis," *American Journal of Political Science* 24 (November 1980): 652-673; Jarol B. Manheim and William W. Lammers, "The News Conference and Presidential Leadership of Public Opinion: Does the Tail Wag the Dog?" *Presidential Studies Quarterly* 11 (Spring 1981): 177-188; John H. Kessel, *The Domestic Presidency: Decision-Making in the White House* (North Scituate, Mass.: Duxbury Press, 1975); and John H. Kessel, "The Structures of the Reagan White House," *American Journal of Political Science* 28 (May 1984): 231-258.

25. Some very interesting survey work has been done on bureaucratic dispositions. See Joel D. Aberbach and Bert A. Rockman, "Clashing Beliefs within the Executive Branch: The Nixon Administration Bureaucracy," *American Political Science Review* 70 (June 1976): 456-468; and Richard L. Cole and David A. Caputo, "Presidential Control of the Senior Civil Service: Assessing the Strategies of the Nixon Years," *American Political Science Review* 73 (June 1979): 399-413.

26. For a discussion of these studies, see Edwards, *The Public Presidency*, 257-260.
27. For more on legal analysis of the presidency, see Louis Fisher, "Making Use of Legal Sources," in *Studying the Presidency*, 182-198.
28. Norman C. Thomas, "Case Studies," in *Studying the Presidency*, 50-78.
29. Alexander L. George, "The Case for Multiple Advocacy in Making Foreign Policy," *American Political Science Review* 66 (September 1972): 765-781; George C. Edwards III, *Implementing Public Policy* (Washington, D.C.: CQ Press, 1980); and Ryan J. Barilleaux, "Evaluating Presidential Performance in Foreign Affairs," in *The Presidency and Public Policy Making*, 114-129.
30. Janis, *Groupthink*.
31. Bruce Miroff, "Presidential Leverage over Social Movements: The Johnson White House and Civil Rights," *Journal of Politics* 43 (February 1981): 2-23.
32. Neustadt, *Presidential Power*.
33. Graham T. Allison, *Essence of Decision: Explaining the Cuban Missile Crisis* (Boston: Little, Brown, 1971).

3. THE INTERPRETABLE PRESIDENCY

Jeffrey K. Tulis

The argument that presidential studies is an immature or undeveloped subfield of political science has been made so well that it would be hard to improve upon it. In 1969 Aaron Wildavsky complained in the introduction to his anthology, *The Presidency,* about the lack of substantial "social science analys[es]." Anthony King, Joseph Pika, and most recently, Bert Rockman have all echoed the claim, albeit with slightly differing diagnoses and prescriptions.[1]

Although the charge against presidential studies has taken hold in the discipline, it also is true that from the perspective of social science some progress has been made since 1969. Indeed, when Wildavsky published a second anthology in 1975 he wrote: "There is no need today as there was when *The Presidency* first appeared to say that the presidency is the most important and least studied institution in American political life. Now there is no shortage of willing voices." And Rockman states, "The thrust of my review . . . is that more and more answers to soluble questions are being given, especially where analysis is susceptible to multivariate quantitative inquiry." The virtues of, and progress from, urging presidency scholars to "catch up" with other subfields of American politics are well stated in George Edwards' essay in this volume.[2]

Rather than develop a variation on the chorus of claims in behalf of classical social science, this chapter calls attention to a new constellation of presidency studies, and therewith a new kind of political science. Simultaneous with the effort of many presidency scholars to catch up with classical social science has been a change in the way social science is practiced. This new way of thinking about politics and society is not necessarily a repudiation or rebuttal of classical social science; it can best be viewed as a fruitful addition to more familiar modes of research. Often referred to as "the interpretive turn" in social science, some of the most exciting recent work on the presidency grows out of and contributes to this new disposition.

Classical social science refers to the once controversial, now commonplace, search for verifiable explanations of political behavior through the construction and testing of hypotheses on the model of the "hard" sciences. Although political science has had little success in establishing a ruling paradigm or a widely shared and cumulative set of findings,[3] its aspiration to science has resulted in a considerable number of individually insightful studies. But the commitment to science also has configured the range of subjects suitable for study by prescribing the form in which analysis should be conducted. The twin commitments to the analysis of causation and to the measurement of causes has disposed political scientists to look at some subjects more than others. Until recently it was commonplace among political scientists to use *rigor* as a term of praise only for political analyses that approached the scientific ideal. It is in the context of this commitment to classical social science that the laments about the presidency subfield were expressed and its progress assessed.

Recently, however, social science has begun another of its periodic revolutions. Fortunately, this one, the interpretive turn, appears to be less contentious and less divisive than the "behavioral revolution" that legitimized classical social science several decades ago. The new enterprise takes its bearing and inspiration from the interpretive side of philosophy rather than from the positivist tradition. Noted anthropologist Clifford Geertz describes the new disposition in his recent book *Local Knowledge:*

> It has dawned on social scientists that they did not need to be mimic physicists or closet humanists or to invent some new realm of being to serve as the object of their investigations. Instead they could proceed with their vocation, trying to discover order in collective life ... many of them have taken an essentially hermeneutic or if that word frightens, interpretive approach to their task. Interpretive explanation—and it is a form of explanation, not just exalted glossography—trains its attention on what institutions, actions, images, utterances, events, customs, all the usual objects of social science interest, mean to those whose institutions, actions, customs, and so on they are.[4]

What we have then is more a search for meaning than for causes, more a concern for significance than for laws, more a quest for coherence than for certainty. One must stress the *more*. Social science has always had two impulses—an aspiration to certainty and demonstration, for establishment of the "facts," and an aspiration to significance, or answers to the "so what" question. What has occurred with the interpretive turn is a shift of emphasis from the former to the latter, along with the recognition that one can be rigorous about meaning and significance, just as one can be rigorous about the facts.

This shift in emphasis on the part of some scholars has occurred in tandem with the progress and continued professionalization of classical social science. So we have emerging a healthy pluralism of perspectives rather than the demise of classical social science. According to Geertz:

> The refiguration of social theory represents, or will if it continues, a sea change in our notion not so much of what knowledge is but of what it is we want to know. Social events do have causes and social institutions effects; but it just may be that the road to discovering what we assert in asserting this lies less through postulating forces and measuring them than through noting expressions and inspecting them.[5]

What has all this to do with the study of the presidency? The presidency is a subject ill suited for the old social science but well suited for the new. The fatal flaw of a small N (roughly forty presidents), combined with a tremendous variety of idiosyncratic differences among them, traditionally lent itself to anecdotes, biography, and what Pika has bemoaned, the "personalization" of the office.[6] To overcome this situation, many scholars turned their attention to links between presidents and other phenomena, such as Congress and public opinion, that are better suited to the sorts of generalizations prescribed by classical social science. In other words, the subject was redefined to be amenable to the questions best answered by political science. Study of the presidency was made ancillary to the study of Congress through roll call analyses or to public opinion understood as tabulated responses to surveys.

To be sure, much work on the presidency in the 1950s and before was anecdotal and uninformative; the drive to generalization that followed is an improvement, even if a change in subject. But it should be remembered that a number of fine legal and historical studies, for all intents and purposes, were banned intellectually, allegedly because they were bad for classical social science.[7] In truth, of course, they were good for what they were. One indication of the emergence of a "new" political science is that such writings are being read again and cited for the insights rather than the foils that they provide.[8]

Recently, there has been a small renaissance of research on the presidency. Scholars as diverse as Stephen Skowronek,[9] James Ceaser,[10] Michael Rogin,[11] Nelson Polsby,[12] and Theodore Lowi,[13] have written important books about the American executive that cannot be reasonably described as scientific, or as aspiring to be scientific. Instead, each of these scholars, and others like them, has attempted to interpret the American political system and the principles that animate it.[14]

The unreconstructed presidency—the one with the small N—is well suited for the emerging interpretive persuasion in political science for at least three reasons.

First, the very features of the presidency that make for poor law-like generalizations help account for the office's cultural significance. Being a visible *one,* the chieftainship of state and government both, the presidency is a repository for the polity's aspirations and disenchantments. Students of American political culture can't help but be drawn to the institution. And indeed they are. Both Rogin's studies of Andrew Jackson, Abraham Lincoln, Woodrow Wilson, and Ronald Reagan and Skowronek's account of regime changes look to the presidency as a crucible in which changing standards of political legitimacy take shape. It is not only the president as an agent of political or policy change that is important from this perspective but also the broader interpretive value of the presidency. Just as Sacvan Bercovitch has used churchly and literary expressions of the "jeremiad" to interpret American political culture and to account for American exceptionalism, so may political scientists view presidents as reflectors and carriers of America's political self-understanding.[15]

Second, presidents themselves offer interpretations of the political order. These interpretations are constituent features of presidential behavior, which most paradigms of the presidency and American politics have treated as mere epiphenomena. Moreover, a presidential interpretation may be interesting in its own right—that is, informative by virtue of the questions to which it points or the problems that it raises. [16]

This seemingly naive view is supported by two important developments in the study of constitutional interpretation. A number of scholars have argued that the Supreme Court is not the sole authoritative interpreter of the Constitution. Particularly in disputes with each other, the president and Congress are also legitimate interpreters.[17] The enterprise of constitutional interpretation thus is confined no longer to the study of judicial opinion. At the same time, constitutional theorists increasingly draw upon the methods and techniques of literary criticism, semiotics, and symbolic anthropology.[18] It is safe to predict that the "text" soon will supplement, if not supplant, the metaphor of the biological "system" in the study of American politics. Taken together, these two developments enhance the value of studying the presidency as a fit window upon a polity that might usefully be treated as a "text." As the public, rhetorical aspects of the presidency become ever more pronounced, so does the suitability of the institution for interpretive endeavors.[19]

Third, more than with other institutions of American politics, literature on the presidency has traditionally been a forum for intellectual reconsiderations of the political order as a whole. The recurrent, and important, discussion of the merits of parliamentary versus presidential systems, worries about the balance of power between president and Congress, and concerns about "governability" are all staples in what Hugh Heclo has called the didactic literature on the presidency. It is true that some discussions of these sorts of concerns are superficial and, as King points out, all too familiar. But the continued hold that such systemic questions have on students and scholars (including seemingly new, but actually well worn, questions, such as the character and autonomy of the state), suggest their intrinsic political interest.[20]

"Old" political science aimed to replace these citizens' concerns with new questions that were amenable to the answers it could provide. The "new" political science offers the prospect of rigorous reinterpretation of the recurrent concerns, concerns that emerge from the practice of politics itself rather than from the formal requirements of analysis.[21] Rigor is essential: presidency scholars have always offered interpretations of the political order as a whole, but often these interpretations were unselfconscious and implied, occasionally unintended. Now more and more accounts of the institution are appearing that are self-conscious interpretations of the larger political system.[22]

The longstanding concern of presidency scholarship for political interpretation, even when aspiring to science, affirms again the necessary overlap between the classical and interpretive perspectives on social science. The two perspectives are mutually dependent. Sound interpretive endeavors depend upon careful articulation of the facts, sometimes careful quantitative analysis. Sound science rests upon the quality of the questions it is asked to answer, questions often provided by interpretation.

Several years ago, the Ford Foundation commissioned Hugh Heclo to review the presidency field and recommend needed research. Heclo urged scholars to dig into the vast archival holdings that had developed with the modern presidency. The good result of this initiative was a series of new, solid interpretations of executive politics. The best of these studies reveal the practical symbiosis of scientific and interpretive aspirations. Note especially Fred Greenstein's reinterpretation of Eisenhower's political style and of leadership more generally, and Peri Arnold's study of the politics and development of presidential reorganization efforts.[23]

But although it is true that the old and new perspectives often depend upon one another, there also are very real differences between them that indicate different ways of thinking about future research.[24]

The old and new presidency scholarship both seem to offer systemic perspectives. In the past, systemic considerations were often presented unselfconsciously. Rockman urges fellow scientists to become fully self-conscious about systemic concerns.[25] Nevertheless, students of the presidency persist in viewing the American political system from the president's vantage point. Virtually all of the "scientific" literature on the presidency follows Richard Neustadt in this respect: the view of the world is from "over the President's shoulder." [26] To be sure, a number of scholars point to structural infirmities in the presidency, and many no longer call for "strong" presidents. Yet even these voices are sobered by their concern for what is good for the presidency, in their case, a more restricted and therefore more effective station. A truly systemic perspective would explore the character or inherent contradictions of republican government.[27] Of course, this problem of vantage point, which can be called "institutional partisanship," is not peculiar to students of the presidency. It is true also of scholars of Congress and the judiciary whose seeming desire is to defend the prerogatives of their institution in its contests with other actors in American politics.

The new social science may remedy this problem for two reasons: first, a truly systemic perspective stands at a juncture between the study of institutions and of American political thought. Political interpretation aims to illuminate just that sort of juncture, the meaning of the mutual dependence of thought and politics. Moreover, because of its interdisciplinary object, the new enterprise attracts many scholars who see themselves not as presidency specialists but rather as students of theoretical problems that point them to the presidency, or to some other institution. These scholars are moved to write by larger political problems and developments they perceive rather than by the requirements of any subdiscipline. Indeed, many studies that can be cited as excellent contributions to our field easily could be classified as contributions to other subfields, such as party politics, the bureaucracy, or psychology and politics. Thus, the idea that presidency scholarship ought to be thought of as a field is implicitly challenged by some of the most illuminating recent studies of the presidency.[28]

Finally, the interpretive turn offers a prospect to scholars who adopt it that is diametrically different than that offered by the good reviews of the presidency literature cited at the outset of this essay. Students of the presidency are now in a theoretical posture that is suitable for the illumination of big questions and the articulation of new ways of thinking about American politics as a whole. Rather than playing catch-up with the rest of political science, a role conducive to self-contempt, presidency scholars are at last well positioned to lead.

Notes

1. Aaron Wildavsky, *The Presidency* (Boston: Little, Brown, 1969); Anthony King, "Executives," in *Handbook of Political Science: Governmental Institutions and Processes,* ed. Fred I. Greenstein and Nelson Polsby, vol. 5 (Reading, Mass.: Addison-Wesley, 1975), 173-255; and Joseph Pika, "Moving beyond the Oval Office: Problems in Studying the Presidency," *Congress and the Presidency* 9 (Winter 1981-82): 17-36. Bert A. Rockman, "Presidential and Executive Studies: The One, the Few, and the Many," in *Political Science: The Science of Politics,* ed. Herbert S. Weisberg (New York: Agathon Press, 1986), 105-140.
2. Aaron Wildavsky, *Perspectives on the Presidency* (Boston: Little, Brown, 1975), v; Rockman, "Presidential and Executive Studies," 133-134; see also George Edwards and Stephen Wayne, *Studying the Presidency* (Knoxville: University of Tennessee Press, 1983). For a comprehensive bibliography of studies of the modern presidency, see Fred I. Greenstein, Larry Berman, and Alvin Felzenberg, *Evolution of the Modern Presidency* (Washington, D.C.: American Enterprise Institute, 1978).
3. David M. Ricci, *The Tragedy of Political Science* (New Haven: Yale University Press, 1984).
4. Clifford Geertz, *Local Knowledge* (New York: Basic Books, 1985), 22; see also Theodore Lowi, *The Personal President* (Ithaca, N.Y.: Cornell University Press, 1985), 80: "The issue of concern is first to describe the phenomenon and then to assess its consequences, not search for its causes."
5. Geertz, *Local Knowledge,* 34.
6. Pika, "Moving beyond the Oval Office," 17-36.
7. Charles Thach, *The Creation of the Presidency* (Baltimore: Johns Hopkins University Press, 1923; reprinted edition, 1969); Edward Corwin, *The President: Office and Powers* (New York: New York University Press, 1957); and Norman Small, *Some Presidential Interpretations of the Presidency* (Baltimore: Johns Hopkins University Press, 1930).
8. See Douglas Hoekstra, "Presidential Power and Presidential Purpose," *Review of Politics* 47 (October 1985); Christopher H. Pyle and Richard Pious, *The President, Congress, and the Constitution* (New York: Free Press, 1984); and Louis Fisher, *Constitutional Conflict between Congress and the President* (Princeton: Princeton University Press, 1985).
9. Stephen Skowronek, *Building the New American State* (Cambridge: Cambridge University Press, 1982); see also his "Presidential Leadership in Political Time," in this volume, and "Notes on the Presidency and Political Development," *Studies in American Political Development,* vol. 1 (1987): 286-302.
10. James W. Ceaser, *Presidential Selection: Theory and Development* (Princeton: Princeton University Press, 1979); see also his *Reforming the Reforms* (Cambridge, Mass.: Ballinger, 1983); and "The Theory of Governance of the Reagan Administration," in *The Reagan Presidency and the Governing of America,* ed. Lester M. Salamon and Michael S. Lund (Washington, D.C.: Urban Institute Press, 1984).
11. Michael Rogin, *Ronald Reagan, the Movie and Other Episodes in Political Demonology* (Berkeley: University of California Press, 1987); and *Fathers and Children: Andrew Jackson and the Subjugation of the Indians* (New York: Knopf, 1975). See also Rogin, "Max Weber and Woodrow Wilson: The Iron Cage in Germany and America," *Polity* 3 (Summer 1971): 557-575.

12. Nelson Polsby, *Consequences of Party Reform* (New York: Oxford University Press, 1983). In the preface Polsby writes, "I count myself as one of those who as a result of the Watergate era have undertaken to attend on a more or less regular basis to the state of the American political system as a whole."

13. Lowi, *The Personal President;* see also his "Ronald Reagan—Revolutionary?" in *The Reagan Presidency.*

14. Other recent studies include: Don K. Price, *America's Unwritten Constitution* (Baton Rouge: Louisiana State University Press, 1983); Bert Rockman, *The Leadership Question* (New York: Praeger, 1984); and Peri Arnold, *The Making of the Managerial Presidency* (Princeton: Princeton University Press, 1986).

15. Sacvan Bercovitch, *The American Jeremiad* (Madison: University of Wisconsin Press, 1979); see also Anne Norton, *Alternative Americas: A Reading of Antebellum Political Culture* (Chicago: University of Chicago Press, 1986).

16. Glen E. Thurow, *Abraham Lincoln and American Political Religion* (Albany: State University of New York Press, 1977).

17. Walter F. Murphy, "Who Shall Interpret? The Quest for the Ultimate Constitutional Interpreter," *Review of Politics* 48 (July 1986): 401-423; Sotirios A. Barber, *On What the Constitution Means* (Baltimore: Johns Hopkins University Press, 1943).

18. William F. Harris II, "Bonding Word and Polity: The Logic of American Constitutionalism," *American Political Science Review* 76 (March 1982): 34-45. Harris's forthcoming book, *The Interpretable Constitution,* suggested the title for the present essay. Ronald Dworkin, "Law as Interpretation," in *The Politics of Interpretation,* ed. W. J. T. Mitchell (Chicago: University of Chicago Press, 1982); Sanford Levinson, "Law as Literature," *Texas Law Review* 60 (March 1982): 373-403; see also Norton, *Alternative Americas,* on the treatment of America as a text.

19. Jeffrey K. Tulis, *The Rhetorical Presidency* (Princeton: Princeton University Press, 1987).

20. Hugh Heclo, *Studying the Presidency* (New York: Ford Foundation, 1977); King, "Executives," pp. 173-175; and James Sundquist, *Constitutional Reform and Effective Government* (Washington, D.C.: Brookings Institution, 1986). See also Peter Evans, Dietrich Rueschemeyer, and Theda Skocpol, eds., *Bringing the State Back In* (New York: Cambridge University Press, 1985).

21. Paradoxically, the progress toward formal analysis in classical social science was concomitant with the denial of the relevance of forms as they appear in political life (for example, constitutional forms). See Harvey C. Mansfield, Jr., "Social Science and the Constitution" (unpublished manuscript, Harvard University, 1987).

22. This point is developed at length in Sotirios A. Barber and Jeffrey K. Tulis, "The Reemergence of Constitutional Theory and the Study of American Politics" (paper presented to the Conference Group on Jurisprudence, American Political Science Association, Washington, D.C., Aug. 1986). Self-conscious constitutional approaches are a subset of studies that manifest the interpretive disposition.

23. Heclo, *Studying the Presidency;* Fred I. Greenstein, *The Hidden Hand Presidency* (New York: Basic Books, 1982); Arnold, *The Making of the Managerial Presidency;* see also Jeff Fishel, *Presidents and Promises* (Washington, D.C.: CQ Press, 1985).

24. This essay highlights some of the differences between interpretation and science. One of the reasons that the new disposition may not prove to be as disruptive as the old is that *interpretation* embraces a number of approaches that differ from each other epistemologically. For example, some interpretivists are moral realists; others

share the value skepticism characteristic of old social science. On this point see Michael Moore, "Moral Reality," *Wisconsin Law Review* 1982 (March 1983): 1061-1156; and Moore, "A Natural Law Theory of Interpretation," *Southern California Law Review* 58 (January 1985): 277-398.

25. Rockman, "Presidential and Executive Studies," 105-140.
26. Richard Neustadt, *Presidential Power* (New York: Wiley, 1980; orig. publ. 1960), vi.
27. See for example, Samuel Kernell, *Going Public: New Strategies of Presidential Leadership* (Washington, D.C.: CQ Press, 1986).
28. It would be useful for presidency scholars to consider the harm as well as the obvious benefit that attends the professionalization, institutionalization, and indeed the defining of the subfield.

4. THE AMERICAN PRESIDENCY
IN COMPARATIVE PERSPECTIVE:
SYSTEMS, SITUATIONS, AND LEADERS

Bert A. Rockman

What does the American presidency look like when viewed from the perspective of other types of political systems? How does it differ from other leadership posts? What differences are the consequence of the varying characteristics of states—their political systems, governmental arrangements, and political cultures? This *systems* comparison is essential to understanding the presidency in comparative perspective because it helps us compare situations that leaders confront and the nature of leadership roles themselves.

Thus, one way that we are able to assess the presidency as an office is by looking at some of the conditions that act to expand or diminish its capacities, and in so doing also compare across political systems conditions that are relevant to the exercise of political leadership. What kinds of *situations,* in other words, make presidents more or less powerful?

Another form of comparison is to look at leadership roles as these differ across systems as well as at differences in the styles of *leaders* within similar roles. Definitions of the job vary to some degree with the individuals who fill it. Their styles of leadership shape its contours. Yet those styles interact with, and are shaped by, situational circumstances as well as by political system characteristics. In short, the elements of comparison, to a degree, are intertwined.

However interactive these elements inevitably are, systems, situations, and leaders are organized in this chapter to provide distinctive bases for a comparative perspective on the presidency. These focal points thus lead us to such questions as: How do systems structure leadership roles? What situational circumstances influence the possibilities for leadership, and to what extent are certain situations largely a function of the nature of the political system? How do leaders themselves vary? How are they selected and their roles defined? From such an exercise, inexact as it may be, we should be able to develop a more sophisticated perspective on the American presidency as a leadership role.

Systems

If American political rhetoric tends to celebrate the system of government to excess, there is a corresponding tendency among scholars of American government to think that their system can be governed better. The scholar's critical perspective becomes especially prominent during times that challenge complacency, whether because of stark presidential aggrandizement or, more frequently, sustained policy stalemate.

These occasions tend to produce a rash of reform proposals. Some—indeed, many—are meant to emulate what are perceived to be more effective forms of governance in other democracies. For a long time, the British system of party government provided the model. Political turmoil and the waning economic fortunes of the United Kingdom, however, have suggested some limits to this model, although most reformers still are drawn to it as if by magnetic force. The Scandinavian model (Sweden and Norway more than Denmark) of social corporatism and rationalized politics also has seemed attractive, yet admittedly far more difficult to emulate because it would require not just institutional alteration but also a vast and probably impossible restructuring of American society and of American social and political norms. The Japanese success story is most recently attractive to Americans. The appeal here, however, has been based on business and industrial management techniques rather than politics and government, which remain very difficult to comprehend and which feature a powerful bureaucracy and a dominant conservative party of several highly institutionalized, yet also personal, factions.

To gain comparative perspective on the American presidency is to see how it and the larger political system differ from other top leadership roles and political systems and also how similar they may be in other respects. That entails not a proclamation of the virtues of one institutional form over the other, but an exploration of their nuances. Thus, we begin with several broadly organized features of systems to guide our analysis, beginning with the power attributes of the nation and concluding with the role of political culture and public expectation.

Power Attributes

The great military and economic power of the United States provides it with resources for political power. The actual use of these political resources is another matter, but there is no doubt that on the world scene, whether at economic summits, NATO meetings, or other settings, the United States still is the principal actor—not unchallenged as it was in the generation after World War II, but still more powerful than any other actor in international military, economic, and political spheres.

Under these circumstances, it is nearly impossible for an American president to be anything less than important. The president, of course, is not a free agent in world politics, which is perceived increasingly as being deeply interconnected with domestic matters in any case. But a president does more or less get to define what a crisis is, and in these matters, he has a freer hand. Since an international crisis that involves the United States inevitably involves far more than the United States, this inherently makes the American president a powerful figure and the presidency an exceedingly important vantage point. To the question, what do presidents do when they are refraining from lobbing nuclear bombs, the answer is they need do nothing else for the job to be of paramount importance.

This powerful presence also makes for powerful expectations at home and abroad. The leader's power naturally must be measured in relation to his objectives and to the expectations that are built around his role. These are larger and greater for American presidents than for virtually any other national leader—greater, no doubt, than the prospects that they can be met.

The simple point here is that it is necessary to distinguish between importance and power. The president of the United States is important because his country has, and is seen to have, great power and influence on world politics. But that does not necessarily make the president a powerful actor in relation to his goals or to the expectations of various domestic and international audiences.

The Size of Government

The size of the enterprise over which the president sits says something about his power, or at least about the tools and instruments at his disposal. Presumably, the greater the government share of societal resources, the more leverage government has in negotiations between public policy makers and private interests.

Two points need to be stressed. One is that the public sphere in the United States historically has been small relative to those in Western European democracies. The other is that the premises underlying the notion that big government makes for easier direction are not necessarily correct.

In an astute analysis of the capacities of the American president, Richard Rose examines the issue of governmental size from a variety of perspectives.[1] One of these is the resource extraction, or taxing, arm of government—which is an indication of the relative size of the public sphere, although not of the distribution of activities within it. (A far higher proportion of government expenditures goes to the defense sector in the United States than in European countries.) In 1980, compared with European nations, the United States ranked next to last in extracting resources for the public sphere, with only Switzerland taxing less. Since then, the extractive reach of the American federal government has diminished a bit as a result of the tax cuts that were passed in 1981. Although the federal government is very large in absolute terms, it is, in relation to the private sector, comparatively small. By itself, however, big government does not necessarily make for a dominating government.

A large state also can be less than responsive to political direction from the top, especially if many of its expenditures lie in the form of past program commitments. Leaders, ideally, wish to set agendas free of past commitments. The accumulation of such commitments over time obviously sets stark limits on directional adaptations. In the present climate, in which privatizing government and the free market have become the common themes of conservatives, whether in America, Britain, or France, a large state is viewed by top political leaders more as an impediment than as a resource.

In sum, a big state is not inherently powerful or capable of being led. Just as it is clear that the global importance of the United States does not imply that a president will be a powerful actor in world affairs in addition simply to having an important presence, so it also is clear that the relatively small American state need not diminish the leadership capacities of the American president.

Centralization

Centralization of resources and authority are believed to provide capability to central political leaders. Yet different forms of centralization need to be taken into consideration. One form is the level of financial and political resources that are available to the central government relative to other units of government. A reasonable presumption is that the higher the ratio of central government resources to regional and local government resources, the greater the leverage of central political leaders. A second form is the centralization of the party apparatus that provides the political power the leadership needs to govern. (The extreme example is the Leninist dogma of "democratic centrism," which means that once a decision is made at the top, discussion ceases and it is carried out.) A third form of centralization has to do with the relationship between the leader at the top and the cabinet "team."

Beginning with the relative centralization of government, we note that by almost any criterion, the resources commanded by the central government in the United States are considerably less than those in European states.[2] The American system is a federal one that grants a considerable amount of autonomy to the state governments, stemming from the original unification of the American government and its embodiment in the constitutional doctrine of residual powers for states. The two European federal states, West Germany and Switzerland, respectively, claim a slightly higher (70 percent) and somewhat lower (59 percent) share of total governmental revenues for their central governments than does the United States (68 percent). But far more European states—those with unitary governments—keep a substantially greater share of revenues at the center, averaging 86 percent.[3]

These data have consequences for national political leaders. In 1981, for example, when Ronald Reagan launched his successful campaign to cut federal taxes, it was thought by the supply-siders that the dollars saved by the private sector would be used to stimulate investment and, therefore, growth in the national economy. State governments, however, commonly reacted to federal spending cuts by increasing their own taxes.[4] Although the net effect of these countervailing activities is unclear, certainly the intended macroeconomic effects of presidential fiscal and tax policies were blunted.

Of course, as we have said, such outcomes are part of a federal system. Yet the American federal system is exceptionally decentralized and, unlike the German federal system, for instance, has little ability to coordinate and homogenize public policies and budgets among the states. Virtually every American president has found his administration in the middle of conflicts between federal policy and one or more states or regions. In the post-World War II era, the most notable of these conflicts was with southern states and communities over civil rights issues, especially school desegregation. More recently, they have had to do mainly with land use in the West; energy production in several states, notably Texas; and, in the Reagan era, the tax policies and rates of the higher tax states of the Northeast and upper Midwest. The states often prevail in such conflicts because of their ability to marshal political resources in Congress.

Unitary governments, to be sure, are no panacea for central policies that meet with deep regional unpopularity. Moreover, from Japan to Italy, the essence of grass-roots politics at the local level is securing pork from the central government pork barrel. Still, an American president who is intent on pursuing "national" policies will find that goal more difficult to achieve than will his counterparts in Western Europe. This, no doubt, is at least as much a function of the great size and territorial diversity of the United States as it is a consequence of its institutions. But the institutions, for better or worse, give direct expression to this diversity.

Another, more finely grained, form of centralizing resources for political leadership is the ability to enforce political discipline from the top. The model for such discipline, according to Rose, is the "party government" model, which he defines as the "unique . . . claim to have the right to choose what solutions shall be binding upon the whole of society." [5]

The effective—and proper, in one view—role of political parties, however, may be to inhibit the leader either from straying beyond the party orbit or from creating a personal political machine.[6] To the extent that a party is highly institutionalized, it may be able to exert as much pressure on the leader to adhere to party interests and values as the leader is to command disciplined support from the party. Harold Wilson, for example, was a vintage conciliator of intraparty conflict in Great Britain, while Margaret Thatcher, with uncertain success, sought to recast the Conservative party in her own image. When the party plays a dominating role, it limits the boundaries of leadership behavior. A scholar of Soviet leadership, for instance, points out that support from the Communist party rests upon ritualized incantations about the party role, which by implication means the role of the massive party apparatus.[7]

Party support, in other words, comes at a high price and limits a leader's pursuit of innovations that stray across accepted party policies and constituencies. No matter how centralized the political machinery may be, leaders have to build and sustain coalitions. In this regard, American presidents are not alone. In fact, because of the limited institutionalization of the parties in the United States, American presidents often are able to penetrate their official party organizations pretty thoroughly and thus ensure the responsiveness of the national party machinery to them. Party members in Congress, of course, have much more independence but they are not untouched by strong currents of presidential popularity.

Another, even more finely grained, form that centralization can take is the relative concentration of resources that surround the office of the leader. It is, however, no straightforward matter to describe precisely what a resource is. That the British prime minister inhabits an office staffed with very few people who are personally subordinate to her does not mean that she is an inherently less powerful person than an American president. Although many people work for the president and are thus accountable to him, size and directability are not equivalents.

That said, and despite the build-up of staff around central leaders in other countries, most notably West Germany and Canada, the modern American presidency is both more munificently staffed than any other leadership post and, perhaps, less institutionalized.[8] This reflects yet another irony. In relation to the other institutions of American government, the president is an important but, constitutionally, not a preeminent actor. In relation to the rest of the executive branch, though, the president is preeminent. Cabinet secretaries are a president's subordinates, not his colleagues.

In addition, the growth of the modern White House staff has reflected the need, as seen by most presidents, for presidential integration and direction of an otherwise fragmented government. The staff and other coordinating, budgetary, and monitoring organs of the Executive Office of the President (EOP) enhance the president's ability to counter the centrifugal tendencies of the departments and their political constituencies as expressed through Congress. It may be that this is a false kind of centralization, one that arises because without it presidents would be completely at the mercy of these centrifugal forces and subgovernmental arrangements. Yet presidents are given a kind of proprietary right (or have come to assume it) over the executive branch. The White House staff embodies that assumption in a government of which the division of turf among many significant institutional actors is never very clear.

Presidential and Parliamentary Systems

What difference, per se, does a difference in governing structure make? In comparing the presidential and parliamentary systems most attention probably has been given to the different role played by the president and by the cabinet-government as legislative initiator. It is reasonable to suppose that presidents are more inhibited than prime ministers because of the independence of the legislature from the executive. But that supposition is in need of review.

Advocates, such as former presidential adviser Lloyd Cutler,[9] have assumed that either parliamentary government or some well-disguised form of it will produce the cohesion and authority that is necessary for presidents to govern according to their agendas. In doing so, they probably are honing in on the wrong signals. The assumption of such advocates is that unified party government, rather than government by a coalition of parties (the far more frequent case) would prevail. They further assume that in a majority party government, few divisions would be of an intraparty nature. Finally, they assume away the relevance of other actors—interest groups, for example, who in a party government system would ply their influence within the parties and in the bureaucracy rather than in the legislature.

Although political machinery does have some effect on how

matters are handled, issues that deeply divide on the basis of interests or values are not resolved simply through majoritarian rituals. Probably the most significant difference between the presidential and parliamentary systems is the nature of the struggle among many interests and political factions to shape the national agenda. The president tends to maximize and expand the agenda in public, partly to accord with his goals and partly to accord with the goals of relevant party constituencies. Because of the separation between the executive and the legislature, his efforts to construct legislative majorities are necessarily open and visible. They generate confrontation, which makes presidents look more vulnerable when they lose and more potent when they win. A potential prime minister, on the other hand, more typically is engaged in striking inter- or intraparty bargains that the government will be able to carry forward.[10] To be sure, once an agenda is formed, it is almost certain, assuming bargains are adhered to, that its most important elements will gain parliamentary approval. But that can be misleading because most of the cutting, shaping, and limitation of the agenda has occurred before the legislative stage. What is preshaped and thus basically certain of passage in a parliamentary system is shaped later in the presidential system and with more uncertainty about its ultimate disposition. In the final analysis, that is the real difference between the two systems.

Accountability

What forms of accountability undergird the systems that presidents and prime ministers lead? A broad summary of these accountability relationships is portrayed in Table 4-1. The overall pattern suggests that more of an insider's political game exists under a parliamentary-cabinet arrangement than under the American presidential arrangement.

Table 4-1   Sources of Prime Ministerial and Presidential Accountability

| | *Extent of accountability* | |
Source of accountability	*Prime ministers*	*Presidents*
Party	Strong	Moderate to weak
Cabinet	Strong	Nonexistent
Legislature	Weak	Strong
Mass public	Strong	Very strong

For both kinds of leaders, of course, mass political accountability is strong. In the parliamentary system, the electoral verdict is, to a greater extent than in the presidential, about the parties, but it is also influenced by leading personalities. It is up to the party to decide on its leadership based on mass political signals. Such signals usually are followed if political disaster looms. Although the president does not start from scratch to build a coalition, his party's support cannot be taken for granted. This makes him more susceptible, consequently, to fluctuations in public opinion than are prime ministers.

Presidents depend very little on cabinet or party approval, but they are greatly dependent on Congress, assuming, of course, that their activities require legislative approval. For prime ministers, however, party and cabinet are intimately connected—a connection that is much fainter in the United States, where the structures are less clearly demarcated to begin with. The president's cabinet is not a collegial body of peers or fellow party leaders. Its members are decidedly his underlings and presidents often rely more deeply for counsel on friends (Bebe Rebozo to Richard M. Nixon, Charles Kirbo to Jimmy Carter), White House staff (Henry Kissinger to Nixon, Zbigniew Brzezinski and Hamilton Jordan to Carter), or Washington icons (Averell Harriman and Clark Clifford to various Democratic presidents).

Party structures also differ. A president can control the formal party machinery at the national level but, even though the national party organizations very recently have become more prominent, most of the action in political parties remains at the state and local level. Prime ministers, on the other hand, are much more dependent on—and therefore more accountable to—their cabinets and their parties.

In sum, presidents usually are less inhibited than prime ministers, not more. However, they also tend to be vulnerable to a process that is more visible and open, and not easily controlled through prearranged agreements. Again, the systems tend to create different behavioral incentives. Naturally, leaders will differ as to how they interpret them.

A Unitary or Collective Executive

The idea that presidents should not be inhibited in the execution of their executive powers is quite firmly asserted in *The Federalist,* no. 70, where Hamilton argued:

> Those politicians and statesmen who have been the most celebrated for the soundness of their principles and for the justness of their views have declared in favor of a single executive and a numerous legislature. . . . Decision, activity, secrecy, and dispatch will generally characterize the proceedings of one man in a much more eminent degree than the proceedings of any greater number.[11]

The concept of a cabinet with collective decision-making responsibilities was not fully comprehended until many years later in the evolution of parliamentary government. The idea required the development of mass-based political parties, which could serve as the energy source for modern parliamentary democracy.

Ironically, the energy produced by the modern mass political party apparently has been more powerful than the Hamiltonian conception of the unitary executive. As a collectivity, the cabinets of modern parliamentary governments, which represent the leading elements of a political party or coalition, provide a governing team that stands or falls together. The cabinet must be brought along by the prime minister and different positions reconciled. If that is done, parliamentary support then can typically be assumed.

In the presidential system, almost the exact opposite holds true. Here, the cabinet members, being the president's subordinates, almost never make collective decisions; that is the president's responsibility, even if he feels compelled to use interdepartmental committees in making them. In this sense, the presidency is indeed the focus of governing energy that Hamilton had hoped to generate. But although the president need not put together agreements in the cabinet (still worrying, of course, about leaks from the disgruntled), his difficulties begin when he must ask and persuade Congress to act on his behalf. Unity in the executive, without the use of other tools, merely displaces the locus of coalition building, making it more open and thus more likely to dissipate presidential energies in embarrassing political defeats.

The collective executive, in short, works through the modern political party. The unitary executive, however, cannot so easily channel energies in that form. Even if the president is deeply partisan, he cannot always count on support from the leaders of his party in Congress; they, in turn, may or may not be in a position to help him work out agreements. In a Constitution that was written before the advent of mass political parties, it was natural to assume, as Hamilton did, that one person could produce sufficient executive energy. Over the long haul, that appears to be a misplaced aspiration.

Selection Processes and Selectorates

The process of presidential candidate selection in the United States is a virtual three-ring circus, but the rings are concentric. They move from smaller audiences to bigger ones in an extraordinarily protracted process.

In modern politics, to get somewhere politicians have to draw attention to themselves or to their roles as political advocates. With the modest exception of France on the center-right, European and Japanese politics are organized exclusively around party organization as the stream through which political ambition is spawned—a condition that once held in the United States, especially in the nineteenth and early twentieth centuries. Party is now, however, only one of the channels through which politicians can beam their messages and, above all, direct their ambitions. As the recent case of Carter, and the more distant ones of Eisenhower and Wendell Willkie make clear, party is not always the dominant channel.

Two pertinent questions arise from this difference in the organization of leadership selection. First, who are the selectors? Next, what difference does the nature of the "selectorate" make for candidates and their behavior?

There is a relatively simple answer to the first question, but the simplicity is mostly superficial. The simple response is that selection is far more party-controlled in other democratic polities than in the United States. The direct primary, a uniquely American phenomenon, tends to remove an especially important lever from party organization—the capacity to select candidates. But although the selectorate is, therefore, broader for American presidential aspirants than for those who aspire to equivalent posts in Europe, it is not precisely clear what the consequences are. Organization and money are important in American primary elections, and candidates who appeal to party activists often are able to generate more of both. In this sense, the primary election process actually can strengthen ideological consonance between candidates and party activists, especially when the traditional party apparatus is more dedicated to the patronage and particularistic elements of politics.

Thus, it is much easier to assert that American processes of candidate selection differ from those in other political democracies than it is to say what those differences mean. The American process of candidate selection is both visible and lengthy. It requires a lot of money and sustained public interest. The process produces a larger number and possibly greater variety of candidates; and it is inevitably less controlled and predictable. When an incumbent seeks reelection, the attention of the president (and therefore of the government) is riveted on creating effective political defenses (or attacks) for the numerous political judgment days ahead. When a sitting president is ineligible to run again or chooses not to, attention drifts from his administration to the succession.

There also are functional similarities between American and other democratic polities, however differently these are manifested. All politicians with aspirations for leadership must build bases for support so that when the opportunity strikes they are in a position to take advantage of it. Politicking, in this sense, does not occur all of a sudden. Rather, it is a continuous process. Moreover, the inside game does not necessarily produce inside leaders, as the case of Thatcher indicates. Her major claim to fame, in the view of Anthony King, was that she was not Ted Heath, her predecessor as Conservative party leader.[12] Had she been an insider's politician, it is unlikely that she would have been so injudicious as to have taken Heath on. After James Callaghan's retirement, the Labour party made an unusual choice, too, when Michael Foote, an eccentric leftist, was selected as a compromise between the party's vote-maximizing wing and its ideologically doctrinaire wing.

When reformers look for a fix, selection processes seem to be the natural target. One assumption that various reformers make is that altering the nature of the selectorates presumably will make the selected more moderate, more responsive, more likely to be victorious, more experienced, and more predictable. But this is less than obvious, even if one could define all of those virtues more sharply. The greater likelihood is that those who are selected will vary widely within any selection process.

Political Culture and Expectations

Expectations about leadership are said to run high in the United States,[13] partly because of the high level of trust that Americans invest in their political and governing institutions compared to citizens of other democratic polities.[14] Even while the political alienation of Americans was a much discussed area of social research in the late 1960s and the 1970s, confidence in government, although diminished, remained higher than among citizens of other democratic polities.

It may be that Americans are incurable optimists or simply naive innocents in regard to what political authority plausibly can achieve. Whatever the case, the irony is considerable. For the higher the expectations, the greater the fall when they are not met.

Before emphasizing, and possibly overemphasizing, peculiarities of the American environment and system, we need to mention first some important comparabilities about modern mass politics. One is that the role of public expectation appears to be a generalized phenomenon of modern political life in all industrially advanced democratic polities. Mass expectations and governing realities are not often compatible, particularly when times are bad. To sustain political support appears to be a difficult undertaking in any system when bad news outraces the good. Denis Kavanagh, for example, reports that only two postwar British prime ministers maintained the support of more than half of the

British public for two years or more.[15] Treating several European countries, Michael Lewis-Beck has shown that the fortunes of political leaders rest greatly on public perceptions of the state of the economy.[16]

To be certain, the styles, structures, and norms of politics are not everywhere the same. Shared norms tend to moderate expectations and provide avenues for molding agreements, as in Norway and Sweden. (In Japan, the meliorating effect of shared norms is reinforced by the dominance of the Liberal Democratic party.) But the flow of events still tends to dictate the margin of political safety for the incumbent leadership. The Swedes, for example, do not share the American political style of braggadocio, power seeking, brashness, and exaggeration, but social turmoil and inflation did affect the stability of their prevailing political coalitions in the 1970s and 1980s.

The great problem of modern democratic accountability is that mass publics typically are results oriented and lack a realistic perspective on what governments can achieve at what cost. As a result, while political leaders normally seek to satisfy such expectations, they are less likely to be held to account (except among other elites) for those behaviors for which they realistically can be held to account. Regardless of what goes into the decision, it is the outcome that counts. This is no peculiarly American malady.

The great-power status of the United States, however, does generate some unique expectations. So does the physical isolation of the United States from its main global rival—an isolation that Europeans often think breeds rashness. Great-power status in an era of mass political consciousness may well lead to episodic jingoism, but without much staying power; the combination makes the worst of all possible worlds. The American mass public is not of a single mind by any means, but its dominant tendency appears to be isolationist when engagement is likely to entail serious costs. Like other modern mass publics, Americans seem unanxious to be greatly disturbed. Yet, although interventionism is more typically an elite-induced phenomenon, mass opinion, when it perceives America to be provoked, often will support strong words and decisive (and, above all, immediately successful) actions. Keep the peace, talk tough when necessary, but get it over with fast.

Beyond the unusual considerations attendant to great-power status, two additional and related aspects of the American system tend to enhance unrealistic expectations about presidents. One is, as Hugh Heclo has suggested, the illusion of national unity that is created by presidential candidates who are trying to build electoral coalitions independent of their party base. The other is the false but widespread belief that the president is the whole of government.

In regard to the illusion of unity, Heclo's argument amounts to the following: presidential nominees are not apprenticed through their party organization. Although they must play to partisans to gain support in primary elections and state caucuses, in a system in which party has a lesser and, indeed, lessening hold on voters, the general election evokes a broad public to which a candidate is apt to make only faintly partisan appeals.[17] Thus, according to Heclo:

> By fleetingly raising expectations concerning the leader's unifying and governing powers, the selection process in the United States may actually make credible government all the more difficult. In popular conception the president is selected to reign in supreme command; in reality he will often be pulling strings and hoping that something somewhere will jump.[18]

Heclo's discussion of the consequences of the American presidential selection process—its lack of political apprenticeship, and its emphasis, therefore, on individualistic political entrepreneurship—resonates with recent critiques of the American presidency.[19] These critiques portray a presidential office divorced from collective responsibility but also without the sustaining power of collective institutions. Thus, public aspirations, centered in a single individual, only rarely can be fulfilled. Because of the mismatch between aspirations and actual assets, presidents, or those who speak for them and act on their behalf, will seek to expand their resources and gain control over other institutions, notably the bureaucracy.[20] The costs of this inflation of the presidency are probably twofold: a loss of judgment by presidents and a loss of authority in the presidency.

In sum, expectations about leadership are founded essentially in the modern democratic ethos. Whether or not Americans hold excessively high expectations about what leadership and government can accomplish, they do not hold their institutions in lesser esteem than other publics. In spite of this, a view has developed that the American presidency is beset by unusually high expectations. Partly this is because of the American projection of power in the world and the accompanying expectation that the president will keep intact both peace and national pride. But much of the diagnosis is grounded in the institutional nature of the American political system in general and the presidency in particular. The individualized and plebiscitary character of the presidency makes of it an office whose occupant typically has been linked to neither party organizations in politics nor senior civil servants in government. It draws attention to the person more than to the institution's capacities for governance, where governance means something more than the mere exertion of presidential will.

The American system creates incentives for a raw form of bottom-line accountability. Such incentives also can readily stimulate irresponsible behavior. Reformers' concerns over the president's abilities to exercise power often have neglected the issue of how such power would and should be exercised. Cut off from the sources of counsel to which most prime ministers can avail themselves, presidents more likely would be granted power unrestrained by prudence. The direction of reform too often unbalances the equation: more powers for political mobilization and fewer incentives for prudent behavior.

Situations

The analysis of systemic differences helps to illuminate differences in the situations or contexts in which leaders find themselves. Our quick tour of some of these varying situations includes: (1) short-run political coalitions; (2) long-run political coalitions; and (3) the role of crisis and foreign policy initiation.

Short-run Coalitions

As noted earlier, the afficionados of party government in the United States typically have in mind the clear majority rule situation, the Westminster model. But majority party government is relatively rare in parliamentary systems across the democratic world. At a minimum, it rests upon a first-past-the-post voting system that gives a seat to the candidate with a plurality. That condition helps create a majority rule situation but guarantees it only when no more than two parties compete.

In most countries, various kinds of coalition arrangements prevail. The tendency of such coalitions (since the coalition patterns tend to be stable) is to provide a certain degree of stability to government. The tiny liberal Free Democratic party in West Germany, for instance, largely has controlled or otherwise deeply influenced economic and foreign policy under both Christian Democratic and Social Democratic governments. Similarly, the small bloc of religious parties in Israel has consistently controlled policy and ministerial posts that deal with religious affairs. Such stability, of course, can turn into deadlock when new forces outside the interparty coalition arise to challenge the status quo. It also gives a small political minority unusually great power.

Under normal circumstances, American presidents are in a complex coalition arrangement in spite of their presumptive control of the executive and the existence of only two parties in Congress. But unlike the coalition-based prime minister, a president's coalitions are fluid rather than wholly structured by party. What remains unclear is whether his position is any more disadvantageous than the head of a coalition government, who is certainly constrained by arrangements agreed on by the parties forming a government. A president can ask for more, but with greater risk of failure. Continued failure, or more importantly the perception of failure, corrodes his political standing.

In any event, rarely in American politics do elections create even a moment of party government. But such moments do occur and when they do there usually are momentous legislative and policy consequences. One of the most critical conditions for producing party government has to do with the generation, dissipation, and regeneration of long-run political coalitions.

Long-run Coalitions

The American political party system is both the oldest and most volatile competitive party system in the world. Democrats and Republicans (and the latter's ancestors) have held different positions and taken on different constituencies during different eras of American history.[21] The process by which the partisan plates beneath the political surface shift over a period of time is referred to in the vocabulary of American politics as the cycle of realignment. The traditional pattern of realignment requires the slow exhaustion of prior party alignments, the emergence of new political appeals and constituencies between the parties, and, ultimately, new patterns of voting. Typically, realigning moments are associated with unusual clarity in mass political cleavages and in partisan divisions among elites.[22] Considerable policy innovation usually occurs because of the relative ease of mobilizing political support in contrast to more normal times. These rare moments of realignment, in classic form, produce a kind of party government for a time in which substantial majorities in Congress are assembled in support of a party program. In modern times, this has meant support of the president's program.

These classic symptoms of realignment are uniquely American, although the more general phenomenon of coalition shift is not. The symptoms are unique because of the independence of the governing branches in the United States and the absence of the party discipline that is found in parliamentary systems. However, long-term and substantial coalition shifts occur in other systems and effectively alter the political equation. For instance, the erosion of the French Communist party (which lost more than half its electoral support in a thirty-year period) has enhanced the prospects of the democratic Left in French politics. The rise of the centrist Liberal-Social Democratic alliance in Britain, whatever its long run prospects, places pressure on the Labour party to moderate its appeals.

During briefer periods of time, too, there can be an exhaustion of political initiative that results from the decay of a prevailing coalition or party. The capacity to cope with larger problems declines. Such symptoms arose in the final years of the various Conservative governments in Britain that ruled between 1951 and 1964 and, again, during the sunset of the tattered Labour government in the late 1970s—a government that was sustained only by the forbearance of smaller parties in not bringing the Callaghan government to an end. Similarly, the victory of the Likud coalition in Israel in 1977 reflected the development of new political forces at a time when the Israeli Labor coalition also had lost its energy and direction.

The life cycle of political coalitions cannot have exactly the same symptoms in parliamentary systems as it does in the United States because parliamentary party discipline is the accepted norm under all conditions. The processes of energizing, of ennervation, and of revitalization go on everywhere, however. As the political forces that generate a government wind down, initiative declines, caution replaces risk taking, survivability displaces direction. Intraparty and intragovernmental rifts become more noticeable. In short, the prospects for governing on behalf of clear goals diminish.

In an absolute pinch, of course, an exhausted government usually can be saved in parliament, if not with the electorate. That, of course, is an advantage that presidents rarely have. Regime exhaustion and political travail are more directly and overtly connected in the American system. But even though party discipline can buffet some of the most severe challenges to a government, its ultimate effects on political vitality are far more limited than a purely legislative comparison between systems would suggest. Harold MacMillan in 1957-59 was not in the same situation as Alec Douglas-Home in 1964; nor was Helmut Schmidt in 1981-82 able to embark upon the initiatives that Willy Brandt had in 1969-71. "Political time"—the life cycle of regime creation and dissolution—needs different indicators across political systems, but the basic concept has universal properties.[23]

Crisis

Can the American president act quickly and decisively in the face of crisis? Is there any inherent difference between the president's ability to do so and that of a cabinet-parliamentary government? The word *inherent* in this formulation is important; but first we need to determine what a crisis is. A crisis generally is what someone in a leadership position declares it to be, but only if widespread agreement follows.

Usually, crisis entails the existence of a new and unanticipated situation that carries with it strong decisional costs and risks. The Argentine invasion of the Falklands/Malvinas in 1982 produced a crisis in London because the costs of any reaction would be strong and risk bearing. Either the fleet would go to war and risk defeat thousands of miles away or it would stay home and the Thatcher government, along with the British nation, would risk political humiliation.

Foreign policy crises are apt to generate greater support of leadership responses because they engage the whole of the nation. The American reaction to the Soviet invasion of Afghanistan indicated, though, how closely foreign and domestic interests are linked, when grain farmers and their representatives in Washington protested against the embargo of American wheat to the Soviet Union that was imposed by the Carter administration. Domestic crises are less likely to meet with agreement on an appropriate response because they engage the attention of diverse interests that see their concerns linked positively or, more often, adversely to proposed solutions.

Two aspects of crisis management stand out, however, as a consequence of the differences between presidential and parliamentary systems. In the American system, the ability to initiate action decisively is a presidential advantage, and, if the crisis is exceptionally brief, decision and action usually can be implemented to some resolution. If, however, the president's action requires congressional approval or if there is litigation, the system of separation of powers can be limiting. For example, the Supreme Court's rejection of Truman's seizure of the steel mills in the midst of a steelworkers' strike during the Korean War is an obvious case of the blunting of presidential initiative. Prime ministers, on the other hand, tend to feel the limits of response early because they have to carry their cabinet with them, especially if the government is a multiparty coalition. Granted, presidents have an advantage when decisive and brief action is possible before others have much of an opportunity to act. But the more protracted the action, the more the complexity of the American system tends to take effect and the greater the tendency of normal politics to prevail. In parliamentary systems, the advantages and disadvantages appear to be the mirror image of the presidential system: initial action involves a fair amount of consultation but fewer impediments arise thereafter.

Although system does structure how crises are managed, more is likely to depend both upon the individual leader's definition of what the crisis is and upon the leader's temperament when making decisions under stress. In this regard, because of the status of the president as decision maker in chief, presidents vary more than prime ministers. Some presidents, such as Nixon, will have an obsession with secrecy; others, like Eisenhower, will make more use of consultative processes. The political system itself, however, is unlikely to influence the probabilities for successful outcomes. In Suez, Eden acted decisively and failed; in the Falklands/Malvinas crisis, Thatcher acted decisively and succeeded. In the *Mayaguez* incident of 1975, Ford acted decisively and, reputedly at least, won, even though more were killed than were rescued from the revolutionary Cambodian forces. Five years later, a similar, although much more complicated, rescue effort failed, probably sealing Carter's political fate.

In sum, the American president can act quickly and decisively in a crisis. That does not mean that he will. Kennedy took his time during the Cuban missile crisis, both to size up alternatives and to reach a consensus among his advisers. Nor does it mean that, after he acts, the president's initiatives will be accepted by the other branches of government. Above all, decisiveness does not necessarily mean success. Machiavelli may be a better guide here than Montesquieu. That consideration leads us naturally enough to leaders and to leadership roles.

Leaders

Leadership Roles

The American president, Clinton Rossiter pointed out in his classic book on the presidency, wears many hats.[24] He plays more roles than top leaders in other systems. Despite the familiar separation-of-powers system, American institutions do not differentiate sharply in their roles. Rather, they share power. Modern European political institutions, to the contrary, differentiate roles while concentrating power.[25]

Among the many hats worn by the American president, according to Rossiter, are those of chief of state, chief executive, chief diplomat, commander-in-chief, and chief legislator. Yet these are only the constitutional roles. To them Rossiter adds several others that have been grafted onto the modern presidency through practice: party chief, opinion leader and representative, manager of prosperity, leader of the Western alliance, and chief administrator. Of the five formal roles, the one that is fixed on most readily, in contrasting the American system with others—usually, as rendered, to the detriment of the American system—is that of chief legislator.

We have noted that presidents as party leaders normally embody their party and penetrate the apparatus of its national organization. Even the exceptions to this rule—Truman and Ford, who as vice-presidential successors had difficulties controlling their parties, and Carter—ultimately were able to secure the apparatus and to win over the minds if not the hearts of their party elites. In general, the personalized control of a party is more difficult to attain for parliamentary political leaders, whose parties are far better organized and institutionalized than their American equivalents. On the whole, within their parties European prime ministers are at least as much a representative or internal mediator as the dominant leader. In countries as different as Italy and Japan, for example, the larger parties have distinctive factions. In Japan, these are formalized. The factions encourage deal cutting, logrolling, and rotation.

Some of the American president's many roles—notably, commander-in-chief, chief diplomat, alliance leader, and prosperity manager (in an increasingly internationalized economy)—result from, or have become more important because of, the central role that the United States plays in world affairs. As chief executive and administrator, it is the president's name rather than his presence that counts. Since 1956, when Rossiter published *The American Presidency,* the role of the White House staff and the EOP have grown markedly in importance. The example of the Reagan presidency in the halcyon days before the Iran-contra scandal emerged seemed to suggest that it was far more important that a president be a chief than a chief executive.[26] In the aftermath of this episode, however, we are reminded that a president also cannot avoid being a chief executive.

Presidents come wrapped in the cloak of the state and are not merely the heads of governments, as are prime ministers. That could be one reason why presidents' elections are so often greeted as a process of national legitimation and unity instead of just the outcome of a partisan struggle. Efforts to diminish the pomp of the chief-of-state role also strip away the notion that the occupant of the office is someone special. Playing on populist sentiments and, perhaps, his own instincts, Carter managed, to his detriment, to strip away all illusions of state majesty from the presidency. Ford and Truman also thought better of humility than majesty (each followed particularly "royal" presidencies). But as Rossiter put it, the American presidency is both the most and the least political of offices.[27] In its guise as chief of state, it is the least directly political, although, of course, astute presidents know how to extract maximum political mileage from this aspect of the presidential role.

All political leaders have been placed in the position of "managing prosperity." Their fortunes are tied to their success or sheer luck with the economy. Yet economic interdependence and the emergence of a global economy has made the economic forces to be managed less obviously manipulable.

It is in the role of chief legislator and opinion leader and representative that, aside from the party leadership role, institutional differences are at their purest. As we have seen, one of the main differences between a president and a prime minister is that the former builds political coalitions after legislation is introduced and the latter, who serves in a parliamentary-cabinet government where political party discipline is paramount and assumed, is involved in building coalitions beforehand. A president is constantly engaged in calculating and recalculating legislative prospects and strategies. This requires, in a highly unpredictable environment, a form of continuous political mobilization.

Blending the roles of opinion leader (spokesman for the people), chief of state, and keeper of the peace and the economy with more overt political roles such as chief legislator and party leader means that highly diverse skills must be brought to the presidency by the person who holds the office. A good compass and the ability to articulate direction are, clearly, crucial requirements of the job; the test, however, as Rossiter himself observed, was how well all of these diverse elements could be blended and integrated—if they could. Surely, in this regard, the president's job is the most complex of all leadership positions. That is because it contains elements that provide it with both unusual power and unusual vulnerability.

Leaders

In view of the complexity of any leadership position, especially the American presidency, how can one define the job? And to what extent can leadership definitions make a difference?

Any leader in any organization of both reasonable complexity and competing goals and strategies is hostage to the priorities of others. However self-starting a leader may be, a president or prime minister is running a kind of variety show with different acts commanding attention. Some acts are staples, others vary according to the momentary rise of certain issues or perceived needs. As every variety show host needs a stand-up comedian and a vocalist, so every governmental leader needs a finance or budget minister and a foreign minister. But a health or education minister, like a juggler or dancing bear, does not have to be a constant booking for the leader.[28] The person at the top must have one and may desire to have the other.

There are, of course, differences between hosts and, thus, between variety shows. During television's first two decades in the United States, there were two enormously successful variety shows, one hosted by Ed Sullivan, a show business columnist for one of the New York tabloids, the other by Bob Hope, one of the most popular comedians of the era. Ed Sullivan had no discernible skills as an entertainer. His acts dominated the show; he merely introduced them. On the other hand, Bob Hope was a big part of his show. People tuned in to watch him. The acts kept him from being exhausted by filling up an hour's space.

Consider the analogy to leadership styles: Harold Wilson, Jimmy Carter, or Helmut Kohl as Ed Sullivan, mostly serving as host to the agendas of others, Margaret Thatcher, Ronald Reagan, or Willy Brandt fulfilling the Bob Hope role, proving unmistakable direction and flavor to the operation of government. Thatcher and Reagan are both endowed with a strong sense of what they want done and the ability to articulate their purposes with stunning clarity. It is difficult to misperceive their signals. For various reasons, neither Wilson nor Carter was clearly directive. Their parties, of course, were divided, but where Thatcher dumped the dissidents overboard, Wilson attempted to smooth over even deeper intraparty differences. Unlike Reagan, who knows his mind from conviction, Carter was open to facts or arguments that could move a decision this way or that, thus creating uncertainty as well as providing an invitation for more acts to gain a spot on his "show."

Holding individual differences constant, however, there also is something different about the presidential and prime ministerial roles that makes the president more of a host for others' agendas (an Ed Sullivan) than is the prime minister. Partly, this is because the prime minister is a party leader first, a government leader second, and the president is the reverse. Much of the agenda-pressing for a prime minister is done inside the party. A great deal also is done inside the cabinet or in forming it. Presidents may face pressures at their party conventions but only in rare instances (Ford in 1976, Carter, to a much lesser degree, in 1980) do the nominees fail to control the convention's platform. But a president, once installed, is theoretically at the head of an executive hierarchy. Whatever the reality, the expectation is that the buck will stop there, not with the secretary of some department. For an administration bent on booking many acts and pleasing a wide array of its party's contradictory constituencies, such as the Carter administration, the Ed Sullivan model becomes overwhelming.[29] Little direction is seen to be forthcoming, whether or not the president really is possessed of any. Unlike Ed Sullivan, such presidents rarely are returned by popular demand.

What difference, finally, does leadership make? The question tantalizes because we have no clear way of connecting leadership behavior to outcomes. We can begin at either end of this problem—the behavioral side or the results side. The behavioral side, we quickly see, depends greatly on which aspects of leadership we deem to be situationally appropriate. In the context of energizing government, simplicity is of the essence. One need not be a philosopher-king, but one needs to be a king (or queen). That, at least, appears to be the lesson we derive from those who have succeeded at giving direction to government, regardless of its ultimate wisdom. In this context, the extent to which constraints fail to paralyze choice is partly a consequence of the willingness to take risks. The more risk-averse leaders are, the greater the constraints will seem to be.

On the results side, we can infer the effects of leadership if we look carefully. Robert Putnam and his colleagues, for instance, illustrate both the limitations and the possibilities of leadership.[30] By studying various Italian regional governments, they conclude that performance is predicted almost perfectly by very broad indicators of regional, social, economic, and historical characteristics. However, when they look at regions with similar characteristics, they note differences from the expected prediction. The greater the difference, the more it appears that entrepreneurial leadership (or, alternatively, its absence) has made a difference in the region's performance.

Clearly, there is a tendency in modern democracies to expect too much from leaders. The Putnam et al. story is sobering in that regard. Yet, we can err excessively in the opposite direction too. And the Putnam et al. saga equally well suggests that possibility. What remains clouded, unfortunately, is the connection between outcomes and institutional factors, situations, and leadership styles.

A Final Word

Comparison is the basis of judgment. False comparisons idealize at least one of the alternatives or generalize from momentary discomforts. The perspective provided by sound comparative analysis makes complex what seemed so simple. The stark contrasts recede on closer inspection. More often, rather than difference in result, institutions give us differences in form.

The American political system generates a good deal of overt but often uncrystallized conflict. Because so much agenda generating and coalition building is done in the open in the United States, conflict is more visible and presidents often appear to be stymied. But governing is nowhere an easy matter. That perspective is necessary if we are to refine our questions and avoid drifting off into idealized alternatives.

Notes

1. Richard Rose, *The Capacity of the President: A Comparative Analysis* (Strathclyde: Centre for the Study of Public Policy, 1984), 14-15.
2. Ibid.
3. Ibid., 14-15.

4. Richard P. Nathan and Fred C. Doolittle, "The Untold Story of Reagan's 'New Federalism,' " *The Public Interest* 77 (Fall 1984): 96-105.
5. Richard Rose, "The Variability of Party Government: A Theoretical and Empirical Critique," *Political Studies* 17 (December 1969): 414.
6. James W. Ceaser, "Political Parties and Presidential Ambition," *Journal of Politics* 40 (August 1978): 708-741.
7. George W. Breslauer, *Khrushchev and Brezhnev as Leaders: Building Authority in Soviet Politics* (London: George Allen & Unwin, 1982).
8. See, for example, Colin Campbell, S. J., *Governments under Stress: Political Executives and Key Bureaucrats in Washington, London, and Ottawa* (Toronto: University of Toronto Press, 1983); and Margaret J. Wyszomirski, "The De-Institutionalization of Presidential Staff Agencies," *Public Administration Review* 42 (1982): 448-457.
9. Lloyd N. Cutler, "To Form a Government," *Foreign Affairs* 59 (Fall 1980): 126-143.
10. Rose, "The Variability of Party Government"; see also Anthony King, "Political Parties in Western Democracies: Some Skeptical Reflections," *Polity* 2 (Fall 1969): 111-141.
11. Alexander Hamilton, in *The Federalist Papers,* ed. Clinton Rossiter (New York: New American Library, 1961), no. 70, 424.
12. Anthony King, "Margaret Thatcher: The Style of a Prime Minister," in *The British Prime Minister,* 2d ed., ed. Anthony King (Durham, N.C.: Duke University Press, 1985), 96-140.
13. See, for example, Theodore J. Lowi, *The Personal President: Power Invested, Promise Unfulfilled* (Ithaca, N.Y.: Cornell University Press, 1985); and Bert A. Rockman, *The Leadership Question: The Presidency and the American System* (New York: Praeger, 1984).
14. See, for instance, Rose, *The Capacity of the President,* 62-78.
15. Dennis Kavanagh, "From Gentlemen to Players: Changes in Political Leadership," in *Britain: Progress and Decline,* ed. William L. Gwyn and Richard Rose, Tulane Studies in Political Science, vol. 17 (1980), 90-91; see also Rose, *The Capacity of the President,* 72-73.
16. Michael Lewis-Beck, "Comparative Economic Voting: Britain, France, Germany, Italy," *American Journal of Political Science* 30 (May 1986): 315-346.
17. On the declining grip of parties, see, for instance, Martin P. Wattenberg, *The Decline of American Political Parties, 1952-1980* (Cambridge, Mass.: Harvard University Press, 1984). On the "unifying" aspects of American presidential elections, see John H. Kessel, "The Seasons of Presidential Politics," *Social Science Quarterly* 58 (December 1977): 419-435; and Hugh Heclo, "Presidential and Prime Ministerial Selection," in *Perspectives on Presidential Selection,* ed. Donald R. Matthews (Washington, D.C.: Brookings Institution, 1973): 19-48.
18. Heclo, "Presidential and Prime Ministerial Selection," 48.
19. Rose, *The Capacity of the President;* Lowi, *The Personal President;* and Rockman, *The Leadership Question.*
20. See, for example, Joel D. Aberbach and Bert A. Rockman, "Clashing Beliefs within the Executive Branch: The Nixon Administration Bureaucracy," *American Political Science Review* 70 (June 1976): 456-468. A lengthy discussion of Reagan administration efforts to gain control of the bureaucracy is in Bert A. Rockman, "USA: Government under President Reagan," in *Jahrbuch zur Staats- und Verwaltungswissenschaft,* ed. Thomas Ellwein et al. (Baden-Baden: Nomos Verlag, 1987): 286-308.

21. See, for instance, Benjamin Ginsberg, *The Consequences of Consent: Elections, Citizen Control and Popular Acquiescence* (Reading, Mass.: Addison-Wesley, 1982).
22. For example, see Paul Allen Beck, "The Electoral Cycle and Patterns of American Politics," *British Journal of Political Science* 9 (April 1979): 129-156; and David W. Brady, "Critical Elections, Congressional Parties and Clusters of Policy Changes," *British Journal of Political Science* 8 (January 1978): 79-99.
23. Stephen Skowronek, "Presidential Leadership in Political Time," in this volume.
24. Clinton Rossiter, *The American Presidency* (New York: Mentor Books, 1956).
25. Samuel P. Huntington, "Political Modernization: America vs. Europe," in *Political Order in Changing Societies,* ed. Samuel P. Huntington (New Haven: Yale University Press, 1968), 93-139.
26. Richard Rose, "The President: A Chief but Not an Executive," *Presidential Studies Quarterly* 7 (Winter 1977): 5-20.
27. Rossiter, *The American Presidency.*
28. See, in this regard, Richard Rose, "British Government: The Job at the Top," in *Presidents and Prime Ministers,* ed. Richard Rose and Ezra N. Suleiman (Washington, D.C.: American Enterprise Institute, 1980), 1-49.
29. According to Heclo, the White House Office of Public Liaison virtually became another interest group making claims on the presidential agenda. See Hugh Heclo, "The Changing Presidential Office," in *Politics and The Oval Office: Towards Presidential Governance,* ed. Arnold J. Meltsner (San Francisco: Institute for Contemporary Studies, 1981), 161-184.
30. Robert D. Putnam, et al., "Explaining Institutional Success: The Case of Italian Regional Government," *American Political Science Review* 77 (March 1983): 55-74.

Part II

ELEMENTS OF PRESIDENTIAL POWER

A longstanding issue in the life sciences is the "nature-nurture" or heredity versus environment controversy. Do people turn out as they do because of their genetic makeup at birth or because of external forces that influence their lives afterward? Theologians argue a third position, free will: we are masters, not prisoners, of our fate. In truth, of course, the answer is some blend of "all of the above": our lives are determined by what we bring into the world, what happens to us later, and what choices we make. So it is with the power of the presidency, which is shaped first by the Constitution—the presidency's "genetic code"; second, by the political environment in which the presidency functions; and third, by a free will element—the political skills and personality that each president brings to the office.

To many students of government and politics, the most impressive thing about the American political system has been the capacity of the Constitution to endure by adapting to changing conditions. In Chapter 5, Jeffrey Tulis traces the development of "The Two Constitutional Presidencies"—the enduring one that the framers defined in 1787 and whose formal provisions remain substantially unaltered, and the adapted one that Woodrow Wilson prescribed and that most twentieth-century presidents have practiced.

Tulis is less than sanguine about the harmony of the blend between the two constitutions. Both the framers and Wilson, he shows, defined the presidency in terms of "energy"—a "vigorous executive," in Alexander Hamilton's phrase.[1] But in the framers' view, presidential energy was to derive from the Constitution itself, particularly its provisions for a unitary executive with ample enumerated powers and the prospect for reelection. Popular leadership by the president, which to the framers was a synonym for demagoguery, was to be avoided at all costs. In the second constitutional presidency, however, popular leadership is regarded as the very essence of energy in the presidency: "Woodrow Wilson prescribes" what "*The Federalist* and the Constitution proscribe." In Tulis's view, "Many of the dilemmas and frustrations of the modern presidency may be traced to the president's anbiguous constitutional station, a vantage place composed of conflicting elements."

Because the constitutional, environmental, and skill elements of presidential power are parts of a unified institution, it is not surprising that Tulis's discussion of the presidency and the Constitution leads him to consider the relationship between the presidency and the people. Stephen Skowronek's concern in "Presidential Leadership in Political Time" is with the political environment more broadly defined: not just the people, but also legislators, interest groups, and other political elites.

Skowronek argues that "a broad view of American political development reveals patterned sequences of political change with corresponding patterns in presidential performance." A sequence begins when voters hand the old ruling coalition a stunning electoral defeat. The challenge for the newly elected president is to undermine the "institutional support for opposition interests," restructure "institutional relations between state and society," and secure "the dominant position of a new political coalition"—in short, to build a "regime" that will survive his administration. Some presidents who came to office after such an election failed to meet this challenge, and even for those who succeeded, their accomplishment contained the ingredients of its own eventual demise. Each "success created a new establishment," concludes Skowronek, which eventually became old and politically vulnerable.

In what Skowronek calls "political time," the Jacksonian regime of the nineteenth century corresponds to the New Deal regime of the twentieth. The election of 1828 comes at a "parallel juncture" with the election of 1932, Andrew Jackson with Franklin D. Roosevelt, James K. Polk with John F. Kennedy, and Franklin Pierce with Jimmy Carter. President and system—accent on the system—are the basic ingredients of Skowronek's understanding of the American presidency.

President and system—accent on the president—is the concern of those who write about the third element of presidential power: the political skills and personalities of individual presidents. Most students of presidential skill have dwelled on technique: bargaining, persuasion, rhetoric, management, and the like. Paul J. Quirk looks instead at "Presidential Competence" to exercise such skills, asking "what must a president know?" Quirk rejects the widely advocated "self-reliant" model of presidential competence as impossibly demanding and the "minimalist" or "chairman of the board" model as not demanding enough. His own model calls for "strategic competence": presidents need not know everything if they know how to find what they need to know. Specifically, Quirk argues, presidents must pay enough attention to the substantive debates about important national issues so that they can evaluate policy recommendations and must keep the policy process sufficiently fluid that they hear a wide range of such recommendations. They also must have—or obtain the services of others who have—Washington experience, the better to promote their policy decisions once they make them.

Quirk's final point in his essay—that voters and commentators should study presidential candidates for signs of strategic competence—is not unlike James David Barber's first point in *The Presidential Character*, which urges them to examine candidates for evidence of psychological health. In Barber's view, presidential success depends above all on the president's having an "active-positive" personality.[2] But according to Chapter 8, "The Psychological Presidency," history belies his claim: only a modest share of the "great" presidents have been active-positives. This essay, which applauds Barber for drawing attention to the psychological aspects of the presidency, concludes by assessing his theory of presidential elections, the subject of Part III.

Whatever the relative weight of the constitutional, environmental, and skill elements may be—and the mix certainly will vary from president to president—presidential power as a whole tends to be less in second terms than in first terms, according to Michael Grossman, Martha Kumar, and Francis Rourke, the authors of "Second-term Presidencies." The roots of second-term weakness lie in presidential reelection campaigns, which usually are devoid of substance, in difficulties in keeping and recruiting talented officials to manage the bureaucracy, in cavalier treatment of Congress, and in overconfidence about the public's support. Underlying a reelected president's woes, of course, is the "immutable reality of . . . the Twenty-second Amendment," which defines second-term presidents as lame duck presidents.

Notes

1. Alexander Hamilton, James Madison, and John Jay, *The Federalist Papers*, with an introduction by Clinton Rossiter (New York: New American Library, 1961), no. 70, 423.
2. James David Barber, *The Presidential Character: Predicting Performance in the White House*, 3d ed. (Englewood Cliffs, N.J.: Prentice Hall, 1985).

5. THE TWO CONSTITUTIONAL PRESIDENCIES

Jeffrey K. Tulis

The modern presidency is buffeted by two "constitutions." Presidential action continues to be constrained and presidential behavior shaped by the institutions created by the original Constitution. The core structures established in 1789 and debated during the founding era remain essentially unchanged. For the most part, later amendments to the Constitution have left intact the basic features of the executive, legislative, and judicial branches of government. Great questions, such as the merits of unity or plurality in the executive, have not been seriously reopened. Because most of the structure persists, it seems plausible that the theory upon which the presidency was constructed remains relevant to its current functioning.[1]

Presidential and public understanding of the character of the constitutional system and of the president's place in it have changed, however. This new understanding is the "second constitution" under whose auspices presidents attempt to govern. Central to this second constitution is a view of statecraft that is in tension with the original Constitution—indeed is opposed to the founders' understanding of the presidency's place in the political system. The second constitution, which puts a premium on active and continuous presidential leadership of popular opinion, is buttressed by several institutional, although extraconstitutional, developments. These include the proliferation of presidential primaries as a mode of selection and the emergence of the mass media as a pervasive force.[2]

Many of the dilemmas and frustrations of the modern presidency may be traced to the president's ambiguous constitutional station, a vantage place composed of conflicting elements. The purpose of this chapter is to lay bare the theoretical core of each of the two constitutions in order to highlight those elements that are in tension between them.

To uncover the principles that underlie the original Constitution, this chapter relies heavily upon *The Federalist*, a set of papers justifying the Constitution that was written by three of its most articulate proponents, Alexander Hamilton, James Madison, and John Jay. The purpose of this journey back to the founders is not to point to their authority or to lament change. Neither is it meant to imply that all the supporters of the Constitution agreed with each of their arguments. *The Federalist* does represent, however, the most coherent articulation of the implications of, and interconnections among, the principles and practices that were generally agreed upon when the Constitution was ratified.[3]

The political thought of Woodrow Wilson is explored to outline the principles of the second constitution. Wilson self-consciously attacked *The Federalist* in his writings; as president he tried to act according to the dictates of his reinterpretation of the American political system. Presidents have continued to follow his example, and presidential scholars tend to repeat his arguments. Of course, most presidents have not thought through the issues Wilson discussed—they are too busy for that. But if pushed and questioned, modern presidents probably would (and occasionally do) justify their behavior with arguments that echo Wilson's. Just as *The Federalist* represents the deepest and most coherent articulation of generally held nineteenth-century understandings of the presidency, Wilson offers the most comprehensive theory in support of contemporary impulses and practices.

The Founding Perspective

Perhaps the most striking feature of the founding perspective, particularly in comparison with contemporary political analyses, is its synoptic character. The founders' task was to create a whole government, one in which the executive would play an important part, but only a part. By contrast, contemporary scholars of American politics often study institutions individually and thus tend to be partisans of "their institution" in its contests with other actors in American politics.[4] Presidency scholars often restrict their inquiries to the strategic concerns of presidents as they quest for power. Recovering the founding perspective gives one a way to think about the systemic legitimacy and utility of presidential power as well. To uncover such a synoptic vision, one must range widely in search of the principles that guided or justified the founders' view of the executive. Some of these principles are discussed most thoroughly in *The Federalist* in the context of other institutions, such as Congress or the judiciary.

The founders' general and far-reaching institutional analysis was preceded by a more fundamental decision of enormous import. Federalists and Anti-Federalists alike sought a government devoted to limited ends. In contrast to polities that attempt to shape the souls of its

citizenry and foster certain excellences or moral
deeply into the "private" sphere, the founders
to be limited to ~~~~ 'ishing and securin~~~~   s
would extend only u~~~~   ~~~~ of pro~~~~   and
fostering liberty for the ex~~~~   would still
be necessary, but it would ~~~~   ~~~~ rather than
imposed upon them.

Proponents and critics of the Constitution agreed about the proper
ends of government, but they disagreed over the best institutional means
to secure them.[5] Some critics of the Constitution worried that its
institutions actually would undermine or subvert its limited liberal
ends. While these kinds of arguments were settled *politically* by the
federalist victory, *The Federalist* concedes that they were not resolved
fundamentally, since they continued as problems built into the structure
of American politics.

"[Is] a vigorous executive . . . inconsistent with the genius of
republican government"? The founders hoped that executive energy
and republican freedom were compatible, but they were not certain.[6]

Demagoguery

The founders worried especially about the danger that a powerful
executive might pose to the system if his power were derived from the
role of popular leader.[7] For most Federalists *demagogue* and *popular
leader* were synonyms, and nearly all references to popular leaders in
their writings are pejorative. Demagoguery, combined with majority
tyranny, was regarded as the peculiar vice to which democracies were
susceptible. While much historical evidence supported this insight, the
founders were made more acutely aware of the problem by the presence
in their own midst of popular leaders such as Daniel Shays, who led an
insurrection in Massachusetts. The founders' preoccupation with
demagoguery may appear today as quaint, yet it may be that we do not
fear it today because the founders were so successful in institutionally
proscribing some forms of it.

The original Greek meaning of *demagogue* was simply "leader of
the people," and the term was applied in premodern times to
champions of the people's claim to rule as against aristocrats and
monarchs. As James Ceaser points out, the term has been more
characteristically applied to a certain *quality* of leadership—that which
attempts to sway popular passions. Since most speech contains a mix of
rational and passionate appeals, it is difficult to specify demagoguery
with precision. But as Ceaser argues, one cannot ignore the phenomenon because it is difficult to define, and he suggests that it possesses at
least enough intuitive clarity that few would label Dwight Eisenhower,

for example, a demagogue, while most would not hesitate to so label Joseph McCarthy. The key characteristic of demagoguery seems to be an *excess* of passionate appeals. Ceaser categorizes demagogues according to the kinds of passions that are summoned, dividing these into "soft" and "hard" types.

The soft demagogue tends to flatter his constituents, "by claiming that they know what is best, and makes a point of claiming his closeness (to them) by manner or gesture." [8] The hard demagogue attempts to create or encourage divisions among the people in order to build and maintain his constituency. Typically, this sort of appeal employs extremist rhetoric that ministers to fear. James Madison worried about the possibility of class appeals that would pit the poor against the wealthy. But the hard demagogue might appeal to a very different passion. "Excessive encouragement of morality and hope" might be employed to create a division between those alleged to be compassionate, moral, or progressive, and those thought insensitive, selfish, or backward. Hard demagogues are not restricted to the right or to the left. [9]

Demagogues also can be classified by their object. Here the issue becomes more complicated. Demagoguery might be good if it were a means to a good end, such as preservation of a decent nation or successful prosecution of a just war. The difficulty is to ensure by institutional means that demagoguery would be employed only for good ends and not simply to satisfy the overweening ambition of an immoral leader or potential tyrant. How are political structures created that permit demagoguery when appeals to passion are needed but proscribe it for normal politics?

The founders did not have a straightforward answer to this problem, perhaps because there is no unproblematic institutional solution. Yet they did address it indirectly in two ways: they attempted both to narrow the range of acceptable demagogic appeals through the architectonic act of founding itself and to mitigate the effects of such appeals in the day-to-day conduct of governance through the particular institutions they created. Certainly they did not choose to make provision for the institutional encouragement of demagoguery in time of crisis, refusing to adopt, for example, the Roman model of constitutional dictatorship for emergencies. [10] Behind their indirect approach may have been the thought that excessive ambition needs no institutional support and the faith that in extraordinary circumstances popular rhetoric, even forceful demagoguery, would gain legitimacy through the pressure of necessity.

Many references in *The Federalist* and in the ratification debates over the Constitution warn of demagogues of the hard variety who through divisive appeals would aim at tyranny. *The Federalist* literally begins and ends with this issue. In the final paper Hamilton offers "a lesson of moderation to all sincere lovers of the Union [that] ought to put them on their guard against hazarding anarchy, civil war, a perpetual alienation of the states from each other, and perhaps the military despotism of a victorious demagogue." [11] The founders' concern with "hard" demagoguery was not merely, though it was partly, a rhetorical device designed to facilitate passage of the Constitution. It also reveals a concern to address the kinds of divisions and issues exploited by hard demagoguery. From this perspective, the founding can be understood as an attempt to *settle* the large issue of whether the one, few, or many ruled (in favor of the many "through" a constitution), to reconfirm the *limited* purposes of government (security, prosperity, and the protection of rights), and thereby give effect to the distinction between public and private life. At the founding, these large questions were still matters of political dispute. Hamilton argued that adoption of the Constitution would settle these perenially devisive questions for Americans, replacing those questions with smaller, less contentious issues. Hamilton called this new American politics a politics of "administration," distinguishing it from the traditional politics of disputed ends. If politics were transformed and narrowed in this way, thought Hamilton, demagogues would be deprived of part of their once powerful arsenal of rhetorical weapons because certain topics would be rendered illegitimate for public discussion. By constituting an American understanding of politics, the founding would also reconstitute the problem of demagoguery. [12]

If the overriding concern about demagoguery in the extraordinary period before the ratification of the Constitution was to prevent social disruption, division, and possibly tyranny, the concerns expressed through the Constitution for normal times were broader: to create institutions that would be most likely to generate and execute good policy or be most likely to resist bad policy. Underlying the institutional structures and powers created by the Constitution are three principles designed to address this broad concern: representation, independence of the executive, and separation of powers.

Representation

As the founders realized, the problem with any simple distinction between good and bad law is that it is difficult to provide clear criteria to distinguish the two in any particular instance. It will not do to suggest that in a democracy good legislation reflects the majority will. A majority may tyrannize a minority, violating its rights; even a non-tyrannical majority may be a foolish one, preferring policies that do not further its interests. These considerations lay behind the founders' distrust of "direct" or "pure" democracy.[13]

Yet an alternative understanding—that legislation is good if it objectively furthers the limited ends of the polity—is also problematic. It is perhaps impossible to assess the "interests" of a nation without giving considerable attention to what the citizenry considers its interests to be. This consideration lies behind the founders' animus toward monarchy and aristocracy.[14] Identifying and embodying the proper weight to be given popular opinion and the appropriate institutional reflections of it is one of the characteristic problems of democratic constitutionalism. The founders' understanding of republicanism as representative government reveals this problem and the Constitution's attempted solution.

Practically, the founders attempted to accommodate these two requisites of good government by four devices. First, they established popular election as the fundamental basis of the Constitution and of the government's legitimacy. They modified that requirement by allowing "indirect" selection for some institutions (for example, the Senate, Court, and presidency), that is, selection by others who were themselves chosen by the people. With respect to the president, the founders wanted to elicit the "sense of the people," but they feared an inability to do so if the people acted in a "collective capacity." They worried that the dynamics of mass politics would at best produce poorly qualified presidents and at worst open the door to demagoguery and regime instability. At the same time, the founders wanted to give popular opinion a greater role in presidential selection than it would have if Congress chose the executive. The institutional solution to these concerns was the Electoral College, originally designed as a semi-autonomous locus of decision for presidential selection, and chosen by state legislatures at each election.[15]

Second, the founders established differing lengths of tenure for officeholders in the major national institutions, which corresponded to the institutions' varying "proximity" to the people. House members were to face reelection every two years, thus making them more responsive to constituent pressure than members of the other national institutions. The president was given a four-year term, sufficient time, it was thought, to "contribute to the firmness of the executive" without justifying "any alarm for the public liberty." [16]

Third, the founders derived the authority and formal power of the institutions and their officers ultimately from the people but immediately from the Constitution, thus insulating officials from day-to-day currents of public opinion, while allowing assertion of deeply felt and widely shared public opinion through constitutional amendment.

Finally, the founders envisioned that the extent of the nation itself would insulate governing officials from sudden shifts of public opinion. In his well-known arguments for an extended republic, Madison reasoned that large size would improve democracy by making the formation of majority factions difficult. But again, argued Madison, extent of the territory and diversity of factions would not prevent the formation of a majority if the issue was an important one.[17]

It is the brakes upon public opinion rather than the provision for its influence that causes skepticism today.[18] Because popular leadership is so central to modern theories of presidency, the rationale behind the founders' distrust of "direct democracy" should be noted specifically. This issue is raised dramatically in *The Federalist* no. 49, in which Madison addresses Jefferson's suggestion that "whenever two of the three branches of government shall concur in [the] opinion ... that a convention is necessary for altering the Constitution, *or correcting breaches of it,* a convention shall be called for the purpose." Madison recounts Jefferson's reasoning: because the Constitution was formed by the people it rightfully ought to be modified by them. Madison admits "that a constitutional road to the decision of the people ought to be marked out and kept open for great and extraordinary occasions." But he objects to bringing directly to the people disputes among the branches about the extent of their authority. In the normal course of governance, such disputes could be expected to arise fairly often. In our day they would include, for example, the war powers controversy, the impoundment controversy, and the issue of executive privilege.

Madison objects to recourse to "the people" on three basic grounds. First, popular appeals would imply "some defect" in the government: "Frequent appeals would, in great measure, deprive the government of that veneration which time bestows on everything, and without which perhaps the wisest and freest governments would not possess the requisite stability." *The Federalist* points to the institutional benefits of popular veneration—stability of government and the enhanced authority of its constitutional officers. Second, the tranquility of the society as a whole might be disturbed. Madison expresses the fear that an enterprising demagogue might reopen disputes over "great national questions" in a political context less favorable to their resolution than the Constitutional Convention.

Finally, Madison voices "the greatest objection of all" to frequent appeals to the people: "The decisions which would probably result from such appeals would not answer the purpose of maintaining the constitutional equilibrium of government." The executive might face political difficulties if frequent appeals to the people were permitted because other features of his office (his singularity, independence, and

e powers) would leave him at a rhetorical disadvantage in
ith the legislature. Presidents will be "generally the objects of
their administrations ... liable to be discolored and
jular," Madison argued. "The Members of the legisla-
tures on the other hand are numerous. . . . Their connections of blood,
of friendship, and of acquaintance embrace a great proportion of the
most influential part of society. The nature of their public trust implies
a personal influence among the people." [19]

Madison realizes that there may be circumstances "less adverse to
the executive and judiciary departments." If the executive power were
"in the hands of a peculiar favorite of the people ... the public decision
might be less swayed in favor of the [legislature]. But still it could never
be expected to turn on the true merits of the question." The ultimate
reason for the rejection of "frequent popular appeals" is that they
would undermine *deliberation,* and result in bad public policy:

> The *passions,* not the *reason,* of the public would sit in judgment.
> But it is the reason alone, of the public, that ought to control and
> regulate the government. The passions ought to be controlled and
> regulated by the government.[20]

There are two frequent misunderstandings of the founders'
opinion on the deliberative function of representation. The first is that
they naively believed that deliberation constituted the whole of legislative politics—that there would be no bargaining, logrolling, or nonde-
liberative rhetorical appeals. The discussion of Congress in *The
Federalist* nos. 52 to 68 and in the Constitutional Convention debates
reveals quite clearly that the founders understood that the legislative
process would involve a mixture of these elements. The founding task
was to create an institutional context that made deliberation most
likely, not to assume that it would occur "naturally" or, even in the best
of legislatures, predominantly.[21]

The second common error, prevalent in leading historical accounts
of the period, is to interpret the deliberative elements of the founders'
design as an attempt to rid the legislative councils of "common men"
and replace them with "better sorts"—more educated and, above all,
more propertied individuals.[22] Deliberation, in this view, is the
byproduct of the kind of person elected to office. The public's opinions
are "refined and enlarged" because refined individuals do the governing. While this view finds some support in *The Federalist* and was a
worry of several Anti-Federalists, the founders' Constitution places
much greater emphasis upon the formal structures of the national
institutions than upon the backgrounds of officeholders.[23] Indeed, good
character and high intelligence, they reasoned, would be of little help to

the government if it resembled a direct democracy: "In all very numerous assemblies, of whatever characters composed, passion never fails to wrest the sceptre from reason. Had every Athenian citizen been a Socrates, every Athenian assembly would still have been a mob." [24]

The presidency thus was intended to be representative of the people, but not merely responsive to popular will. Drawn from the people through an election (albeit an indirect one), the president was to be free enough from the daily shifts in public opinion so that he could refine it and, paradoxically, better serve popular interests. Hamilton expresses well this element of the theory in a passage in which he links the problem of representation to that of demagoguery:

> There are those who would be inclined to regard the servile pliancy of the executive to a prevailing current in the community of the legislature as its best recommendation. But such men entertain very crude notions, as well of the purposes for which government was instituted, as of the true means by which public happiness may be promoted. The republican principle demands that the deliberative sense of the community should govern the conduct of those to whom they intrust the management of the affairs; but it does not require an unqualified complaisance to every transient impulse which the people may receive from the arts of men, who flatter their prejudices to betray their interests. . . . When occasions present themselves in which the interests of the people are at variance with their inclinations, it is the duty of the persons whom they have appointed to be the guardians of those interests to withstand the temporary delusion in order to give them time and opportunity for more cool and sedate reflection.[25]

Independence of the Executive

To "withstand the temporary delusions" of popular opinion, the executive was made independent. The office would draw its authority from the Constitution rather than from another governmental branch. The framers were led to this decision from their knowledge of the states, where according to John Marshall, the governments (with the exception of New York) lacked any structure "which could resist the wild projects of the moment, give the people an opportunity to reflect and allow the good sense of the nation time for exertion." As Madison stated at the convention, "Experience had proved a tendency in our governments to throw all power into the legislative vortex. The executives of the states are in general little more than Cyphers; the legislatures omnipotent."

While independence from Congress was the immediate practical need, it was a need based upon the close connection between legislatures and popular opinion. Because independence from public opinion was the source of the concern about the legislatures, the founders rejected James Wilson's arguments on behalf of popular election as a means of making the president independent of Congress.[26]

Independence of the executive created the conditions under which presidents would be most likely to adopt a different perspective from Congress on matters of public policy. Congress would be dominated by local factions that, according to plan, would give great weight to constituent opinion. The president, as Thomas Jefferson was to argue, was the only national officer "who commanded a view of the whole ground." Metaphorically, independence gave the president his own space within, and his own angle of vision upon the polity. According to the founding theory, these constituent features of discretion are entailed by the twin activities of executing the will of the legislature *and* leading a legislature to construct good laws to be executed, laws that would be responsive to long-term needs of the nation at large.[27]

Separation of Powers

The constitutional role of the president in lawmaking raises the question of the meaning and purpose of separation of powers. What is the sense of separation of power if power is shared among the branches of government? Clearly, legalists are wrong who have assumed that the founders wished to distinguish so carefully among executive, legislative, and judicial power as to make each the exclusive preserve of a particular branch. However, their error has given rise to another.

Political scientists, following Richard Neustadt, have assumed that since powers were not divided according to the principle of "one branch, one function," the founders made no principled distinction among kinds of power. Instead, according to Neustadt, they created "separate institutions sharing power." [28] The premise of that claim is that power is an entity that can be divided up to prevent any one branch from having enough to rule another. In this view, the sole purpose of separation of powers is to preserve liberty by preventing the arbitrary rule of any one center of power.

The Neustadt perspective finds some support in the founders' deliberations, and in the Constitution. Much attention was given to making each branch "weighty" enough to resist encroachment by the others. Yet this "checks and balances" view of separation of powers can be understood better in tandem with an alternative understanding of the concept: Powers were separated and structures of each branch differentiated in order to equip each branch to perform different tasks. Each branch would be superior (although not the sole power) in its own sphere and in its own way. The purpose of separation of powers was to make effective governance more likely.[29]

Ensuring the protection of liberty and individual rights was one element of effective governance as conceived by the founders, but not the only one. Government also needed to ensure the security of the nation and to craft policies that reflected popular will.[30] These three governmental objectives may conflict; for example, popular opinion might favor policies that violated rights. Separation of powers was thought to be an institutional way of accommodating the tensions between governmental objectives.

Table 5-1 presents a simplified view of the purposes behind the separation of powers. Note that the three objectives of government—popular will, popular rights, and self-preservation—are mixed twice in the Constitution; they are mixed among the branches and within each branch so that each objective is given priority in one branch. Congress and the president were to concern themselves with all three, but the priority of their concern differs, with "self preservation" or national security of utmost concern to the president.

The term "separation of powers" perhaps has obstructed understanding of the extent to which different structures were designed to give each branch the special quality needed to secure its governmental objectives. Thus, while the founders were not so naive as to expect that

Table 5-1   Separation of Powers

Objectives (in order of priority)	*Special qualities and functions (to be aimed at)*	*Structures and means*
Congress 1. Popular will 2. Popular rights 3. Self-preservation	Deliberation	a. Plurality b. Proximity (frequent House elections) c. Bicameralism d. Competent powers
President 1. Self-preservation 2. Popular rights 3. Popular will	Energy and "steady administration of law"	a. Unity b. Four-year term and reeligibility c. Competent powers
Court 1. Popular rights	"Judgment, not will"	a. Small collegial body b. Life tenure c. Power linked to argument

Congress would be simply "deliberative," they hoped that its plural membership and bicameral structure would provide necessary, if not sufficient, conditions for deliberation to emerge. Similarly, the president's "energy," it was hoped, would be enhanced by unity, the prospect of reelection, and substantial discretion. As we all know, the Court does not simply "judge" dispassionately; it also makes policies and exercises will. But the founders believed that it made no sense to have a Court if it were intended to be just like a Congress. The judiciary was structured to make the dispassionate protection of rights more likely, if by no means certain.

The founders differentiated powers as well as structures in the original design. These powers ("the executive power" vested in the president in Article II and "all legislative power herein granted," given to Congress in Article I) overlap and sometimes conflict. Yet both the legalists' view of power as "parchment distinction" and the political scientists' view of "separate institutions sharing power" provide inadequate guides to what happens and what was thought ought to happen when power collided. The founders urged that "line drawing" among spheres of authority be the product of political conflict among the branches, not the result of dispassionate legal analysis. Contrary to more contemporary views, they did not believe that such conflict would lead to deadlock or stalemate.[31]

Consider the disputes that sometimes arise from claims of "executive privilege." [32] Presidents occasionally refuse to provide information to Congress that its members deem necessary to carry out their special functions. They usually justify assertions of executive privilege on the grounds of either national security or the need to maintain the conditions necessary to sound execution, including the unfettered canvassing of opinions.

Both Congress and the president have legitimate constitutional prerogatives at stake: Congress has a right to know and the president a need for secrecy. How does one discover whether in any particular instance the president's claim is more or less weighty than Congress's? The answer will depend upon the circumstances—for example, the importance of the particular piece of legislation in the congressional agenda versus the importance of the particular secret to the executive. There is no formula independent of political circumstance with which to weigh such competing institutional claims. The most knowledgeable observers of those political conflicts are the parties themselves: Congress and the president.

Each branch has weapons at its disposal to use against the other. Congress can threaten to hold up legislation or appointments important to the president. Ultimately, it could impeach and convict him. For his part, a president may continue to "stonewall"; he may veto bills or fail to support legislation of interest to his legislative opponents; he may delay political appointments; and he may put the issue to public test, even submitting to an impeachment inquiry for his own advantage. The lengths to which presidents and Congresses are willing to go was thought to be a rough measure of the importance of their respective constitutional claims. Nearly always, executive-legislative disputes are resolved at a relatively low stage of potential conflict. In 1981, for example, President Ronald Reagan ordered Interior Secretary James Watt to release information to a Senate committee after the committee had agreed to maintain confidentiality. The compromise was reached after public debate and "contempt of Congress" hearings were held.

It is important to note that this political process is dynamic. Viewed at particular moments, the system may appear deadlocked; considered over time, considerable movement becomes apparent. Similar scenarios could be constructed for the other issues over which congressional and presidential claims to authority conflict, such as the use of executive agreements in place of treaties, the deployment of military force, or the executive impoundment of appropriated monies.[33]

While conflict may continue to be institutionally fostered or constrained in ways that were intended by the founders, one still may wonder whether their broad objectives have been secured and whether their priorities should be ours. At the outset of the present century, Woodrow Wilson mounted an attack on the founders' design, convinced that it had not secured its objectives. More importantly, his attack resulted in a reordering of these objectives in the understandings that presidents have of their roles. His theory underlies the second constitution that buffets the presidency.

The Modern Perspective

Woodrow Wilson's influential critique of *The Federalist* contains another synoptic vision. Yet his comprehensive reinterpretation of the constitutional order appears, at first glance, to be internally inconsistent. Between writing his classic dissertation, *Congressional Government,* in 1885, and the publication of his well-known series of lectures, *Constitutional Government in the United States,* in 1908, Wilson shifted his position on important structural features of the constitutional system.

Early in his career Wilson depicted the House of Representatives as the potential motive force in American politics and urged reforms to make it more unified and energetic. He paid little attention to the presidency or judiciary. In later years he focused his attention on the presidency. In his early writings Wilson urged a plethora of constitutional amendments that were designed to emulate the British parliamentary system, including proposals to synchronize the terms of representatives and senators with that of the president and to require presidents to choose leaders of the majority party as cabinet secretaries. Later Wilson abandoned formal amendment as a strategy, urging instead that the existing Constitution be reinterpreted to encompass his parliamentary views.

Wilson also altered his views at a deeper theoretical level. Christopher Wolfe has shown that while the "early" Wilson held a "traditional" view of the Constitution as a document whose meaning persists over time, the "later" Wilson adopted a historicist understanding, claiming that the meaning of the Constitution changed as a reflection of the prevailing thought of successive generations.[34]

As interesting as these shifts in Wilson's thought are, they all rest upon an underlying critique of the American polity that he maintained consistently throughout his career. Wilson's altered constitutional proposals, indeed his altered understanding of constitutionalism itself, ought to be viewed as a series of strategic moves designed to remedy the same alleged systemic defects. Our task here is to review Wilson's understanding of those defects and to outline the doctrine he developed to contend with them—a doctrine whose centerpiece would ultimately be the rhetorical presidency.

Wilson's doctrine can be nicely counterpoised to the founders' understanding of demagoguery, representation, independence of the executive, and separation of powers. For clarity, these principles will be examined here in a slightly different order than before: separation of powers, representation, independence of the executive, and demagoguery.

Separation of Powers

For Wilson, separation of powers was the central defect of American politics. He was the first and most sophisticated proponent of the now conventional argument that separation of powers is a synonym for "checks and balances," the negation of power by one branch over another. Yet Wilson's view was more sophisticated than its progeny because his ultimate indictment of the founders' conception was a functionalist one. Wilson claimed that under the auspices of the founders' view, formal and informal political institutions failed to promote true deliberation in the legislature and impeded energy in the executive.

Wilson characterized the founders' understanding as "Newtonian," a yearning for equipoise and balance in a machinelike system:

The admirable positions of the *Federalist* read like thoughtful applications of Montesquieu to the political needs and circumstances of America. They are full of the theory of checks and balances. The President is balanced off against Congress, Congress against the President, and each against the Court. . . . Politics is turned into mechanics under [Montesquieu's] touch. The theory of gravitation is supreme.[35]

The accuracy of Wilson's portrayal of the founders may be questioned. He reasoned backward from the malfunctioning system as he found it to how they must have intended it. Wilson's depiction of the system rather than his interpretation of the founders' intentions is of present concern.

Rather than equipoise and balance, Wilson found a system dominated by Congress, with several attendant functional infirmities: major legislation frustrated by narrow-minded committees, lack of coordination and direction of policies, a general breakdown of deliberation, and an absence of leadership. Extraconstitutional institutions— boss-led political parties chief among them—had sprung up to assume the functions not performed by Congress or the president, but they had not performed them well. Wilson also acknowledged that the formal institutions had not always performed badly, that some prior Congresses (those of Webster and Clay) and some presidencies (those of Washington, Adams, Jefferson, Jackson, Lincoln, Roosevelt, and, surprisingly, Madison) had been examples of forceful leadership.[36]

These two strands of thought—the growth of extraconstitutional institutions and the periodic excellence of the constitutional structures—led Wilson to conclude that the founders had mischaracterized their own system. The founders' rhetoric was "Newtonian," but their constitutional structure, like all government, was actually 'Darwinian." Wilson explains:

The trouble with the Newtonian theory is that government is not a machine but a living thing. It falls, not under the theory of the universe, but under the theory of organic life. It is accountable to Darwin, not to Newton. It is modified by its environment, necessitated by its tasks, shaped to its functions by the sheer pressure of life.[37]

The founders' doctrine had affected the working of the structure to the extent that the power of the political branches was interpreted mechanically and that many of the structural features reflected the Newtonian yearning. A tension arose between the "organic" core of the system and the "mechanical" understanding of it by politicians and citizens. Thus, "the constitutional structure of the government has hampered and limited [the president's] actions but it has not prevented [them.]" Wilson tried to resolve the tension between the understanding of American politics as Newtonian and its actual Darwinian character to make the evolution self-conscious and thereby more rational and effective.[38]

Wilson attacked the founders for relying on mere "parchment barriers" to effectuate a separation of powers. This claim is an obvious distortion of founding views. In *Federalist* nos. 47 and 48, the argument is precisely that the federal constitution, unlike earlier state constitutions, would *not* rely primarily upon parchment distinctions of power but upon differentiation of institutional structures.[39] However, through Wilson's discussion of parchment barriers an important difference between his and the founders' view of the same problem becomes visible. Both worried over the tendency of legislatures to dominate in republican systems.

To mitigate the danger posed by legislatures, the founders had relied primarily upon an independent president with an office structured to give its occupant the personal incentive and means to stand up to Congress when it exceeded its authority. These structural features included a nonlegislative mode of election, constitutionally fixed salary, qualified veto, four-year term, and indefinite reeligibility. Although the parchment powers of the Congress and president overlapped (contrary to Wilson's depiction of them), the demarcation of powers proper to each branch would result primarily from political interplay and conflict between the political branches rather than from a theoretical drawing of lines by the judiciary.[40]

Wilson offered a quite different view. First, he claimed that because of the inadequacy of mere parchment barriers, Congress, in the latter half of the nineteenth century, had encroached uncontested upon the executive sphere. Second, he contended that when the president's institutional check was employed it took the form of a "negative"— prevention of a bad outcome rather than provision for a good one. In this view separation of powers hindered efficient, coordinated, well-led policy.[41]

Wilson did not wish to bolster structures to thwart the legislature. He preferred that the president and Congress should be fully integrated into, and implicated in, each other's activities. Rather than merely assail Congress, Wilson would tame or, as it were, domesticate it. Separation would be replaced by institutionally structured cooperation. Cooperation was especially necessary because the president lacked the energy he needed, energy that could be provided only by policy backed by Congress and its majority. Although Congress had failed as a deliberative body, it could now be restored to its true function by presidential leadership that raised and defended key policies.

These latter two claims actually represent the major purposes of the Wilsonian theory: leadership and deliberation. Unlike the founders, who saw these two functions in conflict, Wilson regarded them as dependent upon each other. In "Leaderless Government" he stated:

> I take it for granted that when one is speaking of a representative legislature he means by an "efficient organization" an organization which provides for deliberate, and deliberative, action and which enables the nation to affix responsibility for what is done and what is not done. The Senate is deliberate enough; but it is hardly deliberative after its ancient and better manner. . . . The House of Representatives is neither deliberate nor deliberative. We have not forgotten that one of the most energetic of its recent Speakers thanked God, in his frankness, that the House was not a deliberative body. It has not the time for the leadership of argument. . . . For debate and leadership of that sort the House must have a party organization and discipline such as it has never had.[42]

At this point, it appears that the founders and Wilson differed on the means to common ends. Both wanted "deliberation" and an "energetic" executive, but each proposed different constitutional arrangements to secure those objectives. In fact, their differences went much deeper, for each theory defined deliberation and energy to mean different things. These differences, hinted at in the above quotation, will become clearer as we examine Wilson's reinterpretation of representation and independence of the executive.

Representation

In the discussion of the founding perspective, the competing requirements of popular consent and insulation from public opinion as a requisite of impartial judgment were canvassed. Woodrow Wilson gave much greater weight to the role of public opinion in the ordinary conduct of representative government than did the founders. Some scholars have suggested that Wilson's rhetoric and the institutional practices he established (especially regarding the nomination of presidential candidates) are the major sources of contemporary efforts toward a more "participatory" democracy. However, Wilson's understanding of representation, like his views on separation of powers, is more sophisticated than his followers'.[43]

Wilson categorically rejected the Burkean view of the legislator who is elected for his quality of judgment and position on a few issues and then left free to exercise that judgment:

> It used to be thought that legislation was an affair to be conducted by the few who were instructed for the benefit of the many who were uninstructed: that statesmanship was a function of

origination for which only trained and instructed men were fit. Those who actually conducted legislation and conducted affairs were rather whimsically chosen by Fortune to illustrate this theory, but such was the ruling thought in politics. The Sovereignty of the People, however . . . has created a very different practice. . . . It is a dignified proposition with us—is it not?—that as is the majority, so ought the government to be.[44]

Wilson did not think that his view was equivalent to "direct democracy" or to subservience to public opinion (understood, as it often is today, as response to public opinion polls). He favored an interplay between representative and constituent that would, in fact, educate the constituent. This process differed, at least in theory, from the older attempts to "form" public opinion: it did not begin in the minds of the elite but in the hearts of the mass. Wilson called the process of fathoming the people's desires (often only vaguely known to the people until instructed) "interpretation." Interpretation was the core of leadership for him.[45] Before we explore its meaning further, it will be useful to dwell upon Wilson's notion of the desired interplay between the "leader interpreter" and the people so that we may see how his understanding of deliberation differed from the founders'.

For the founders, deliberation meant reasoning on the merits of policy. The character and content of deliberation thus would vary with the character of the policy at issue. In "normal" times, there would be squabbles by competing interests. Deliberation would occur to the extent that such interests were compelled to offer and respond to arguments made by the others. The arguments might be relatively crude, specialized, and technical or they might involve matters of legal or constitutional propriety. But in none of these instances would they resemble the great debates over fundamental principles—for example, over the question whether to promote interests in the first place. Great questions were the stuff of crisis politics and the founders placed much hope in securing the distinction between crisis and normal political life.

Wilson effaced the distinction between "crisis" and "normal" political argument.

Crises give birth and a new growth to statesmanship because they are peculiarly periods of action . . . [and] also of unusual opportunity for gaining leadership and a controlling and guiding influence. . . . And we thus come upon the principle . . . that governmental forms will call to the work of the administration able minds and strong hearts constantly or infrequently, according as they do or do not afford *at all times* an opportunity of gaining and retaining a commanding authority and an undisputed leadership in the nation's councils.[46]

Woodrow Wilson's lament that little deliberation took place in Congress was not that the merits of policies were left unexplored but rather that because the discussions were not elevated to the level of major contests of principle the public generally did not interest itself. True deliberation, he urged, would rivet the attention of press and public, while what substituted for it in his day were virtually secret contests of interest-based factions. Wilson rested this view on three observations. First, the congressional workload was parceled among specialized standing committees, whose decisions usually were ratified by the respective houses without any general debate. Second, the arguments that did take place in committee were technical and structured by the "special pleadings" of interest groups, whose advocates adopted the model of legal litigation as their mode of discussion. As Wilson characterized committee debates:

> They have about them none of the searching, critical, illuminating character of the higher order of parliamentary debate, in which men are pitted against each other as equals, and urged to sharp contest and masterful strife by the inspiration of political principle and personal ambition, through the rivalry of parties and the competition of policies. They represent a joust between antagonistic interests, not a contest of principles.[47]

Finally, because debates were hidden away in committee, technical, and interest-based, the public cared little about them. "The ordinary citizen cannot be induced to pay much heed to the details, or even the main principles of lawmaking," Wilson wrote, "unless something more interesting than the law itself be involved in the pending decision of the lawmaker." For the founders this would not have been disturbing, but for Wilson the very heart of representative government was the principle of publicity: "The informing function of Congress should be preferred even to its legislative function." The informing function was to be preferred both as an end in itself and because the accountability of public officials required policies that were connected with one another and explained to the people. Argument from "principle" would connect policy and present constellations of policies as coherent wholes to be approved or disapproved by the people. "Principles, as statesmen conceive them, are threads to the labyrinth of circumstances." [48]

Wilson attacked separation of powers in an effort to improve leadership for the purpose of fostering deliberation. "Congress cannot, under our present system ... be effective for the instruction of public opinion, or the cleansing of political action." As mentioned at the outset of this chapter, Wilson first looked to Congress itself, specifically to its

Speaker, for such leadership. Several years after the publication of *Congressional Government,* Wilson turned his attention to the president. "There is no trouble now about getting the president's speeches printed and read, every word," he wrote at the turn of the century.[49]

Independence of the Executive

The attempt to bring the president into more intimate contact with Congress and the people raises the question of the president's "independence." Wilson altered the meaning of this notion, which originally had been that the president's special authority came independently from the Constitution, not from Congress or the people. The president's station thus afforded him the possibility and responsibility of taking a perspective on policy different from either Congress or the people. Wilson urged us to consider the president as receiving his authority independently through a mandate from the people. For Wilson, the president remained "special," but now because he was the only governmental officer with a national mandate.[50]

Political scientists today have difficulty in finding mandates in election years, let alone between them, because of the great number of issues and the lack of public consensus on them. Wilson understood this problem and urged the leader to sift through the multifarious currents of opinion to find a core of issues that he believed reflected majority will even if the majority was not yet fully aware of it. The leader's rhetoric could translate the people's felt desires into public policy. Wilson cited Daniel Webster as an example of such an interpreter of the public will:

> The nation lay as it were unconscious of its unity and purpose, and he called it into full consciousness. It could never again be anything less than what he said it was. It is at such moments and in the mouths of such interpreters that nations spring from age to age in their development.[51]

"Interpretation" involves two skills. First, the leader must understand the true majority sentiment underneath the contradictory positions of factions and the discordant views of the mass. Second, the leader must explain the people's true desires to them in a way that is easily comprehended and convincing.

Wilson's desire to raise politics to the level of rational disputation and his professed aim to have leaders educate the mass are contradictory. Candidly, he acknowledges that the power to command would require simplification of the arguments to accommodate the mass: "The arguments which induce popular action must always be broad and obvious arguments; only a very gross substance of concrete conception can make any impression on the minds of the masses." [52] Not only is argument simplified, but disseminating "information"—a common concern of contemporary democratic theory—is not the function of a deliberative leader in Wilson's view:

> Men are not led by being told what they don't know. Persuasion is a force, but not information; and persuasion is accomplished by creeping into the confidence of those you would lead. . . . Mark the simplicity and directness of the arguments and ideas of true leaders. The motives which they urge are elemental; the morality which they seek to enforce is large and obvious; the policy they emphasize, purged of all subtlety.[53]

Demagoguery

Wilson's understanding of leadership raises again the problem of demagoguery. What distinguishes a leader-interpreter from a demagogue? Who is to make this distinction? The founders feared that there was no institutionally effective way to exclude the demagogue if popular oratory during "normal" times was encouraged. Indeed the term *leader,* which appears a dozen times in *The Federalist,* is used disparagingly in all but one instance, and that one is a reference to leaders of the Revolution.[54]

Wilson was sensitive to this problem. "The most despotic of governments under the control of wise statesmen is preferable to the freest ruled by demagogues," he wrote. Wilson relied upon two criteria to distinguish the demagogue from the leader, one based upon the nature of the appeal, the other upon the character of the leader. The demagogue appeals to "the momentary and whimsical popular mood, the transitory or popular passion," while the leader appeals to "true" and durable majority sentiment. The demagogue is motivated by the desire to augment personal power, while the leader is more interested in fostering the permanent interests of the community. "The one [trims] to the inclinations of the moment, the other [is] obedient to the permanent purposes of the public mind." [55]

Theoretically, there are a number of difficulties with these distinctions. If popular opinion is the source of the leader's rhetoric, what basis apart from popular opinion itself is there to distinguish the "permanent" from the "transient?" If popular opinion is constantly evolving, what sense is there to the notion of "the permanent purposes of the public mind?" Yet the most serious difficulties are practical ones. Assuming it theoretically possible to distinguish the leader from the demagogue, how is that distinction to be incorporated into the daily operation of political institutions? Wilson offered a threefold response to this query.

First, he claimed that his doctrine contained an ethic that could be passed on to future leaders. Wilson hoped that politicians' altered understanding of what constituted success and fame could provide some security. He constantly pointed to British parliamentary practice, urging that long training in debate had produced generations of leaders and few demagogues. Wilson had taught at Johns Hopkins, Bryn Mawr, Wesleyan, and Princeton, and at each of those institutions he established debating societies modeled on the Oxford Union.[56]

Second, Wilson placed some reliance upon the public's ability to judge character:

> Men can scarcely be orators without that force of character, that readiness of resource, that cleverness of vision, that grasp of intellect, that courage of conviction, that correctness of purpose, and that instinct and capacity for leadership which are the eight horses that draw the triumphal chariot of every leader and ruler of freemen. We could not object to being ruled by such men.[57]

According to Wilson, the public need not appeal to a complex standard or theory to distinguish demagoguery from leadership, but could easily recognize "courage," "intelligence," and "correctness of purpose"— signs that the leader was not a demagogue. Wilson does not tell us why prior publics *have* fallen prey to enterprising demagogues, but the major difficulty with this second source of restraint is that public understanding of the leader's character would come from his oratory rather than from a history of his political activity or from direct contact with him. The public's understanding of character might be based solely on words.

Finally, Wilson suggests that the natural conservatism of public opinion, its resistance to innovation that is not consonant with the speed and direction of its own movement, will afford still more safety:

> Practical leadership may not beckon to the slow masses of men from beyond some dim, unexplored space or some intervening chasm: it must daily feel the road to the goal proposed, knowing that it is a slow, very slow, evolution to the wings, and that for the present, and for a very long future also, Society must walk, dependent upon practicable paths, incapable of scaling sudden heights.[58]

Woodrow Wilson's assurances of security against demagogues may seem unsatisfactory because they do not adequately distinguish the polity in which he worked from others in which demagogues have prevailed, including some southern states in this country. However, his arguments should be considered as much for the theoretical direction and emphases that they imply as for the particular weaknesses they reveal. Wilson's doctrine stands on the premise that the need for more energy in the political system is greater than the risk incurred through the possibility of demagoguery.[59] This represents a major shift, indeed a reversal, of the founding perspective. If Wilson's argument regarding demagoguery is strained or inadequate, it was a price he was willing to pay to remedy what he regarded as the founders' inadequate provision for an energetic executive.

Conclusion

Both constitutions were designed to secure an energetic president, but they differ over the legitimate sources and alleged virtues of popular leadership. For the founders, the president draws his energy from his authority. His authority rests upon his independent constitutional position. For Woodrow Wilson and for presidents ever since, power and authority are conferred directly by the people. *The Federalist* and the Constitution proscribe popular leadership. Woodrow Wilson prescribes it. Indeed, Wilson urges the president to minister continually to the moods of the people as a preparation for action. The founders' president was to look to the people, but less frequently, and to be judged by them, but usually after acting.

The second constitution gained legitimacy because presidents were thought to lack the resources necessary for the energy that was promised but not delivered by the first constitution. The second constitution did not replace the first, however. Because many of the founding structures persist while our understanding of the president's legitimate role has changed, the new view should be thought of as superimposed upon the old, altering without obliterating the original structure.

Many commentators have noted the tendency of recent presidents to raise public expectations about what they can achieve. Indeed, public disenchantment with government altogether may stem largely from disappointment in presidential performance, since the presidency is the most visible and important American political institution. Yet, rather than being the result of the peculiar personality traits of particular presidents, raised expectations are grounded in an institutional dilemma common to all modern presidents. Under the auspices of the second constitution, presidents continually must craft rhetoric that pleases their popular audience. But although presidents are always in a position to promise more, the only additional resource they have to secure their promises is public opinion itself. Because Congress retains the independent status conferred upon it by the first constitution, it can resist the president.

Of course, presidents who are exceptionally popular or gifted as orators can overcome the resistance of the legislature. For the political system as a whole this possibility is both good and bad. To the extent that the system requires periodic renewal through synoptic policies that reconstitute the political agenda, it is good. But the very qualities that are necessary to secure such large scale change tend to subvert the deliberative process, which makes unwise legislation or incoherent policy more likely.

Ronald Reagan's major political victories as president illustrate both sides of this systemic dilemma.[60] Without the second constitution, it would be difficult to imagine Reagan's success at winning tax reform legislation. His skillful coordination of a rhetorical and a legislative strategy overcame the resistance of thousands of lobbies that sought to preserve advantageous provisions of the existing tax code. Similarly, Social Security and other large policies that were initiated by Franklin D. Roosevelt during the New Deal may not have been possible without the second constitution.

On the other hand, Reagan's first budget victory in 1981 and the Strategic Defense Initiative (known as "Star Wars") illustrate how popular leadership can subvert the deliberative process or produce incoherent policy. The budget cuts of 1981 were secured with virtually no congressional debate. Among their effects was the gutting of virtually all of the Great Society programs passed by Lyndon B. Johnson, which themselves were the product of a popular campaign that circumvented the deliberative process.

When Congress does deliberate, as it has on Star Wars, the debate is often structured by contradictory forms of rhetoric, the product of the two constitutions. Presidents make different arguments to the people than they make to Congress. To the people President Reagan promised to strive for a new defense technology that would make nuclear deterrence obsolete. But to Congress, his administration argued that Star Wars was needed to supplement, not supplant, deterrence.[61] Each kind of argument can be used to impeach the other. Jimmy Carter found himself in the same bind on energy policy. When he urged the American people to support his energy plan, Carter contended that it was necessary to remedy an existing crisis. But to Congress he argued that the same policy was necessary to forestall a crisis.[62]

The second constitution promises energy, which is said to be inadequately provided by the first constitution. This suggests that the two constitutions fit together to form a more complete whole. Unfortunately, over the long run, the tendency of the second constitution to make extraordinary power routine undermines, rather than completes, the logic of the original constitution. Garry Wills has described how presidents, since John F. Kennedy, attempt to pit public opinion against their own executive establishment. Successors to a charismatic leader then inherit "a delegitimated set of procedures" and are themselves compelled "to go outside of procedures—further delegitimating the very office they [hold.]" [63] In President Reagan's case, this cycle was reinforced by an ideology opposed to big government. "In the present crisis," Reagan said at his inaugural, "government is not the solution to our problem; government *is* the problem." Although fiascoes like the Iran-contra affair are not inevitable, they are made more likely by the logic and legitimacy of the second constitution.

Notes

1. Notable structural changes in the Constitution are the Twelfth, Seventeenth, Twentieth, and Twenty-second Amendments, which deal respectively with change in the Electoral College system, the election of senators, presidential succession, and presidential reeligibility. While all are interesting, only the last seems manifestly inconsistent with the founders' plan. For a defense of the relevance of the constitutional theory of the presidency to contemporary practice, see Joseph M. Bessette and Jeffrey Tulis, eds., *The Presidency in the Constitutional Order* (Baton Rouge: Louisiana State University Press, 1981).
2. James W. Ceaser, *Presidential Selection: Theory and Development* (Princeton: Princeton University Press, 1979); Nelson Polsby, *Consequences of Party Reform* (New York: Oxford University Press, 1983); Doris Graber, *Mass Media and American Politics*, 2d ed. (Washington, D.C.: CQ Press, 1984); David L. Paletz and Robert M. Entman, *Media, Power, Politics* (New York: Free Press, 1981); and Harvey C. Mansfield, Jr., "The Media World and Democratic Representation," *Government and Opposition* 14 (Summer 1979): 35-45.
3. This essay does not reveal the founders' personal and political motives except as they were self-consciously incorporated into the reasons offered for their constitution. The founders' views are treated on their own terms, as a constitutional theory; Hamilton's statement in the first number of *The Federalist* is taken seriously: "My motives must remain in the depository of my own breast. My arguments will be open to all and may be judged by all." James Madison, Alexander Hamilton, and John Jay, *The Federalist Papers*, ed. Clinton Rossiter (New York: New American Library, 1961), no. 1, 36. For a good discussion of the literature on the political motives of the founding fathers, see Erwin Hargrove and Michael Nelson, *Presidents, Politics, and Policy* (New York: Knopf, 1984), chap. 2.
4. The most influential study of the presidency is by Richard Neustadt. See *Presidential Power: The Politics of Leadership from FDR to Carter* (New York: John Wiley & Sons, 1979, originally published 1960), vi: "One must try to view the Presidency from over the President's shoulder, looking out and down with the perspective of *his* place."
5. Herbert J. Storing, *What the Anti-Federalists Were For* (Chicago: University of Chicago Press, 1981), 83*n*.
6. *The Federalist*, no. 70, 423.
7. *The Federalist* literally begins and ends with this issue. In the first number "Publius" warns "that of those men who have overturned the liberties of republics, the greatest number have begun their career by paying obsequious court to the people, commending demagogues and ending tyrants." And in the last essay,

"These judicious reflections contain a lesson of moderation to all the sincere lovers of the Union, and ought to put them upon their guard against hazarding anarchy, civil war, and perhaps the military despotism of a victorious demagogue, in the pursuit of what they are' not likely to obtain, but from TIME and EXPERI-ENCE."

8. Ceaser, *Presidential Selection*, 12, 54-60, 166-167, 318-327. See also V. O. Key, *The Responsible Electorate* (New York: Random House, 1966), chap. 2; Stanley Kelley, Jr., *Political Campaigning: Problems in Creating an Informed Electorate* (Washington, D.C.: Brookings Institution, 1960), 93; and Pendleton E. Herring, *Presidential Leadership* (New York: Holt, Rinehart & Winston, 1940), 70; and *The Federalist*, no. 71, 432.

9. *The Federalist*, no. 10, 82; and Ceaser, *Presidential Selection*, 324.

10. Clinton Rossiter, *Constitutional Dictatorship: Crisis Government in the Modern Democracies* (Princeton: Princeton University Press, 1948), chap. 3.

11. *The Federalist*, no. 85, 527.

12. Harvey Flaumenhaft, "Hamilton's Administrative Republic and the American Presidency," in *The Presidency in the Constitutional Order*, 65-114. Of course, the Civil War and turn of the century progressive politics show that Hamilton's "administrative republic" has been punctuated with the sorts of crises and politics Hamilton sought to avoid.

13. *The Federalist*, no. 10, 77; no. 43, 276; no. 51, 323-325; no. 63, 384; and no. 73, 443. Moreover, the factual quest to find a "majority" may be no less contestable than dispute over the merits of proposals. Contemporary political scientists provide ample support for the latter worry when they suggest that it is often both theoretically and practically impossible to discover a majority will—that is, to count it up—due to the manifold differences of intensity of preferences and the plethora of possible hierarchies of preferences. Kenneth Arrow, *Social Choice and Individual Values* (New York: John Wiley & Sons, 1963); and Benjamin I. Page, *Choices and Echoes in Presidential Elections* (Chicago: University of Chicago Press, 1978), chap. 2.

14. *The Federalist*, no. 39, 241; see also Martin Diamond, "Democracy and the Federalist: A Reconsideration of the Framers' Intent," *American Political Science Review* 53 (March 1959): 52-68.

15. *The Federalist*, no. 39, 241; no. 68, 412-423. See also James Ceaser, "Presidential Selection," in *The Presidency in the Constitutional Order*, 234-282. Ironically, the founders were proudest of this institutional creation; the Electoral College was their most original contrivance. Moreover, it escaped the censure and even won a good deal of praise from antifederal opponents of the Constitution. Because electors were chosen by state legislatures for the sole purpose of selecting a president, the process was thought *more* democratic than potential alternatives, such as selection by Congress.

16. *The Federalist*, no. 72, 435. The empirical judgment that four years would serve the purpose of insulating the president is not as important for this discussion as the *principle* reflected in that choice, a principle that has fueled recent calls for a six-year term.

17. *The Federalist*, nos. 9 and 10.

18. Gordon Wood, *The Creation of the American Republic: 1776-1787* (New York: W. W. Norton, 1969); Michael Parenti, "The Constitution as an Elitist Document," in *How Democratic is the Constitution?* ed. Robert Goldwin (Washington, D.C.: American Enterprise Institute, 1980), 39-58; and Charles Lindblom, *Politics and Markets* (New York: Basic Books, 1979), conclusion.

19. *The Federalist,* no. 49, 313-317.
20. Ibid., 317.
21. See *The Federalist,* no. 57; Joseph M. Bessette, "Deliberative Democracy," in *How Democratic is the Constitution?* 102-116; and Michael Malbin, "What Did the Founders Want Congress to Be—and Who Cares?" (Paper presented to the annual meeting of the American Political Science Association, Denver, Colo., September 2, 1982). On the status of legislative deliberation today, see Joseph M. Bessette, "Deliberation in Congress" (Ph.D. diss., University of Chicago, 1978); William Muir, *Legislature* (Chicago: University of Chicago Press, 1982); and Arthur Maas, *Congress and the Common Good* (New York: Basic Books, 1983).
22. Wood, *Creation of the American Republic,* chap. 5; and Ceaser, *Presidential Selection,* 48.
23. *The Federalist,* no. 62; no. 63, 376-390; and Storing, *What the Anti-Federalists Were For,* chap. 7.
24. *The Federalist,* no. 55, 342; Max Farrand, ed., *The Records of the Federal Convention of 1787,* 4 vols. (New Haven: Yale University Press, 1966), vol. 1, 53.
25. *The Federalist,* no. 71, 432; Madison expresses almost the identical position in no. 63, where he states, "As the cool and deliberate sense of the community, ought in all governments, and actually will in all free governments, ultimately prevail over the views of its rulers; so there are particular moments in public affairs when the people, stimulated by some irregular passion, of some illicit advantage, or misled by the artful misrepresentations of interested men, may call for measures which they themselves will afterwards be most ready to lament and condemn. In these critical moments how salutary will be [a Senate]."
26. John Marshall, *Life of George Washington,* quoted in Charles Thatch, *The Creation of the Presidency,* reprint ed. (Baltimore: Johns Hopkins University Press, 1969), 51; and Farrand, *Records,* vol. 2, 35, 22, and 32.
27. *The Federalist,* no. 68, 413; no. 71, 433; and no. 73, 442; see also Storing, "Introduction," in *Creation of the Presidency,* vi-viii. Thomas Jefferson, "Inaugural Address," March 4, 1801, in *The Life and Writings of Thomas Jefferson,* ed. Adrienne Koch and William Peden (New York: Modern Library, 1944), 325.
28. Neustadt, *Presidential Power,* 26, 28-30, 170, 176, 204. See also James Sterling Young, *The Washington Community* (New York: Columbia University Press, 1964), 53. This insight has been the basis of numerous critiques of the American "pluralist" system which, it is alleged, frustrates leadership as it forces politicians through a complicated political obstacle course.
29. Farrand, *Records,* vol. 1, 66-67; *The Federalist,* no. 47, 360-380; see also U.S. Congress, *Annals of Congress,* vol. 1, 384-412, 476-608. See generally Louis Fisher, *Constitutional Conflict between Congress and the President* (Princeton: Princeton University Press, 1985).
30. In many discussions of separation of powers today, the meaning of *effectiveness* is restricted to only one of these objectives—the implementation of policy that reflects popular will. See, for example, Donald Robinson, ed., *Reforming American Government* (Boulder, Colo.: Westview Press, 1985).
31. See, for example, Lloyd Cutler, "To Form a Government," *Foreign Affairs* (Fall 1980): 126-143.
32. Gary J. Schmitt, "Executive Privilege: Presidential Power to Withhold Information from Congress," in *Presidency in the Constitutional Order,* 154-194.
33. Richard Pious, *The American Presidency* (New York: Basic Books, 1979), 372-415; Gary J. Schmitt, "Separation of Powers: Introduction to the Study of

Executive Agreements," *American Journal of Jurisprudence* 27 (1982): 114-138; Louis Fisher, *Presidential Spending Power* (Princeton: Princeton University Press, 1975), 147-201.

34. Woodrow Wilson, *Congressional Government: A Study in American Politics* (1884; reprint, Gloucester, Mass.: Peter Smith, 1973), preface to 15th printing, introduction; Wilson, *Constitutional Government in the United States* (New York: Columbia University Press, 1908); and Christopher Wolfe, "Woodrow Wilson: Interpreting the Constitution," *Review of Politics* 41 (January 1979): 131. See also Woodrow Wilson, "Cabinet Government in the United States," in *College and State*, ed. Ray Stannard Baker and William E. Dodd, 2 vols. (New York: Harper & Brothers, 1925), vol. 1, 19-42; Paul Eidelberg, *A Discourse on Statesmanship* (Urbana: University of Illinois Press, 1974), chaps. 8 and 9; Harry Clor, "Woodrow Wilson," in *American Political Thought*, ed. Morton J. Frisch and Richard G. Stevens (New York: Scribner's, 1971); and Robert Eden, *Political Leadership and Nihilism* (Gainesville, Fla.: University of Florida Press, 1984), chap. 1.
35. Wilson, *Constitutional Government*, 56, 22; Wilson, "Leaderless Government," in *College and State*, 337.
36. Wilson, *Congressional Government*, 141, 149, 164, 195.
37. Wilson, *Constitutional Government*, 56.
38. Ibid., 60; see also Wilson, *Congressional Government*, 28, 30, 31, 187.
39. *The Federalist*, nos. 47 and 48, 300-313. Consider Madison's statement in *Federalist* no. 48, 308-309:

    Will it be sufficient to mark with precision, the boundaries of these departments in the Constitution of the government, and to trust to these parchment barriers against the encroaching spirit of power? This is the security which appears to have been principally relied upon by the compilers of most of the American Constitutions. But experience assures us that the efficacy of the provision has been greatly overrated; and that some more adequate defense is indispensably necessary for the more feeble against the more powerful members of the government. The legislative department is everywhere extending the sphere of its activity and drawing all power into its impetuous vortex.
40. Schmitt, "Executive Privilege."
41. Woodrow Wilson, "Leaderless Government," 340, 357; Wilson, *Congressional Government*, 158, 201; and Wilson, "Cabinet Government," 24-25
42. Wilson, "Leaderless Government," 346; at the time he wrote this, Wilson was thinking of leadership internal to the House, but he later came to see the president performing this same role. Wilson, *Constitutional Government*, 69-77; see also Wilson, *Congressional Government*, 76, 97-98.
43. Eidelberg, *Discourse on Statesmanship*, chaps. 8 and 9; and Ceaser, *Presidential Selection*, chap. 4, conclusion.
44. Woodrow Wilson, *Leaders of Men*, ed. T. H. Vail Motter (Princeton: Princeton University Press, 1952), 39. This is the manuscript of an oft-repeated lecture that Wilson delivered in the 1890s. See also Wilson, *Congressional Government*, 195, 214.
45. Wilson, *Leaders of Men*, 39; and Wilson, *Constitutional Government*, 49. See also Wilson, *Congressional Government*, 78, 136-137.
46. Wilson, "Cabinet Government," 34-35. See also Wilson, "Leaderless Government," 354; and Wilson, *Congressional Government*, 72, 136-137.
47. Wilson, *Congressional Government*, 69, 72.
48. Ibid., 72, 82, 197-198; Wilson, "Cabinet Government," 20, 28-32; and Wilson,

Leaders of Men, 46.
49. Wilson, *Congressional Government*, 76; ibid., preface to 15th printing, pp. 22-23.
50. Ibid., 187.
51. Wilson, *Constitutional Government*, 49. Today, the idea of a mandate as objective assessment of the will of the people has been fused with the idea of leader as interpreter. Presidents regularly appeal to the results of elections as legitimizing those policies that they believe ought to reflect majority opinion. On the "false" claims to represent popular will, see Stanley Kelley, Jr., *Interpreting Elections* (Princeton: Princeton University Press, 1984).
52. Wilson, *Leaders of Men*, 20, 26.
53. Ibid., 29.
54. I am indebted to Robert Eden for the point about *The Federalist*. See also Ceaser, *Presidential Selection*, 192-197.
55. Wilson, "Cabinet Government," 37; and Wilson, *Leaders of Men*, 45-46.
56. See for example, Wilson, *Congressional Government*, 143-147.
57. Ibid., 144.
58. Wilson, *Leaders of Men*, 45.
59. Wilson, *Congressional Government*, 144.
60. I discuss this and other dilemmas more fully in *The Rhetorical Presidency* (Princeton: Princeton University Press, 1987).
61. Steven E. Miller and Stephen Van Evera, eds., *The Star Wars Controversy* (Princeton: Princeton University Press, 1986), preface.
62. Sanford Weiner and Aaron Wildavsky, "The Prophylactic Presidency," *The Public Interest* 52 (Summer 1978): 1-18.
63. Garry Wills, "The Kennedy Imprisonment: The Prisoner of Charisma," *Atlantic*, January 1982, 34; and H. H. Gerth and C. Wright Mills, eds., *From Max Weber* (New York: Oxford University Press, 1958), 247-248.

6. PRESIDENTIAL LEADERSHIP
IN POLITICAL TIME

Stephen Skowronek

Three general dynamics are evident in presidential history. The locus of the first is the constitutional separation of powers. It links presidents past and present in a timeless and constant struggle over the definition of their institutional prerogatives and suggests that although much has changed in two hundred years, the basic structure of presidential action has remained essentially the same. A second dynamic can be traced through the modernization of the nation. It links presidents past and present in an evolutionary sequence culminating in the expanded powers and governing responsibilities of the "modern presidency," and it suggests that the post-World War II incumbents stand apart—their shared leadership situation distinguished from that of earlier presidents by the scope of governmental concerns, the complexity of national and international issues, and the sheer size of the institutional apparatus. The third dynamic is less well attended by students of the American presidency. Its locus is the changing shape of the political regimes that have organized state-society relations for broad periods of American history, and it links presidents past and present at parallel junctures in "political time." [1] This third dynamic is the point of departure for our investigation.

To read American history with an eye toward the dynamics of political change is to see that within the sequence of national development there have been many beginnings and many endings. Periods are marked by the rise to power of new political coalitions, one of which comes to exert a dominant influence over the federal government. The dominant coalition operates the federal government and perpetuates its position through the development of a distinctive set of institutional arrangements and approaches to public policy questions. Once established, however, coalition interests have an enervating effect on the governing capacities of these political-institutional regimes. From the outset, conflicts among interests within the dominant coalition threaten to cause political disaffection and may weaken regime support. Then, beyond the problems posed by conflicts among established interests,

115

more basic questions arise concerning the nature of the interests themselves. Not only does the nation change in ways that the old ruling coalition finds increasingly difficult to address, but as disaffection within the coalition makes the mobilization of political support more difficult, the regime becomes increasingly dependent on sectarian interests with myopic demands and momentary loyalties. Generally speaking, the longer a regime survives, the more its approach to national affairs becomes encumbered and distorted. Its political energies dissipate, and it becomes less competent in addressing the manifest governing demands of the day.

Thinking in terms of regime sequences rather than linear national development, one can distinguish many different political contexts for presidential leadership *within* a given historical period. Leadership situations might be distinguished by whether or not the president is affiliated with the dominant political coalition. Looking at the modern Democratic period, regime outsiders like Republicans Dwight D. Eisenhower and Richard M. Nixon might be said to have faced a different political problem in leading the nation than regime insiders like John F. Kennedy and Lyndon B. Johnson. Leadership situations also might be distinguished in political time, that is, by when in a regime sequence the president engages the political-institutional order. Thus, Presidents Franklin D. Roosevelt, John F. Kennedy, and Jimmy Carter—all Democrats who enjoyed Democratic majorities in Congress—may be said to have faced different problems in leading the nation as they were arrayed along a sequence of political change that encompassed the generation and degeneration of the New Deal order.

It is not difficult to relate this view of the changing relationship between the presidency and the political system to certain outstanding patterns in presidential leadership across American history. First, the presidents who traditionally make the historians' roster of America's greatest—George Washington, Thomas Jefferson, Andrew Jackson, Abraham Lincoln, Woodrow Wilson, and Franklin D. Roosevelt—all came to power in an abrupt break from a long-established political-institutional regime, and each led an infusion of new political interests into control of the federal government.[2] Second, after the initial break with the past and the consolidation of a new system of government control, a general decline in the political effectiveness of regime insiders is notable. Take, for example, the sequence of Jeffersonians. After the galvanizing performance of Jefferson's first term, we observe increasing political division and a managerial-style presidency under James Madison. Asserting the sanctity of an indivisible Republican majority, James Monroe opened his administration to unbridled sectarianism and oversaw a debilitating fragmentation of the federal establishment.

A complete political and institutional breakdown marked the shortened tenure of John Quincy Adams.

But is it possible to go beyond these general observations and elaborate a historical-structural dimension of political leadership in the presidency? What are the characteristic political challenges that face a leader at any given stage in a regime sequence? How is the quality of presidential performance related to the changing shape of the political-institutional order? These questions call for an investigation that breaks presidential history into regime segments and then compares leadership problems and presidential performances at similar stages in regime development across historical periods. Taking different regimes into account simultaneously, this essay will group presidents together on the basis of the parallel positions they hold in political time.

The analysis focuses on three pairs of presidents drawn from the New Deal and Jacksonian regimes: Franklin D. Roosevelt and Andrew Jackson; John F. Kennedy and James K. Polk; and Jimmy Carter and Franklin Pierce. All were Democrats and thus affiliated with the dominant coalition of their respective periods. None took a passive, caretaker view of his office. Indeed, each aspired to great national leadership. Paired comparisons have been formed by slicing into these two regime sequences at corresponding junctures and exposing a shared relationship between the presidency and the political system.

We begin with two beginnings—the presidency of Franklin D. Roosevelt and its counterpart in political time, the presidency of Andrew Jackson. Coming to power upon the displacement of an old ruling coalition, these presidents became mired in remarkably similar political struggles. Although separated by more than a century of history, they both faced the distinctive challenge of regime construction. Leadership became a matter of securing the political and institutional infrastructure of a new governmental order.

Beyond the challenges of regime construction lie the ever more perplexing problems of managing an established regime in changing times. The regime manager is constrained on one side by the political imperatives of coalition maintenance and on the other by deepening factional divisions within the ranks. Leadership does not penetrate to the basics of political and institutional reconstruction. It is caught up in the difficulties of satisfying regime commitments while stemming the tide of internal disaffection. Consequently, the president is challenged at the level of interest control and conflict manipulation. Our examination of the manager's dilemma focuses on John F. Kennedy and his counterpart in political time, James K. Polk.

Finally, we come to the paradoxes of establishing a credible leadership posture in an enervated regime. Jimmy Carter and Franklin

Pierce came to power at a time when the dominant coalition had degenerated into myopic sects that appeared impervious to the most basic problems facing the nation. Neither of these presidents penetrated to the level of managing coalition interests. Each found himself caught in the widening disjunction between established power and political legitimacy. Their affiliation with the old order in a new age turned their respective bids for leadership into awkward and superficial struggles to escape the stigma of their own irrelevance.

All six of these presidents had to grapple with the erosion of political support that inevitably comes with executive action. But, while this problem plagued them all, the initial relationship between the leader and his supporters was not the same, and the terms of presidential interaction with the political system changed sequentially from stage to stage. Looking within these pairs, we can identify performance challenges that are shared by leaders who addressed the political system at a similar juncture. Looking across the pairs, we observe an ever more tenuous leadership situation, an ever more constricted universe of political action, and an ever more superficial penetration of the political system.

Jackson and Roosevelt: Political Repudiation and the Challenge of Regime Construction

The presidencies of Andrew Jackson and Franklin D. Roosevelt were both launched on the heels of a major political upheaval. Preceding the election of each, a party long established as the dominant and controlling power within the federal government had begun to flounder and fragment in an atmosphere of national crisis. Finally, the old ruling party suffered a stunning defeat at the polls, losing its dominant position in Congress as well as its control of the presidency. Jackson and Roosevelt assumed the office of chief executive with the old ruling coalition thoroughly discredited by the electorate and, at least temporarily, displaced from political power. They each led into control of the federal establishment a movement based on general discontent with the previously established order of things.

Of the two, Jackson's election in 1828 presents this crisis of the old order in a more purely political form. New economic and social conflicts had been festering in America since the financial panic of 1819, but Jackson's campaign gained its special meaning from the confusion and outrage unleashed by the election of 1824. In that election, the Congressional Caucus collapsed as the engine of national political unity. The once monolithic Republican party disintegrated into warring factions during the campaign, and after an extended period of political maneuvering, an alliance between John Quincy

Adams and Henry Clay secured Adams a presidential victory in the House of Representatives despite Jackson's pluralities in both popular and electoral votes. The Adams administration was immediately and permanently engulfed in charges of conspiracy, intrigue, and profligacy in high places. Jackson, the hero of 1815, became a hero wronged in 1824. The Jackson campaign of 1828 launched a broadside assault on the degrading "corruption of manners" that had consumed Washington and on the conspiracy of interests that had captured the federal government from the people.[3]

In the election of 1932, the collapse of the old ruling party dovetailed with and was overshadowed by the Great Depression. The Democratic party of 1932 offered nothing if not hope for economic recovery, and in this Roosevelt's candidacy found its special meaning almost in spite of the candidate's own rather conservative campaign rhetoric. The depression had made a mockery of President Herbert Hoover's early identification of his party with prosperity, and the challenge of formulating a response to the crisis broke the Republican ranks and threw the party into disarray. The Roosevelt appeal was grounded not in substantive proposals or even partisan ideology, but in a widespread perception of Republican incompetence, if not intransigence, in the face of national economic calamity. As future secretary of state Cordell Hull outlined Roosevelt's leadership situation in January 1933: "No political party at Washington [is] in control of Congress or even itself . . . there [is] no cohesive nationwide sentiment behind any fundamental policy or idea today. The election was an overwhelmingly negative affair. . . ."[4]

Thus, Jackson and Roosevelt each engaged a political system cut from its moorings by a wave of popular discontent. Old commitments of ideology and interest suddenly had been thrown into question. New commitments were as yet only vague appeals to some essential American value (republican virtue, economic opportunity) that had been lost in the indulgences of the old order. With old political alliances in disarray and new political energies infused into Congress, these presidents had an extraordinary opportunity to set a new course in public policy and to redefine the terms of national political debate. They recaptured the experience of being first.

But this situation is not without its characteristic leadership challenge. The leader who is propelled into office by a political upheaval in governmental control ultimately confronts the imperatives of establishing a new order in government and politics. This challenge is presented directly by the favored interests and residual institutional supports of the old order; once the challenge has been posed, the unencumbered leadership environment that was created by the initial break with the past quickly fades. The president is faced with the choice of either abandoning his new departure or consolidating it with structural reforms. Situated just beyond the old order, presidential leadership crystallizes as a problem of regime construction.

The president as regime builder grapples with the fundamentals of political regeneration—institutional reconstruction and party building. At these moments, when national political power has been shaken to its foundational elements, we see the president join at center stage a set of activities that other leaders, less favorably situated, engage only indirectly or piecemeal—destroying residual institutional support for opposition interests, restructuring institutional relations between state and society, and securing the dominant position of a new political coalition. Success in these tasks is hardly guaranteed. Wilson had to abandon this course when the Republicans reunited and preempted his efforts to broaden the Democratic base. Lincoln was assassinated just as the most critical questions of party building and institutional reconstruction were to be addressed. This disaster ushered in a devastating confrontation between president and Congress and left the emergent Republican regime hanging in a politically precarious position for the next three decades. Even Jackson and Roosevelt—America's quintessential regime builders—were not uniformly successful. Neither could keep the dual offensives of party building and institutional reconstruction moving in tandem long enough to complete them both.

Andrew Jackson

Republican renewal was the keynote of Jackson's first term. The president was determined to ferret out the political and institutional corruption that he believed had befallen the Jeffersonian regime. This meant purging incompetence and profligacy from the civil service, initiating fiscal retrenchment in national projects, and reviving federalism as a system of vigorous state-based government.[5] Jackson's appeal for a return to Jefferson's original ideas about government certainly posed a potent indictment of the recent state of national affairs and a clear challenge to long-established interests. But there was a studied political restraint in his initial repudiation of the past that defied the attempts of his opponents to characterize it as revolutionary.[6] Indeed, while holding out an attractive standard with which to rally supporters, Jackson was careful to yield his opposition precious little ground upon which to mount an effective counterattack. He used the initial upheaval in governmental control to cultivate an unreproachable political position as the nation's crusader in reform.

Significantly, the transformation of Jackson's presidency from a moral crusade into a radical program of political repudiation and institutional reconstruction was instigated, not by the president himself, but by the premier institution of the old regime, the Bank of the United States.[7] At the time of Jackson's election, the bank was long established as both the most powerful institution in America and the most important link between state and society. It dominated that nation's credit system, maintained extensive ties of material interest with political elites, and actively involved itself in electoral campaigns to sustain its own political support. It embodied all the problems of institutional corruption and political degradation toward which Jackson addressed his administration. The bank was a concentration of political and economic power able to tyrannize over people's lives and to control the will of their elected representatives.

During his first years in office, Jackson spoke vaguely of the need for some modification of the bank's charter. But since the charter did not expire until 1836, there appeared to be plenty of time to consider appropriate changes. Indeed, although Jackson was personally inclined toward radical hard-money views, he recognized the dangers of impromptu tinkering with an institution so firmly entrenched in the economic life of the nation and hesitated at embracing untested alternatives. Moreover, Jackson foresaw an overwhelming reelection endorsement for his early achievements and knew that to press the bank issue before the election of 1832 could only hurt him politically. After a rout of Henry Clay, the architect of the bank and the obvious challenger in the upcoming campaign, Jackson would have a free hand to deal with the institution as he saw fit.

But Jackson's apparent commitment to some kind of bank reform and the obvious political calculations surrounding the issue led the bank president, Nicholas Biddle, to join Henry Clay in a preelection push to recharter the institution without any reforms a full four years before its charter expired. Biddle feared for the bank's future in Jackson's second term. Clay needed to break Jackson's unreproachable image as a national leader and to expose his political weaknesses. An early recharter bill promised to splinter Jackson's support in Congress. If the president signed the bill, his integrity as a reformer would be destroyed; if he vetoed it, he would provide a sorely needed coherence to anti-Jackson sentiment.

As expected, the recharter bill threw Jackson enthusiasts into a quandary and passed through Congress. The bill pushed Jackson beyond the possibility of controlling the modification of extant institutions without significant opposition, and forced him to choose between retreat and an irrevocable break with established governmental arrangements. He saw the bill not only as a blatant attempt by those attached to the old order to destroy him politically, but also as proof certain that the bank's political power threatened the very survival of republican government. Accepting the challenge, he set out to destroy the bank. The 1828 crusade for republican renewal became in 1832 an all-fronts offensive for the establishment of an entirely new political and institutional order.

The president's veto of the recharter bill clearly marked this transition. The political themes of 1828 were turned against the bank with a vengeance. Jackson defined his stand as one that would extricate the federal government from the interests of the privileged and protect the states from encroaching federal domination. He appealed directly to the interests of the nation's farmers, mechanics, and laborers, claiming that this great political majority stood to lose control over the government to the influential few. This call to the "common man" for a defense of the republic had long been a Jacksonian theme, but now it carried the portent of sweeping governmental changes. Jackson not only was declaring open war on the premier institution of the old order, he was challenging long-settled questions of governance. The Supreme Court, for example, had upheld the constitutionality of the bank decades before. Jackson's veto challenged the assumption of executive deference to the Court and asserted presidential authority to make an independent and contrary judgment about judicial decisions. Jackson also challenged executive deference to Congress, perhaps the central operating principle of the Jeffersonian regime. His veto message went beyond constitutional objections to the recharter bill and asserted the president's authority to make an independent evaluation of the social, economic, and political implications of congressional action. In all, the message was a regime builder's manifesto that looked toward fusing a broad-based political coalition, shattering established institutional relationships between state and society, and transforming power arrangements within the government itself.

Of course, new political regimes are not built by presidential proclamation. Jackson had his work cut out for him at the beginning of his second term. His victory over Clay in 1832 was certainly sweeping enough to reaffirm his leadership position, and having used the veto as a campaign document, Jackson could claim a strong mandate to complete the work it outlined. But the veto also had been used as an issue by Clay, and the threat to the bank was fueling organized political opposition in all sections of the country.[8] More important still, the Senate, which had been shaky enough in Jackson's first term, moved completely beyond his control in 1833, and his party's majority in the House returned in a highly volatile condition. Finally, the bank's charter still had three years to run, and bank president Biddle had every intention of exploiting Jackson's political vulnerabilities in hope of securing his own future.

Thus, the election victory drew Jackson deeper into the politics of reconstruction. To maintain his leadership position he needed to neutralize the significance of the bank for the remainder of its charter and prevent any new recharter movement from emerging in Congress. His plan was to have the deposits of the federal government removed from the bank on his own authority and transferred to a select group of politically friendly state banks. The president would thus circumvent his opponents and, at the same time, offer the nation an alternative banking system. The new banking structure had several potential advantages. It promised to work under the direct supervision of the executive branch, to forge direct institutional connections between the presidency and local centers of political power, and to secure broad political support against a revival of the national bank.

This plan faced formidable opposition from the Treasury Department, the Senate, and most of all from the Bank of the United States. Biddle responded to the removal of federal deposits with an abrupt and severe curtailment of loans. By squeezing the nation into a financial panic, Biddle hoped to turn public opinion against Jackson. The Senate followed suit with a formal censure of the president, denouncing his pretensions to independent action on the presumption of a direct mandate from the people.

The so-called Panic Session of Congress (1833-34) posed the ultimate test of Jackson's resolve to forge a new regime. Success now hinged on consolidating the Democratic party in Congress and reaffirming its control over the national government. The president moved quickly to deflect blame for the panic onto the bank. Destroying Biddle's credibility, he was able by the spring of 1834 to solidify Democratic support in the House and gain an endorsement of his actions (and implicitly, his authority to act) from that chamber. Then, undertaking a major grass-roots party-building effort in the midterm elections of 1834, Jackson and his political lieutenants were able to secure a loyal Democratic majority in the Senate. The struggle was over, and in a final acknowledgment of the legitimacy of the new order, the Democratic Senate expunged its censure of the president from the record.

But even as Congress was falling into line, the limitations of the president's achievement were manifesting themselves throughout the nation at large. Jackson had successfully repudiated the old governmental order, consolidated a new political party behind his policies, secured that party's control over the entire federal establishment, and redefined the position of the presidency in its relations with Congress, the courts, the states, and the electorate. But his institutional alternative for reconstructing financial relations between state and society—the state deposit system—was proving a dismal failure.

In truth, Jackson had latched onto the deposit banking scheme out of political necessity as much as principle. The president had been caught between his opponents' determination to save the bank and his supporters' need for a clear and attractive alternative to it. Opposition to Biddle and Clay merged with opposition to any national banking structure, and the interim experiment with state banking quickly became a political commitment. Unfortunately, the infusion of federal deposits into the pet state banks fueled a speculative boom and threatened a major financial collapse.

Hoping to stem the tide of this disaster, the Treasury Department began to choose banks of deposit less for their political soundness than for their financial soundness, and Jackson threw his support behind a gradual conversion to hard money. In the end, however, the president was forced to accept the grim irony of his success as a regime builder. As Congress moved more solidly behind him, its members began to see for themselves the special political attractions of the state deposit system. With the passage of the Deposit Act of 1836, Congress expanded the number of state depositories and explicitly limited executive discretion in controlling them.[9]

Thus, although Jackson had reconstructed American government and politics, he merely substituted one irresponsible and uncontrollable financial system for another. Institutional ties between state and society emerged as the weak link in the new order. Jackson's chosen successor, Martin Van Buren, understood this all too well as he struggled to extricate the federal government from the state banks in the midst of the nation's first great depression.

Franklin D. Roosevelt

As a political personality, the moralistic, vindictive, and tortured Jackson stands in marked contrast to the pragmatic, engaging, and buoyant Franklin D. Roosevelt. Yet, their initial triumphs over long-established ruling parties and the sustained popular enthusiasm that accompanied their triumphs propelled each into grappling with a similar set of leadership challenges. By late 1934, Roosevelt himself seemed to sense the parallels. To Vice President John Nance Garner he wrote, "The more I learn about Andy Jackson, the more I love him." [10]

The interesting thing about this remark is its timing. In 1934 and 1935, Roosevelt faced mounting discontent with the emergency program he had implemented from the favored interests of the old order. Moreover, he saw that the residual bulwark of institutional support for that order was capable of simply sweeping his programs aside. Like Jackson in 1832, Roosevelt was being challenged either to reconstruct the political and institutional foundations of the national government or to abandon the initiative he had sustained virtually without opposition in his early years of power.

The revival of the economy had been the keynote of Roosevelt's early program.[11] Although collectivist in approach and bold in their assertion of a positive role for the federal government, the policies of the early New Deal did not present a broadside challenge to long-established political and economic interests. Roosevelt had adopted the role of a bipartisan national leader reaching out to all interests in a time of crisis. He carefully courted the southern Bourbons, who controlled the old Democratic party, and directly incorporated big business into the government's recovery program. But if Roosevelt's program did not ignore the interests attached to and supported by the governmental arrangements of the past, it did implicate those interests in a broader coalition. The New Deal had also bestowed legitimacy on the interests of organized labor, the poor, and the unemployed, leaving southern Bourbons and northern industrialists feeling threatened and increasingly insecure.

This sense of unease manifested itself politically in the summer of 1934 with the organization of the American Liberty League. Though the league mounted an aggressive assault on Roosevelt and the New Deal, Roosevelt's party received a resounding endorsement in the midterm elections, actually broadening the base of enthusiastic New Dealers in Congress. The congressional elections vividly demonstrated the futility of political opposition, but in the spring of 1935, a more potent adversary arose within the government itself. The Supreme Court, keeper of the rules of governance for the old regime, handed down a series of anti-New Deal decisions. The most important of these nullified the centerpiece of Roosevelt's recovery program, the National Industrial Recovery Act. With the American Liberty League clarifying the stakes of the New Deal departure and the Court pulling the rug out from under the cooperative approach to economic recovery, Roosevelt turned his administration toward structural reform. If he could no longer lead all interests toward economic recovery, he could still secure the interests of a great political majority within the new governmental order.

Roosevelt began the transition from national leader to regime builder with a considerable advantage over Jackson. He could restructure institutional relations between state and society simply by reaching out to the radical and irrepressibly zealous Seventy-fourth Congress (1935-37), and offering it sorely needed coherence and direction. The result was a second round of New Deal legislation. The federal government extended new services and permanent institutional supports to organized labor, the small businessman, the aged, the unemployed, and later, the rural poor. At the same time, the president revealed a new approach to big business and the affluent by pressing for tighter regulation and graduated taxation.[12]

In their scope and vision, these achievements far surpassed the makeshift and flawed arrangements that Jackson had improvised to restructure institutional relations between state and society in the bank war. But Roosevelt's comparatively early and more thoroughgoing success on this score proved a dubious advantage in subsequent efforts to consolidate the new order. After his overwhelming reelection victory in 1936, Roosevelt pressed a series of consolidation initiatives. Like Jackson in his second term, he began with an effort to neutralize the remaining threat within the government.

Roosevelt's target, of course, was the Supreme Court. He was wise not to follow Jackson's example in the bank war by launching a direct ideological attack on the Court. After all, Roosevelt was challenging a constitutional branch of government and hardly could succeed in labeling that branch a threat to the survival of the republic. The president decided instead to kill his institutional opposition with kindness. He called for an increase in the size of the Court, ostensibly to ease the burden on the elder justices and increase overall efficiency. Unfortunately, the real stakes of the contest never were made explicit, and the chief justice deflected the attack by simply denying the need for help. More importantly, the Court, unlike the bank, did not further exacerbate the situation. Instead, it reversed course in the middle of the battle and displayed a willingness to accept the policies of the second New Deal.

The Court's turnabout was a great victory for the new regime, for it relegated to an irretrievable past the old strictures surrounding legitimate governmental activity that Roosevelt had been repudiating from the outset of his presidency. But in so doing, it eliminated even the implicit justification for Roosevelt's proposed judicial reforms. With the constituent services of the New Deal secure, Congress had little reason to challenge the integrity of the Court. Bound by his own inefficiency arguments, Roosevelt did not withdraw his proposal. Although stalwart liberals stood by the president to the end, traditional Democratic conservatives deserted him. A bipartisan opposition took open ground against Roosevelt, defeated the "Court packing" scheme, and divided the ranks of the New Deal coalition. It was a rebuke every bit as portentous as the formal censure of Jackson by the Senate.

With Roosevelt, as with Jackson, the third congressional election of his tenure called forth a major party-building initiative. Stung by the Court defeat, the president sought to reaffirm his hold over the Democratic party and to strengthen its liberal commitments. Ironically, this effort was handicapped by the sweeping character of Roosevelt's early successes. Unlike Jackson in 1834, Roosevelt in 1938 could not point to any immediate threat to his governing coalition. The liberal program was already in place. The Court had capitulated, and despite deep fissures manifested during the Court battle, the overwhelming Democratic majorities in Congress gave no indication of abandoning the New Deal. Even the southern delegations in Congress maintained majority support for Roosevelt's domestic reform initiatives.[13] Under these conditions, party building took on an aura of presidential self-indulgence. Although enormously important from the standpoint of future regime coherence, at the time it looked like heavy-handed and selective punishment for the ungrateful defectors. In this guise, it evoked little popular support, let alone enthusiasm.

The party-building initiative failed. Virtually all of the conservative Democrats targeted for defeat were reelected, and the Republicans showed a resurgence of strength. As two-party politics returned to the national scene, the awkward division within the majority party between the old southern conservatism and the new liberal orthodoxy became a permanent feature of the new regime.

Despite these setbacks, Roosevelt pressed forward with the business of consolidating a new order, and a final effort met with considerable success. In 1939, Roosevelt received congressional approval of a package of administrative reforms that promised to bolster the position of the president in his relations with the other branches of government. Following the precepts of his Committee on Administrative Management, the president had asked for new executive offices to provide planning and direction for governmental operations. The Congress endorsed a modest version of the scheme, but while deflating Roosevelt's grand design, it clearly acknowledged the new governing demands presented by the large federal programs and permanent bureaucratic apparatus he had forged. The establishment of the Executive Office of the President closed the New Deal with a fitting symbol of the new state of affairs.[14]

Polk and Kennedy: Political Reaffirmation and the Dilemma of Interest Management

The administrations of Jackson and Roosevelt shared much in both the political conditions of leadership and the challenges undertaken. An initial upheaval, the ensuing political confusion, and the widespread support for a decisive break from the institutional strictures

of the past framed America's quintessential regime-building presidencies. Opposition from the favored interests of the old order and their residual institutional supports eventually pushed these presidents from an
original program to meet the immediate crisis at hand into structural
reforms that promised to place institutional relations between state and
society on an entirely new footing. After a second landslide election,
Jackson and Roosevelt each moved to consolidate their new order by
eliminating the institutional opposition and forging a more coherent
base of party support. As the nation redivided politically, they secured a
new ruling coalition, reset the political agenda, and institutionalized a
new position of power for the presidency itself.

It is evident from a comparison of these performances that where
Rooseveltian regime building was triumphant, Jacksonian regime
building faltered and vice versa: Roosevelt left institutional relations
between state and society thoroughly reconstructed but his performance
as a party builder was weak and his achievement flawed; Jackson left
institutional relations between state and society in a dangerous disarray
but his performance and achievement as a party builder remain
unparalleled. The more important point, however, lies beyond these
comparisons. It is that few presidents can engage in a wholesale
political repudiation of the past and address the political system at the
level of institutional reconstruction and party building. Most presidents
must use their skills and resources—however extensive these may be—
to work within the already established governmental order.

The successful regime builder leaves in his wake a more constricted universe for political leadership. To his partisan successors, in
particular, he leaves the difficult task of keeping faith with a ruling coalition. In an established regime, the majority-party president comes to
power as a representative of the dominant political alliance and is
expected to offer a representative's service in delegate style. Commitments of ideology and interest are all too clear, and the fusion of
national political legitimacy with established power relationships argues against any attempt to tinker with the basics of government and
politics. The leader is challenged not to break down the old order and
forge a new one, but to complete the unfinished business, adapt the
agenda to changing times, and defuse the potentially explosive choices
among competing obligations. He is partner to a highly structured
regime politics, and to keep the partnership working, he must sustain a
preemptive control over impending disruptions. The political problem
is to get innovation without repudiation and to present creativity as a
vindication of orthodoxy.

The presidencies of James K. Polk and John F. Kennedy clearly
illustrate the problems and prospects of leadership that is circumscribed

by the challenge of managing an established coalition. Both men came to the presidency after an interval of opposition-party control and divided government. The intervening years had seen some significant changes in the tenor of public policy, but there had been no systemic transformations of government and politics. Ushering in a second era of majority-party government, Polk and Kennedy promised at once to reaffirm the commitments and revitalize the program of the dominant regime.

Neither Polk nor Kennedy could claim the leadership of any major party faction. Indeed, their credibility as regime managers rested largely on their second-rank status in regular party circles. Each schooled himself in the task of allaying mutual suspicions among the great centers of party strength. Their nominations to the presidency were the result of skillful dancing around the conflicts that divided contending party factions. What they lacked in deep political loyalites, they made up for with their freedom to cultivate the support of all interests.

Once the office was attained, the challenge of interest management was magnified. Each of these presidents had accepted one especially virulent bit of orthodoxy that claimed majority support within the party as a necessary part of the new regime agenda. Their ability to endorse their party's most divisive enthusiasm (Texas annexation, civil rights) without losing their broad base of credibility within it was fitting testimony to their early education in the art of aggressive maintenance. But their mediating skills did not alter the fact that each came into office with a clear commitment to act on an issue which had long threatened to split the party apart. In addition, Polk and Kennedy each won astonishingly close elections. There was no clear mandate for action, no discernible tide of national discontent, no mass rejection of what had gone before. The hairbreadth Democratic victories of 1844 and 1960 suggested that the opposition could continue to make a serious claim to the presidency and reinforced an already highly developed sense of executive dependence on all parts of the party coalition. With maintenance at a premium and an ideological rupture within the ranks at hand, Polk and Kennedy carried the full weight of the leadership dilemma that confronts the majority-party president of an established regime.

James K. Polk

For the Democratic party of 1844, the long-festering issue was the annexation of Texas with its implicit threat of prompting a war of aggression for the expansion of slave territory.[15] Andrew Jackson, an ardent nationalist with a passion for annexation, had steered clear of any definitive action on Texas during the last years of his presidency. The threat of dividing along sectional lines the national party he had just consolidated argued for a passive posture of merely anticipating the inevitable.[16] Democratic loyalists followed Jackson's lead until 1843, when the partyless "mongrel president," John Tyler, desperate to build an independent political base of support for himself, latched onto the annexation issue and presented a formal proposal on the subject to Congress. With Texas finally pushed to the forefront, expansionist fever heated up in the South and the West and antislavery agitation accelerated in the North.

Jackson's political nightmare became reality on the eve of his party's nominating convention in 1844. Martin Van Buren, Jackson's successor to the presidency in 1837 and still the nominal head of the democracy, risked an all but certain nomination by coming out against the *immediate* annexation of Texas. Despite its carefully worded attention to orthodoxy as Jackson had originally defined it, the New Yorker's pronouncement fused a formidable opposition in the southern and western wings of the party and left the convention deadlocked through eight ballots. With Van Buren holding a large bloc of delegates but unable to get the leaders of the South and West to relinquish the necessary two-thirds majority, it became clear that only a "new man" could save the party from disaster. That man had to be firm on immediate annexation without being openly opposed to Van Buren. On the ninth ballot, James Knox Polk became the Democratic nominee.

Polk was a second-choice candidate, and he knew it. As leader of the Democratic party in Tennessee, he had the unimpeachable credentials of a stalwart friend of Andrew Jackson. He had served loyally as floor leader of the House during the critical days of the bank war, and he had gone on to win his state's governorship. But after Polk tried and failed to gain his party's vice-presidential nomination in 1840, his political career fell on hard times. Calculating his strategy for a political comeback in 1844, Polk made full use of his second-rank standing in high party circles. Again he posed as the perfect vice-presidential candidate and cultivated his ties to Van Buren. Knowing that this time Van Buren's nomination would be difficult, Polk also understood the special advantages of being a Texas enthusiast with Van Buren connections. As soon as that calculation paid off, Polk ventured another. In accepting the presidential nomination, he pledged that, if elected, he would not seek a second term. Although he thus declared himself a lame duck even before he was elected, Polk reckoned that he would not serve any time in office at all unless the frustrated party giants in all sections of the nation expended every last ounce of energy for the campaign, which they might not do if it meant foreclosing their own prospects for eight years.[17]

The one-term declaration was a bid for party unity and a pledge of party maintenance. But the divisions that were exposed at the convention of 1844 and their uncertain resolution in a Texas platform and a dark-horse nomination suggested that the party was likely to chew itself up under a passive caretaker presidency. If Polk was to avoid a disastrous schism in the party of Jackson, he would have to order, balance, and service the major contending interests in turn. He would have to enlist each contingent within the party in support of the policy interests of all the others. Polk submerged himself in a high-risk strategy of aggressive maintenance in which the goal was to satisfy each faction of his party enough to keep the whole from falling apart. The scheme was at once pragmatic and holistic, hard-headed and fantastic. The most startling thing of all is how well it worked.

The president opened his administration (appropriately enough) with a declaration that he would "know no divisions of the Democratic party." He promised "equal and exact justice to every portion." [18] His first action, however, indicated that the going would be rough. Scrutinizing the cabinet selection process, Van Buren (whose electoral efforts had put Polk over the top) judged that his interests in New York had not been sufficiently recognized. The frustrated ex-president presumed a determination on the new president's part to turn the party toward the slave South. Polk tried to appease Van Buren with other patronage offers, but relations between them did not improve. From the outset Van Buren's loyalty was tinged with a heavy dose of suspicion.

The outcry over patronage distribution indicated that any action the president took would cloud Polk's orthodoxy in charges of betrayal. Van Buren's was but the first in an incessant barrage of such charges.[19] But Polk was not powerless in the face of disaffection. He had an irresistible agenda for party government to bolster his precarious political position.

Polk's program elaborated the theme of equal justice for all coalition interests. On the domestic side, he reached out to the South with support for a lower tariff, to the Northwest with support for land price reform, to the Northeast by endorsing a warehouse storage system advantageous to import merchants, and to the old Jackson radicals with a commitment to a return to hard money and a reinstatement of the independent treasury. (Van Buren had dedicated his entire administration to establishing the independent treasury as a solution to Jackson's banking dilemma, but his work had been undermined in the intervening four years.) It was in foreign affairs, however, that the president placed the highest hopes for his administration. Superimposed on his carefully balanced program of party service in the domestic arena was a missionary embrace of Manifest Destiny. Reaching out to the South, Polk promised to annex Texas; to the Northwest, he promised Oregon; and to bind the whole nation together, he made a secret promise to himself to acquire California. In all, the president would complete the orthodox Jacksonian program of party services and fuse popular passions in an irresistible jingoistic campaign to extend the Jacksonian Republic across the continent.

Driven by a keen sense of the dual imperatives of maintenance and leadership, Polk embarked on a course of action designed to transform the nation without changing its politics. Party loyalty was the key to success, but it would take more than just a series of favorable party votes to make this strategy of aggressive maintenance work. The sequence, pace, and symbolism of Polk's initiatives had to be assiduously controlled and coordinated with difficult foreign negotiations so that the explosive moral issues inherent in the program would not enter the debate. Sectional paranoia and ideological heresies had to be held in constant check. Mutual self-interest had to remain at the forefront so that reciprocal party obligations could be reinforced. Polk's program was much more than a laundry list of party commitments. If he did not get everything he promised in the order he promised it, he risked a major political rupture that would threaten whatever he did achieve. Here, at the level of executive management and interest control, the president faltered.

After the patronage tiff with Van Buren demonstrated Polk's problems with the eastern radicals, disaffection over the Oregon boundary settlement exposed his difficulties in striking an agreeable balance between western and southern expansionists. The president moved forward immediately and simultaneously on his promises to acquire Oregon and Texas. In each case he pressed an aggressive, indeed belligerent, border claim. He demanded "all of Oregon" (extending north to the 54° 40′ parallel) from Great Britain and "Greater Texas" (extending south below the Nueces River to the Rio Grande) from Mexico.

The pledge to get "all of Oregon" unleashed a tidal wave of popular enthusiasm in the Northwest. But Great Britain refused to play according to the presidential plan, and a potent peace movement spread across the South and the East out of fear of impending war over the Oregon boundary. Polk used the belligerence of the "54° 40′ or fight" faction to counter the peace movement and to prod the British into coming to terms, but he knew the risks of war on that front. An impending war with Mexico over the Texas boundary promised to yield California in short order, but a war with both Mexico and Great Britain promised disaster.

When the British finally agreed to settle the Oregon boundary at the forty-ninth parallel, Polk accepted the compromise. Then, after an appropriate display of Mexican aggression on the Texas border, he asked Congress for a declaration of war against that nation. Abandoned, the 54° 40′ men turned on the president, mercilessly accusing him of selling out to the South and picking on defenseless Mexico instead of standing honorably against the British. A huge part of the Oregon territory had been added to the Union, but a vociferous bloc of westerners now joined the Van Burenites in judging the president to be willfully deceptive and dangerously prosouthern. Polk had miscalculated both British determination and western pride. His accomplishment deviated from the pace and scope of his grand design and in so doing undermined the delicate party balance.

Polk's designs were further complicated by the effects of wartime sensibilities on his carefully balanced legislative program. The independent treasury and warehouse storage bills were enacted easily, but old matters of principle and simple matters of interest were not enough to calm agitated eastern Democrats. They demanded the president's assurance that he was not involved in a war of conquest in the southwest. Polk responded with a vague and evasive definition of war aims. There was little else he could do to ease suspicions.

More portentous still was the influence of the tariff initiative on wartime politics. Polk had to court northwestern Democrats to make up for expected eastern defections on a vote for a major downward revision of rates. To do so, he not only held out his promised land price reform as an incentive to bring debate to a close, he also withheld his objections to a legislative initiative brewing among representatives of the South and West to develop the Mississippi River system. The northwesterners swallowed their pride over Oregon in hopeful expectation and threw their support behind the tariff bill.

After the tariff bill was enacted, Polk vetoed the internal improvement bill. It had never been a part of his program, and it was an offense to all orthodox Jacksonians. Needless to say, the deviousness of the president's maneuverings was an offense to the West that all but eclipsed the veto's stalwart affirmation of Jacksonian principles. To make matters worse, the land bill failed. The president made good his pledge to press the measure, but he could not secure enactment. Burned three times after offering loyal support to southern interests, the northwesterners no longer were willing to heed the counsels of mutual restraint. The president's effort to bring the war to a quick and triumphant conclusion provided them with their opportunity to strike back.

The war with Mexico was in fact only a few months old, but that already was too long for the president and his party. To speed the peace, Polk decided to ask Congress for a $2 million appropriation to settle the Texas boundary dispute and to pay "for any concessions which may be made by Mexico." This open offer of money for land was the first clear indication that the United States was engaged in— perhaps had consciously provoked—a war of conquest in the Southwest. With it, the latent issue of 1844 manifested itself with a vengeance. Northern Democrats, faced with the growing threat of antislavery agitation at home, saw unequal treatment in the administration's handling of matters of interest, intolerable duplicity in presidential action, and an insufferable southern bias in national policy. They were ready to take their stand on matters of principle.

It is ironic that Polk's implicit acknowledgment of the drive for California, with its promise of fulfilling the nationalistic continental vision, would fan the fires of sectional conflict. Surely he had intended just the opposite. The president was, in fact, correct in calculating that no section of the party would oppose the great national passion for expansion to the Pacific. But he simply could not stem the tide of party disaffection in the East, and unfulfilled expectations fueled disaffection in the West. He was thus left to watch in dismay as the disaffected joined forces to take their revenge on the South.

Northern Democrats loyally offered to support the president's effort to buy peace and land, but added a demand that slavery be prohibited from entering any of the territory that might thus be acquired. This condition, known as the "Wilmot Proviso" after Pennsylvania Democrat David Wilmot, splintered the party along the dreaded sectional cleavage. An appropriation bill with the proviso was passed in the House, but it failed in the Senate when an effort to remove the proviso was filibustered successfully. Now it was Polk's turn to be bitter. In a grim confession of the failure of his grand design, he claimed that he could not comprehend "what connection slavery had with making peace with Mexico." [20]

Ultimately, Polk got his peace with Mexico, and with it he added California and the greater Southwest to the Union. He also delivered on tariff revision, the independent treasury, the warehouse storage system, Oregon, and Texas. Interest management by Polk had extorted a monumental program of party service from established sources of power in remarkably short order. Indeed, except for the conclusion of peace with Mexico, everything had been put in place between the spring of 1845 and the summer of 1846. But the Jacksonian party had ruptured under the pressures of enacting this most orthodox of party programs. Polk's monument to Jacksonian nationalism proved a breeding ground for sectional heresy, and his golden age of policy achievement was undercut at its political foundations.

The failure of interest management to serve the dual goals of political maintenance and policy achievement manifested itself in political disaster for the Democratic party. By the fall of 1846, the New York party had divided into two irreconcilable camps, with Van Buren leading the radicals who were sympathetic to the Wilmot Proviso and opposed to the administration. While Polk maintained an official stance of neutrality toward the schism, party regulars rallied behind Lewis Cass, a westerner opposed to the proviso. Cass's alternative—"popular" or "squatter" sovereignty in the territories—promised to hold together the larger portion of the majority party by absolving the federal government of any role in resolving the questions of slavery extension and regional balance that were raised by Polk's transformation of the nation. When the Democrats nominated Cass in 1848, the Van Buren delegation bolted the convention. Joining "Conscience Whigs" and "Liberty party" men, they formed the Free Soil party, dedicated it to the principles of the Wilmot Proviso, and nominated Van Buren as their presidential candidate.[21]

After the convention, Polk abandoned his studied neutrality. In the waning months of his administration, he withdrew administration favors from Free Soil sympathizers and threw his support behind the party regulars.[22] But it was Van Buren who had the last word. Four years after putting aside personal defeat, loyally supporting the party, and electing Polk, he emerged as the leader of the "heretics" and defeated Cass.

John F. Kennedy

John F. Kennedy had every intention of spending eight years in the White House, but this ambition only compounded the leadership dilemma inherent in his initial political situation. Kennedy's presidential campaign harkened back to Rooseveltian images of direction and energy in government. It stigmatized Republican rule as a lethargic, aimless muddle, and roused the people with a promise to "get the country moving again." At the same time, however, the party of Roosevelt maintained its awkward division between northern liberals and southern conservatives. The candidate assiduously courted both wings, and the narrowness of his victory reinforced his debts to each. The president's prospects for eight years in the White House seemed to hinge on whether or not he could, in his first four, vindicate the promise of vigorous national leadership without undermining the established foundations of national political power.

Kennedy's New Frontier was eminently suited to these demands for aggressive maintenance. It looked outward toward placing a man on the moon and protecting the free world from communist aggression. It looked inward toward pragmatic adaptations and selected adjustments of the New Deal consensus. Leadership in the international arena would fuse the entire nation together behind bold demonstrations of American power and determination. Leadership in the domestic arena would contain party conflict through presidential management and executive-controlled initiatives.

This leadership design shared more in common with Polk's pursuits than a frontier imagery. Both presidents gave primacy to foreign enthusiasms and hoped that the nation would do the same. Facing a politically divided people and an internally factionalized party, they set out to tap the unifying potential of America's missionary stance in the world and to rivet national attention on aggressive (even provocative) international adventures. By so doing, they claimed the high ground as men of truly national vision. At the same time, each countered deepening conflicts of principle within the ruling coalition with an attempt to balance interests. They were engaged in a constant struggle to mute the passions that divided their supporters and stem the tide of coalition disaffection. Resisting the notion of irreconcilable differences within the ranks, Polk and Kennedy held out their support to all interests and demanded in return the acquiescence of each in executive determination of the range, substance, and timing of policy initiatives.

Of course, there are some notable differences in the way these presidents approached regime management. Kennedy, who was not unaware of Polk's failings, avoided Polk's tactics.[23] Polk had gone after as much as possible as quickly as possible for as many as possible in the hope that conflicts among interests could be submerged through the ordered satisfaction of each. Kennedy seemed to feel that conflicts could be avoided best by refraining from unnecessarily divisive action. He was more circumspect in his choice of initiatives and more cautious in their pursuit. Interest balance translated into legislative restraint and aggressive maintenance became contained advocacy. Kennedy's "politics of expectation" kept fulfillment of the liberal agenda at the level of anticipation.[24]

At the heart of Kennedy's political dilemma was the long-festering issue of civil rights for black Americans. Roosevelt had seen the fight for civil rights coming, but he refused to make it his own, fearing the devastating effect it would have on the precarious sectional balance in his newly established party coalition.[25] Harry S Truman had seen the fight break out and temporarily rupture the party in 1948.[26] His response was a balance of executive amelioration and legislative caution. When the Republicans made gains in southern cities during the 1950s, the prudent course Truman had outlined appeared more persuasive than ever. But by 1961, black migration into northern cities, Supreme Court support for civil rights demands, and an ever more aggressive civil rights movement in the South had made it increasingly difficult for a Democratic president to resist a more definitive commitment.

In his early campaign for the presidential nomination, Kennedy developed a posture of inoffensive support on civil rights.[27] While keeping himself abreast of the liberal position, he held back from leadership and avoided pressing the cause upon southern conservatives. Such maneuvering became considerably more difficult at the party convention of 1960. The liberal-controlled platform committee presented a civil rights plank that all but committed the nominee to take the offensive. It pledged presidential leadership on behalf of new legislation, vigorous enforcement of existing laws, and reforms in congressional procedures to remove impediments to such action. Adding insult to injury, the plank lent party sanction to the civil rights demonstrations that had been accelerating throughout the South.

Although the Democratic platform tied Kennedy to the cause that had ruptured the party in 1948, it did not dampen his determination to hold on to the South. Once nominated, he reached out to the offended region and identified himself with more traditional Democratic strategies. Indeed, by offering the vice-presidential nomination to Lyndon B. Johnson, he risked a serious offense to the left. Johnson was not only the South's first choice and Kennedy's chief rival for the presidential nomination, but his national reputation was punctuated by conspicuous efforts on behalf of ameliorative civil rights action in the Senate. Kennedy himself seems to have been a bit surprised by Johnson's acceptance of second place. The liberals were disheartened.[28] Together, however, Kennedy and Johnson made a formidable team of regime managers. Riding the horns of their party's dilemma, they balanced the boldest Democratic commitment ever on civil rights with a determination not to lose the support of its most passionate opponents. Their narrow victory owed as much to those who were promised a new level of action as to those who were promised continued moderation.

The president's inaugural and State of the Union addresses directed national attention to imminent international dangers and America's world responsibilities. Civil rights received only passing mention. Stressing the need for containment in the international arena, these speeches also reflected the president's commitment to containment in the domestic arena. In the months before the inauguration, Kennedy had decided to keep civil rights off his legislative agenda. Instead, he would prod Congress along on other liberal issues, such as minimum wage, housing, area redevelopment, aid to education, mass transit, and health care. The plan was not difficult to rationalize. If the president pressed for civil rights legislation and failed, his entire legislative program would be placed in jeopardy, and executive efforts on behalf of blacks would be subject to even closer scrutiny. If, on the other hand, he withheld the civil rights issue from Congress, southerners might show their appreciation for the president's circumspection. His other measures might have a better chance for enactment, and blacks would reap the benefits of this selected expansion of the liberal legislation as well as the benefits of Kennedy's executive-controlled civil rights initiatives.

Accordingly, Kennedy avoided personal involvement in a preinaugural fight in the Senate over the liberalization of the rules of debate. The effort failed. He did lend his support to a liberal attempt to expand the House Rules Committee, but this was a prerequisite to House action on Kennedy's chosen legislative program. The Rules effort succeeded, but the new committee members gave no indication of an impending civil rights offensive.[29]

Feelings of resentment and betrayal among civil rights leaders inevitably followed the decision to forgo the bold legislative actions suggested in the party platform. But by giving substance to the promise of aggressive executive action, the president sought to allay this resentment and persuasively demonstrate a new level of federal commitment. The administration moved forward on several fronts. The centerpiece of its strategy was to use the Justice Department to promote and protect black voter registration drives in the South. This promised to give blacks the power to secure their rights and also to minimize the electoral costs of any further Democratic defections among southern whites. On other fronts, the president liberalized the old Civil Rights Commission and created the Committee on Equal Employment Opportunity to investigate job discrimination. When Congress moved to eliminate the poll tax, the president lent his support. When demonstrations threatened to disrupt southern transportation terminals, Attorney General Robert Kennedy enlisted the cooperation of the Interstate Commerce Commission in desegregating the facilities. When black applicant James Meredith asserted his right to enroll at the University of Mississippi, the administration responded with protection and crisis mediation. Even more visibly, the president appointed a record number of blacks to high civil service positions.

Kennedy pressed executive action on behalf of civil rights with more vigor and greater effect than any of his predecessors. Still, civil rights enthusiasts were left with unfulfilled expectations and mounting suspicions. Ever mindful of the political imperatives of containing advocacy, the president was trying not only to serve the interests of blacks but also to manage those interests and serve the interests of civil rights opponents. Indeed, there seemed to be a deceptive qualification in each display of principle. For example, the president's patronage policies brought blacks into positions of influence in government, but they also brought new segregationist federal judges to the South. The FBI that provided support for the voter registration drive also tapped the phone of civil rights activist Martin Luther King, Jr. The poll tax was eliminated with administration support, but the administration backed away from a contest over literacy tests. Kennedy liberalized the Civil Rights Commission, but he refused to endorse its controversial report recommending the withholding of federal funds from states that violated the Constitution. While he encouraged the desegregation of interstate transportation terminals, the president put off action on a key campaign pledge to promote the desegregation of housing by executive order. (When the housing order was finally issued, it adopted the narrowest possible application and was not made retroactive.) And although the administration ultimately saw to the integration of the University of Mississippi, the attorney general first tried to find some way to allow the racist governor of the state to save face.

Executive management allowed Kennedy to juggle contradictory expectations for two years. But as an exercise in forestalling a schism within the ranks, the administration's efforts to control advocacy and balance interests ultimately satisfied no one and offered no real hope of resolving the issue at hand. The weaknesses in the president's position became more and more apparent early in 1963 as civil rights leaders pressed ahead with their own timetable for action.

Although civil rights leaders clearly needed the president's support, they steadfastly refused to compromise their demands and relinquish de facto control over their movement to presidential management. The president and his brother became extremely agitated when movement leaders contended that the administration was not doing all that it could for blacks. Civil rights groups, in turn, were outraged at the implication that the movement represented an interest like any other and that claims of moral right could be pragmatically "balanced" against the power of racism and bigotry in a purely political calculus. Independent action already had blurred the line between contained advocacy and reactive accommodation in the administration's response to the movement.

Continued independence and intensified action promised to limit the president's room to maneuver still further and to force him to shift his course from interest balancing to moral choice. The first sign of a shift came on February 28, 1963. After a season of rising criticism of presidential tokenism, embarrassing civil rights advocacy by liberal

Republicans in Congress, and pretentious planning for spring demonstrations in the most racially sensitive parts of the South, the
president recommended some mild civil rights measures to Congress.
His message acknowledged that civil rights was indeed a moral issue
and indicated that it no longer could be treated simply as another
interest. But this shift was one of words more than action. Kennedy did
not follow up his legislative request in any significant way.

Although civil rights agitation clearly was spilling over the
channels of presidential containment, the prospect for passing civil
rights legislation in Congress had improved little since the president
had taken office. Kennedy's circumspect attitude on civil rights matters
during the first two years of his administration had been only
moderately successful in winning support from southern Democrats for
his other social and economic measures. Several of the administration's
most important successes—minimum wage, housing, and area redevelopment legislation—clearly indicated the significance of southern
support. On the other hand, the president already had seen southern
Democrats defect in droves to defeat his proposed Department of
Urban Affairs, presumably because the first department head was to be
black.[30] If Kennedy no longer could hope to contain the civil rights
issue, he still faced the problem of containing the political damage that
inevitably would come from spearheading legislative action.

Kennedy's approach to this problem was to press legislation as an
irresistible counsel of moderation. This meant holding back still longer,
waiting for the extreme positions to manifest themselves fully, then
offering real change as the only prudent course available. He did not
have to wait long. A wave of spring civil rights demonstrations that began in Birmingham, Alabama, and extended throughout the South
brought mass arrests and ugly displays of police brutality to the center
of public attention. Capitalizing on the specter of social disintegration,
the administration argued that a new legislative initiative was essential
to the restoration of order and sought bipartisan support for it on this
basis. Congressional Republicans were enlisted with the argument that
the only way to get the protesters off the streets was to provide them
with new legal remedies in the courts. Kennedy then seized an
opportunity to isolate the radical right. On the evening of the day Gov.
George Wallace made his symbolic gesture in defiance of federal
authority at the University of Alabama (physically barring the entrance
of a prospective black student), the president gave a hastily prepared
but impassioned television address on the need for new civil rights
legislation.

In late June the administration sent its new legislative proposal to
Congress. The bill went far beyond the mild measures offered in

February. It contained significantly expanded voting rights protections and for the first time called for federal protection to enforce school desegregation and to guarantee equal access to public facilities. But even with this full bow to liberal commitments, the struggle for containment continued. The administration tried to counter the zeal of urban Democrats by searching for compromise in order to hold a bipartisan coalition of civil rights support. When civil rights leaders planned a march on Washington in the midst of the legislative battle, the president tried without success to dissuade them.

Containing the zeal of the left was the least of the president's problems. Kennedy had struggled continually to moderate his party's liberal commitments and thus avoid a rupture on the right. Now as a landmark piece of civil rights legislation inched its way through Congress, the president turned to face the dreaded party schism. His popularity had plummeted in the South. George Wallace was contemplating a national campaign to challenge liberal control of the Democratic party, and an ugly white backlash in the North made the prospects for such a campaign brighter than ever. Conservative reaction, party schism, and the need to hold a base in the South were foremost in the president's thinking as he embarked on his fateful trip to Texas in November 1963.

Pierce and Carter:
Political Enervation and the Struggle for Credibility

For Polk and Kennedy, leadership was circumscribed by a political test of aggressive maintenance and the corresponding dilemmas of interest management. With a preemptive assertion of executive control, each attempted to orchestrate a course and pace for regime development that would change the nation without changing its politics. Their governing strategies involved them in convoluted conflict manipulations calculated to reconcile conflicting coalition interests, stave off a political rupture, and move forward on outstanding regime commitments. Grounded in established power, leadership cast a dark cloud of duplicity over its greatest achievements.

Indeed, it would be difficult to choose the greater of these two performances. Polk was able to deliver on an impressive array of policy promises, but his success was premised on excluding from the political arena the basic moral issue raised by these policies. Kennedy delivered little in the way of outstanding policy, but ultimately he did acknowledge the great moral choice he confronted and made a moral decision of enormous national significance. These differences notwithstanding, it is evident that Polk and Kennedy dealt with the unraveling of interest management in similar ways. Executive control and a promise of delivering significant policy support to all the interests of the majority party gave way within two years to an effort to limit the effects of an open rupture. When interest management no longer could stave off disaffection and hold the old coalition together, these presidents took their stand with the larger part and tried to isolate the heretics.

The irony in these performances is that while upholding their respective regime commitments and affirming their party orthodoxies, Polk and Kennedy raised serious questions about the future terms of regime survival and thus left orthodoxy itself politically insecure. Because Polk's nationalism and Kennedy's liberalism ultimately came at the expense of the old majority coalition, a new appeal to the political interests of the nation seemed imperative. In vindicating orthodoxy, Polk and Kennedy set in motion a pivotal turn toward sectarianism in regime development.

For the Jacksonian Democrats, the turn toward sectarianism grew out of a political defeat. The election of 1848 exposed the weaknesses of stalwart Jacksonian nationalism and spurred party managers to overcome the political damage wrought by sectional divisiveness. In 1850, Democratic votes secured passage of a bipartisan legislative package designed to smooth the disruptions that had rumbled out of the Polk administration.[31] This incongruous series of measures, collectively labeled the Compromise of 1850, repackaged moderation in a way that many hoped would isolate the extremes and lead to the creation of a new Union party. But the dream of a Union party failed to spark widespread interest, and Democratic managers grasped the sectarian alternative. Using the compromise as a point of departure, they set out to reassemble the disparate parts of their broken coalition. While supporting governmental policies that were designed to silence ideological conflict, they renewed a partnership in power with interests at the ideological extremes.[32]

For the New Deal regime, the turn came on the heels of a great electoral victory. Running against a Republican extremist, Lyndon B. Johnson swept the nation. But the disaffection stemming from the Kennedy administration was clearly visible: southern Democrat Johnson lost five states in his own region to the Republican outlier. In 1965 and 1966, Johnson tried to fuse a new consensus with policies that ranged across the extremes of ideology and interest. He dreamed of superseding the New Deal with a Great Society, but his vast expansion of services to interests added more to governmental fragmentation than to regime coherence. He also hoped to supersede the old Democratic party with a "party for all Americans," but his extension of regime commitments did more to scatter political loyalties than to unify them.[33]

By the time of the next incarnation of majority-party government (1852 and 1976, respectively), the challenge of presidential leadership had shifted categorically once again. By 1852, the nationalism of Jackson had degenerated into a patchwork of suspect compromises sitting atop a seething sectional division. By 1976, the liberalism of Roosevelt had become a grab bag of special interest services all too vulnerable to political charges of burdening a troubled economy with bureaucratic overhead. Expedience eclipsed enthusiasm in the bond between the regime and the nation. Supporters of orthodoxy were placed on the defensive. The energies that once came from advancing great national purposes had dissipated. A rule of myopic sects defied the very notion of governmental authority.

Expedience also eclipsed enthusiasm in the bond between the majority party and its president. Franklin Pierce and Jimmy Carter each took the term *dark horse* to new depths of obscurity. Each was a minor local figure, far removed from the centers of party strength and interest. Indeed, each hailed from the region of greatest erosion in majority-party support. Pierce, a former governor of New Hampshire, was called to head the Democratic ticket in 1852 after forty-eight convention ballots failed to yield a consensus on anyone who might have been expected to actually lead the party. His appeal within regular party circles (if it may be so called) lay first in his uniquely inoffensive availability, and second, in his potential to bring northeastern Free Soil Democrats back to the standard they so recently had branded as proslavery. Carter, a former governor of Georgia, was chosen to head the Democratic ticket in 1976 after mounting a broadside assault on the national political establishment. To say that he appealed to regular party circles would be to mistake the nature of his campaign and to exaggerate the coherence of the Democratic organization at that time. Still, Carter offered the Democrats a candidate untainted by two decades of divisive national politics, and one capable of bringing the South back to the party of liberalism.

The successful reassembling of broken coalitions left Pierce and Carter to ponder the peculiar challenge of leading an enervated regime. These presidents engaged the political system at a step removed from a claim to the management of coalition interests and the orchestration of agenda fulfillment. Tenuously attached to a governmental establishment that itself appeared dangerously out of step with the most pressing problems of the day, their leadership turned on a question so narrow that it really is perquisite to leadership—that of their own credibility. Despite determined efforts to establish credibility, neither Pierce nor Carter could reconcile his own awkward position in the old order with the awkward position of the old order in the nation at large. Caught between the incessant demands of regime interests and the bankruptcy of the assumptions about the government and the nation that had supported those interests in the past, neither could find secure ground on which to make a stand and limit the inevitable political unraveling that comes with executive action. What began in expedience simply dissolved into irrelevance.

Franklin Pierce

In 1852, Franklin Pierce carried twenty-seven of the thirty-one states for a hefty 250 out of 296 electoral votes.[34] In the process, the Democratic party strengthened its hold over both houses of Congress. Still, the Pierce landslide was more apparent than real, and the election was anything but a mandate for action. As a presidential candidate, Pierce had simply endorsed the past work of a bipartisan group of Senate moderates. His campaign had been confined to a simple declaration of support for the Compromise of 1850 and a pledge to resist any further agitation on slavery, the issue that underlay all other national concerns. The Pierce campaign was nothing if not a dutiful bow to senatorial authority and moderate political opinion.

It is possible that the new president might have enhanced his position at the start of his term by taking a second bow to the center and placing the largesse of his office at the disposal of the Senate moderates. But there were other aspects of the election that argued against this approach. Pierce actually had received less than 51 percent of the popular vote. He had won the presidency not because the moderate center of national opinion had rallied to his standard but because the party managers working in the field had reassembled support at the extremes of Democratic party opinion. To the extremists, the Compromise of 1850 was a source of suspicion rather than satisfaction; it was a matter of reluctant acquiescence rather than loyal support.

Pierce was sensitive to the precariousness of his victory but thought the logic of his situation was fairly clear. He believed that the election of 1848 had demonstrated that it was not enough for the Democratic party to stand with the moderates and let the extremes go their own way and that the narrow victory of 1852 amply demonstrated the electoral imperative of consolidating party loyalties across the spectrum of party opinion. Pierce was gratified by the election's renewed display of party loyalty—however reluctantly given—and he found far-fetched and unimpressive the possibility that the centrists of both parties might join him on independent ground in a kind of national coalition government. He therefore decided to reach out to the old party coalition and to try to heal the wounds of 1848 once and for all.

In a bold bid for leadership, Pierce held himself aloof from the moderate senators and set out to rebuild the political machinery of Jacksonian government under presidential auspices. As the mastermind of a party restoration, he hoped to gain a position of respectability in his dealings with Congress, to take charge of national affairs, and ultimately—in 1856—to lay claim to the mantle of Andrew Jackson. The basic problem with this plan for establishing a credible leadership posture was that no interest of any significance depended on the president's success. Pierce had exhausted his party's national strength and legitimacy simply by letting the various party leaders elect him. These leaders had no stake in following their own creation and no intention of withholding their mutual suspicions in order to enhance the president's position. Pierce quickly discovered that his claim to the office of Andrew Jackson had no political foundation, and that by asserting his independence at the outset, he had robbed the alternative strategy—a bow to senatorial power—of any possible advantage.

As for political vision, Pierce's goal of resuscitating the old party machinery was ideologically and programmatically vacuous. It was conceived as a purely mechanical exercise in repairing and perfecting the core institutional apparatus of the regime and thereby restoring its operational vitality. There was no reference to any of the substantive concerns that had caused the vitality of the party apparatus to dissipate in the first place. Those concerns were simply to be forgotten. Pierce recalled Polk's dictum of "equal and exact justice" for every portion of the party, but not the wide-ranging appeal to unfinished party business that had driven Polk's administration. He held up to the nation the vision of a political machine restored and purged of all political content.[35]

The rapid unraveling of the Pierce administration began with the president's initital offer to forget the Free Soil heresy of 1848 and provide all party factions in the North their due measure of presidential favor for support given in 1852. Much to the president's dismay, many of the New York Democrats who had remained loyal in 1848 refused to forgive the heretics and share the bounty. The New York party disintegrated at a touch, and the Whigs swept the state's elections in 1853.

Within months of Pierce's inauguration, then, his strategy for establishing credibility as a leader was in a shambles. The president's key appointment to the Collectorship of the Port of New York had yet to be confirmed by the Senate, and if the party leaders withheld their endorsement—a prospect that Pierce's early standoffishness and the New York electoral debacle made all too real—the rebuke to the fledgling administration would be devastating. But Pierce not only had placed himself at the mercy of the Senate, he had also placed the Senate at the mercy of the radical states' rights advocates of the South. This small but potent faction of southern senators felt shortchanged by the distribution of patronage in their own region and resolved to use the president's appeal for the restoration of Free Soilers as a basis to seek their revenge. They characterized the distribution of rewards in the North as representing a heightened level of commitment to the Free Soil element, and they challenged their more moderate southern cohorts to extract an equal measure of new commitment for their region as well.

The radical southerners found their opportunity in Illinois senator Stephen Douglas's bill to organize the Nebraska territory. Douglas pushed the Nebraska bill because it would open a transcontinental railroad route through the center of his own political base. His bill followed the orthodox party posture, a posture confirmed in the Compromise of 1850, stipulating that the new territory would be organized without reference to slavery and that the people of the territory would decide the issue. Southerners who ostensibly had accepted this formula for settling new lands by electing Pierce in 1852 were offended by the president's northern political strategy in 1853 and felt compelled to raise the price of their support in 1854. They demanded that the Douglas bill include a repeal of the Missouri compromise of 1820 and thus explicitly acknowledge that slavery could become permanently established anywhere in the national domain. Douglas evidently convinced himself that the expected benefits of his Nebraska bill were worth the price extracted by the South. After all, it could be argued that the repeal would only articulate something already implicit in the doctrine of squatter sovereignty. The change in the formal terms of sectional peace would be more symbolic than real. In any case, Douglas accepted the repeal, and by dividing the Nebraska territory in two (Nebraska and Kansas) hinted that both sections might peacefully lay claim to part of the new land.

In January 1854, less than a year into Pierce's administration, Douglas led his southern collaborators to the White House to secure a presidential endorsement for the Kansas-Nebraska bill. With Douglas's railroad and the confirmation of Pierce's New York collector nominee hanging in the balance, the cornerstone of the Pierce presidency gave way. In his very first legislative decision, the president was being told to disregard his electoral pledge not to reopen the issue of slavery and to tie his leadership to the repudiation of the Missouri Compromise. To endorse the handiwork of the party leaders was to risk his credibility in the nation at large. But if he chose to stand by his pledge, he was certain to lose all credibility within the party. Pierce chose to stand with the party leaders. Like Douglas, he apparently convinced himself that the Kansas-Nebraska bill was consistent enough with the spirit of the Compromise of 1850 to not raise any new issues concerning slavery. He then offered to help Douglas convince the northern wing of the party. The administration's candidate for collector of the Port of New York was confirmed.

Between March 1853 and January 1854, Pierce had tried and failed to prove himself to his party on his own terms; between January and May of 1854, he struggled to prove himself to his party on the Senate's terms. The president threw all the resources of the administration behind passage of the Kansas-Nebraska bill in the House. Despite a Democratic majority of 159 to 76, he fought a no-win battle to discipline a party vote. Midway into the proceedings, 66 of the 90 northern Democrats stood in open revolt against this northern Democratic president. A no-holds-barred use of presidential patronage ultimately persuaded 44 to give a final assent. Instead of perfecting the political machine, Pierce found himself defying a political revolution. Passage of the bill was secured through the support of southern Whigs. Forty-two northern Democrats openly voted no. Not one northern Whig voted yes.[36]

In the winter of 1854, Pierce lost his gamble with national credibility. Exhausted after the passage of Douglas's bill, the administration turned to reap northern revenge for the broken pledge of 1852. The Democrats lost every northern state except New Hampshire and California in the elections of 1854. The once huge Democratic majority in the House disappeared, and a curious new amalgamation of political forces prepared to take over. Adding to the rebuke was the threat of civil war in the territories. Free Soil and slave factions rushed into Kansas and squared off in a contest for control. The president called for order, but the call was ignored.

Pierce never gave up hope that his party would turn to him. But once the North had rejected his administration, the South had no more use for him, and the party Pierce so desperately had wanted to lead became increasingly anxious to get rid of him. Ironically, when faced with the unmitigated failure of his leadership and his political impotence at midterm, Pierce seemed to gain his first sense of a higher purpose. He threw his hat into the ring for a second term with a spirited defense of the Kansas-Nebraska Act and a biting indictment of the critics of the Missouri Compromise repeal. He appealed to the nation to reject treason in Kansas. He wrapped his party in the Constitution and cast its enemies in the role of uncompromising disunionists bent on civil war.[37]

This was the president's shining hour. Rejecting the specter of party illegitimacy and the stigma of his own irrelevance, standing firm with the establishment against the forces that would destroy it, Pierce pressed the case for his party in the nation and with it, his own case for party leadership. Still, there was no rally of political support. The party took up the "friends of the Constitution" sentiment, but it hastened to bury the memory of the man who had articulated it. Pierce's unceasing effort to prove his significance to those who had called him to power never bore fruit. The Democratic convention was an "anybody but Pierce" affair.

Jimmy Carter

There is no better rationale for Jimmy Carter's mugwumpish approach to political leadership than Franklin Pierce's unmitigated failure. No sooner had Pierce identified his prospects for gaining credibility as a national leader with the revitalization of the old party machinery under presidential auspices than he fell victim to party interests so factious that the desperate state of national affairs was all but ignored. Gripped by myopic sects, the party of Jackson proved itself bankrupt as a governing instrument. Its operators no longer were capable even of recognizing that they were toying with moral issues of explosive significance for the nation as a whole. Pierce's plan for claiming party leadership first and then taking charge of the nation dissolved with its initial action, pushing the president down a path as demoralizing for the nation as it was degrading to the office. The quest for credibility degenerated into saving face with the Senate over patronage appointments, toeing the line on explosive territorial legislation for the sake of Douglas's railroad, and forswearing a solemn pledge to the nation.

It was Jimmy Carter's peculiar genius to treat his remoteness from his party and its institutional power centers as a distinctive asset rather than his chief liability in his quest for a credible leadership posture. He called attention to moral degeneration in government and politics, made it his issue, and then compelled the political coalition that had built that government to indulge his crusade against it. In a style reminiscent of Andrew Jackson, Carter identified himself with popular disillusionment with political insiders, entrenched special interests, and the corruption of manners that consumed Washington. He let the liberals of the Democratic party flounder in their own internal disarray until it became clear that liberalism no longer could take the political offensive on its own terms. Then, in the 1976 Florida primary, Carter pressed his southern advantage. The party either had to fall in line behind his campaign against the establishment or risk another confrontation with the still greater heresies of George Wallace.

The obvious problem in Carter's approach to the presidency was that while it claimed a high moral stance of detachment from the establishment, it also positioned itself within an established governing coalition. This curiosity afforded neither the regime outsider's freedom to oppose established interests nor the regime insider's freedom to support them. The tension in Carter's campaign between an effort to reassemble the core constituencies of the traditional Democratic regime and his promise to reform the governmental order that served it suggested the difficulties he would face establishing a credible leadership posture in office. Carter's narrow victory in the election magnified those difficulties by showing the regime's supporters in Congress to be a good deal more secure politically than their strange new affiliate in the executive mansion.

On what terms, then, did Carter propose to reconcile his outsider's appeal with his position within the old order? The answer of the campaign lay in Carter's preoccupation with problems of form, procedure, and discipline rather than in the substantive content of the old order. It was not bureaucratic *programs,* Carter argued, but bureaucratic *inefficiency* that left the people estranged from their government. It was not the system per se that was at fault but the way it was being run. In the eyes of this late-regime Democrat, the stifling weight and moral decay of the federal government presented problems of technique and personnel rather than problems of substance.

Like Jackson's early efforts, Carter's reform program called for governmental reorganization, civil service reform, and fiscal retrenchment. But coming from an outsider affiliated with the old order, the political force and ideological energy of this program for revitalization were largely nullified. What Jackson presented as an ideological indictment of the old order and a buttress for supporters newly arrived in power, Carter presented as institutional engineering plain and simple. Carter's Jackson-like appeal to the nation translated into an ideologically passionless vision of reorganizing the old order without challenging any of its core concerns.[38]

It is in this respect that the shaky ground on which Carter staked his credibility as a leader begins to appear a good deal more like that claimed by Franklin Pierce than their different party postures would at first lead us to suppose. Both pinned their hopes on the perfectability of machinery. Carter would do for the bureaucratic apparatus of the liberal regime what Pierce had intended to do for the party apparatus of the Jacksonian regime—repair the mechanical defects and realize a new level of operational efficiency. With their perfection of the apparatus, they hoped to save the old regime from its own self-destructive impulses and, at the same time, eliminate the need to make any substantive choices among interests. Political vitality was to be restored simply by making the engines of power run more efficiently.

Sharing this vision, Pierce and Carter also shared a problem of action. Neither could point to any interest of political significance that depended on his success in reorganization. Carter's plan for instilling a new level of bureaucratic discipline was not the stuff to stir the enthusiasm of established Democrats, and once the plan became concrete action, there was plenty for party interests to vehemently oppose. Carter's vision of institutional efficiency dissolved in a matter of weeks into institutional confrontation.

The Carter administration immediately engaged the nation in an elaborate display of symbolism that was designed to build a reservoir of popular faith in the president's intentions and confidence in his ability to change the tenor of government.[39] The economic difficulties the old regime faced in simply maintaining its programmatic commitments at current levels dampened whatever enthusiasm there was for reaching out to the interests with expansive new programs in orthodox Democratic style. The impulse to lead thus focused on an early redemption of the pledge to be different. With his "strategy of symbols," the president bypassed Congress and claimed authority in government as an extension of his personal credibility in the nation at large.

The first material test of this strategy came in February 1977, when Carter decided to cut nineteen local water projects from the 1978 budget. As mundane as this bid for leadership was, it placed the disjunction between the president's appeal to the nation and his political support in government in the starkest possible light. For the president, the water projects were a prime example of the wasteful and unnecessary expenditures inherent in the old ways government did business. The cuts offered Carter a well-founded and much needed opportunity to demonstrate to the nation how an outsider with no attachments to established routines could bring a thrifty discipline to government without really threatening any of its programmatic concerns. Congress—and, in particular, the Democratic leadership in the Senate—saw the matter quite differently. The president's gesture was received as an irresponsible and politically pretentious assault on the bread and butter of congressional careers. Its only real purpose was to enhance the president's public standing, yet its victims were those upon whom presidential success in government must ultimately depend. The Democratic leaders of the Senate pressed the confrontation. They reinstated the threatened water projects on a presidentially sponsored public works jobs bill. Carter threatened to stand his ground, and majority-party government floundered at the impasse.

As relations with Congress grew tense, the president's bid for national leadership became even more dependent on public faith and confidence in his administration's integrity. By standing aloof from politics as usual, the administration saddled itself with a moral standard that any would find difficult to sustain. A hint of shady dealing surfaced in the summer of 1977, and by the fall, the symbolic supports of Carter's leadership were a shambles.

Like the water projects debacle, the Bert Lance affair is remarkable for its substantive insignificance. The administration's "scandal" amounted to an investigation of financial indiscretions by one official before he took office. But the Carter administration was nothing if not the embodiment of a higher morality, and the budget director was the president's most important and trusted political appointee. The exposé of shady dealings on the part of the man whose hand was on the tiller of the bureaucratic machine not only indicted the administration on the very ground that it had asserted a distinctive purpose, but also made a sham of the Democratic Senate's nomination review process. Shorn of its pretentions to a higher standard of conduct, the outsider status of the administration became a dubious asset. Attention now was directed to the apparent inability of the outsiders to make the government work and address the nation's manifest problems.

Despite these first-year difficulties in establishing a credible leadership posture on his own terms, Carter still refused to abdicate to the party leaders. Indeed, as time went on the intransigence of the nation's economic difficulties seemed to stiffen the president's resistance to social policy enthusiasms he felt the nation could no longer afford to support. There was to be no alliance between Carter and Sen. Edward M. Kennedy to recapitulate the Pierce-Douglas disaster. But what of the prospects for continued resistance? The core constituencies of the Democratic party—blacks and organized labor in particular—found the president's program of governmental reorganization and fiscal retrenchment tangential to their concerns at best. They had little use for a Democratic president who seemed to govern like a Republican, and their disillusionment added to the dismay of the congressional leadership. Stalwart liberals admonished the president not to forsake the traditional interests but to rally them and, in Kennedy's words, "sail against the wind." [40] If the shaky state of the economy made this message perilous for the president to embrace, his awkward political position made it equally perilous to ignore.

Following the Lance affair, Carter did attempt to dispel disillusionment with an appeal to the neoliberal theme of consumerism. He had identified himself with consumer issues during his campaign and opened the second year of his administration with a drive to establish a consumer protection agency. The proposal hardly could be said to address the demands of the old Democratic constituencies, but it had enthusiastic backing from consumer groups, a general appeal in the nation at large, support from the Democratic leadership in Congress, and the rare promise of serving all these at little direct cost to the government. In consumer protection, Carter found the makings of a great victory, one that would not only wash away the memory of the first year but also define his own brand of political leadership. But the legislation failed, and with the failure his prospects for leadership all but collapsed.

Indeed, this defeat underscored the paradox that plagued Carter's never-ending struggle for credibility. Opposition fueled by business interests turned the consumer protection issue against the administration with devastating effect. Identifying governmental regulation of industry with the grim state of the national economy, business made Carter's neoliberalism appear symptomatic of the problem and counterproductive to any real solution.[41] Carter's own critique of undisciplined governmental expansion actually became the property of his critics, and the distinctions he had drawn between himself and the old liberal establishment became hopelessly blurred. While this most distant of Democratic presidents was alienating the liberal establishment by his neglect of its priorities, he was being inextricably linked to it in a conservative assault on the manifest failings of the New Deal liberal regime as a whole. Carter's liberalism-with-a-difference simply could not stand its ground in the sectarian controversies that racked the liberal order in the 1970s. It was as vulnerable to the conservatives for being more of the same as it was vulnerable to the liberals for being different.

As tensions between the old regime politics and new economic realities intensified, all sense of political definition was eclipsed. Notable administration victories—the Senate's ratification of a bitterly contested treaty with Panama, the endorsement of a version of the much heralded administrative reorganization, the negotiation of an accord between Israel and Egypt—offered precious little upon which to vindicate the promise of revitalization. Moreover, the president's mugwumpish resolve to find his own way through deepening crises increasingly came to be perceived as rootless floundering. His attempt to assert forceful leadership through a major cabinet shakeup in the summer of 1979 only added credence to the image of an administration out of control. His determination to support a policy of inducing recession to fight inflation shattered the political symbolism of decades past by saddling a Democratic administration with a counsel of austerity and sacrifice and passing to the Republicans the traditional Democratic promise of economic recovery and sustained prosperity.

The administration was aware of its failure to engage the political system in a meaningful way well before these momentous decisions. By early 1979, the president had turned introspective. It was readily apparent that his credibility had to be established anew and that an identification of the administration with some clear and compelling purpose was imperative. Carter's response to the eclipse of political definition was not, of course, a Piercelike defense of the old order and its principles. It was, if anything, a sharpened attack on the old order and a renewed declaration of presidential political independence.

In what was to be his most dramatic public moment, Carter appeared in a nationally televised appeal to the people in July 1979 with a revised assessment of the crisis facing the nation.[42] This new bid for leadership credibility began with an acknowledgment of widespread disillusionment with the administration and its "mixed success" with Congress. But the president detached himself from the "paralysis, stagnation, and drift" that had marked his tenure. He issued a strong denunciation of the legislative process and reasserted his campaign image as an outsider continuing the people's fight against degenerate politics. Attempting to restore the people's faith in themselves and to rally them to his cause, Carter all but declared the bankruptcy of the federal government as he found it. Thirty months in office only seemed to reveal to him how deeply rooted the government's incapacities were. It was the system itself, not simply its inefficiencies, that the president now placed in question.

Trying once again to identify his leadership with the alienation of the people from the government, Carter again exposed himself as the one with the most paralyzing case of estrangement. The awkward truth in this presidential homily lent credence to the regime's most vehement opponents by indicting the establishment controlled by the president's ostensible allies. On the face of it, Carter had come to embrace a leadership challenge of the greatest moment—the repudiation of an entire political-institutional order—but beneath the challenge lay the hopeless paradox of his political position. The Democratic party tore itself apart in a revolt against him and the sentiments he articulated. It rejected his message, discredited his efforts, and then, in its most pathetic display of impotence, revealed to the nation that it had nothing more to offer. Carter finally may have seen the gravity of the problems he confronted, but as the people saw it, he was not part of the solution.

Rethinking the Politics of Leadership

The politics of leadership often is pictured as a contest between the man and the system. Timeless forces of political fragmentation and institutional intransigence threaten to frustrate the would-be leader at every turn. Success is reserved for the exceptional individual. It takes a person of rare political skill to penetrate the system and manipulate the government in politically effective ways. It takes a person of rare character to give those manipulations national meaning and constructive purpose.

Although the significance of the particular person in office cannot be doubted, this perspective on leadership presents a rather one-sided view of the interplay between the presidency and the political system. It is highly sensitive to differences among individual incumbents, but it tends to obscure differences in the political situations in which they act. If presidential leadership is indeed something of a struggle between the individual and the system, it must be recognized that the system changes as well as the incumbent. The changing universe of political action is an oft-noted but seldom explored dimension of the leadership problem.

While changes in the political conditions and challenges of presidential leadership have been incessant, they have not been entirely erratic. A broad view of American political development reveals patterned sequences of political change with corresponding patterns in presidential performance. Presidential history in this reading has been episodic rather than evolutionary, with leadership opportunities gradually dissipating after an initial upheaval in political control over government. Presidents intervene in—and their leadership is mediated by—the generation and degeneration of political orders. The clock at work in presidential leadership keeps political rather than historical time.

The leaders who stand out at a glance—Washington, Jefferson, Jackson, Lincoln, Wilson, and Roosevelt—are closer to each other in the political conditions of leadership than they are to any of their respective neighbors in historical time. In *political* time each was first. As the analysis of the Jacksonian and New Deal regimes has shown, successive incarnations of majority-party government produced progressively more tenuous leadership situations. Presidents approached ever more perplexing problems of regime governance with ever more superficial governing solutions; regime supporters approached ever more perplexing leadership choices with ever less forbearance.

The regime builders rode into power on an upheaval in governmental control and tested their leadership in efforts to secure a political and institutional infrastructure for a new governing coalition. Their success created a new establishment, thrust their partisan successors into the position of regime managers, and posed the test of aggressive maintenance. Ultimately, visions of regime management dissolved into politically vacuous mechanical contrivances, and leadership was preempted in the political contradictions of simply establishing presidential credibility.

As actors in political time, then, presidents of the same historical epoch can face radically different opportunities and challenges in attempting to lead the nation. But beyond specifying these differences, the perspective of political time also offers a more general understanding of the problem of historical action in a national institutional context and thus of presidency as a position of political leadership. The critical issue running through our six cases has not been success or failure in enacting some momentous piece of contentious legislation. After all, Franklin Pierce succeeded in pitched battle in enacting the Kansas-Nebraska Act but failed miserably as a political leader. Nor has the critical issue been the success of the policies enacted in solving the nation's problems. After all, the New Deal failed to pull the nation out of the Depression and Andrew Jackson's alternative banking scheme exacerbated an economic depression. The critical issue here has been the president's authority to define the terms of an ongoing political discourse, and thereby to control the meaning of the historical moment at hand. A president's authority over the political meaning of historical action changes with the passage of political time and hinges in large measure on the structured disposition of the incumbent toward the governing commitments of the immediate past.[43]

All leaders seek to shape the future with creative responses to contemporary problems. In a national institutional context, however, shaping the future requires repudiating commitments of ideology and interest embedded in previously established governing arrangements. The paradigmatic expressions of political leadership in the presidency thus come from incumbents, such as Jackson and Roosevelt, who stand free of commitments to the immediate past and who are able to define their leadership projects against the backdrop of the manifest failures of a recently displaced governing coalition. The structured capacity of the incumbent to exploit the repudiative thrust of presidential leadership is the crucial variable. More than anything else, it is this that determines the president's success or failure in resetting the boundaries of legitimate governmental action on its own terms.

Both Jackson and Roosevelt fashioned a place in political history that served as a source of legitimacy for a generation of successors. In doing so, they placed their successors, especially those leading reincarnations of majority party government, at cross purposes. For Polk and Kennedy, whose ascension to power reaffirmed the commitments of the past—and, to an even greater extent, for Pierce and Carter, whose challenge was to repair the political machinery of the old order—leadership was caught between the demands for innovation and the dangers of repudiation. Innovation posed a threat to the political foundations of the incumbent's power.

For presidents affiliated with the established governing coalition, the inherent hostility between leadership and the prevailing political order must be submerged in self-denying rationalizations and subtle explanations of the chosen course of action. As these explanations become more subtle, it grows increasingly difficult for the president to sustain his political definition of the moment. The integrity of innovation—if it may be so called—is compromised by attachment to old orthodoxies, and political achievement raises more questions about political legitimacy than it forecloses.

Affirmation or repudiation, orthodoxy or innovation, commitment or betrayal—these are the choices and trade-offs of a president's intervention into the political system. Thematically, they capture the political stakes of historical action in a national institutional context. Structured in time and place, they shape the president's leadership project and determine his significance as a national political leader.

As in the historical pairings of Adams and Jackson, Buchanan and Lincoln, and Hoover and Roosevelt, we have seen again, in more recent years, that presidents who face similar national problems do not lay claim to the same political authority, and that solving problems may be a less essential part of presidential leadership than is the authority to relegate the political past to the realm of discredited history. The abrupt turn from Jimmy Carter's stillborn struggle for political credibility to the commanding heights of political authority enjoyed by Ronald Reagan in his first term displays the significance to presidential leadership of political structure and political time vis-à-vis individual capacities. We may never know to what degree Reagan's personal limitations contributed to the diminished potency of the most portentous moment for political leadership in the past fifty years. But today, with those limitations now fully exposed, Reagan's hold over American politics in his first six years appears all the more astounding. As of this writing, it is by no means certain whether the unraveling of the Reagan administration after the 1986 elections will revive what Reagan so explicitly repudiated, or whether his ultimate achievement will be to have made conservatism safe for Democrats.

Notes

The author would like to thank Karen Orren for her contributions to this revised version of an article by the same name that appeared in the first edition of this collection.

1. Other recent works investigating distinctly political patterns in presidential history include Erwin C. Hargrove and Michael Nelson, *Presidents, Politics, and Policy*

(New York: Knopf, 1984); and James David Barber, *The Pulse of Politics: Electing Presidents in the Media Age* (New York: W. W. Norton, 1980).

2. Thomas A. Bailey, *Presidential Greatness: The Image and the Man from George Washington to the Present* (New York: Appleton-Century-Croft, 1966), 23-24. Bailey critically discusses the ratings by professional historians. The important point here, however, is that the presidents who rated highest in the Schlesinger surveys of 1948 and 1962 all shared this peculiarly structured leadership situation at the outset of their terms.

3. Robert Remini, *Andrew Jackson and the Course of American Freedom, 1822-1832,* vol. 2 (New York: Harper & Row, 1981), 12-38, 74-142.

4. Quoted in Frank Freidel, *FDR and the South* (Baton Rouge: Louisiana State University Press, 1965), 42.

5. Remini, *Andrew Jackson,* 152-202, 248-256.

6. The famous veto of the Maysfield Road, for example, was notable for its limited implications. It challenged federal support for *intrastate* projects and was specifically selected as an example for its location in Henry Clay's Kentucky. On Jackson's objectives in civil service reform, see Albert Somit, "Andrew Jackson as an Administrative Reformer," *Tennessee Historical Quarterly* 13 (September 1954): 204-223; and Eric McKinley Erickson, "The Federal Civil Service under President Jackson," *Mississippi Valley Historical Review,* 13 (March 1927): 517-540. Also significant in this regard is Richard G. Miller, "The Tariff of 1832: The Issue That Failed," *Filson Club History Quarterly* 49 (July 1975): 221-230.

7. The analysis in this and the following paragraphs draws on the following works: Remini, *Andrew Jackson;* Robert Remini, *Andrew Jackson and the Bank War: A Study in the Growth of Presidential Power* (New York: W. W. Norton, 1967); Marquis James, *Andrew Jackson: Portrait of a President* (New York: Grosset & Dunlap, 1937), 283-303, 350-385; and Arthur Schlesinger, Jr., *The Age of Jackson* (Boston: Little, Brown, 1945), 74-131.

8. Charles Sellers, Jr., "Who Were the Southern Whigs?" *American Historical Review* 49 (January 1954): 335-346.

9. Harry Scheiber, "The Pet Banks in Jacksonian Politics and Finance, 1833-1841," *Journal of Economic History* 23 (June 1963): 196-214; Frank Otto Gatell, "Spoils of the Bank War: Political Bias in the Selection of Pet Banks," *American Historical Review* 70 (October 1964): 35-58; and Frank Otto Gatell, "Secretary Taney and the Baltimore Pets: A Study in Banking and Politics," *Business History Review* 39 (Summer 1965): 205-227.

10. Quoted in James MacGregor Burns, *Roosevelt: The Lion and the Fox* (New York: Harcourt, Brace & World, 1956), 208.

11. The analysis in this and the following paragraphs draws on Burns, *Roosevelt;* and Freidel, *FDR and the South.*

12. Burns, *Roosevelt,* 223-241.

13. Freidel, *FDR and the South.*

14. Richard Polenberg, *Reorganizing Roosevelt's Government: The Controversy over Executive Reorganization, 1936-1939* (Cambridge, Mass.: Harvard University Press, 1966).

15. The analysis in this and the following paragraphs draws on the following works: Charles Sellers, *James K. Polk: Continentalist, 1843-1846* (Princeton: Princeton University Press, 1966); John Schroeder, *Mr. Polk's War: American Opposition and Dissent, 1846-1848* (Madison: University of Wisconsin Press, 1973); Norman A. Graebner, "James Polk," in *America's Ten Greatest Presidents,* ed. Morton Borden (Chicago: Rand McNally, 1961), 113-138; and Charles McCoy, *Polk and*

the Presidency (Austin: University of Texas Press, 1960).

16. Sellers, *James K. Polk*, 50.

17. Ibid., 113-114, 123.

18. Ibid., 282-283.

19. Ibid., 162-164; Joseph G. Raybeck, "Martin Van Buren's Break with James K. Polk: The Record," *New York History* 36 (January 1955): 51-62; and Norman A. Graebner, "James K. Polk: A Study in Federal Patronage," *Mississippi Valley Historical Review* 38 (March 1952): 613-632.

20. Sellers, *James K. Polk*, 483.

21. Frederick J. Blue, *The Free Soilers: Third Party Politics, 1848-54* (Urbana: University of Illinois Press, 1973), 16-80; and John Mayfield, *Rehearsal for Republicanism: Free Soil and the Politics of Antislavery* (Port Washington, N.Y.: Kennikat Press, 1980), 80-125.

22. McCoy, *Polk and the Presidency*, 197-198, 203-204.

23. Arthur M. Schlesinger, Jr., *A Thousand Days: John F. Kennedy in the White House* (Boston: Houghton Mifflin, 1965), 675-676.

24. Carroll Kilpatrick, "The Kennedy Style and Congress," *Virginia Quarterly Review* 39 (Winter 1963): 1-11; and Henry Fairlie, *The Kennedy Promise: The Politics of Expectation* (New York: Doubleday, 1973), especially 235-263.

25. Freidel, *FDR and the South*, 71-102.

26. Herbert S. Parmet, *The Democrats: The Years after FDR* (New York: Oxford University Press, 1976), 80-82.

27. The analysis in this and the following paragraphs draws on material presented in the following works: Carl M. Bauer, *John F. Kennedy and the Second Reconstruction* (New York: Columbia University Press, 1977); Schlesinger, *A Thousand Days;* Parmet, *The Democrats*, 193-247; Bruce Miroff, *Pragmatic Illusions: The Presidential Politics of John F. Kennedy* (New York: David McKay, 1976), 223-270; and Fairlie, *The Kennedy Promise*, 235-263.

28. Bauer, *John F. Kennedy*, 30-38; and Schlesinger, *A Thousand Days*, 47-52.

29. Bauer, *John F. Kennedy*, 61-88; and Schlesinger, *A Thousand Days*, 30-31.

30. Parmet, *The Democrats*, 211; and Bauer, *John F. Kennedy*, 128-130.

31. Holman Hamilton, *Prologue to Conflict: The Crisis and Compromise of 1850* (Lexington: University of Kentucky Press, 1964), especially 156-164.

32. Roy F. Nichols, *The Democratic Machine, 1850-54* (New York: AMS Press, 1967).

33. Parmet, *The Democrats*, 220-228.

34. The analysis in this and the following paragraphs draws on Roy F. Nichols, *Franklin Pierce: Young Hickory of Granite Hills* (Philadelphia: University of Pennsylvania Press, 1969); and Nichols, *The Democratic Machine*, 147-226.

35. Nichols, *Franklin Pierce*, 292-293, 308-310; and Nichols, *The Democratic Machine*, 224.

36. Roy F. Nichols, "The Kansas-Nebraska Act: A Century of Historiography," *Mississippi Valley Historical Review* 43 (September 1956): 187-212; and Nichols, *Franklin Pierce*, 292-324, 333-338.

37. Nichols, *Franklin Pierce*, 360-365, 425-434.

38. Jack Knott and Aaron Wildavsky, "Skepticism and Dogma in the White House: Jimmy Carter's Theory of Governing," *Wilson Quarterly* 1 (Winter 1977): 49-68; and James Fallows, "The Passionless Presidency: The Trouble with Jimmy Carter's Administration," *Atlantic Monthly*, May 1979, 33-58, and June 1979, 75-81.

39. The analysis in this and the following paragraphs draws on the following works: Robert Shogun, *Promises to Keep: Carter's First Hundred Days* (New York: Thomas Y. Crowell, 1977); Haynes Johnson, *In the Absence of Power: Governing America* (New York: Viking, 1980); Robert Shogun, *None of the Above: Why Presidents Fail and What Can Be Done about It* (New York: New American Library, 1982), 177-250; Thomas Ferguson and Joel Rogers, eds., *The Hidden Election: Politics and Economics in the 1980 Presidential Campaign* (New York: Pantheon, 1981), 200-230; and Alan Wolfe, *America's Impasse: The Rise and Fall of the Politics of Growth* (New York: Pantheon, 1981), 200-230.

40. Shogun, *None of the Above,* 220.

41. Johnson, *In the Absence of Power,* 233-245.

42. *New York Times,* July 16, 1979, 1, 10.

43. See Stephen Skowronek, "Notes on the Presidency in the Political Order," in *Studies in American Political Development,* vol. 1, ed. Karen Orren and Stephen Skowronek (New Haven: Yale University Press, 1986).

7. PRESIDENTIAL COMPETENCE

Paul J. Quirk

The performance of Ronald Reagan in the White House raises a basic, yet rarely examined, question about the presidency: To succeed politically and serve the country well, what must a president know? To what extent must a president be his own expert in governing, whatever that entails, and to what extent can he rely on other officials to supply the necessary knowledge and understanding to do the job? The Reagan presidency puts this question in an unusual light because from the start he was criticized as inattentive and uninformed; because the White House has never denied that he has been much less studious and involved in substantive debate than most presidents; and because, despite two periods of severe difficulty (a recession in the first term and a foreign policy scandal in the second), he nevertheless often has been described as a successful president.[1]

Although the requirements for a competent presidency cannot be reduced to a formula, they should be possible to define in general terms. This chapter examines three distinct and competing conceptions of the president's personal tasks and expertise, that is, of presidential competence. It criticizes two of them—one an orthodox approach of long standing, the other mainly associated with Reagan—as defective. It then presents a third model, based on a notion of "strategic competence," and discusses the requirements of that model in three major areas of presidential activity. At the end, it turns briefly to the question of the competence and success of President Reagan.

The Self-reliant Presidency

Most commentary on the presidency assumes a conception of the president's personal tasks that borders on the heroic. Stated simply, the president must strive to be self-reliant and bear personally a large share of the burden of governing. And he therefore must meet intellectual requirements that are correspondingly rigorous.

The classic argument for the self-reliant presidency is presented in Richard Neustadt's *Presidential Power.*[2] In arguing for an enlarged conception on the presidential role, Neustadt stressed that the president's political interests, and therefore his perspective on decisions, are unique. Only the president has political stakes that correspond with the national interest somehow construed. For no other government official is individual achievement so closely identified with the well-being of the entire nation. Thus a president's chances for success depend on what he can do for himself: his direct involvement in decisions, his personal reputation and skill, his control over subordinates.[3]

It is in this spirit that students of the presidency often hold up Franklin D. Roosevelt as the exemplary modern president—if not for his specific policies or administrative practices, at least for his personal orientation to the job. A perfect "active-positive" in James David Barber's typology of presidential personalities,[4] Roosevelt made strenuous efforts to increase his control and to improve his grasp of issues and situations. For example, he would set up duplicate channels within the government to provide him information and advice, and when this did not seem enough, he looked outside the government for persons who could offer additional perspectives.[5] The ideal president, in short, is one with a consuming passion for control, and thus for information.

This image of the president—as one who makes the major decisions himself, depends on others only in lesser matters, and firmly controls his subordinates—appeals to the general public, which seems to evaluate presidents partly by how well they live up to it. But is the self-reliant presidency sensible, even as an ideal? Both experience and the elementary facts of contemporary government indicate strongly that it is not.

Even for Roosevelt, self-reliance carried certain costs. In an admiring description of Roosevelt's administrative practices, Arthur Schlesinger, Jr., concedes that his methods hampered performance in some respects. Roosevelt's creation of unstructured, competitive relationships among subordinates, a method he used for control, caused "confusion and exasperation on the operating level"; it was "nerve-wracking and often positively demoralizing." Because Roosevelt reserved so many decisions to himself, he could not make all of them promptly, and aides often had to contend with troublesome delays.[6] The overall effect of Roosevelt's self-reliant decision making on the design, operation, and success of New Deal programs is open to question. Indeed, the New Deal is revered (by those who do) mainly for its broad assertion of governmental responsibility for the nation's well-being, not for the effectiveness of its specific programs. Roosevelt took pride in an observer's estimate that for each decision made by Calvin Coolidge, he was making at least thirty-five. Perhaps some smaller ratio would have been better.

In later administrations the weaknesses of the self-reliant presidency have emerged more clearly. Presidents who have aspired to self-reliance have ended up leaving serious responsibilities badly neglected. Lyndon B. Johnson, another president with prodigious energy and a need for control, gravitated naturally to the self-reliant approach.[7] Eventually, however, he directed his efforts narrowly and obsessively to the Vietnam War. Meeting daily with the officers in charge, Johnson directed the military strategy from the Oval Office, going into such detail, at times, as to select specific targets for bombing. Every other area of presidential concern he virtually set aside. Although such detailed involvement would have been unobjectionable had there been any cause to believe it would help to resolve the conflict, the reverse seems more likely. Guided by the president's civilian subordinates, the military officers themselves should have been able to decide matters of strategy at least as well as the president, probably better. Moreover, Johnson's direct operational control of military strategy may have impaired his ability to take a broader, "presidential" perspective. After all, doing a general's job, to some inevitable degree, means thinking like a general. Johnson illustrated a dangerous tendency for self-reliance to become an end in itself.

Jimmy Carter, although less a driven personality than Johnson, preferred self-reliance as a matter of conviction. It led him toward a narrowness of a different kind. From the first month in office, Carter signaled his intention to be thoroughly involved, completely informed, and prompt. "Unless there's a holocaust," he told the staff, "I'll take care of everything the same day it comes in." Thus he spent long hours daily poring over stacks of memoranda and took thick briefing books with him for weekends at Camp David. Initially, he even checked arithmetic in budget documents. Later he complained mildly about the number of memoranda and their length, but he still made no genuine effort to curb the flow.[8] Carter's extreme attention to detail cannot have contributed more than very marginally to the quality of his administration's decisions. Yet it took his attention from other, more essential tasks. Carter was criticized as having failed to articulate the broad themes or ideals that would give his presidency a sense of purpose—a natural oversight, if true, for a president who was wallowing in detail. He certainly neglected the crucial task of nurturing constructive relationships with other leaders in Washington.[9]

The main defect of the self-reliant presidency, however, is none of these particular risks, but rather the blunt, physical impossibility of carrying it out. Perhaps Roosevelt, an extraordinary man who served when government was still relatively manageable, could achieve some sort of approximation of the ideal. But the larger and more complex government has become, the more presidents have been forced to depend on the judgments of others. Today, any single important policy question produces enough pertinent studies, positions, and proposals to keep a conscientious policy maker fully occupied. In any remotely literal sense, therefore, presidential self-reliance is not so much inadvisable as inconceivable.

Even as an inspirational ideal (like perfect virtue), the self-reliant presidency is more misleading than helpful. It can lead to an obsessive narrowness, and it is too far removed from reality to offer any concrete guidance. Rather than such an ideal, presidents need a conception of what a competent, successful performance would really consist of—one that takes the nature of government and the limits of human ability as they exist.

The Minimalist Presidency

A second approach to presidential competence rejects the heroic demands of self-reliance altogether. In this approach, the president requires little or no understanding of specific issues and problems and instead can rely almost entirely on subordinates to resolve them. Although rarely if ever advocated by commentators, the "minimalist" approach commands close attention if only because of the Reagan administration's attempt to use it.

Minimalism does not imply a passive conception of the presidency as an institution, the view of some nineteenth-century American presidents. Accepting the "Whig theory of government," they believed that Congress, as the most representative branch, should lead the country, and thus they left it to Congress to shape and pass legislation without much presidential advice.[10] The Whig theory has been abandoned in the twentieth century, and minimalism, as here defined, is not an attempt to restore it. With the help of a large personal staff, the Office of Management and Budget (OMB), and other presidential agencies in the Executive Office of the President, a minimalist president can exercise his powers as expansively as any.

Nor does minimalism describe the "hidden-hand" leadership ascribed to Dwight D. Eisenhower in the notable reinterpretation of his presidency by Fred Greenstein.[11] Long viewed as a passive president, who reigned rather than ruled, Eisenhower has been thoroughly misinterpreted, according to Greenstein's provocative thesis. In truth, Eisenhower, seeing a political advantage, merely cultivated this image. He worked longer hours, gave closer attention to issues, and exercised more influence than the public was allowed to notice. His methods of influence were indirect. In the long dispute between the administration and Joseph McCarthy over the senator's charges of Communist infiltration of the government, Eisenhower resolutely withheld any public criticism of McCarthy by name. Privately, however, the president and his aides arranged the format of the Senate's Army-McCarthy hearings and plotted strategy for the executive branch, which ultimately led to the senator's downfall.[12]

The hidden-hand style, Greenstein argues, generally permitted Eisenhower to get what he wanted, yet insulated him from politically harmful controversy. By remaining "above politics," Eisenhower could achieve a political feat as yet unmatched by any of his successors— serving two complete four-year terms, popular to the end. Eisenhower was no minimalist, in short; he was merely a closet activist.

The only recent minimalist president has been Ronald Reagan, whose administration often flatly rejected the self-reliant approach. President Reagan's role in decision making, his spokesmen said during the first year, would be that of a chairman of the board. He would personally establish the general policies and goals of his administration, select cabinet and other key personnel who shared his commitments, then delegate broad authority to them so that they could work out the particulars.[13]

In part, the very limited role for the president was clearly designed to accommodate Reagan's particular limitations—especially his disinclination to do much reading or sit through lengthy briefings—and to answer critics who questioned his fitness for office. By expounding a minimalist theory, the Reagan administration was able to defend the president's frequent lapses and inaccuracies in news conferences as harmless and irrelevant. It is a "fantasy of the press," said communications director David Gergen, that an occasional "blooper" in a news conference has any real importance.[14]

Nevertheless, the administration presented this minimalist model not merely as an ad hoc accommodation but as a sensible way in general for a president to operate. The model has at least one claim to be taken seriously: unlike self-reliance, it has the merit of being attainable. For several reasons, however, it can neither be defended in general nor even judged satisfactory in Reagan's case.

First, chairman-of-the-board notions notwithstanding, a minimalist president and his administration will have serious difficulties reaching intelligent decisions. This is so if only because a minimalist president—or rather, the sort of president to whom minimalism might be suited—will not fully appreciate his own limitations. By never paying attention to the complexities of careful policy arguments, one never comes to understand the importance of thorough analysis. In politics and government, at least, people generally do not place a high value on discourse that is much more sophisticated than their own habitual mode of thought.

That President Reagan has shown no particular humility about his ability to make policy judgments has been most apparent in his decisions about budgets, taxes, and the federal deficit. In late 1981, Reagan's key economic policy makers—OMB director David A. Stockman, Treasury Secretary Donald Regan, and White House Chief of Staff James Baker—recommended unanimously that the president propose a modest tax increase to keep the budget deficit to an acceptable level. After the last holdout, Regan, came on board, the press began to treat the president's concurrence as a foregone conclusion. To the humiliation of his advisers, however, Reagan instead followed his own instinct not to retreat and rejected their recommendation. The resulting 1983 presidential budget was so far in deficit that it was dismissed out of hand even by the Republican Senate, and the president ended up accepting a package of "revenue enhancements" that Congress virtually forced upon him. In 1983 and 1984 Reagan repeatedly rejected pleas for a deficit-reducing tax increase that were made by Stockman and Martin Feldstein, the administration's second chairman of the Council of Economic Advisers (CEA) and its most distinguished economist.

Second, even if a minimalist president is willing to delegate authority and accept advice, his aides and cabinet members cannot make up for his limitations. Rather, as they compete for the president's favor, they will tend to assume his likeness. That is, they will take cues from his rhetoric and descend to his level of argumentation; advocates will emerge for almost any policy he is inclined to support. Such imitation apparently produced the scandals in the Environmental Protection Agency (EPA) that embarrassed the Reagan administration during the first term and led to the removal of numerous high-level officials. These officials, including Administrator Anne Gorsuch Burford, interpreted Reagan's sweeping antiregulatory rhetoric to mean that, requirements of the law notwithstanding, they should do hardly any regulating at all. Similarly, because Reagan had made a campaign promise to restore tax exemptions for racially segregated private schools, Treasury and Justice Department officials who should have known that such a policy was legally and politically indefensible proposed a regulation to grant the exemptions. The result was widespread charges that the administration opposed civil rights, months of harmful publicity, and the eventual rejection of the administration's position by an eight-to-one vote of the Supreme Court.[15]

The effect of Reagan's relaxed approach to policy decisions on the quality of debate in his administration is illustrated by a September 1981 White House meeting on the defense budget, recounted in

Stockman's mean-spirited but revealing memoir.[16] OMB was proposing a moderate reduction in the planned growth of defense spending—
still giving the Pentagon an inflation-adjusted increase of 52 percent
over five years and 92 percent of its original request. In a presentation
that Stockman calls "a masterpiece of obfuscation," Secretary of
Defense Caspar W. Weinberger compared American and Soviet
capabilities as if OMB was refusing to endorse any increase. Almost all
of his comparisons, displayed in elaborate charts, concerned weapons
categories that Stockman wasn't trying to cut. Weinberger stressed that
the B-52 bomber was outdated, even though OMB supported full
funding for the B-1 and Stealth bombers that were planned to replace
it; and he detailed the superiority of Warsaw Pact forces in numbers of
divisions, even though OMB had agreed to buy the full complement of
sixteen active divisions the Pentagon wanted. (The secretary concluded
all of this by showing a blown-up cartoon depicting the OMB budget
as "a four-eyed wimp who looked like Woody Allen, carrying a tiny ri-
fle.") In the end, Weinberger got his way. Whatever the merits of the
decision, a well-prepared, attentive president would have dismissed
such a presentation as largely irrelevant to what was actually in
dispute. A defense secretary who anticipated such a response would
have felt compelled to address the real issues.

Finally, if a president openly delegates significant decisions or
almost always accepts subordinates' advice, the press is likely to
comment adversely and make this a source of embarrassment for him.
Because the public likes presidents who seem in command, it makes
good copy for a reporter to suggest that aides are assuming the
president's job—even though relying heavily upon them may be a
sensible adaptation to the president's personal limitations. The press
has sometimes challenged Reagan to demonstrate his involvement in
decisions, and this may have led him to make more decisions in certain
areas than he would have otherwise. During Reagan's summit meetings with Soviet Premier Mikhail Gorbachev, for example, the president negotiated with the Soviet leader one-to-one on arms control, a
subject of daunting complexity for any president.

Neither self-reliance nor minimalism offers a reliable, or even a
plausible, route to presidential competence. The question is whether
there is another possible model that corrects the defects of both—
making feasible demands on the president yet allowing for competent
performance.

Strategic Competence

The third conception of presidential competence, set forth in the
rest of this chapter, lies between the two extremes of minimalism and

self-reliance. But it does not represent merely a vague compromise between them. It is based on a notion of *strategic competence,* from which it derives definition.

Strategic competence does not refer to the correct but not very helpful observation that presidents need to be competent in the choice of strategies. It refers primarily to the idea that, in order to achieve competence, presidents must have a well-designed (even if mostly implicit) strategy *for* competence. This strategy, it seems, must take into account three basic elements of the president's situation.

1. The president's time, energy, and talent, and thus his capacity for direct, personal competence, must be regarded as a scarce resource. *Choices must be made concerning what things a president will attempt to know.*
2. Depending on the task (for example, deciding issues, promoting policies), the president's ability to substitute the judgment and expertise of others for his own and still get satisfactory results varies considerably. *Delegation works better for some tasks than for others.*
3. The success of such substitutions will depend on a relatively small number of presidential actions and decisions concerning the selection of subordinates, the general instructions they are given, and the president's limited interactions with them. *How well delegation works depends on how it is done.*

Achieving competent performance, then, can be viewed as a problem of allocating resources. The president's personal abilities and time to use them are the scarce resources. For each task, the possibilities and requirements for effective delegation determine how much of these resources should be used, and how they should be employed.

The rest of this chapter will work out the implications of strategic competence in three major areas of presidential activity: policy decisions, policy processes, and policy promotion.[17] The test of the model is twofold. For each area of presidential activity, does it provide adequately for competent performance? Taken as a whole, does it call for a level of expertise and attentiveness that an average president can be expected to meet?

Policy Decisions

When it comes to substantive issues, vast presidential ignorance is simply inevitable. No one understands more than a few significant issues very well. Fortunately, presidents can get by—controlling subordinates reasonably well and minimizing the risk of policy disasters—on far less than a thorough mastery. Some prior preparation, however, is required.

As a matter of course, each president has a general outlook or philosophy of government. The principal requirement beyond this is for the president to be familiar enough with the substantive policy debates in each major area to recognize the signs of responsible argument. This especially includes having enough exposure to the work of policy analysts and experts in each area to know, if only in general terms, how they reach conclusions and the contribution they make. The point is not that the president will then be able to work through all the pertinent materials on an issue, evaluate them properly, and reach a sound, independent conclusion—that is ruled out if only for lack of time. However, as he evaluates policy advice, the president will at least be able to tell which of his subordinates are making sense. Whatever the subject at hand, the president will be able to judge: Is an advocate bringing to bear the right kinds of evidence, considerations, and arguments, and citing appropriate authorities?

One can observe the importance of this ability by comparing two, in some respects similar, episodes. Both John F. Kennedy in 1963 and Ronald Reagan in 1981 proposed large, controversial reductions of the individual income tax, each in some sense unorthodox. But in the role played by respectable economic opinion, the two cases could not be more different.

Kennedy brought to bear the prescriptions of Keynesian economics, which by then had been the dominant school of professional economic thought for nearly three decades. The Kennedy administration took office when the economy was in a deep recession. From the beginning, therefore, Walter Heller, a leading academic economist and Kennedy's CEA chairman, sought tax reductions to promote economic growth—the appropriate Keynesian response even though it might increase the federal deficit. Already aware of the rationale for stimulation, Kennedy did not require persuasion on the economic merits, but he did have political reservations. "I understand the case for a tax cut," he told Heller, "but it doesn't fit my call for sacrifice." Nor did it fit the economic views of Congress or the general public—both of which remained faithful on the whole to the traditional belief in an annually balanced budget. But the CEA continued lobbying, and Kennedy—first partially, later completely—went along. Finally, in 1963 Kennedy proposed to reduce income taxes substantially.

The novelty of this proposal, with the economy already recovering and the budget in deficit, alarmed traditionalists. "What can those people in Washington be thinking about?" asked former president Eisenhower in a magazine article. "Why would they deliberately do this to our country?" Congress, which also had doubts, moved slowly but eventually passed the tax cut in 1964. The Keynesian deficits proved right for the time: the tax cut stimulated enough economic activity that revenues, instead of declining, actually increased.[18]

Aside from being a tax cut and being radical, Reagan's proposal bore little resemblance to Kennedy's. Pushed through Congress in the summer of 1981, the Kemp-Roth tax bill (named for its congressional sponsors Rep. Jack F. Kemp and Sen. William V. Roth, Jr.) represented an explicit break with mainstream economic thinking, both liberal and conservative. The bill embodied the ideas of a small fringe group of economists whose views conservative Republican economist Herbert Stein dismissed in the *Wall Street Journal* as "punk supply side economics." In selling the bill to Congress, which was submissive in the aftermath of the Reagan election landslide, the administration made bold, unsupported claims. Despite tax rate reductions of 25 percent in a three-year period, it promised, the bill would so stimulate investment that revenues would increase and deficits decline. This resembled the claims for the Kennedy bill except that, under the prevailing conditions, nothing in conventional economic models or empirical estimates remotely justified the optimistic predictions. Senate Republican leader Howard Baker, a reluctant supporter, termed the bill "a riverboat gamble." The gamble did not pay off. Within a year, policy makers were contemplating deficits in the $200 billion range— twice what they had considered intolerable a short time earlier and enough, nearly all agreed, to damage the economy severely.[19]

A president with some measure of sophistication about economic policy would have dismissed as economic demagoguery the extraordinary claims made for the Kemp-Roth bill.[20] He would have become aware of several things: that mainstream economists have worked out methods for estimating the effects of tax policies; that these estimates are imprecise and subject to a certain range of disagreement; but that, nevertheless, they are the best estimates anybody has. President Reagan undoubtedly knew (it would have been impossible not to) that most economists did not endorse Kemp-Roth. But it seems he had never paid enough attention to economic debate to recognize an important distinction between ideological faith and empirical measurement.

None of this is to suggest that presidents should set aside their ideologies and simply defer to experts, conceived somehow as ideologically neutral. Gerald Ford, the most conservative recent president next to Reagan, had an abiding commitment to the free market and assembled a cabinet and staff largely from individuals who shared his perspective. Yet the Ford administration also insisted that sound professional analysis underlie its decisions and took pains to consider a variety of views. Ford's CEA chairman, Alan Greenspan, was a devout conservative, but he encouraged the president to meet with diverse groups of outside economists (including former advisers in liberal Democratic administrations). He relied on conventional economic models and forecasting methods to fashion his own advice to the president. None of this prevented Ford's conservatism from shaping the policies of his administration, which held down government spending, stressed controlling inflation more than reducing unemployment, and started the process of deregulation.[21]

In much the same way, Reagan achieved conservative goals (cutting tax rates and reducing governmental distortion of economic decisions)—along with some liberal ones (tax relief for low-income people)—in the historic Tax Reform Act of 1986. The president's proposal was based on a massive study of the tax system by economists and tax specialists in the Treasury Department, which had advocated such reforms since the 1960s, and it embodied a consensual judgment among experts both inside and outside of government that the proliferation of credits, exemptions, and deductions in the federal tax code was harmful to the economy.[22]

An adequate level of policy expertise cannot be acquired in a hurry. A president needs to have been over the years the kind of politician who participates responsibly in decision making and debate and who does his homework. This means occasionally taking the time to read some of the advocacy documents (such as hearing testimony and committee reports) that are prepared especially for politicians and their staff. Such documents tend to be pitched toward the politician's sophistication and tolerance for detail, and yet can provide a fairly rigorous education.

If properly prepared, a president need not spend long hours immersed in memoranda, the way Jimmy Carter did. If, after a thorough briefing on a decision of ordinary importance, the president still does not see which course he prefers, he is probably just as well off delegating the decision or taking a vote of his advisers. Other tasks will make more of a contribution to his success than further reading or discussion on a decision that is a close call anyway.

Policy Processes

In addition to policy issues, presidents must be competent in the processes of policy making.[23] Most presidential policy decisions are based on advice from several agencies or advisory groups in the executive branch, each with different responsibilities and points of view. To be useful to the president, all the advice must be brought together in a timely, intelligible way, with proper attention to all the significant viewpoints and considerations. Unfortunately, complex organizational and group decision processes like these have a notorious capacity to produce self-defeating and morally unacceptable results. The specific ways in which they go awry are numerous, but in general terms there are three major threats: intelligence failures, in which critical information is filtered out at lower organizational levels (sometimes because subordinates think the president would be upset by or disagree with it),[24] group-think, in which a decision-making group commits itself to a course of action prematurely and adheres to it because of social pressures to conform,[25] and noncoordination, which may occur in formulating advice, in handling interdependent issues, or in carrying out decisions.[26]

Many of the frustrations of the Carter administration resulted from its failure to organize decision processes with sufficient care and skill. Carter's original energy proposals, which affected numerous federal programs, were nonetheless formulated by a single drafting group under the direction of Energy Secretary James Schlesinger. The group worked in secrecy and isolation, as well as under severe time pressure, which the president had imposed. The resulting proposals had serious flaws that, combined with resentment of the secrecy, led to a fiasco in Congress. Such problems were typical. The Carter administration's system of interagency task forces for domestic policy making generally was chaotic and not well controlled by the White House.[27] Moreover, the White House itself was weakly coordinated. Not only did Carter's White House have fewer high-level coordinators than Reagan's, but, as John Kessel's comparative study has shown, those it did have were less active in communicating with the rest of the staff.[28]

In foreign policy, the major criticisms of the Carter administration concerned its propensity for vacillation and incoherence. Those tendencies resulted largely from its failure to manage the conflict between national security assistant Zbigniew Brzezinski and Secretary of State Cyrus Vance. Despite their different approaches to foreign policy, neither their respective roles nor the administration's operative doctrines were ever adequately clear. One crucial issue was whether the American stance toward negotiating with the Soviets on strategic arms would be linked with Soviet activities in the Horn of Africa (as Brzezinski wanted), or decided solely for its direct effects on American strategic interests (the preference of Vance). Instead of being reconciled, both policies were stated in public, each by the official who favored it, which cast doubt on America's ability to act consistently on either of them.[29] In part this problem resulted from Carter's personal unwillingness to discipline subordinates—to insist, for example, that Brzezinski abide by the more modest role that in theory had been assigned to him.

In short, serious presidential failures often will result not from individual ignorance—his own or that of his advisers—but from their collective failure to maintain reliable processes for decision. But what must a president know to avoid this danger, and how can he learn it?

The effort to design the best possible organization for presidential coordination of the executive branch is exceedingly complex and uncertain—fundamentally a matter of hard trade-offs and guesses, not elegant solutions. Rather than adopt any one organizational plan or carefully study the debates about them, a president needs to have a high degree of generalized *process sensibility*. He should be generally conversant with the risks and impediments to effective decision making and strongly committed to avoiding them; he should recognize the potentially decisive effects of structure, procedures, and leadership methods; and he should be prepared to assign these matters a high priority. In short, the president should see organization and procedure as matters both difficult and vital.

The main operational requirements are straightforward. One or more of the president's top-level staff should be a process specialist— someone with experience managing large organizations, ideally the White House, and whose role is defined primarily as a manager and guardian of the decision process, not as an adviser on politics and policy.[30] Certainly one such person is needed in the position of White House chief of staff; others, perhaps much lower in rank, are needed to manage each major area of policy. A suitable person is one who is sophisticated about the problems of organizational design and the subtleties of human relationships—in addition to just being orderly. The president should invest such a person with the support and authority needed to impose a decision-making structure and help him insist on adherence to it. Since any organizational arrangement will have weaknesses, some of them unexpected, the president and other senior officials must give the decision-making process continual attention—monitoring its performance, and making adjustments.

Finally, if any of this is to work, the president also must be willing to discipline his own manner of participation. A well-managed, reliable decision-making process sometimes requires the president to perform, so to speak, unnatural acts. For example, in the heat of debate about a major decision, the inclination to enforce general plans about structures and roles does not come naturally. A "point-of-order" about procedures appears to distract from urgent decisions. In any case, the president's temptation is to react according to the substantive outcome he thinks he prefers: if an official who is supposed to be a neutral coordinator has a viewpoint the president likes, let him be heard; if an agency will make trouble over a decision that seems inevitable, let it stay out of it.

Whatever the established procedures, senior officials sometimes will try to bypass them—asking for more control of a certain issue or ignoring channels to give the president direct advice.

On important decisions that require intensive discussion—decisions in major foreign policy crises, for example—the requirements are even more unnatural. In order to avoid serious mistakes, it is crucial not to suppress disagreement or close off debate prematurely. Thus, it is important for the president to assume a neutral stance until the time comes to decide. According to psychologist Irving Janis's study of the Kennedy administration's disastrous decision to invade the Bay of Pigs, the president unwittingly inhibited debate just by his tone and manner of asking questions, which made it obvious that he believed, or wanted to believe, the invasion would work.[31] The president must restrain tendencies that are perfectly normal: to form opinions, perhaps optimistic ones, before all the evidence is in, and then want others to relieve his anxiety by agreeing. He must have a strong process sensibility if only because without it he would lack the motivation to do his own part.

The performance of Reagan and his aides in organization and policy managment has been mixed. In establishing effective advisory systems, especially at the outset of the administration, they did well. The administration's principal device for making policy decisions, a system of "cabinet councils," was planned and run largely by Chief of Staff James Baker, who had a knack for organization and previous experience in the Ford administration.[32] Each cabinet council was a subcommittee of the full cabinet, staffed by the White House and chaired by a cabinet member or sometimes the president. The system generally worked well in blending departmental and White House perspectives and reaching decisions in a timely manner, and it kept cabinet members attuned to the president's goals. Inevitably, adjustments were made with the passage of time. A White House Legislative Strategy Group (LSG) ended up making many of the decisions. Among the cabinet councils, the one assigned to coordinate economic policy, chaired by Treasury Secretary Regan, assumed a broad jurisdiction. To a degree, Reagan played his part in making these arrangements work. He enforced roles—removing a secretary of state, Alexander Haig, who was prone to exceed the limits of his charter—and invested the chief of staff with the authority to run an orderly process.

Nevertheless, the Reagan administration often has failed to make decisions through a reasonably sound, deliberate process. One difficulty has been that some of the officials Reagan has selected to manage decision making have lacked the appropriate skills or disposition for the task. In 1985 he allowed an exhausted Baker and an ambitious Regan to switch jobs. Although Regan by then had plenty of experience, he was less suited than Baker to the coordinating role of a chief of staff, and he soon came under attack for surrounding himself with weak subordinates and seeking to dominate the decision process. Until the appointment of Frank D. Carlucci in December 1986, the administration went through a series of four undistinguished national security advisers—one of them, William P. Clark, a long-time associate of Reagan's with minimal experience in foreign policy.

On a number of occasions an even more important source of difficulty was the conduct of the president himself. Instead of exercising self-restraint and fostering discussion, Reagan gave his own impulses free rein. He ignored bad news and responded with anger to unwelcome advice.[33] His role in decisions was unpredictable. Reagan's announcement in March 1983 of the effort to develop a "Star Wars" missile defense system was made, as Steinbrunner says, "without prior staff work or technical definition ... [and] rather astonished professional security bureaucracies throughout the world."[34] The Star Wars program is profoundly controversial on grounds of cost, feasibility, and strategic value; yet the president acted without even a cursory canvassing of opinion in the executive branch. During the 1986 summit meeting in Reykjavik, Iceland, Reagan again acted without prior staff work as he tentatively accepted a surprise Soviet proposal to do away with long-range nuclear weapons—a Utopian notion that ignored the vast superiority of Soviet conventional forces and was soon disavowed by the administration.

Finally, a lack of concern for the integrity of the decision process figured prominently in the Iran-contra scandal that emerged in late 1986, a disaster for U.S. foreign policy and the worst political crisis of the Reagan presidency. Intended largely to gain the release of American hostages held in Lebanon, the secret arms sales to Iran were vehemently opposed by Secretary of State George P. Shultz and Defense Secretary Weinberger, who wrote on his copy of the White House memorandum proposing the plan that it was "almost too absurd for comment." To get around their resistance, the White House largely excluded the two officials from further discussions and carried out the sales, in some degree, without their knowledge. Moreover, to escape the normal congressional oversight of covert activities, the transfers were handled directly by the staff of the National Security Council (NSC), theoretically an advisory unit, instead of the Defense Department (DOD) or the Central Intelligence Agency (CIA). In short, the White House deprived itself of the advice of the two principal cabinet members in foreign policy, the congressional leadership on intelligence matters, and the operational staff of DOD and the CIA—any of whom would have been likely to point out, aside from other serious objections, that the weapons transfers almost inevitably would become public. After the story broke, the transfers were all but universally condemned, and a White House aide was moved to ask his colleagues, "Can't we even think of a good reason for the arms sale—not one to justify it, but a reason good enough that people wouldn't think we're crazy?" [35]

The scandal became even deeper and more complex when it was revealed that some of the proceeds from the sale apparently were diverted, illegally, to the contra forces seeking to overthrow the Marxist government of Nicaragua. At a minimum, this aspect of the scandal indicates a marked failure of managerial control of the NSC staff.

Policy Promotion

Good policy decisions, carefully made, are not enough. Presidents also need competence in policy promotion—the ability to get things done in Washington and especially in Congress. For no other major presidential task, it seems, is the necessary knowledge any more complicated or esoteric. Nevertheless, it is also a task in which delegation can largely substitute for the president's own judgment and thus one in which strategic competence places a modest burden on the president. [36]

To promote his policies effectively, a president must act upon good judgment on complex, highly uncertain problems of strategy and tactics. Which presidential policy goals are politically feasible and which must be deferred? With which groups or congressional leaders should coalitions be formed? When resistance is met, should the president stand firm, perhaps taking the issue to the public, or should he compromise? In all these matters what is the proper timing? Such decisions call for a form of political expertise that has several related elements (all of them different from winning elections): a solid knowledge of the main coalitions, influence relations, and rivalries among groups and individuals in Washington; personal acquaintance with a considerable number of important or well-informed individuals; and a fine-grained, practical understanding of how the political institutions work. This expertise can be acquired, clearly enough, only through substantial and recent experience in Washington. For a president who happens to lack this experience, however, this need not pose much difficulty. Like any technical skill, which in a sense it is, it can easily be hired; the president needs merely to see his need for it.

Because the government has many jobs that require political skill, people with the requisite experience abound. Many of them (to state the matter politely) would be willing to serve in the White House, and by asking around it is not hard to get good readings on their effectiveness. Most importantly, having hired experienced Washington operatives, a president can delegate to them the critical judgments about feasibility, strategy, and political technique. It is not that such judgments are clear-cut, of course. But unlike questions of policy, in these matters there is no difficult boundary to discern between the realm of expertise and that of values and ideology. Political strategy, in the narrow sense of how to achieve given policy objectives to the greatest possible extent, is ideologically neutral. It is even nonpartisan: Republican and Democratic presidents attempt to influence Congress in much the same way.[37] In any case, a political expert's performance in the White House can be measured primarily by short-term results, that is, by how much the administration's policy goals are actually being achieved.

Both the value and the necessity of delegating policy promotion emerge from a comparison of Carter and Reagan—the two recent presidents who had no prior Washington experience. If there was a single, root cause of the failure of the Carter administration (underlying even its mismanagement of decision making), it was its refusal to recruit people with successful experience in Washington politics for top advisory and political jobs in the White House.

One of the more unfortunate choices was that of Frank Moore to direct legislative liaison. Although he had held the same job in Georgia when Carter was governor, Moore had no experience in Washington and came to be regarded in Congress as out of his depth. Among Moore's initial staff, which consisted mostly of Georgians, two of the five professionals had worked neither in Congress nor as a lobbyist. In organizing them, Moore chose a plan that had been opposed by the former Democratic liaison officials asked for advice. Instead of using the conventional division by chambers and major congressional groups, Moore assigned each lobbyist to specialize in an area of policy. This kept them from developing the stable relationships with individual members of Congress that would enhance trust, and it ignored the straightforward consideration that not all the issues in which the lobbyists specialized would be actively considered at the same time.[38] The Carter administration's reputed incompetence in dealing with Congress might have been predicted: the best of the many Georgians on the Carter staff were able and effective, but others were not, and collectively they lacked the orientation to operate well in Washington.[39]

After this widely condemned failure of his immediate predecessor, it is not surprising that President Reagan did not make the same mistake. But it is still impressive how thoroughly he applied the lesson, even setting aside sectarian considerations for some of the top White

House positions. James Baker, who was mainly responsible for political operations during the first term, not only had been a Ford administration appointee and campaign manager for George Bush, but was considered too moderate for a high-level position by many of Reagan's conservative supporters. The congressional liaison director, Max Friedersdorf, was a mainstream Republican who had worked on congressional relations for Nixon and Ford.[40] In short, the political strategy by which the "Reagan Revolution" was pushed through Congress in 1981 was devised and executed by hired hands who were latecomers, at most, to Reaganism. Although there was some change in personnel in subsequent years, including the job switch by Baker and Regan, the organization and management of this function was essentially stable.[41]

Although the task of formulating strategy for policy promotion can be delegated, much of the hard work cannot. Nothing can draw attention to a proposal and build public support like a well-presented speech by the president. Further, there are always certain votes available in Congress if the president makes the necessary phone calls or meets with the right members. The latter task is often tedious, however, if not somewhat degrading—pleading for support, repeating the same pitch over and over, and promising favors to some while evading requests from others. Presidents therefore often neglect this duty, a source of frustration for their staffs. Carter "went all over the country for two years asking everybody he saw to vote for him," his press secretary complained, "but he doesn't like to call up a Congressman and ask for his support on a bill." Reagan, in contrast, spared no personal effort to pass his program. During the debate on funding for the MX missile in 1985, he had face-to-face meetings with more than two hundred members of Congress, and followed up with dozens of phone calls. When House Republicans felt they were being ignored in negotiations on tax reform, he went to the Hill to make amends. Of course, a president's effectiveness in lobbying and making speeches depends very much on his basic skills in persuasive communication. A lack of such skills cannot be made up by presidential aides; nor can it be overcome to any great extent by additional learning.

The Possibility of Competence

The presidency is not an impossible job. The requirements for personal knowledge, attention, and expertise on the president's part seem wholly manageable—but only if the president has a *strategy* for competence that puts his own, inherently limited capacities to use where and how they are most needed.

With regard to the substance of *policy decisions*, it is enough if the president over the years has given reasonably serious attention to the major national issues and thus is able to recognize the elements of responsible debate. Waking before sunrise to read stacks of policy memoranda is neither necessary nor especially productive. To maintain an effective *policy process,* the president needs mainly to have a strong process sensibility, that is, a clear sense of the need for careful and self-conscious management of decision making and a willingness to discipline himself as he participates in it. He need not claim any facility in drawing the boxes and arrows of organization charts himself. Although this substantive and procedural competence will not ensure that the president will always make the "right" decision—the one he would make with perfect understanding of the issues—it will minimize the likelihood of decisions that are intolerably far off the mark. Finally, and easiest of all, the president must know enough to avail himself of the assistance of persons experienced in *policy promotion* in the political environment of Washington, and especially in dealing with Congress—whether they have been long-time supporters or not. Then he must respect their advice and do the work they ask of him.

J̃udged in these terms, as we have seen, President Reagan has performed well in some ways but not in others. His most consistently competent performance has been in promoting policies, where he has obtained the services of people with the requisite experience; relied, generally, on their judgment; and contributed generously of his own effort. In some respects he has shown appropriate concern for the decision process. At least his administration had a carefully designed advisory system. But Reagan has failed to meet the requirements of competence in two related ways. In making decisions, he sometimes has ignored substantive debate or dismissed expert opinion as irrelevant—even in matters, such as macroeconomic policy, clearly subject to expertise. And he has undermined reliable decision processes, not only overruling but actively suppressing unwelcome advice. In short, he has shown how a minimalist president may assume a dangerously large role in making the decisions of his administration.

In some ways Reagan has been an impressively successful president, achieving many of his policy goals and generally maintaining the public's confidence—at least until the Iran-contra affair caused a dramatic drop in his public standing. This may seem to suggest that for the most part he has gotten away with whatever weaknesses he has had as a decision maker. That conclusion, however, would be premature. Some of Reagan's initial policies—his blunt rejection of environmentalism, confrontational stance toward the Soviet Union, and accommodating stance toward South Africa—were so politically unacceptable they eventually were abandoned. Other policies—those that have created and locked into place an enormous budget deficit; that have produced a vast expansion of military spending, most of it poured into nuclear weaponry; and that seek to commit a sizable share of the nation's resources to a missile defense system with uncertain feasibility and strategic value—are still in place. It can be said without exaggeration that there have been deeper concerns about the fundamental soundness and long-term consequences of these policies, shared by a wider spectrum of informed opinion, than were evoked by the policies of any previous modern president.[43]

Notes

This chapter is an extensively revised and elaborated version of "What Must a President Know?" by Paul J. Quirk in *Transaction/SOCIETY,* no. 23 (January/February 1983) © 1983 by Transaction Publishers. The author would like to acknowledge the following people for their very helpful advice: Stella Herriges Quirk, Irving Louis Horowitz, A. James Reichley, Robert A. Katzmann, Martha Derthick, and Michael Nelson.

1. This judgment is, of course, controversial. Surveyed in 1985, before the Iran-contra crisis, on how history would rate Reagan, members of a group of political scientists who study the presidency showed a wide range of opinion. The opinions of the 109 persons who gave usable responses were as follows: "great," 8; "near great," 3; "good," 56; "fair," 23; "poor," 19. The journalist who did the survey was impressed that a solid majority (61 percent) graded Reagan as "good" or better. However, since "good" was the middle category—a position normally reserved for a neutral response—it is just as pertinent that an even larger majority (82 percent) graded him as "good" or worse. Almost four times as many respondents chose one of the two bottom categories as one of the two top ones. It should be added that political scientists, like other social scientists, are generally liberal in their politics. Don Bonafede, "Presidential Scholars Expect History to Treat the Reagan Presidency Kindly," *National Journal,* April 6, 1985, 743. See also Bruce Buchanan, *The Citizen's Presidency* (Washington, D.C.: CQ Press, 1987).
2. Richard E. Neustadt, *Presidential Power: The Politics of Leadership* (New York: John Wiley & Sons, 1960). Later editions, most recently in 1980, have updated the analysis and in some ways modified the argument.
3. Ibid., chap. 7.
4. James David Barber, *The Presidential Character: Predicting Performance in the White House,* 2d ed. (Englewood Cliffs, N.J.: Prentice-Hall, 1977).
5. Arthur M. Schlesinger, Jr., "Roosevelt as Administrator," in *Bureaucratic Power in National Politics,* 2d ed., ed. Francis E. Rourke (Boston: Little, Brown, 1972), 126-138.
6. Ibid., 132-133, 137.
7. On Johnson's personality and his presidency, see Doris Kearns, *Lyndon Johnson and the American Dream* (New York: Harper & Row, 1976).
8. James Fallows, "The Passionless Presidency," *Atlantic,* May 1979, 33-48.
9. See Nelson W. Polsby, *The Consequences of Party Reform* (New York: Oxford University Press, 1983), 108-109.

10. On the Whig theory and the changing conceptions of the presidency as an institution, see James L. Sundquist, *The Decline and Resurgence of Congress* (Washington, D.C.: Brookings Institution, 1981), chap. 2.

11. Fred I. Greenstein, *The Hidden-Hand Presidency: Eisenhower as Leader* (New York: Basic Books, 1982).

12. Ibid., 61, 155-227.

13. Dick Kirschten, "White House Strategy," *National Journal,* February 21, 1981, 300-303.

14. John Herbers, "The Presidency and the Press Corps," *New York Times Magazine,* May 9, 1982, 45ff.

15. The case was *Bob Jones University v. United States* (1983).

16. David A. Stockman, *The Triumph of Politics: How the Reagan Revolution Failed* (New York: Harper & Row, 1986), 276-295.

17. For the sake of brevity, I omit the president's problems and potential strategies for managing policy implementation by the bureaucracy. See Richard P. Nathan, *The Administrative Presidency* (New York: John Wiley & Sons, 1983). This function depends heavily on the appropriate selection of political executives. See G. Calvin Mackenzie, *The Politics of Presidential Appointments* (New York: Free Press, 1980).

18. Arthur M. Schlesinger, Jr., *A Thousand Days: John F. Kennedy in the White House* (Boston: Houghton Mifflin, 1965), 628-630, 1002-1008.

19. At least one Reagan administration leader has been candid about the role of faith in its 1981 economic proposals. See William Greider, "The Education of David Stockman," *Atlantic,* December 1981, 27ff.

20. The same cannot be said of members of Congress, whom one expects to be more prone to demagoguery, and who came under intense political pressure, stimulated in large part by the president.

21. See A. James Reichley, *Conservatives in an Age of Change: The Nixon and Ford Administrations* (Washington, D.C.: Brookings Institution, 1981), chap. 18; Roger Porter, *Presidential Decision Making: The Economic Policy Board* (New York: Cambridge University Press, 1980), chap. 3; and Martha Derthick and Paul J. Quirk, *The Politics of Deregulation* (Washington, D.C.: Brookings Institution, 1985), chap. 2.

22. Timothy B. Clark, "Strange Bedfellows," *National Journal,* February 2, 1985. For a penetrating study of the politics of taxation, see John F. Witte, *The Politics and Development of the Federal Income Tax* (Madison: University of Wisconsin Press, 1985).

23. The president's task in managing decision making is more difficult than that of chief executives in some of the parliamentary democracies because they have more elaborate and better institutionalized coordinating machinery. See Colin Campbell and George J. Szablowski, *The Super-Bureaucrats: Structure and Behavior in Central Agencies* (New York: New York University Press, 1979).

24. Harold Wilensky, *Organizational Intelligence: Knowledge and Policy in Government and Industry* (New York: Basic Books, 1967).

25. Irving Janis, *Victims of GroupThink: A Psychological Study of Foreign-Policy Decisions and Fiascoes* (Boston: Houghton Mifflin, 1972).

26. Fundamentally, all organization theory concerns the problem of coordination. See Anthony Downs, *Inside Bureaucracy* (Boston: Little, Brown, 1967), chap. 11; and Jay R. Galbraith, *Organization Design* (Reading, Mass.: Addison Wesley, 1977). Problems of coordination in the executive branch are emphasized in I. M. Destler,

Making Foreign Economic Policy (Washington, D.C.: Brookings Institution, 1980).

27. Lester M. Salamon, "The Presidency and Domestic Policy Formulation," in *The Illusion of Presidential Government,* ed. Hugh Heclo and Lester Salamon (Boulder, Colo.: Westview Press, 1982), 177-212.

28. For this and other Reagan-Carter comparisons, see John H. Kessel, "The Structures of the Reagan White House" (Paper delivered at the annual meeting of the American Political Science Association, Chicago, September 1-4, 1983). More generally on Carter, however, see Kessel, "The Structures of the Carter White House," *American Journal of Political Science* 22 (August 1983).

29. The resulting mutual recriminations constitute leading themes in the recently published memoirs of the two officials. See Cyrus Vance, *Hard Choices: Critical Years in America's Foreign Policy* (New York: Simon & Schuster, 1983); and Zbigniew Brzezinski, *Power and Principle: Memoirs of the National Security Advisor, 1977-1981* (New York: Farrar, Straus & Giroux, 1983).

30. An influential argument for separating the roles of process manager and policy adviser is in Alexander George, "The Case for Multiple Advocacy in Making Foreign Policy," *American Political Science Review* 66 (September 1972): 751-785; see also George, *Presidential Decision Making: The Effective Use of Information and Advice* (Boulder, Colo.: Westview Press, 1980).

31. Janis, *Victims of GroupThink,* chap. 2.

32. For an account of the Reagan administration's organizational strategy, see James P. Pfiffner, "White House Staff versus the Cabinet: Centripetal and Centrifugal Roles," *Presidential Studies Quarterly* 16 (Fall 1986): 666-690.

33. Reagan's capacity for ignoring bad news is documented in Stockman, *The Triumph of Politics;* and Laurence I. Barrett, *Gambling With History: Reagan in the White House* (New York: Penguin Books, 1984), especially 174.

34. John D. Steinbrunner, "Security Policy," in *The New Direction in American Politics,* ed. John E. Chubb and Paul E. Peterson (Washington, D.C.: Brookings Institution, 1985), 351.

35. *Los Angeles Times,* December 31, 1986. Even though the arms sale had no prominent defenders outside the administration, and only a few within it, the president refused to admit that the decision was a mistake; he conceded only that errors had been made in its implementation.

36. On the president's relations with Congress, see Anthony King, ed., *Both Ends of the Avenue: The Presidency, the Executive Branch, and Congress in the 1980s* (Washington, D.C.: American Enterprise Institute, 1983).

37. For a historical treatment and analysis of organization for White House liaison, see Stephen J. Wayne, *The Legislative Presidency* (New York: Harper & Row, 1978).

38. Eric L. Davis, "Legislative Liaison in the Carter Administration," *Political Science Quarterly* 95 (Summer 1979): 287-302. Eventually, organization of the staff by issues was dropped.

39. In *Consequences of Party Reform,* 105-114, Polsby details the Carter administration's major mistakes in dealing with Congress and argues persuasively that its difficulties were not importantly the result of internal changes in Congress.

40. Dick Kirschten, "Second Term Legislative Strategy Shifts to Foreign Policy and Defense Issues," *National Journal,* March 30, 1985, 696-699.

41. Samuel Kernell, *Going Public: New Strategies of Presidential Leadership* (Washington, D.C.: CQ Press, 1986); and Theodore J. Lowi, *The Personal President:*

Power Invested, Promise Unfulfilled (Ithaca, N.Y.: Cornell University Press, 1985).

42. Quoted in Polsby, *Consequences of Party Reform,* 109.
43. The Vietnam War, which was probably the worst policy mistake of modern times, was fought and then gradually abandoned by a series of presidents whose policies generally were in rough correspondence with the changing tides of national opinion. To broaden the comparison, the one president of the twentieth century who encountered more doubt than Reagan was Herbert Hoover, whose passive approach to dealing with the Depression was rejected overwhelmingly by informed opinion and the general public.

8. THE PSYCHOLOGICAL PRESIDENCY

Michael Nelson

The United States elects its president every four years, which makes it unique among democratic nations. During almost every recent election campaign, *Time* magazine has run a story about James David Barber, which makes him equally singular among political scientists. The two quadrennial oddities are not unrelated.

The first *Time* article was about Barber's just published book *The Presidential Character: Predicting Performance in the White House,* in which he argued that presidents could be divided into four psychological types: "active-positive," "active-negative," "passive-positive," and "passive-negative." What's more, according to Barber via *Time,* with "a hard look at men before they reach the White House," voters could tell in advance what candidates would be like if elected: healthily "ambitious out of exuberance," like the active-positives; or pathologically "ambitious out of anxiety," "compliant and other-directed," or "dutiful and self-denying," like the three other, lesser types, respectively. In the 1972 election, Barber told *Time,* the choice was between an active-positive, George McGovern, and a psychologically defective active-negative, Richard Nixon.[1]

Nixon won the election, but Barber's early insights into Nixon's personality won notoriety for both him and his theory, especially in the wake of Watergate. So prominent had Barber become by 1976 that Hugh Sidey used his entire "Presidency" column in the October 4 *Time* just to tell readers that Barber was refusing to type candidates Gerald R. Ford and Jimmy Carter this time around. "Barber is deep into an academic study of this election and its participants, and he is pledged to restraint until it is over," Sidey reported solemnly.[2] (Actually, more than a year before, Barber had told interviewers from *U.S. News & World Report* that he considered Ford an active-positive.)[3] Carter, who read Barber's book twice when it came out, was left to tell the *Washington Post* that active-positive is "what I would like to be. That's what I hope I prove to be."[4] And so Carter would, wrote Barber in a special postelection column for *Time.*[5]

The 1980 election campaign witnessed the appearance of another Barber book, *The Pulse of Politics: Electing Presidents in the Media Age,* and in honor of the occasion, two *Time* articles. This was all to the good, because the first, a Sidey column in March, offered more gush than information: "The first words encountered in the new book by Duke's Professor James David Barber are stunning: 'A revolution in presidential politics is underway.'. . . Barber has made political history before." [6] A more substantive piece in the May 19 "Nation" section described the new book's cycle theory of twentieth-century presidential elections: since 1900, steady four-year "beats" in the public's psychological mood, or "pulse," have caused a recurring alternation among elections of "conflict," "conscience," and "conciliation." *Time* went on to stress, although not explain, Barber's view of the importance of the mass media, both as a reinforcer of this cycle and as a potential mechanism for helping the nation to break out of it. [7]

Time's infatuation with Barber brought him fame that comes rarely to scholars, more rarely still to political scientists. For Barber, it has come at some cost. Although widely known, his ideas are little understood. The media's cursory treatment of them has made them appear superficial or even foolish—instantly appealing to the naive, instantly odious to the thoughtful. Partly as a result, Barber's reputation in the intellectual community as an *homme sérieux* has suffered. In the backrooms and corridors of scholarly gatherings, one hears "journalistic" and "popularizer," the worst academic epithets, muttered along with his name.

This situation is in need of remedy. Barber's theories may be seriously flawed, but they are serious theories. For all their limitations—some of them self-confessed—they offer one of the more significant contributions a scholar can make: an unfamiliar but useful way of looking at a familiar thing that we no longer see very clearly. In Barber's case, the familiar thing is the American presidency, and the unfamiliar way of looking at it is through the lenses of psychology.

Psychological Perspectives on the Presidency

Constitutional Perspectives

To look at politics in general, or the American presidency in particular, from a psychological perspective is not new. Although deprived of the insights (and spared the nonsense) of twentieth-century psychology, the framers of the Constitution constructed their plan of government on a foundation of Hobbesian assumptions about what motivates political man. James Madison and most of his colleagues at the Constitutional Convention assumed that "men are instruments of their desires"; that "one such desire is the desire for power"; and that "if unrestrained by external checks, any individual or group of individuals will tyrannize over others." [8] Because the framers believed these things, a basic tenet of their political philosophy was that the government they were designing should be a "governmer' of laws and not of men." Not just psychology but recent history had taught them to associate liberty with law and tyranny with rulers who departed from law, as had George III and his colonial governors.

In the end the convention yielded to those who urged, on grounds of "energy in the executive," that the Constitution lodge the powers of the executive branch in a single person, the president.[9] There are several explanations for why the framers were willing to put aside their doubts and inject such a powerful dose of individual "character," in both the moral and the psychological senses of the word, into their new plan of government. The first is the framers' certain knowledge that George Washington would be the first president. They knew that Washington aroused powerful and, from the standpoint of winning the nation's support for the new government, vital psychological reactions from the people. As Seymour Martin Lipset has shown, Washington was a classic example of Max Weber's charismatic leader, a man "treated [by the people] as endowed with supernatural, superhuman, or at least specifically exceptional powers or qualities." [10] Marcus Cunliffe notes that

> babies were being christened after him as early as 1775, and while he was still President, his countrymen paid to see him in waxwork effigy. To his admirers he was "godlike Washington," and his detractors complained to one another that he was looked upon as a "demigod" who it was treasonous to criticize. "Oh Washington!" declared Ezra Stiles of Yale (in a sermon of 1783). "How I do love thy name! How have I often adored and blessed thy God, for creating and forming thee the great ornament of human kind!" [11]

Just as Washington's charismatic "gift of grace" would legitimize the new government, the framers believed, so would his personal character ensure its republican nature. The powers of the president in the Constitution "are full great," wrote South Carolina convention delegate Pierce Butler to a British kinsman,

> and greater than I was disposed to make them. Nor, entre nous, do I believe they would have been so great had not many of the delegates cast their eyes towards General Washington as President; and shaped their Ideas of the Powers to be given to a President, by their opinions of his Virtue.[12]

The framers were not so naive or short-sighted as to invest everything in Washington. To protect the nation from power-mad tyrants after he left office, they provided that the election of presidents, whether by electors or members of the House of Representatives, would involve selection by peers—personal acquaintances of the candidates who could screen out those of defective character. And even if someone of low character slipped through the net and became president, the framers felt that they had structured the office to keep the nation from harm. "The founders' deliberation over the provision for indefinite reeligibility," writes Jeffrey Tulis, "illustrates how they believed self-interest could sometimes be elevated." [13] Whether motivated by "avarice," "ambition," or "the love of fame," argues Alexander Hamilton in the *Federalist,* a president will behave responsibly in order to secure reelection to the office that allows him to fulfill his desire.[14] Underlying this confidence was the assurance that in a relatively slow paced world, a mad or wicked president could do only so much damage before corrective action could remove him. As John Jay explains, "So far as the fear of punishment and disgrace can operate, that motive to good behavior is amply afforded by the article on the subject of impeachment." [15]

Scholarly Perspectives

The framers' decision to inject personality into the presidency was a conscious one. But it was made for reasons that eventually ceased to pertain, the last of them crumbling on August 6, 1945, when on orders of an American president, an atomic bomb was dropped on Hiroshima. The destructive powers at a modern president's disposal are ultimate and swift; the impeachment process now seems uncertain and slow. Peer review never took hold in the Electoral College. The rise of the national broadcast media makes the president's personality all the more pervasive. In sum, the framers' carefully conceived defenses against a president of defective character are gone.

Clearly, then, a sophisticated psychological perspective on the presidency was overdue in the late 1960s, when Barber began offering one in a series of articles and papers that culminated in *The Presidential Character.*[16] Presidential scholars long had taken as axiomatic that the American presidency is an institution shaped in some measure by the personalities of individual presidents. But rarely had the literature of personality *theory* been brought to bear, in large part because scholars of the post-Franklin D. Roosevelt period no longer seemed to share the framers' assumptions about human nature, at least as far as the presidency was concerned. As we saw in Chapter 1, historians and political scientists exalted not only presidential power, but also presidents who were ambitious for power. Richard Neustadt's influential book *Presidential Power,* published in 1960, was typical in this regard:

> The contributions that a president can make to government are indispensable. Assuming that he knows what power is and wants it, those contributions cannot help but be forthcoming in some measure as by-products of his search for personal influence.[17]

As Erwin Hargrove reflected in post-Vietnam, post-Watergate 1974, this line of reasoning was the source of startling deficiencies in scholarly understandings of the office: "We had assumed that ideological purpose was sufficient to purify the drive for power, but we forgot the importance of character." [18]

Scholars also had recognized for some time that Americans' attitudes about the presidency, like presidents' actions, are psychologically as well as politically rooted. Studies of schoolchildren indicated that they first come into political awareness by learning of, and feeling fondly toward, the president. As adults, they "rally" to the president's support, both when they inaugurate a new one and in times of crisis.[19] Popular nationalistic emotions, which in constitutional monarchies are directed toward the king or queen, are deflected in American society onto the presidency. Again, however, scholars' awareness of these psychological forces manifested itself more in casual observation (Dwight D. Eisenhower was a "father figure"; the "public mood" is fickle) than in systematic thought.

The presidencies of John F. Kennedy, Lyndon B. Johnson, and Richard M. Nixon altered this state of scholarly quiescence. Surveys taken shortly after the Kennedy assassination recorded the startling depth of the feelings that citizens have about the presidency. A large share of the population experienced symptoms classically associated with grief over the death of a loved one. Historical evidence suggests that the public has responded similarly to the deaths of all sitting presidents, popular or not, by murder or natural causes.[20]

If Kennedy's death illustrated the deep psychological ties of the public to the presidency, the experiences of his successors showed even more clearly the importance of psychology in understanding the connection between president and presidency. Johnson, the peace candidate who rigidly pursued a self-defeating policy of war, and Nixon, who promised "lower voices" only to angrily turn political disagreements into personal crises, projected their personalities onto policy in ways that were both obvious and destructive. The events of this period brought students of the presidency up short. As they paused to consider the nature of the "psychological presidency," they found Barber standing at the ready with the foundation and first floor of a full-blown theory.

James David Barber and the Psychological Presidency

Barber's theory offers a model of the presidency as an institution shaped largely by the psychological mix between the personalities of individual presidents and the public's deep feelings about the office. It also proposes methods of predicting what those personalities and feelings are likely to be in given instances. These considerations govern *The Presidential Character* and *The Pulse of Politics,* books that we shall examine in turn. The question of how we can become masters of our own and of the presidency's psychological fate also is treated in these books but it receives fuller exposition in other works by Barber.

Presidential Psychology

> The primary danger of the Nixon administration will be that the President will grasp some line of policy or method of operation and pursue it in spite of its failure. . . . How will Nixon respond to challenges to the morality of his regime, to charges of scandal and/or corruption? First such charges strike a raw nerve, not only from the Checkers business, but also from deep within the personality in which the demands of the superego are so harsh and hard. . . . The first impulse will be to hush it up, to conceal it, bring down the blinds. If it breaks open and Nixon cannot avoid commenting on it, there is a real setup here for another crisis. . . .

James David Barber is more than a little proud of that prediction, primarily because he made it in a talk he gave at Stanford University on January 19, 1969, the eve of Richard Nixon's first inauguration. It was among the first in a series of speeches, papers, and articles whose purpose was to explain his theory of presidential personality and how to predict it, always with his forecast for Nixon's future prominently, and thus riskily, displayed. The theory received its fullest statement in *The Presidential Character.*

"Character," in Barber's usage, is not quite a synonym for personality.[21] A politician's psychological constitution also includes two other components: his adolescence-born "world view," which Barber defines as his "primary, politically relevant beliefs, particularly his conceptions of social causality, human nature, and the central moral conflicts of the time"; and his "style," or "habitual way of performing three political roles: rhetoric, personal relations, and homework," which develops in early adulthood. But clearly Barber regards character, which forms in childhood and shapes the later development of style and world view, to be "the most important thing to know about a president or candidate." As he defines the term, "character is the way the President orients himself toward life—not for the moment, but enduringly." It "grows out of the child's experiments in relating to parents, brothers and sisters, and peers at play and in school, as well as to his own body and the objects around it." Through these experiences, the child—and thus the man to be—arrives subconsciously at a deep and private understanding of his fundamental worth.

For some, this process results in high self-esteem, the vital ingredient for psychological health and political productiveness. Others must search outside themselves for evidence of worth that at best will be a partial substitute. Depending on the source and nature of their limited self-esteem, Barber suggests, they will concentrate their search in one of three areas: the affection from others that compliant and agreeable behavior brings, the sense of usefulness that comes from performing a widely respected duty, or the deference attendant with dominance and control over other people. Because politics is a vocation rich in opportunities to find all three of these things—affection from cheering crowds and backslapping colleagues, usefulness from public service in a civic cause, dominance through official power—it is not surprising that some insecure people are attracted to a political career.

This makes for a problem, Barber argues: if public officials, especially presidents, use their office to compensate for private doubts and demons, it follows that they will not always use it for public purposes. Affection-seekers will be so concerned with preserving the good will of those around them that they rarely will challenge the status quo or otherwise rock the boat. The duty-doers will be similarly inert, although in their case inertia will result from their feeling that to be "useful" they must be diligent guardians of time-honored practices and procedures. Passive presidents of both kinds may provide the nation with "breathing spells, times of recovery in our frantic political life," or even "a refreshing hopefulness and at least some sense of sharing and caring." Still, in Barber's view, their main effect is to "divert popular attention from the hard realities of politics," thus leaving the country to "drift." And "what passive presidents ignore, active presidents inherit." [22]

Power-driven presidents pose the greatest danger. They will seek their psychological compensation not in inaction but in intense efforts to maintain or extend their personal sense of domination and control through public channels. When things are going well for the power-driven president and he feels that he has the upper hand on his political opponents, there may be no problem. But when things cease to go his way, as eventually they must in a democratic system, such a president's response almost certainly will take destructive forms, such as rigid defensiveness or aggression against opponents. Only those with high self-esteem will be secure enough to lead as democratic political leaders must lead, with persuasion and flexibility as well as action and initiative.

Perhaps more important than the theoretical underpinnings of Barber's character analysis is the practical purpose that animates *The Presidential Character:* to help citizens choose their presidents wisely. The book's first words herald this purpose:

> When a citizen votes for a presidential candidate he makes, in effect, a prediction. He chooses from among the contenders the one he thinks (or feels, or guesses) would be the best president. . . . This book is meant to help citizens and those who advise them cut through the confusion and get at some clear criteria for choosing presidents.

How, though, in the heat and haste of a presidential election, with candidates notably unwilling to bare their souls publicly for psychological inspection, are we to find out what they are really like? Easy enough, argues Barber. To answer the difficult question of what motivates a political man, just answer two simpler ones in its stead: Is he active or passive? ("How much energy does the man invest in his presidency?"); and is he positive or negative? ("Relatively speaking, does he seem to experience his political life as happy or sad, enjoyable or discouraging, positive or negative in its main effect?") According to Barber, the four possible combinations of answers to these questions turn out to be almost synonymous with the four psychological strategies people use to enhance self-esteem. The active-positive is the healthy one in the group. His high sense of self-worth enables him to work hard at politics, have fun at what he does, and thus be fairly good at it. Of the four eighteenth- and nineteenth-century presidents and the fourteen twentieth-century presidents whom Barber has typed, he places Thomas Jefferson, Franklin D. Roosevelt, Harry S Truman, Kennedy, Ford, and Carter in this category. The passive-positive (James Madison, William H. Taft, Warren G. Harding, Ronald Reagan) is the affection-seeker; although not especially hard-working, he enjoys the office. The passive-negative (Washington, Calvin Coolidge, Eisenhower) neither works nor plays; it is duty, not pleasure or zest, that gets him into politics. Finally, there is the power-seeking active-negative, who compulsively throws himself into his presidential chores with little satisfaction. In Barber's view, active-negative presidents John Adams, Woodrow Wilson, Herbert Hoover, Johnson, and Nixon all shared one important personality-rooted quality: they persisted in disastrous courses of action (Adams's repressive Alien and Sedition Acts, Wilson's League of Nations battle, Hoover's Depression policy, Johnson's Vietnam, Nixon's Watergate) because to have conceded that they were wrong would have been to cede their sense of control, something their psychological constitutions could not allow.[23] Table 8-1 summarizes Barber's four types and his categorizations of individual presidents.

Not surprisingly, *The Presidential Character* was extremely controversial when it came out in 1972. Many argued that Barber's theory was too simple, that his four types did not begin to cover the range of human complexity. At one level, this criticism is as trivial as it is true. In spelling out his theory, Barber states very clearly that "we are talking about tendencies, broad directions; no individual man exactly fits a category." His typology is offered as a method for sizing up potential presidents, not for diagnosing and treating them. Given the nature of election campaigning, a reasonably accurate shorthand device is about all we can hope for. The real question, then, is whether Barber's shorthand device is reasonably accurate.

Barber's intellectual defense of his typology's soundness, quoted here in full, is not altogether comforting:

> Why might we expect these two simple dimensions [active-passive, positive-negative] to outline the main character types? Because they stand for two central features of anyone's orientation toward life. In nearly every study of personality, some form of the active-passive contrast is critical; the general tendency to act or be acted upon is evident in such concepts as dominance-submission, extraversion-introversion, aggression-timidity, attack-defense, fight-flight, engagement-withdrawal, approach-avoidance. In every life we sense quickly the general energy output of the people we deal with. Similarly we catch on fairly quickly to the affect dimension— whether the person seems to be optimistic or pessimistic, hopeful or skeptical, happy or sad. The two baselines are clear and they are also independent of one another: all of us know people who are very active but seem discouraged, others who are quite passive but seem happy, and so forth. The activity baseline refers to what one does, the affect baseline to how one feels about what he does.
>
> Both are crude clues to character. They are leads into four basic character patterns long familiar in psychological research.[24]

In the library copy of *The Presidential Character* from which I copied this passage, there is a handwritten note in the margin: "Footnote, man!" But there was no footnote to the psychological literature, here or anywhere else in the book. Casual readers might take this to mean that none is necessary, and they would be right if Barber's types really were "long familiar in psychological research" and "appeared in nearly every study of personality." [25] But they aren't and they don't; as Alexander George has pointed out, personality theory itself is a "quagmire" in which "the term 'character' in practice is applied loosely and means many different things." [26] Barber's real

Table 8-1   Barber's Character Typology, with Presidents
Categorized According to Type

Affect toward the Presidency

Energy Directed toward the Presidency	Positive	Negative
Active	Thomas Jefferson Franklin Roosevelt Harry Truman John Kennedy Gerald Ford Jimmy Carter "consistency between much activity and the enjoyment of it, indicating relatively high self-esteem and relative success in relating to the environment ... shows an orientation to productiveness as a value and an ability to use his styles flexibly, adaptively"	John Adams Woodrow Wilson Herbert Hoover Lyndon Johnson Richard Nixon "activity has a compulsive quality, as if the man were trying to make up for something or escape from anxiety into hard work ... seems ambitious, striving upward, power-seeking ... stance toward the environment is aggressive and has a problem in managing his aggressive feelings."
Passive	James Madison William Taft Warren Harding Ronald Reagan "receptive, compliant, other-directed character whose life is a search for affection as a reward for being agreeable and co-operative ... low self-esteem (on grounds of being unlovable)."	George Washington Calvin Coolidge Dwight Eisenhower "low self-esteem based on a sense of uselessness ... in politics because they think they ought to be ... tendency is to withdraw, to escape from the conflict and uncertainty of politics by emphasizing vague principles (especially prohibitions) and procedural arrangements."

SOURCE: Barber's discussions of all presidents are in *The Presidential Character: Predicting Performance in the White House*, 3d ed. (Englewood Cliffs, N.J.: Prentice-Hall, 1985).

defense of his theory—that it works; witness Nixon—is not to be dismissed, but one wishes he had explained better why he thinks it works.[27]

Interestingly, Barber's typology also has been criticized for not being simple enough, at least not for purposes of accurate preelection application. Where, exactly, is one to look to decide if candidate Jones is, deep down, the energetic, buoyant fellow his image makers say he is? Barber is quite right in warning analysts away from their usual hunting ground—the candidate's recent performances in other high offices. These offices "are all much more restrictive than the Presidency is, much more set by institutional requirements," [28] and thus much less fertile cultures for psychopathologies to grow in. (This is Barber's only real mention of what might be considered a third, coequal component of the psychological presidency: the rarefied, court-like atmosphere—so well described in George Reedy's *The Twilight of the Presidency*[29]— that surrounds presidents and allows those whose psychological constitutions so move them to seal themselves off from harsh political realities.)

Barber's alternative—a study of the candidate's "first independent political success," or "fips," in which he found his personal formula for success in politics—is not very helpful either. How, for example, is one to tell which "ips" was first? According to Barber's appropriately broad definition of *political*, Johnson's first success was not his election to Congress, but his work as a student assistant to his college president. Hoover's was his incumbency as student body treasurer at Stanford. Sorting through someone's life with the thoroughness necessary to arrive at such a determination may or may not be an essential task. But clearly it is not a straightforward one.

Some scholars question not only the technical basis or practical applicability of Barber's psychological theory of presidential behavior, but also the importance of psychological explanation itself. Psychology appears to be almost everything to Barber, as this statement from his research design reveals:

> What is de-emphasized in this scheme? Everything which does not lend itself to the production of potentially testable generalizations about presidential behavior. Thus we shall be less concerned with the substance or content of particular issues . . . less concern[ed] for distant phenomena, such as relationships among other political actors affecting events without much reference to the president, public opinion, broad economic or historical trends, etc.—except insofar as these enter into the president's own approach to decision-making.[30]

But is personality all that matters? Provocative though it may be, Barber's theory seems to unravel even as he applies it. A "healthy" political personality turns out not to be a guarantor of presidential success: Barber classed Ford and Carter early in their presidencies as active-positives, for example. Carter, in fact, seemed to take flexibility—a virtue characteristic of active-positives—to such an extreme that it approached vacillation and inconsistency, almost as if in reading *The Presidential Character* he had learned its lessons too well.

Nor, as Table 8-2 shows, does Barber's notion of psychological unsuitability seem to correspond to failure in office. The ranks of the most successful presidents in three recent surveys by historians include some whom Barber classified as active-positives (Jefferson, Truman, and Franklin Roosevelt), but an equal number of active-negatives (Wilson, Lyndon Johnson, and John Adams), and others whom Barber labeled passive-negatives (Washington and Eisenhower).[31] The most perverse result of classifying presidents by this standard involves Abraham Lincoln, whom Jeffrey Tulis, correctly applying Barber's theory, found to be an active-negative.[32]

Clearly, personality is not all that matters in the modern presidency. As Tulis notes, Lincoln's behavior as president can be explained much better by his political philosophy and skills than by his personality. Similarly, one need not resort to psychology to explain the failures of active-negatives Hoover and, in the latter years of his presidency, Lyndon Johnson. Hoover's unbending resistance to federal relief in the face of the Depression may have stemmed more from ideological beliefs than psychological rigidity. Johnson's refusal to change the administration's policy in Vietnam could be interpreted as

Table 8-2   "Great" Presidents and Barber's Character Typology

	Positive	Negative
Active	Thomas Jefferson Franklin Roosevelt Harry Truman	John Adams Woodrow Wilson Lyndon Johnson [Abraham Lincoln]
Passive		George Washington Dwight Eisenhower

NOTE: For the purposes of this table, a "great" president is defined as one who ranked among the first ten in at least one of these three polls of historians: Steve Neal, "Our Best and Worst Presidents," *Chicago Tribune Magazine*, January 10, 1982, 9-18; Robert K. Murray and Tim H. Blessing, "The Presidential Performance Study: A Progress Report," *Journal of American History* (December 1983): 535-555; and David L. Porter, letter to author, January 15, 1982. Four others who achieved this ranking (Jackson, Polk, T. Roosevelt, and McKinley) are not included because Barber did not classify them according to his typology. Lincoln's name is bracketed because Jeffrey Tulis classified him using Barber's typology.

the action of a self-styled consensus leader trying to steer a moderate course between hawks who wanted full-scale military involvement and doves who wanted unilateral withdrawal.[33] These presidents' actions were ineffective, but not necessarily irrational.

The theoretical and practical criticisms that have been mentioned are important ones, and they do not exhaust the list. (Observer bias, for example. Since Barber's published writings provide no clear checklist of criteria by which to type candidates, subjectivity is absolutely inherent.) But they should not blind us to his major contributions in *The Presidential Character:* a concentration (albeit an overconcentration) on the importance of presidential personality in explaining presidential behavior, a sensitivity to its nature as a variable (power does not always corrupt; nor does the office always make the man), and a boldness in approaching the problems voters face in predicting what candidates will be like if elected.

Public Psychology

The other side of the psychological presidency—the public's side—is Barber's concern in *The Pulse of Politics: Electing Presidents in the Media Age.* The book focuses on elections, those occasions when, because citizens are filling the presidential office, they presumably feel (presidential deaths aside) their emotional attachment to it most deeply. Again Barber presents us with a typology. The public's election moods come in three variations: *conflict* ("we itch for adventure, . . . [a] blood-and-guts political contest"), *conscience* ("the call goes out for a revival of social conscience, the restoration of the constitutional covenant"), and *conciliation* ("the public yearns for solace, for domestic tranquility").[34] This time the types appear in recurring order as well, over twelve-year cycles.

Barber's question—What is the nature of "the swirl of emotions" with which Americans surround the presidency?—is as important and original as the questions he posed in *The Presidential Character.* But again, his answer is as puzzling as it is provocative. Although Barber's theory applies only to American presidential elections in this century, he seems to feel that the psychological "pulse" has beaten deeply, if softly, in all humankind for all time. Barber finds conflict, conscience, and conciliation in the "old sagas" of early man and in "the psychological paradigm that dominates the modern age: the *ego,* instrument for coping with the struggles of the external world [conflict]; the *superego,* warning against harmful violations [conscience]; the *id,* longing after the thrill and ease of sexual satisfaction [conciliation]." He finds it firmly reinforced in American history. Conflict is reflected in our emphasis on the war story ("In isolated America, the warmakers repeatedly confronted the special problem of arousing the martial spirit against distant enemies. . . . Thus our history vibrates with *talk* about war"); conscience is displayed in America's sense of itself as an instrument of divine providence ("our conscience has never been satisfied by government as a mere practical arrangement"); and conciliation shows up in our efforts to live with each other in a heterogeneous "nation of nationalities." In the twentieth century, Barber argues, these themes became the controlling force in the political psychology of the American electorate, so controlling that every presidential election since the conflict of 1900 has fit its place within the cycle (conscience in 1904, conciliation in 1908, conflict again in 1912, and so on). What caused the pulse to start beating this strongly, he feels, was the rise of national mass media.

The modern newspaper came first, just before the turn of the century. "In a remarkable historical conjunction," writes Barber, "the sudden surge into mass popularity of the American daily newspaper coincided with the Spanish-American War." Since war stories sold papers, daily journalists also wrote about "politics as war" or conflict. In the early 1900s, national mass circulation magazines arrived on the scene, taking their cues from the Progressive reformers who dominated that period. "The 'muckrakers'—actually positive thinkers out to build America, not destroy reputations"—wrote of "politics as a moral enterprise," an enterprise of conscience. Then came the broadcast media, radio in the 1920s and television in the 1950s. What set them apart was their commercial need to reach not just a wide audience but the widest possible audience. "Broadcasting aimed to please, wrapping politics in fun and games . . . conveying with unmatched reach and power its core message of conciliation."

As for the cyclic pulse, the recurring appearance of the three public moods in the same precise order, Barber suggests that the dynamic is internal: each type of public mood generates the next. After a conflict election ("a battle for power . . . a rousing call to arms"), a reaction sets in. Conscience calls for "the cleansing of the temple of democracy." But "the troubles do not go away," and four years later "the public yearns for solace," conciliation. After another four years, Barber claims, "the time for a fight will come around again," and so on.

In *The Pulse of Politics,* difficulties arise not in applying the theory (a calendar will do: if it's 1988, this must be a conscience election), but from the theory itself. Barber needs an even more secure intellectual foundation here than in his character theory, for this time he not only classifies all presidential elections into three types, but also asserts that they will recur in a fixed order. Once again, however, there are no footnotes; if Barber is grounding his theory in external sources, it is impossible to tell—and hard to imagine—what they are. Nor does the theory stand up sturdily under its own weight. If, for example, radio and television are agents of conciliation, why did we not have fewer conciliating elections before they became our dominant political media and more since? Perhaps that is why some of the "postdictions" Barber's theory leads to are as questionable as they are easy to make: Did conflict typify the 1924 Coolidge-Davis election, conscience the Eisenhower-Stevenson election in 1952, and conciliation the 1968 contest between Nixon, Humphrey, and Wallace?

The most interesting criticism pertinent to Barber's pulse theory, however, was made in 1972 by a political scientist concerned with the public's presidential psychology, which he described in terms of a "climate of expectations" that "shifts and changes." This scholar wrote: "Wars, depressions, and other national events contribute to that change, but there is also a rough cycle, from an emphasis on action (which begins to look too 'political') to an emphasis on legitimacy (the moral uplift of which creates its own strains) to an emphasis on reassurance and rest (which comes to seem like drift) and back to action again. One need not be astrological about it." (A year earlier this scholar had written that although "the mystic could see the series . . . marching in fateful repetition beginning in 1900 . . . the pattern is too astrological to be convincing.") Careful readers will recognize the identity between the cycles of action-legitimacy-reassurance and conflict-conscience-conciliation. Clever ones will realize that the passages above were written by James David Barber.[35]

Man, Mood, and the Psychological Presidency

There is, in fact, a good deal about the public's political psychology sprinkled through *The Presidential Character,* and the more of it one discovers, the more curious things get. Most significant is the brief concluding chapter, "Presidential Character and the Moods of the Eighth Decade" (reprinted in the 1977 second edition and the 1985 third edition), which contains Barber's bold suggestion of a close fit between the two sides of his model. For each type of public psychological climate, Barber posits a "resonant" type of presidential personality. This seems to be a central point in his theory of the presidency: "Much of what [a president] is remembered for," he argues, "will depend on the fit between the dominant forces in his character and the dominant feelings in his constituency." Further, "the dangers of discord in that resonance are great."[36]

What is the precise nature of this fit? When the public cry is for action (conflict), Barber argues, "it comes through loudest to the active-negative type, whose inner struggle between aggression and control resonates with the popular plea for toughness.... [The active-negative's] temptation to stand and fight receives wide support from the culture." In the public's reassurance (conciliation) mood, he writes, "they want a friend," a passive-positive. As for the "appeal for a moral cleansing of the Presidency," or legitimacy (conscience), Barber suggests that it "resonates with the passive-negative character in its emphasis on *not doing* certain things." This leaves the active-positive, Barber's president for all seasons.[37] Blessed with a "character firmly rooted in self-recognition and self-love," Barber's "active-positive can not only *perform* lovingly or aggressively or with detachment, he can *feel* those ways." [38]

What Barber first offered in *The Presidential Character*, then, was the foundation of a model of the psychological presidency that was not only two-sided but integrated as well, one in which the "tuning, the resonance—or lack of it" between the public's "climate of expectations" and the president's personality "sets in motion the dynamic of his Presidency." He concentrated on the personality half of his model in *The Presidential Character*, then firmed it up and filled in the other half—the public's—in *The Pulse of Politics*. And here is where things get so curious. Most authors, when they complete a multivolume opus, trumpet their accomplishment. Barber does not. In fact, one finds in *The Pulse of Politics* no mention at all of presidential character, of public climates of expectations, or of "the resonance—or lack of it" between them.[39]

At first blush, this seems doubly strange, because there is a strong surface fit between the separate halves of Barber's model. As Table 8-3 indicates, in the twenty elections since Taft's in 1908 (Barber did not type twentieth-century presidents before Taft), presidential character and public mood resonated thirteen times. The exceptions—active-negative Wilson's election in the conscience year of 1916, passive-negative Coolidge's in conflictual 1924, active-negative Hoover's in the conscience election of 1928, passive-negative Eisenhower's in the conciliating election of 1956, active-negative Johnson's in conscience-oriented 1964, active-negative Nixon's in conciliating 1968, and passive-positive Reagan's in conflict-dominated 1984—perhaps could be explained in terms of successful campaign image management by the winners, an argument that also would support Barber's view of the media's power in presidential politics. In that case, a test of Barber's model would be: Did these "inappropriate" presidents lose the public's support when it found out what they were really like after the election? In every presidency but those of Coolidge, Eisenhower, and possibly Reagan, the answer would have been yes.

On closer inspection it also turns out that in every case but these,

Table 8-3 Resonance of Character Type and Public Mood in Presidential Elections, 1908-84

	Election		Winning Presidential Candidate	
Year	Public mood	*"Resonant" character types*	Name	Character type
1908	Conciliation	Passive-positive (Active-positive)	Taft	Passive-positive
1912	Conflict	Active-negative (Active-positive)	Wilson	Active-negative
1916	Conscience	Passive-negative (Active-positive)	Wilson	Active-negative
1920	Conciliation	Passive-positive (Active-positive)	Harding	Passive-positive
1924	Conflict	Active-negative (Active-positive)	Coolidge	Passive-negative
1928	Conscience	Passive-negative (Active-positive)	Hoover	Active-negative
1932	Conciliation	Passive-positive (Active-positive)	Roosevelt	Active-positive
1936	Conflict	Active-negative (Active-positive)	Roosevelt	Active-positive
1940	Conscience	Passive-negative (Active-positive)	Roosevelt	Active-positive
1944	Conciliation	Passive-positive (Active-positive)	Roosevelt	Active-positive
1948	Conflict	Active-negative (Active-positive)	Truman	Active-positive
1952	Conscience	Passive-negative (Active-positive)	Eisenhower	Passive-negative
1956	Conciliation	Passive-positive (Active-positive)	Eisenhower	Passive-negative
1960	Conflict	Active-negative (Active-positive)	Kennedy	Active-positive
1964	Conscience	Passive-negative (Active-positive)	Johnson	Active-negative
1968	Conciliation	Passive-positive (Active-positive)	Nixon	Active-negative
1972	Conflict	Active-negative (Active-positive)	Nixon	Active-negative
1976	Conscience	Passive-negative (Active-positive)	Carter	Active-positive
1980	Conciliation	Passive-positive (Active-positive)	Reagan	Passive-positive
1984	Conflict	Active-negative (Active-positive)	Reagan	Passive-positive

the presidents whose administrations were unsuccessful were active-negatives, whom Barber tells us will fail for reasons that have nothing to do with the public mood. As for the overall thirteen for twenty success rate for Barber's model, it includes seven elections that were won by active-positives, whom he says resonate with every public mood. A good hand in a wild-card game is not necessarily a good hand in straight poker; Barber's success rate in the elections not won by active-positives is only six of thirteen. In the case of conscience elections, only once did a representative of the resonant type (passive-negative) win, while purportedly less suitable active-negatives won three times.

Barber's Prescriptions

In *The Presidential Character* and *The Pulse of Politics* Barber developed a suggestive and relatively complete model of the psychological presidency. Why he has failed even to acknowledge the connection between the theories in each book, much less present them as a unified whole, remains unclear. Perhaps he feared that the lack of fit between his mood and personality types—the public and presidential components—would have distracted critics from his larger points.

In any event, the theoretical and predictive elements of Barber's theory of the presidency are sufficiently provocative as to warrant him a hearing for his prescriptions for change. Barber's primary goal for the psychological presidency is that it be "de-psychopathologized." He wants to keep active-negatives out and put healthy active-positives in. He wants the public to become the master of its own political fate, breaking out of its electoral mood cycle, which is essentially a cycle of psychological dependency. Freed of their inner chains, the presidency and the public, Barber claims, will be able to forge a "creative politics" or "politics of persuasion," as he has variously dubbed it. Just what this kind of politics would be like is not clear, but apparently it would involve greater sensitivity on the part of both presidents and citizens to the ideas of the other.[40]

It will not surprise readers to learn that Barber, by and large, dismisses constitutional reform as a method for achieving his goals: if the presidency is as shaped by psychological forces as he says it is, then institutional tinkering will be, almost by definition, beside the point.[41] Change, to be effective, will have to come in the thoughts and feelings of people: in the information they get about politics, the way they think about it, and the way they feel about what they think. Because of this, Barber believes, the central agent of change will have to be the most pervasive—media journalism—and its central channel, the coverage of presidential elections.[42]

It is here, in his prescriptive writings, that Barber is on most solid ground, here that his answers are as good as his questions. Unlike many media critics, he does not assume imperiously that the sole purpose of newspapers, magazines, and television is to elevate the masses. Barber recognizes that the media is made up of commercial enterprises that must sell papers and attract viewers. He recognizes, too, that the basic format of news coverage is the story, not the scholarly treatise. His singular contribution is his argument that the media can improve the way it does all of these things at the same time, that better election stories will attract bigger audiences in more enlightening ways.

The first key to better stories, Barber argues, is greater attention to the candidates. Election coverage that ignores the motivations, developmental histories, and basic beliefs of its protagonists is as lifeless as dramas or novels that did so would be. It also is uninformative; elections are, after all, choices among people, and as Barber has shown, the kinds of people candidates are influences the kinds of presidents they would be. Good journalism, according to Barber, would "focus on the person as embodying his historical development, playing out a character born and bred in another place, connecting an old identity with a new persona—the stuff of intriguing drama from Joseph in Egypt on down. That can be done explicitly in biographical stories." [43]

Barber is commendably diffident here; he does not expect reporters to master and apply his own character typology. But he does want them to search the candidates' lives for recurring patterns of behavior, particularly the rigidity that is characteristic of his active-negatives. (Of all behavior patterns, rigidity, he feels, "is probably the easiest one to spot and the most dangerous one to elect.") [44] With public interest ever high in "people" stories and psychology, Barber probably is right in thinking that this kind of reporting would not only inform readers but engage their interest as well.

This goal—engaging readers' interest—is Barber's second key to better journalism. He finds reporters and editors notably, sometimes belligerently, ignorant of their audiences. "I really don't know and I'm not interested . . . ," he quotes Richard Salant of CBS News. "Our job is to give people not what they want, but what we decide they ought to have." Barber suggests that what often is lost in such a stance is an awareness of what voters need to make voting decisions, namely, information about who the candidates are and what they believe. According to a study of network evening news coverage of the 1972 election campaign, which he cites, almost as much time was devoted to the polls, strategies, rallies, and other "horse-race" elements of the election as to the candidates' personal qualifications and issue stands combined. As Barber notes, "The viewer tuning in for facts to guide his choice would, therefore, have to pick his political nuggets from a great gravel pile of political irrelevancy." [45] Critics who doubt the public's interest in long, fleshed-out stories about what candidates think, what they are like, and what great problems they would face as president would do well to check the ratings of CBS's "60 Minutes."

An electorate whose latent but powerful interest in politics is engaged by the media will become an informed electorate because it wants to, not because it is supposed to. This is Barber's strong belief. So sensible a statement of the problem is this, and so attractive a vision of its solution, that one can forgive him for cluttering it up with types and terminologies.

Notes

1. "Candidate on the Couch," *Time,* June 19, 1972, 15-17; James David Barber, *The Presidential Character: Predicting Performance in the White House* (Englewood Cliffs, N.J.: Prentice-Hall, 1972); a second edition was published in 1977, a third edition in 1985. Unless otherwise indicated, the quotations cited in this essay appear in all three editions, with page numbers drawn from the first edition.
2. Hugh Sidey, "The Active-Positive Searching," *Time,* October 4, 1976, 23.
3. "After Eight Months in Office—How Ford Rates Now," *U.S. News & World Report*, April 28, 1975, 28.
4. David S. Broder, "Carter Would Like to Be an 'Active Positive,'" *Washington Post,* July 16, 1976, A12.
5. James David Barber, "An Active-Positive Character," *Time,* January 3, 1977, 17.
6. Hugh Sidey, "'A Revolution Is Under Way,'" *Time,* March 31, 1980, 20.
7. "Cycle Races," *Time,* May 19, 1980, 29.
8. Robert A. Dahl, *A Preface to Democratic Theory* (Chicago: University of Chicago Press, 1956), 6-8.
9. The phrase is Alexander Hamilton's. See Alexander Hamilton, James Madison, and John Jay, *The Federalist Papers,* with an introduction by Clinton Rossiter (New York: New American Library, 1961), nos. 70, 423.
10. Seymour Martin Lipset, *The First New Nation* (New York: Basic Books, 1963), chap. 1; and Max Weber, *The Theory of Social and Economic Organization* (New York: Oxford University Press, 1947), 358.
11. Marcus Cunliffe, *George Washington: Man and Monument* (New York: New American Library, 1958), 15.
12. Max Farrand, *The Records of the Federal Conventions of 1787,* 4 vols. (New Haven: Yale University Press, 1966), I: 65.
13. Jeffrey Tulis, "On Presidential Character," in *The Presidency in the Constitutional Order,* ed. Jeffrey Tulis and Joseph M. Bessette (Baton Rouge: Louisiana State University Press, 1981), 287.
14. *Federalist,* nos. 71 and 72, 431-440.
15. *Federalist,* no. 64, 396.
16. See, for example, James David Barber, "Adult Identity and Presidential Style: The Rhetorical Emphasis," *Daedalus* (Summer 1968): 938-968; Barber, "Classifying and Predicting Presidential Styles: Two 'Weak' Presidents," *Journal*

of Social Issues (July 1968): 51-80; Barber, "The President and His Friends" (Paper presented at the annual meeting of the American Political Science Association, New York, September 1969); and Barber, "The Interplay of Presidential Character and Style: A Paradigm and Five Illustrations," in *A Source Book for the Study of Personality and Politics,* ed. Fred I. Greenstein and Michael Lerner (Chicago: Markham, 1971), 383-408.

17. Richard E. Neustadt, *Presidential Power: The Politics of Leadership* (New York: John Wiley & Sons, 1960), 185.

18. Erwin C. Hargrove, *The Power of the Modern Presidency* (New York: Knopf, 1974), 33.

19. See, for example, Fred I. Greenstein, *Children and Politics* (New Haven: Yale University Press, 1965); and John E. Mueller, *War, Presidents, and Public Opinion* (New York: John Wiley & Sons, 1973).

20. Paul B. Sheatsley and Jacob J. Feldman, "The Assassination of President Kennedy: Public Reactions," *Public Opinion Quarterly* (Summer 1964): 189-215.

21. Unless otherwise indicated, all quotes from Barber in this section are from *The Presidential Character,* chap. 1.

22. Ibid., 145, 206. In more recent writings, Barber's assessment of presidential passivity has grown more harsh. A passive-positive, for example, "may . . . preside over the cruelest of regimes." *Presidential Character,* 3d ed., 529-530.

23. The third edition of *The Presidential Character* contains Barber's discussions of all presidents, including Ford, Carter, and Reagan.

24. Barber, *Presidential Character,* 12.

25. Thirteen years after *The Presidential Character* was first published, in an appendix to the third edition, Barber described a variety of works to show that his character types "are not a product of one author's fevered imagination," but rather keep "popping up in study after study." In truth, most of the cited works are not scholarly studies of psychological character at all, nor are they claimed to be by their authors.

26. Alexander George, "Assessing Presidential Character," *World Politics* (January 1974): 234-282.

27. Ibid. George argues that Nixon's behavior was not of a kind that Barber's theory would lead one to predict.

28. Barber, *Presidential Character,* 99.

29. George Reedy, *The Twilight of the Presidency* (New York: New American Library, 1970). See also Bruce Buchanan, *The Presidential Experience: What the Office Does to the Man* (Englewood Cliffs: Prentice-Hall, 1978).

30. James David Barber, "Coding Scheme for Presidential Biographies," January 1968, mimeographed, 3.

31. The surveys are reported in Steve Neal, "Our Best and Worst Presidents," *Chicago Tribune Magazine,* January 10, 1982, 9-18; Robert K. Murray and Tim H. Blessing, "The Presidential Performance Study: A Progress Report," *Journal of American History* (December 1983): 535-555; and David L. Porter, letter to author, January 15, 1982.

32. Tulis, "On Presidential Character."

33. Erwin C. Hargrove, "Presidential Personality and Revisionist Views of the Presidency," *Midwest Journal of Political Science* (November 1973): 819-836.

34. James David Barber, *The Pulse of Politics: Electing Presidents in the Media Age* (New York: W. W. Norton, 1980). Unless otherwise indicated, all quotes from Barber in this section are from chapters 1 and 2.

35. The first quote appears in *The Presidential Character,* 9; the second in "Interplay

of Presidential Character and Style," footnote 2.

36. Barber, *Presidential Character,* 446.
37. Ibid., 446, 448, 451.
38. Ibid., 243.
39. Barber did draw a connection between the public's desire for conciliation and its choice of a passive-positive in the 1980 election: "Sometimes people want a fighter in the White House and sometimes a saint. But the time comes when all we want is a friend, a pal, a guy to reassure us that the story is going to come out all right. In 1980, that need found just the right promise in Ronald Reagan, the smiling American." James David Barber, "Reagan's Sheer Personal Likability Faces Its Sternest Test," *Washington Post,* January 20, 1981, 8.
40. James David Barber, "Tone-Deaf in the Oval Office," *Saturday Review/World,* January 12, 1974, 10-14.
41. James David Barber, "The Presidency after Watergate," *World,* July 31, 1973, 16-19.
42. Barber, *Pulse of Politics,* chap. 15. For other statements of his views on how the press should cover politics and the presidency, see James David Barber, ed. *Race for the Presidency: The Media and the Nominating Process* (Englewood Cliffs: Prentice-Hall, 1978), chaps. 5-7; and idem, "Not Quite the New York Times: What Network News Should Be," *The Washington Monthly,* September 1979, 14-21.
43. Barber, *Race for the Presidency,* 145.
44. Ibid., 171, 162-164.
45. Ibid., 174, 182-183.

9. SECOND-TERM PRESIDENCIES: THE AGING OF ADMINISTRATIONS

Michael B. Grossman, Martha Joynt Kumar, and Francis E. Rourke

The reelection of a president, particularly after he has soundly defeatd his challenger, might be expected to inaugurate a period of success at governing parallel to his success at the polls. In fact, the opposite more often has been true. Each modern president's second term has been more difficult than his first. The second terms of Harry S Truman, Lyndon B. Johnson, and Richard M. Nixon were marked by outright failure, while those of Franklin D. Roosevelt and Dwight D. Eisenhower were far less productive for them and the country than their first terms. What an English commentator once wrote about Roosevelt also could be applied to many of his successors: "The Roosevelt coalition was a formidable machine for re-electing Franklin Roosevelt. It was less reliable as a means for organizing radical change." [1]

Several presidents have reflected on the problem of the second term. "Generally speaking," Nixon said in a Camp David meeting with reporters shortly after his 1972 victory, "whether they are Democratic administrations or Republican administrations, the tendency is for an administration to run out of steam after the first four years, and then to coast and usually coast downhill." [2] Although Nixon had been returned to office with the largest popular majority in history, it was the potential decline of his powers in the days ahead that was most on his mind. A month after Ronald Reagan's overwhelming reelection in 1984, then-White House Counselor Edwin Meese announced that a planning group had been formed by the president to evaluate the reasons for past second-term declines. [3]

Of course, Nixon and Meese may have been trying to provide an alibi in advance for future shortcomings, but the record supports their basic concern. Roosevelt fell short in his efforts to enlarge the Supreme Court and to purge his conservative opponents from the Democratic party, and he ultimately had to abandon the main reform impulse of his New Deal program. Truman was unable to move his Fair Deal legislation forward, was locked into the Korean War, and barely avoided a constitutional crisis after he relieved the highly popular Gen. Douglas MacArthur from his command of United Nations forces in Korea. Eisenhower gave up on his goal of trimming back the reforms of the New Deal and was forced to fend off the legislative and budget programs of his congressional adversaries, who won a tremendous victory in the 1958 midterm election. Johnson left office in 1968, brought down by domestic unrest and conflict over the Vietnam War. Nixon resigned in disgrace because of the Watergate crisis and barely escaped indictment.

Why do presidents decline in power and influence during their second terms? To what extent are the patterns of decline predictable? Are they inevitable or reversible? In this chapter, we examine the ways in which second-term presidents have lost their ability to dominate the political process, their responses to the winding down of their administrations, and some strategies through which presidents could improve their position during the second term. We do so by discussing four aspects of the second-term experience: (1) the reelection campaign; (2) the relationship between the president and his administration; (3) patterns of cooperation and conflict with Congress; and (4) efforts to reach out to the public. Finally, we examine the record of Ronald Reagan, who, some analysts once thought, would avoid the setbacks that other presidents suffered as their second terms progressed.

The Reelection Campaign

Most incumbent presidents who run for reelection win by very large margins, usually much larger than the plurality they obtained when they were first elected. Sitting presidents have been candidates in sixteen of the twenty-two presidential elections held during the twentieth century; in twelve of those elections, they were victorious. In eight elections, the incumbent president won by an overwhelming majority. These included the reelections of William McKinley in 1900, Theodore Roosevelt in 1904, Calvin Coolidge in 1924, Franklin Roosevelt in 1936, Eisenhower in 1956, Johnson in 1964, Nixon in 1972, and Reagan in 1984. Franklin Roosevelt's third and fourth victories, in 1940 and 1944, were by comfortable if not overwhelming majorities. The two other winners, Truman in 1948 and Woodrow Wilson in 1916, were reelected by narrow pluralities. Four sitting presidents lost: William H. Taft, Herbert Hoover, Gerald R. Ford, and Jimmy Carter. Taft's defeat was largely the product of a major split in the Republican party in 1912, while Hoover lost at the height of the great depression in 1932. Only two presidents, Ford in 1976 and Carter in 1980, lost in circumstances that did not seem altogether beyond their control.

The exceptional margins of victory that so many incumbent presidents received did not lead to exceptional accomplishments in office. In each case the president and his aides seemed to assume that the reelection gave him a strong personal mandate from the people. No credence was given to a more limited interpretation—that the public, although endorsing the incumbent's request to continue to exercise governing authority, nonetheless reserved the right to follow opposition leaders on issues on which they disagreed with the president.

Several common elements of presidential reelection campaigns have had a negative influence on the second term. These characteristics include the vacuous and unfocused nature of the campaign; the use of a "Rose Garden" strategy to keep the president away from contentious settings; the separation of the president's campaign from those of party colleagues in Congress; and the increase in ticket splitting by voters.

The Vacuous Nature of the Campaign

In almost every reelection effort by an incumbent, the president's advisers design the campaign as a referendum on the president's performance during the first term. The intent is to persuade voters to compare his term to the bad old days of Hoover, Truman, Carter, or some other widely unpopular figure from the past. In no case have a reelection-seeking president's aides urged him to propose a specific set of programs or a definite agenda for after the election. In 1956, 1972, and 1984, the only references to the second term during the campaign were vague promises of greater achievements to come, as exemplified by Reagan's slogan, "You ain't seen nothing yet." Although such a strategy probably increases the president's margin of victory, it also contributes to his governing problems in the second term by making it easier for adversaries to separate opposition to his programs from opposition to him.

The main result of the vacuous campaign has been a stalled agenda after the reelection. Eisenhower and Nixon had virtually no new proposals to make at the beginning of their second terms. Both found themselves reacting to the proposals and agendas of others. These presidents discovered, as Erwin Hargrove and Michael Nelson suggest, that

> the only real vaccine against domestic policy stalemate in the second term is that it be ushered in by an achievement-style re-election—a landslide victory for the president and large gains for his congressional party in response to a campaign whose theme is dramatic policy innovation.[4]

The Rose Garden Strategy

Incumbent presidents have tried to maximize their electoral support by presenting themselves to the voters as the nation's chief executive rather than as a political party's candidate. Campaign advisers endeavor both to keep the president distant from his party and to minimize his exposure in settings where unexpected and unpleasant confrontations may occur. Instead, presidents typically appear in the White House Rose Garden, where photo opportunities abound and hecklers seldom are heard. The charisma of the office, they and their campaign advisers correctly assume, counts for more than presidential appearances in settings that are difficult to arrange and thus may make him look like a "mere politician."

For all its electoral virtues, however, an important result of the Rose Garden strategy is to detach the president from meaningful interchanges with the public and the media. A genuine campaign can place the president in contact with sectors of public opinion with which he is not familiar. In contrast, even for the most open of presidents, the White House provides a rarefied atmosphere that warning signals of difficulties ahead are slow to penetrate. An isolated president who has received a large electoral victory may be especially unprepared for the troubles that await him in the second term.

Separation from Congressional Campaigns

Since the 1950s, incumbent presidents have tended to centralize their campaign's financial and organizational resources behind their own reelection. The welfare of their party's candidates for Congress and other offices has taken a distant second place. As a result, members of Congress feel no obligation to support a reelected president if he should get into trouble during the second term. Nixon, for example, found it very difficult to rally Republicans in Congress to his side during his Watergate troubles, having lent them only nominal support during his successful second-term campaign in 1972.

Moreover, incumbent presidents now use personal rather than party organizations to run their reelection campaigns. Nixon's Committee for the Re-Election of the President, the President Ford Committee, the President Carter Committee, and the President Reagan Committee gave directions and orders to the Republican and Democratic national committees. In addition, the directors of the White House campaign organizations separated the president from the congressional campaigns. In 1972 Nixon's committee raised $64 million—none of it shared with Republican congressional candidates— in an election many felt the president could have won by spending only a fraction of that amount. Republican senator Gordon Allott, for example, was left with no funds at the end of a close campaign that he lost in Colorado. Small wonder that some of Nixon's long-time allies could no longer be counted on to support him when he ran into trouble. Since 1972, federal financing of presidential elections has reduced the competition for funds between the presidential and congressional organizations, but conflicts still occur. Presidential renomination campaigns—even when the president is unopposed—raise millions of dollars that could go to his party's congressional candidates, as do "independent" expenditures for the president in the general election. When a president fails to use his political capital to help his party during the reelection campaign, he loses a chance to establish a useful and important bond that could help him govern during the second term.

Ticket Splitting

In 1900 only 3.4 percent of the nation's congressional districts were carried by a presidential candidate of one party and a congressional candidate of the other.[5] Because more voters now split their tickets, incumbent presidential candidates believe they can increase the size of their own majority by disengaging themselves from local contests. To do so, however, further loosens the electoral bonds between the president and his party and makes it easier for members of Congress to go their own way after the election. Although ticket splitting has increased generally during the past thirty years, the change has been particularly noticeable from first- to second-term presidential elections. For example, the percentage of districts that split rose from 19.3 to 29.9 percent for Eisenhower between 1952 and 1956 and from 32 to 44.1 percent for Nixon between 1968 and 1972. In 1984 Reagan carried 372 of 435 congressional districts, but Republican House candidates carried only 181. More than half the congressional districts that voted for Reagan also electd a Democrat to Congress.[6]

Executive Branch Internal Relations

A president's reelection campaign will affect the second term, but the way he handles the everyday work of the government once he has been reelected is even more important. One requirement for effective leadership by any president is that he build a successful relationship with the network of executive departments and agencies. Whatever grand designs presidents may have for innovations in policy when they enter office, they soon discover that it is the executive apparatus that must carry out most of the goals they seek to achieve. Thus, it has become imperative for every president that he control the executive branch in a way that ensures that it will serve his purposes, not its own interests or those of the groups that are its principal clients.

The main avenue through which a president builds a working relationship with the rest of the executive branch is his power to appoint the officials, from the cabinet on down, who will oversee and direct the activities of the departments and agencies. The White House expects that its appointees not only will share the president's goals in their areas of responsibility, but also will have sufficient professional competence to command the respect of both their subordinates and the groups their agency serves. Theoretically, at least, a second-term president should find the appointment process to be far easier to influence than when he first came to office and had to depend on the advice of many other people in making so many decisions in such a short time. There are fewer appointments to be made during the second term; the president is more knowledgeable about the skills particular jobs require; and within his own administration he now has a pool of experienced administrators whose loyalties and abilities already have been measured. In firm control of the appointments process, a president thus should be able to establish a relationship with other officials and organizations within the executive branch that will enhance his prospects for effective leadership during the second term.

Unfortunately, the record suggests that as presidential control over the appointment process increases during the second term, the quality of appointments actually decreases. Of course, some appointments that presidents have made at the end of their tenure were widely regarded as being of a very high caliber. Johnson's selection of Clark Clifford as secretary of defense during the last year of his presidency clearly falls into this category. But the picture that emerges from a close study of the entire Johnson appointment record is quite different.[7] At the beginning of the Johnson presidency, John Macy, the chairman of the Civil Service Commission, also served the president as special assistant for personnel management. His role was to ensure that Johnson's appointees were professionally qualified for their jobs. The rest of the White House staff set itself the task of determining whether those considered for appointment were sufficiently loyal to the president and his policies. As time wore on, however, Johnson's presidency was increasingly beset by the twin traumas of Vietnam and domestic violence. Macy's participation in the appointment process gradually diminished and the White House role expanded. Loyalty to the president rather than professional competence became the principal standard by which prospective appointees were judged in an administration under heavy political attack because of its policies.

Other administrations have faced a different recruitment problem toward the end of their tenure. As one study suggests:

> It becomes increasingly difficult near the end of any presidential administration to bring to government service persons of as high caliber as had been attracted in the beginning. Candidates are less willing to make financial and other sacrifices for an appointment of merely a year or two, and much of the excitement and challenge of being part of a new administration have dissipated. There is, in short, a kind of natural cycle, a decline in quality, in the twilight of an administration.[8]

The coping mechanism that modern presidents usually employ to deal with recruitment problems in the latter days of their administration is to name senior career civil servants to high positions in executive agencies and departments when vacancies occur. As a result, the administration in its second term may gradually become a government of technocrats, far removed in spirit as well as flesh from the heady days of the beginning of the president's first term, when the new people in charge of the executive branch believed that anything was possible.

The willingness to appoint career officials to high executive posts is one manifestation of a reconciliation that typically takes place between the political and the bureaucratic sectors of the executive branch as an administration matures in office. This reconciliation reflects movement and change by officials in both arenas. By the time an administration nears the end of its term in office, political appointees, especially those working in departments and agencies rather than the White House, have lost much of their initial distrust of bureaucracy. They have discovered that bureaucrats can save them from mistakes or even help them achieve successes for which they can claim credit. Although political appointees may not actually "marry the natives," as their critics in the White House commonly allege, they do become accustomed to living very comfortably with them.[9] White House officials, in contrast, adapt to bureaucracy in a somewhat different way—by developing a variety of techniques for making or carrying out policies that bypass the permanent government.

Bureaucrats also undergo a metamorphosis. As the president's tenure unfolds, they find that their most dire forebodings about the damage the administration may inflict on their agency or its programs are not realized. The president's appointees may even prove to be effective advocates of the agency's cause with Congress and the public at large. Moreover, these executives control access to perquisites dear to the bureaucratic heart, such as promotions or better job assignments.

Practical considerations, then, dictate a rapprochement within every administration between political and career officials, usually on terms favorable to the president. In a study they undertook of the political attitudes of higher civil servants during the Nixon administration, Richard Cole and David Caputo found a very strong tendency among senior career officials to move toward the political orientation of the administration in office.[10] During Nixon's tenure as president the number of senior officials identifying themselves as Democrats declined, while the number of those who defined themselves as independents or Republicans increased. In part, this shift occurred because Nixon was able to bring Republicans into the senior civil service. But part of it also reflected a conversion effect. Many Democratic careerists shifted their political affiliation from Democratic to independent during the Nixon years.

For all the good it may do a president, the reconciliation with bureaucracy that an administration ordinarily achieves during a second term does little to arrest the political decline from which it is simultaneously suffering. What a president loses in the way of influence with Congress and the public as a result of his lame duck status can not be repaired or offset entirely by improving his relations with the bureaucracy. Indeed, to the extent that a president loses support among Congress and the public, he may suffer a corresponding loss within the executive branch itself. It is, as Richard Neustadt has noted, a settled custom in Washington for bureaucrats to align their view of the president with the views that others take of him.[11]

Much of presidents' loss of influence may occur within the ranks of career officials, as bureaucrats begin to play a waiting game with the second-term incumbent, gradually turning their attention to speculations about what the next administration will be like. The president's own appointees may also give him trouble toward the end of his administration. Cabinet members may begin to steer a very independent course of action—even to the point of defying a direct presidential order, as did Johnson's secretary of labor, Willard Wirtz. More commonly, however, a president's main problem with his second-term appointees is not so much defiance as desertion. Almost from the beginning of the second term, but accelerating near the end, many of the most experienced and able presidential appointees reach for lucrative positions in the private sector, knowing they can still trade on their White House connection. Their loss can be very damaging to the president, especially when, as in Michael Deaver's case during the Reagan presidency, a former White House staff member seems to be exploiting his connections for personal profit.

This exodus from the administration's upper echelons presents the president with the problem of finding replacements, which is no easy task when individuals outside of government know that their tenure in office will be relatively brief and that they will have small opportunity to blaze new policy trails as public officials. In the latter days of the

Eisenhower administration, John Kessel reports, "some 70 persons were considered or approached about the secretaryship of defense—before Thomas S. Gates was promoted from Secretary of the Navy." [12]

Moreover, since a president's political capital dwindles during his second term, he must make doubly sure that anyone he nominates for an executive position will be acceptable to Congress and to the constituency with which the nominee will be working. In the first flush of his election victory in 1980, Reagan was able to appoint James Watt as secretary of the interior and Anne Burford as administrator of the Environmental Protection Agency; both were widely viewed by the environmental movement as unfriendly to their cause. He also appointed Ray Donovan, a man regarded with some hostility by the AFL-CIO, as secretary of labor. It would be difficult to imagine Reagan securing approval for similar second-term nominations. Indeed, these officials were replaced by appointees who were much more acceptable to the constituencies that their agencies normally serve.

Toward the end of his days in office, a president often acts in less partisan ways than he earlier did. Looking ahead to retirement, and increasingly interested in cultivating his historical reputation, he becomes more detached from the political and policy maneuvering that were his concern when he first took office. The president becomes preoccupied with gathering materials for his memoirs or with making plans for the library and museum with which his time in office will be memorialized. Eisenhower adopted this stance in 1960, as did Johnson in 1968.

Executive-Legislative Relations

Executive Policy Making

Recent presidencies have been marked by recurring patterns of policy development. At the beginning of the first term, a president finds that he is expected to do something about the major issues that were raised during the election campaign. Although he may have tried to avoid making clear commitments about what he would do, an agenda of action is anticipated. The president usually responds by quickly introducing a program of domestic policy initiatives. If he is slow to obtain results from Congress, as was the case with Kennedy and Carter, his failure is regarded as a sign of weakness. Kennedy's and Carter's mistake was to appear to be committed to programs that had little chance of passing in a Congress that they were in no position to confront. Most presidents have chosen to do battle over issues on which the opposition is less securely entrenched and then have gone all out to win.

Second terms, as a general rule, have been times when presidents emphasized foreign policy. To build a majority on domestic issues is more difficult in the second term than in the first because potential supporters demand a larger reward for their support and opponents become more effective. In foreign policy, a patriotic tide may be easier to rouse and ride. Foreign policy also requires less congressional cooperation. The bad news for presidents, however, is that although foreign policy still lies largely within their prerogative, Congress has begun to insinuate itself into this area very energetically, often described in a negative way by the White House as "micro-management." For example, presidents face a more active Congress today in the foreign aid process and in the approval of arms sales. Congress approved Reagan's proposals for arms sales to Saudi Arabia and aid to the contra rebels in Nicaragua, but only after fierce battles and eventual compromises on the part of the White House.

Managing Congressional Relations

After four years a president has had the opportunity to learn about informal networks of information and influence in Congress whose existence is not immediately apparent to the novice. Thus, presidents in their second term might be expected to have fewer problems with Congress than they did in their first. In fact, they usually have more. The explanation lies not in their lack of ability in the small skills of managing congressional relations but in their insistence on regarding their reelection as a popular mandate to carryout highly controversial policies without prior consultation with Congress.

Roosevelt's effort in 1937 to increase the size of the Supreme Court might have generated more support if he had tried to build a consensus beforehand in Congress and in the legal community. Because he acted in what seemed to many to be a highhanded manner, his opponents defeated him by rallying support in Congress, the legal profession, the media, and various state governments. Roosevelt responded to this defeat by trying to purge from Congress Democrats who had opposed his court-packing proposal and other measures; his futile effort to do so ultimately contributed to the erosion of congressional support for his domestic reforms.

Truman's second-term difficulties included a hostile congressional reaction to what some leaders of the opposition regarded as rash actions on his part. His decision to enter and fight the Korean War without their partnership left Truman vulnerable to criticism when he got into trouble by firing MacArthur and trying to take over the steel mills. These unilateral and self-damaging actions stand in sharp contrast to his success in building a legislative coalition for European recovery and rearmament after he succeeded to the presidency in 1945.

The second-term presidents who suffered most by pursuing highly controversial policies were Johnson and Nixon. Congress's resentment of Johnson grew as the president escalated the Vietnam War and was manifest in the hostile atmosphere of hearings that were conducted by committee chairmen of his own party. Although his legislative mastery in domestic policy continued, congressional opposition to the war was a major factor leading to Johnson's decision not to stand for reelection in 1968. Nixon encountered even greater resistance when hostile bills such as the War Powers Resolution were passed over his veto. As he defended himself against charges stemming from the Watergate scandal, Nixon's support dwindled to the point that he could avert impeachment only by resigning.

Congress as Gladiator

Because a president's legislative fortunes are closely related to his party's strength in Congress, losses in the midterm elections limit his chances for success. Only Theodore Roosevelt had more members of his own party in either the House or the Senate when he left office than when he entered, and his case is a statistical fluke, because both Houses were enlarged during his second term.

As Table 9-1 shows, the midterm elections of the second term have brought especially severe losses to the president's party.[13] These losses have been accompanied by comparable declines in presidential support in Congress from the first to the last years in office on issues where the president took a clear-cut stand, as data in Table 9-2 from the Eisenhower, Johnson, Nixon, and Reagan administrations reveal.[14]

Although all presidents have experienced a larger number of failures as their second terms progressed, three elements seem to be important in determining the extent of the setbacks: whether Congress and the public think the president is basing his proposals on definite goals that they can support; the ability of the White House staff to rally the president's supporters to his cause; and the skill of the president's opponents in mobilizing opposition to his policies. Of Eisenhower, Reagan, Nixon, and Johnson, only the last was working with a concrete agenda—the unfinished business of the New Deal. None of these presidents' staffs were as effective in their last years in office as they had earlier been.

The Public and the Media

Having won reelection, a victorious White House tends to be overconfident about the degree of public support it enjoys. In the heady atmosphere of victory, it is easy for presidents and their closest aides to ignore signals that warn of public unease or resistance to specific presidential programs and tactics. They may even dismiss signals as an effort by the media to subvert the election returns. From this attitude it is a short step to regarding news organizations and their representatives as the president's enemies.

As their press problems grow, presidents and their aides usually try to recapture the levels of public support they believe they enjoyed on election day, often by flaying the press. But favorable coverage no longer can be taken for granted. Instead, journalists, now viewing themselves as under attack, take joy in uncovering the president's mistakes and highlighting what they regard as the failures and contradictions of his administration. News organizations can provide a harsh and unflattering view of any administration, and when a president is weakening, their attacks may seem cruel and relentless. Stephen Wayne has cited two "rules of the media: Never kick anyone unless they're down. Once they're down, don't stop kicking." [15]

Content analysis of White House store is from 1953 to 1978 in *The New York Times* and *Time* and from 1968 to 1978 on *The CBS Evening News* suggests that even though news organizations continued to produce more favorable than unfavorable stories about presidents, the proportion of favorable stories fell during each president's tenure in

Table 9-1   Gains or Losses of President's Party in Midterm Elections (in Number of Seats)

President	Year	House	Senate
T. Roosevelt	1902	+9	+2
	1906	−28	−3
Wilson	1914	−59	+5
	1918	−19	−6
F. D. Roosevelt	1934	+9	+10
	1938	−71	−6
Eisenhower	1954	−18	−1
	1958	−47	−13
Nixon	1970	−12	+2
	1974	−48	−5
Reagan	1982	−26	+1
	1986	−5	−8

SOURCE: Norman J. Ornstein, Michael J. Malbin, Allen Schick, and John F. Bibby, *Vital Statistics on Congress,* 1984-85 edition (Washington, D.C.: American Enterprise Institute, 1984), 56.

office.[16] Favorable stories declined by more than 20 percent from the first to the last years of the Eisenhower, Johnson, and Nixon administrations, while the percentage of unfavorable stories increased nearly 10 percent for Eisenhower and Johnson and nearly 30 percent for Nixon.[17]

As noted earlier, a president usually responds to a weakened influence on domestic matters by turning to foreign policy. Presidents find it easier to win public support when they appear to be protecting the United States or advancing the cause of democracy around the world. Because the public usually supports the president on foreign policy issues, Congress has been very amenable to White House direction on both national security and defense issues. Reagan was able to win votes from a previously reluctant Congress for the MX missile and the Strategic Defense Initiative in 1985 and 1986 because some legislators feared a public backlash if they denied him support when he was about to begin delicate negotiations with Soviet leaders.

Representing the United States abroad, a president appears statesmanlike rather than partisan. He can invoke the symbolism of national security to induce the public to "rally round the flag." Moreover, political leaders abroad, both of America's allies and its adversaries, generally are impressed by evidence that a president enjoys strong public support at home. World response to Reagan's sweeping reelection victory in 1984 strengthened his position as leader of the western alliance, particularly because the political position of many European leaders was far less secure in office at that time.

Still, second-term presidents who turn to foreign affairs as a respite from domestic difficulties risk becoming the victims of interna-

Table 9-2 Presidential Victories on Votes in Congress

President	Year	Victories
Eisenhower	1953	89.2%
	1960	65.1
Johnson	1964	87.9
	1968	74.5
Nixon	1969	74.8
	1974	59.6
Reagan	1981	81.9
	1986	56.5

SOURCE: *Congressional Quarterly Weekly Report,* October 25, 1986, 2687. The last year shown for Reagan (1986) is the last year for which data were available at press time.

tional forces and events that are beyond their control. During Wilson's second term he expanded the nation's role in international affairs by leading the United States to enter and help win World War I, but issues connected with the post-war settlement ultimately caused his presidency to collapse. Truman and Johnson lost public support as a result of the disappointing consequences of their second-term commitment of American troops to Korea and Vietnam, respectively. And nothing in Ronald Reagan's presidency brought him more grief than his ill-starred effort to win freedom for American hostages seized in Lebanon by secretly sending arms to Iran, even as his administration was trying to prevent other nations from doing so.

The Aging of the Reagan Administration

Until his troubles with Iran began, Reagan appeared to many observers to have escaped the kind of decline suffered by other two-term presidents. Most striking was the president's high level of public approval as measured by the polls, which seemed to defy precedent. Through most of 1986 his approval ranged above 60 percent, in contrast to the low 40 percent range it had reached during much of his first two years in office. Since the 1940s (the period for which we have poll data) only one other president, Eisenhower, received a similarly high rating so late during his tenure. No other post-World War II president has shown a higher approval rating in the later years of his tenure than at its beginning.

Reagan's high level of public support was the main argument for his supporters' claim that he did not become a lame duck after the election of 1984. Evaluating this argument depends somewhat on what is meant by *lame duck*. It certainly is true that Reagan did not become a "dead duck," as nearly invisible as Johnson after he announced his coming retirement in the spring of 1968 or as almost all presidents become during the postelection period of transition to their successor. But lame duck status usually has not been thought to mean that the president loses all power. What the term rather refers to is the president's diminished ability to shape the national policy agenda during his second term or to impose his will on Congress and the rest of the political community in policy disputes.

If we turn from Reagan's approval in the polls to his ability to influence the public, we see a much less successful president, long before the Iran-contra affair began to take its toll. In early 1986 Reagan hoped to reverse the trend of sixty-year losses for the president's party in the midterm elections. During frequent campaign swings that year, he asked voters to regard continued Republican control of the Senate as an endorsement of his stewardship. Instead, the Democrats swept to a surprisingly easy victory, picking up eight seats to win control of the Senate and maintaining their comfortable majority in the House.

But even before the midterm elections damaged his reputation for political invincibility, Reagan was suffering from second-term decline. In Congress, the president quickly found himself bucking Republicans as well as Democrats on the issues of entitlement programs and import quotas. He was forced to yield to the opposition much more frequently than in his first term. This was evident when he accepted full funding for the Superfund for toxic wastes, a measure he originally had opposed, and when congressional resistance to his "free market" farm policies forced him to reverse course and support a proposal to pay farmers to take 15 percent of their land out of production. Even tax reform, widely touted as Reagan's major second-term domestic achievement, passed only after congressional leaders of both parties wrenched the legislation away from him. House Democrats, led by Ways and Means chairman Dan Rostenkowski, and a bipartisan coalition of senators, led by Republican Finance Committee chairman Robert Packwood, wrote a bill that the president felt compelled to sign, even though he had promised House Republicans that he would veto a very similar bill.

Like his predecessors, Reagan also found that a president's opponents retaliate in the second term for the rough manner in which he treated them when he was riding high. In 1981, for example, Reagan used Congress's reconciliation procedures, originally intended to be a means of achieving greater legislative supervision over the budget, as a vehicle to dominate policy making. According to Reagan's budget director, David Stockman, the president permitted his aides to bring inaccurate budget figures to Congress.[18] Thus, with his early success, Reagan sowed seeds of opposition that later made him one of the least influential recent presidents in the budget process. By 1985 the president no longer could muster a majority even of Republican votes in the House for his budget proposals.

Moreover, the Reagan Revolution, the president's attempt to reduce government's role in American life, has not been at the center of congressional debate during the second term. In early 1986, months before the Republican party lost control of the Senate in the midterm elections, the president was forced to swallow previously unacceptable defense cuts as part of the Gramm-Rudman-Hollings deficit reduction measure. A majority of Republican senators broke with Reagan on the issue of South African sanctions. And it was the chairman of the Senate Foreign Relations Committee, Republican Richard Lugar, who shaped American policy toward the Philippine revolution early in 1986, not the White House.

In the final analysis, Reagan has been different from other second-term presidents only in his administration's superior management of political communications and in its exploitation of the symbolic properties of the presidency. Particularly striking (prior to the Iran-contra affair) was Reagan's ability to remain untarred when things went badly, the so-called Teflon effect. Few presidents could have escaped unscathed, as Reagan did, from the debris of the summit meeting with Soviet Premier Mikhail Gorbachev in 1986.

One aspect of the way news organizations usually present critical stories about political leaders has helped Reagan to manage communications and to escape criticism during the early part of the second term. Most of what appears as criticism of any president in the media is based on the willingness of his political opponents to speak out. When the opposition is weak or silent, as it was during this period, the president benefits. As Richard Cohen of the *Washington Post* suggests:

> Without Congress and the larger political community adding resonance, the press sounds shrill when it sets off on its own. It did that early on with Ronald Reagan, detailing his press conference mistakes. That's hardly done anymore because Congress, sensing the man's popularity, remained mum; the all-important second day story never materialized.[19]

Because Reagan remained popular at a stage of his presidency when his predecessors had begun to look shopworn, opponents withheld or lowered the level of their public criticism for fear of invoking the anger of his supporters. Here, as elsewhere, the "tyranny of the majority" made itself felt. Elected officials of both parties were quick to assure their constituents that they back the president when he is "right" or when he is "representing America."

Nevertheless, Reagan's success with the voters and the news media, however remarkable, was isolated, even before Iran upset his applecart. In 1986 the *Congressional Quarterly Weekly Report* wrote that only 56 percent of the bills that the president favored passed Congress, some 20 percent below Eisenhower's and Johnson's success rates at similar stages of their tenure in office. In 1974, the year he was forced to resign, Nixon's success rate with Congress was three percentage points higher than Reagan's in 1986. The 1986 Reagan figure represents the fourth lowest score recorded in the thirty-four years that Congressional Quarterly has been tabulating presidential success.

In sum, Reagan's ability to shape the political agenda was in decline from the beginning of his second term. His difficulties were compounded by the Iran-contra affair, but they did not begin with that unhappy development. Moreover, once the Iran story broke, the many-sided investigation of the affair by the Tower Commission, the two branches of Congress, and the special prosecutor guaranteed that stories unflattering to the administration would appear regularly in the press whether or not members of Congress summoned up the courage to criticize the White House.

The Second-Term Decline: Can Anything Stop It?

What underlies the problems of second-term presidents? First, many of the events that occur at any point in an administration are beyond the president's control. Luck enters in. But if a president must suffer a stroke of ill fortune, it is better that it occur sooner rather than later, so that he will have more time to recover politically. The recession of 1981-82 hurt Reagan far less than the recession of 1958-59 hurt Eisenhower.

Second terms also have been marked by a certain loss of vitality in the White House. A new administration draws much of its energy from the apparent endorsement its agenda received in the election from the American people. The entire Washington community genuflects when it seems that public opinion had spoken in favor of a new president. In the second term, however, the White House cannot draw similar energy from a reelection campaign in which, as we have seen, it has avoided discussion and clarification of its objectives for the following four years. As a result, the administration must make more concessions to other political actors, who soon decide that it may be both safe and profitable to defy the president. Presidents who refuse to bow to this necessity, and go it alone, such as Truman and Nixon, only aggravate their appearance of weakness.

Of course, the experience an administration brings to its second term carries certain advantages for the president. After four years of governing, he should be relatively comfortable in the job. He has demonstrated his staying power to the political establishment. He has learned (or should have learned) techniques of coalition building that may enable him to consolidate a network of supporters who think they have a stake in the continuing success of his policies. Because he does not have to stand again for election, he no longer is as likely to feel constrained by interest groups that previously could have threatened to embarrass his reelection efforts. Finally, he is less likely to commit errors of youth and inexperience. Truman, ascending to the office in 1945, made a quick decision to use the atom bomb against Japan, a decision that still is the subject of ethical and political debate in this and other countries. Kennedy, in 1961, three months after becoming president, launched the ill-fated invasion of Cuba at the Bay of Pigs. In political as in other human affairs, there appear to be the follies of youth as well as the follies of age.

The immutable reality of the second term is the Twenty-second Amendment, which, by limiting the president's tenure, guarantees that public attention will be diverted to the competition to elect his successor. What a president can do is to avoid aggravating the problems that the aging of his administration inevitably will bring. In the second term even more than in the first, a president must adjust to those aspects of his situation that cannot be changed, while remaining alert for opportunities to exercise leadership when the tides of public opinion are running his way.

Notes

1. Godfrey Hodgson, *All Things to All Men: The False Promise of the Modern American Presidency* (New York: Simon and Schuster, 1980), 66.
2. *Public Papers of the Presidents of the United States: Richard Nixon, 1972* (Washington, D.C.: U.S. Government Printing Office, 1974), 1150.
3. Edwin Meese, speaking at the Leadership Conference, Center for the Study of the Presidency, St. Louis, Mo., Dec. 7, 1984.
4. Erwin C. Hargrove and Michael Nelson, "The Presidency: Reagan and the Cycle of Politics and Policy," in *The Elections of 1984,* ed. Michael Nelson (Washington, D.C.: CQ Press, 1985), 206.
5. Norman J. Ornstein, Michael J. Malbin, Allen Schick, and John F. Bibby, *Vital Statistics on Congress, 1984-85 Edition* (Washington, D.C.: American Enterprise Institute, 1984), 56.
6. Ibid.
7. See Richard L. Schott and Dagmar S. Hamilton, *People, Positions, and Power* (Chicago: University of Chicago Press, 1983).
8. Ibid., 27.
9. The term *natives* refers in this case to an agency's career employees and the groups they serve.
10. Richard L. Cole and David A. Caputo, "Presidential Control of the Senior Civil Service: Assessing the Strategies of the Nixon Years," *American Political Science Review* 73 (June 1979): 399-413.
11. Richard E. Neustadt, *Presidential Power* (New York: John Wiley and Sons, 1980).
12. John H. Kessel, *Presidential Parties* (Homewood, Ill.: Dorsey Press, 1984), 67.
13. Ornstein et al., *Vital Statistics,* 44.
14. Jacqueline Calmes, "Hill Support for President Drops to Ten Year Low," *Congressional Quarterly Weekly Report,* Oct. 25, 1986, 2687.
15. Stephen Wayne, speaking at the 1985 Annual Meeting of the American Political Science Association, New Orleans, La.
16. For a fuller presentation of this content analysis, see Martha Joynt Kumar and Michael Baruch Grossman, "Images of the White House in the Media," in *The President and The Public,* ed. Doris A. Graber (Philadelphia: ISHI, 1982).

17. Michael Baruch Grossman and Martha Joynt Kumar, *Portraying the President* (Baltimore, Md.: Johns Hopkins University Press, 1981), 262, figs. 4 and 5.
18. See especially David A. Stockman, *The Triumph of Politics: Why the Reagan Revolution Failed* (New York: Harper and Row, 1985), 79-204; and William Greider, *The Education of David Stockman*, rev. ed. (New York: E. F Dutton, 1986), 14-43.
19. Richard Cohen, book review, *Columbia Journalism Review*, March-April 1986, 62.

Part III

PRESIDENTIAL SELECTION

F ew contrasts in American politics seem sharper than that between the presidential selection process that existed through the election of 1968 and the process since then. In 1968, only seventeen states held presidential primaries; by 1984, twenty-nine states did. In 1968, two-thirds of the national convention delegates were not chosen in primaries; most of them were appointed by each state's party chair or governor. In 1984, less than half were chosen outside the primary system, most at open party caucuses. At the 1968 Democratic convention, 5 percent of the delegates were black and 13 percent were women, compared with 18 percent and 50 percent, respectively, in 1984. The party's 1968 nominee was Hubert Humphrey, who had not entered a single primary. In 1984, as in 1972, 1976, and 1980, the presidential candidates of both major parties received their nominations because they had won most of the primaries, especially the early ones. During the fall campaign of 1968, each candidate was free to raise and spend as much money as he could; in 1984, each received—and was limited to—a check from the federal treasury. In 1968, debates between the Republican and Democratic candidates remained the exception; by 1980, they were the rule.

Dramatic historical changes like these cry out for explanations that are rooted in equally dramatic causes. Scholars and journalists commonly have offered the Democratic party's 1969 McGovern-Fraser Commission on party reform, which opened up the nominating process to wider public participation, as the only event that possibly could account for the recent changes in presidential politics. The first chapter in this part suggests that H. L. Mencken's aphorism is applicable to that line of analysis: "There is a simple explanation for everything, and it is wrong."

In "The Presidency and the Nominating System," Mark Peterson and Jack Walker describe the McGovern-Fraser reforms and those that were instituted by subsequent party commissions, both Democratic and Republican. But according to Peterson and Walker, the effects of these changes in the rules are less important than their causes, which can be understood only by placing them in an appropriately broad context. "American society is in the midst of an extraordinary period of social change and economic transformation that has been underway since World War II," they write. These changes have triggered new styles of political mobilization among the citizenry—demonstrations, ideological interest groups, referendums, and other forms of participatory politics. Alterations in the presidential nominating system have reflected these deeper tides of change. "There will be no returning to the 'good old days' of the 1950s, which were marked by relative calm and political predictability," the authors conclude.

Peterson and Walker's emphasis on the context in which presidential selection takes place is complemented nicely by the concern that John Aldrich and Thomas Weko show for the contest itself, as well as for its consequences. In "The Presidency and the Election Process," Aldrich and Weko describe the goals of voters, the strategies of candidates, and the effects of elections on governance.

According to Aldrich and Weko, most voters have "a meaningful vision of what the nation should be and what is wrong with it." To win, candidates must convince voters that they share this vision and are capable of fulfilling it as president. This is no simple task: candidates are constrained, after all, by the efforts of their opponents and by "reality"—their public records, national conditions, and the like. Campaigns, then, become complex efforts to "frame" the choice of voters in a way that is most likely to win votes. Yet even though the more successful framer will win the election, if the basis of victory is backward-looking and devoid of policy appeals, it will be hard to govern successfully.

10. THE PRESIDENCY AND THE NOMINATING SYSTEM

Mark A. Peterson and
Jack L. Walker

"Where's the beef?" That question, borrowed from the advertising campaign of a national hamburger chain, became the signature of the Democratic party's presidential nomination campaign in 1984. With it, former vice president Walter Mondale challenged the basis of the "bold new ideas" theme on which Sen. Gary Hart, Mondale's most serious rival, was building his quest for the nomination. For Hart, Mondale's simple but biting challenge represented a bitter irony. Little more than a decade earlier, Hart had begun his political career as one of the renegades of the 1960s and 1970s, who rode the forces of the anti-Vietnam War, civil rights, and environmental movements against the establishment politicians of the Democratic party. Their aim, personified in the 1972 presidential campaign of Sen. George McGovern (which Hart managed), was to make the Democratic party more representative and principled. But by 1984—as a candidate—Hart found himself following the advice of his pollster, using the new nominating process to bolster his political viability, not to define and debate the issues.

What had gone wrong in the ensuing years? First, of course, Hart had changed. He was now part of the establishment, with a vested interest in winning, not just in maintaining ideological coherence. More important, like all institutional reforms, those directed at the nominating process after 1968 had both desired effects and unintended consequences, many of which could not have been anticipated. What happened in 1984 is probably not what any reformer would have desired. For many observers, the question of "Where's the beef?" could have been applied to the nominating process as a whole, with its exhausting and seemingly interminable steeplechase of caucuses and primaries that elevated style over substance, endurance over rectitude, and electability over governability. Personality and television presence seemed paramount in campaigns for party nominations, with little of the deliberation that critics argue is essential to build governing coalitions.[1] More varied categories of people are now explicitly represented in the nominating conventions of the two parties, but they have less influence on the choices of their parties.

Nevertheless, the impetus for reform continues. Each change in the rules of the nominating process has effects that the next group of reformers wishes to rectify. If reforms introduced in one year prove detrimental to a candidate, that candidate's supporters will seek further changes to reward that candidate's electoral strengths. More generally, American society is in a constant state of flux, as new groups take on political significance and ultimately stimulate their opponents to mobilize. When forces within the society change, pressure is brought to bear on all national institutions, including the political parties, to reflect those transformations. The accepted electoral procedures of one era quickly come to be regarded as serious injustices in need of change. Each new wave of reforms alters the rules and procedures, helping to define what is politically and programmatically possible in the American system. Rules structure the incentives that candidates face, influence the results of presidential elections, and contribute to the constraints and opportunities for leadership that presidents encounter in office.

Pressure for Reform

Criticism of the procedures used to nominate presidential candidates is hardly confined to the 1980s. The elaborate process, based upon the Electoral College, that was provided for in the Constitution was one of the first aspects of the constitutional system to be changed with the Twelfth Amendment in 1804. The Electoral College was short-circuited during the early nineteenth century by members of Congress who decided to choose presidential candidates for their parties at meetings of their own. The choices were routinely endorsed by the electors, but this system, labeled "King Caucus" by its critics, was itself supplanted a few decades later by a system of national nominating conventions. Staged by the political parties, the conventions brought together state and local party leaders and elected officials from across the country. The Progressive reformers of the early twentieth century denounced the nondemocratic and sometimes corrupt methods used to select delegates to the nominating conventions. They introduced in a few states the procedure of selecting delegates in direct primaries, a system they felt would be more responsive to the public will. In recent years the conventions have lost their deliberative character almost entirely; nominations have been made on the first ballot of every convention since 1952.

Since 1968 the Democratic party has been debating further, and sometimes offsetting, changes in its nominating procedures. The results have been the spread of direct primaries, the selection of more women and minorities as delegates, the elimination of winner-take-all selection systems, and the adoption of requirements that delegates be legally bound to carry out their pledges to vote for candidates at the convention. Republicans, preferring to leave such discretion to the state party organizations, have been much slower to change their nominating procedures and have avoided wholesale reforms at the national level. But, pulled along by the Democrats, they often have been affected against their wishes when Democratic-controlled state legislatures have passed legislation requiring the use of direct primaries to select convention delegates or have mandated other changes in party rules.

The process of change is still under way, partly in reaction to the unanticipated consequences of earlier reforms. In response to complaints about the 1984 nominating process, the Democratic party established the Fairness Commission to review the rules for 1988. The commission recommended some changes in the nominating procedures, but this time the Democratic party chose to maintain most of the far-reaching reforms established in 1984. Nevertheless, reforming the candidate selection process remains at the forefront of political debate, and it seems unlikely that the rules governing presidential nominations in 1988 will satisfy the critics.[2]

Social Changes in the Electorate

Why is there such widespread dissatisfaction among both liberals and conservatives with the procedures used in nominating presidential candidates? Can we identify any social or political trends that have led to the enactment of so many procedural reforms? Have the new rules produced the outcomes expected by the reformer? If even more changes are to be attempted, can we establish any guidelines for evaluating proposals? Whose interests should be served by change, and more important, what should be the overriding goal or central purpose of reform?

The first thing any aspiring reformer must recognize is that there will be no returning to the "good old days" of the 1950s, which were marked by relative calm and political predictability. American society is in the midst of an extraordinary period of social change and economic transformation that has been under way since World War II. Massive population shifts to the South and West, and the end of several decades of black migration to the North, have created a new regional balance of political power. As many as ten million Hispanics have moved into the United States from Mexico, Cuba, and elsewhere in Latin America, touching off political changes and creating social tensions in many southern and southwestern states. The fast pace of urbanization and suburbanization has redued the share of the population living in rural areas from 34 percent in 1950 to 26 percent in 1980. All of these rapid changes have unsettled state and local political systems and altered the relative power of states and regions in Congress. For those concerned with the performance of the political system, however, the most significant long-term change in the American electorate during the past three decades has been the truly revolutionary increase in average educational attainments, a development that has greatly expanded the pool of potential civic activists.

Only 15 percent of the electorate that chose Dwight D. Eisenhower for president in 1952 had ever attended college, and more than 40 percent had received only an elementary-school education. In 1984, 41 percent of the electorate had attended college—almost triple the number of three decades earlier—and those with only elementary educations had shrunk to 11 percent. Evidence that these trends will continue can be seen among voters born since World War II, only 2 percent of whom have stopped with elementary educations and 46 percent of whom have attended college.[3]

Social researchers have found that one of the most powerful influences on political attitudes and behavior in any population is its level of education. The more education people have, the more tolerant they are likely to be of new ideas, the more willing they will be to associate with members of other social or ethnic groups, and the more they will engage in political activity of all kinds.[4] As education has increased in the United States, so has public awareness of abstract questions of public policy, and with it the amount of pressure members of Congress feel from their constituents. The percentage of adults reporting that they had written letters to public officials about policy questions grew from 17 percent in 1964 to 28 percent in 1976. As members of this active political stratum have become more involved in the governmental process, they also have been more willing to reinforce their opinions with financial contributions. Surveys reveal that more than 12 percent of the electorate—representing some twenty-two million people—reported making campaign contributions in 1984, compared with only 4 percent in 1952.[5]

The entry of greater numbers of well-educated citizens into the potential electorate has unsettled the political system and created many surprises for unsuspecting candidates, as well as opportunities for new kinds of office seekers. As voters gather more information on their own about the candidates and issues in elections, they are more likely to ignore party loyalties and split their ballots. A large, shifting, independent political force is emerging that all candidates seek to influence through the mass media.

Much publicity has been given to declines in voter turnout since the early 1960s. Only 53.3 percent of the eligible voters turned out to vote in 1984, a result in part of the large proportion of young people in the potential electorate and also the restrictive systems of voter registration employed in many states.[6] But not nearly enough attention has been paid to the steady expansion during this same period in the American electorate's active core and the variety of political activities in which its members engage. These new, better educated voters can be reached by appeals to broad ideological principles and are willing to consider unconventional solutions to social problems. This volatile electorate, increasingly dominated by the post-World War II baby-boom generation, already has reshaped the American political landscape and promises even more change in future years. In some regions, the expansion of the naturalized immigrant population and the more effectively mobilized black community ensures even more pronounced deviations from the past.

Political Mobilization in the 1960s and 1970s

The American public's extraordinary propensity to write letters to its representatives is not entirely an outgrowth of rising educational levels, nor is the increase in financial contributions caused only by growing affluence. Citizens are being encouraged to engage in these activities through their memberships in organized groups. Since 1950 a national process of political mobilization has been under way in which new groups and civic organizations have been formed at an unprecedented rate, bringing many formerly quiescent elements of the population into closer contact with the nation's political leaders.

Social Protests

The recent burst of organizational activity began in 1955 with the Montgomery, Alabama, bus boycott to protest segregation and continued with the sit-ins, freedom rides, and protest marches of the civil rights movement, events that eventually led to the transformation of the American political system. Armed with the symbolic authority of affirmative decisions from the Supreme Court, and backed by a broad coalition of liberal religious groups, labor unions, and civic leaders from the white community, the civil rights movement called into question the moral foundations upon which political leadership had been based in the postwar years.

The demand of the civil rights movement for the immediate implementation of the promises of political equality that were fundamental parts of the American democratic creed led many other groups in the population, who also believed they were victims of discrimination, to make similar appeals, using class-action law suits, acts of civil disobedience, and initiatives and referenda, as well as conventional electoral politics. These actions involved the same mixture of tactics that had been pioneered by the civil rights movement, thus spurring on the process of mobilization. White college students who were veterans of the early years of protest, for example, came home from the Mississippi Freedom Summer in 1964 and immediately made efforts to convince their fellow students that they were somehow members of an oppressed class in need of liberation.[7]

The 1960s were marked by the formation of a series of movements involving women, Hispanics, the elderly, the handicapped, homosexuals, and many other formerly unmobilized and often despised segments of society. Hundreds of groups were formed in attempts to make the same kind of gains for their constituents that they believed blacks were achieving through the civil rights movement. The National Organization for Women (NOW) has been described as the "NAACP of the women's movement."[8] The Mexican-American Legal Defense and Education Fund (MALDEF), one of the most active of the new Hispanic groups, was incorporated by a former staff member of the NAACP.[9] Established institutions were placed under great pressure as one group after another engaged in angry egalitarian polemics against the customary procedures used for hiring employees or measuring achievement. Most of the society's fundamental assumptions about human relations and the bases of authority were subjected to searching criticism.

Once this process of political mobilization of the disadvantaged sectors of the society was well under way, other kinds of social movements, mainly from the educated middle class, began to arise. Many of the groups were founded early in this century and slowly developed broad public support. They were dedicated to forwarding the rights of consumers against the power of large businesses, placing restraints on the ability of businesses and individuals to exploit the environment, or granting the government extensive powers to ensure higher standards of industrial health and safety. The formation of all of these groups, abetted by the patronage of sympathetic government agencies, wealthy individuals, private foundations, and other institutions, not only increased the scope of the interest group community but also helped generate an entirely new cleavage in American politics. With the power of organized labor diminished by declining union memberships and by economic pressures that forced it to stress bread-and-butter interests compatible with those of business, the once fundamental political and economic division between business and labor largely gave way to a split between business and the organizations mobilized around the new issues generated in the 1960s and 1970s. Ideological feuds, lack of money, or personality clashes destroyed some of the new issue organizations, but politicians began to pay heed, and so did the voters.

Technological Advances

In the 1970s several technological advances facilitated the task of organizing large groups with national memberships. Computerized systems that could store and classify millions of names and addresses permitted associations to target mailings to the individuals most likely to contribute money or communicate with their elected representatives. The country's long distance telephone network, which expanded rapidly after World War II, allowed organizations to reach members almost instantly at little cost. The art of public opinon polling also was perfected and put into widespread use. Combined with the nearly total penetration of American homes by radio and television and the increased sophistication of the broadcast news media, the newly emerging groups had ready means for challenging the status quo. Even organizations without explicit memberships, such as the various centers created by consumer activist Ralph Nader, could use new technological tools to mobilize supporters and put pressure on government institutions.

Public Pressures

Through elaborate networks of associations and advocacy groups, public preferences and opinions can be both molded and transmitted to political leaders. The degree to which these groups have transformed the political system was graphically illustrated by the striking differences in the reactions of the American public to the wars in Korea and Vietnam. If public opinion polls that measured support for the war in Korea in the 1950s are compared with polls about the war in Vietnam, the patterns are remarkably similar. As casualties mounted and frustration grew over the limited goals of American forces in both conflicts, the number of citizens expressing disapproval of the war effort began to rise at about the same rate.[10] President Harry S Truman's public approval rating, as measured by the Gallup poll, dropped rapidly to less than 25 percent as the war dragged on, just as Lyndon B. Johnson's declined to its lowest point toward the end of his term.[11] Voters in the national elections of 1952 and 1968 shifted toward the candidates who promised to end the fighting.

In the 1960s, however, the more highly mobilized public, accustomed to unconventional forms of political expression, voiced its dissatisfaction with the war more forcefully than had the previous generation. Once public support for the war in Vietnam began to evaporate during 1968 and 1969, political leaders begin to feel pressure almost immediately, in the form of letters from constituents, visits from delegations of concerned citizens, negative testimony in Congress, and protest demonstrations in cities and towns across the country. Leaders found that they were no longer as insulated as they had been from the shifting tides of public opinion, a trend that continued into the 1980s. Even a president as popular as Ronald Reagan saw his interventionist policies in Central America constrained by public concerns about military involvement, and his diplomatic approach to ending South Africa's policy of apartheid threatened by a well mobilized public calling for more stringent measures.

Conservative Countermovements

Most of the groups that formed in the 1950s and 1960s were dedicated to liberal causes, but they were matched almost immediately by conservative countermovements that grew even stronger in the 1970s. Planned Parenthood, Inc., was soon confronted by the National Right to Life Committee; the Fellowship of Reconciliation encountered the Committee on the Present Danger; the National Council of Churches was matched by the Moral Majority. Through an extension of the process of political mobilization begun with the Montgomery bus boycott of 1955, these new conservative groups began campaigns of opposition to most of the central policies of the Kennedy-Johnson years, often employing techniques perfected by the liberals, such as computer-assisted direct-mail solicitations for funds. Several new policy initiatives were launched by this rapidly growing network; some, such as the tax limitation movement, began to have a major influence on national political debate. Conservative movements, like the liberal ones that preceded them, roused many elements of the population—housewives concerned about abortion, new groups of business executives, and Protestant evangelicals—into active participation in political life for the first time.

With the help of sympathetic business firms and foundations, an imposing network of think tanks, public interest law firms, and conservative political magazines was created. Organizations like the Heritage Foundation, once a fledgling operation compared to its liberal counterparts, became major institutions in American politics and policy making. In concert with the Reagan administration, they helped to bring about a fundamental shift in the public agenda away from government regulation and domestic commitments and toward a more antagonistic approach to the Soviet Union and its allies.[12]

The Reformers' Response to Political Mobilization

Faced with the pressures that were generated by the surge of political mobilization and the rising ideological conflict of the 1960s and 1970s, political leaders responded with an extraordinary series of legal and constitutional changes in society's central institutions. Such far-reaching reforms had not been implemented since the introduction at the turn of the century of the secret ballot, the direct primary, the referendum and recall, nonpartisan elections, and the city manager form of government.

Like the Progressives of the early 1900s, the reformers of the 1960s and 1970s wanted to increase participation in the deliberative processes of government. Their first impulse was to bring to the bargaining table those who were pursuing their interests through protests and threats of violence. The reformers hoped that procedural changes eventually would lead to changes in public policy. They also wished to reestablish order and accommodate pressures for change so that the legitimacy of the American political system might be restored. These were not entirely compatible goals, as events in the late 1960s were to reveal, but they were the principal motives behind the many far-reaching changes that were made in the rules of the political game during this period. The system for nominating presidential candidates was only one of many different areas that the reformers of the 1960s and 1970s marked for change.

Reapportionment

Three landmark reforms stand out in this period that laid the groundwork for efforts to change the system of presidential nomination. First, the Supreme Court decided in *Baker v. Carr* (1962), *Reynolds v. Sims* (1964), *Westberry v. Sanders* (1964), and subsequent rulings that state legislatures, local city councils, and U.S. congressional districts must be apportioned according to equal population size. In the words of the Court, "[O]ne man's vote is to be worth as much as another's." [13]

The immediate result of reapportionment was rapid turnover in all representative bodies. Prior to reapportionment, 20 percent of those elected to the state Senate in the 1959 general election in New Jersey were new members; in 1967, soon after reapportionment, 75 percent of those chosen were serving for the first time. No sooner was the issue settled than the 1970 census figures became available, requiring yet another round of district drawing. The Tennessee state legislature, for example, was redistricted six times in the nine years from 1963 to 1972.

The constant shifting of district lines allowed newly organized political forces, centered in the suburbs and central cities, to exert a much greater voice in state politics and led to the unsettling of state political systems for more than a decade.[14] Reapportionment decisions had their greatest effects on southern states, such as Georgia and Mississippi, which had long been controlled by the Democratic party, or in states such as New Jersey and Michigan, where carefully constructed political coalitions based in rural regions and small towns had prevented urban areas from having proportional representation.

Voting Rights

The second landmark reform was a double-barreled assault on voting restrictions, the effect of which was felt mainly in the South. Ratification of the Twenty-fourth Amendment in 1964 eliminated the poll tax in Alabama, Arkansas, Mississippi, Texas, and Virginia, and the passage of the Voting Rights Act of 1965 barred the use of literacy tests and sent federal examiners to register blacks in southern counties where their voting participation was below a specified level. These were the final strokes that ended a century of formal discrimination against black voters. Within a decade, the black vote in most southern states doubled. In 1964 only 28,500 blacks were registered to vote in Mississippi, compared with 525,000 whites; in 1974 there were 286,000 registered blacks and 690,000 registered whites. Complete political equality was still far off, but this tenfold increase in eligible black voters almost immediately changed the political culture of the state, leading in 1974 to the election of 191 blacks to public office—an unthinkable event prior to 1965—and to open courting of black voters by all candidates for statewide office.[15]

Beginning in the late 1960s, the new political role of blacks and the new legislative influence of cities and suburbs led to vigorous two-party competition for statewide offices in the South for the first time in the twentieth century. Republicans were elected to the U.S. Senate in North Carolina, Florida, and Alabama, and liberal Democratic governors such as Reubin Askew of Florida, Jimmy Carter of Georgia, and later even George Wallace of Alabama—once a militant segregationist—ran successfully on platforms that made straightforward appeals to blacks and to the interest of cities and suburbs. The potential for black voter mobilization became even more apparent in 1984 with the campaign of Jesse Jackson for the Democratic presidential nomination. With a black candidate available on the ballot for the first time, turnout in caucuses and primary elections increased dramatically in areas with heavy concentrations of black voters. The procedural reforms of the 1960s finally caused a true reconstruction of southern politics, a century after the end of the Civil War.

The Eighteen-Year-Old Vote

The third landmark reform affected the entire country, although its effects were not as large as many reformers had expected. Eighteen-to-twenty-year-olds were granted the right to vote in 1971 with the Twenty-sixth Amendment to the Constitution, thus bringing about the largest expansion of the electorate since 1920, when suffrage was extended to women. Democrats made special efforts to cultivate these new voters in 1972 but were disappointed to find that they were hard to register and get to the polls. Only 48 percent of all eighteen-to-twenty-year-olds voted in the 1972 election, compared with 71 percent of those aged forty-five to fifty-four. Even more than their parents, they tended to avoid firm ties to the Democratic or Republican parties; nor did they vote as a cohesive bloc.[16]

In the 1980s, however, the competition between the two parties for young voters developed new urgency. Contrary to the pattern of every previous election since 1952, Reagan's popularity permitted the Republicans in 1984 to capture a majority of votes cast by those aged eighteen to twenty-four. The Democrats hope to reclaim their hold on the young electorate, however, by reinforcing the antagonism many young people feel toward the social agenda of conservative Republicans.

Conclusion

Reapportionment, voting rights, and the eighteen-year-old vote—all of these unsettling reforms contributed to the collapse of many local party machines and opened the political system to participation by elements of the population that had been excluded in the past. It was inevitable that, having successfully transformed state and local party organizations, reformers would begin to press for similar changes in the processes through which the party's most important national leader was chosen.

Presidential Nomination Reforms

The process of reform in presidential nominations began in earnest in the wake of the Democratic party's stormy 1968 nominating convention in Chicago. The campaign for the nomination, set against the background of urban riots and Vietnam protests, had already been upset by Johnson's surprise announcement that he would not run for reelection and the tragic assassinations of civil rights leader Martin Luther King, Jr., and presidential contender Robert Kennedy. The convention itself was marked by a steady stream of angry complaints about the rules governing the meeting, by near-violent disputes among delegates on the convention floor, and by what an investigating commission later described as a "police riot" in the streets of Chicago.[17]

As the convention drew to a close, a resolution was passed that, for the first time in the modern history of the party system, called for a commission to establish new rules to govern the 1972 convention. This body, chaired in the beginning by Sen. George McGovern and later by Rep. Donald Fraser, was followed by an unprecedented succession of reform commissions. First came the one chaired by Rep. Barbara Mikulski to establish the rules for 1976. Morley Winograd, state chairman of the Michigan Democratic party, chaired the subsequent commission to set the 1980 rules. A commission to change the rules for 1984, chaired by Gov. James Hunt of North Carolina, was followed by the Fairness Commission, which introduced modest changes for the 1988 campaign. The Republicans have adopted the spirit of many of the proposed reforms, although largely informally, after the Democrats took the initiative. It is the work of the Democratic commissions, therefore, that has transformed the nominating process.

The most dramatic change in nomination procedures after 1968 was the rapid increase in the number of states holding direct primaries to choose their delegates to the national nominating conventions. There were seventeen state primaries in 1968, twenty-three in 1972, thirty in 1976, and thirty-six in 1980. Members of the McGovern-Fraser Commission had not intended to encourage this swift departure from the traditional system of caucuses and conventions, but the complicated rules they created for the conduct of caucuses had this effect. Many state party leaders, afraid that if they continued to use the caucus system they would lose all control over their party apparatus to volunteers representing various candidates, adopted the primary system as the lesser evil.[18]

The Democrats also transformed the makeup of state delegations by requiring that at least one-half of the delegates be women, no matter what system was used to choose them, and that all states develop plans to increase the number of delegates chosen from among racial minorities, although no quotas were established. As a result of these reforms, women rose as a proportion of total delegates at Democratic conventions from 13 percent in 1968 to 49 percent in 1984, and blacks from 5 percent in 1968 to 18 percent in 1984. Republicans did not enact similar rules concerning delegate representativeness, and the proportion of black delegates at Republican conventions remained steady at about 3 percent of the total. Even without explicit quotas, however, the proportion of female delegates at Republican conventions steadily increased from 16 percent in 1968 to 44 percent in 1984.[19]

Despite this attention to the racial and sexual makeup of state delegations, the real effect of the reforms was to reduce the autonomy of convention delegates. Biological traits aside, delegates now were chosen in most states not because of their personal qualifications but because of their support for certain presidential candidates. The Democrats prohibited any state from using a winner-take-all system to allocate delegates after a primary. The Republicans did not require states to follow this practice, but soon both parties in most states apportioned delegates in rough accordance with the proportion of votes each candidate received in the primary. Delegates also were legally bound to vote for their candidate on at least the first ballot of the convention, regardless of the circumstances.

In 1982 the Hunt Commission suggested far-reaching changes in the rules for the nominating process in 1984. Responding to the perceived weaknesses of the previous reforms—which made the party susceptible to capture by little-known outsiders such as Carter—the rules for 1984 were designed to favor establishment candidates and to regenerate the influence of the party's leaders and elected officials. Instead of a drawn-out sequence of caucuses and primaries that could give an outsider a chance to build momentum, the period for selecting delegates was shortened by almost two months. Other provisions of the 1984 nominating rules retreated from the previous strict adherence to proportional representation in allocating delegates among candidates. States were permitted to use procedures that rewarded the largest vote-getter, and candidates receiving less than 20 percent of the vote could be denied delegates. Finally, where the reforms of the previous decade had often made the party's convention hostile territory for state party leaders, governors, and members of Congress, the rules in 1984 specifically reserved 14 percent of the delegate seats for party officials and officeholders, known as "superdelegates." Among the objectives of the reforms for 1984, according to Governor Hunt, was "our goal to nominate a candidate who can win, and after winning, can govern effectively." [20] The reforms seemed especially well suited to Mondale and Sen. Edward Kennedy, the two most likely inside candidates when the new rules were ratified.

The revised nominating process did not satisfy everyone, however, especially Gary Hart and Jesse Jackson, the two runners-up to Mondale in 1984. Many observers complained that the Hunt Commission reforms had done nothing to limit the length and shallowness of the campaign. The media, with its concern for the horse race and visual images, seemed as dominant as ever. More important from the standpoint of the vanquished candidates of 1984, however, was their perception that the Hunt Commission reforms had gone too far. The increased use of caucuses instead of primaries for delegate selection, the 20 percent threshold requirement, and the existence of the superdelegates directed the nominating process away from the "democratic" impulses of the previous reforms. With the cumulative effect of these rules changes giving Mondale a majority of delegates even though he won less than 40 percent of the vote in the primaries, Jesse Jackson decried the "move away from primaries and one-man, one-vote and a move to back-room politics." [21]

These complaints inspired the Democratic party to form yet another commission, the Fairness Commission, to redesign the nominating procedures for 1988. As the product of considerable dissatisfaction with the nominating process, the commission began its labors in the now-traditional pattern of the party reform movement. However, once the commission was formed, its chairman selected (Donald Fowler, former Democratic party chairman in South Carolina), and its work begun, a dramatic change occurred in the politics of reform. According to an adviser in the Fairness Commission, "The general consensus is that the party has got to stop mucking around with the nominating process." [22] Minor changes were made to address some of the critics' concerns, but no fundamental reforms were proposed or enacted. The rules established for the nominating process in 1988 reinforced rather than rejected the patterns of the previous election.

Campaign Finance Reforms

The movement for electoral reform was not confined to the parties. Another extremely important part of the package of reforms was the passage by Congress during the 1970s of a series of laws governing campaign finance, the most important of which was the Campaign Finance Act of 1974.

This reform, which went into effect with the 1976 election, made extensive changes in this fundamental element of the political process. To regulate the participation of trade unions, businesses, and interest groups in national political campaigns, the law established procedures for forming political action committees (PACs), the only legal means through which these groups could provide financial resources to candidates. The campaign act also established limits on the permissible size of individual and organizational contributions to candidates— $1,000 for individuals, $5,000 for the PACs—and required candidates to report the source of all contributions from PACs and all individual contributions of more than $200 to a newly created regulatory agency, the Federal Election Commission.

Reporting laws had been enacted before, but this one included several other, more significant provisions. Most important, it provided for an equal match from public funds, dollar for dollar, of all individual contributions under $250, up to a limit to be established in each election

($10.1 million in 1984). Political action committees were excluded from the matching provisions. Candidates were not required to accept public funding, but if they decided to do so—as have all thirty-five major party presidential candidates since the law took effect, except for John Connally in 1980—they also were required to accept limitations both upon the total amount of money they could spend and upon the amount they could spend in each state.

Although the overall limitations on campaign expenditures are generous ($20.2 million in 1984 and $22.2 million for 1988, plus 20 percent for fund-raising costs), reformers still saw this law as a significant step in limiting the control of large vested interests over the outcome of party nominations. Critics of the reform feared that it would create a rash of candidates running highly divisive campaigns centered on narrow controversial issues, all at public expense. In order to guard against that possibility, candidates were not eligible for federal matching funds until they had already raised $100,000 in individual contributions, including at least $5,000 from each of twenty different states in individual contributions of no more than $250. Any candidate who failed to receive as much as 10 percent of the vote in two consecutive primary elections would stop receiving public funds. Vast amounts of money were needed to conduct national presidential campaigns through the mass media. With public financing, the creation of the PACs, strict reporting provisions, and limits on expenditures, the reformers were trying to provide the necessary funds and at the same time maintain an important measure of competitive equity.

Campaigning from 1972 to 1988

After the reforms of the early 1970s, particularly those that produced a dramatic increase in the number of primaries and that favored proportional rules in allocating delegates, the nominating process could have led to a stalemate among several candidates, with none of them able to build a majority. This result would have revived the convention as the instrument of choice. But as the Democrats' nominations of McGovern in 1972, Carter in 1976, and Mondale in 1984 demonstrated, the reformed system not only prevented stalemate but also led to ultimately convincing victories for the front runner. Candidates who won or did better than the press expected in the early primaries were able to drain away from their competitors financial contributions, volunteer workers, and exposure on the national television networks. The popularity of these "thrusting candidates" sometimes began to sag toward the end of the long primary season, as Carter's did in both 1976 and 1980, but by then they had already gained enough pledged delegates to win the nomination easily on the first ballot at the convention. In 1984, however, rules changes designed to aid the inside front runner almost backfired on Mondale. The condensed primary schedule, rather than preventing the development of momentum by an outsider, nearly denied Mondale enough time to make a comeback after Hart's surprise victory in the New Hampshire primary.

Public financing for primary campaigns in 1976, 1980, and 1984 also had surprising effects. It increased the importance of private contributions, the opposite of what the reformers intended. Federal matching dollars greatly benefited candidates whose popularity accelerated after early successes by doubling the surge of contributions that they received in the wake of their primary victories.[23]

Once it became evident that their early successes were the key to victory in the reformed system, the marathon campaign was born. To win, candidates needed to devote two years or more to the exhausting, nearly full time pursuit of publicity and support. Candidates with heavy responsibilities in government, such as members of the leadership in the House or Senate or state governors—positions that provide the experience a successful president may need—were virtually precluded from consideration because their duties did not allow them enough time to campaign. Mondale, who as a U.S. senator in 1974 said he was unwilling to make the necessary commitment to a life of campaigning and Holiday Inns, found the requisite time and energy as a former officeholder in 1984. From 1976 to 1984, every major party nominee has been either an incumbent president seeking reelection or an "unemployed" politician.

Reagan's success in the 1980 race for the Republican nomination, however, stands as a reminder that there are limits to the effectiveness of marathon campaigning by little-known candidates. Reagan was defeated in his first confrontation with George Bush in the highly publicized Iowa caucuses but was able to recover quickly and win the nomination once he increased his efforts in later primaries. Despite his early defeat, Reagan was a near-consensus choice within his party by the time the primaries began in 1980. He had built a dedicated following during fifteen years of advocacy and two efforts to win the office in earlier elections, a kind of "supermarathon" campaign. Mondale's experience—with his initial short-lived bid for office in 1976 and his ultimate come-from-behind nomination victory in 1984—reveals a similar pattern.

Incumbent presidents evidently have some of these same advantages in nomination contests, as shown by the successful campaigns of Ford in 1976 and Carter in 1980 against powerful opponents. The new system, however, encourages challengers to incumbent presidents to develop within their own party. The challenger enjoys public exposure and notoriety that may set the stage for victory in later elections, while the incumbent president is presented with a serious distraction that threatens to transform every official announcement or policy decision during the final two years of the four-year term into a partisan campaign gesture.[24]

The 1988 race for the presidency both highlights the patterns that were established in the reform era and serves as a significant juncture for any analysis of the nominating process, the effects of reforms, and the consequences of reforms for the American political system. Ironically, the only significant change in the nominating process introduced for the 1988 election was one crafted by officials outside the national party, not by the Fairness Commission. In order to get Democratic candidates for the presidency to be responsive to the needs and interests of the South, southern party leaders established a "megaprimary" comprised of southern states. By having most of the old Confederacy choose its delegates on the same day, fairly early in the campaign season, they hoped to have more influence in determining the nominee of the party—preferably one with a more conservative bent than previous party nominees.

The southern primary, however, may test the proposition that reforms can produce dramatic unintended consequences. Almost a fifth of southern voters are black. As demonstrated in 1984, black voters are willing to be active in support of an attractive candidate, one who is likely to trumpet liberal issues, not the more conservative agenda favored by southern party leaders. Because it is the first regional primary, experience with the southern megaprimary will shape future debate about the appropriateness of requiring such primaries, a reform that is often discussed.

The results of the 1988 election also put recent reforms to a severe test in other ways. For the first time since the party reform movement began in 1968, the nominating process is not influenced by the reelection campaign of an incumbent president. The election also provides another opportunity to see how well sitting governors and members of Congress fare against those without current governmental responsibilities. Some candidates decided to remain in office, harried by the affairs of government but able to remain in the limelight. In any future election, the nomination of candidates who retained their official posts will require the reevaluation of concerns about the marathon campaign.

Finally, in many respects the outcome of the 1988 election is more important for the Republican party. It marks only the third time since 1956 that its candidates have sought the support of voters without the advantage of incumbency. Only in 1964 did the Republicans endure the kind of severe trial that the Democrats experienced in 1968, which led to the long series of reforms in the nominating process. It is not clear how long the Republicans can continue to escape similar difficulties. The New Right and the Christian Right gained prominence during the Reagan years, but much of their social agenda remains unrealized. Their links to the Republican party have always been tenuous, and their activism tests both the responsiveness of the party and the pragmatism of its right wing.

Reform and the Conduct of the Presidency

What have been the effects of more than a decade of reforms in the presidential nomination process? Critics have charged that by changing the rules and bringing new, sometimes volatile constituencies into the electorate, the reformers seriously eroded the ability of the parties to build durable coalitions, mediate among contending factions, and decide what the issues would be in an election campaign.[25] The new rules also made possible, in the case of Jimmy Carter, the selection as president of a party outsider who sometimes was unable to gain the cooperation of other powerful leaders in Washington.

Reformers have responded that no set of rules could have offset the enormous effects on presidential fortunes of the civil rights movement, the war in Vietnam, the Watergate crisis, and disputes over environmental pollution, abortion, inflation, and the declining competitiveness of American industry. With so many pressures pulling in so many different directions at once, it is doubtful that any president could have exercised strong, consistent leadership during the 1970s, no matter what procedures were employed by the political parties to nominate their candidates. The response of reformers to these intense pressures was to open the system to larger and larger numbers of people so that the country could make a safe passage through one of the most turbulent periods in the history of the United States with its democratic traditions still intact. Evidence of their success can be found among the scores of former McGovern campaign insurgents and social movement activists who now are embedded in the Democratic party establishment.

The controversy over the rules governing presidential nominations reveals a central paradox that exists at the heart of all democratic systems of government, a paradox that often frustrates the best efforts of both reformers and party leaders. The principal force that diffuses authority and fragments power in a democracy—active citizen participation—is also the fundamental justification for authority and leadership. The same process that provides the system its reason for being can render it so unmanageable that no collective goals can be reached. The process of participation itself can deteriorate into a selfish, aimless scramble for private gain.

The principal aim of reformers in the 1960s and 1970s was to recognize newly mobilized elements of American society and peacefully resolve social conflicts that could easily have led to widespread violence or bloodshed. Had the events of these tumultuous years been mismanaged, the governmental system could have been engulfed in an uncontrollable political rampage that might have undermined the country's democratic traditions. Reformers were willing to trade away some of the political leadership's capacity to aggregate preferences, establish agendas, and even determine presidential nominees in order to increase the participation of women, blacks, and other minorities that had not been adequately consulted in the past. They also intended to force onto the political agenda a number of controversial new questions of public policy that they believed had been ignored or suppressed by the established party leadership. The process is being repeated in the 1980s to accommodate the pent-up demands of conservative movements in American society. That is the essence of politics in an open democratic process. Disruptive ideological impulses, however unnerving they may be to established leaders, must be provided some legitimate outlet if they are not to challenge directly the basic precepts of the polity.

The stability of American democracy ultimately depends upon the willingness of elected officials, and of party and interest group leaders of all persuasions, to exercise self-restraint and engage in compromise. Although this willingness can never be entirely a product of formal procedures, rules are extremely important. Whatever rules future reformers may enact, they must be evaluated by a dual standard that grows out of democracy's central paradox. First, the public must be convinced that the procedures governing election campaigns are not unfairly tilted toward some predetermined outcome. Second, leaders must be given enough political and administrative resources so that after the election the government can actually reach the goals the voters have set for it. Reformers have vacillated between the seemingly conflicting demands of legitimacy and effectiveness, but in the end the two are linked and neither can safely be ignored. A democratic government that is "effective" but not legitimate violates the political creed of the society. A government paralyzed by a torrent of unmanageable demands loses its legitimacy. In short, the overriding purpose of procedural reform in a democracy is to encourage enough citizen participation in government to create a legitimate moral basis for the effective exercise of political authority.

Notes

1. Terry Sanford presents a good summary of contemporary critics of reform in *A Danger of Democracy: The Presidential Nominating Process* (Boulder, Colo.: Westview Press, 1981).
2. See, for example, George Grassmuck, ed. *Before Nomination: Our Primary Problems* (Washington, D.C.: American Enterprise Institute, 1985).
3. These figures came from random samples of the adult U.S. population surveyed by the Center for Political Studies of the University of Michigan. Results are reported in Warren E. Miller, Arthur H. Miller, and Edward J. Schneider, eds., *American National Election Data Sourcebook: 1952-1978* (Cambridge, Mass.: Harvard University Press, 1980). The most recent figures are from the 1984 National Election Study, Center for Political Studies, the University of Michigan.
4. For an insightful discussion of the importance of education in determining political behavior, see Philip E. Converse, "Change in the American Electors," in *The Human Meaning of Social Change,* ed. Angus Campbell and Philip Converse (New York: Russell Sage, 1972), 263-338.
5. Miller, Miller, and Schneider, *American National Election Data Sourcebook;* and 1984 National Election Study.
6. Raymond E. Wolfinger and Steven J. Rosenstone. *Who Votes?* (New Haven: Yale University Press, 1980).
7. Thousands of college students from across the country worked in southern communities during that summer to register black voters. The project was organized by the Student Nonviolent Coordinating Committee (SNCC), and the work was often dangerous. On June 21, 1964, three civil rights workers, one a New York college student, were brutally killed in Philadelphia, Mississippi. On July 14, the bodies of two nineteen-year-old black students were found in the Mississippi River.
8. Maren Lockwood Carden, *The New Feminist Movement* (New York: Russell Sage, 1974), 103-118.
9. David S. Broder, *Changing of the Guard: Power and Leadership in America* (New York: Simon & Schuster, 1980), 283.
10. For an analysis of these data, see John E. Mueller, *Wars, Presidents and Public Opinion* (New York: John Wiley & Sons, 1973).
11. *Gallup Opinion Index,* report no. 182 (October-November 1980).
12. Thomas Byrne Edsall, *The New Politics of Inequality* (New York: W. W. Norton, 1984); and Alan Crawford, *Thunder on the Right* (New York: Pantheon Books, 1980).
13. *Westberry v. Sanders* 376 U.S. 1 (1964).
14. Timothy G. O'Rourke, *The Impact of Reapportionment* (New Brunswick, N.J.: Transaction Books, 1980).
15. Richard E. Cohen, "Changing Racial Conditions May Shape 1975 Voting Rights Act," *National Journal,* October 26, 1974, 1606-1613.
16. "Whatever Happened to the Youth Vote?" *Congressional Quarterly Weekly Report,* July 15, 1978, 1792-1795.
17. Daniel Walker, *Rights in Conflict* (Report of the National Commission on the Causes and Prevention of Violence, Chicago Study Team, 1968).
18. Patricia Bonom, James MacGregor Burns, and Austin Ranney, eds., *The American Constitutional System under Strong and Weak Parties* (New York: Praeger, 1981), 97-114.

19. James W. Ceaser, *Reforming the Reforms: A Critical Analysis of the Presidential Selection Process* (Cambridge, Mass.: Ballinger, 1982), 52. The most recent figures were supplied by the Democratic National Committee and the Republican National Committee.

20. Michael J. Malbin, "Democratic Rules Makers Want to Bring Party Leaders Back to the Conventions," *National Journal,* January 2, 1982, 26.

21. "Back-Room Party Caucuses Draw Fire from Mondale Foes," *Congressional Quarterly Weekly Report,* June 2, 1984, 1315.

22. ·Thomas Mann, quoted in Rhodes Cook, "Many Democrats Cool to Redoing Party Rules," *Congressional Quarterly Weekly Report,* August 24, 1985, 1687.

23. William R. Keech and Donald R. Matthews, *The Party's Choice* (Washington, D.C.: Brookings Institution, 1976); and John H. Aldrich, *Before the Convention: Strategies and Choices in Presidential Nomination Campaigns* (Chicago: University of Chicago Press, 1980).

24. During his final year in the White House, Ford spent over 20 percent of his working time engaged directly in campaigning for renomination. See Ford's testimony at the Duke University-Woodrow Wilson Center Forum on Presidential Nominations, May 11, 1981.

25. Nelson W. Polsby, *Consequences of Party Reform* (New York: Oxford University Press, 1983).

11. THE PRESIDENCY AND THE ELECTION PROCESS: CAMPAIGN STRATEGY, VOTING, AND GOVERNANCE

John H. Aldrich and Thomas Weko

Jack Germond and Jules Witcover entitled their books about the 1980 and 1984 presidential election campaign *Blue Smoke and Mirrors* and *Wake Us When It's Over*.[1] The titles reflect a widely shared view of general election campaigns and candidates' campaign strategies: they are irrelevant. In this essay, we argue that campaign strategy matters. It materially affects the public and its behavior, and it helps to shape and constrain presidential governance for the victor.

Decades of research have shown that voters are relatively ill informed about most political matters, including presidential elections. Yet they do have goals concerning the governance of the nation and the problems they think should be solved. They vote, therefore, for the candidate they believe is most likely to achieve those goals and solve those problems.

Presidential candidates design their campaign strategies to convince a majority of the public that they would make the better president. Their strategies are constrained by current political realities, their own and their opponents' natures and political histories, and the competitive environment of an election (most notably the opposition's attempts to lead voters to opposite conclusions). Yet the complexity that faces voters as they attempt to decide who would make a better president gives the candidates room to maneuver strategically.

Candidates design their strategies to "frame" the voters' choice in terms that are favorable to their candidacy. In 1980, for instance, Ronald Reagan tried to persuade voters to see the choice as "Why return a failed incumbent?" while Jimmy Carter tried to make them see it as "Whatever my failures, Reagan will be worse." The successful candidate, then, is that candidate who benefits from current political realities and the other constraints noted above *and* who can frame the voters' choice more successfully.

Campaign strategy not only helps to frame the choices of the electorate, it also helps to frame the victor's postelection political agenda. Reagan was successful with Congress early in his first term because his policy proposals were central to his campaign. Four years later, Reagan held less sway over Congress, despite an even larger margin of victory, because his campaign did not frame a legislative agenda.

The rest of this essay expands on these arguments and applies them to recent presidential campaigns and administrations. We begin by considering the nature of the public's choice in presidential elections.

The Public's Choice

Voters have basic goals and values in relation to politics and governance. They have, that is, a meaningful vision of what the nation should be and what is wrong with it. As others have suggested, the public's basic concerns include peace, prosperity, and tranquility, and it holds presidents responsible for achieving (or failing to achieve) these ends.[2] Moreover, these concerns are rooted in actual conditions, and they are also shaped by the flow of information in the mass media. Thus, the public's concerns change with changes in the conditions it experiences and the flow of information it receives about the world.

Another attribute of voters is that they choose the presidential candidate they consider better. More than 90 percent vote for the candidate they rank higher on the National Election Studies (NES) "feeling thermometer." And, as Stanley Kelley and Thad Mirer have shown, there is an equally direct translation of the voter's "likings" and "dislikings" of the candidates to their vote.[3] So clear and obvious is this relationship that Kelley and Mirer entitled their study "The Simple Act of Voting."

Thus far we have established that voters have basic goals and concerns, and that they support the candidate they prefer. But do voters bring their goals and concerns to bear in deciding which candidate is better? That is, do voters prefer one candidate to the other because they believe the candidate is better able to handle the concerns that are most important to them? Consider the data in Table 11-1, which are drawn from a national election survey conducted by the Gallup organization for John Aldrich, Eugene Borgida, and John Sullivan. The survey asked respondents what problem they felt was most important to the nation and what national problem was personally most important to them. It also asked which candidate was better, in the voter's opinion, at handling these national and personal problems. As Table 11-1 indicates, there is a remarkably strong correspondence between the candidate the respondent judged as better to handle these problems and how he or she voted. Virtually every respondent who thought one candidate would be better than his opponent at handling the problem most important personally or to the nation (or both) voted for that candidate.

Table 11-1 Percentage Voting for Candidate Viewed as Better to Handle the Most Important Problem Facing the Country and the Most Important Political Problem to the Person, 1984

	Candidate better on nationally and personally most important problem						
	Reagan better on both	Reagan once neither once	Neither on both	Reagan on one Mondale on other	Mondale once neither once	Mondale on both	Total % (N)
Reported vote for Reagan	100%	94.6%	52.9%	43.6%	10.5%	2.9%	59.9% (371)
Reported vote for Mondale	0	5.4	47.1	56.4	89.5	97.1	40.1 (249)
Total % (N)	42.8 (266)	9.0 (56)	8.2 (51)	6.3 (39)	6.1 (38)	27.5 (171)	100.0 (621)

SOURCE: Gallup post-election survey, 1984, conducted for Aldrich, Borgida, and Sullivan. Reprinted with permission.

Those who thought neither Reagan nor Walter Mondale would better handle their most important concerns split their vote evenly, as did those who thought Reagan would be better for one concern and Mondale for the other. Reagan won because most voters thought he would handle their chief concerns better than Mondale.

The strategic problem of the candidate, then, consists of three elements. First, the candidate must identify the public's concerns and, where useful and possible, heighten the salience of these concerns. Second, the candidate must identify himself as the candidate who most shares the public's concerns. Third, the public must be convinced that the candidate is better able to handle its concerns than the opponent. Thus, Reagan's strategy in 1984 consisted, in large part, of highlighting the importance of economic recovery, something for which he could conceivably take credit and for which Mondale could not. Mondale, in turn, sought to increase the salience of budget deficits, to associate himself with the issue, and to persuade the public that he was better able to solve this problem than Reagan.

Citizens, of course, are not willing to listen to preposterous claims. The candidates' room to maneuver in campaigns is constrained. It is constrained by the concerns and goals of the electorate. It is constrained, even in an era of weakened partisan ties, by the attachment that a majority of the electorate still feels, some of them strongly, to a party. And it is constrained by the nature of the candidates. A candidate brings to the contest a public record, often a long one, that cannot be easily or credibly disavowed, a set of longstanding political commitments, an airing of skills, talents, and incapacities, and, for better or worse, a tie to the political party that nominated him. An incumbent, of course, is especially constrained by a record, a very public record, of his actions and achievements in office and by a host of national conditions for which he may or may not be responsible, but for which the public may hold him responsible. But even nonincumbent candidates are constrained by their pasts. For example, Reagan brought to the 1980 contest almost three decades of experience as a spokesman for conservative causes. In 1984 Mondale brought longstanding commitments from—and to—organized labor and other liberal Democratic causes that he could not believably disavow, had he wanted to.

The Candidate's Choice of Strategies

However important the constraints on a candidate's ability to maneuver may be, they are not so powerful as to leave a candidate only one strategy. Thus, the question for each candidate is, simply, Which strategy should be chosen? The answer comes in two parts.

First, part of the raw material from which candidates fashion their strategies is "reality," the setting in which the campaign is conducted. This setting includes the condition of the nation (is inflation high, is the nation at war?), the basic concerns of the public, and the candidate's political history. The choices of candidates, like those of voters, are made under conditions of uncertainty; they cannot be sure about the concerns of the public or how to shape them, much less how to move voters in the preferred direction. They face an opponent who is seeking to lead voters to opposite conclusions, and they must deal with news media that may challenge central elements of the campaign strategy.

Secondly, given the constraints considered above, strategies are chosen in light of the candidate's goals. Candidates have two basic goals. First, candidates (at least all major-party nominees) want to be elected. Even those who face massive defeat, such as Mondale, George McGovern, or Barry Goldwater, persist in the hope of victory, and, more important, they act accordingly. Second, candidates, like citizens (indeed, as citizens), have a set of beliefs and values about how the government should operate, about the problems they see facing the government, and about the policies appropriate to solve these problems.

How do the candidates seek to achieve their goals, given the constraints they face? The answer is that they attempt to frame the decision for the voters. Mondale could not campaign on the grounds that he could ameliorate severe economic conditions; such a claim was not believable. He could not run on a platform that promised a return to the Great Society; such a claim would not win him the election. He would not design a campaign around sharp cuts in domestic programs, such a claim was personally unpalatable. Nonetheless, he did have room to maneuver. There were issues on which he could reasonably hope to compete with Reagan, thereby convincing voters that he was better suited to the presidency than the incumbent. The public had concerns, including the deficit and the arms race, that were not auspicious to Reagan and on which Mondale, given his background, could at least hope to convince voters that he would be the better president. The problem for Mondale was to convince the public to see the choice on grounds that were favorable to him, not on the grounds on which Reagan wanted the public to choose.

Why is it possible for candidates to shape the voters' choice, and hence partly control their own electoral fortunes? Because individuals cope with complexity and uncertainty by simplifying. Research has established that people who are placed in complex decision settings— even experts—tend to choose on the basis of a very limited set of criteria. They do so by adopting a variety of "heuristics," informational and decisional shortcuts that diminish the complexity of the choice.[4] In the language of social psychologists, individuals who are confronted with complex and uncertain choices, such as voters, "frame" their decision. Each candidate's strategy can be seen, then, as an attempt to manipulate the voters' information and criteria in terms that are favorable to the candidate. In short, they try to shape the voters' framing of their electoral choice.

No candidate frames the choice of voters unilaterally. Reality and believability—that is, consistency with actual political conditions and with the candidate's political background—are constraints because people will not adopt an unrealistic or unbelievable frame. The campaign is also contested, which means that the voters can choose between the two candidates' frames (or construct frames of their own). Not all campaigns are the same, of course. In 1984 Reagan held a distinct advantage as a popular incumbent. This advantage afforded him not only greater room to maneuver but also the ability to set the agenda and tone of the campaign. In effect, Reagan got to move first, while Mondale was forced to react to his campaign strategy. Reagan was the leader in the 1984 campaign, and Mondale was the follower.

As a general rule, the incumbent's advantage in an election is, in part, the advantage of being the leader to whom the challenger must react. The elections of 1976 and 1980, however, were exceptions to this rule. In both caes, the incumbent was in a relatively weak position, obviating many of the advantages of incumbency, including being the campaign leader. In 1976 the incumbent, Gerald R. Ford, was an unelected president who had been in office barely two years. The national economy was not strong. Although Ford had received high marks for putting Watergate and the resignation of Richard M. Nixon behind, his pardon of Nixon had diluted much of the benefit. As a result, he trailed Carter going into the campaign. By 1980, because of domestic economic woes and Iran's holding Americans hostage, Carter found himself in roughly the same position as Ford.

Reagan's more typical situation in 1984 allows us to consider the position of the leader in the strategic game, more nearly able to frame the voters' decision almost independently of the strategy of the opponent. We begin an analysis of the asymmetric 1984 contest with Reagan's strategic problem. We then look at the follower's problem in 1984, and, finally the more nearly balanced, and hence more directly competitive, strategic problem in 1980.

A One-Candidate, or Leader, Framing Strategy: Reagan in 1984

The reality that confronted Reagan in 1984 consisted of three central and related elements. First, he enjoyed a level of public approval of his incumbency that was virtually without precedent. Second, national and international conditions were especially favorable to him.

The nation was at peace, and there were no international crises comparable to the Iranian crisis in 1980. The economy was performing handsomely. Real disposable income had grown by 5.8 percent in the year before the election; unemployment had fallen by 1.5 percent; and the consumer price index had increased by only 3.6 percent.[5] More to the point, most voters concluded that they were better off financially. In the NES surveys, 44 percent said they were better off in 1984 than in the year before, compared to 27 percent who said they were worse off. Finally, Reagan enjoyed a comfortable fifteen-point lead over Mondale in early trial polls.

At the outset of the campaign Reagan had a number of feasible re-election strategies to choose from. These could be roughly divided into two categories: run on his record (that is, maintain the status quo), or talk about the future (that is, provide voters with a new frame for their decision). He and his advisers actively considered these two very different strategies.[6]

To run on his record is a relatively low risk strategy for a popular incumbent. To execute this strategy, Reagan would articulate few new goals, thereby leaving undisturbed the frame already employed by the electorate in giving him such high marks for job performance and a substantial lead in the trial heats. More precisely, he would encourage voters to contrast his successful performance with the uncertain prospect of choosing the nonincumbent Mondale. Such a strategy would not actively seek out converts from those who already supported Mondale. But with a large lead, it would be better, or at least less risky, to ensure the continued support of already favorable voters than to risk some portion of that majority by wooing the minority that favored Mondale.

Still, Reagan could have chosen a different strategy than running on his record. Usually, such strategies consist of announcing and emphasizing new policy initiatives for the future. In this case, the strategy would have been to articulate a second installment of the Reagan Revolution. To do so, of course, would risk his lead (to an unknown degree) because it would encourage the electorate to substitute a frame of unknown advantage for one that was clearly to Reagan's benefit.

The first, "safe" strategy had two additional advantages. First, the Reagan camp would not need to know why Reagan was popular; it sufficed simply to know that he was. To present a new frame would require them to make inferences about how people would choose under new and uncertain conditions. Second, running on his record had the advantage of precedent: both Dwight D. Eisenhower (in 1956) and Nixon (in 1972) had employed similar strategies under similar circumstances and with great success.

Electorally, then, a strategy that undergirded Reagan's claim that "You ain't seen nothin' yet!" with specifics seemed to offer no advantage. Why was such a strategy considered and, at least by some advisers, forcefully advocated? In his first election Reagan had followed a policy-initiative strategy, then claimed that his victory was an issue referendum. Although evidence indicates that (in the voters' minds, at least) it was not, this claim was crucial in his subsequent success with Congress.[7] A reelection campaign that promised a second installment of the Reagan Revolution would create, some aides anticipated, an opportunity to repeat their early legislative successes.

The tradeoff facing Reagan was clear: to run on his record would enhance his chances of a major victory but reduce the prospects for legislative victories in the second term. Or, he could point to the future, taking a greater electoral risk but with the hope of being able to achieve more in office.

Reagan decided to play it safe. In fact, he was so studious in executing this low-risk strategy that some were disgruntled by his failure to discuss plans for a second term. As Germond and Witcover lamented just days after the November election:

> Like President Nixon in 1972, Reagan bluffed his way to reelection in an antiseptic, stagy, and shallow campaign in which both the man and his plans for the next four years were carefully sheltered from the voters and the accompanying news media. . . . He promised . . . [that] "America is back," is "standing tall," is "going for the gold" and hence, "You ain't seen nothin' yet." That last Reagan line . . . defines the problem. We ain't heard nothin' yet either about what the President really intends to do in his second term.[8]

Reporters and pundits, however, have different concerns than the electorate; they believe that a campaign should feature a dramatic clash of issues. Voters, in contrast, want a campaign that will help them choose the better candidate for president. Does a campaign in which a successful incumbent runs simply on the basis of his record permit voters to discern which candidate would make the better president? The 1984 campaign, by all indications, permitted voters to decide this question more quickly and conclusively than did that of 1980, even though it may appear to have been more "antiseptic, stagy, and shallow" than the earlier contest.

By all indications, Reagan's framing strategy worked exactly as intended. In 1984, 64 percent of the respondents to the NES surveys said they approved of the way Reagan was handling his job as president, and 87 percent of these approvers voted for him.[9] That arithmetic by itself translates into 56 percent of the two-candidate vote, enough by far to win without picking up any votes from those who did not approve. It is further evidence of the success of his strategy that Reagan received a larger degree of support from those who approved of his job performance than any of the three preceding incumbents. Finally, Reagan made no attempt to garner support among those who disapproved of his performance. Here, too, his strategy was "successful." Reagan received the votes of only 7 percent of those who disapproved, the smallest percentage received by an incumbent from disapprovers in the last four elections. Reagan simply sought to reinforce the favorable frame that prevailed at the outset of the campaign; the survey indicates that he was very successful.

The Follower Strategy: Mondale in 1984

Mondale found himself in an unenviable position in the late summer of 1984. Reagan was popular, and Mondale was forced to react to his strategy, which was designed to give Mondale as little room to maneuver as possible. Moreover, Mondale, like all nonincumbents, was less well known to the public. Therefore, to alter the voters' terms of choice, Mondale had to locate weaknesses in Reagan's record (since Reagan was not offering any new plans to attack), inform the public about these weaknesses, and convince them that he was better than Reagan on those grounds. Only then would he be in a position to attempt to convince the public to frame their decision on his and not Reagan's terms.

Mondale followed a two-pronged strategy: leadership and policy. First, though the public evaluated Reagan favorably as a leader in many ways, he was relatively vulnerable—and Mondale was potentially stronger—on matters of fairness, concern, and compassion. Second, and more important, Mondale believed that Reagan was vulnerable on the issues of budget deficits and of nuclear weapons and arms negotiations with the Soviet Union. Mondale lamented that he could win if only people voted on the issues. In truth, he was largely correct. When asked to locate themselves and candidates on seven issue dimensions, respondents perceived that they were, on the average, equally distant from Reagan's and from Mondale's issue positions.[10] Moreover, Mondale was competitive on policy issues that were prominent concerns of the electorate, such as budget deficits and nuclear weapons and the arms race. Nuclear weapons and the arms race was selected more often than any of the other twelve alternatives as the most important problem facing the nation (by 25 percent), with budget deficits ranking third (12.6 percent). These problems were also cited with some regularity as the personally most important political problem (14 percent and 6 percent, respectively), according to the

Aldrich, Borgida, and Sullivan data. The only other concern that was cited frequently as nationally important was unemployment (24 percent), and one may venture that a liberal Democrat such as Mondale would benefit from that concern, too.

Although Mondale's strategy was feasible, in order for him to win everything would have had to work: he would have to convince the public that his terms, not Reagan's, were the appropriate terms on which to make their choice and that he would be better at handling their concerns than Reagan. The only real chance of the strategy's working would come if Reagan altered his own strategy, which is precisely what Mondale sought in challenging Reagan to reveal his deficit-reduction plans. Mondale's claim that his plan was superior to Reagan's could be convincing only if Reagan were to reveal a plan. Absent a comparison of plans, many voters would be led to choose on grounds other than the budget deficit—grounds that probably would be favorable to Reagan. Further, since any deficit-reduction plan necessarily promised pain and cost to the electorate, without a Reagan deficit plan the electorate's choice would be between the sure prospect of higher taxes under Mondale and an uncertain future under Reagan.

In view of Reagan's resolve and ability to follow his low-risk strategy consistently, what happened in the election? As the data in Table 11-2 show, on questions of leadership, Mondale was, indeed, regarded as much more fair, compassionate, and concerned, but Reagan was seen, by large margins, as more inspiring, commanding of respect, and capable of providing strong leadership. Did Mondale's leadership strategy work, then? It is unlikely that he expected his strategy to reshape the grounds of comparison completely. His emphasis on fairness, concern, and compassion at best could reduce the initial advantage that Reagan held on leadership evaluations—and in this Mondale succeeded.

On policy, however, Mondale's strategy was rather less successful. As already noted, nuclear weapons and the arms race and budget deficits were regarded by many as the most important problems facing the country. Thus, Mondale was shrewd to try to frame the choice on problems that the public already believed to be crucial, and to associate himself with those concerns. Mondale was unsuccessful, however, in convincing the public that he was better able to resolve the problems they cared about. As the data in Table 11-3 illustrate, voters, by a margin of ten percentage points, thought Reagan the better candidate to deal with nuclear weapons and the arms race; three times as many voters thought Reagan could better handle the budget deficit. (The same was true of those who cited taxes, which Mondale attempted to relate to the budget deficits.) As Mondale had hoped, there was a very

Table 11-2 Percentage Reporting that Various Candidate
Characteristics Describe Mondale and Reagan
Extremely or Quite Well

Characteristic	Describing Mondale	Describing Reagan	Difference: Mondale − Reagan
Compassion and concern			
Compassionate	78.9%	58.9%	+19.0%
Really cares about people like you	63.9	47.0	+16.0
Understands people like you	58.9	43.1	+15.8
Fair	76.5	57.8	+18.7
In touch with ordinary people	66.2	36.4	+29.8
(Average difference)			(+20.0)
Political Leadership			
Commands respect	59.2	78.7	−19.5
Inspiring	43.5	59.5	−16.0
Provides strong leadership	48.8	71.1	−22.3
(Average difference)			(−19.3)

SOURCE: National Election Studies, 1984 election survey, compiled by authors.

strong relationship between the candidate voters thought would be better at handling each of these problems and their vote. The central failing in Mondale's strategy was his inability to convince the public that he would be the better president to handle those problems.

Table 11-3 also includes data for those who cited unemployment as the most important problem facing the nation. One would expect unemployment to work to the advantage of the Democratic candidate— a candidate long associated with liberal, Democratic concerns, such as Mondale. But Mondale did not make unemployment a central part of his campaign strategy, so although he fared better on this concern than on many others, Reagan still was seen as better able to handle this problem by those who were concerned about it.

In sum, Mondale did have some room to maneuver strategically. He emphasized two of the problems that concerned many people, he was in a potentially strong position on the third (unemployment), and he was in an even stronger position on several others, including racial discrimination. Yet his strategic room was limited. Mondale had to convince large majorities that he would be the better risk on each concern, and he was unable to do so.

The widespread perception among voters that Reagan had done a

Table 11-3   Perceptions of Candidate Better on Selected Problem and the Vote, 1984

A. Candidate seen as better at handling selected most important problems facing the country

Most important problem cited is:	Candidate better			N
	Reagan	*Neither*	*Mondale*	
Nuclear weapons and the arms race	47.5%	15.4	37.1	336
Budget deficits	59.1%	22.7	18.2	176
Taxes	59.2%	19.7	21.1	76
Unemployment	43.4%	23.4	33.2	316

B. Two-candidate vote for Reagan among those citing candidate as better at handling selected problems

Most important problem cited is:	Candidate better			N	Tau-C [a]
	Reagan	*Neither*	*Mondale*		
Nuclear weapons and the arms race	84.9%	9.5	5.6	250	.848
Budget deficits	84.8%	13.1	2.0	143	.725
Taxes	94.6%	5.4	0.0	53	.776
Unemployment	81.6%	13.2	5.3	223	.875

SOURCE: Gallup postelection survey, 1984, conducted for Aldrich, Borgida, and Sullivan. Compiled by authors.

[a] Correlation between candidate cited as better at handling problem and candidate for whom respondent voted.

good job in the office of president in his first term, combined with a Reagan strategy that aimed to leave their framing of the electoral choice intact, meant that Mondale simply was unconvincing in his pleas to voters to see the choice between Reagan and himself on his terms, rather than on Reagan's. As the nearly daily polls that were conducted by Richard Wirthlin for Reagan's campaign indicated, Mondale never was able to make any significant or lasting inroads into Reagan's initial lead.

Competitive Framing: Carter and Reagan in 1980

The 1984 campaign is best understood as an asymmetric contest between an incumbent leader and a nonincumbent follower. The 1980 campaign, in contrast, was a more nearly symmetric contest in which the two candidates began on a virtually equal competitive footing.

Carter had all but dissipated the potential advantages of incumbency. His popular standing was low; the NES survey reveals that 59 percent disapproved of his performance. He possessed a meager one percentage point lead over Reagan in early trial heats, and carried the scars of a hard-fought renomination campaign. During the prior year, the consumer price index had risen 12.6 percent, real disposable income grew by a paltry 0.7 percent, and unemployment had risen 1.6 points to a level of 6.9 percent.[11] Election day marked a full year of the Iranian hostage crisis. Carter was notably unsuccessful in dealing with Congress, and media commentary regularly referred to his leadership as "rudderless."

Strategically, Carter's diminished incumbency not only made the 1980 contest more nearly a battle of equals, but also greatly limited the range of feasible and believable strategies that were available to him. In the post-Watergate 1976 election, Carter had campaigned on the strength of his personal integrity and trustworthiness. In 1980 these remained his areas of greatest strength with the electorate. Moreover, Carter could reasonably hope to portray Reagan as the opposite: someone who could not be trusted with the presidency. His campaign, therefore, had to emphasize the personal aspects of the voters' decision. He could not run on the record of his administration, and a future-oriented policy campaign was vulnerable to the challenge, "Why didn't you do this already?" Thus, Carter's best hope was to make people think of Reagan as irresponsible, as they had thought of Goldwater sixteen years earlier.

Carter launched an essentially negative, personality-based campaign. One Carter aide summarized the strategy in this way:

> A campaign strategy can reinforce perceptions the public already has. We are trying to reinforce certain perceptions the public already has about Reagan [that is, his riskiness and extremism]. . . . [These attacks] also put Mr. Reagan on the defensive on a series of issues, and had pushed aside discussion of the economy, which is the most vulnerable issue for Mr. Carter himself.[12]

Not surprisingly, this attempt to frame the voters' decision elicited many complaints of meanness from the press; it also required that Carter put his stock of trust, goodwill, and integrity at risk. As one Carter aide remarked: "We thought we were trading off in our area of greatest strength in exchange for a payoff on Reagan's greatest weakness. We thought it was a good deal."[13]

Reagan's greatest electoral strength was that he was not Carter. But any nonincumbent must provide a positive reason for the voters to support him; he must persuade them that they are not abandoning the frying pan for the fire. Thus, Reagan's strategy had to be twofold.

First, he had to—and did—remind the voters of the record of the past four years. Against that backdrop, however, he also had to convince them that he could do better. Reagan's approach was to offer the public a clearly defined set of policy proposals that, he claimed, would resolve the problems that Carter had created or failed to solve. Specifically, he proposed a tax cut, reductions in domestic spending, and increased spending for defense as his plan to solve the nation's economic woes and to reestablish its international strength.

Thus, the public was offered two quite different ways of framing their decision in 1980. The voters need not have chosen on either basis, of course. Still, candidates do frame the choice in large part, especially when the electorate is volatile and uncertain. (In 1980, for example, the number of voters who made up their minds at almost the last minute was as high as has ever been recorded in public opinion surveys.) Each candidate tried, of course, to deflect the charges of—and the frame offered by—his opponent. In this, Reagan had the distinct advantage. He was able to appear to the public in person (especially in the televised debates) and attempt to demonstrate that he was not the sort of person Carter portrayed him to be. He did so with considerable success. Carter's attempt to deflect the charge of incompetency, on the other hand, seemed to fly in the face of economic reality and the continuing hostage crisis.[14]

Campaign Strategy and Governance

The candidates' campaign strategies help the voters frame their choice in an election and, thus, affect the outcome—this we have shown. But presidential campaign strategy also frames the choice process for Congress after the election.

A campaign framing strategy offers an implicit sort of contract: "If elected I promise to. . . ." By placing a set of policy promises at the center of the campaign, for instance, the candidate is committed to try to achieve them once in office. Moreover, such policy framing also helps to frame the choices of others, such as legislators, when the president takes office.

The advantage, in other words, of making commitments on policy during the campaign, aside from any electoral advantage, is that Congress and other members of the Washington community are likely to interpret the results of the election in the terms that were specified by the victor during the campaign. Thus, the president is more likely to control the policy agenda and to be able to get Congress to do what he wants in those areas he made most central to his campaign.

At one extreme in this regard is Carter, who won in 1976 without centering his campaign on major policy proposals. Instead, he won a largely personal victory, based on his ability to convince the public of his personal integrity, compassion, and trustworthiness. There was no major policy initiative that Congress "owed" to Carter on the strength of his electoral victory, and they gave him none. At the other end of the continuum, Reagan was successful with Congress in his first term largely because he campaigned in 1980 on issues that he subsequently took to Congress: tax and domestic spending cuts and an increase in defense spending. The lesson is that although a campaign based on "nonpromises" may entail smaller electoral risks, it also will yield smaller policy payoffs later on.

Although a president needs to use a policy-based campaign to be able to frame the legislative agenda, he will not succeed on that basis alone. As Erwin Hargrove and Michael Nelson suggest, "presidencies of achievement," such as Reagan's first administration, must join the ideas of the campaign frame to appropriate leadership skills and an election outcome that will persuade members of Congress that cooperation with the president is politically desirable or necessary. What kind of election does this? The answer, it appears, is an election in which the president has "coattails," that is, in which his party gains a large number of seats in Congress.[15] Such elections not only sweep new members of the president's party into Congress—members who are predisposed to cooperate with "their" president—but also persuade incumbent legislators that to cooperate with the president is politically wise and opposition is risky. Gary Jacobson, analyzing the effect of a presidential election without coattails, writes: "A landslide without coattails [such as 1984] leaves the claim of a mandate ... open to serious doubt"; it permits members of the opposition to "refuse to recognize a mandate" and confronts them with "little psychological or political pressure to cooperate with the president on his own terms." [16]

Reagan's victory in 1980 met all the conditions for a framing election in Congress. Even Democrats in the House of Representatives believed that they had little choice but to accept Reagan's campaign frame as the starting point for their deliberations. His policy promises defined the agenda. An aide to Speaker Thomas P. O'Neill, Jr., said:

> What the Democrats did, in extraordinary fashion, was to recognize the cataclysmic nature of the 1980 election results. The American public wanted this new president to be given a chance to try out his programs. We aren't going to come across as being obstructionists.[17]

In 1984 Reagan ran on his record. The consequences of his refusal to spell out new policy initiatives and his inability to elect many new Republicans to the House or Senate were immediately apparent. If House Democrats had been willing in 1981 to bow to Reagan's agenda, in late 1984 and early 1985 even members of Reagan's own party (especially in the Senate) were unwilling to submit to his policy leadership. His budget was pronounced "dead on arrival" by Senate Republicans. Tax reform, which he urged Congress to take up as the first order of business, was pushed behind the budget deficit on the agenda. The resulting Gramm-Rudman-Hollings deficit reduction bill was a congressional initiative. And when, finally, "tax simplification" legislation passed, it neither originated solely with Reagan nor owed its adoption simply to his efforts. Indeed, what enabled the plan to be adopted was that no one in particular could plausibly claim credit for it; it was bipartisanship that brought about its adoption, not presidential control of the agenda. In sum, Reagan's sway over Congress was far less impressive in the wake of his issueless landslide reelection than it had been in the year after his narrower, but policy-framed, 1980 electoral victory.

Conclusion

Convention has it that electoral campaigns have little effect on the outcome of presidential elections or on governance. The opposite is more nearly true.

Of course, strategy alone does not determine what happens in the election or, afterward, in Congress; there are many reasons that people vote the way they do and why presidents win or lose in their struggles with Congress. Campaign strategies are, nonetheless, important. Strategy matters because it tells the public and Congress, "This is who I am, what I stand for, and what I will do in office." Candidates provide, at the core of their complex day-to-day strategy, a frame that guides voters in their electoral choice and that helps, therefore, to determine the electoral outcome. And, no less important, the frame they present both helps to determine how the election is subsequently understood and interpreted and shapes the legislative agenda and policy struggles of the next four years.

Notes

Data reported in this paper were made available by the Interuniversity Consortium for Political and Social Research, National Election Studies, and by Aldrich, Eugene Borgida, and John L. Sullivan. The analysis and interpretation are due solely to the authors.

1. Jack W. Germond and Jules Witcover, *Blue Smoke and Mirrors: How Reagan Won and Why Carter Lost the Election of 1980* (New York: Viking, 1981); and *Wake Us When It's Over: Presidential Politics of 1984* (New York: Macmillan, 1985).

2. See, for example, Charles W. Ostrom, Jr., and Dennis M. Simon, "Promise and Performance: A Dynamic Model of Presidential Popularity," *American Political Science Review*, 79 (June 1985): 334-358.
3. Stanley Kelley, Jr., and Thad W. Mirer, "The Simple Act of Voting," *American Political Science Review* 68 (June 1974): 572-591. See also Stanley Kelley, Jr., *Interpreting Elections* (Princeton: Princeton University Press, 1983).
4. See Daniel Kahneman, Paul Slovic, and Amos Tversky, eds., *Judgment under Uncertainty: Heuristics and Biases* (New York: Cambridge University Press, 1982). See also John Zaller, "Toward a Theory of the Survey Response" (Paper delivered at the annual meeting of the American Political Science Association, Washington, D.C., Sept. 1984).
5. These figures are taken from D. Roderick Kiewiet and Douglas Rivers, "The Economic Basis of Reagan's Appeal," in *The New Direction in American Politics*, ed. John E. Chubb and Paul E. Peterson (Washington, D.C.: Brookings Institution, 1985), 69-90.
6. See Germond and Witcover, *Wake Us When It's Over;* and Peter Goldman and Tony Fuller, with others, *The Quest for the Presidency—1984* (New York: Bantam Books, 1985).
7. See, for example, Paul R. Abramson, John H. Aldrich, and David W. Rohde, *Change and Continuity in the 1980 Elections,* rev. ed. (Washington, D.C.: CQ Press, 1983).
8. Jack W. Germond and Jules Witcover, "On Reagan's Second-Term Plans, the Public 'Ain't Heard Nothin' Yet,' " *National Journal,* November 10, 1984, 2176.
9. Paul R. Abramson, John H. Aldrich, and David W. Rohde, *Change and Continuity in the 1984 Elections* (Washington, D.C.: CQ Press, 1986), 199.
10. Ibid.
11. Kiewiet and Rivers, "The Economic Basis of Reagan's Appeal," 69-72.
12. Quoted in Jeff Greenfield, *The Real Campaign: How the Media Missed the Story of the 1980 Campaign* (New York: Summit Books, 1982), 286-287.
13. Quoted in Germond and Witcover, *Blue Smoke and Mirrors,* 254.
14. Our analysis is confirmed by Michael M. Gant, "Citizens' Evaluations of the 1980 Presidential Candidates: Influence of Campaign Strategies," *American Politics Quarterly* 11 (July 1983): 327-348.
15. See Erwin C. Hargrove and Michael Nelson, *Presidents, Politics, and Policy* (Baltimore: Johns Hopkins University Press, 1984); and their "The Presidency: Reagan and the Cycle of Politics and Policy, in *The Elections of 1984,* ed. Michael Nelson (Washington, D.C.: CQ Press, 1985), 189-213. As Jacobson points out, political scientists and officeholders have different definitions of *coattails.* Since we want to explain the behavior of officeholders, and their behavior is based upon their interpretation of events, we follow their definition. Gary C. Jacobson, "Congress: Politics after a Landslide without Coattails," in *Elections of 1984,* 215-237.
16. Jacobson, "Congress: Politics after a Landslide," 228-229.
17. Quoted in Hargrove and Nelson, "The Presidency," 200.

Part IV

PRESIDENTS AND POLITICS

A fter two or more years of relentless campaigning, a newly elected president may earnestly hope that "politics" is over and "government" can begin. The endless search for popular votes, the constant cultivation of the press, the ceaseless wooing of interest group support, the steady accumulation of debts to the political party—all this is behind, he may hope, with only the most serious matters of state ahead. In practice, of course, the presidency does not work that way. To deal effectively with the great issues, presidents need the cooperation of others in government, cooperation that is most likely to be forthcoming when presidential popularity is high, the press accepts the president's policy agenda, interest groups are mobilized, and the party is faithful.

The need that presidents have for political support is not new. What is new is the extent to which they work to achieve such support. As Bruce Miroff argues in "The Presidency and the Public," the modern president "not only responds to popular demands and passions but actively reaches out to shape and mold them." He does so both in speeches or appearances that promote particular goals of his administration and in symbol-ridden events (Miroff calls them spectacles) whose purpose is to dramatize the president's qualities as a leader. Viewed in its proper light as a spectacle, for example, the highly popular invasion of the tiny island of Grenada that Ronald Reagan launched in October 1983 resembles nothing so much as a professional wrestling match, in which the audience (read: citizenry) is gratified merely by the sight of good overpowering evil, apart from any concern about the inherent insignificance of the event.

Miroff's analysis of the presidency and the public implicitly challenges one tenet of the conventional wisdom of political science, namely, that citizens are so fickle and demanding that any president is almost destined to disappoint them. In "The Presidency and the Press," James Fallows takes on an even more familiar stereotype: the media as an adversary of the president. To be sure, Fallows notes, there are certain subjects on which the White House press corps feels sufficiently

confident to offer an independent, and thus sometimes critical, assessment of a president: suspected scandal, dissension within the administration, tactical blunders, and "politics in the narrow sense: the business
of winning elections and gaining points in the opinion polls." Such
stories often vex the White House and prompt charges that the press is
antagonistic to the president. But according to Fallows, when it comes
to substantive issues—"the *what* of government"—presidents generally
are able to secure the press's acquiescence to their policy agenda. "If
you listen to the press secretary make his morning announcement," he
writes, "you know—barring scandal or gaffe—what the lead will be on
the evening news that night."

Interest groups are another oft-cited thorn in the side of modern
presidents. Jimmy Carter, in his farewell address as president, listed
the selfish and demanding nature of interest group politics as one of the
greatest dangers that was facing the nation. But, Benjamin Ginsberg
and Martin Shefter argue in "The Presidency and the Organization of
Interests," certain presidents are able to "enhance their own power and
promote their own policy aims by constructing a new, more congenial
configuration of social forces." Carter's successor, Ronald Reagan,
attempted to be one such president. (Franklin D. Roosevelt was
another.) Rather than accepting as givens the usual political demands
of three historically Democratic groups—white southerners, urban
ethnics, and middle class voters—Reagan successfully altered the
national political agenda in an effort to transform these groups,
respectively, from "rednecks to evangelicals, . . . workers to patriots and
right-to-lifers, . . . [and] beneficiaries to taxpayers." In all cases, the
new identities of these traditional groups made them more likely to
support Reagan and his policies.

Finally, modern presidents seem to have tried less to transform
political parties (as they did with interest groups) or manipulate them
(as with the public and the press) than to emasculate them, according to
Sidney Milkis in "The Presidency and Political Parties." To Franklin
Roosevelt and most of his successors, the traditional party system was
too grounded in state and local organizations to be of much help in the
effort to forge national programs and policies. Indeed, to the extent that
the parties exercised influence through Congress, they were perceived
as an impediment to presidential leadership. Roosevelt, Lyndon B.
Johnson, and Richard M. Nixon each took steps to replace party
influence with centralized administration, both in the federal bureaucracy and the White House itself. Yet, Milkis argues, Reagan, who has
been so innovative in his manipulation of the public, the press, and the
interests, actually has tried to restore some of the traditional roles of the
political parties.

12. THE PRESIDENCY AND THE PUBLIC: LEADERSHIP AS SPECTACLE

Bruce Miroff

The framers of the United States Constitution envisioned a president substantially insulated from the demands and passions of the people by the long duration of his term and the dignity of his office. The modern president, in contrast, not only responds to popular demands and passions but actively reaches out to shape and mold them. Both the possibilities that were opened up by modern technology and the problems presented by the increased fragility of parties and institutional coalitions lead presidents to turn to the public for support and strength. To maintain popular backing, the indispensable requirement is that the public believe in the president's qualities of leadership.

Observers of presidential politics increasingly are recognizing the centrality of the president's relationship with the American public. George Edwards speaks of "the public presidency" and argues that the "greatest source of influence for the president is public approval." [1] Samuel Kernell suggests that presidential appeals for popular favor now overshadow more traditional methods of seeking influence, especially bargaining. Presidents today, Kernell argues, are "going public"; he demonstrates their propensity to cultivate popular support by recording the mounting frequency of their public addresses, public appearances, and political trips. These constitute, he claims, "the repertoire of modern leadership." [2]

This new understanding of presidential leadership can be carried further. A president's approach to, and impact upon, public perceptions is not limited to overt appeals in speeches and appearances. Much of what the modern presidency does, in fact, involves the projection of images whose purpose is to shape public understanding and gain popular support. A significant—and growing—part of the presidency revolves around the enactment of leadership as a *spectacle*.

To examine the presidency as a spectacle is to ask not only how a president seeks to appear but also what it is that the public sees. We are accustomed to gauging the public's responses to a president with polls that measure approval and disapproval of the president's overall performance in office and his effectiveness in managing the economy and foreign policy. Yet these evaluative categories may say more about the information desired by politicians or academic researchers who construct them than about the terms in which most members of a president's audience actually view him. A public that responds mainly to presidential spectacles will not ignore the president's performance, but its understanding of that performance, as well as its sense of the more overarching and intangible strengths and weaknesses of the administration, will be colored by the terms of the spectacle.

The Presidency as Spectacle

A spectacle is a kind of symbolic event, one in which particular details stand for broader and deeper meanings. What differentiates a spectacle from other kinds of symbolic events is the centrality of character and action. A spectacle presents intriguing and often dominating characters not in static poses but through actions that establish their public identities.

Spectacle implies a clear division between actors and spectators. As Daniel Dayan and Elihu Katz have noted, a spectacle possesses "a narrowness of focus, a limited set of appropriate responses, and ... a minimal level of interaction. What there is to see is very clearly exhibited; spectacle implies a distinction between the roles of performers and audience." [3] A spectacle does not permit the audience to interrupt the action and redirect its meaning. Spectators can become absorbed in a spectacle or can find it unconvincing, but they cannot become performers. A spectacle is not designed for mass participation; it is not, by nature, a democratic event.

Perhaps the most distinctive characteristic of a spectacle is that the actions that comprise it are meaningful not for what they achieve but for what they signify. Actions in a spectacle are gestures rather than means to an end. What is important is that they be understandable and impressive to the spectators. This distinction between gestures and means is illustrated by Roland Barthes in his classic discussion of professional wrestling as a spectacle. Barthes shows that professional wrestling is completely unlike professional boxing. Boxing is a form of competition, a contest of skill in a situation of uncertainty. What matters is the outcome; because this is in doubt, we can wager on it. But in professional wrestling, the outcome is preordained: it would be senseless to bet on who is going to win. What matters in professional wrestling are the gestures made during the match, gestures by performers portraying distinctive characters, gestures that carry moral significance. In a typical match, an evil character threatens a good character, knocks him down on the canvas, abuses him with dirty tricks, but ultimately loses when the good character rises up to exact a just revenge.[4]

It may seem odd to approach the presidency through an analogy with boxing and wrestling, but let us pursue it for a moment. Much of what presidents do is analagous to what boxers do—they engage in contests of power and policy with other political actors, contests in which the outcomes are uncertain. But a growing amount of presidential activity is akin to wrestling. The contemporary presidency is presented by the White House (with the collaboration of the media) as a series of spectacles in which a larger-than-life main character, along with his supporting team, engages in emblematic bouts with immoral or dangerous adversaries.

A number of recent developments have converged to foster the rise of spectacle in the modern presidency. The mass media have become the principal vehicle for presidential spectacle. Directing more of their coverage to the president than to any other person or institution in American life, the media keep him constantly before the public and give him unmatched opportunities to display his leadership qualities. Television provides the view most amenable to spectacle; by favoring the visual and the dramatic, it promotes stories with simple plot lines over complex analyses of causes and consequences. But other kinds of media are not fundamentally different. As David Paletz and Robert Entman have shown, American journalists "define events from a short-term, anti-historical perspective; see individual or group action, not structural or other impersonal long run forces, at the root of most occurrences; and simplify and reduce stories to conventional symbols for easy assimilation by audiences." [5]

The mass media are not, to be sure, always reliable vehicles for presidential spectacles. Reporters may frame their stories in terms that undermine the meanings the White House intends to convey. Their desire for controversy can feed off presidential spectacles, but it also can destroy them. As we will see in the case of Jimmy Carter, the media can contribute to spectacular failures in the presidency as well as to successful spectacles.

Spectacle has also been fostered by the president's rise to primacy in the American political system. A political order originally centered on institutions has given way, especially in the public mind, to a political order that centers on the person of the president. Theodore Lowi writes, "Since the president has become the embodiment of government, it seems perfectly normal for millions upon millions of Americans to concentrate their hopes and fears directly and personally upon him." [6] The "personal president" that Lowi describes is the object of popular expectations; these expectations, Stephen Wayne and Thomas Cronin have shown, are both excessive and contradictory.[7]

The president must attempt to satisfy the public by delivering tangible benefits, such as economic growth, but these almost never will be enough. Not surprisingly, then, presidents turn to the gestures of the spectacle to satisfy their audience.

To understand the modern presidency as a form of spectacle, we must consider the presentation of the president as a spectacular character, his team's role as supporting performers, and the arrangement of gestures that convey to the audience the meaning of his actions.

A contemporary president is, to borrow a phrase from Guy Debord, "the spectacular representation of a living human being. . . ." [8] An enormous amount of attention is given to the president as a public character; every deed, quality, and foible is regarded as fascinating and important. The American public may not learn the details of policy formation, but they know that Gerald R. Ford bumps his head on helicopter doorframes and that Ronald Reagan likes jellybeans. In a spectacle, a president's character possesses intrinsic as well as symbolic value; it is to be appreciated for its own sake. The spectators do not press the president to specify what economic or social benefits he is providing or denying them; nor do they closely inquire into the truthfulness of the claims he makes. (To the extent that they do evaluate the president in such terms, they step outside the terms of the spectacle.) His featured qualities are presented as benefits in themselves. Thus, John F. Kennedy's glamour casts his whole era in a romanticized glow, while Reagan's amiability relieves the grim national mood that had developed under his predecessor.

The qualities of the presidential character must not only be appealing; they must also be magnified by the spectacle. The spectacle makes the president appear exceptionally decisive, tough, courageous, prescient, or prudent. Whether he is in fact all or any of these things is obscured. What matters is that he is presented as having these qualities, in magnitudes far beyond what ordinary citizens can imagine themselves to possess. The president must appear confident and masterful before spectators whose very position, as onlookers, denies the possibility of mastery. [9]

The most likely presidential qualities to be magnified will be ones that contrast dramatically with those attributes that drew criticism to the previous president. Thus, Kennedy, who followed a president perceived as elderly and inactive, was featured in spectacles of youth and vigor. Carter, coming after a Nixon administration that was disgraced for its power-hungry immorality, was featured in spectacles of modesty and honesty. Reagan, coming after a president perceived as weak, was featured in spectacles that highlighted his potency.

The president is the principal figure in presidential spectacles, but he has the help of aides and advisers. The star performer is surrounded by a team. Members of the president's team can, through the supporting parts they play, enhance or detract from the spectacle's effect upon the audience. For a president's team to enhance his spectacles, its members should project attractive qualities that either resemble the featured attributes of the president or make up for the president's perceived deficiencies. A team will diminish presidential spectacles if its members project qualities that underscore the president's weaknesses.

A performance team, Erving Goffman has shown, contains "a set of individuals whose intimate cooperation is required if a given projected definition of the situation is to be maintained." [10] There are a number of ways the team can disrupt presidential spectacles. A member of the team can call too much attention to himself, partially upstaging the president. This was one of the disruptive practices that made the Reagan White House eager to be rid of Secretary of State Alexander Haig. He can give away important secrets to the audience; Budget Director David Stockman's famous confessions about supply-side economics to a reporter for *The Atlantic* jeopardized the mystique of economic innovation that the Reagan administration had created in 1981. Worst of all, a member of the team can, perhaps inadvertently, discredit the central meanings that a presidential spectacle has been designed to establish. Thus, revelations of Budget Director Bert Lance's questionable banking practices deflated the lofty moral tone that was established at the outset of the Carter presidency.

Spectacles require not only larger-than-life main characters and supporting players, but actions. These actions are to be understood as gestures, important not for what they accomplish but for the messages and meanings they convey. The gestures in a presidential spectacle are magnified; they must be clear and unmistakable. Thus, not only will the president be reported to have made a fateful decision; if possible, he will be shown, perhaps in a "photo opportunity," as the decision maker.

The audience watching a presidential spectacle is, the White House hopes, as impressed by gestures as by results. Indeed, the gestures are sometimes preferable to the results. Thus, a "show" of force by the president is preferable to the death and destruction that are the results of force. The ways in which the invasion of Grenada in 1983 and the bombing of Libya in 1986 were portrayed to the American public suggest an eagerness in the White House to present the image of military toughness but not the casualties from military conflict—even when they are the enemy's casualties.

Gestures overshadow results. They also overshadow facts. But facts are not obliterated in a presidential spectacle. Not only do they remain present; they are needed, in a sense, to nurture the gestures. Without real events, presidential spectacles would not be impressive; they would seem contrived, mere pseudoevents. However, some of the facts that emerge in the course of an event might discredit its presentation as spectacle. Therefore, a successful spectacle, such as Reagan's "liberation" of Grenada, must be more powerful than any of the facts upon which it draws. Rising above contradictory or disconfirming details, the spectacle must transfigure the more pliant facts and make them carriers of its most spectacular gestures.

Presidential spectacles are seldom pure spectacles, in the sense that a wrestling match can be a pure spectacle. Although they may involve a good deal of advance planning and careful calculation of gestures, they cannot be completely scripted in advance. Unexpected and unpredictable events will emerge during a presidential spectacle. If the White House is fortunate and skillful, it can capitalize upon some of these events by using them to enhance the spectacle. If the White House is not so lucky or talented, unanticipated events can detract from, or even undermine, the spectacle.

Also unlike wrestling or other pure spectacles, presidential spectacles often have more than one audience. Their primary purpose is to construct meanings for the American public. But they also can direct messages to those whom the White House has identified as its foes or the sources of its problems. In 1981, when Reagan fired members of the Professional Air Traffic Controllers' Organization (PATCO) because they engaged in an illegal strike, he presented to the public the spectacle of a tough, determined president who would uphold the law and, unlike his predecessor, would not be pushed around by grasping interest groups. The spectacle also conveyed to organized labor that the White House knew how to feed popular suspicions of unions and could make things difficult for a labor movement that remained too assertive.

As the PATCO firing shows, some presidential spectacles retain important policy components. One could construct a continuum in which one end represented pure policy and the other pure spectacle. Toward the policy end one would find behind-the-scenes presidential actions, including quiet bargaining over domestic policies (such as Lyndon B. Johnson's lining up of Republican support for civil rights legislation) and covert actions in foreign affairs (the Nixon administration's use of the CIA to "destabilize" a socialist regime in Chile). Toward the spectacle end would be presidential posturing at home (law-and-order and drugs have been handy topics) and dramatic foreign travel (since 1972, China has been a particular presidential favorite). Most of the president's actions are a mix of policy and spectacle.

What forms have presidential spectacles taken? The remainder of this essay examines the emergence of spectacle in the presidency of John F. Kennedy, the failure of spectacle in the presidency of Jimmy Carter, and the triumph of spectacle in the presidency of Ronald Reagan.

The Possibilities of Spectacle and Spectacular Failure: John F. Kennedy and Jimmy Carter

It was the administration of John F. Kennedy that first disclosed the possibilities in presidential spectacle. Certainly there were precursors to Kennedy in this regard—especially the two Roosevelts—but the coming together of vast media coverage, inflated popular expectations, and talent at producing spectacle is first evident in the New Frontier. To be sure, the possibilities of spectacle were too new, and the pull of important policy issues too great, for spectacle to be at the center of the most important events of the Kennedy presidency. But spectacle nonetheless was present even in those events—and more evident still in secondary undertakings.

Kennedy became, in the course of his brief presidency, a remarkable spectacle character. His candidacy had evoked doubts about his age, experience, and qualifications. But these seeming handicaps were turned into virtues. His would be a presidency that projected youth, vigor, and novelty, that recast the institution itself as a headquarters for intelligence and masterful will. Qualities of the president that signified power were supplemented by other qualities—wealth, physical attractiveness, and wit—that signified glamour. Kennedy's character was portrayed by the media as pleasurable in its own right. Yet it also carried symbolic value, representing, on the surface, the national will to excellence, and, at a deeper level, the nation's excitement with its status as a great imperial power.

Although some of the glitter of Kennedy's character has been rubbed off by later revelations, his winning attributes became the model for many of his successors. Even if other presidents could not hope to emulate all of his appealing features, they could strive for that grace in being president that was Kennedy's ultimate charm. Nixon had some talent at producing spectacles—witness the handling of his 1972 trip to China—but the grace of Kennedy continued to elude him. Nixon and his advisers recognized, for example, the value in all those photographs of Kennedy walking along the beach or sailing at Hyannis Port. But their attempt to project the same relaxed grace produced comedy rather than spectacle. When photographers were taken out to snap pictures of the president walking at San Clemente, they found Nixon "traipsing along the beach in an ill-fitting windbreaker, a pair of dress trousers, and *street* shoes." [11]

The Kennedy team also received exceptional media coverage—and revealed thereby that the people surrounding the president could contribute their own spectacle value. Members of Kennedy's staff and cabinet were portrayed as a "ministry of talent," a constellation of exceptionally intelligent and able men revolving around a brilliant star. Even more engaging was the image, favored by Kennedy himself, of his team as a "band of brothers." In reality, Patrick Anderson has shown, Kennedy's staff "hummed with an undercurrent of jealousy, rivalry, and friction." [12] But what the public saw was a team of youthful, impressive men bound together by their dedication to an equally young and impressive leader. Kennedy's team thus served as an extension of its leader, magnifying his qualities to add to his luster.

Intelligence and toughness were particularly featured in the area of foreign policy. With McGeorge Bundy as the president's special assistant for national security affairs and Robert McNamara as his secretary of defense, Kennedy had team members who underscored his own claim to foreign-policy mastery. McNamara became a legend for his analytical and statistical sharpness, while Bundy, the former Harvard dean, came across, in the words of David Halberstam, as "the sharpest intellect of a generation, a repository of national intelligence." [13] Each projected unflagging drive and steely determination; as Halberstam wrote of McNamara: "He was a man of force, moving, pushing, getting things done . . . the can-do man in the can-do society, in the can-do era." [14] McNamara and Bundy seemed to be running the national security apparatus as extensions of Kennedy.

An even more direct extension of John Kennedy was his brother, the attorney general. Not only did Robert Kennedy's intelligence and drive recall those of the president; his special closeness to his brother made their strengths seem intertwined. Yet Robert also projected intensity and what his detractors dubbed ruthlessness, qualities that could undercut his brother's charm. John Kennedy was not tarnished by his brother or any other aide, however, both because of his own self-deprecating wit and because his team included an especially good-humored team member. Press Secretary Pierre Salinger became one of the best known of the New Frontiersmen not because he shared their vaunted strengths but because he supplied comic leavening. As Anderson has written, Salinger "was Kennedy's Falstaff and he made the most of the role." [15]

The most dramatic actions of the Kennedy presidency were designed to produce results rather than to feature gestures; spectacle was not yet a very deliberate motive. Yet even in such actions as the steel crisis of 1962, the civil rights struggle of 1963, and the recurring Berlin and Cuban crises, the Kennedy administration provided moments of spectacle that would impress its successors and help shape future media expectations. Sometimes it was the image of the president at the center of a White House command post, personally making cool and effective decisions in the heat of crisis. There also was the image of the president denouncing the greed of steel company executives and invoking a higher public interest before a national television audience.

When spectacle predominated in the New Frontier, it was in peripheral areas. The space race was one such area; Kennedy's public pledge to send a man to the moon had little to do with scientific advancement, but a great deal to do with demonstrating the superiority of America's (and the president's) spirit in the face of the communist challenge. Physical fitness was a minor spectacle; much-publicized fifty-mile hikes by New Frontiersmen highlighted the theme of restoring vigor to American life. The presidential press conference was adapted to the purposes of spectacle and became one of Kennedy's greatest successes. As the first president to permit live television coverage of his press conferences, Kennedy used this forum to demonstrate to the public his mastery of facts, quick intelligence, and sense of humor. What was said during Kennedy's press conferences was less important than his appealing way of saying it, the press a less important audience than the wider public.

By the time of Jimmy Carter's administration, spectacle had moved closer to the center of the presidency. As a sign of its rise, spectacle specialists—pollster/adviser Patrick Caddell and advertising expert Gerald Rafshoon—now were prominent members of the president's team. The Carter presidency began with what appeared to be highly effective gestures to enhance the stature of its star. Yet its capacity to mount an appealing spectacle soon proved to be surprisingly weak. Carter thus provides an instructive example of spectacular failure.

As a spectacle character, the Carter portrayed in the media was unstable. The attractive images that graced his dark-horse campaign and presidential honeymoon were supplanted by a predominantly negative set of images during the summer and fall of his first year in office. The initial Jimmy Carter was the White House version. The picture of the president that the media conveyed included a nice blend of "soft" and "hard" features. Against the background of Vietnam and Watergate, the soft Carter was reassuring; this gentle, relaxed, open, and moral man would banish the specter of the imperial presidency. Yet soft would not come across as weak because of the complementary qualities of hardness in Carter's makeup. This tough, self-assured, smart, managerial president would satisfy the continuing American hunger for strong leadership. Most members of the media were impressed by Carter at first—and reported a similarly favorable perception among the public. *Time* observed that Carter "is winning converts by the millions with his revivalist, meet-the-masses approach to the presidency. . . ."

But once the Bert Lance affair, along with a swarm of later administration difficulties in domestic and foreign affairs, began to preoccupy the press, the Carter character began to change. Revelations about Lance's banking practices prior to his selection as budget director, including questionable loans and overdraft privileges for himself and his friends, were made to seem even worse by Carter's handling of the ensuing scandal. Carter made a premature proclamation of Lance's innocence, then had to watch in embarrassment as troubling details continued to surface. The White House lost control of how its star was projected as the media—partly on its own and partly as a conduit for Carter's congressional and partisan critics—reassembled his features into an unflattering portrait. A highly moral president was tarnished by the Lance affair, brought down into "the pit of politics as usual." A self-assured president now appeared stubborn and isolated, "drawing the wagons around himself and his beleaguered friend" Lance in a manner reminiscent of Johnson and Nixon. A president earlier portrayed as exceptionally bright now was characterized as intellectually adrift and devoid of priorities.

Worst of all for Carter was the appearance of ineptitude. Carter was first saddled with this image in the fall of 1977. Hostile columnists, such as Evans and Novak, began to label him a "political incompetent." More neutral sources broadcast the image in stories with headlines like: "Can Jimmy Carter Cope?" *(Newsweek)*. Talk of a "one-term president" conjured up impressions of a doomed administration. If Carter and his team had succeeded initially in presenting a refreshingly decent yet still potent presidential character, the character who acted out the remainder of his term was no longer refreshing and seemed disturbingly weak to most observers. A towering political figure in a spectacle of his own making, he came to appear too small for his job in a spectacle of failure.[16]

Carter's team could not rescue his character or strengthen his capacity to carry out engaging spectacles. Indeed, the team contributed mightily to his failure. The chief culprits were his closest aides, Hamilton Jordan and Jody Powell. During Carter's honeymoon, the press had wondered about the youth and inexperience of the president's aides but had played up their colorful features. A cover story in *Time*, entitled "The President's Boys," advised readers to "just call 'em Ham and Jody," and depicted them as "the living image" of the Carter administration's "down-home style." [17]

The southern charm of Carter's "boys" soon wore thin as spectacle. Jordan, in particular, developed an image that was a political albatross to his boss. As he grew in power, first as Carter's de facto, then as his official, chief of staff, Jordan became the emblem of a confused and disorganized administration. Aaron Latham depicted him as "one of the most disorderly people ever to serve in the White House. . . . He sits at the center of the White House radiating chaos. And that is just what seems to be crippling this administration: a sense that no one is in charge, that no one knows what to do. . . ." [18] Jordan also became notorious for making enemies on Capitol Hill (a sign of political ineptitude) and for "turning up as the Administration's most-often-mentioned figure in Washington's gossip columns" (a sign of personal immaturity).[19] In the spectacles of the Carter years, the president's closest aides came across as callow and maladroit. A president who had such apparent nobodies working for him was hardly a president who could project an image of commanding skill and presence.

If Jordan and Powell were damaging to Carter as a spectacle character, the rest of his team simply had little spectacle value. No one in the Carter administration achieved the media stature of a Robert McNamara, a Robert Kennedy, or even a Pierre Salinger. Even before scandal brought him low, Lance came across as a small-town banker rather than a distinguished financier. Zbigniew Brzezinski, the president's national security adviser, looked like an ersatz Henry Kissinger. The administration did contain figures, such as Joseph Califano and Cyrus Vance, who could have supplied some of the aura of Washington experience and expertise it so badly lacked, but they were kept at arm's length by the White House and eventually departed under unpleasant circumstances.

During Carter's presidential honeymoon, his administration's awareness of the possibilities of spectacle was frequently demonstrated. The gestures of a modest, open, democratic presidency were numerous: the inaugural walk with his wife down Pennsylvania Avenue, the casual "fireside chat," the town meetings in representative American communities. That these gestures were symbolic rather than substantive was obvious to the press. Garry Trudeau, in his "Doonesbury" comic strip, quickly satirized them by having the president create a new post, Secretary of Symbolism. Nonetheless, most journalists were impressed. *Newsweek* saw in Carter "a gift for imagery"; *Time* proclaimed him a "master of the symbolic act." [20]

Once Carter's imagery of the democratic, post-imperial president faded and was replaced by the new image of weakness and ineptitude, however, the White House no longer could come up with fresh spectacles to refurbish his character. Their most memorable effort, the spectacle of the president descending from a two-week stay at his Camp David mountaintop retreat to warn the American people of "a crisis of the American spirit," turned into a spectacular flop. The spectacle originated when, with his standing in the polls sinking to disastrous lows and his energy proposals encountering vast public indifference, Carter recognized, as he acknowledged in his memoirs, that he "had to do something to get the attention of the news media and the public." [21] So, in the words of *Newsweek,* the president "created his own attention-catching theatrics—his abrupt and messy cancellation of an earlier TV speech on energy, his disappearance into the woodsy silence of the Catoctins, his consultations with the relays of counselors delivered daily to his mountain by clattering Marine helicopters." [22] At last, coming down from Camp David to deliver a televised address, Carter framed his newest proposals on energy with a sermon that diagnosed the nation's supposed malaise and called for the public to support him in restoring American confidence.

Carter's "crisis of confidence" speech is mainly remembered as a gloomy jeremiad that compares poorly in popular appeal to the upbeat rhetoric of Reagan. In fact, the speech was well received at the time. *Newsweek,* for example, called it "the best speech of his Presidency," and reported that subsequent polling found 75 percent of the American people in agreement with the president's argument.[23] Yet the apologetic and negative tone of the speech was risky. If this spectacle was to work, Carter would have to give further signs that he deserved public confidence.

What happened instead was a classic case of the maladroit handling of spectacle. Three days after his speech, Carter purged several members of his cabinet. Designed as a display of strength and mastery, the firings gave off an air of desperation and made Carter seem even weaker. Having implied in his speech that the American people might be largely to blame for the nation's problems, Carter now seemed to foist off on his cabinet the blame for his own problems. The purge was carried out awkwardly; a particularly disastrous gesture was the distribution of a new White House personnel form that seemed to value loyalty to the president over competence. Whatever momentum Carter had gained from his speech was lost in the purge. His poll ratings quickly dropped back down to their pre-speech level, and the whole affair left his presidency even further eviscerated. Carter was not, as it turned out, a "master of the symbolic act"; on the contrary, his administration became the standard for failure in the art of presenting a presidential spectacle.

The Triumph of Spectacle: Ronald Reagan

The Reagan presidency was a triumph of spectacle. In the realm of substantive policy, it was marked by striking failures as well as significant successes. Its penchant for secrecy and covert action led it into a disastrous policy of arms sales to Iran and diversion of funds to the Nicaraguan contras, which, once exposed to public view in late 1986, proved too egregious to be counteracted by the arts of the spectacle specialists. Until then, however, the Reagan presidency had largely floated above the consequences of its flawed processes or failed policies, secure in the brilliant glow of its successful spectacles.

The basis of this success was the character of Ronald Reagan. His previous career in movies and television made Reagan comfortable with and adept at spectacles; he moved easily from one kind to another.[24] Reagan presented to his audience a multifaceted character, funny yet powerful, ordinary yet heroic, individual yet representative. He was a character richer even than Kennedy in mythic resonance.

Coming into office after a president who was widely perceived as weak, Reagan as a spectacle character projected potency. His administration featured a number of spectacles in which Reagan displayed his decisiveness, forcefulness, and will to prevail. The image of masculine toughness was played up repeatedly. The American people saw a president who, even though in his seventies, rode horses and exercised vigorously, a president who liked to cite (and thereby identify himself with) movie tough guys such as Clint Eastwood and Sylvester Stallone. Yet Reagan's strength was nicely balanced by his amiability: his aggressiveness was rendered benign by his characteristic one-line quips. The warm grin took the edge off, removed any intimations of callousness or violence.

Quickly dubbed the Great Communicator, Reagan presented his character not through eloquent rhetoric but through storytelling. As Paul Erickson has demonstrated, Reagan liked to tell tales of "stock symbolic characters," figures whose values and behavior were "heavily colored with Reagan's ideological and emotional principles." [25] Although the villains in these tales ranged from Washington bureaucrats to Marxist dictators, the heroes, whether ordinary people or inspirational figures like Knute Rockne, shared a belief in America. Examined more closely, these heroes turned out to resemble Reagan himself. Praising the heroism of Americans, Reagan, as representative American, praised himself.

The power of Reagan's character rested not only on its intrinsic attractiveness but also on its symbolic appeal. The spectacle specialists who worked for Reagan seized upon the idea of making him an emblem for the American identity. In a June 1984 memo, White House aide Richard Darman sketched a campaign strategy that revolved around the president's mythic role: "Paint RR as the personification of all that is right with or heroized by America. Leave [Walter] Mondale in a position where an attack on Reagan is tantamount to an attack on America's idealized image of itself. . . ." [26] Having come into office at a time of considerable anxiety, with many Americans uncertain (according to polls and interviews) about the economy, their future, and America itself, Reagan was an immensely reassuring character. He had not been marked by the shocks of recent American history, and he even denied those shocks had meaning. He told Americans that the Vietnam War was noble rather than appalling, that Watergate was forgotten, that racial conflict was a thing of the distant past, and that the economy still offered the American dream to any aspiring individual. Reagan (the character) and America (the country) were presented in the spectacles of the Reagan presidency as timeless, above the decay of aging and the difficulties of history.

The Reagan team assumed special importance because Reagan ran what Lou Cannon has called "the delegated presidency." [27] His team members carried on, as was well known to the public, most of the business of government; Reagan's own work habits were decidedly relaxed. Reagan's team did not contain many performers who reinforced the president's character, as did Kennedy's New Frontiersmen. But it featured several figures whose spectacle role was to compensate for Reagan's deficiencies or to carry on his mission with a greater air of vigor than the amiable president usually conveyed. The Reagan presidency was not free of disruptive characters—Alexander Haig's and James Watt's unattractive features and gestures called the president's spectacle into question. Unlike the Carter presidency, however, it removed these characters before too much damage had been done.

David Stockman was the most publicized supporting player in the first months of 1981. His image in the media was formidable. *Newsweek*, for example, marveled at how "his buzz-saw intellect has helped him stage a series of bravura performances before Congress," and acclaimed him "the Reagan Administration's boy wonder. . . ." [28] There was spectacle appeal in the sight of the nation's youngest-ever budget director serving as the right arm of the nation's oldest-ever chief executive. More important, Stockman's appearance as the master of budget numbers compensated for a president who was notoriously uninterested in data. Stockman faded in spectacle value after his disastrous *Atlantic* confessions in the fall of 1981. His admission that budget numbers had been doctored to show the results the administration wanted, and that the across-the-board tax cut of 1981 was a "Trojan horse" to make politically palatable a large reduction in the rates paid by the wealthiest taxpayers, left his credibility wounded. But Stockman's contribution had been substantial when it was most needed, in the crucial budget and tax battles of Reagan's early months as president.

As Reagan's longtime aide, Edwin Meese was one of the most prominent members of the president's team. Meese's principal spectacle role was not as a White House manager but as a cop. Even before he moved from the White House to the Justice Department, Meese became the voice and the symbol of the administration's commitment to a tough stance on law-and-order issues. Although the president sometimes spoke about law and order, Meese took on the issue with a vigor that his more benign boss could not convey.

In foreign affairs, the Reagan administration developed an effective balance of images in the persons of Caspar Weinberger and George Shultz. Weinberger quickly became the administration's most visible cold war hard-liner. As the tireless spokesman and unbudging champion of a soaring defense budget, he was a handy symbol for the Reagan military buildup. Nicholas Lemann notes that while "Weinberger's predecessor, Harold Brown, devoted himself almost completely to management, Weinberger . . . operated more and more on the theatrical side." [29] His grim, hawklike visage was as much a reminder of the Soviet threat as the alarming paperback reports on the Russian behemoth that his Defense Department issued every year. Yet Weinberger could seem too alarming, feeding the fears of those who worried about Reagan's warmaking proclivities.

Once Haig was pushed out as secretary of state, however, the Reagan administration found the ideal counterpoint to Weinberger in George Shultz. In contrast to both Haig and Weinberger, Shultz was a reassuring figure. He was portrayed in the media in soothing terms: low-key, quiet, conciliatory. In form and demeanor, he came across, in the words of *Time*, "as a good gray diplomat." [30] Shultz was taken to be a voice of foreign policy moderation in an administration otherwise dominated by hard-liners. Actually, Shultz had better cold war credentials than Weinberger, having been a founding member of the hard-line Committee on the Present Danger in 1976. And he was more inclined to support the use of military force than was the secretary of defense, who reflected the caution of a Pentagon that had been burned by the Vietnam experience. But Shultz's real views were less evident than his spectacle role as the gentle diplomat.

The Reagan presidency benefited not only from a spectacular main character and a useful team but also from talent and good fortune at enacting spectacle gestures. It is not difficult to find events during the Reagan years—the PATCO strike, the Geneva summit, the Libyan bombing, and others—whose significance primarily lay in their spectacle value. The most striking Reagan spectacle of all was the invasion of Grenada. Grenada deserves a close look; it can serve as the archetype of a successful presidential spectacle.

American forces invaded the island of Grenada in October 1983. Relations between the Reagan administration and the Marxist regime of Grenada's Maurice Bishop had been increasingly tense. When Bishop was overthrown and murdered by a clique of more militant Marxists, the Reagan administration began to consider military action. It was urged to invade by the Organization of Eastern Caribbean States, composed of Grenada's island neighbors. And it had a pretext for action in the safety of the Americans—most of them medical students—on the island. Once the decision to invade was made, American troops landed in force, evacuated most of the students, and seized the island after encountering unexpectedly stiff resistance. Reagan administration officials announced that in the course of securing the island U.S. forces had discovered large caches of military supplies and documents, indicating that Cuba planned to turn Grenada into a base for the export of revolution and terror.

Examination of the details that eventually came to light cast doubt upon the Reagan administration's claims of a threat to the American students and a buildup of "sophisticated" Cuban weaponry on the island. Beyond such details, there was a sheer incongruity between the importance bestowed on Grenada by the Reagan administration and the insignificance that the facts seemed to suggest. Grenada is a tiny island, with a population of 100,000, a land area of 133 square miles, and an economy whose exports totaled $19 million in 1981.[31] That American troops could secure it was never in question; as Richard Gabriel has noted, "In terms of actual combat forces, the U.S. outnumbered the island's defenders approximately ten to one." [32] Grenada's importance did not derive from the facts of the event, or from the military, political, and economic implications of America's actions, but from its value as a spectacle.

What was the spectacle of Grenada about? Its meaning was articulated by a triumphant President Reagan: "Our days of weakness are over. Our military forces are back on their feet and standing tall." [33] In truth, Reagan, even more than the American military, came across in the media as "standing tall" in Grenada.

The spectacle actually began with the president on a weekend golfing vacation in Augusta, Georgia. His vacation was interrupted first by reports on planning for an invasion of Grenada and then by news that the Marine barracks in Beirut, Lebanon, had been bombed. Once the news of the Grenada landings replaced the tragedy in Beirut on the front page and television screen, the golfing angle proved to be an apt beginning for a spectacle. It was used to dramatize the ability of a relaxed and laid-back president to rise to a grave challenge. And it supplied the White House with an unusual backdrop to present the president in charge, with members of his team by his side. As Francis X. Clines reported in the *New York Times:*

> The White House offered the public some graphic tableaux, snapped by the White House photographer over the weekend, depicting the President at the center of various conferences. He is seen in bathrobe and slippers being briefed by Mr. Shultz and Mr. McFarlane, then out on the Augusta fairway, pausing at the wheel of his golf cart as he receives another dispatch. Mr. Shultz is getting the latest word in another, holding the special security phone with a golf glove on.[34]

Pictures of the president as decision maker were particularly effective because pictures from Grenada itself were lacking; the American press had been barred by the Reagan administration from covering the invasion. This outraged the press, but was extremely useful to the spectacle, which would not have been furthered by pictures of dead bodies or civilian casualties, or by independent sources of information with which congressional critics could raise unpleasant questions.

The initial meaning of the Grenada spectacle was established by Reagan in his announcement of the invasion. The enemy was suitably evil: "a brutal group of leftist thugs. . . ." American objectives were purely moral—to protect the lives of innocent people, namely American medical students, on the island, and to restore democracy to the people of Grenada. And the actions taken were unmistakably forceful: "The United States had no choice but to act strongly and decisively. . . ."[35]

But the spectacle of Grenada soon expanded beyond this initial definition. The evacuation of the medical students provided one of those unanticipated occurrences that heighten the power of spectacle: when several of the students kissed the airport tarmac to express their relief and joy at returning to American soil, the resulting pictures on television and in the newspapers were better than anything the administration could have orchestrated. They provided the spectacle with historical as well as emotional resonance. Here was a second hostage crisis—but where Carter had been helpless to release captive Americans, Reagan had swiftly come to the rescue.

Rescue of the students quickly took second place, however, to a new theme: the claim that U.S. forces had uncovered and uprooted a hidden Soviet-Cuban base for adventurism and terrorism. In his nationally televised address, Reagan did not ignore the Iran analogy: "The nightmare of our hostages in Iran must never be repeated." But he stressed the greater drama of defeating a sinister communist plot. "Grenada, we were told, was a friendly island paradise for tourism. Well, it wasn't. It was a Soviet-Cuban colony being readied as a major military bastion to export terror and undermine democracy. We got there just in time." [36] Grenada was turning out to be an even better spectacle for Reagan: he had rescued not only the students but the people of all the Americas as well. (Later there would be another bonus: the happiness of the Grenadian people at the overthrow of the military clique that had murdered Maurice Bishop. Reagan thus became not just rescuer but liberator.)

As the spectacle expanded and grew more heroic, public approval increased. The president's standing in the polls went up. *Time* reported that "a post-invasion poll taken by the *Washington Post* and ABC News showed that 63% of Americans approve the way Reagan is handling the presidency, the highest level in two years, and attributed his gain largely to the Grenada intervention." [37] Congressional critics, although skeptical of many of the claims made by the administration, began to stifle their doubts and chime in with endorsements in accordance with the polls. An unnamed White House aide, quoted in *Newsweek*, drew the obvious lesson: "You can scream and shout and gnash your teeth all you want, but the folks out there like it. It was done right and done with dispatch." [38]

In its final gestures, the Grenada spectacle commemorated itself. Reagan invited the medical students to the White House, and, predictably, basked in their praise and cheering. The Pentagon contributed its symbolic share, awarding some eight thousand medals for the Grenada operation—more than the number of American troops that set foot on the island. In actuality, Gabriel has shown, "the operation was marred by a number of military failures." [39] Yet these were obscured by the triumphant appearances of the spectacle.

That the spectacle of Grenada was more potent, and would prove more lasting in its effects, than any disconfirming facts possibly could, was observed at the time by Anthony Lewis. Reagan "knew the facts would come out eventually," wrote Lewis. "But if that day could be postponed, it might make a great political difference. People would be left with their first impression that this was a decisive President fighting communism." [40] Grenada became for most Americans a highlight of Reagan's first term. Insignificant in military or diplomatic terms, it was, as spectacle, one of the most successful acts of the Reagan presidency.

Conclusion

It is tempting to blame the growth of spectacle on individual presidents, their calculating advisers, or compliant journalists. It is more accurate, however, to attribute the growth of spectacle to larger forces: the extreme personalization of the modern presidency, the excessive expectations of the president that most Americans possess, and the voluminous media coverage that fixes on presidents and treats American politics largely as a report of their adventures. Presidential spectacles even can be linked to a culture of consumption in which spectacle is the predominant form relating the few to the many.

Spectacle, then, is more a structural feature of the contemporary presidency than a strategy of deception adopted by particular presidents. In running for the presidency, and then carrying out its tasks, any contemporary chief executive is likely to turn to spectacle. It has become institutionalized, as spectacle specialists in the White House routinely devise performances for a vast press corps that is eager to report every colorful detail. Spectacle is expected by the public, as the most visible manifestation of presidential leadership. A president who deliberately eschewed its possibilities probably would encounter the same kinds of difficulties as a president who, like Carter, failed at it.

Still, the rise of spectacle in the presidency remains a disturbing development. It is harmful to presidents, promoting gesture over accomplishment and appearance over fact. It is even more harmful to the public, since it obfuscates presidential activity, undermines executive accountability, and encourages passivity on the part of citizens. The presentation of leadership as spectacle has little in common with the kind of leadership that American democratic values imply.

Notes

1. George C. Edwards III, *The Public Presidency: The Pursuit of Popular Support* (New York: St. Martin's, 1983), 1.
2. Samuel Kernell, *Going Public: New Strategies of Presidential Leadership* (Washington, D.C.: CQ Press, 1986), 84.
3. Daniel Dayan and Elihu Katz, "Electronic Ceremonies: Television Performs a Royal Wedding," in *On Signs*, ed. Marshall Blonsky (Baltimore: Johns Hopkins University Press, 1985), 16.
4. Roland Barthes, *Mythologies* (New York: Hill & Wang, 1972), 15-25.
5. David L. Paletz and Robert M. Entman, *Media Power Politics* (New York: Free Press, 1981), 21.

6. Theodore J. Lowi, *The Personal President* (Ithaca, N.Y: Cornell University Press, 1985), 96.

7. See Stephen J. Wayne, "Great Expectations: What People Want from Presidents," in *Rethinking the Presidency,* ed. Thomas E. Cronin (Boston: Little, Brown, 1982), 185-199; and Thomas E. Cronin, *The State of the Presidency,* 2d ed. (Boston: Little, Brown, 1980), 2-25. Cronin was one of the first to recognize the relationship between inflated public expectations and the emergence of public relations strategies at the center of presidential politics. See his "The Presidency Public Relations Script," in *The Presidency Reappraised,* ed. Rexford G. Tugwell and Thomas E. Cronin (New York: Praeger, 1974), 168-183.

8. Guy Debord, *Society of the Spectacle* (Detroit: Black & Red, 1983), para. 60.

9. On the confidence of the public personality and the anxiety of his audience, see Richard Sennett, *The Fall of Public Man* (New York: Knopf, 1977).

10. Erving Goffman, *The Presentation of Self in Everyday Life* (Garden City, N.Y.: Anchor Books, 1959), 104.

11. Dan Rather and Gary Paul Gates, *The Palace Guard* (New York: Warner Books, 1975), 285.

12. Patrick Anderson, *The President's Men* (Garden City, N.Y.: Anchor Books, 1969), 239.

13. David Halberstam, *The Best and the Brightest* (Greenwich, Conn.: Fawcett Crest Books, 1973), 57.

14. Ibid., 265.

15. Anderson, *The President's Men,* 279.

16. Material in the preceding three paragraphs is adapted from Bruce Miroff, "The Media and Presidential Symbolism: The Woes of Jimmy Carter" (Paper delivered at the annual meeting of the American Political Science Association, New York, September 3-6, 1981).

17. "The President's Boys," *Time,* June 6, 1977.

18. Aaron Latham, "Hamilton Jordan: A Slob in the White House," *Esquire,* March 28, 1978, 77.

19. "Ham Jordan: Carter's Unorthodox 'Right Arm,'" *U.S. News & World Report,* February 27, 1978.

20. *Newsweek,* May 2, 1977; and *Time,* February 14, 1977.

21. Jimmy Carter, *Keeping Faith: Memoirs of a President* (New York: Bantam Books, 1982), 115.

22. "To Lift a Nation's Spirit," *Newsweek,* July 23, 1979.

23. "Jimmy Carter's Cabinet Purge," *Newsweek,* July 30, 1979.

24. For a discussion of how his movie roles helped transform Reagan's character, see Michael Rogin, "'Ronald Reagan': The Movie" (Paper delivered at the annual meeting of the American Political Science Association, New Orleans, August 29-September 1, 1985).

25. Paul D. Erickson, *Reagan Speaks: The Making of an American Myth* (New York: New York University Press, 1985), 51, 52, 49.

26. Quoted in ibid., 100.

27. Lou Cannon, *Reagan* (New York: G. P. Putnam's Sons, 1982), 371-401.

28. "Meet David Stockman," *Newsweek,* February 16, 1981.

29. Nicholas Lemann, "The Peacetime War," *Atlantic,* October 1984, 88.

30. "Cooly Taking Charge," *Time,* September 6, 1982.

31. "From Bad to Worse for U.S. in Grenada," *U.S. News & World Report,* October 31, 1983.

32. Richard A. Gabriel, *Military Incompetence: Why the American Military Doesn't Win* (New York: Hill & Wang, 1985), 154.
33. Quoted in "Fare Well, Grenada," *Time,* December 26, 1983.
34. *New York Times,* October 26, 1983.
35. Ibid.
36. Ibid., October 28, 1983.
37. "Getting Back to Normal," *Time,* November 21, 1983.
38. " 'We Will Not Be Intimidated,' " *Newsweek,* November 14, 1983.
39. Gabriel, *Military Incompetence,* 186.
40. Anthony Lewis, "What Was He Hiding?" *New York Times,* October 31, 1983.

13. THE PRESIDENCY AND THE PRESS

James Fallows

In January 1983, halfway through his first term, Ronald Reagan paid an impromptu call on a neighborhood tavern while on a tour of Boston. After raising a glass with the other, startled customers, the president made one of the off-the-cuff remarks about national policy that had caused him political difficulty in the previous few months. Some people thought that the Reagan Revolution was on the wane, that the president could not recapture the mandate for bold innovation he had enjoyed in his first year in office. He didn't agree, the president said; he had lots of new projects he'd like to undertake. He proceeded to give his listeners an example. Although he guessed he'd probably kick himself in the morning for saying so, President Reagan said he thought it might make sense to abolish the corporate income tax.

His premonition about regretting the remark showed how well Ronald Reagan had come to understand the press. In the week after his statement, newspapers and television news reports were full of stories about his comments, nearly all of them unfavorable. Many of the accounts treated Reagan's remarks as a gaffe: here was one more piece of evidence that Ronald Reagan could say almost anything, once he slipped the leash usually held by his handlers in the White House. Other accounts dwelt on the political meaning of the incident. The biggest threat to the administration, according to this reasoning, was the "fairness issue," the idea that Reagan's policies took from the poor and gave to the rich. Abolishing the corporate income tax, at a time when more than ten million people were out of work, offered a caricature of a president in anguish over the burdens borne by giant corporations but indifferent to the downtrodden.

Many of these analyses were intelligently presented. From the political point of view, they might even have been correct. But what was missing from nearly all of them was the conception that the president's proposal might possibly have been a good idea.

On this as on so many other questions of public policy, economists disagree. But a strong faction within the profession has argued for many years that the corporate income tax serves no reasonable public purpose. Among other things—this faction argues—the corporate tax drives big companies even farther from the healthy rigors of the competitive market system. In corporate life as in personal life, expenses that are tax-deductible cost less than they seem to. Why should a profitable company really worry about spending a thousand dollars for an executive's country club membership or agreeing to an unrealistic wage agreement with a union? Even if management won a fight to save money on such items, nearly half the savings would be taxed away. But if there were no corporate income tax, a dollar saved would be a dollar earned; market forces would be strengthened, and companies would be more efficient as a result.

There are sound economic arguments on the other side, too; the point is that there *is* a lively debate on the merits of the corporate income tax. In that debate, many who are known as liberals, such as Lester Thurow of MIT, take the same side as the president.

Why was this perspective missing from the coverage of Ronald Reagan's remarks? If it had been included, the event certainly would have looked better for the president. Its absence, therefore, might have reflected the press's liberal bias against a conservative administration. That is precisely the explanation that probably seemed most plausible to members of the White House staff. Similarly, Jimmy Carter's assistants thought that nasty news stories reflected the press's Washington-insider bias against southerners and outsiders. Members of Gerald R. Ford's entourage thought the press held a biased view of Ford as a dolt. Richard Nixon, of course, thought himself the victim of an unending smear campaign by the press. Lyndon B. Johnson believed he got bad coverage because of a bias against his Texas-usurper ways.

As this long list of comparable complaints might indicate, the corporate-tax story suggests that there is something more complicated, and more disturbing, at play than the tensions between left-wing reporters and a right-wing president. It illustrates, instead, a kind of bias that rises above merely partisan disputes. It reveals reporters' clear preference to write about *politics,* rather than about the history, the substance, or the day-by-day truths of government's operation. Sometimes this bias works to the president's advantage, sometimes to his disadvantage. But in all cases, the public is disserved.

Press Definitions of News: Government as Politics

In its broadest sense, of course, *politics* embraces everything that matters about a citizen's relationship with his government. It is the web of connections between elected leaders and the diverse national factions whose interests they must meld. It is the long history of previous choices that restrict the choices that are available today. It is the setting of world history and economic change that forces one administration to confront dilemmas that its predecessors had ignored.

But in this chapter politics will be considered as the press defines it: in its narrowest sense, the sense most akin to sports. Newspaper sports pages have improved dramatically in the last generation. On a typical day the reader will find discussions of great sophistication about the why and how of sports. Will the new football or soccer or team-tennis league survive? How did a certain coach win a crucial game? Why was Russell greater than Chamberlain? Why are baseball players paid so much? Who are the future greats in the high school leagues? If the answers aren't available in the newspapers, there is always *Sports Illustrated*.

Behind the sophistication, however, there is ... nothing. Sports has no ultimate purpose apart from the skill of its execution. And that is its crucial difference from politics. Like sports, politics has a dimension of pure tactics, skill, wins, and losses: the horse race among candidates for the presidency or other offices, the long pennant race, in which campaign organizations gain ground on one another. But in politics, unlike sports, there is something else beyond these details of execution. The game of politics is played not for its own sake but to manage the social, economic, and at times military forces that affect the nation. If the game is played poorly, lives can be lost, societies ruined. Yet the stakes in the game are the missing element in most of what we read about government, and nowhere more so than in coverage of the White House.

Explaining why this is so is not hard. Reporters, like others whose performance is open to public view, are wary of falling on their faces. In the news business, there is usually more to be lost through a big mistake than there is to be gained through a display of unusual insight. Reporters naturally minimize their risks by concentrating on the areas where they are most confident. For members of the White House press corps, that almost always means horse-race politics. When it comes to economics or the workings of the domestic bureaucracy, the White House correspondent probably will feel unsure about discriminating between the trends that matter and those that do not. He will not lack that confidence about politics. Many of the reporters, especially for the television networks, qualify for the White House beat by covering a presidential campaign. As a result, White House reporters typically pour more of themselves into the attempt to explain the politics of a new development than its substance.

During the last year and a half of the Carter administration, for example, one of the biggest political stories was the contest between

President Carter and Sen. Edward Kennedy to be the Democratic nominee. By the middle of 1980, it had become clear that Carter would run away with the nomination, but in 1979 it looked like a close, and therefore exciting, race.

In July of 1979, Carter went on television to discuss the latest version of his energy-conservation plans. Shortly afterward, Kennedy held a press conference to describe an energy program of his own. The major newspapers assigned their crack political reporters to the story and covered it as yet another warmup to the 1980 race. The *Wall Street Journal* headline, typical of the others, was "Kennedy Offers $58 Billion Energy Plan as Prospect for 1980 Election Seems Likelier." Twelve of the fifteen paragraphs in the story were devoted to handicapping the next election; only three, to the plan itself.

That kind of coverage may have made perfect sense to the members of the Kennedy and Carter campaign teams. Assessing the effects of each new event on the 1980 election was exactly what they did each day. But from the public point of view, even from the viewpoint of those who are abundantly interested in the horse-race aspect of politics, there was a more important story to be done, or at least started, that day. It was a story that would compare the two energy plans, seriously appraise their consequences, dig out the differences between them and the alternatives that exist. In the end, it might be a more profoundly "political" form of coverage; for, unlike another recap of developments among the campaign teams, it would give the public more information on which to base its choices among the candidates.

An equivalent episode in the Reagan administration was the portrayal of the battle over Reaganomics in 1981. In many press accounts the economic decisions were depicted as grudge matches, fought on many fronts. The executive branch locked horns with the legislative; Ronald Reagan faced off against Tip O'Neill, David Stockman fought with Caspar Weinberger; the advocates of pure supply side economics fought against those who would betray the faith. Meanwhile, Edward Meese, James Baker, and Michael Deaver struggled for the upper hand. The play-by-play of each of these contests was lavishly and expertly reported.

In fairness, by the end of that same year, many newspapers, news magazines, and networks *had* begun to complement their reports of political jockeying among the supply-siders with an examination of the economic consequences. From the Reagan administration's point of view, much of the resulting coverage must have seemed vexatious. In dwelling on the extreme cases—the ailing pensioners whose disability checks were cut off, the steel and auto workers who lost their jobs—the coverage may have appeared, to the administration, to distort the meaning of the long-range changes the new policies were designed to promote. But even if we assume, for the moment, that the complaint was correct, the new direction in economic coverage was still a plus because it directed attention to the results of political struggles, not to the struggles themselves.

This changed emphasis may have been a natural response to the administration's bold claims that it was setting a decisively different course. Perhaps, as many conservatives suspected, it arose from liberal reporters' and editors' hostility to the Reagan administration's goals. But it also could have meant that journalists were broadening their conception of politics to embrace more than the play-by-play of Washington infighting. If so, the reading public—Republicans as well as Democrats—has reason to cheer.

The other great public controversy of the 1980s concerned the control of nuclear weapons. Here, as with economic policy, press reports gradually evolved away from the sports-page approach. Eventually, there were informative discussions of the strategic and technical foundations on which the nuclear arsenals had been built, of the risks and consequences of different approaches. Still, these "documentaries" and "special series," admirable and constructive as they were, seemed to represent special, unsustainable exertions. When not pushing themselves to unusual effort, most members of the White House press fell back to viewing nuclear policy as the Sugar Bowl and economic policy as the Rose Bowl. What really mattered to them was how well the teams played the game.

One clear illustration of this tendency was the treatment of Kenneth Adelman. In January 1983, Adelman was nominated to direct the Arms Control and Disarmament Agency, succeeding Eugene Rostow, whom President Reagan had dismissed. Over the next three months, Adelman's nomination became the object of a bitter, partisan fight in the Senate.

At one level, the fight reflected fundamental disagreements about the course of arms control policy. On the administration's left, many advocates of the Strategic Arms Limitation Treaties (known as SALT I and SALT II) feared irreparable rupture between the Soviet Union and the United States. The two treaties might not have accomplished miracles, these advocates would concede; but if the two great nuclear powers stopped talking about controlling nuclear weapons, who could say what horrors would follow?

From the administration's right came an argument made with equal passion and intensity. Those who saw the early 1980s as a parallel to the late 1930s thought that Western governments, even the one led by Ronald Reagan, were in danger of appeasing a ruthlessly aggressive power, as the English and French had done with Hitler, to the world's lasting regret. In the shuffling of Rostow and Adelman, they saw a battle for the administration's soul. The question, in their minds, was whether the United States would regain the moral courage necessary to speak the truth about Soviet intentions in general, and their violation of arms control treaties in particular.

Some press reports on the Adelman nomination depicted this clash of world views. The journalists who took this tack often had a reflexively partisan outlook. Conservatives overlooked the reasonable complaints that could be made about Adelman's credentials for the job; liberals exaggerated how much difference this one nominee could make in the administration's policy. But most accounts portrayed the nomination struggle as just another contest, another test of the administration's power and dexterity. Adelman himself took on a sports-page identity, as the error-prone shortstop who keeps muffing easy grounders. In the first of his three appearances before the Senate Foreign Relations Committee, which was considering his nomination, Adelman discussed the administration's goals in arms control and outlined the philosophical premises that led the Reagan administration to its specific arms control proposals. But he also responded "I don't know" or "I haven't thought about it" to several questions, and when the television networks covered his testimony, they ran those answers—the bobbled grounders—back to back.

From that point on, the Adelman nomination story had less to do with arms control than with arguments about this particular player, and whether he ever would learn big-league skills. When his nomination was finally confirmed, the White House and Capitol Hill reporters chalked it up as another extra-innings win for the big right-hander, Dutch Reagan. Most reports were as unrevealing about the real stakes in arms control as the controversy over Anne Gorsuch Burford, the director of the Environmental Protection Agency, was about environmental protection.

The Reykjavik summit of 1986 offers another, even more remarkable, example of how the press elevates political skill over policy substance in its coverage of arms control. President Reagan left his meeting with Soviet premier Mikhail Gorbachev grim—and, on television, grim-faced—with disappointment over his failure to reach an agreement on nuclear weapons. In a post-summit press conference, Secretary of State George Shultz called the meeting a "failure."

But as Air Force One headed back to Washington, Reagan's advisers decided that the situation was salvageable, at least politically: all the White House had to do was start smiling and declare victory. The summit had not failed, according to the new administration interpretation. Instead, Reagan had stared down the Soviets on the Strategic Defense Initiative ("Star Wars") and established the framework for a better arms agreement in the near future. To sell this argument, Shultz, Chief of Staff Donald Regan, national security adviser John Poindexter, and other administration officials spent a solid week appearing on television news shows and talking to journalists—smiling, upbeat, and aggressive all the while. The press, marveling at the audacious shrewdness of this exercise in "spin control," changed the emphasis in its coverage from "Failure at Reykjavik" to "President Stands Tall."

Presidential Advantages

From the president's point of view, the press's predisposition to cover government as politics has some clear advantages. If he understands the reporters' preference for sports-style political coverage, it becomes far easier for him to control the kind of reports that are written about him. The pioneer in this area was Richard Nixon, who in 1968 laid down the rules for running a presidential campaign in the modern (that is to say, the television-dominated) era.

Nixon understood that in the three or four months between the national convention and the general election, a candidate no longer had to worry about getting *enough* coverage, as he had during the primaries. He was going to get all the news he could handle, the most important of which would be two or three minutes on the network broadcasts each evening. The challenge was to make those few minutes turn out right, to get as much of the candidate's own material across as possible, with the minimum of distraction. Nixon knew that the television reporters would find some way to fill those minutes each day—and that they would leap on misstatements and blunders, like so many fielding errors, if given the chance.

Aware of these hazards, Nixon developed the appropriate plan. To put out his message, he gave one big speech a day, no later than the very early afternoon and in plenty of time for the evening news. Then he did nothing else—nothing, since every extra event increased the danger of tripping over your own news, making a mistake, giving the correspondents too much choice about what to use. He wouldn't give interviews promiscuously, or speak off the cuff, or make any unnecessary noise. The people whose town he was visiting might complain, and the press occasionally grumbled about his attempts to "manage the news." But these criticisms were dwarfed by Nixon's success—even more dramatic in 1972 than in 1968—in getting his point across.

Two of Nixon's successors demonstrated, in opposite ways, the effectiveness of his approach. Jimmy Carter and his entourage in the

1976 presidential campaign were determined to avoid doing anything that smacked of resemblance to Nixon; they were hardly the only Americans with such feelings at the time. After Carter had won the party's nomination, he stuck with the approach that had proven so phenomenally successful during the primary campaigns. This was a campaign style based on making news rather than controlling it— on maximum personal contact with individual voters through endless extemporaneous speeches, countless town meetings, and numerous rallies in a single day. During the primary elections, this approach had worked well. In Iowa and New Hampshire, a candidate could visit enough towns and give enough speeches to physically *see* a significant share of the voters.

The general election campaign was different: no matter how hard he tried, a candidate could never meet more than a tiny fraction of the national electorate. To communicate with the rest, he would have to rely on newspapers and, especially, television. But Carter stuck with his original approach. He made one big speech, sometimes at nine in the morning and sometimes at nine at night. Whenever it came, it was accompanied by a handful of other pronouncements and performances during the day—brief remarks and impromptu interviews that reinforced the candidate's image as accessible and open.

As human qualities, these may have been more appealing than Nixon's isolation; but as a matter of political tactics, they nearly cost Carter the election. Whenever someone stuck a microphone near Carter's mouth and asked him a question, he would get an answer. Since those answeres were so much more juicy than the points Carter wanted to make in his speeches about nuclear proliferation or crime, they dominated the story on the evening news. For days and days, reporters kept asking—and Carter kept answering—questions about an interview with *Playboy* magazine, in which he had discussed, among other subjects, his "lust in my heart" for women other than his wife. This interview was covered to death, but Carter was able to deliver one speech on inflation, in virtually unchanged form, three different times without any detectable news coverage. Partly as a result, Carter sank during the four-month general election campaign from an enormous lead over Ford to a hairbreadth victory.

Four years later, Reagan began walking down the same road Carter had taken earlier, making off-the-cuff remarks about evolution and the Ku Klux Klan. But unlike Carter, he recovered quickly enough to return to the Nixon approach of 1968. His tactics were not the only, or even the major, explanation for his sweeping victory. A change in political ideology, and widespread revulsion against Carter, were certainly at least as important. But Reagan's approach enabled him to stop hurting himself, a trick that Carter mastered only imperfectly and too late.

The principles of news management during presidential campaigns apply even more once a candidate has reached the White House. There he has physical control over the main sources of news. His assistants, instead of riding on the campaign airplane with the reporters, work in office buildings, protected by guards and security barriers from reporters who hope to drop by for a chat. The president has at his disposal the machinery of the entire federal government, which means that he can "generate news"—by greeting a foreign leader or forming a presidential commission—at will.

Presidential Disadvantages

If their knowledge of the press's preference for politics gives them all these advantages, why, then, are presidents from both parties united in their belief that the White House press has given them a bad deal? Because their control is always limited: it determines subject matter, not tone.

A president is least able to control the news, and a reader is most likely to enjoy the benefits of an independent, critical assessment, when reporters move onto terrain where they feel comfortable. When given a chance to cover a subject they know well and can handle confidently, reporters will use their powers to observe, inquire, and appraise. Unfortunately, for most of the White House reporters there are only four such subjects.

The first is anything that smacks of indictable criminal scandal. The regulars of the White House press corps, aware that they had been burned by accepting President Nixon's protestations of innocence too quickly, will not let any potential scandal go unexamined. Nor will any ambitious young reporter, aware of how life has changed for the Messrs. Woodward and Bernstein. Little "judgment" or discretion is required in pursuing these stories because of the reporter's confidence that the standard of criminality will be clear. With enough digging, the reporter feels, he may turn up the incriminating photo, the signed document. Such expectations—so necessary in the courtroom, so misleading in understanding real political life—were intensified by the Watergate scandal. There, contrary to the whole human history of high-level political scheming, clear-cut evidence of misbehavior *did* come to light, when the White House tapes revealed that President Nixon had been involved in a conspiracy to thwart justice. This evidence was referred to as the "smoking gun," which linked a suspect to his crime.

The search for the smoking gun is the theme that unites many

White House stories since Watergate, even if the immediate subject is as trivial as the behavior of Carter staffer Hamilton Jordan, who was accused (but later cleared) of snorting cocaine or the Reagan campaign's acquisition of Jimmy Carter's debate briefing book. During the Kenneth Adelman controversy, the senators who opposed the nominee, and the reporters covering the case, really dug in only twice—once to determine whether Adelman had used the word *sham* in a newspaper interview conducted two years before his nomination and once to find out whether he had studied a memorandum recommending personnel changes, contrary to his assertion that he had not made any decisions about hiring or firing. Both of these controversies proved dramatic, at least for a little while; both carried a connotation of lying or other provable misbehavior. But neither had much to do with the supposed purpose of the confirmation hearings, which was to determine the nominee's philosophy on nuclear weaponry.

The Iran-contra affair that plagued Reagan's second term illustrates both the smoking-gun syndrome and one of its corollaries, namely, that scandal is a license for recycling old criticisms and making new ones. The Reagan administration's practice of trading arms for hostages with Iran, then sending the profits to the contra rebels in Nicaragua was outrage enough, since it violated both the administration's own policy and several laws. But reporters went beyond the events themselves to question Reagan's very competence as president, even his awareness of what he and his aides had done in his name. Press criticism of the president's lackadaisical work habits was not new, but it previously had been ineffective: if Reagan was too lazy, his defenders invariably rejoined, then why was he so successful? The Iran-contra affair offered reporters a way of saying, See, we told you all along.

Politicians sometimes claim that reporters are doing "the easy thing" when they concentrate on scandal. That complaint is imprecise, at least as far as sheer man-hours are concerned. Searching for scandals and smoking guns is exhausting work. It is easy only in that it relieves the reporter of the burden of explaining why a certain policy or decision is important. If he can show that it *broke the law,* his work is done.

Understanding this about reporters, shrewd presidents are compelled to deal with potential scandal the way Reagan dealt with his first national security adviser, Richard Allen (who was accused of accepting watches from Japanese businessmen), and not the way Jimmy Carter dealt with budget director Bert Lance. As soon as one of his associates is tainted, a president must jettison him promptly—as Reagan did Allen. Otherwise, the story may drag on for months, as it did when

Carter stood by Lance, who was accused of financial improprieties. When the briefing-book story broke in the summer of 1983, President Reagan initially compounded his troubles by attempting to pooh-pooh the whole thing, but then tried to recover by turning over great volumes of documents in hopes of deflecting stories of a cover-up. He was less adroit in handling the Iran-contra affair. During the first several weeks, Reagan did nothing but blunder: he told several easily refutable lies about the nature of the arms-for-hostages dealings; called Lt. Col. Oliver North, the chief perpetrator in the affair, a "national hero"; and refused to fire Chief of Staff Regan.

The second area where reporters will make the news, rather than follow it, includes stories of dissension, internal rivalry, unhappy passengers rocking the boat. This is why Midge Costanza, a controversial White House assistant, became the most famous member of the Carter administration during its first year, even though she returned to anonymity soon afterward. Similarly, it is why the reported rivalry between President Reagan's three principal first-term assistants, James Baker, Edwin Meese, and Michael Deaver, became the subplot of much White House reporting in 1981 and 1982. Two assistants on the next-lower rung in the White House, David Gergen and Richard Darman, became household words, at least in Washington, largely because reports of the top-level rivalry prominently featured them.

The Reagan administration's second-term soap opera involved Regan and Nancy Reagan, who wanted the chief of staff fired. Every slight by Regan that the first lady chose to reveal to reporters (usually to NBC's Chris Wallace, on a not-for-attribution basis, of course) became the day's main story, including an account of how he had hung up on her. The *coup de grâce* came when Mrs. Reagan publicly praised her husband's appointment of Howard Baker as chief of staff, even before Regan was told that he was to be replaced.

Politicians well understand that reporters love stories about internal feuds. Therefore, the first test of loyalty within any administration is to avoid making comments that could prop up a "dissent from within" article. If anonymous quotes from the State Department suggest that the secretary of state doesn't like the national security adviser, if second-level assistants at the Pentagon are complaining about the White House staff, reporters will eagerly convey details of the controversy to their readers. But if an administration can manage to present a unified face to the world—or at least that portion of the world represented by the White House press—reporters are less likely to draw harsh conclusions for themselves.

The third area is the gaffe, or tactical blunder. In most cases the substance of the mistake matters very little; what counts is that the fielder dropped the ball. During his debate with Jimmy Carter in the 1976 presidential campaign, Gerald Ford made an inept comment, roughly summarized as "Poland is not dominated by the Soviet Union." No one aware of the history of the Republican party or of Ford's mainstream anticommunism could have mistaken the remark as anything other than a bit of unfortunate phrasing. What Ford was trying to say, as everyone knew, was the the Poles were proud and independent people whose spirit had not been broken. Indeed, as the Polish labor movement expressed its independence in the next three years, Ford's comments began to appear somewhat prescient. In the harshest interpretation, they might have been taken as further evidence that he was not always quick on his feet—but not that he was soft on communism or ignorant of the shape of the post-1945 world.

But because this presidential debate, like many other events in a president's public career, was interpreted by many reporters as a gaffe-avoidance contest, Ford "lost" the debate in a big way. For nearly two weeks after the episode, the Carter campaign reveled in (and encouraged) lurid coverage of the blunder. From Hamtramck to Buffalo, network correspondents interviewed Polish-Americans-in-the-street and asked, in apparent seriousness, whether they had grown more concerned about the administration's commitment to the Captive Nations of Eastern Europe.

A little more than a year later, Jimmy Carter went to Warsaw and had his own taste of a Polish gaffe. When he arrived at the Warsaw airport, he made standard welcoming remarks in English—and then stood by as a State Department official translated them into Polish. Almost immediately, a controversy broke out over the "mistakes" in the translation. On calm, later reflection, it turned out that the mistakes were nowhere near as glaring as initial reports had implied. One crucial sentence, for example, had read in English, "I have come here to understand your desire for the future." For *desire,* the translator used a Polish word, *pozadania,* whose carnal connotations are more pronounced than those of *desire.* But the translator never said some of the things that were reported, as fact, in the American press. (For example, "I lust after the Poles.") In any case, the whole episode was simply silly, since it made no dent in Polish-American relations or in the business the president had come to transact.

As his comments on the corporate income tax, mentioned at the beginning of this chapter, might indicate, Ronald Reagan also suffered from the press's concentration on gaffes. During his first year in office, he would offer in his press conferences an inventive history of the partition of Vietnam, or an interpretation of federal law for which no legal support could be found. Each time this happened, analyses of the gaffes would overshadow whatever other news the president hoped to produce at the press conference.

For a time, the gaffe stories all but disappeared. The explanation was not so much that Reagan had grown more precise in his language as that his imprecision had become old news. Because his misstatements were so common, he drained them of news value. But when the Iran-contra affair surfaced, reporters once again began to harp on every seemingly confused, inaccurate, or uninformed remark by the president. Indeed, some stories took on a new cast—directly or indirectly, reporters asked, Is Ronald Reagan senile?

Fourth, there is politics in the narrow sense: the business of winning elections and gaining points in the opinion polls. Reporters will apply their highest powers of analysis and put their reputations on the line to predict whether George Bush or Gary Hart or some other candidate is most likely to serve as president in 1989. Washington journalism boasts three dozen men and women who can tell their readers, with authority and with hard-won facts, *how* any politician is doing: in his local campaign organizations, while working the crowd, in staying on top of the popular trend. Most people in Washington, myself included, will read these stories first when they open the paper. The only thing the stories omit is the *what:* what effect the candidates' promises would have, if implemented, what happened the last time a similar approach was tried. In the prelude to the 1988 election, for example, readers saw expert analyses of whether "competitiveness" was a potent enough issue to give Rep. Richard Gephardt, Sen. Joseph Biden, or some other little-known presidential candidate a chance for the Democratic nomination. They had very little opportunity to learn what their plans for making America competitive might be, or to read informed analyses of whether the proposals were likely to work.

The *what* of government is usually missing from White House stories because of the same imbalance in the reporters' knowledge mentioned earlier. When it comes to stories about scandal, dissension, gaffes, and horse-race politics, most reporters have both the interest and the confidence necessary to set the agenda by themselves. They will break a story, even if official spokesmen tell them it's not important. They will move beyond presenting a balanced set of pro and con quotations, if they are convinced that the quotations fail to give the reader a full appreciation of the truth. If the subject is the prospect for the Iowa caucus vote, a good White House reporter would laugh at any colleague who interviewed each side's campaign manager and thought he'd told all there was to tell. The expert political reporter would want to get out and make his own judgments, by talking to the voters, probing the different levels of the campaign organization, seeing for himself how the candidate came across. These are the tools of appraisal, but the same reporters who use them so adroitly in political stories hesitate to do so on questions of substance.

In this preference, the best White House reporters resemble their counterparts on the president's staff. A Hamilton Jordan in Jimmy Carter's White House or a Lyn Nofziger in Ronald Reagan's might look on a Sam Donaldson or Jack Germond as a creature from another culture, with opposite loyalties, on the other side of the fence. But in the most important ways, they are the same: intelligent pros, gifted handicappers, in love with the skill and detail of politics and faintly interested in anything else.

Conclusion

The result of the reporters' uneven confidence is an important division of labor between president and press. When a story falls into one of the four categories, the reporters determine how much prominence it will have, and how long it will be pursued. But when it falls outside the categories—that is, when it concerns what the government actually does—then the White House controls the topic of the news. Over drinks, during slow moments on the beat, White House reporters will complain bitterly about their status as the press room's trained seals. They describe how confining it all is, how little their editors understand the pointlessness of their beat, how they detest waiting in the press room for Jody Powell or Marlin Fitzwater to show up with the day's press releases.

Nonetheless, if you listen to the press secretary make his morning announcement, you know—barring scandal or gaffe—what the lead will be on the evening news that night. During the Carter years, his appointments staff prepared weekly summaries of the president's schedule. For each day, they listed what the likely "news event" would be. Under normal circumstances, the predictions almost always came true. If the president was making an announcement about the U.S. Forest Service, the Forest Service would get that day's news—and would not be in the news again until another announcement was planned, or until it was the scene of scandal or internal dispute.

But, having accepted the president's chosen topic, reporters treat it in their own chosen way, usually with reflexive cynicism about an administration's intentions. The true lesson of the Watergate scandal was the value of hard digging—not only into scandals, but everywhere else. The *perceived* lesson of Watergate in the White House press room is the Dan Rather lesson: that a surly attitude—such as Rather, then a White House correspondent, displayed toward Nixon—can take the place of facts or analysis. Since the days of Watergate, reporters often have proved their tough-mindedness by asking insulting questions at presidential news conferences. TV correspondents feel they've paid their homage to the shade of Bob Woodward by ending their reports not with intelligent criticism but with a mock-significant twist. "The administration says its plans will work, but the true result is *still to be seen.* Dan Daring, NBC News, the White House."

The Public's Stake

The peculiarities of the White House press corps obviously matter to the few Americans who are presidents, candidates for president, or members of the White House staff. But do they matter to anybody else? They do because they shape the citizen's view of his government and of the public choices to be made in his name. The reporters' most important effect comes through the things their dispatches leave out.

One of those missing ingredients is a sense of history. By history, I do not mean ostentatious references to the Tariff of Abominations or the XYZ Affair. Rather, I mean a prudent awareness that others have walked many of the same paths before and that, by learning from the errors, we may be spared errors of our own.

For example, in the summer of 1979, Jimmy Carter decreed a sudden shake-up in his cabinet. He fired secretaries of several departments and shifted others to new jobs. The press coverage left no doubt in readers' minds that this was more than gaffe, it was disaster. Such turbulence had only one precedent, the reports implied—one that deepened the stain on Carter. On the day after his reelection in 1972, Nixon had demanded resignation letters from everyone on his staff.

In fact, there were many other precedents, less automatically damning to Carter. In 1830, the second year of Andrew Jackson's first term, tensions between two factions in his administration grew acute. The disputes were personified in the bitter rivalry between Martin Van Buren, then secretary of state, and John C. Calhoun, the vice president. Both men hoped to succeed Jackson as president. As the hostility became intolerable, Van Buren offered his resignation, and Jackson seized the opportunity to dissolve the whole cabinet, replacing it with one in which Calhoun's influence was diminished. Four years later, shortly after beginning his second term, Jackson juggled his cabinet again. To end bickering over economic policy, he fired and transferred half a dozen secretaries. Afterward, wrote Arthur M. Schlesinger, Jr., in *The Age of Jackson,* "the administration was streamlined for action."

Jackson's case was not an exact parallel to Carter's but it resembled the Carter changes more than did any of Nixon's acts. Had such a suggestion informed the frantic press commentary in the first days after Carter's firings (or had the administration thought to steer reporters to anecdotes like these), it might have indicated that changing a cabinet was not necessarily a sign of desperation or mental instability.

The nonhistorical approach of White House reporting is, if anything, more important when it comes to the consideration of public issues than to perceptions of a president's performance. By ignoring past attempts to grapple with enduring problems, the press can make presidents look less competent than they are, while misleading the public about the real choices that are available.

The safest bet about any administration's foreign policy is that, sooner or later, it will be the subject of stories about "Split in Middle East Policy." Reagan's administration was plagued by such stories, as was Carter's before it, and Nixon's and Ford's before that. Anything else would be a surprise, since American policy toward the Middle East has been divided at least since Israel became a nation in 1948.

The struggles between President Harry S Truman and James Forrestal, which eventually led to Forrestal's removal as secretary of defense in 1949 and his suicide five days later, can be read in part as a history of disagreement over the Zionist cause. American policy toward the Middle East always has been divided because, by American standards, there is something to be said for the claims of each side. To present this deep-seated dilemma as an indication of chaos in a particular administration is to undermine public comprehension of the problem and to diminish the chances of solving it.

The same pattern applies to discussions of nuclear policy. Since the early seventies, each president has been accused of ordering a "drastic" or "radical" change in America's retaliatory strategy. In the Ford administration, the change was the "counterforce" strategy announced by James Schlesinger, then the secretary of defense. In the Carter administration, it was "Presidential Directive 59." And in the Reagan administration it was the proposal to improve "command and control" systems and inaugurate a "nuclear war-fighting" capacity. What these decisions had in common, to judge by the coverage, was a stark departure from past practice. Before the change, according to the stories, the United States had stood by the policy of deterrence, in which its threat to destroy the Soviet population prevented the Soviet Union from destroying ours. After the change, it was said, the United States had seemingly made nuclear warfare more likely, by viewing it less cataclysmically.

In fact, at least since the early sixties, American policy has contained both "counterforce" and "countervalue" elements. (*Counterforce* implies attacking an enemy's military systems; *countervalue*, attacking the cities.) The technical and political premises that underly this strategy may be flawed, or they may be sound. But the public debate over nuclear strategy is distorted or retarded each time a new story emphasizes what is new in a particular administration's approach, rather than what has been constant for several decades.

Other illustrations abound. They include the plans to "reform" welfare or the civil service, which each new president announces on arrival, before running into the same obstacles that stopped his predecessors' plans. They also include the commitment to "cabinet government" that the last four presidents have made as they began their terms, only to abandon it two or three years later for reasons that were perfectly predictable to those who had studied the previous administration.

Presidents and their assistants are slow to learn from recent history because of the arrogance that naturally surrounds those who have just won a national election. If the old gang had so much to teach, why did it get beaten? Carter was elected largely on the strength of anti-Nixon sentiment, and Reagan on anti-Carter feelings. It would have been as unnatural for Carter and his advisers to think that Nixon's experience with cabinet government might instruct them as for Reagan's advisers to stop and learn from Carter's record.

This indifference to past experience is often reflected within the White House press, which suggests to its readers that each campaign, each inauguration, wipes the historical slate clean. This leaves the reading public in the same position as a teenaged boy on the verge of puberty, unaware of the powerful hormones that will soon be coursing through his body. As those hormones take hold and work their predictable effect, the young man will not understand the strange things happening to him.

The problems most likely to embroil an administration, from controlling the threat of nuclear war, to containing conflict in the Middle East, to reenergizing the great public and private bureaucracies on which the nation depends for schooling and medical care and economic expansion, did not start on one inauguration day, and they will not be solved by the next. The best an administration can hope for is steady progress. But if there is to be progress, rather than cycles of making the same mistakes every four years, each president must build on the work already done. That, in turn, requires a public that understands why the "Social Security problem" is more than a slogan for Democrats to use against Republicans at campaign time, why reinvigorating the federal bureaucracy involves more than denouncing it in speeches, and why the crucial issue in defense spending is not whether the Republicans are too wasteful and the Democrats too stingy but how the military organization really works. And where will most of the information necessary for citizens to understand these choices come from, if not from the press?

Many political reporters, echoing many politicians, would respond that such an emphasis on the "what" of government would take them too far away from their mission of "objectively" covering the news. There is a place for objectivity, in the sense of giving all sides to a political dispute a fair hearing; but political reporters unhesitatingly step beyond the strictures of objectivity when it comes to analyzing a campaign or pursuing a scandal. They do not see themselves as editorializing; instead, they are trying hard to give the reader a fuller understanding of the truth, as they have been able to discern it. Is it not at least as important for them to do so about the military budget or Medicare? An objective story about Medicare might report that its budget rose faster than that of any other major program during the late 1970s and early 1980s. That story is essential; but the reader also should be exposed to other stories, which explain why the increase occurred, how it might be contained, and whether proposed reforms have worked, when tried elsewhere.

This is not a call for reporters to vent their untutored opinions; on the contrary, reporters ought to apply the hard standards of appraisal and analysis to the substance of government. One illustration of this approach occurred in 1983. After a presidential commission declared that the American education system was failing, some political reporters converted "the education issue" into one more ingredient in the political horse race. But at many newspapers and magazines, reporters took a close look at *education*, not the politics of education. They compared schools where test scores were rising with ones where they were falling; they asked whether teachers' unions were serving students' interests, and whether and where more money would help. No single, simple answer emerged from these stories, but they gave their readers a way to think more constructively about improving schools.

Stories about gaffes and scandals, campaigns and internal dissent, do no harm in themselves. They may distort the meaning of presidential leadership, as the unremitting violence and conspiracy of television dramas distort the nature of day-by-day American life. The damage comes only from the neglect of the stories these reports displace, the ones that would help readers understand the public business that remains to be done.

White House reporters are ever suspicious about a president's efforts to manipulate them in an attempt to make himself look good. They deserve to be more worried about another form of manipulation: the campaign, in which press and president unintentionally collude, to keep citizens from understanding how their government works.

14. THE PRESIDENCY AND THE ORGANIZATION OF INTERESTS

Benjamin Ginsberg and Martin Shefter

A central concern of students of American politics is the capacity of contending economic interests and social forces to influence governmental institutions and policies. Thus scholars who are concerned with the presidency frequently explore the response of presidents to the electoral strategies, lobbying campaigns, or partisan efforts of organized groups. But whatever the precise topic of their research, almost all scholars take the interests, groups, and forces that compete for influence in the United States as givens. They assume that presidents must contend with, struggle against, or construct alliances from among whatever groups they find in society.

Presidents, however, are not in fact limited to dealing with some predefined or fixed constellation of forces. At times, presidents can reorganize interests, destroy established centers of power, and even call new groups into being. Thus, rather than simply contend with existing groups, presidents can attempt to enhance their own power and promote their own policy aims by constructing a new, more congenial configuration of social forces. That is, under the appropriate circumstances, presidents need not deal with the social universe exactly as they find it, but may instead reconstitute society. Presidents can do this by redefining the agenda of national politics, so as to reshape established political identities and alignments. They can mobilize new political forces and demobilize existing ones. And by altering the distribution of public benefits and burdens, presidents may be able to create new, politically relevant, interests.

Obviously, presidents cannot simply wish away obdurate opposing forces and create friendlier ones at will. Their capacity to reshape interests varies with political conditions.[1] Success is most likely during periods of political crisis when existing alliances, identities, and organizations are weakened. When the old order collapses, political leaders have their best opportunity to redefine the terms on which individuals are reintegrated into political life. Thus was Franklin D. Roosevelt able, during the crisis engendered by the Great Depression, to reshape the American political universe. He redefined the agenda of national politics by converting the federal government from a night watchman to a provider of services. By so doing Roosevelt promoted the formation of new groups seeking their share. In addition, the New Deal created the institutional mechanisms through which new interests, notably organized labor, could be mobilized into politics.

There are three ways in which presidents can attempt to reconstruct or reorganize the constellation of interests that play a significant role in the political process. First, presidents may be able to transform the political identities of established groups. Second, they may create new social and political forces by dividing existing groups. Finally, they may seek to construct new interests by uniting previously disparate elements. To return to the example of the New Deal, Roosevelt, through his old-age assistance programs, was able to transform the elderly, a social group that previously had no political relevance, into "senior citizens," a political force organized to defend and extend Social Security benefits. Through its regulatory and trade policies, the New Deal divided American business by encouraging businessmen to identify their interests more closely with their sector of the economy than with their economic class. This enabled the Democrats to establish significant enclaves of support within a business community that previously had been overwhelmingly Republican.[2] And through his social welfare programs, Roosevelt united previously disparate ethnic groups into a politically more coherent working class than ever had existed in American politics.

In sum, Roosevelt brought into being new social forces that would support his programs and bolster his power while disorganizing at least some of the interests that opposed him. Thus, the New Deal could be seen as involving not only the reorientation of American government and policy but also the reorganization of American society into the form with which his administration and its successors were thereafter to contend.

The regime created by Roosevelt collapsed during the 1960s and 1970s as a result of conflicts sparked by the Vietnam War, the civil rights revolution, and America's decline in the world economy. During the 1980s, forces led by Ronald Reagan sought to promote another enduring reconstitution of American government and politics. Following Roosevelt's example, the Reaganites sought to reorganize American society in order to create a stable foundation for their rule. The president's landslide reelection victory in 1984 seemed to indicate that the political forces he had called into being had become ascendant in American politics.

The Iran-contra controversy that erupted in 1986, however,

seriously threatened Reagan's personal standing and threw his administration into disarray. Nevertheless, a number of the new political groupings that were created during Reagan's first six years as president may continue to be important in American politics after his departure from office. This, at least, is the judgment of the Democratic Leadership Council (DLC), an influential group of public officials who argue that the Democratic party must accommodate the new forces of the Reaganite order. The DLC resembles the moderate wing of the post-Roosevelt Republican party, whose members asserted that their party's only hope for success was to come to terms with the groups created by the New Deal. Just as Roosevelt's Republican successors had to contend with organized labor and other political offshoots of the New Deal, so too may Ronald Reagan's Democratic successors live in a political world that bears the imprint of the Reaganites' effort to manipulate established social and political forces, transforming some, dividing or uniting others.

Transforming Political Identities

The Reaganites undertook to transform the political identities of three groups that had been associated with the Democratic party: white southerners, urban ethnics, and middle class voters. In each of these cases, the Reaganites did not simply base their appeal on the group's traditional political concerns. Instead, they attempted to change fundamentally and permanently the terms under which—and the institutions through which—the group's members were integrated into politics.

From Rednecks to Evangelicals

Reagan and his supporters sought to transform white southerners from rednecks, that is, individuals integrated into the political process mainly on the basis of their racial concerns, into evangelicals who are integrated into politics primarily through their religious orientations. For a century after the Civil War, white southerners had participated in politics through the Democratic party, which had defended the southern caste system. Southern whites were linked to the Democrats not simply by their racial attitudes, but also by local political institutions that were connected with the party—county commissions, sheriffs, judges, voting registrars, and the like. These institutions gave whites preferential access to governmental services and guaranteed white political power by excluding blacks from participation in government and politics.[3]

The civil rights revolution and, in particular, the Voting Rights Act of 1965 destroyed the institutional foundations of the traditional southern Democratic regime by preventing local governmental institutions from being used to maintain white privilege at the expense of black political subordination. The disruption of this system gave the Republicans an opportunity to win the support of southern whites. In their effort to woo southern white voters permanently into the Republican party, however, the Reaganites did not copy the traditional southern Democratic tactic of emphasizing racial issues. Instead, they relied upon another, still vital, set of southern institutions, namely, the evangelical churches that are such a prominent feature of the southern landscape. By appealing to southern whites on the basis of their religious beliefs, the Reaganites hoped to use these churches to forge enduring links between white voters and the Republican party. The essence of their appeal was to politicize the moral concerns of white southerners by concentrating on such issues as abortion, school prayer, and pornography. At the same time, Reagan and his followers made evangelical churches, in effect, organizational components of the new Republican party. For example, funds and organizational support were provided to these churches for voter registration activities.

As a result of the Reaganites' efforts, southern whites increasingly have been integrated into politics on the basis of their evangelical religious affiliations rather than their racial concerns. This shift has helped to give the Republicans a firm social base in the white South for the first time in the party's 130-year history. In 1984, for example, Reagan received the votes of 67 percent of those white southerners who described themselves as "born again." [4]

From Workers to Patriots and Right-to-Lifers

In their efforts to strengthen the electoral base of the Republican party, Reagan and his supporters also had a great deal of success in transforming members of urban ethnic groups from workers, who were integrated into political life on the basis of their economic status, into patriots and right-to-lifers. By *patriots* we mean individuals whose political identities and affiliations are shaped by nationalistic senti- ments. Right-to-lifers are those whose political attitudes and activities are based upon moral, usually religious, values.

In their capacity as workers, urban ethnics had been integrated into politics during the New Deal era by organizations that were affiliated with the Democratic party: trade unions, political machines, and urban service bureaucracies, which increasingly had come to perform the functions of political machines. These institutions provided members of urban ethnic groups with access to public and private employment at relatively high wages, with social services, and with preferential access to locally administered federal programs. At the same time, trade unions and urban machines and bureaucracies functioned as the local institutional foundations of the national Democratic party, mobilizing urban ethnics to support Democratic candidates.[5]

The Reaganites weakened the links between the Democrats and urban ethnics by attacking these institutions. The administration undermined organized labor by encouraging employers to engage in antiunion practices; indeed, it set an example by destroying the Professional Air Traffic Controllers Organization when the group conducted a strike in 1981.[6] In addition, Reagan appointed commissioners hostile to organized labor to the National Labor Relations Board, an agency formerly dominated by labor sympathizers. Moreover, the administration supported policies of deregulation that provide business firms with a strong incentive to rid themselves of their unions. Finally, the Reagan administration's fiscal and monetary policies, by driving up real interest rates and the value of the dollar, eroded the competitiveness of many sectors of American industry in domestic and world markets, thereby increasing unemployment in these sectors and reducing labor's bargaining power.

The Reagan administration attacked urban political machines and service bureaucracies mainly through its domestic spending reductions. The programs whose budgets have suffered the most under Reagan are precisely those that once provided urban governments with substantial revenues and allowed them to dispense a large number of jobs, such as the comprehensive employment and training program (CETA). The Justice Department also attacked urban machines and bureaucracies by launching a series of investigations of corruption in municipal government (for example, Operation Graylord), whose primary targets were large cities controlled by the Democrats.[7]

The attack on labor unions, political machines, and municipal bureaucracies diminished these institutions' ability to provide benefits to members of urban ethnic groups, and thus undermined the institutional linkage between these voters and the Democratic party. As in the case of southern whites, the disruption of these institutional foundations gave the Republicans an opportunity to win the support of what formerly had been a staunch Democratic constituency.

In appealing to urban ethnics, Reagan was handicapped in one way: in their capacity as workers many of these voters were seriously hurt by his administration's economic and tax programs, which were designed mainly to serve the interests of the upper middle class and certain segments of the business community. Instead of seeking to appeal to members of urban ethnic groups on economic grounds, however, the Reaganites attempted to secure and institutionalize their support on two other bases. First, they used Catholic and, to a lesser extent, conservative Protestant churches to link urban ethnics, like white southerners, to the Republican party on the basis of their moral and religious convictions. The president's supporters sought to politicize these concerns by taking up so-called family issues—above all, the issue of abortion. At the same time, just as they made southern evangelical churches organizational components of the Republican party, the Reaganites sought to use Catholic and conservative Protestant churches in the North, some of which have made it their business to rally the faithful against proabortion candidates, for organizational support and voter mobilization.[8] The importance of this political transformation was indicated by the 1984 election. White working class voters who belonged to trade unions but did not regularly attend a church gave Reagan only 46 percent of their votes. By contrast, among white working class voters who attended a church regularly but did not belong to a union, Reagan received 67 percent of the vote.

In addition to using moral appeals, the Reaganites also attempted to politicize the patriotic sentiments of urban ethnics. In this effort, the president was for a time able to harness the national media—an institution whose editorial pages and televised commentary were frequently hostile to his policies—by creating news events filled with patriotic symbols and appeals that the media could neither attack nor ignore. The spectacle created to accompany the unveiling of the refurbished Statue of Liberty in 1986 is a prime example. In addition, where the risks of failure were low, the Reagan administration used military force abroad not only to demonstrate America's resolve to foreigners but to reinforce national pride among Americans as well. Again, the media were the president's unwilling allies in this effort, as indicated, for example, by news coverage of the 1986 bombing of Libya. Of course, Reagan's capacity to use the media in this way was not unlimited. Eventually, in the Iran-contra affair, the president's opponents were able to harness the media for their own purposes and, through a series of journalistic investigations and disclosures, seriously damage Reagan's political standing.

From Beneficiaries to Taxpayers

Finally, the Reagan administration sought to convince many middle income urban and suburban voters to regard themselves less as beneficiaries of federal programs than as taxpayers, whose chief concern is the cost of government. After World War II many middle income voters were integrated into the political process and linked to the Democratic party by federal programs that subsidized mortgages, expanded access to higer education, and, not least important, promoted social peace with welfare programs that placated the poor and labor programs that reduced working class militancy. In exchange, middle class voters gave their support to the various expenditure programs through which the Democratic party channeled public funds to its other constituent groups: crop subsidies for farmers, maritime subsidies for the shipping industry, and so on. This elaborate logrolling arrangement—termed "interest group liberalism" by Theodore Lowi—enabled the Democratic party to accommodate the claims of the host of disparate groups it sought to include in its electoral coalition.[9]

During the 1960s and 1970s, many of the benefits that middle income voters had come to expect from federal programs and policies were sharply curtailed. For example, rising mortgage interest rates increased housing costs, affirmative action programs seemed to threaten the middle class's privileged access to higher education, and social peace was disrupted by urban violence and riots. The curtailment of these benefits undermined the political basis of the support that many middle income voters had given to the Democratic party. This provided the Republicans with an opportunity to win their loyalty.[10]

In wooing middle income voters, the Republicans chose not to base their appeal on new federal benefits. (To be sure, the Republicans did not repeal any existing middle class benefit programs.) Instead, the president and his followers sought to link these voters to the Republican party in their capacity as taxpayers. That is, Reagan declared tax relief to be a central political issue and, in 1981, his administration provided middle and upper income votes with a sizable reduction in federal income tax rates. In 1984, an important element in the president's successful campaign against Walter Mondale was his warning to middle income voters that the Democrats wanted to take their tax cuts away. Thus, although in 1976 only 2 percent of middle class voters identified taxes and spending as important national problems, by 1984, 23 percent of voters with above average incomes did so. Of these voters, 67 percent cast their ballots for Reagan.

The main reason that the Reaganites sought to appeal to middle income voters as taxpayers rather than as beneficiaries was that they hoped in this way to erode middle class support for domestic expenditures in general. From the president's perspective, transforming middle class voters into taxpayers was an important step not only in linking these voters to the Republican party, but also in undermining the entire apparatus of interest group liberalism through which the Democrats had maintained the allegiance of their various constituencies. Joined to the transformation of southerners into evangelicals and of urban ethnics into patriots and right-to-lifers, the transformation of middle income voters into taxpayers promised to disorganize the Democrats' political base.

318 Ginsberg and Shefter

Dividing Established Political Forces

At the same time that they sought to transform the identities of established political forces, the Reaganites also attempted to divide a number of groups that had been more or less allied with one another and with the Democrats during the New Deal era, and to attach some of those groups to the Republican party. Many Reagan administration efforts to alter longstanding public policies can be understood in this light. A major technique the New Dealers and their successors had employed to build a solid base of support was to fashion public policies and political practices that not only linked disparate political forces together, but prevented conflicts from emerging to disrupt the regime over which the Democrats presided. Reagan and his allies attempted to destroy these accommodations through their policies of business deregulation, tax reduction, and domestic spending cuts.

Business Deregulation

During the New Deal period the federal government established or extended a regime of regulation over numerous sectors of the American economy: airlines, telecommunications, petroleum, coal, banking, securities, and interstate trucking. Characteristically, these regulations restricted price competition among firms within the regulated industry, and in some cases erected barriers to the entry of new firms. To the extent that firms within these industries could pass added costs on to their customers without having to worry about being undersold by competitors, they lost an incentive to control their labor costs. Consequently, union-management relations in most regulated industries were less adversarial than cooperative in character: rather than fight one another over wages and work rules, unions and employers entered the political arena as allies to defend and extend the regulatory regime and to secure direct or indirect public subsidies for their industry.

During the late 1970s an unlikely coalition of conservatives and consumer advocates, asserting that these business-labor accommodations served "special interests" at the expense of the "public interest," secured a substantial measure of deregulation.[11] Through deregulation, conservatives sought to get business to break its accommodations with organized labor; consumer advocates, for their part, wanted to weaken the labor unions and business interests that were among their main rivals for influence within the Democratic party. Conservatives have had more reason to be satisfied with the consequences of deregulation. Especially in airlines, telecommunications, and trucking, deregulation has led to the emergence of nonunion firms that undersell the established giants in their industry, which in turn has compelled those giants to demand give-backs from their unions to lower their own labor costs.

It is little wonder, then, that the Reagan administration sought to maintain the momentum of deregulation. Deregulation led many in business to abandon their alliance with union leaders and join other corporate executives to support patterns of labor relations and public policy—and to support politicians—consonant with the new order that the Reaganites are seeking to construct.

Tax Reduction

Another group that gave substantial support to the Democrats during the 1960s and 1970s—college-educated professionals—has experienced deep political divisions as a result of the Reagan administration's fiscal policies. Socially this group is quite heterogeneous, ranging from ill-paid social workers to lavishly compensated attorneys—so much so, in fact, that sociologists have debated whether it is meaningful to speak of this "new class" as a coherent social and political force.[12] But groups are constituted in the political realm, and during the 1960s and 1970s political entrepreneurs were able to mobilize large numbers of professionals on behalf of liberalism by using the issues of Vietnam and environmentalism.

Reagan sought to divide the new class by shifting the political debate to the issues of tax and budget cuts. The 1981 tax cut was promoted as a means of stimulating the private sector; the tax reform plan that the president made the centerpiece of his second administration was especially beneficial to professionals with high salaries. Professionals in a position to take advantage of the new opportunities—namely, those who work in the private sector—were attracted into the Republican party.

At the same time, the administration's reductions in federal domestic expenditures restricted opportunities for one category of professionals—namely, those who work in the public and nonprofit sectors. The Reaganites, however, were not in the least unhappy to see elementary school teachers, social workers, and university professors try to defend their interests by becoming increasingly active in Democrat party politics. They calculated that the more committed the Democrats became to the cause of boosting domestic expenditures, the firmer would become the commitment of middle-income taxpayers, business owners, and private sector professionals to the Republican party.

The Reaganite strategy was quite successful in 1984. College graduates working in the public sector awarded Reagan only 40 percent of their votes. On the other hand, college graduates in the private sector supported Reagan by the overwhelming margin of 68 percent to Mondale's 32 percent. In terms of party identification, among college graduates in the public sector, Democrats outnumbered Republicans 54 percent to 20 percent. By contrast, among private sector college graduates, 40 percent identified with the Republican party and only 29 percent with the Democrats.

Domestic Spending Cuts

Reaganite fiscal policies divided another set of forces that had been tacitly allied with one another from the 1930s to the 1970s—the beneficiaries of federal expenditure programs. Under the New Deal system, the claims that disparate groups made upon the federal treasury all were accommodated through logrolling arrangements that characteristically were negotiated by the Democratic leaders in Congress. These logrolling arrangements entailed a steady growth of the public sector through a process of budgetary "incrementalism," as Aaron Wildavsky termed it at the time.[13] This pattern of policy making depended in turn upon a steady expansion of public revenues, which was achieved without the political conflict that would have resulted from repeated increases in nominal tax rates by allowing inflation to steadily increase real rates of federal income taxation through what came to be called "bracket creep."

By slashing federal tax rates and introducing indexation to prevent bracket creep, the Reaganites undermined the fiscal foundations of the New Deal pattern of accommodations among the beneficiaries of federal expenditure programs. The enormous deficit that was created by the administration's fiscal policies came to exert constant pressure upon the domestic programs' funding levels and even their survival. To protect their favorite programs in this fiscal environment, groups such as farmers, organized labor, and advocates of welfare spending were compelled to engage in zero-sum conflict, in contrast to the positive-sum politics of the New Deal system: one group's gain now was another group's loss.[14] Divorced from their former coalition partners, many members of these groups moved toward the Republican camp—often, as we saw earlier, on the basis of appeals quite different from those that had linked them to the Democrats.

Unifying Disparate Groups

Not only did the Reagan administration seek to transform the political identities of established groups and divide others, it also created new interests to support the Republican party by uniting several previously disparate groups. Three such alliances were especially important: the Reaganites united Catholic and Protestant religious conservatives; they forged linkages among business owners, managers and upper-income professionals, essentially restoring the political unity of the bourgeoisie; and, they politically reunified American business and attached it to the Republican party.

Uniting Religious Conservatives

Conservatives used family issues, particularly abortion, to promote an alliance between Catholics and evangelical Protestants and to attach both to the Republican party. Indeed, what came to be called the right-to-life issue was quite consciously invented for this purpose by Richard Vigurie, Paul Weyrich, Howard Phillips, and other conservative activists.[15] Seeking to take advantage of the furor caused by the Supreme Court's pro-choice decision in *Roe v. Wade,* these politicians first used the issue, as we saw, to promote the political transformation of southen whites and urban ethnics. They then convinced Catholic and evangelical Protestant leaders (and even some Orthodox Jews) that they had common interests, and worked with these leaders to arouse public opposition to abortion. The first step in this process was to shift public sympathy away from victims of the "epidemic of teenage pregnancy" and toward the fetuses of women who have abortions. Fetuses were renamed "the unborn," emphasizing their humanity, and the feelings—and rights—of other human beings were attributed to them.[16]

To dramatize the plight of the unborn, right-to-life leaders sponsored well-publicized Senate hearings at which testimony, photographs, and other exhibits were presented to illustrate the violent effects of abortion upon its innocent victims. At the same time, publicists for the movement produced leaflets, articles, books, and films, such as *The Silent Scream,* to highlight the agony said to be felt by the unborn as they were aborted. All this underscored the movement's claim that abortion was nothing less than the savage murder of millions of innocent human beings. Finally, Catholic and evangelical Protestant religious leaders were roused to denounce abortion from their pulpits and on televised religious programs, especially on the Christian Broadcasting Network (CBN). Right-to-life activists also organized demonstrations and disruptions at abortion clinics throughout the nation. This well-organized campaign struck a responsive chord among millions of Americans and played a role in Reagan's victories in the 1980 and 1984 presidential elections. With the right-to-life issue, conservative politicians thus united two forces, Catholics and Protestant evangelicals, that had been bitter opponents through much of American history.

Reconstituting the Bourgeoisie

The Reaganites also sought to reunite upper middle class professionals with business owners and managers. During the 1960s and 1970s, as mentioned earlier, upper middle class professionals had been important components of the New Politics movement. This movement imposed substantial burdens on business, especially through environmental, consumer, and occupational health and safety legislation that limited the goods manufacturers could produce and the ways they could produce them, and that required corporations to invest capital in equipment to promote a cleaner environment, safer products, and healthier workplaces.

Through its tax programs and domestic budget cuts, the Reagan administration sought to divide the New Politics movement and to win the support of upper middle class professionals working in the private sector. The main difficulty the Reaganites faced in this endeavor was the tension between their desire to win the support of middle class voters with substantial tax cuts, and the president's simultaneous pledge to initiate dramatic increases in defense spending. The administration sought to resolve this apparent contradiction by adopting an economic theory and a fiscal policy that would link the interests of upper middle class professionals and business through the Republican party.

The economic theory was, of course, the supply-side doctrine proposed by conservative economist Arthur Laffer. The economic details of the theory need not concern us; indeed, most orthodox economists ridiculed it. However, supply-side economics was more important as a political theory than as an economic doctrine. Supply-side theory purported to show that it was possible to cut taxes and increase spending simultaneously. In adopting it, Reagan was asserting, first, that upper middle class professionals and those segments of the business community that benefited from military spending had common interests, and, second, that his administration's programs would be oriented to those areas of shared interest.

The fiscal policies Reagan pursued after taking office fulfilled his political goals. The administration's tax cuts gave capital-intensive industries very generous depreciation allowances; its military spending greatly benefited the defense industry and thousands of subcontractors; and the fiscal stimulus of the ensuing deficit boosted corporate profits, especially in service industries. At the same time, Reaganite fiscal policies gave high-income professionals substantial tax cuts, access to foreign goods at low prices, and historically high rates of return on the securities the government sold to investors to finance its deficits.

In linking both upper-income professionals and business to the Republican party, the Reaganites have politically reunited the bourgeoisie. The political division between business and professionals during the 1960s and early 1970s had opened the way for the enactment of policies that were detrimental to the economic interests of both groups—policies that fostered inflation and subjected business to hostile forms of regulation. The reunification of the bourgeoisie has enabled business and professionals to pursue interests they have in common and has provided the Republicans with the support of a class that, when united, constitutes what is arguably the nation's most powerful political force.

Reunifying Business

Before Reagan and his followers could fully reunify the bourgeoisie they faced the task of uniting the business community itself. During the decades after the New Deal the Democrats had reached an accommodation with many segments of big business—internationally competitive firms that benefited from the Roosevelt administration's free trade policies, firms in capital-intensive industries that found it relatively easy to make concessions to organized labor, and defense contractors that benefited from a foreign policy of internationalism.[17] However, proprietors of smaller firms that were not involved in international markets often found Democratic labor and social programs onerous, and characteristically aligned themselves with the Republican party. This breach between Wall Street and Main Street undermined the political potency of American business.

During the 1970s the accommodation between big business and the Democratic party was severely strained by two developments that Reagan sought to exploit. The erosion of America's position in the world economy caused firms that previously had accepted the high labor costs and taxes associated with the Democrats to be no longer willing to do so. And Democratic support for environmental, consumer, and other new regulatory programs further alienated many of the party's allies in the business community. In campaigning for the presidency, Reagan appealed for the support of business by indicating that he would trim costly social programs, weaken the influence of organized labor, and relax the environmental rules and other forms of regulation that had been sponsored by Democratic politicians during the 1960s and 1970s. Moreover, Reagan offered the thousands of firms that could benefit from military contracts substantial increases in defense spending.

These Reaganite policies have brought about the political reunification of American business under Republican auspices.[18] This reunification was a critical element in the 1980 and 1984 elections as well as a significant portent for the future of American politics. It contributes to the Republican party's recent six-to-one advantage over the Democrats in raising campaign funds: in 1985-86, for example, the Republicans raised $146 million to the Democrats' $25 million.[19] These campaign funds, in turn, give the Reublicans a decisive edge in the use of expensive new political technologies—computers, phone banks, polls, and television advertising—that are important ingredients of political success in the 1980s.

To retain the support of the newly united business community, the Republican party must continue to foster prosperity. If the Republicans have had an Achilles' heel it has been the enormous budget and trade deficits that were generated by the combination of major tax cuts and major increases in military spending. During the early years of Reagan's presidency the budget deficit kept real interest rates at historically high levels and contributed to the dollar's reaching record high levels as well. High interest rates, in turn, restricted business investment, and the high dollar reduced the competitiveness of American firms in both domestic and foreign markets.

During the course of the Reagan presidency, however, foreign capital began to flood into the United States, helping to finance both the federal deficit and American business investment. Foreign investors now purchase more than 20 percent of all U.S. government securities; markets in these securities have developed in Tokyo and London, with daily trading volumes exceeding $1 billion. A major reason for this inflow of capital was that every time Reagan denounced the Soviet Union and announced his support for a major weapons system, foreign investors concluded that the United States was the safest place in the world to invest their funds. In this way, Reaganism was a seamless web: its politics helped make it economically viable, and its economics helped make it politically viable.

Moreover, the budget and trade deficits produced by the Reagan administration's fiscal policies were not simply problems. These deficits also provided the Reaganites with important political benefits and opportunities. First, by making it difficult for politicians to appeal for votes with new public expenditure programs, the budget deficit impeded efforts by the Democrats to reconstruct their political base.[20] More important, the deficits functioned as a novel revenue-collection apparatus that, at least in the short run, enabled the Reaganites to finance government expenditures without raising taxes and alienating their political constituency.

This apparatus worked as follows. By increasing the value of the dollar, the Reagan administration's fiscal policies encouraged Americans to purchase foreign, mainly Japanese, goods. At the same time, America's high interest rates and political stability encouraged foreign bankers—again, most notably the Japanese—to purchase U.S. Treasury securities with the profits their nation's manufacturers make selling goods in the United States. Thus, during the 1980s, what might be called "Toyota dollars" or "autodollars" were recycled by Japanese banks, much as "petrodollars" were recycled by American banks in the 1970s. These autodollars, invested in U.S. government securities, were used to help finance the Reagan deficits. In essence, Japanese industrialists and bankers served as tax collectors for the Reagan administration. Although Americans, in their capacity as voters, demonstrated in 1984 that they opposed increased taxation as a means of financing the federal government's expenditure, as consumers they willingly—indeed, enthusiastically—handed over billions of dollars for this purpose whenever they purchased Japanese and other foreign-made goods. The costs of this revenue system were borne by unemployed workers in the manufacturing sector, and by employers who failed to restructure their firms to meet foreign competition.

Not all business interests, however, were happy with these fiscal policies and practices. Reagan's program produced a conflict between what might be termed the traditionalist and supply-side camps within the Republican party. The traditionalists, whose chief spokesman was Republican senator Robert Dole, asserted that the nation's first economic priority must be to reduce the deficit—through budget cuts, and, if necessary, tax increases. The supply-siders, whose leaders included Representative Jack Kemp, were prepared to accept continuing budget deficits in order to protect Reaganite tax cuts, and thus to avoid reductions in defense spending and in politically popular programs that benefited middle class constituencies.

The conflict between traditionalists and supply-siders had two sources. The first was a difference in economic and political perspectives. Traditionalist Republicans feared that continuing huge deficits would wreck the economy, and hence their party's electoral fortunes. Supply-siders asserted that the deficit posed no immediate threat to the economy, and they feared that the steps the traditionalists proposed to cut the deficit—such as reducing Social Security benefits and raising taxes—could severely damage Republican electoral prospects.

The second source of conflict between traditionalists and supply-siders was a cleavage between two sets of interests in the Republican party. Large deficits, high interest rates, and high dollars hurt sectors of the economy that produced goods in the United States for export (such as agriculture), that faced competition in the American market from goods produced abroad (such as steel), or that were adversely affected by high real estate rates (such as local banks and thrift institutions). These interests were the mainstays of the traditionalist camp. Other sectors of American business, however, benefited from Reaganite fiscal policies. For example, firms that manufactured goods abroad for sale in the United States, including much of the computer and telecommunications industries, benefited from high dollars, as did domestic importers of goods produced by foreign manufacturers. In addition, firms in the service sector were not severely affected by interest rates or the value of the dollar, but did benefit greatly from the macroeconomic stimulus provided by budget deficits. At one time, the national banking and financial communities probably would have supported the traditionalists. However, the banking industry in the 1980s was neither as vigorous nor as united as in earlier party battles. Banking deregulation and the development of new financial instruments, such as interest-rate and foreign-currency futures, enabled large financial institutions to hedge against adverse interest- and exchange-rate fluctuations, thereby reducing their fear of government deficits. Although the financial community was not enthusiastic about deficit spending, concern about budget deficits was not its first political priority—as Wall Street's overwhelming support for Reagan in 1984 indicated.

Even without the ardent support of the banking industry, the traditionalists were able to force the Reagan administration to alter its tax and fiscal policies significantly. In December 1985 Republican traditionalists joined with congressional Democrats to secure the enactment of the Gramm-Rudman-Hollings deficit reduction act. This act set deficit reduction targets and provided for across-the-board cuts in defense and domestic programs if the targets were not met. Calculating that the president would be unwilling to accept reductions in military spending, the Democrats saw Gramm-Rudman-Hollings as a way to compel him to accept tax increases. Republican traditionalists, on the other hand, were willing to take either tax increases or spending cuts—their goal was simply to reduce the budget deficit by whatever means necessary. The act also was supported by some supply-siders, including Sen. Philip Gramm himself, who wished both to prevent their political opponents from capitalizing on the deficit issue and to force Congress to accept further domestic spending cuts.

Reagan signed the Gramm-Rudman-Hollings Act into law, but at the same time his administration moved to eliminate the sources of traditionalist opposition to its policies by working aggressively to lower the value of the American dollar relative to foreign currencies, in particular the Japanese yen. Reagan's appointees on the Federal Reserve Board led one prong of this effort by reducing U.S. interest rates. In the so-called Plaza agreement of September 1985, Treasury

Secretary James Baker and Federal Reserve Board chairman Paul Volcker led the other by persuading their foreign counterparts to intervene in world currency markets to lower the dollar. They were able to do so by urging that this would provide the best hope for meeting the threat of protectionist legislation in Congress. Reducing the value of the dollar was expected to make American goods more competitive abroad and foreign (mainly Japanese) goods less competitive in the American market. By helping American producers meet foreign competition in both the domestic and the export arenas the Reagan administration sought to placate the traditionalists.

Of course, a reduction of the trade deficit, for all it might do to mollify the traditionalists, threatened to undermine the very mechanism through which the Reagan administration funded its budget deficit. The tax reform act that was signed into law by the president in 1986, however, promised a solution to this problem. Tax reform sought to finance a reduction in individual federal income tax rates by restricting some business tax preferences. To the extent that corporate tax increases could be passed on to consumers, tax reform would result in American corporations supplanting Japanese corporations as revenue agents for the American state. In effect, then, the Reagan administration moved to finance its expenditures through a "Chevy levy" rather than a Toyota tax.[21] To be sure, increased taxes on American manufacturing corporations could threaten the competitiveness of the nation's products, reducing the proceeds from any such fiscal arrangement. However, the U.S. Treasury could seek to reduce the value of the dollar, as it did in 1987, to lower the prices of American products abroad and pressure foreign governments to pursue policies that would increase the market for U.S. manufactured goods.[22] Such a strategy might overcome the division between supply-side and traditionalist interests, thereby cementing the reunification of American business under Republican auspices. To achieve this outcome the Republican party might be willing to forgo some of the political advantages it previously derived from the budget deficit.

Conclusion

By transforming, dividing, and unifying different preexisting groups and interests, Ronald Reagan and his associates attempted both to undermine a number of political forces that otherwise might enhance their opponents' base of political support and to create new groups that would strengthen their own social base. In so doing, they sought to create a new constellation of forces in American politics, one that would be more consonant with the president's programmatic and partisan goals and that would increase the probability of the Reagan regime's enduring. Rather than shape his policies to meet the demands of society, Reagan undertook to reconstitute society to fit his policies. In essence, to build a more secure foundation for their supply-side regime, the Reaganites sought to transform the United States into a supply-side society.

The presidency, however, is not the only institution available to political entrepreneurs in their efforts to govern the nation and reshape American society. During the late 1960s and early 1970s, opponents of the policies and practices of the Johnson and Nixon administrations used congressional investigations, media exposés, and judicial processes to attack the White House, drive Johnson and Nixon from office, and impose limits on the power of the presidency. The institutions that triumphed over the White House in these conflicts themselves became major centers of power and counterweights to the presidency.[23]

Reagan's efforts to circumvent the limitations these institutions imposed upon presidential power—in particular, congressional restrictions on and media exposure of covert intelligence operations—precipitated the Iran-contra affair and provided his opponents an opportunity to launch a full-scale attack upon his administration. It is striking that after the controversy erupted, all the major actors in the political system—including the administration itself—took for granted that the appropriate response was for Congress to establish special investigating committees, for the national news media to deploy reporters, and for the federal judiciary to appoint an independent counsel to investigate, expose, and prosecute the officials who were involved in the affair. This response indicates the extent to which the role of these institutions as counterweights to the presidency has become institutionalized. Equally striking was how rapidly the Reagan administration was thrown into disarray by their attack.

Although Reagan's opponents very effectively used congressional, media, and judicial investigations to disrupt his administration, it remains an open question whether they will be able to undo the political transformations he fostered. Some Democrats would like to rebuild the New Deal coalition but, as noted earlier, the influential Democratic Leadership Council argues that the party can hope to be successful only by coming to terms with the new political forces that were created by Reaganism. Like members of the moderate wing of the post-New Deal Republican party—derided by Old Guard conservatives as "me-too" Republicans—who presented themselves to voters as the most competent administrators of the welfare state, the "me-too" Democrats of the DLC seek to convince the political interests created by Reaganism that the Democrats can better protect the economic gains they achieved during the 1980s and manage the nation's foreign affairs more prudently. In other words, the DLC is seeking to use the institutions that have emerged as a counterweight to the presidency not to disrupt or disorganize these new political interests but rather to weaken their attachment to the Republicans.

Thus, efforts by presidents to refashion the constellation of political forces with which they and their successors must deal are open to challenge and are not always successful. Moreover, political conditions do not permit most presidents even to attempt to reconstruct society in this way. But even though society is not often amenable to presidential reconstruction, the groups and forces with which U.S. chief executives contend ultimately are a product not simply of autonomous social processes but also of struggles between presidents and their opponents. In the United States it is through conflicts between the presidency and other political institutions that society is shaped by politics. This is the true significance of the presidency in American political life.

Notes

1. Stephen Skowronek, "Presidential Leadership in Political Time," Chapter 6 in this volume.
2. Compare E. E. Schattschneider, *The Semi-Sovereign People* (New York: Holt, 1960), especially pp. 78-96, with Thomas Ferguson, "From Normalcy to New Deal: Industrial Structure, Party Competition and American Public Policy in the Great Depression," *International Organization* 38 (Winter 1984): 42-94.
3. V. O. Key, Jr., *Southern Politics* (New York: Random House, 1949). Also J. Morgan Kousser, *The Shaping of Southern Politics* (New Haven: Yale University Press, 1974).
4. These and other 1984 election data in this chapter are from the National Election Survey of the University of Michigan's Center for Political Studies. On the role of evangelicalism in the contemporary Republican coalition, see Gillian Peele, *Revival and Reaction* (New York: Oxford University Press, 1985); see also Loch Johnson and Charle S. Bullock III, "The New Religious Right and the 1980 Election," in *Do Elections Matter?*, ed. Benjamin Ginsberg and Alan Stone (New York: M. E. Sharpe, 1986), 148-163.
5. John Mollenkopf, *The Contested City* (Princeton: Princeton University Press, 1983), chap. 2.
6. Michael Goldfield, *The Decline of Unions in the United States* (Chicago: University of Chicago Press, 1987). See also Thomas Edsall, *The New Politics of Inequality* (New York: W. W. Norton, 1985), chap. 4.
7. Martin Shefter, *Political Crisis/Fiscal Crisis* (New York: Basic Books, 1987), xi-xx.
8. Connie Paige, *The Right to Lifers* (New York: Summit, 1983).
9. Theodore J. Lowi, *The End of Liberalism* (New York: W. W. Norton, 1966).
10. Mike Davis, *Prisoners of the American Dream* (London: Verso, 1986), chaps. 4 and 5.

11. Martha Derthick and Paul Quirk, *The Politics of Deregulation* (Washington, D.C.: Brookings Institution, 1985).
12. Steven Brint, " 'New Class' and Cumulative Trend Explanations of the Liberal Political Attitudes of Professionals," *American Journal of Sociology* 90 (July 1984): 30-71.
13. Aaron Wildavsky, *The Politics of the Budgetary Process* (Boston: Little, Brown, 1964).
14. John Ferejohn, "Congress and Redistribution," in *Making Economic Policy in Congress,* ed. Allen Schick (Washington, D.C.: American Enterprise Institute, 1983).
15. Paige, *The Right to Lifers.*
16. Benjamin Ginsberg, *The Captive Public* (New York: Basic Books, 1986), chap. 4.
17. Peter Gourevitch, *Politics in Hard Times* (Ithaca, N.Y.: Cornell University Press, 1986), chap. 4.
18. Edsall, *New Politics of Inequality,* chap. 3; see also Thomas Ferguson and Joel Rogers, *Right Turn* (New York: Hill and Wang, 1986).
19. Thomas Edsall, "Both Parties Get the Company's Money—but the Boss Backs the GOP," *Washington Post National Weekly Edition,* September 16, 1986, 14.
20. Paul Peterson and John Chubb, *The New Direction in American Politics* (Washington, D.C.: Brookings Institution, 1985), chap. 13.
21. To cope with the falling dollar and the threat of American protectionism many foreign manufacturers, most notably the Japanese, built factories in the United States. As a consequence, the American subsidiaries of foreign firms also came to serve as revenue agents for the Reagan regime. See *New York Times,* August 9, 1986, 1.
22. *New York Times,* January 23, 1987, 1.
23. Benjamin Ginsberg and Martin Shefter, "A Critical Realignment? The New Politics, the Reconstituted Right, and the 1984 Election," in *The Elections of 1984,* ed. Michael Nelson (Washington, D.C.: CQ Press, 1985).

15. THE PRESIDENCY AND POLITICAL PARTIES

Sidney M. Milkis

The relationship between the presidency and the American party system has always been a difficult one. The architects of the Constitution established a nonpartisan president who, with the support of the judiciary, was intended to play the leading institutional role in checking and controlling the "violence of faction" that the framers feared would destroy the fabric of representative democracy. Even after the presidency became a more partisan office during the early part of the nineteenth century, its authority continued to depend upon an ability to rise above partisanship. The president is nominated by a party but, unlike the British prime minister, is not elected by it.

The inherent tension between the presidency and the party system reached a critical point during the 1930s. The creation of the modern presidency, arguably the most significant institutional legacy of Franklin D. Roosevelt's New Deal, ruptured severely the limited, albeit significant, bond that linked presidents to their parties. In fact, the modern presidency was crafted with the intention of reducing the influence of the party system on American politics. In this sense Roosevelt's extraordinary party leadership contributed to the decline of the American party system. This decline continued—even accelerated—under the administrations of subsequent modern presidents, notably Lyndon B. Johnson and Richard M. Nixon. Under Ronald Reagan, however, the party system has shown at least some signs of transformation and renewal.

New Deal Party Politics, Presidential Reform, and the Decline of the American Party System

The New Deal seriously questioned the adequacy of the traditional natural rights liberalism of John Locke and the framers, which emphasized the need to limit constitutionally the scope of government's responsibilities.[1] The modern liberalism that became the public philosophy of the New Deal entailed a fundamental reappraisal of the concept of rights. As Roosevelt first indicated in his 1932 campaign speech at the Commonwealth Club in San Francisco, effective political reform would require, at minimum, the development of "an economic declaration of rights, an economic constitutional order," grounded in a commitment to guarantee a decent level of economic welfare for the American people. Although equality of opportunity traditionally had been promoted by limited government interference in society, certain economic and social changes in society, such as the closing of the frontiers and the growth of industrial combinations, demanded that America now recognize "the new terms of the old social contract."

The establishment of such a new constitutional order would require a reordering of the political process. The traditional patterns of American politics, characterized by constitutional mechanisms that impeded collective action, would have to give way to a more centralized and administrative governmental order. As Roosevelt put it, "The day of enlightened administration has come." [2]

The concerns expressed in the Commonwealth Club speech are an important guide to understanding the New Deal and its effects on the party system. The pursuit of an economic constitutional order presupposed a fundamental change in the relationship between the presidency and the party system. In Roosevelt's view, the party system, which was essentially based upon state and local organizations and interests and thus was suited to congressional primacy, would have to be transformed into a national, executive-oriented system organized on the basis of public issues.

In this understanding Roosevelt no doubt was influenced by the thought of Woodrow Wilson. The reform of parties, Wilson believed, depended upon extending the influence of the presidency. The limits on partisanship inherent in American constitutional government notwithstanding, the president represented his party's "vital link of connection" with the nation: "He can dominate his party by being spokesman for the real sentiment and purpose of the country, by giving the country at once the information and statements of policy which will enable it to form its judgments alike of parties and men." [3]

Wilson's words spoke louder than his actions; like all presidents after 1800, he reconciled himself to the strong fissures within his party. [4] Roosevelt, however, was less committed to working through existing partisan channels and, more important, the New Deal represented a more fundamental departure than did Wilsonian Progressivism from traditional Democratic policies of individual autonomy, limited government, and states' rights.

As President-elect, Roosevelt began preparations to modify the partisan practices of previous administrations. For example, feeling that Wilson's adherence to traditional partisan politics in staffing the federal government was unfortunate, Roosevelt expressed to Attorney General Homer Cummings his desire to proceed along somewhat different lines, with a view, according to the latter's diary, "to building up a national organization rather than allowing patronage to be used merely to build Senatorial and Congressional machines." [5] Roosevelt followed traditional patronage practices during his first term, allowing Democratic Chairman James Farley to coordinate appointments in response to local organizations and Democratic senators, but the recommendations of organization people were not followed as closely after his reelection. Beginning in 1938, especially, as Ed Flynn, who became Democratic chairman in 1940, indicated in his memoirs, "The President turned more and more frequently to the so-called New Dealers," so that "many of the appointments in Washington went to men who were supporters of the President and believed in what he was trying to do, but who were not Democrats in many instances, and in all instances were not organization Democrats." [6]

Moreover, whereas Wilson took care to consult with legislative party leaders in the development of his policy program, Roosevelt relegated his party in Congress to a decidedly subordinate status. He offended legislators by his use of press conferences to announce important decisions and, again unlike Wilson, eschewed the use of the party caucus in Congress. Roosevelt rejected as impractical, for example, the suggestion of Rep. Alfred Phillips, Jr., "that those sharing the burden of responsibility of party government should regularly and often be called into caucus and that such caucuses should evolve party policies and choice of party leaders." [7]

The most dramatic aspect of Roosevelt's effort to remake the Democratic party was his intervention in a dozen congressional primary campaigns in 1938 in an effort to unseat entrenched conservative Democrats. Such intervention was not unprecedented; in particular, William H. Taft and Wilson had made limited efforts to cleanse their parties of recalcitrant members. Yet Roosevelt's campaign took place on an unprecedentedly large scale and, unlike previous efforts, made no attempt to work through the regular party organization. The degree to which his action was viewed as a shocking departure from the norm is indicated by the press's labeling of it as "the purge," a term associated with Adolf Hitler's attempt to weed out dissension in the German Nazi party and Joseph Stalin's elimination of "disloyal" party members from the Soviet Communist party.

Finally, in 1936 the Roosevelt administration successfully pushed for the abolition of the two-thirds rule for Democratic national conventions, which required support from two-thirds of the delegates for the nomination of president and vice president. This rule had been defended in the past because it guarded the most loyal Democratic section—the South—against the imposition of an unwanted ticket by the less habitually Democratic North, East, and West.[8] To eliminate it, therefore, both weakened the influence of southern democracy, which the journalist Thomas Stokes described as "the ball and chain which hobbled the Party's forward march," and facilitated the adoption of a national reform program.[9]

After the 1938 purge campaign, the columnist Raymond Clapper noted that "no President ever has gone as far as Mr. Roosevelt in striving to stamp his policies upon his party." [10] This massive partisan effort began a process whereby the party system eventually was transformed from local to national and programmatic party organizations. At the same time, the New Deal made partisanship less important. Roosevelt's partisan leadership, although it did effect important changes in the Democratic party organization, ultimately envisioned a personal link with the public that would better enable him to make use of his position as leader of the nation, not just of the party governing the nation.[11] For example, in all but one of the 1938 primary campaigns in which he personally participated, Roosevelt chose to make a direct appeal to public opinion rather than attempt to work through or reform the regular party apparatus. This strategy was encouraged by earlier reforms, especially the direct primary, which had begun to weaken greatly the grip of party organizations on the voters. Radio broadcasting also had made direct presidential appeals an enticing strategy, especially for as popular a president with as fine a radio presence as Roosevelt. After his close associate Felix Frankfurter urged him to go to the country in August 1937 to explain the issues that gave rise to the bitter Court-packing controversy, Roosevelt, perhaps in anticipation of the purge campaign, responded: "You are absolutely right about the radio. I feel like saying to the country—'You will hear from me soon and often. This is not a threat but a promise.' " [12]

In the final analysis, the "benign dictatorship" that Roosevelt sought to impose on the Democratic party was more conducive to corroding the American party system than to reforming it. Wilson's prescription for party reform—extraordinary presidential leadership—posed a serious, if not intractable, dilemma: on the one hand, the decentralized character of politics in the United States can be modified only by strong presidential leadership; on the other, a president determined to alter fundamentally the connection between the executive and his party eventually will shatter party unity.[13]

Roosevelt, in fact, was always aware that the extent to which his purposes could be achieved by party leadership was limited. He felt that a full revamping of partisan politics was impractical, given the obstacles to party government that are so deeply ingrained in the American political experience. The enormity of the failure of the purge campaign reinforced this view.[14] Moreover, New Dealers did not view the welfare state as a partisan issue. The reform program of the 1930s was conceived as a "second bill of rights," which should be established as much as possible in permanent programs beyond the vagaries of public opinion and elections.[15]

Thus, the most significant institutional reforms of the New Deal did not promote party government, but fostered instead a program that would help the president govern in the absence of party government. This program, as embodied in the 1937 executive reorganization bill, would have greatly extended presidential authority over the executive branch, including the independent regulatory commissions. The President and executive agencies also would be delegated extensive authority to govern, making unnecessary the constant cooperation of party members in Congress. As the *Report of the President's Committee on Administrative Management* put it, with administrative reform the "brief exultant commitment" to progressive government that was expressed in the elections of 1932 and, especially, 1936 now would be more firmly established in "persistent, determined, competent, day by day administration." [16]

Interestingly, the administrative reform program, which was directed to making politics less necessary, became, at Roosevelt's urging, a party government-style "vote of confidence" in the administration. Roosevelt initially lost this vote in 1938 when the reorganization bill was defeated in the House, but he did manage, through the purge campaign and other partisan actions, to keep administrative reform sufficiently prominent in party councils that a compromise measure passed in 1939. Although considerably weaker than Roosevelt's original proposal, the 1939 Executive Reorganization Act was a significant measure, which provided authority for the creation of the White House Office and the Executive Office of the President, and enhanced the president's control over bureaucratic agencies. As such, the 1939 administrative reform program represents the genesis of the institutional presidency, which was better equipped to govern independently of the regular political process.

The civil service reform carried out by the Roosevelt administration was another important part of the effort to displace partisan politics with executive administration. The original reorganization proposals of 1937 contained provisions to make the administration of the civil service more effective and to extend the merit system. The reorganization bill passed in 1939 was shorn of this controversial feature; but Roosevelt found it possible to accomplish extensive civil service reform by executive order. Although the purpose of administrative reform ostensibly was to strengthen the presidency, the extension of the merit system "upward, outward and downward" cast an especially New Deal hue over government machinery. This entailed extending merit protection beginning in June 1938 to the personnel appointed by the Roosevelt administration during its first term; four-fifths of these had been brought into government outside of regular merit channels.[17] Administrative reform, therefore, was pursued to politicize, rather than simply professionalize, the bureaucracy, albeit in a nonpartisan way.

Roosevelt's leadership and the administrative reform program of the New Deal transformed the Democratic party into a temporary way station on the road to administrative government. As the presidency developed into an elaborate and ubiquitous institution, it preempted party leaders in many of their limited, but significant, duties: providing a link to interest groups, staffing the executive department, contributing to policy development, and organizing campaign support. Moreover, New Deal administrative reform was not directed to creating presidential government per se, but to imbedding progressive principles, which were considered tantamount to political rights, in a bureaucratic structure that would insulate reform and reformers from electoral change.

Lyndon Johnson's Great Society and the Transcendence of Partisan Politics

Presidential leadership during the New Deal helped to set the tone for the post-1950 resumption of party decline by preparing the executive branch to be a government unto itself, and establishing the presidency rather than the party as the locus of political responsibility. But the modern presidency was created to chart the course for, and direct the voyage to, a more liberal America. Roosevelt's pronouncement of a "second bill of rights" proclaimed and began this task, but it fell to Johnson to "codify the New Deal vision of a good society." [18]

Johnson's attempt to create the Great Society marked not only the completion and significant extension of programmatic liberalism, but also accelerated the effort to transcend partisan politics. Roosevelt's ill-fated efforts to guide the affairs of his party were well remembered by Johnson, who came to Congress in 1937 in a special House election as an enthusiastic supporter of the New Deal. He took Roosevelt's experience to be the best example of the generally ephemeral nature of party government in the United States, and he fully expected the cohesive Democratic support he received from Congress after the 1964 elections to be temporary.[19] Thus Johnson, like Roosevelt, looked beyond the party system toward the politics of "enlightened administration."

Although Johnson avoided any sort of purge campaign and worked closely with Democratic congressional leaders, he took strong action to deemphasize the role of the traditional party organization. For example, the Johnson administration undertook a ruthless attack on the Democratic National Committee (DNC) beginning in late 1965, slashing its budget to the bone and eliminating several of its important programs, such as the highly successful voter registration division. The president also ignored the pleas of several advisers to replace the amiable but ineffective John Bailey as DNC chairman. Instead, he humiliated Bailey, keeping him on but turning over control of the scaled-back committee activities to the White House political liaison, Marvin Watson.[20]

Journalists and scholars generally have explained Johnson's lack of support for the regular party organization in terms of his political background and personality. Some have suggested that Johnson was afraid the DNC might be built into a power center capable of challenging his authority in behalf of the Kennedy wing of the party.[21] Others have pointed to Johnson's roots in the one-party system in Texas, an experience that inclined him to emphasize a consensus style of politics, based on support from diverse elements of the electorate that spanned traditional party lines.[22]

These explanations are surely not without merit. Yet to view Johnson's failures as a party leader in purely personal terms is to ignore the imperative of policy reform that also influenced his administration. Like Roosevelt, Johnson "had always regarded political parties, strongly rooted in states and localities, capable of holding him accountable, as intruders on the business of government."[23] Moreover, from the beginning of his presidency Johnson envisioned the creation of an ambitious program that would leave its mark on history in the areas of government organization, conservation, education, and urban affairs. Such efforts to advance not only the New Deal goal of economic security but also the "quality of American life" necessarily brought Johnson into sharp conflict with the Democratic party.[24]

There is considerable evidence of the Johnson administration's lack of confidence in the ability of the Democratic party to act as an intermediary between the White House and the American people. For example, an aide to Vice President Hubert Humphrey wrote Marvin Watson that "out in the country most Democrats at the State and local level are not intellectually equipped to help on such critical issues as Vietnam and the riots." After a meeting with Queens, New York, district leaders, the White House domestic adviser Joseph Califano reported that "they were ... totally unfamiliar with the dramatic increases in the poverty, health, education and manpower training areas." [25] The uneasy relationship between the Johnson presidency and the Democratic party was particularly aggravated by the administration's aggressive commitment to civil rights, which created considerable friction with local party organizations, especially, but not exclusively, in the South. It is little wonder, then, that when trouble erupted in the cities, the president, in order to find out what was going on, had his special assistants spend time in the ghettos around the country, instead of relying on the reports of local party leaders. [26]

Lack of trust in the Democratic party encouraged the Johnson administration to renew the New Deal pattern of institutional reform. In the area of policy development, one of the most significant innovations of the Johnson administration was to create several task forces under the supervision of the White House Office and the Bureau of the Budget to establish the basic blueprint of the Great Society. These working groups were made up of leading academics throughout the country who prepared reports during the Johnson presidency in virtually all areas of public policy. The specific proposals that came out of these meetings, such as the Education Task Force's elementary-education proposal, formed the heart of the Great Society program. The administration took great care to protect the task forces from political pressures, even keeping them secret. Moreover, members were told to pay no attention to political considerations; they were not to worry about whether their recommendations would be acceptable to Congress and party leaders. [27]

The deemphasis on partisan politics that marked the creation of the Great Society was also apparent in the personnel policy of the Johnson presidency. As his main talent scout Johnson chose not a political adviser but John Macy, who was also chairman of the Civil Service Commission. Macy did work closely with the White House staff, but, especially during the earlier days of the adminstration, he was responsible for making direct recommendations to the president. As the White House staff rather grudgingly admitted, Macy's "wheel ground exceedingly slow but exceedingly fine." [28] Candidates with impressive credentials and experience were uncovered after careful national searches.

The strong commitment to merit in the Johnson administration greatly disturbed certain advisers who were responsible for maintaining the president's political support. James Rowe, who was Johnson's campaign director in both 1964 and 1968, constantly hounded Macy, without success, to consider political loyalists more carefully. Rowe believed that Johnson's personnel policy was gratuitously inattentive to political exigencies. At one point he ended a memo to Macy by saying, "Perhaps you can train some of those career men to run the political campaign in 1968. (It ain't as easy as you government people appear to think it is.)" Macy never responded, but the president called the next day to defend the policies of his personnel director and to give Rowe hell for seeking to interfere in the appointment process.[29]

The rupture between the presidency and the party made it difficult to sustain political enthusiasm and organizational support for the Great Society. The Democrats' very poor showing in the 1966 congressional elections precipitated a firestorm of criticism about the president's inattention to party politics, criticism that continued until Johnson withdrew from the 1968 campaign. Yet Johnson and most of his advisers felt that this deemphasis on partisanship was necessary if the administration were to achieve programmatic reform and coordinate more effectively the increasingly unwieldy activities of government. During the early days of the Johnson presidency, one of his more thoughtful aides, Horace Busby, wrote Johnson a long memo in which he stressed the importance of establishing an institutional basis for the Great Society. About a year later, that same aide expressed great satisfaction that the Johnson presidency had confounded its critics in achieving notable institutional changes. In fact, these changes seemed to mark the full triumph of the Democrats as the party to end party politics:

> Most startling is that while all recognize Johnson as a great politician his appointments have been the most consistently free of politics of any President—in the Cabinet or at lower levels.
> On record, history will remember this as the most important era of non-partisanship since the "Era of Good Feeling" more than a century ago at the start of the nineteenth century. Absence of politics and partisanship is one reason the GOP is having a hard time mounting any respectable offense against either Johnson or his program.[30]

As in the case of the New Deal, however, the institutional innovations of the Great Society did not truly eliminate "politics" from the activities of the executive branch. Rather, the Great Society extended the merging of politics and administration that had characterized executive reform during the 1930s. Each of the outside task forces generated proposals that conformed with Johnson's vision of a Great Society. Moreover, each included both government officials and professors, in order to provide an umbilical cord from the campus to Washington. Finally, all task force proposals as well as all appointments were carefully imbued with the political concerns of the executive office of the president so that Johnson could put forth a reasonably comprehensive program that established his political iden-tity. As White House aide Bill Moyers urged in a memo to Johnson re-garding appointments to the newly created Department of Housing and Urban Development, the goal of the Great Society was to renew "some of the zeal—coupled with sound, tough executive management of the New Deal Days." [31]

The legacy of Johnson's assault on party politics was apparent in the 1968 election. By 1966, Democratic leaders no longer felt that they were part of a national coalition. As 1968 approached, the Johnson administration was preparing a campaign task force that would work independently of the regular party apparatus.[32] These actions greatly accelerated the breakdown of the state and local Democratic machinery, placing organizations in acute distress in nearly every large state.[33] By the time Johnson withdrew from the election in March 1968, the Democratic party was already in the midst of a lengthy period of decay that was accentuated, but not really caused, by the conflict over the Vietnam War.

Thus, the events that took place at the tumultuous 1968 Demo-cratic convention and the party reforms that followed in the wake of those events should be viewed as the culmination of longstanding efforts to free the presidency from traditional partisan influences. In many respects, the expansion of presidential primaries and other changes in nomination politics that were initiated by the McGovern-Fraser Commission were a logical extension of the modern presidency. The very "quietness" of the "revolution" in party rules that took place during the 1970s is evidence in itself that the party system was forlorn by the end of the Johnson era.[34]

Johnson was well aware that forces were in place for the collapse of the regular party apparatus by 1968. From 1966 on, his aides virtually bombarded him with memos warning him of the disarray in the Democratic party organization. Johnson was also informed that reform forces in the states were creating "a new ball game with new rules." These memos indicated that the exploitation of a weakened party apparatus by insurgents would allow someone with as little national prominence as antiwar senator Eugene McCarthy to mount a head-on challenge, which could not be easily fended off by the power of incumbency.[35] The president expressed his own recognition of the decline of party politics in a private meeting he had with Humphrey on April 3, 1968, a few days after announcing his decision not to run. Al-though indicating an intention to remain publicly neutral, Johnson wished his vice president well. But he expressed concern about Humphrey's ability to win the support of the party organization: "The president cannot assure the Vice President because he could not assure it for himself." [36] Like Roosevelt, Johnson had greatly diminished his political capital in pursuit of programmatic innovation.

Richard Nixon, Nonpartisanship, and the Demise of the Modern Presidency

Considering that the New Deal and Great Society were established upon a strategy to replace traditional party politics with administration, it is not surprising that when a conservative challenge to liberal reform emerged, it entailed the development of a conservative "administrative presidency." [37] This further contributed to the decline of partisan politics.

Until the 1960s, opponents of the welfare state generally were opposed to the modern presidency, which had served as a fulcrum of liberal reform. Nevertheless, by the end of the Johnson administration, it became clear that a strong conservative movement would require an activist program of retrenchment in order to counteract the enduring effects of the New Deal and Great Society. Once the opponents of liberal public policy, primarily housed in the Republican party, recognized this, they looked to the possibility that the modern presidency could be a two-edged sword, which could cut in a conservative as well as a liberal direction. Fred Greenstein argues that even Dwight D. Eisenhower, who talked of "restoring the balance," quickly became a defender of the accrued responsibilities of the modern presidency.[38]

With the Nixon administration especially, conservatives began to use the presidency as a lever to effect fundamental policy change in a rightward direction. Although Nixon emphasized a legislative strategy to achieve policy goals during the first two years of his presidency, faced with few legislative achievements, he later attempted to carry out his policies by executive administration. The administrative actions of the Nixon presidency were, of course, a logical extension of the practices of Roosevelt and Johnson. The centralization of authority in the White House and the reduction of the regular Republican organization to perfunctory status during the Nixon years was hardly new.[39] The complete autonomy of the Committee for the Re-Election of the President (CREEP) from the regular Republican organization in the 1972 campaign was but the final stage of a long process of White House preemption of the political responsibilities of the national committee. And the administration reform program that was pursued after Nixon's reelection, in which executive authority was concentrated in the hands of White House operatives and four cabinet "supersecretaries," was the culmination of a longstanding tendency in the modern presidency to reconstitute the executive branch as a more formidable and independent instrument of government.[40]

Thus, just as Roosevelt's presidency anticipated the Great Society, Johnson's presidency anticipated the administrative presidency of Richard Nixon. Ironically, the strategy of pursuing policy goals through administrative capacities that had been created for the most part by Democratic presidents was considered especially suitable by a minority Republican president who faced a hostile Congress and bureaucracy intent upon preserving those presidents' programs. Nixon, actually, surpassed previous modern presidents in viewing the party system as an obstacle to effective governance.

In many respects, however, the conservative administrative presidency was ill-conceived. The centralization of responsibility within the presidency originally had been instituted to build a more liberal America. As a program of the Democratic party, the modern presidency depended upon broad agreement among Congress, the bureaucracy, and eventually the courts to expand the welfare state; a formidable politics of executive administration depended, then, upon a consensus that powers should be delegated to the executive. Once such a system was in place, any conservative assault on the welfare state, such as that intended by Nixon, needed to be more intense and calculated than those of the earlier, liberal presidents. Yet, mainly because of Watergate, Nixon's presidency had the effect of strengthening opposition to the unilateral use of presidential power, while further attenuating the bonds that linked presidents to the party system. The evolution of the modern presidency now left it in complete political isolation.

This isolation continued during the Ford and Carter years, so much so that by the end of the 1970s, statesmen and scholars were lamenting the demise of the presidency as well as of the party system. The ability of the political parties to facilitate consensus and redirect policy seemed to be a thing of the past. The modern presidency, which was developed to alleviate the need for parties in the political process, now seemed burdened by an overload of responsibilities and a lack of organizational support. Although in the past critical realignments had restored the vigor of democratic politics in the United States and provided opportunities for extraordinary presidential leadership, American government now seemed stricken by a "dealignment," the disintegration rather than the renewal of the polity.[41]

The Reagan Presidency and Beyond

Although the traditional party system was severely weakened by the emergence of the modern presidency, a phoenix may yet emerge from the ashes. The erosion of old-style partisan politics has opened up the possibility for the development of a more national and issue-oriented party system, which may provide the foundation for closer ties between presidents and their parties.

The Republican party, in particular, has developed a strong organizational apparatus, which displays unprecedented strength, for an American party, at the national level. Since 1976, the Republican National Committee and the other two national Republican campaign organizations, the National Republican Senatorial Committee and the National Republican Congressional Committee, have greatly expanded their efforts to raise funds and provide services for party candidates. Moreover, these efforts have carried the national party into activities, such as the publication of a public policy quarterly, *Commonsense,* that demonstrate its interest in generating programmatic proposals. The Democrats have lagged behind in party-building efforts, but the losses they suffered in the 1980 elections encouraged them to modernize the national party machinery, openly imitating some of the devices employed by the Republicans.[42] As a result, the traditional party apparatus, based upon patronage and state and local organizations, has given way to a more programmatic party politics based on the national organization. These developments have led some to suggest that there is not simply a revitalization but a reconstruction of political parties as more formidable organizations.[43] Perhaps, therefore, a party system has finally evolved that is compatible with the national polity forged on the anvil of the New Deal.

The revival of the Republican party as a force against executive administration may complete the development of a new American party system. The nomination and election of Ronald Reagan, a far more ideological conservative than Nixon, has galvanized the Republican commitment to programs, such as "regulatory relief" and "new federalism," that challenge severely the institutional legacy of the New Deal. If such a trend continues, the circumvention of the regular political process by administrative action may be displaced by the sort of full-scale debate about political questions usually associated with political realignments.

It is also significant that the Reagan administration has made a concerted effort to strengthen the Republican party.[44] In order to enhance cooperation among the White House, the national committee, and the congressional campaign organizations, Reagan chose his close personal friend, Nevada senator Paul Laxalt, to fill a newly created position—general party chairman. Laxalt's close associate Frank Fahrenkopf, former chairman of the Nevada Republican party, was given the traditional post of the Republican National Committee chair. The White House, with Laxalt's support, then actively intervened to replace the head of the National Republican Senatorial Committee, Senator Robert Packwood of Oregon, a frequent Reagan critic, with a more reliable political ally, Senator Richard Lugar of Indiana.[45] These developments enabled the Reagan administration to improve the coordination of campaigns and policy development within the party without undermining Republican organizational strength. Reagan himself surprised even his own political director with his "total readiness" to shoulder such partisan responsibilities as making numerous fund-raising appearances for the party and its candidates.[46] Apparently, after spending the first fifty years of his life as a Democrat, Reagan brings to Republican activities the enthusiasm of a convert.

Future presidents may lack Reagan's political skill or motivation to support their parties, which will mean a return to the decline of party politics in the United States. Yet the recent institutionalization of the national committees and the strengthening of the campaign committees in Congress have created the foundation for a national party organization that is no longer exclusively absorbed in presidential politics.[47] This may increase the distance between the regular party apparatus and the presidency in one sense, but it also makes possible a strengthened alliance. Because the reconstitution of the party system has been associated with issues and sophisticated fund-raising techniques rather than with the patronage that served as the lifeblood of traditional party politics, it may pose less of an obstacle than did the traditional apparatus to the personal and programmatic ambitions of presidents. For example, leading members of the modern party organization are likely to be more sensitive than were traditional party operatives to exigencies of governance that prevent presidents from adhering strictly to partisanship. As William Greener, the deputy chief of staff for political operations at the Republican National Committee, put it:

> It is unreasonable to expect a President to be a partisan in all respects. Maybe twenty years ago complete partisanship made sense. But the scope of what government undertakes now is much greater. You could not strictly speaking use the party as a spoils system.[48]

The experience of the Reagan administration suggests how the relationship between the president and the party can be mutually beneficial. Republican party strength provided Reagan with the support of a formidable institution, solidifying his personal popularity and facilitating the support of his program in Congress. As a result, the Reagan presidency has been able to suspend the paralysis that seemed to afflict American government in the 1970s, even though the Republicans never attained control of the House of Representatives. In turn, the president's popularity has served the party by strengthening its fund-raising efforts and promoting a shift in voters' party loyalties, placing the Republicans in a position of virtual parity with the Democrats for the first time since the 1940s.[49] It may be, then, that the 1980s will mark the watershed of a new political era, as well as of a renewed link between presidents and the party system.

Nevertheless, the separated character of political institutions in the United States provides a precarious setting for comprehensive party programs. The Reagan White House, intent upon a conservative revolution, has fought to impose a program of reform that necessarily looks beyond the limited agreements that can be worked out in the fragmented structure of American party politics. It is unlikely that the emergence of national parties will fundamtentally alter these processes, a condition that will continue to encourage modern presidents, particularly those intent upon ambitious policy reform, to emphasize popular appeals and administrative action rather than collective responsibility. It is not surprising, therefore, that the Reagan presidency has frequently pursued its program by acts of administrative discretion that short-circuit the legislative process, particularly in the realm of government regulation.[50]

The restoration of partisanship in the presidency is also likely to be retarded by the modern nominating process, which is the legacy of the McGovern-Fraser reforms. There have been important efforts to "reform the reforms," and the decline of party caused by its loss of control over nominations has been ameliorated by the strengthening of the financial and organizational capacity of the national and congressional committees. Yet the process of selecting presidential candidates by a series of state primaries and caucuses is so permeable that it may be virtually impossible to sustain any substantial spirit of partisan community.

Finally, it must be recognized that the revival of partisanship may require presidents who are committed to lessening the influence of the White House in favor of shared responsibility with the diverse elements of the party. Even if such leadership makes sense politically, it remains to be seen whether future presidents will recognize its wisdom. As Alexis de Tocqueville noted about the forces tending toward centralization in a democracy, "The only public men in democracies who favor decentralization are, almost invariably, either very disinterested or extremely mediocre; the former are scarce and the latter are powerless." [51]

Notes

1. For a more detailed discussion of the arguments presented in this section, see Sidney M. Milkis, "Franklin D. Roosevelt and the Transcendence of Partisan Politics," *Political Science Quarterly* 100 (Fall 1985): 479-504; and Milkis, "The New Deal, Administrative Reform, and the Transcendence of Partisan Politics," *Administration and Society* 18 (February 1987): 433-472.

2. Franklin D. Roosevelt, *Public Papers and Addresses,* 13 vols. (New York: Random House, 1938-1950), vol. 1, 751-752.

3. Woodrow Wilson, *Constitutional Government in the United States* (New York: Columbia University Press, 1908), 68-69.

4. Arthur S. Link, "Woodrow Wilson and the Democratic Party," *Review of Politics* 18 (April 1956): 146-156.

5. Personal and Political Diary of Homer Cummings, January 5, 1933, box 234, No. 2, p. 90, Homer Cummings Papers (no. 9973), Manuscripts Department, University of Virginia Library, Charlottesville, Virginia.

6. Edward J. Flynn, *You're the Boss* (New York: Viking, 1947), 153.

7. Alfred Phillips, Jr., to Franklin D. Roosevelt, June 9, 1937; and Roosevelt to Phillips, June 16, 1937, President's Personal File, 2666, Franklin D. Roosevelt Library, Hyde Park, New York.

8. Franklin Clarkin, "Two-Thirds Rule Facing Abolition," *New York Times,* January 5, 1936, sec. 4, 10.

9. Thomas Stokes, *Chip Off My Shoulder* (Princeton: Princeton University Press, 1940), 503.

10. Raymond Clapper, "Roosevelt Tries the Primaries," *Current History,* October 1938, 16.

11. Morton Frisch, *Franklin D. Roosevelt: The Contribution of the New Deal to American Political Thought and Practice* (Boston: St. Wayne, 1975), 79.

12. Frankfurter to Roosevelt, August 9, 1937, box 210, The Papers of Thomas G. Corcoran; Roosevelt to Frankfurter, August 12, 1937, box 60, Felix Frankfurter Papers; both in Manuscript Division, Library of Congress, Washington, D.C.

13. Herbert Croly, a fellow Progressive, criticized Wilson's concept of presidential party leadership along these lines. See *Progressive Democracy* (New York: Macmillan, 1914), 346.

14. In the dozen states where the president acted against entrenched incumbents, he was successful in only two—Oregon and New York. Moreover, the purge campaign galvanized opposition throughout the nation, apparently contributing to the heavy losses the Democrats sustained in the 1938 general elections.

15. The term "second bill of rights" comes from Roosevelt's 1944 State of the Union message, which reaffirmed the New Deal's commitment to an economic constitutional order. Roosevelt, *Public Papers and Addresses,* vol. 13, 40.

16. *Report of the President's Committee on Administrative Management* (Washington, D.C.: Government Printing Office, 1937), 53. The President's Committee on Administrative Management, headed by Louis Brownlow, played a central role in the planning and politics of executive reorganization from 1936 to 1940. For a full analysis of the commission, see Barry Karl, *Executive Reorganization and Reform in the New Deal* (Cambridge, Mass.: Harvard University Press, 1963).

17. Richard Polenberg, *Reorganizing Roosevelt's Government* (Cambridge, Mass.: Harvard University Press, 1966), 22-23, 184. The merging of politics and administration took an interesting course as a result of the passage of the Hatch Act in 1939. Until the passage of this bill, which barred most federal employees from

participating in campaigns, the Roosevelt administration was making use of the growing army of federal workers in state and local political activity, including some of the purge campaigns. The Hatch Act demolished the national Roosevelt political machine as distinct from the regular Democratic organization. Yet Roosevelt was more interested in orienting the executive branch as an instrument of programmatic reform than he was in developing a national political machine, and the insulation of federal officials from party politics was not incompatible with such a task. This explains why Roosevelt, although he fought against passage of the Hatch bill, decided to sign it.

18. For an account of the influence of Roosevelt and the New Deal on Johnson's presidency, see William E. Leuchtenburg, *In the Shadow of FDR: From Harry Truman to Ronald Reagan*, rev. ed. (Ithaca, N.Y.: Cornell University Press, 1985), chap. 4.

19. Lyndon Baines Johnson, *The Vantage Point: Perspectives of the Presidency, 1963-1969* (New York: Holt, Rinehart and Winston, 1971), 323.

20. Theodore White, *The Making of a President, 1968* (New York: Atheneum, 1969), 107.

21. Rowland Evans and Robert Novak, "Too Late for LBJ," *Boston Globe*, December 21, 1966, 27.

22. David Broder, "Consensus Politics: End of An Experiment," *Atlantic Monthly*, October 1966, 62.

23. Doris Kearns, *Lyndon Johnson and the American Dream* (New York: New American Library), 256.

24. Larry O'Brien, Johnson's chief legislative aide, gives an interesting report on one of the early strategy sessions that led to the Great Society in a November 1964 memo, which expresses concern about the acute political problems he anticipated would result from such an ambitious program. Memorandum, Larry O'Brien to Henry Wilson, November 24, 1964, Henry Wilson Papers, box 4, Lyndon Baines Johnson Library, Austin, Texas.

25. Memorandum, William Connel to Martin Watson, August 27, 1967, Marvin Watson Files, box 31; Memorandum, Joe Califano to the President, March 27, 1968, Office Files of the President (Dorothy Territo), box 10; both in Johnson Library.

26. Memorandum, Harry C. McPherson, Jr., and Clifford L. Alexander, for the president, February 11, 1967, Office Files of Harry McPherson; Sherwin J. Markmam, Oral History, by Dorothy Pierce McSweeny, tape 1, May 21, 1969, 24-36; both in Johnson Library. Many local Democrats felt threatened by the community action program with its provision for "maximum feasible participation." See Daniel P. Moynihan, *Maximum Feasible Misunderstanding* (New York: Free Press, 1970), 144-145.

27. William E. Leuchtenburg, "The Genesis of the Great Society," *Reporter*, April 21, 1966, 38.

28. Memorandum, Hayes Redmon to Bill Moyers, May 5, 1966, box 12, Office Files of Bill Moyers, Johnson Library. For an excellent book-length treatment of Johnson's personnel policy, see Richard L. Schott and Dagmar S. Hamilton, *People, Positions and Power: The Political Appointments of Lyndon Johnson* (Chicago: University of Chicago Press, 1983).

29. Memorandum, James Rowe for John W. Macy, Jr., April 28, 1965, John Macy Papers, box 504; James H. Rowe, Oral History, by Joe B. Frantz, interview 2, September 16, 1969, 46-47; both in Johnson Library. Rowe's battles with Macy are noteworthy and ironic, for as a charter member of the White House Office he

performed Macy's role for the Roosevelt administration, upholding the principle of merit against the patronage requests of DNC chairman James Farley and his successor, Ed Flynn.

30. Draft memorandum, Horace Busby to Mr. Johnson, no date (June 1964), box 52, folder of Memos to Mr. Johnson, June 1964; Memorandum, Horace Busby for the president, September 21, 1965, box 51, Office Files of Horace Busby, Johnson Library.

31. Leuchtenburg, "Genesis of the Great Society," 37-38; and Memorandum, Bill Moyers for the president, December 11, 1965, box 11, Office Files of Bill Moyers, Johnson Library.

32. James Rowe became quite concerned upon hearing of the task force proposal. He warned the White House staff that this might further weaken the regular party apparatus, which was "already suffering from shellshock both in Washington and around the country because of its impotent status." James Rowe, "A White Paper for the President on the 1968 Presidential Campaign," no date, Marvin Watson Files, box 20, Folder of Rowe, O'Brien, Cooke, Griswell Operation, Johnson Library.

33. Allan Otten, "The Incumbent's Edge," *Wall Street Journal,* December 28, 1967.

34. Byron E. Shafer, *Quiet Revolution: The Struggle for the Democratic Party and the Shaping of Post-Reform Politics* (New York: Russell Sage Foundation, 1983). For a discussion on the long-term forces underlying the McGovern-Fraser reforms, see David B. Truman, "Party Reform, Party Atrophy and Constitutional Change," *Political Science Quarterly* 99 (Winter 1984-85): 637-655.

35. Memorandum, John P. Roche for the president, December 4, 1967, *White House Central Files,* folder of PL (Political Affairs); Memorandum, Ben Wattenberg for the president, December 13, 1967, Marvin Watson Files, box 10; Memorandum, Ben Wattenberg for the President, March 13, 1968, Marvin Watson Files, box 11; all in Johnson Library.

36. Memorandum of conversation, April 5, 1968, White House Famous Names, box 6, Folder of Robert F. Kennedy, 1968 Campaign, Johnson Library.

37. Richard Nathan, *The Administrative Presidency* (New York: John Wiley & Sons, 1983).

38. Fred Greenstein, "Nine Presidents in Search of a Modern Presidency," in *The New American Political System,* 2d ed., ed. Anthony King (Washington, D.C.: American Enterprise Institute, in press).

39. On Nixon's party leadership as president, see the Ripon Society and Clifford Brown, *Jaws of Victory* (Boston: Little, Brown, 1973), 226-242.

40. Nathan, *Administrative Presidency,* 43-56.

41. Walter Dean Burnham, *Critical Elections and the Mainsprings of American Politics* (New York: W. W. Norton, 1970); Everett Carll Ladd, *Transformations of the American Party System,* 2d ed. (New York: W. W. Norton, 1978).

42. A. James Reichley, "The Rise of National Parties," in *The New Direction in American Politics,* ed. John E. Chubb and Paul E. Peterson (Washington, D.C.: Brookings Institution, 1985), 191-195.

43. Ibid., 195-200; Cornelius P. Cotter and John F. Bibby, "Institutionalization of Parties and the Thesis of Party Decline," *Political Science Quarterly* 95 (Spring 1980): 1-27; Joseph A. Schlesinger, "The New American Party System," *American Political Science Review* 79 (December 1985): 1152-1169; and Michael Nelson, "The Case for the Current Nominating Process," in *Before Nomination,* ed. George Grassmuck (Washington, D.C.: American Enterprise Institute, 1985).

44. Rhodes Cook, "Reagan Nurtures His Adopted Party to Strength," *Congressional Quarterly Weekly Report,* September 28, 1985, 1927-1930.
45. Howell Raines, "Laxalt and Political Ally Chosen for G.O.P. Posts," *New York Times,* January 9, 1983, 10; and Steven V. Roberts, "Packwood Loses Party Job in Senate," *New York Times,* December 3, 1982, 19.
46. David S. Broder, "A Party Leader Who Works at It," *Boston Globe,* October 21, 1985, 14; and Personal interview with Mitchell E. Daniels, assistant to the president for political and governmental affairs, June 5, 1986.
47. Cotter and Bibby, "Institutionalization of Parties," 25.
48. Personal interview with William I. Greener III, June 4, 1986.
49. Thomas E. Cavanaugh and James L. Sundquist, "The New Two-Party System," *The New Direction in American Politics.*
50. Michael Fix and George C. Eads, "The Prospects for Regulatory Reform: The Legacy of Reagan's First Term," *Yale Journal on Regulation* 2 (no. 2, 1985): 293-318.
51. Alexis de Tocqueville, *Democracy in America,* ed. J. P. Mayer (New York: Doubleday, 1969), 735.

Part V

PRESIDENTS AND GOVERNMENT

The bicentennial of the writing and ratification of the United States Constitution has rekindled public and scholarly interest in the nation's two centuries of experience with constitutional government. Regarding the presidency, the essays in this part suggest two propositions. The first is that the institutions of government that the framers of the Constitution created—namely, Congress, the judiciary, and the presidency—still relate to each other in rough conformance to the original design. Second, what is most different about modern American government is the array of bureaucratic and staff agencies, unanticipated in the Constitution, that have grown up around the presidency.

The White House staff is the concern of John Burke in "The Institutional Presidency." Not until 1857 did Congress appropriate funds for such a staff—one clerk. More than a half century later, Woodrow Wilson still had only seven full-time aides. Growth in the size of the White House staff began in earnest during the presidency of Franklin D. Roosevelt and, with occasional lapses, has yet to abate. For Roosevelt and his successors, the challenge has been to keep up with the activities of the ever-growing federal bureaucracy, of which the president is, constitutionally, chief executive. Ironically, Burke argues, the size and complexity of the modern staff have caused it to take on "the character of a bureaucratic organization" itself.

The framers would have been startled by the prominence of the president's staff, but no more than by the bureaucracy that prompted its development. The Constitution refers obliquely to "departments" and "officers," but those references are in no way commensurate to their importance in modern government. Contending with the bureaucracy is in many ways more vexing to presidents than haggling with Congress or the courts, as Elizabeth Sanders notes in "The Presidency and the Bureaucratic State." Yet mastery is not impossible, as many have come to believe. "Without any significant increase in statutory powers," Sanders argues, "and despite some serious excesses and missteps, the Reagan presidency has impressively demonstrated the potential of the chief executive to reshape both public policy and the modus operandi of the federal bureaucracy." Whether Reagan's particular combination of administrative tools—budgetary reallocations, central clearance of bureaucratic rules and regulations, vigorous personnel policies, and encouragement of devolution and privatization of federal tasks—would appeal to or work for future presidents is less certain.

However tangential the Constitution may be to presidential activities within the executive branch, 1787 remains the operative year for understanding "The Presidency and Congress," according to Morris Fiorina. The Constitutional Convention, he notes, not only created an executive that was formally independent of the legislature, but also separated the two branches electorally. Members of Congress represent small parts of the nation, the president the whole; congressional elections sometimes coincide with presidential elections, sometimes they do not. Historically, political parties—another extraconstitutional innovation—have helped to bridge this separation by giving reelection-minded members of Congress "a compelling personal incentive," as Fiorina describes it, ". . . to do what they could to see that a national administration of their party was perceived as effective." This incentive can exist, however, only as long as voters link their choices for Congress with their choices for president. In the post-World War II era, much as the framers probably intended, fewer and fewer voters have been making that link, and presidents have had a harder and harder time bridging the constitutional gap between the White House and Capitol Hill.

The Constitution also continues to shape the relationship between "The Presidency and the Judiciary," argues Robert Scigliano. Delegates to the Constitutional Convention feared legislative power and tried to encourage what Scigliano calls a "limited alliance" between the executive and the judiciary that would restrain it. In the framers' plan, "the hope was that these two 'weaker branches' of government would support each other against congressional encroachments on themselves and against legislative oppressions originating in the people." Through most of American history, the limited alliance seemed to hold.

The past half century, Scigliano shows, has been marked by greater conflict between the presidency and the judiciary, particularly the Supreme Court. But this may represent a fulfillment of the framers' real concern, which was that no one branch outstrip the others. In recent times, it has been the presidency whose power most often has seemed ascendant, and it should not surprise us that the modern judiciary has been more inclined to restrain presidential power than to buttress it.

Which of our two propositions about the Constitution—that it provides little direction for the White House staff and the bureaucracy but much for the president's relations with Congress and the judiciary—applies to the vice presidency? Neither and both. The constitutional vice presidency has virtually no powers and, in truth, vice presidents historically have been almost without influence. But in recent decades a number of informal political and policy-making roles have been played by vice presidents. The difficulty of determining how much the office has changed is captured in the equivocal title of Joseph Pika's chapter: "A New Vice Presidency?"

16. THE INSTITUTIONAL PRESIDENCY

John P. Burke

To most scholars of the American presidency, the tenure of
Franklin D. Roosevelt marks a dramatic shift in the character of the of-
fice. Beginning with his request for an emergency banking act on
March 9, 1933, five days after his inauguration,[1] continuing with the
Agricultural Adjustment Act on March 16, the creation of the Civilian
Conservation Corps on March 21, the Federal Emergency Relief Act
on March 21, another banking bill on March 29, the massive Muscle
Shoals/Tennessee Valley project on April 10, an emergency railroad
act on May 4, and culminating in the National Industrial Recovery Act
on May 17 (the capstone of Roosevelt's hectic "hundred days"),
Roosevelt's New Deal fundamentally altered the relationship between
government and the economy. Moreover, as a result of Roosevelt's
programs, government increasingly touched the daily lives of American
citizens. By 1935, in the midst of the Great Depression, the budget of
the federal government had climbed to $6.65 billion, more than double
its expenditures of $3.1 billion in 1929.

The significance of Roosevelt's legislative accomplishments should
not be minimized. But for presidency scholars, Roosevelt's legacy rests
also in the effects of his administration upon the office of president, not
simply in the particular policies and programs he fostered. One
important facet of the Roosevelt administration that sets it off from its
predecessors is indeed that for which history remembers Roosevelt most
vividly: the ability of the president to put his mark on the nation's
political agenda. But other characteristics of his presidency are also
significant: greater presidential power to make decisions and act on the
president's own initiative, greater visibility as the central actor in
American politics, and enhanced resources through the creation of a
large White House staff.[2]

Undoubtedly all of these changes have interacted to produce a
qualitatively different kind of presidency, but at least three of them are
not unique to the presidency that began to emerge in the 1930s. Many
earlier presidents had sought to put their stamp on the nation's political

agenda: Andrew Jackson's "democracy," Theodore Roosevelt's "trust busting," and Woodrow Wilson's "progressivism," to name merely a few of the more prominent examples. Earlier presidents also had exercised great power on their own initiative: John Adams attempted to stock the federal judiciary with his supporters in the aftermath of his election loss to Thomas Jefferson, Jefferson purchased the Louisiana Territory without full congressional authorization, Jackson battled Congress over the National Bank, and Abraham Lincoln suspended the writ of habeas corpus during the Civil War. Even without the electronic media, nineteenth and early twentieth century presidents were highly visible to the nation during their terms of office; early presidents still predominate in lists of great presidents.[3]

What does mark a unique change in the presidency of Franklin Roosevelt and the presidents who have succeeded him is the presence of a large staff to aid and assist the president. Jefferson served in office with only one messenger and one secretary. Ulysses S. Grant had three staff assistants. Even as late as Wilson's administration, only seven persons were assigned to the president as full-time administrative aides. Not until 1857 did Congress appropriate money for a presidential clerk—one. As recently as the presidency of Calvin Coolidge the entire budget for the White House staff, including office expenses, was less than $80,000.[4]

As demands on the president mounted, more help was needed. Roosevelt's solution was to muddle through, borrowing staff from existing departments and agencies. In fact, the legislative whirlwind of Roosevelt's first hundred days was the product of precisely such a loosely organized group of assistants, many of whom did not have formal positions on the White House staff. Roosevelt especially liked to use departmental assistant secretaries, since "no specific duties were required by law."[5] In fact, two members of his "brain trust" had appointments of this sort. Rexford Tugwell and Raymond Moley both left the faculty of Columbia University to join the new administration. Since there were few positions available on the White House staff, Roosevelt made them assistant secretaries in regular cabinet-level departments—Tugwell in the Department of Agriculture, Moley at State—but had them report directly to him, employing their talents as he saw fit. In Roosevelt's second term, one of his closest assistants, Thomas P. Corcoran, held the rather unprepossessing position of counsel to the Reconstruction Finance Corporation.

Other members of Roosevelt's brain trust did not even join him in Washington: although they served as influential advisers, Adolf Berle, Jr., remained on the faculty at Columbia and Judge Sam Rosenman, at least in the early years, stayed on the New York bench. What few staff positions Roosevelt could fill went to other long-time aides. Louis Howe was given the title of secretary to the president, with Steven Early serving as press secretary, Marvin McIntyre as appointments secretary, and "Missy" LeHand as the president's personal secretary.

Roosevelt's patchwork staff worked, but just barely. In an interview with a group of reporters in the aftermath of the 1936 election, Roosevelt publicly attributed his success to the failure of Governor Alfred P. Landon of Kansas, his opponent, to seize upon the president's chief weakness. "What is your weakness?" one of the reporters asked. "Administration," replied the President.[6] Clearly, something needed to be done.

In fact, Roosevelt already had taken steps to rectify his administrative problems, forming the Committee on Administrative Management, headed by Louis Brownlow. Concluding that "the President needs help," Brownlow and his associates proposed that in order "to deal with the greatly increased duties of executive management falling upon the president, the White House staff should be expanded."[7] After initial congressional rejection of their then-controversial proposal,[8] the revised recommendations of the Brownlow Committee were passed by Congress in the Reorganization Act of 1939. Significant increases in the staff resources available to the president also followed in the wake of the 1947 Hoover Commission on the Reorganization of the Executive Branch.[9]

From the handful of aides Roosevelt and his predecessors in office could appoint, the numbers have increased steadily in each of the succeeding administrations. By 1953, the size of the immediate White House staff (the White House Office) was about 250. Twenty years later, it had grown to almost 500 persons. In 1977, criticizing the size of the staff as a symptom of the "imperial presidency," Jimmy Carter reduced it by 100 employees, largely through moving them to other parts of the executive branch. By 1980, Carter's last year in office, the size of the staff had inched back upward to 500, larger than that of any of his predecessors; it remained about that size under Ronald Reagan. When other administrative units under direct presidential control (the larger Executive Office of the President) are included—such as the Office of Management and Budget, the National Security Council, and the Council of Economic Advisers[10]—the number swells to more than 1,700 appointees, operating with a budget well above $120 million by 1986. Physically, the Executive Office of the President has spilled out from the east and west wings of the White House to occupy the Old Executive Office Building next door to the White House—once large enough to house the Departments of State, War, and Navy—and then to encompass a New Executive Office Building located on the north side of Pennsylvania Avenue as well as other, smaller buildings in the vicinity.

A marked change in the character of the presidency thus has occurred. By recognizing that the American presidency is an institution, a *presidency*, not merely a *president,* we can better understand the office, how it operates, the kinds of challenges it raises, and how it affects our politics.

The Institutional Presidency

If the presidency is best understood as an institution, then clearly it should embody certain characteristics of an institution. But what do we mean by terms like *institution, institutional,* and *institutionalization?* Our concern here is for the organizational character of the presidency—its growth in size, the complexity of its work ways, and the general way in which it resembles a large, well-organized bureaucracy.[11] Such an institution is complex, in terms both of what it does (its functions) and how it operates (its formal and informal structure). An institution is universalistic and routine in its decision-making and operating procedures: precedent, impersonal codes, and merit govern, not fiat, personal preferences, and favoritism. Finally, an institution is well bounded, differentiated from its environment.[12]

Complex Organization

Institutions are complex: they are relatively large in size; each of their parts performs a specialized function; and some form of central authority coordinates the parts' various contributions to the work of the institution.

The first aspect of complexity—the increase in the size of the institutional presidency—can be easily seen by comparing the White House staff of President Roosevelt in 1939, before adoption of the Brownlow Commission's recommendations for administrative reform, with the staff recently at work in the Reagan White House. The eight individuals that the 1939 Government Manual lists as members of the White House staff (Table 16-1) are clearly dwarfed by the long list of staff members serving under President Reagan (Table 16-2). Moreover, the staff positions listed in Table 16-2 are only the top layer of the five to six hundred aides and assistants at Reagan's immediate disposal, which indicates further complexity in today's presidency.

A comparison of Tables 16-1 and 16-2 also illustrates the second aspect of organizational complexity: increasing specialization of function. Roosevelt's aides were by and large generalists; they were simply called secretary to the president or administrative assistant. In the Reagan presidency, by contrast, we find titles such as Special Assistant

Table 16-1 The White House Office, 1939

Secretary to the President	Stephen Early
Secretary to the President	Brig. Gen. Edwin M. Watson
Secretary to the President	Marvin H. McIntyre
Administrative Assistant	William H. McReynolds
Administrative Assistant	James H. Rowe, Jr.
Administrative Assistant	Lauchlin Currie
Personal Secretary	Marguerite A. LeHand
Executive Clerk	Rudolph Forster

SOURCE: *United States Government Manual, 1939* (Washington, D.C.: Government Printing Office, 1939).

to the President for Public Liaison, Deputy Assistant to the President for Drug Abuse Policy, Executive Secretary of the Cabinet Council on Management and Administration, and Special Assistant to the President for Legislative Affairs (House). Many other units of the president's staff (not listed in Table 16-2) operate within functionally defined, specialized areas, such as national security or environmental quality. In fact, one of the primary causes of the growth of the White House staff has been the addition of these units: the Bureau of the Budget (created in 1921, transferred from the Treasury Department in 1939, and reorganized as the Office of Management and Budget in 1970), Council of Economic Advisers (1946), National Security Council (1947), Office of Special Representative for Trade Negotiations (1963), Office of Policy Development (1970),[13] Council on Environmental Quality (1970), and the Intelligence Oversight Board (1977). All told, the once relatively simple tasks of the president's staff—writing speeches, handling correspondence, and orchestrating his daily schedule—have evolved into substantive duties that affect the policies the president proposes and how he deals with the steadily increasing demands placed upon his office.

The final characteristic of institutional complexity is the presence of some central authority that coordinates the contributions of the institution's functional parts. For the presidency, such authority nominally resides in the president himself. But in recent administrations, coordinating authority has been especially manifest in the increasing importance of a White House chief of staff—Sherman Adams under Dwight D. Eisenhower, Theodore Sorensen under John F. Kennedy, H. R. Haldeman under Richard M. Nixon, Hamilton Jordan under Carter, James Baker, Donald Regan, and Howard Baker under Reagan—each of whom played substantive roles in policy making and

Table 16-2 The White House Office, 1986

Donald T. Regan, *Chief of Staff to the President*

James Scott Brady, *Assistant to the President and Press Secretary*

Patrick J. Buchanan, *Assistant to the President and Director of Communications*

Fred F. Fielding, *Counsel to the President*

Max L. Friedersdorf, *Assistant to the President and Legislative Strategy Coordinator*

Edward V. Hickey, Jr., *Assistant to the President and Director of Special Support Services*

Robert C. McFarlane, *Assistant to the President for National Security Affairs*

M. B. Oglesby, *Assistant to the President for Legislative Affairs*

Edward J. Rollins, *Assistant to the President for Political and Governmental Affairs*

Larry M. Speakes, *Assistant to the President and Principal Deputy Press Secretary*

John A. Svahn, *Assistant to the President for Policy Development*

Bruce Chapman, *Deputy Assistant to the President and Director of the Office of Planning and Evaluation*

Linda Chavez, *Deputy Assistant to the President and Director of the Office of Public Liaison*

David L. Chew, *Staff Secretary and Deputy Assistant to the President*

Roger B. Porter, *Deputy Assistant to the President for Policy Development and Director of the Office of Policy Development*

James S. Rosebush, *Deputy Assistant to the President*

Frederick J. Ryan, Jr., *Deputy Assistant to the President*

Karna Small, *Deputy Assistant to the President for National Security Affairs and Senior Director for Public Affairs, National Security Council*

Carlton E. Turner, *Deputy Assistant to the President for Drug Abuse Policy*

Pamela J. Turner, *Deputy Assistant to the President for Legislative Affairs (Senate)*

Robert H. Tuttle, *Deputy Assistant to the President and Director of Presidential Personnel*

Ronald L. Alvarado, *Special Assistant to the President for Intergovernmental Affairs*

Linda L. Arey, *Special Assistant to the President and Deputy Director of the Office of Public Liaison*

Haley Barbour, *Special Assistant to the President for Political Affairs*

Ralph C. Bledsoe, *Special Assistant to the President and Executive Secretary of the Cabinet Council on Management and Administration*

Melvin L. Bradley, *Special Assistant to the President for Policy Development*

Anne Higgins, *Special Assistant to the President and Director of Correspondence*

John M. Hudson, *Special Assistant to the President for Legislative Affairs*

Mary Jo Jacobi, *Special Assistant to the President for Public Liaison*

Nancy M. Kennedy, *Special Assistant to the President for Legislative Affairs*

James F. Kuhn, *Special Assistant to the President*

Christopher M. Lehman, *Special Assistant to the President for National Security Affairs*

Ronald F. Lehman, *Special Assistant to the President for National Security Affairs*

Frederick D. McClure, *Special Assistant to the President for Legislative Affairs*

William F. Martin, *Special Assistant to the President for National Security Affairs*

John F. Matlock, Jr., *Special Assistant to the President for National Security Affairs*

Constantine C. Menges, *Special Assistant to the President for National Security Affairs*

Margaret Noonan, *Special Assistant to the President for Presidential Speechwriting*

Deborah K. Owen, *Associate Counsel to the President*

Richard Prendergast, *Special Assistant to the President for Legislative Affairs*

Walter Raymond, Jr., *Special Assistant to the President for National Security Affairs*

Mitchell E. Daniels, Jr., *Deputy Assistant to the President and Director, Office of Intergovernmental Affairs*

Thomas C. Dawson, *Executive Assistant to the Chief of Staff and Deputy Assistant to the President*

Bently T. Elliott, *Deputy Assistant to the President and Director of Speechwriting*

Donald R. Fortier, *Deputy Assistant to the President for National Security Affairs*

Richard A. Hauser, *Deputy Counsel to the President*

William Henkel, *Deputy Assistant to the President and Director of the Presidential Advance Office*

Christopher Hicks, *Deputy Assistant to the President for Administration*

Charles D. Hobbs, *Deputy Assistant to the President for Policy Development*

Alfred H. Kingon, *Cabinet Secretary and Deputy Assistant to the President*

Alan M. Kranowitz, *Deputy Assistant to the President for Legislative Affairs (House)*

William B. Lacy, *Deputy Assistant to the President and Director, Office of Political Affairs*

John M. Poindexter, *Deputy Assistant to the President for National Security Affairs*

Albert R. Brashear, *Special Assistant to the President and Deputy Press Secretary for Domestic Affairs*

Marshall J. Breger, *Special Assistant to the President for Public Liaison*

Helen R. Cameron, *Special Assistant to the President for Political Affairs*

Andrew H. Card, Jr., *Special Assistant to the President for Intergovernmental Affairs*

Sherrie M. Cooksey, *Associate Counsel to the President*

James P. Covey, *Special Assistant to the President for National Security Affairs*

Kenneth E. DeGraffenreid, *Special Assistant to the President for National Security Affairs*

Anthony Dolan, *Special Assistant to the President and Chief Speechwriter*

Thomas Donnelly, Jr., *Special Assistant to the President for Legislative Affairs*

Michael A. Driggs, *Special Assistant to the President for Policy Development*

Henry M. Gandy, *Special Assistant to the President for Legislative Affairs*

H. Lawrence Garrett III, *Associate Counsel to the President*

Bryce L. Harlow, *Special Assistant to the President for Legislative Affairs*

Robert R. Reilly, *Special Assistant to the President for Public Liaison*

Nancy J. Risque, *Special Assistant to the President for Legislative Affairs*

John G. Roberts, Jr., *Associate Counsel to the President*

William L. Roper, *Special Assistant to the President for Health Policy*

Peter H. Roussel, *Special Assistant to the President and Deputy Press Secretary*

Gaston J. Sigur, Jr., *Special Assistant to the President for National Security Affairs*

Paul B. Simmons, *Special Assistant to the President and Director of the Office of Policy Development*

Robert B. Sims, *Special Assistant to the President and Deputy Press Secretary for Foreign Affairs*

T. Burton Smith, M.D., *Physician to the President*

Cataline Villalpando, *Special Assistant to the President for Public Liaison*

David B. Waller, *Senior Associate Counsel to the President*

Lyn M. Withey, *Special Assistant to the President for Legislative Affairs*

James L. Hooley, *Special Assistant to the President and Director of Presidential Advance*

SOURCE: *United States Government Manual, 1986–1987* (Washington, D.C.: Government Printing Office, 1986).

in most cases had day-to-day operational authority over the workings of the White House staff.

In fact, the centralization of power within the White House staff in the role of chief of staff seems to be unavoidable, regardless of the president's own wishes. For example, Carter, at the start of his administration, publicly announced that he wanted no chief of staff of the sort Haldeman had been under Nixon. However, by the end of Carter's second year in office Jordan functioned as de facto chief of staff, and by Carter's third year the appointment was official. When Carter spoke of a national "crisis of confidence" in an ill-fated, July 1979 speech, he traced the problem to the nation's moral fabric; but most observers blamed any enfeeblement of leadership on Carter and, especially, on his staff.[14] Carter, moreover, "solved" the crisis by firing a good chunk of his cabinet, several of whom had clashed with the White House staff. More than half the cabinet went, but almost all of Carter's staff, especially the "Georgia mafia," remained. "From now on, the Cabinet will have to clear everything with the White House," declared Stuart Eizenstat, then serving as assistant to the president for domestic affairs.[15]

Universalistic Recruitment Criteria

Comparison of the Reagan and Roosevelt staffs also indicates the second trend toward institutionalization of the presidency: the increasing reliance upon universalistic criteria—especially educational credentials and other job-related skills—for recruitment to the president's staff. For Roosevelt and presidents before him, White House aides were drawn from the ranks of political cronies and other long-time associates. Howe first went to work for then-New York State assemblyman Franklin Roosevelt in 1912. Most of the other aides listed in Table 16-1—Early, McIntyre, and LeHand—first served Roosevelt during his unsuccessful vice-presidential campaign in 1920.

Today, the résumés of presidential aides look a bit different. Long-time associates of a president—such as Edwin Meese and Michael Deaver under Reagan—still make their way onto the president's staff. But once they are transplanted to the hothouse of Washington politics, they often find themselves pushed from positions of real power by individuals who are experienced in national government, possess expertise in substantive policy areas, and are adept at Washington politics. In 1981, for example, President Reagan created an organizational "troika," with authority divided among his top three assistants—Meese, Deaver, and James Baker. Although on paper, Baker's tasks seemed the most difficult and his authority the weakest, his political skills and well-honed Washington expertise enabled him to displace his two rivals—whose political experience had been limited to the environs of Oakland and Sacramento—as the real center of power in the Reagan White House. Not only had Baker been undersecretary of commerce in Gerald R. Ford's administration, he was also national chairman of Ford's 1976 election bid and had managed George Bush's campaign in the 1980 presidential race—both times against then-candidate Reagan.

Even when a Meese or Deaver is visible at the top of the White House staff, the lower levels are filled with relatively young, skilled, and well-educated individuals. For example, among the initial appointees to Reagan's Office of Policy Development, the unit that helps to frame domestic policy proposals, 31 percent held MBAs and other management-related degrees, 31 percent were lawyers, 16 percent had Ph.D.s, and only 23 percent held no advanced degree. The office was headed by Martin Anderson, an economics professor from Stanford.[16]

Differentiation from Environment

The increasing complexity of the presidency and its growing reliance on expert skill and advice have given the presidency its own unique place in the policy process, differentiating it from its political environment. One way this has occurred is through increased White House control over new policy initiatives. Presidents now routinely try to shape the nation's political agenda, and the staff resources they have at their disposal enhance their ability to do so. Kennedy, Lyndon B. Johnson, and especially Nixon, with the creation of the Domestic Council, all emphasized White House control of policy proposals, deemphasizing the involvement of the cabinet and the bureaucracy. Carter and Reagan both began office with calls for more presidential reliance upon the cabinet but quickly found that goal to be unworkable in practice and turned inward to the White House staff for policy advice.

Those outside the White House—Congress, the bureaucracy, the news media, and the public—have responded to presidential direction by expecting more of it. Political lobbying and influence seeking, especially by those directly involved in national politics, are increasingly president-centered. American politics remains highly decentralized, incremental, and with multiple points of access. But those seeking to influence national politics try to cultivate those who have most to do with policy proposals: the White House staff.

A second aspect of the presidency that differentiates it from the surrounding political environment is the way parts of the staff are organized explicitly to manage external relations. The press secretary and his staff coordinate and in many cases control the presidential news that is passed on to the media.[17] Since 1953, specific staff assistants have been assigned solely to lobby Congress on the president's behalf. Today, White House lobbying efforts are organized formally within the large, well-staffed Office of Congressional Relations.

One interesting device that presidents have used to manage relations with the political environment has been the establishment of special channels of influence for important constituent groups. Again, this practice began in the Roosevelt administration, when David Niles became the first staff aide explicitly assigned the task of serving as a liaison for minority groups. Eisenhower hired the first black presidential assistant, Frederic Morrow, and added a special representative from the scientific community as well. In 1970, Nixon created the Office of Public Liaison to serve as the organizational home within the White House staff for the increasing numbers of aides who served as conduits to particular groups. By the time Carter left office, there were special staff members specifically assigned to such diverse groups as consumers, women, the elderly, Jews, Hispanics, white ethnic Catholics, Vietnam veterans, and gays, as well as such traditional constituencies as blacks, labor, and the business community.[18] The increasing differentiation of the presidency as a discrete entity thus complements its increasing complexity and reliance upon expertise as evidence of its status as an institution.

Effects of an Institutional Presidency

Even if the presidency bears the marks of an institution, do its distinctly institutional characteristics—as opposed to the individual styles and practices of each president—matter? Despite the tremendous growth in the size of the president's staff, perhaps it remains mainly a cluster of aides and supporting personnel, their tasks, organization, and tenure varying greatly from administration to administration, even changing within the term of a particular president. After all, both scholarly analysts and journalistic observers of the presidency have noted enormous differences between the Kennedy and Eisenhower White House, between Johnson and Nixon, Carter and Reagan. It is the personality, character, and individual behavior of each of these presidents that has generally attracted the attention of press and public.

Some of these observations are true, but to the extent that the institutionalized daily workings of the presidency transcend the personal ideologies, character, and idiosyncracies of those who work within it (especially the president), it makes sense to analyze the presidency from an institutional perspective. As we will see, not only do many of the presidency's institutional characteristics affect the office, they do so negatively as well as positively.

External Centralization:
Presidential Control over Policy Making

The creation of a large presidential staff has centralized much policy-making power within the confines of the presidency. This development has both positive and negative aspects.

On the positive side, an institutional presidency that centralizes control over policy can protect those programs that presidents wish to foster. The Washington political climate is not receptive to new political initiatives; they must compete for programmatic authority and budget allocations with older programs that generally are well established in agencies and departments, have strong allies on Capitol Hill, and enjoy a supportive clientele of special interest groups.

In creating the Office of Economic Opportunity, Lyndon Johnson, a president whose legislative skills were unsurpassed, recognized precisely this problem. The OEO was designed to be a central component of Johnson's War on Poverty. As Congress was considering the legislation to create the OEO, the departments of Commerce; Labor; and Health, Education, and Welfare all lobbied to have it administratively housed within their respective bailiwicks. Johnson, recognizing that to do so would subordinate the OEO to whatever other goals a department might pursue, lobbied Congress to set up OEO independently so that it would report directly to the president. Johnson was especially swayed by the views of Harvard economist John Kenneth Galbraith, who warned: "Do not bury the program in the departments. Put it in the Executive offices, where people will know what you are doing, where it can have a new staff and a fresh man as director." [19]

Centralization of power in the president's staff has not always redounded to his advantage. One of the worst effects of increasing White House control of the policy process, especially in foreign policy, has been to diminish or even exclude other sources of advice. Since the creation of the National Security Council in 1947, presidents increasingly have relied for policy recommendations upon the Council's staff, especially the president's Special Assistant for National Security. Ironically, Congress's intent in creating the NSC was to check the foreign policy power of the president by creating a deliberative body whose members (set by law) would provide an alternative yet timely source of advice to the president.

Except during Eisenhower's presidency, the NSC has not generally functioned as an effective deliberative body. The reasons why the White House-centered NSC staff and its head, the national security special assistant, have come to dominate the foreign policy-making process are plain: proximity to the Oval Office, readily available staff resources, and a series of presidents whose views about decision-making processes differed from those held by Eisenhower. Beginning with McGeorge Bundy under Kennedy, and continuing with Walt W. Rostow under Johnson, Henry Kissinger under Nixon, and Zbigniew Brzezinski under Carter, national security assistants not only have advocated their own policy views, but also have eclipsed other sources of foreign policy advice, especially the secretary of state and his department.

Perhaps the best testimony to the problems created by centralized control over foreign policy by the NSC staff can be found in the memoirs of two recent secretaries of state. Cyrus Vance, who served under Carter, repeatedly battled with the president's special assistant for national security, Zbigniew Brzezinski. Vance's resignation as secretary of state, in fact, was precipitated by the ill-fated decision— from which Vance and the State Department were effectively excluded—to try to rescue the American hostages in Iran.[20]

Alexander Haig, Reagan's first secretary of state, encountered similar problems with the NSC. In his memoirs, Haig claims he had only secondhand knowledge of many of President Reagan's decisions. In a chapter tellingly entitled "Mr. President, I Want You to Know What's Going on around You," Haig reports:

> William Clark, in his capacity as National Security Adviser to the President, seemed to be conducting a second foreign policy, using separate channels of communications ... bypassing the State Department altogether. Such a system was bound to produce confusion, and it soon did. There were conflicts over votes in the United Nations, differences over communications to heads of state, mixed signals to the combatants in Lebanon. Some of these, in my judgment, represented a danger to the nation.[21]

Haig's successor as secretary of state, George Shultz, also found himself cut out of a number of important policy decisions by the NSC. The most notable was the Reagan administration's secret negotiations with Iran to exchange arms for hostages in Lebanon and its use of the profits generated by the arms sales covertly to fund the contras in Nicaragua. The arms deal violated standing administration policy against negotiating for hostages, and the disclosure of the secret contra funds undermined congressional support for Reagan's policies in Central America. The affair not only indicated Shultz's conflicts with the NSC but was politically damaging to President Reagan.

Internal Centralization: Hierarchy, Gate Keeping, and Presidential Isolation

The general centralization of policy-making power by the White House staff has been accompanied by a centralization of power *within* the staff by one or two chief aides. This internal centralization of authority is further evidence of the institutional character of the presidency. But it can also affect the way the institutional presidency operates, providing both opportunities and risks for a president.

On the positive side, centralization of authority within a well-organized staff system offers clear lines of responsibility, well-demarcated duties, and orderly work ways. When presidents lack a centralized, organized staff system, the policy-making process suffers.

The travails of Franklin Roosevelt's staff well illustrate the problems that can arise from a lack of effective organization. Roosevelt favored a relatively unorganized, competitive staff, one in which the president acted as his own chief of staff. But rather than establishing regular patterns of duties and assignments and an orderly system of reporting and control, Roosevelt often gave his staff assistants the same assignment, in effect pitting them against each other.

Some analysts have argued that redundancy—two or more staff members doing the same thing—can benefit an organization.[22] But in Roosevelt's case, staff resources were minimal. Worse, his staff arrangements generated competitiveness, jealousy, and feelings of insecurity among his aides, none of which is conducive to sound policy advice or effective administration. "Roosevelt used men, squeezed them dry, and ruthlessly discarded them. . . . The requirement [for success] was that they accept criticism without complaint, toil without credit, and accept unquestioningly Roosevelt's moods and machinations." [23]

In addition to making the staff more effective, a system in which one staff member serves as a chief of staff or at least is *primus inter pares* (first among equals) is advantageous to a president for other reasons. It can protect the president's political standing, for example. A highly visible staff member with a significant amount of authority within the White House can act as a kind of lightning rod, deflecting political controversy away from the president and toward himself.

Perhaps the best example of this useful division of labor comes from the Eisenhower presidency. Part of Eisenhower's success as president derives from a leadership style in which he projected himself as a chief of state who was above the political fray, while allowing his assistants, especially the flinty former governor of New Hampshire, Sherman Adams, Eisenhower's chief of staff in the White House, to seem like prime ministers concerned with day-to-day politics. In a

Time magazine feature on Eisenhower's staff, Adams's scrawled "O.K., S.A." was said to be tantamount to presidential approval. Although in reality it was Eisenhower who made the decisions, Adams's reputation as the "abominable 'No!' man" helped "preserve Eisenhower's image as a benevolent national and international leader." [24]

But a well-organized, centralized staff system can also work against a president. There are dangers—especially corruption and the abuse of power—in elevating one assistant to prominence and investing that person with large amounts of power. Adams proved politically embarrassing to Eisenhower when he was accused of accepting gifts from a New England textile manufacturer. Eisenhower found it personally difficult to ask his trusted aide to resign, delegating the job to Vice President Nixon. In fact, the political and personal problems that Eisenhower experienced by relying upon, then having to fire, Adams seem to be part of a recurring pattern: Harry S Truman and Harry Vaughan, Johnson and Walter Jenkins, Nixon and Haldeman, Carter and Bert Lance, Reagan and Richard Allen.

Another two-edged consequence of a centralized staff system is that a highly visible staff assistant with sufficient authority can act as gatekeeper, controlling and filtering the flow of information to and from the president. Both Jordan under Carter and Regan under Reagan were criticized for limiting access to the president and selectively screening the information and advice he received. Joseph Califano, Jr., Carter's secretary of health, education, and welfare, had repeated run-ins with Jordan. While lobbying Rep. Dan Rostenkowski, the influential chairman of the Health Subcommittee of the House Ways and Means Committee, on a hospital cost containment bill, Califano found that Rostenkowski resented the treatment he was receiving from Jordan. "He never returns a phone call, Joe," Rostenkowski complained. "Don't feel slighted," Califano replied. "He treats you exactly as he treats most of the Cabinet." [25] In July 1979, Carter fired Califano and promoted Jordan.

Donald Regan, who succeeded James Baker as Reagan's chief of staff in 1985, acquired tremendous power over domestic policy, played a major role in making important presidential appointments, and even was touted in the media as Reagan's prime minister. Immediately upon taking office, Regan flexed his political muscles by revamping the cumbersome cabinet council system, substituting instead two streamlined bodies: the Economic Policy Council and the Domestic Policy Council. Regan retained control of the two councils' agendas. According to Meese aide Becky Dunlop, "Don Regan more than anyone else has the authority to say this issue has to be dealt with by the Cabinet council. And he does that on a regular basis." Subsequent council reports to President Reagan also flowed through Regan: "The simplified system strengthened Regan's direct control over policy, establishing him as a choke point for issues going to the President." [26] Moreover, Regan became the first chief of staff to play a major role in foreign policy making.

Regan certainly was effective in centralizing power in his own hands, but his attempts to exercise strong control over the policy-making process did not always serve the president's purposes. In the realm of domestic policy, House Republicans frequently were upset by the tactics of Regan and his staff: Regan "had ignored them while shaping a tax bill with House Ways and Means Chairman, Dan Rostenkowski." President Reagan salvaged tax reform with a personal appeal to Congress, "but the specter of the President traveling to Capitol Hill like a supplicant to plead for *Republican* House votes plainly raised doubts about the quality of White House staff work." [27]

In the realm of foreign affairs, Regan was the first chief of staff to play a major role in both making and implementing policy. Regan's attempts to influence foreign policy precipitated the resignation of Robert McFarlane, special assistant to the president for national security, and the selection of Admiral John Poindexter as his replacement. The Regan-dominated, Poindexter-led NSC soon involved the Reagan administration in the politically embarrassing Iran-contra affair.

Centralized authority even of the type Donald Regan practiced is clearly preferable to organizational anarchy. But as hierarchy and centralization develop within the White House staff, presidents can find themselves increasingly isolated, relying on a small, core group of advisers. If that occurs, what information the president gets already will have been selectively filtered and interpreted. What discussions and deliberations occur will take place within an inner circle of likeminded advisers.

Bureaucratization

As the top levels of the White House staff have increased in authority and political visibility, the rest of the staff has taken on the character of a bureaucratic organization. Among its bureaucratic characteristics are complex work routines, which often stifle originality and reduce differences on policy to their lowest common denominator. Drawing on his experience in the Carter White House, Greg Schneiders complains that if one feeds "advice through the system . . . what may have begun as a bold initiative comes out the other end as unrecognizable mush. The system frustrates and alienates the staff and cheats the President and the country." Schneiders also notes that the frustrations of staffers do not end with the paper flow: "There are also the meetings. The incredible, interminable, boring, ever-multiplying meetings. There are staff meetings and task force meetings, trip meetings and general schedule meetings, meetings to make decisions and unmake them and to plan future meetings, where even more decisions will be made."

"All of this might be more tolerable," Schneiders suggests, "if the staff could derive satisfaction vicariously from personal association with the President." But few aides have any direct contact with the president: "even many of those at the highest levels—assistants, deputy assistants, special assistants—don't see the President once a week or speak to him in any substantive way once a month."[28]

What develops as a substitute for work satisfaction or personal contact with the president are typical patterns of bureaucratic behavior: "bureaucratic" and "court" politics. With regard to court politics, for example, White House staff members often compete for assignments and authority that serve as a measure of their standing and prestige on the staff and ultimately with the president. Sometimes these turf battles actually are physical in character, with staff members competing for more office space and closer proximity to central figures in the administration, especially to the president and his Oval Office in the west wing. At the start of each presidential term, there is intense journalistic speculation about the size and location of staff offices; these are taken as signs of relative power and influence by the larger Washington community.

Occasionally something as insignificant as a *the* can make a world of difference to a staff assistant. In 1946, President Truman appointed John Steelman as "Assistant to the President." When Steelman's charter of operations was being drawn up by the Bureau of Budget, he cleverly inserted "The" before his title, telling the budget official, "My understanding is that I am supposed to be the chief of staff of the White House." The article stayed and was printed at the top of Steelman's stationery, thereby enhancing his status with other staff members, as well as among those outside the administration. Truman continued to call him assistant to the president, but other staff members grumbled over Steelman's self-assumed importance.[29]

As the Steelman example also suggests, not only are staff members concerned about their standing within the White House staff, they are attentive to how they are perceived by others. Patterns of behavior—bureaucratic politics—can develop that relate to a staff member's place in the organization: "Where one stands depends upon where one sits." Staff members often develop allies on the outside—members of the press, members of Congress, lobbyists, and other political influentials—who can aid the programs and political causes of particular parts of the institutional presidency or personal careers of staffers. Conversely, they also can create hostility and enmity among those outside the staff who compete for presidential attention. Perhaps the classic example is the "us versus them" attitude that develops in foreign policy making between the NSC staff (inside the White House) and the State Department (outside) and between the Office Policy Development (inside) and the regular departments (outside) domestic policy. In part, such attitudes stem from different orientations and perspectives: "Political appointees seem to want to accomplish goals quickly while careerists opt to accomplish things carefully." [30] But they also may inhere in simple bureaucratic competition and politics, generated by a very complex, quite bureaucratic institution.

Politicization

As a response to the bureaucratization of the White House staff, presidents increasingly are politicizing the institutional presidency. That is, they are attempting to make sure that staff members heed the president's policy directives and serve his, rather than their own, political needs.

In most cases, the president's aim in politicizing the staff is understandable: a president should expect broad agreement among his aides and assistants with his political programs and policy goals. President Nixon, for example, created the Domestic Council as a discrete unit within the White House staff to serve as his principal source of policy advice on domestic affairs; Nixon feared that the agencies and departments were dominated by liberal Democrats who were unsympathetic to his policy aims.[31]

The difficulty for a president comes in determining to what degree he should politicize his staff. Excessive politicization can limit the range of opinions among (and thus advice from) the staff; taken to extremes, politicization may result in a president taking counsel from a phalanx of likeminded yes men.

Excessive politicization can also weaken the objectivity of the policy analysis at the president's disposal; this is especially true when the politicized staff unit has a tradition of neutral competence and professionalism. As Terry Moe summarizes the argument, "Politicization is deplored for its destructive effects on institutional memory, expertise, professionalism, objectivity, communications, continuity, and other bases of organizational competence." [32]

One part of the president's staff in which politicization has been most noticeable—and the debate over politicization most charged—is the Office of Management and Budget (OMB). The same Nixon effort that created the Domestic Council also led to the reorganization of the old Bureau of the Budget into the present OMB. The old bureau, although an arm of the executive branch and certainly not wholly outside politics, was regarded as a place where neutral competence was paramount: "a place where the generalist ethic prevailed ... a place where you were both a representative for the President's particular view and the top objective resource for the continuous institution of the Presidency." [33]

Under Nixon, the number of political appointees in the OMB was increased. Moreover, some functions once assigned to professionals were given to political appointees; presidentially appointed program associate directors, for example, were placed in the examining divisions of the OMB.[34] The effects of these changes have been noticeable: greater personal staff loyalty to political appointees, less cooperation with other parts of the White House staff and with Congress, and reduced impartiality and competence in favor of increased ideology and partisanship. The role of the OMB in the policy process also has changed: it now gives substantive policy advice—not just objective budget estimates—and has taken an active and visible role in lobbying Congress.

The experience of the Reagan administration is particularly revealing about the risks of excessive politicization in an area—budget making—in which expertise and objective analysis must complement the policy goals that are expressed in the president's budget proposal. From the start, Reagan relied heavily on the OMB, especially during the directorship of David Stockman, both in formulating Reaganomics and in trying to get its legislative proposals passed by Congress. Stockman himself has concluded—and announced that conclusion in the title of his memoir recounting his experiences in the Reagan White House—that the "Reagan Revolution has failed." [35] Part of Stockman's thesis is that Reagan was done in by normal Washington politics, which is particularly averse to a budget conscious president. But Stockman's own words reveal a politicized, deprofessionalized OMB, which may not have been able to give the president the kind of objective advice he needed, at times, to win over his critics and political opponents:

> None of us really understands what's going on with all these numbers.... The thing was put together so fast that it probably should have. been put together differently.... We were doing the whole budget-cutting exercise so frenetically ... juggling details, pushing people, and going from one session to another ... the

defense program was just a bunch of numbers written on a piece of paper. And it didn't mesh.[36]

The politicization of the OMB does not explain all of Stockman's difficulties. But as Stockman's account attests, Reagan and his advisers needed hard questioning, objective analysis, and criticism of the sort that the old bureau but not the new OMB could provide a president.

Putting the President Back In

The institutional presidency that has developed during the last fifty years undoubtedly offers the president important resources that he needs to meet the complex policy tasks and expectations of the office. But those same resources can work against the president; as we have seen, the effects of an institutional presidency—centralization of policy making, hierarchy, bureaucratization, and politicization—can detract from as well as serve a president's policy goals.

Presidents are not, however, simply at the mercy of the institution. Having emphasized the institutional character of the presidency, we should not neglect the presidential character of the institution. The presidency takes on a different coloration from administration to administration, from one set of staff advisers to another. Presidents and their staffs are by no means hostage to the institution; often they have been able to benefit from the positive resources it provides while deflecting or overcoming institutional forces that detract from their goals.

For example, in order to retard some of the negative effects of relying on a large White House staff, Eisenhower complemented his use of the formal machinery of the NSC and Adams's office with informal channels of advice. In foreign affairs he turned to his trusted secretary of state, John Foster Dulles, as well as to a network of friends with political knowledge and experience, such as Gen. Alfred Gruenther, supreme Allied commander in Europe. Eisenhower also held regular meetings with his cabinet and with congressional leaders to inform them of his actions and to garner their support, as well as to hear their views and opinions.[37]

When dealing with his staff, Eisenhower encouraged his aides to be candid with him, to feel free to air their disagreements and doubts. Minutes of his NSC meetings reveal a president exposed to the policy splits of his staff, who often engaged in lively discussions with Dulles, Nixon, and others. But Eisenhower was careful to reserve the ultimate power of decision for himself; although they had a voice in the process, neither the NSC nor Adams decided for the president.

Kennedy dismantled most of the national security staff that had existed under Eisenhower, preferring instead to use smaller, more informal and collegial decision-making forums. Kennedy's abandonment of formal procedures may have been unwise, but his experience with the collegial Ex-Com (his executive committee of top foreign policy advisers) offers lessons about how presidents can work effectively through informal patterns of advice seeking and giving. In April 1961, Kennedy's advisers performed poorly, leading him into an ill-conceived, poorly planned, hastily decided, and badly executed invasion of Cuba—the Bay of Pigs disaster. In the aftermath of that fiasco, Kennedy commissioned a study to find out what had gone wrong. On the basis of its findings, Kennedy reorganized his decision-making procedures—even making major changes in the CIA—and explored the faults in his own leadership style. By the time of the Cuban missile crisis in October 1962, Kennedy and his advisers had become an effective decision-making group. Information was readily at hand, the assumptions and implications of policy choices were probed, pressures that could lead to false group consensus were avoided, and Kennedy himself deliberately did not disclose his own policy preference—sometimes absenting himself from meetings—in order to facilitate candid discussion and head off premature decisions.

A president can also take steps to deal with the bureaucratic tendencies that can crop up in his staff. Kennedy's New Frontier agenda, for example, gave his advisers a common set of very unbureaucratic goals; his personal style generated loyalty and trust. Eisenhower lacked the youthful vigor of his successor, but his broad organizational experience made him a good judge of character with a sure instinct for what and how much he could delegate to subordinates. Eisenhower also emphasized to his aides that they worked for him, not for the NSC, Adams, or others on the staff.

Finally, although the tendency toward the centralization of policy-making power within the White House and the politicization of the advisory process has been powerful, all presidents have the capacity to choose how they will act and react within a complex political context that is populated by other powerful political institutions, processes, and participants. Too much politicization weakens any special claims of expertise, experience, and general institutional primacy that the president may make in a particular policy area. Too much centralization eclipses the role of other political actors in a system that is geared to share, rather than exclude, domains of power; it also may set in motion powerful antipresidential forces.

Notes

1. It was only after 1933, following ratification of the Twentieth Amendment to the Constitution, that presidents were inaugurated on January 20.
2. Fred I. Greenstein, "Change and Continuity in the Modern Presidency," in *The New American Political System,* ed. Anthony King (Washington, D.C.: American Enterprise Institute, 1978), 45-86.
3. In a January 10, 1982, *Chicago Tribune* poll, the ten greatest presidents, according to historians, were in rank order, Lincoln, Washington, F. Roosevelt, T. Roosevelt, Jefferson, Wilson, Jackson, Truman, Eisenhower, and Polk. Even in Maranell and Dodder's poll of American historians, only Franklin Roosevelt and Kennedy among recent presidents made the top ten; Garry Maranell and Richard Dodder, "Political Orientation and Evaluation of Presidential Prestige: A Study of American Historians," *Social Science Quarterly* 51 (1970): 418.
4. Steven Wayne, *The Legislative Presidency* (New York: Harper & Row, 1978), 30.
5. Patrick Anderson, *The President's Men* (New York: Doubleday, 1969), 29.
6. Quoted in Louis Brownlow, *A Passion for Anonymity: The Autobiography of Louis Brownlow,* vol. 2 (Chicago: University of Chicago Press, 1958), 392.
7. President's Committee on Administrative Management, *Administrative Management in the Government of the United States* (Washington, D.C.: U.S. Government Printing Office, 1937), 4.
8. The initial Brownlow Committee recommendation for reorganizing the executive branch also included controversial proposals to redefine the jurisdiction of cabinet departments, regroup autonomous and independent agencies and bureaus, and give the president virtually unchecked authority to determine and carry out the reorganization and any needed in the future. These more controversial proposals either were dropped or made more palatable in the reorganization act passed by Congress in 1939.
9. For further discussion of the Brownlow and Hoover commissions, as well as other efforts at reorganizing the presidency, see Peri E. Arnold, *Making the Managerial Presidency: Comprehensive Reorganization Planning, 1905-1980* (Princeton: Princeton University Press, 1986).
10. Other components of the Executive Office of the President include the Council on Environmental Policy, the Office of Science and Technology Policy, and the Office of the U.S. Trade Representative.
11. The reader should note that this sense of *institutional* differs from the way others have used the term. For former Kennedy aide Theodore Sorensen, for example, *institutional* refers to what he took to be the overly formalized and structured staff organization of the Eisenhower presidency, which his boss rejected: "From the outset he [Kennedy] abandoned the notion of a collective, institutionalized presidency. He abandoned the practice of the Cabinet and the National Security Council making group decisions like corporate boards of directors." Theodore Sorensen, *Kennedy* (New York: Bantam, 1966), 281.
12. The characteristics of institutionalization are adapted, in part, from Nelson Polsby, "The Institutionalization of the U.S. House of Representatives," *American Political Science Review* 52 (1968): 144-168. On the notion of the presidency as an institution, see Lester Seligman, "Presidential Leadership: The Inner Circle and Institutionalization," *Journal of Politics* 18 (1956): 410-426; Norman Thomas and Hans Baade, eds., *The Institutionalized Presidency* (Dobbs Ferry, N.Y.: Oceana Press, 1972); Robert S. Gilmour, "The Institutionalized Presidency: A Conceptual Clarification," in *The Presidency in Contemporary Context,* ed. Norman Thomas

(New York: Dodd, Mead, 1975), 147-159; John Kessel, *The Domestic Presidency: Decision-Making in the White House* (North Scituate, Mass.: Duxbury Press, 1975); Lester Seligman, "The Presidency and Political Change," *The Annals* 466 (1983): 179-192; John Kessel, "The Structures of the Carter White House," *American Journal of Political Science* 27 (1983): 431-463; John Kessel, "The Structures of the Reagan White House," *American Journal of Political Science* 28 (1984): 231-258; and Colin Campbell, *Managing the Presidency* (Pittsburgh: University of Pittsburgh Press, 1986).

13. The Office of Policy Development was named the Domestic Council until 1977.

14. See, for example, Dom Bonafede, "Carter Turns on the Drama—But Can He Lead?" *National Journal*, July 28, 1979, 1236-1240. According to Bonafede (p. 1237), "The Cabinet shuffle was provoked, in large measure, by the traditional rivalry between the Cabinet and the White House staff, and by the desire by Carter and his senior assistants to strengthen their grip on the federal bureaucracy."

15. Quoted in Bonafede, "Carter Turns on the Drama," 1238.

16. Reagan data from 1981, "Policy Development Office," *National Journal*, April 25, 1981, 684-687.

17. On White House-press relations, see Michael Baruch Grossman and Martha Joynt Kumar, *Portraying the President: The White House and the News Media* (Baltimore: Johns Hopkins University Press, 1981).

18. For further discussion, see Joseph Pika, "Interest Groups and the Executive: Federal Intervention," *Interest Group Politics*, ed. Allan J. Cigler and Burdett A. Loomis (Washington, D.C.: CQ Press, 1983), 298-323.

19. Galbraith quoted in Lyndon Johnson, *Vantage Point: Perspectives of the Presidency, 1963-69* (New York: Holt, Rinehart and Winston, 1971), 76.

20. Vance had earlier opposed the mission as poorly conceived and difficult to execute, yet while the secretary was on a brief weekend vacation in Florida, Carter hastily called a meeting of his top foreign policy advisers. The meeting was dominated by members of Brzezinski's staff and the military, who favored the rescue attempt. The State Department, which favored a more cautious, diplomatic solution to the hostage crisis, was represented in the meeting only by Vance's undersecretary, Warren Christopher. Christopher reported that he was isolated in his dissent: "Everyone else at the meeting supported the rescue attempt." When Vance returned to Washington on Monday morning, he was "stunned and angry that such a momentous decision had been made in his absence." After several days of "deep personal anguish," he decided to resign. Cyrus Vance, *Hard Choices: Critical Years in America's Foreign Policy* (New York: Simon & Schuster, 1983), 409-410.

22. Martin Landau, "Redundancy, Rationality, and the Problem of Duplication and Overlap," *Public Administration Review* 29 (1969): 346-358.

23. Patrick Anderson, *The President's Men* (Garden City, N.Y.: Anchor, 1969), 10.

24. Fred I. Greenstein, *The Hidden-Hand Presidency: Eisenhower as Leader* (New York: Basic Books, 1982), 147. Adams's counterpart in the field of foreign affairs was Secretary of State John Foster Dulles.

25. Joseph A. Califano, Jr., *Governing America: An Insider's Report from the White House and the Cabinet* (New York: Simon & Schuster, 1981), 148.

26. Ronald Brownstein and Dick Kirschsten, "Cabinet Power," *National Journal*, June 28, 1986, 1589.

27. Bernard Weinraub, "How Donald Regan Runs the White House," *New York Times Magazine*, January 5, 1986, 14.

28. Greg Schneiders, "My Turn: Goodbye to All That," *Newsweek,* September 24, 1979, 23.
29. Ken Hechler, *Working with Truman: A Personal Memoir of the White House Years* (New York: G. P. Putnam's Sons, 1982), 46-47.
30. Thomas P. Murphy, Donald E. Neuchterlein, and Ronald J. Stupak, *Inside the Bureaucracy: The View from the Assistant Secretary's Desk* (Boulder, Colo.: Westview Press, 1978), 181.
31. For evidence, based on a 1970 survey, supporting Nixon's view, see J. D. Aberbach and B. A. Rockman, "Clashing Beliefs within the Executive Branch: The Nixon Administration," *American Political Science Review* 70 (1976): 456-468. In data largely taken from a 1976 survey, Cole and Caputo found that Republicans were more likely to be selected to career positions during the Nixon years and that executives calling themselves independents during that period were more likely to resemble their Republican colleagues in attitudes and values. Richard Cole and David Caputo, "Presidential Control of the Senior Civil Service: Assessing the Strategies of the Nixon Years," *American Political Science Review* 73 (1979): 399-413.
32. Terry M. Moe, "The Politicized Presidency," *The New Direction in American Politics,* ed. John Chubb and Paul Peterson (Washington, D.C.: Brookings Institution, 1985), 235.
33. Hugh Heclo, "OMB and the Presidency: The Problem of "Neutral Competence,'" *Public Interest,* no. 38 (1975): 81.
34. Ibid., 85.
35. David A. Stockman, *The Triumph of Politics: Why the Reagan Revolution Failed* (New York: Harper & Row, 1986).
36. Quoted in William Greider, *The Education of David Stockman and Other Americans* (New York, E. P. Dutton, 1982), 33, 37.
37. On Eisenhower's "binocular" use of informal and formal patterns of advice, see Greenstein, 100-151.

17. THE PRESIDENCY AND THE BUREAUCRATIC STATE

Elizabeth Sanders

Thresholds in the ebb and flow of presidential power may be marked by the sudden realization that once popular anecdotes now seem irrelevant. One of the most quoted stories of recent decades is Richard Neustadt's rendering of a remark Harry S Truman made in 1952 as he mused on his successor's prospects as chief executive: "He'll sit there and he'll say, 'Do this! Do that!' *and nothing will happen.* Poor Ike—it won't be a bit like the Army. He'll find it very frustrating." [1] Equally popular quotations about the presidency include the Brownlow Committee's 1937 complaint that independent agencies and commissions constitute "a headless fourth branch of government," [2] and the remark of the first budget bureau director that "cabinet members . . . are the natural enemies of the president." [3] The vision of the relationship between the presidency and the bureaucracy that these stories evoke—of a bound and progressively enfeebled Prometheus—seemed appropriate as recently as 1980, but they are out of place today.

Reagan and the Bureaucracy

Without any significant increase in statutory powers, and despite some serious excesses and missteps, the Reagan presidency has impressively demonstrated the potential of the chief execuive to reshape both public policy and the modus operandi of the federal bureaucracy. Using constitutional and statutory powers that the office has been endowed with for decades, the national governmental apparatus has been harnessed to a policy agenda sharply different from that of the Democratic regime of Franklin D. Roosevelt and his successors. The principal elements of the Reagan strategy may be grouped under four headings: macroeconomic policy, central clearance of rules and regulations, personnel, and devolution and privatization.

Macroeconomic Policy

The 1974 Budget and Impoundment Act manifested Congress's intention to regain control of national spending. Ironically, the new budget process instead provided an opening for presidential intervention that, since 1981, has yielded unprecedented budgetary power to the president. The new centralization of congressional tax and spending decisions in a single annual budget resolution "offers the president a more cohesive means of monitoring and influencing congressional activity than was possible before the Budget Committees were created." [4] Reagan, using his newly aggressive Office of Management and Budget (OMB), took full advantage of this centralization. Interpreting the 1980 election as a mandate to shrinking the social welfare state and societal expectations that fueled its growth, the administration struck powerful blows at the heart of the state: its central resource extraction and dispensing functions. Welfare state expansion was virtually halted; nondefense program increases barely kept pace with inflation (see Table 17-1). Social program expenditures, which had risen from 5 percent of the gross national product (GNP) in 1961 to almost 11 percent in 1980, began a relative decline after 1982.[5] Conversely, the previous contraction of the defense budget share was reversed, for a $91 billion increase (from 5.2 to 6.3 percent of GNP) over the last Carter budget.[6]

Since total federal government expenditures have grown significantly (from 22.2 percent of GNP in 1981 to 23.7 percent in 1985), the national government clearly has not contracted during Reagan's presidency. Its policy emphasis, however, appears to have changed significantly. The figures in Table 17-1 partially reflect forces other than the president's budget priorities, such as the expansionist momentum of past laws that entitle persons to benefits, and national and international economic conditions, but they roughly embody the interests of the president's regional and ideological constituencies, as well as his decision to spare Social Security recipients the cuts that other social program beneficiaries have experienced.

Although the president has no direct control over monetary policy, the Federal Reserve Board under chairman Paul Volcker (reappointed by Reagan in 1983) has pursued policies consonant with, and undoubtedly influenced by, the administration's agenda. After a sharp, recession-inducing boost early in Reagan's first term, interest rates were brought down a third from their 1980 level and inflation (as measured by the Consumer Price Index) was reduced from 13.5 percent to 3.6 percent per year by 1985.[7] The costs of this reversal in the inflationary spiral were borne by blue collar workers through wage reductions and unemployment.

As a result of administration-sponsored legislation, the personal and corporate tax burden also was reduced significantly, even before the landmark tax reform of 1986. Individual and corporate income

Table 17-1 Budget Outlays by Function, Fiscal 1976-85 (Millions of Dollars)

	1976	1981	1985	Absolute 1981-85 increases
Defense	89,619	157,513 (105,713) [a]	252,748 (142,795)	60.5% (35.1)
Social Security and Medicare	89,736	178,783 (119,989)	254,445 (143,754)	42.3 (19.8)
Agriculture	3,170	11,323 (7,599)	25,565 (14,444)	125.8 (90.1)
Law enforcement/justice	3,324	4,762 (3,196)	6,277 (3,546)	31.8 (11.0)
International affairs	6,433	13,104 (8,795)	16,176 (9,139)	23.4 (3.9)
Science, space, and technology	4,373	6,469 (4,342)	8,627 (4,874)	33.4 (12.3)
Energy	4,204	15,166 (10,179)	5,685 (3,212)	−62.5 (−68.4)
National resources and environment	8,184	13,568 (9,106)	13,357 (7,546)	−1.6 (−17.1)
Commerce and housing credit	7,619	8,206 (5,507)	4,229 (2,389)	−48.5 (−56.6)
Transportation	13,739	23,379 (15,691)	25,838 (14,598)	10.5 (−7.0)
Community and regional development	5,442	10,568 (7,093)	7,680 (4,339)	−27.3 (−38.8)
Education, job training and social services	18,910	33,709 (22,623)	29,342 (16,577)	−13.0 (−26.7)
Health: services, research, and regulation	15,734	26,866 (18,031)	33,542 (18,950)	28.0 (5.1)
Income security (welfare)	60,784	99,723 (66,928)	128,200 (72,429)	28.6 (8.2)
Veterans	18,433	22,991 (15,430)	26,352 (14,888)	14.6 (−3.5)
General government	2,519	4,582 (3,075)	5,228 (2,954)	14.1 (−3.9)
Revenue sharing/general block grants	7,232	6,854 (4,600)	6,353 (3,589)	−7.3 (−22.0)
Interest	26,711	68,734 (46,130)	129,436 (73,128)	88.3 (58.5)

SOURCE: Office of Management and Budget, *Budget of the United States Government,* fiscal years 1986 (Table 20) and 1987 (Table 18). 1976 dollar equivalents are calculated from GNP deflator tables in the appendix to the *Economic Report of the President,* February, 1986, B-3, 257.

[a] Figures in parentheses represent budget amounts and comparison in constant 1976 dollars.

taxes dropped from 12 percent of GNP in 1980 to 9.9 percent in 1984; total tax revenues (including excise, Social Security, and other taxes) fell from 20.1 to 18.6 percent in the same period.[8] The result of large defense spending increases and sharp revenue reductions is a massive federal deficit whose costs are widely borne. But these costs, it seems, are tolerable to the administration, since public and scholarly anxiety about record deficits serves as a powerful psychological restraint on further expansions of the welfare state, and attempts to reduce the deficit through tax increases would be unpopular with voters and campaign contributors.

Reagan's macroeconomic strategy overwhelmed a large number of well-organized interests that had enjoyed long success in protecting their tax advantages and annual budget increases. As Theodore Lowi's policy typology predicts, the shift in policy focus from distributive and regulatory programs to redistributive taxation and budget decisions moved debate out of the congressional committees and bureaucratic units, where interest groups wield power over relatively narrow policies, and onto the floor of Congress, where battles are waged publicly between broad partisan and ideological coalitions. The familiar processes of bureaucratic and committee politics were superseded to an extent few political scientists thought possible a decade ago.

Central Clearance of Rules and Regulations

In 1937 Roosevelt's Brownlow Committee on Administrative Management urged that all executive agencies, "independent"or otherwise, be absorbed into the presidentially supervised cabinet departments. From that time forward, presidents have attempted to bring these various administrative units under centralized direction. The public service intelligentsia—municipal and state administrative careerists, public administration scholars, and public law professors—have been strong supporters of this effort.[9] Such support has put them in the somewhat anomalous position of championing both merit-based public administration by neutral experts[10] and hierarchical control of administration by the president. Their advocacy of presidential control (and its converse, a tendency to disparage congressional influence over administration) was in part the result of the presidency's centrality, urban orientation, and potential to spur rapid reform. It also reflected approval of the liberal programs of the presidents who hired public administration reformers like themselves to help establish control over the expanding executive apparatus. It is ironic, then, that Reagan appears to have succeeded where successive Democratic presidents and their intellectual advisers failed. He has brought the "headless fourth branch of government" under tight White House control, using methods pioneered by previous Democratic presidents.

Prior chief executives had attempted to make of the Bureau of the Budget (OMB's predecessor) both a managerial tool (to minimize program duplication and waste) and a policy-generating and evaluating unit, integrated into the White House advisory staff.[11] Earlier presidents, both Republican and Democratic, also had established central coordinating and review mechanisms to scrutinize the rules and regulations generated by executive agencies. Under Reagan, both processes were merged and brought to fruition by the most powerful budget bureau since the office was created in 1921.

Before Reagan, control of administration was regarded mainly as a problem of staffing and structure—that is, of ensuring the loyalty and cooperation of agency employees and of structuring their interactions with the president, his aides, Congress, and the array of interest groups concerned with the agency's operations. Thus, appointment and reorganization powers were the instruments of choice in presidential attempts to control the bureaucracy. But both were of limited usefulness in dealing with the independent regulatory agencies, whose members, by law, serve fixed, staggered terms and must represent both political parties (see Figure 17-1). Since the first such agency was established in the late nineteenth century (the Interstate Commerce Commission), an administrative lore has accumulated (ratified in court decisions and statutes) granting these bodies a peculiar hybrid status that includes quasi-judicial and quasi-legislative powers, as well as conventional administrative ones. The Supreme Court itself made a major contribution to the "fourth branch" lore by ruling, in 1935, that Roosevelt had no power to remove for political reasons a recalcitrant member of an agency with quasi-legislative and quasi-judicial functions.[12] Even in agencies and departments with standard executive functions the president's appointment powers are limited to the highest-ranking positions, and in filling them he is besieged with patronage requests.

Thus handicapped by their limited power to control personnel in the executive branch, presidents Roosevelt, Truman, Kennedy, and Nixon attempted to bring the agencies under closer supervision by using the limited reorganization authority granted them by a skeptical Congress. One of their major goals was to win the right to designate the chairs of the commissions, and then to enhance the chair's control over staff, budgets, and the organization of work. By the end of the Nixon administration, the president had been empowered to name the chairs of all the major independent agencies, but most attempts to authorize agency heads to delegate decision making to a subset of members or to the professional staff of the agency (a method, perhaps, to bypass certain commissioners) were blocked by congressional opponents.

Figure 17-1 Executive Branch of the United States Government

THE PRESIDENT

Executive Office of the President

White House Office
Office of Management and Budget
Council of Economic Advisers
National Security Council
Office of Policy Development

Office of the United States
   Trade Representative
Council on Environmental Quality
Office of Science and Technology Policy
Office of Administration

THE VICE PRESIDENT

DEPARTMENT OF AGRICULTURE

DEPARTMENT OF COMMERCE

DEPARTMENT OF DEFENSE

DEPARTMENT OF EDUCATION

DEPARTMENT OF ENERGY

DEPARTMENT OF HEALTH AND HUMAN SERVICES

DEPARTMENT OF HOUSING AND URBAN DEVELOPMENT

DEPARTMENT OF THE INTERIOR

DEPARTMENT OF JUSTICE

DEPARTMENT OF LABOR

DEPARTMENT OF STATE

DEPARTMENT OF TRANSPORTATION

DEPARTMENT OF TREASURY

MAJOR INDEPENDENT AGENCIES, GOVERNMENT CORPORATIONS, AND OTHER ESTABLISHMENTS

Independent Regulatory Commissions and Boards[1]	*Independent Executive Agencies*[2]	*Government Corporations, Foundations, and Other*[3]
Board of Governors of the Federal Reserve System	Central Intelligence Agency	Administrative Conference of the U.S.
Commodity Futures Trading Commission	Environmental Protection Agency	Appalachian Regional Commission
Consumer Product Safety Commission	General Services Administration	Export-Import Bank
Equal Employment Opportunity Commission	National Aeronautics and Space Administration	Federal Deposit Insurance Corporation
Federal Communications Commission	Office of Personnel Management	National Credit Union Administration
Federal Election Commission	Peace Corps	National Railroad Passenger Corporation (AMTRAK)
Federal Home Loan Bank Board	U.S. Arms Control and Disarmament Agency	National Science Foundation
Federal Maritime Commission	U.S. International Development Cooperation Agency	Occupational Safety and Health Review Commission
Federal Trade Commission	Veterans Administration	Panama Canal Commission
Interstate Commerce Commission		Pension Benefits Guaranty Corporation
Merit Systems Protection Board		Postal Rate Commission
National Labor Relations Board		Smithsonian Institution
Nuclear Regulatory Commission		Tennessee Valley Authority
Securities Exchange Commission		U.S. Postal Service
U.S. International Trade Commission		

SOURCE: *U.S. Government Manual 1985-86*; and U.S. Senate, Committee on Governmental Affairs, *Policy and Supporting Positions*. 98th Congress, 2d sess. (Committee Print, 1984).

1. Most of these agencies "regulate" privately owned firms; the MSPB, however, "regulates" other federal officials and the USITC has only investigatory and advisory powers. All have multiple directors who serve fixed, overlapping terms, and the composition of all but the NLRB must be bipartisan by law.

2. These agencies have single heads who serve at the president's pleasure. Some (like the VA) are actually larger than some departments but have a narrower mission.

3. Structure is extremely varied here. Directors may be single (although most are multiple), serve fixed or indefinite (presidentially decided) terms, involve state officials, and may be bipartisan by law. Functions range from advice on streamlining regulation (the AC) to running a railroad (AMTRAK) or acting as a specialized administrative court (OSHRC).

Congress also refused reorganization proposals that would absorb independent agencies into cabinet departments or establish formal White House policy guidance for the independent regulatory agencies.[13]

In general, since it first granted the president reorganization powers in 1932, Congress has displayed a niggardly attitude toward the range of the grant. Authorizations typically ran for only a few years at a time, exempted the independent regulatory and other named agencies, prohibited the creation or abolition of departments, and allowed a one- or two-house veto of individual reorganization plans. Truman and Kennedy were forced to expend much staff time and political capital to persuade Congress to make modest changes in administrative structure, and the changes wrung from Congress had to be justified in terms of economy and efficiency in government rather than enhanced presidential control or administrative rationality. In the early 1980s, Congress allowed the reorganization statute to expire; President Reagan did not press the issue, apparently acknowledging that the gains from administrative reorganization are not worth the effort.[14]

The imposition of central clearance of executive agency decisions has an obvious appeal for the president. It transcends personnel and organizational obstacles by creating a final, rigid bottleneck in which administrative actions may be scrutinized for conformity with his policy goals and standards. OMB is ideally situated to perform such a function for the president. It has been authorized to review agencies' budget requests since it was created in 1921 and has supervised their information-gathering activities since 1942.[15] The systematic use of OMB to clear agency and departmental legislative requests (as well as bills passed by Congress) dates from the Truman administration. In the 1970s, as concern grew about the effects of federal regulations on productivity and inflation, presidential reliance on OMB central clearance procedures steadily increased.[16]

The Nixon administration began by instituting "quality of life" reviews, in which health and safety regulations (particularly, as it turned out, those of the Environmental Protection Agency) were examined by OMB and other affected agencies. Gerald R. Ford generalized and intensified the central review process by issuing Executive Order 11821 in 1974. This directive required that all executive branch agencies submit "inflation impact statements" for major new regulations to the Council on Wage and Price Stability (COWPS). Although COWPS was not authorized to block offending regulations, all agencies of the federal bureaucracy were encouraged to judge the efficiency and effectiveness of their actions by a common standard—economic analysis—and to ensure that their activities could withstand the glare of centralized scrutiny.

A more wide ranging review process was instituted by President Jimmy Carter. His 1978 Executive Order 12044 directed each executive agency to revise its internal procedures in order to centralize rule making and make it more cost effective. High-level, presidentially appointed executives in each agency were to be fully informed about regulatory proposals or assessments made at lower levels; in addition, semiannual agendas listing regulations to be developed or reappraised were to be published by the agencies. (The need for these instructions indicates how amorphous the federal bureaucracy had become.) In developing major regulations—the definition of which was ultimately the province of each agency but for which $100 million in resultant costs was a presumptive threshold—the order directed agencies to undertake "a careful examination of alternative approaches ... an analysis of the economic consequences of each ... and a detailed explanation of the reasons for choosing one alternative over the others." Authority was vested in the OMB to oversee agency compliance with the president's directives. The Regulatory Council, consisting of agency and department heads, screened pending and proposed rules for duplicative and contradictory efforts, and the Regulatory Analysis Review Group (RARG)—with a broad ex-officio membership, staffed and led by the chair of the president's Council of Economic Advisers (CEA)—was empowered to select agency rule analyses for independent review. Soon after, RARG objected to a number of preliminary EPA air quality standards as poorly reasoned and excessively costly.[17]

Carter's executive order, like the Reagan directives that replaced it, exempted independent regulatory agencies from the analysis, agenda, and review requirements, although heads of those agencies were free to participate in the Regulatory Council on a voluntary basis. This exemption recognized the peculiar status of the multiheaded, bipartisan boards and commissions, but by the late 1970s it did not pose serious problems for the strategy of bureaucratic control through central clearance. Presidents had discovered that the right appointments could disrupt venerable commission values and procedures, and presidentially backed deregulation statutes had sharply diminished the authority of agencies such as the ICC and Civil Aeronautics Board (CAB). The newer regulatory agencies whose activities had generated so much business opposition, such as EPA, the National Highway Transportation Safety Administration (NHTSA), and the Occupational Safety and Health Administration (OSHA), were of the standard executive form, headed by a single director who was appointed (and removable) by the president or the head of the department in which the agency was housed. In addition, the multitude of rules and regulations produced by the cabinet departments and most of the single-headed, noncabinet agencies (pertaining, for example, to education, public transportation, housing, forestry, air and water pollution, veterans' benefits, strip mining, workplace safety, and oil leasing) posed no clear legal or constitutional obstacles to central clearance.

In sum, the rapidly developing trend of the 1970s was to centralize and scrutinize the issuance of administrative rules and regulations, requiring policies generated by the federal bureaucracy to be evaluated against ever more formal and stringent criteria. In furtherance of that trend, Reagan issued Executive Order 12291 in February 1981, directing that all regulatory proposals from nonexempt agencies be submitted to the OMB well before publication of notice of impending rule making and be accompanied by an elaborate "regulatory impact analysis."

Under Reagan, however, the clearance process has generated so much controversy that, far from prodding Congress to write the OMB review process into law, it has provoked federal court challenges from interest groups and Democratic congressional leaders. These critics charge that, in abrogating to the president control of both procedure and substance, Reagan's central clearance process violates the Administrative Procedure Act of 1946, a multitude of statutes conferring regulatory jurisdiction on federal agencies, and perhaps the constitutional separation of powers itself.[18]

Although the clearance system that was established by Executive Order 12291 and subsequent directives clearly built on earlier practices, it went beyond its predecessors in several ways. Clearance powers were vested in one unit, the OMB, instead of a broad-based, ex-officio council; the OMB, rather than the agencies themselves, was charged with developing uniform standards for identifying major rules and could overrule the agencies' applications of those standards; and OMB applied an explicit, quantitative cost/benefit measure that stood as a barrier to proposed regulations, not just a hortatory goal. The Carter administration had urged agencies to review, and perhaps eliminate, existing regulations and to publish a prospective calendar; Executive Order 12291 went further in mandating that existing regulations be reexamined[19] and in applying cost/benefit tests at the earliest stages of rule development. More fundamentally, central reviewers in the Carter administration were not unsympathetic with the purposes of the rules and regulations generated in the bureaucracy; they mainly attempted to render methods more efficient and less costly. In the Reagan administration the burden of proof is clearly on the agencies to demonstrate that any regulation at all is needed, and to delay "inevitable" rules (NHTSA's passive restraint standard for automobiles, for example) is itself considered an achievement.[20]

The new clearance system, supported by shrunken and more ideologically attuned bureaucracies, has had a measurable impact on agency performance. In early 1981 the administration announced a freeze on several hundred regulations that were pending or approved but not yet in effect, in order to subject them to the new and more stringent cost/benefit standards. By 1984 the administration boasted of a steady contraction in the size of the *Federal Register,* the publication in which rules, regulations, and notice of agency procedings appear. Almost six thousand fewer rules were enacted during Reagan's first term than during the Carter administration; Murray Weidenbaum, Reagan's first CEA chair, estimates that the cancellation, modification, delay, and nongeneration of regulations saved businesses and government several billion dollars. Although these cost-savings claims are flawed by bias and omission, reversal of the earlier trend of regulatory expansion is unmistakable, and much of that contraction probably results from the highly centralized OMB clearance system that was inaugurated in 1981.[21]

Personnel

Staffing the executive branch with agents sympathetic to the president's program is a major weapon in the struggle to control national administration. Personnel strategy has three interrelated aspects: the sheer number of appointments; the ratio of political to civil service positions; and the role of "overhead" units in the Executive Office of the President (EOP), which effect wide-ranging central policy direction.

For presidents (like Reagan) who head political coalitions that seek to limit the reach of the social welfare and regulatory state, reducing the number of federal employees is a predictable priority. Fewer people on the payroll means less "meddlesome" activity and fewer rules and regulations; it also helps to shrink the federal budget. As can be seen in Table 17-2, however, government's human resources have not contracted in the aggregate during the Reagan administration. Rather, as with budget outlays, priorities have been shifted: the ranks of the disapproved welfare and regulatory agencies have been reduced, while civilian employment in the Defense Department and other security-related agencies has grown. The most disadvantaged agencies are those concerned with social services, worker and product safety and health, and the regulation of business prices and competitive practices.[22] Other forms of economic regulation that are essential to the smooth functioning of business and finance, such as the Federal Reserve Board, the securities and commodities exchange commissions, the Patent and

Table 17-2 Employment in Selected Departments and Agencies, 1976, 1981, and 1985 (Number of Full-time Positions)

	1976	1981	1985
Departments			
Defense	951,034	923,559	1,065,551[a]
Energy	—	17,920[b]	16,257[a]
Health and Human Servies, and Education	136,462	151,922[b]	137,377[a]
Housing and Urban Development	14,863	15,122	12,101[a]
Agencies			
Antitrust Division, Department of Justice	856	939	717
Civil Aeronautics Board	758	650	—
Commodity Futures Trading Commission	497	550	567
Consumer Product Safety Commission	890	812	502
Environmental Protection Agency	9,370	10,768	10,307
Equal Employment Opportunity Commission	2,584	3,416	3,107
Federal Communications Commission	2,129	2,004	1,818
Federal Energy Regulatory Commission	1,398[c]	1,742	1,533
Federal Maritime Commission	319	306	212
Federal Trade Commission	1,638	1,587	1,075
Food and Drug Administration	6,597	7,756	7,084
Interstate Commerce Commission	2,237	1,836	839
National Highway Traffic Safety Administration	881	797	640
Nuclear Regulatory Commission	2,289	3,277	3,318
Office of Surface Mining and Reclamation	—	1,036	846
Occupational Safety and Health Administration	2,494	2,988	2,176
Mine Safety and Health Administration	3,149[d]	3,808	2,829
Patent and Trademark Office	3,014	2,834	3,438
Securities and Exchange Commission	2,060	2,023	2,046
Veterans Administration	196,049	214,100[a]	221,292[a]

SOURCES: Office of Management and Budget, *Budget of the U.S. Government*, Summary Tables and Appendix, Fiscal Years 1978, 1983, and 1987. Unfortunately for scholars, Budget figure change categories (from "full-time permanent" to "full-time equivalent" and other counts) making it impossible to use exactly the same categories for all these years.

[a] Full-Time Equivalency Figures. 1981 figure is an OMB estimate.

[b] For the DOEn and DOEd 1982 figures were used, as the FY1983 Budget did not include the two departments in its report. The Department of Education was created in 1979 and the remainder of its parent Health, Education, and Welfare Department renamed Health and Human Services.

[c] Federal Power Commission in 1976.

[d] Mining Enforcement and Safety Administration in 1976.

Trademark Office (and one might include here the Nuclear Regulatory Commission), have been left intact. Overall, the number of civilian employees in the executive branch was in 1985 slightly higher than in 1981.

To maintain ideological or programmatic control presents more problems in areas where government spending and personnel are contracting than in areas where they are expanding. In this sense, Roosevelt was in a very advantageous position. The creation of thousands of new positions and hundreds of new bureaus provided him an opportunity to fill new policy positions with enthusiastic supporters, and to overwhelm any resistance among presumably conservative holdover civil servants. Roosevelt made extensive use of a time-honored practice called "blanketing in." Newly created positions (almost 100,000 by the end of 1934 alone) were filled by political appointment; then, in the late 1930s, when growing dissatisfaction with the administration made a Republican administration more likely, civil service "reform" laws were passed to confer tenure on incumbents.[23]

To impose programmatic control of an agency while reducing employment is more difficult. The RIF (reduction in force made necessary by budget cuts or reorganizations) is a very blunt instrument because civil service regulations prohibit firing employees for ideological reasons and generally require that the most recent employees be dismissed first. For a president who takes office during a political rupture or realignment, that means firing the employees who are most likely to support the new administration and keeping the stalwarts of the old regime. Further, overall limitations on agency employment normally mean fewer political appointments to use either as patronage resources or as a means to establish programmatic control.

In these circumstances, a president who is determined to be master of the federal bureaucracy, especially on the threshold of major policy change, clearly has to maintain a tight rein over the appointments process. Reagan has done so, profiting from the institutionalization of ever more elaborate personnel screening processes by his predecessors and learning from their mistakes. He has also taken advantage of statutory changes that were pioneered by Democratic administrations to enhance presidential control of the civil service.

The presidents who inherited Roosevelt's massive expansion of the federal bureaucracy created and steadily elaborated a personnel recruitment apparatus to help them meet the new task. Truman was the first to have an aide in the White House who specialized in screening prospective appointments—a small but significant shift into the presidential circle of a process that, under Roosevelt, was still geared to dispensing patronage under the aegis of the postmaster general, members of Congress, and state party leaders. What had been a party operation gradually became a presidential function. In the Kennedy administration, control of executive appointments was centralized in the White House under an experienced, professional personnel director. Educational, ethnic, regional, and other characteristics might be designated part of the recruitment process, but the principal test would be loyalty to the president and his program.[24]

Reagan's Presidential Personnel Office has distilled the lessons and employed the institutions of his predecessors. It differs from them mainly in having the president's unflagging support and interest and in avoiding the errors of the Nixon and Carter administrations. Both these presidents had allowed cabinet and agency heads to select lower level appointees, a decision both came to rue and to correct with politically costly housecleanings.[25] Reagan and his aides have consistently assigned a high priority to White House control of appointments, resisting pressures to decentralize the process. Their close screening of assistant, deputy, and under secretaries, general counsels, and directors of major agency subunits has thus assured that loyalty to the president reaches deep inside the departments and agencies. Appointments to independent regulatory agencies, an arena in which members of Congress have been recognized as a major, if not the major, influence on appointments,[26] have been brought fully into the presidential network. The result is that Reagan has achieved a degree of loyalty and coherence in the bureaucracy that other presidents have longed for and public administration reformers have promoted. His practices differ from those of his predecessors in their effectiveness, not their intent.

In the late 1930s, Roosevelt's Brownlow Committee proposed that the bipartisan Civil Service Commission be replaced by a single, presidentially appointed administrator. Congress did not accede to what critics charged was a "power grab" by the president, an attempt to gain political control over the entire civil service.[27] Indeed, in 1939 Republicans and southern Democrats retaliated against Roosevelt's widespread use of federal employees in the 1936 and 1938 elections by passing the Bill to Prevent Pernicious Political Activities, better known as the Hatch Act. By severely restricting civil servants' participation in partisan political activities, Congress denied Roosevelt and subsequent presidents what might have been an important political resource. The Administrative Procedure Act of 1946 was a part of the same campaign by congressional Republicans and rural Democrats to tame the vastly expanded Rooseveltian bureaucracy and wean it from presidential control.[28]

A generation later, the Carter administration achieved some success in reversing the pendulum swing.[29] The Civil Service Reform

Act of 1978 abolished the Civil Service Commission and created the Office of Personnel Management (OPM), headed by a single presidential appointee. To guard against the political exploitation of civil service workers, the Merit Systems Protection Board was established to investigate violations of civil service regulations and hear employee grievances. In addition, civil servants at the GS 13-15 level are now subject to regular performance evaluations on which promotion and raises are based, and it is easier for agency heads to fire, demote, or deny promotions to incompetent employees.[30] The law was designed explicitly to give the president and his managers effective control over a "sluggish," "top-heavy" and "inflexible" bureaucracy.[31]

The most significant provision of the Civil Service Reform Act was the creation of a flexible, performance-based Senior Executive Service (SES). Upper-level civil service employees were now eligible to transfer from the regular civil service into the SES, where cash bonuses of up to 20 percent of base pay could be awarded for high performance ratings from their presidentially appointed supervisors (in contrast to the smaller, semiautomatic raises of the traditional civil service pay system), but where employees were also subject to demotion or transfer for unsatisfactory performance. In addition to the approximately 7,000 SES positions that were created for senior career civil service personnel, the law authorized an additional 800 or so SES positions for individuals from outside the civil service—from business or academia, for example. The 1978 act thus created an elite cadre of administrators that was much more responsive to direction by the president's appointees, and under the supervision of an OPM director who is himself a political appointee. In sum, although the president can only appoint about 600 top administrators, the creation of the SES gave his political appointees an additional 7,800 or so administrators whose performance would be very sensitive to their work standards.[32] The SES is a particularly valuable resource for presidents who, on taking office, confront a bureaucracy staffed by ideologically unsympathetic upper-level bureaucrats.[33] No president ever left his successor a more important institutional legacy than that bequeathed to Reagan by Carter in the Civil Service Reform Act.

Unfortunately for Reagan, Congress in 1980-81 severely limited the number of SES members who could receive performance bonuses, producing widespread demoralization and massive resignations from the service. Recognizing its error, Congress agreed to revise general merit pay provisions in 1984 and restore the original 50 percent SES bonus limitation of the 1978 Act.[34] From the administration's point of view, both higher executive pay scales and performance-based increases are essential to attract noncareer executives and assure the responsiveness of the higher civil service to the president's program.

Critics have charged that Reagan inordinately politicized the civil service, particularly the SES. Rhetorically, the civil service has been portrayed as part of the problem of "runaway government" rather than as an effective instrument of governance. Advocating pay cuts at all but the highest levels, placing political appointees deeper and deeper into the ranks, and allowing threats of RIFs and transfers to demoralize (some would say terrorize) the bureaucracy, the administration pursued control to the point of jeopardizing the policy expertise and institutional memory of civil administration.[35] In past regime shifts, the national government has been a magnet for thousands of enterprising reformers who, while bent on redirecting the state, never doubted that public service was a worthy career. The Reagan administration, however, appeared contemptuous of the apparatus it managed, of both its personnel and its statutory foundation. That attitude was evident in the original appointments of Anne Gorsuch to the EPA and James Watt to the Interior Department, and also in the OMB, where zealous budget-cutters with very little substantive expertise have attempted to override the judgment of agency personnel. The appointment of an aggressive and abrasive OPM director, Donald J. Devine, supported the impression that the administration was intent on enforcing performance standards and programmatic conformity deep inside the bureaucracy and that traditional deference to federal employee unions and affirmative action concerns was clearly subordinate to that goal.[36]

The administration's handling of the civil service generated so much controversy among federal employees and their congressional supporters that Congress blocked until 1985 the implementation of rules that had been proposed by the OPM in 1983 to weigh performance criteria more heavily in RIFs. In 1985, when it became clear that the Senate would not approve his renomination to head OPM, Devine withdrew his name.[37] By the mid-1980s, abrasive radicals had mostly been replaced by smoother administrators—at OPM, OSHA, the Interior Department, and EPA, for example—but the general direction of policy change continued. Although the personal styles of the Reagan agency heads have varied greatly, they have been uniformly loyal to the president's agenda.

Presidents Ford and Carter had demonstrated that zealous reformers could work within the loose confines of discretionary statutes and completely reorient transportation regulatory policy years before there was a solid congressional or public consensus for such changes.[38] Reagan simply followed their example on a much wider scale. His appointees instituted sometimes jolting, sometimes subtle policy changes within their agencies. At OSHA, for example, Reagan appointee

Thorne Auchter engineered a striking shift in the modus operandi of worker health and safety enforcement. Largely abandoning its adversarial posture toward industry, the agency moved from frequent inspections, fines, and orders to an emphasis on voluntary compliance and negotiated settlements. In 1982 OSHA fines were down 69 percent from 1980 and citations for serious hazards had dropped 47 percent. No new rules were issued for more than two-and-a-half years.[39] Similar shifts in enforcement practices took place in the Mine Safety and Health Administration and the NHTSA.[40] Generally, administrators in the regulatory agencies promoted the policies of the president's Task Force on Regulatory Relief (created in 1981 and chaired by Vice President George Bush) and obligingly requested less money and fewer personnel for their agencies. In the social welfare bureaucracy, Reagan appointees dutifully labored to reduce both the range of government services and the number of people receiving benefits. Although Congress—particularly the Democratic House—balked at institutionalizing a number of the administration's policy changes, the bureaucracy itself posed no notable obstacle to their implementation.

The depth of loyalty and activism that Reagan obtained through the appointment power not only contributed to a smooth central clearance process but also blurred the traditional political science distinction between cabinet government and centralized EOP direction of the bureaucracy (see Table 17-3 for a listing of EOP units). This distinction took root in the 1960s, born of studies that contrasted the Eisenhower and Kennedy administrative structures. Eisenhower had relied heavily on his cabinet members, meeting with them frequently and encouraging open debate. Department and agency heads both implemented and participated in the shaping of policies. Such was their loyalty to Eisenhower that—in a manner anticipating the Reagan administration—the president's subordinates took the blame for policies that in fact represented his own preferences.[41]

Kennedy's governing mode was sharply different. The formal structure of Eisenhower's cabinet government struck him as too rigid, confining, and uninventive for an administration bent on broad policy innovation. As a result, Kennedy called cabinet meetings only when absolutely necessary. He relied instead on his special assistants in the White House Office, on likeminded loyalists whom he had placed in the Bureau of the Budget and other EOP agencies and who were treated as special assistants, and on ad hoc task forces. The task forces, consisting of intellectual and political activists (many of whom later found permanent posts in the administration), were appointed during the transition period between Kennedy's election and inauguration to survey a wide range of foreign and domestic problems and propose

Table 17-3 Components of the Executive Office of the President, 1985

Unit	Number of Budgeted Full-time Positions
White House Office[a]	322
Office of Management and Budget	594
Council of Economic Advisers	28
National Security Council	58
Office of Policy Development	45
Office of the U.S. Trade Representative	130
Council on Environmental Quality	11
Office of Science and Technology Policy	15
Office of Administration	139
Office of the Vice President	18

SOURCE: Office of Management and Budget, *Budget of the United States Government,* fiscal year 1987, Appendix I, C1-C14; Office of the Federal Register, *The United States Government Manual 1985-86* (revised, July 1, 1985), 78-80.

Note: Excludes employees at presidential and vice-presidential residences.

[a] Includes, among others, assistants to the president for communications, personnel, legislative strategy, national security affairs, political and governmental affairs, policy development, public liaison, intergovernmental affairs, health policy, and presidential advance; a press secretary, speech writer, and cabinet secretary.

governmental solutions. Later, task forces were convened to deal with crises of the moment, particularly in foreign affairs.[42]

Government by EOP in its extreme form was attained under Nixon. Cabinet members almost never met as a group to engage in meaningful policy debate, and, in fact, seldom saw the president at all. Policy making was a tightly held operation involving only a few White House advisers and other presidential confidants, such as Attorney General John Mitchell. The department heads' marching orders were given by the White House Office, which more than doubled in size between 1968 and 1971.[43] The Bureau of the Budget was reorganized: the Office of Management and Budget assumed the old bureau's traditional functions (budget preparation, clearance, and executive branch management), while the EOP's new Domestic Council (renamed the Office of Policy Development under Reagan) was created to bring about central policy coordination. So centralized and defensive was Nixon's administrative operation, however, that neither policy creativity nor effective management resulted.[44]

Responding to intense public and congressional hostility to Nixon's policy of EOP centralization, Ford and Carter attempted to revive cabinet involvement in policy formulation by integrating the expertise of the departments and agencies into the president-centered network of the EOP. The brief Ford administration, however, overwhelmed by the Watergate legacy (including a swollen Democratic Congress), had little opportunity to demonstrate an effective administrative strategy. As for the Carter administration, it was too fragmented to permit Eisenhower-style delegation to the departments and agencies, and its EOP lacked the coherent sense of mission needed to build broad support for a policy agenda either in Congress or the bureaucracy.

Extreme centralization of budgetary and regulatory review and clearance functions in the OMB suggests, taken alone, that the Reagan administration lies on the Nixon end of the cabinet-EOP organizational spectrum. The powerful roles of former chief of staff Donald Regan and other close presidential advisers, notably Treasury Secretary James Baker and Attorney General Edwin Meese, are also reminiscent of White House government in the early 1970s. But clearly this is not the whole picture. The president remains highly accessible to his cabinet. Although an original system of six cabinet councils proved unwieldy, it was preserved and reorganized in 1985 into two: an economic council headed by Baker and a second council, presided over by Meese, to coordinate policy formation in all other domestic areas. The National Security Council (NSC) provides foreign policy coordination, but cabinet secretaries George Shultz at State and Caspar Weinberger at Defense have been the dominant public policy advisers, whatever the NSC's role in conducting clandestine operations.

Not only are the four major figures in this coordination-and-advice network department heads rather than EOP staffers, but the other department and agency heads also have participated in frequent meetings of their cabinet councils. They have been genuinely encouraged to air their views, criticize the views of others, and run their agencies without constant White House interference.[45]

Here, then, is the paradox: the most cohesive EOP since Nixon co-exists with a cabinet government style of consultation and delegation reminiscent of Eisenhower—both presided over by a president who is confident enough to encourage argument among his subordinates in the style of Roosevelt. This is an interesting hybrid administrative strategy. However, the reasons for the apparent success probably lie outside the administrative system itself. That is, Reagan's administrative system succeeded in providing leadership, coherence, policy innovation, and political sensitivity not because it combined the best elements from an array of past presidential strategies but because of the political context in which he came to power in 1981.

Devolution and Privatization

The fourth leg of the Reagan administration's strategy of bureaucratic control is its effort to pare down the federal budget and bureaucracy by having state and local governments and private business assume increasing responsibilities for the provision of goods and services once provided by the federal government. The administration's original New Federalism initiatives proved too drastic for Congress. They proposed a policy exchange in which the states would take over Aid to Families with Dependent Children (AFDC) and Food Stamp programs, while the federal government would assume the full financial burden of Medicaid. In addition, Reagan proposed that smaller categorical grant programs be consolidated and turned over to the states as block grants, at a somewhat reduced level of funding. In the face of congressional opposition, the AFDC/Medicaid exchange had to be dropped, although the administration responded by implementing tighter federal controls over eligibility and financial penalties for states that failed to cut costs. Congress did agree to make ten block-grant consolidations (replacing about eighty categorical grants), with funding reductions of around 15 percent.[46] Budget pressures make it likely that such consolidations, which effect some administrative savings at both the federal and the state levels, will continue.

Reagan thus revived a process begun by President Nixon and sharpened the break from past Democratic tendencies to expand categorical grants and concomitant federal policy controls. The categorical grant had been the mainstay of the welfare state elaborated by Roosevelt and his Democratic successors. It had generated, by the late 1960s, a kind of "picket-fence" federalism, linking vertical networks of federal and state bureaucrats, policy professionals, and groups of mobilized beneficiaries.[47] These networks not only created entrenched pressures to expand their programs but also threatened presidential control of administration and policy leadership. Reagan's attack on categorical grants therefore served the dual purpose of reinvigorating his own office and disrupting the old federal-state-society linkages in order to reconstruct an alternative national state.

In regulatory policy, the Reagan administration's choices were more complicated. In some arenas, federal abandonment of standard setting and enforcement would simply lead to a proliferation of state regulation that industries with competitive national and international markets would find extremely burdensome. This was evident in 1981, when the administration rescinded its rule for the labeling of toxic substances in the workplace. By 1983, fourteen states had enacted their own diverse labeling laws and the administration was compelled to issue uniform rules.[48]

On the other hand, the responsibility for regulating inherently local strip mining has been handed over to the twenty-five states that operate federally approved programs for surface mining enforcement and reclamation. States are also encouraged to develop their own occupational safety and health programs, and if these are judged at least as effective as the federal program, state workplace inspectors replace OSHA personnel (OSHA then pays half the cost of the state operations and continues to monitor them). By 1984, twenty-five states had instituted such programs. In other areas, the Reagan administration has reduced federal oversight of state regulatory activity and encouraged greater leeway in meeting federal standards.[49] However, state sovereignty, in itself, has not been a central value for the administration. If states can be persuaded to take over controversial programs that necessitate dealing with powerful lobbies and making difficult choices, so much the better—as long as state control does not produce locally popular regulations that penalize the large national and multinational firms that are important constituents of the Republican party.

Private business is the beneficiary, and the federal bureaucracy the target, of a second aspect of the administration's divestment strategy. The president has directed executive agencies to review their activities and pinpoint those that could be performed more efficiently by the private sector on a contract basis. The first such directive was issued in 1955, and the practice of contracting out the provision of federally funded goods and services has been steadily increasing ever since. Reagan's innovation, as with other inherited strategies, was to carry the policy to new extremes. In an August 1983 revision of the contracting-out directive (Circular A-76), the OMB set formal standards for agencies to use in reviewing their activities. Public versus private cost comparisons were simplified in a way that made business involvement more likely. In defending the new guidlines, OMB argued that it was good policy to make government employees "compete for business" with the private sector, and estimated that the government spent at least $20 billion a year in activities that could appropriately be performed by private business. Critics—particularly representatives of the fedeal employee unions—have charged that core governmental functions are being spun off in this way, diminishing the nation's long-term capability for governance.[50] This kind of divestiture of administrative capacity, and the threat it poses to the jobs of civil servants, may be seen as yet another weapon in the arsenal of a regime bent not only on sub- duing the federal bureaucracy but on unraveling a half century of administrative development as well.

When the dust has settled, it is likely that Reagan will have had more influence on the bureaucratic state than any other president except Roosevelt. This is all the more remarkable because Reagan assumed the presidency after a decade of developments—including congressional reorganization, the increased electoral advantage of House incumbency, the decline of party voting, and a bevy of statutes explicitly designed to diminish the president's domestic and foreign policy prerogatives—that were widely perceived as significant hindrances to presidential leadership.[51] The degree of control that Reagan achieved has been condemned by most public administration professionals, but it represents the culmination of the decades-old program of civil service reformers to establish presidential mastery of the bureaucracy. To this end, the reformers backed (1) discretionary legislation within which broadly stated public purposes could be flexibly interpreted and applied by the executive; (2) extensive presidential reorganization powers; (3) an end to the independence of the independent regulatory commissions; (4) the appointment of a civil service director serving at the president's pleasure; (5) the expansion of the White House staff; (6) the establishment of central clearance and budgetary machinery; and (7) the creation of a senior civil service corps sensitive to presidential direction. Reagan was not unconventional in his attempts to use the reformers' methods to establish control of the bureaucracy. He was simply more successful than his predecessors.

The apparent assumption of the civil service reformers that the degree of presidential control they advocated could be achieved without "politicizing" the bureaucracy appears naive. The American national bureaucracy has always been politicized. Unlike European bureaucracies, which sank their roots in a time of monarchical absolutism, national administration in the United States grew up in the rough and tumble of democratic politics. Pushed and pulled to serve alternating partisan, regional, and institutional goals, it has never been able to achieve broad legitimacy as a system for the marshalling of neutral policy expertise.[52] Since it has not been able to carve out for itself an authoritative, autonomous position in governance, the national bureaucracy has always been a battleground where the institutions that do enjoy legitimate authority—president, legislature, and courts—compete for dominance.

Presidential Influence and "Political Time"

As the nation's highest elected official, the president has a legitimate claim to supply the policy agenda to organize the work of the bureaucracy. But Congress can, and often does, dispute that claim.

Studies have demonstrated that agency behavior is systematically influenced by Congress, acting through its jurisdictional committees, as well as by presidential partisanship;[53] that congressional recommendation has been a major path of recruitment into the regulatory agencies,[54] and that members of Congress are much more likely to grant administrative discretion to a president of their own party than to one of the opposition.[55]

There is no necessary contradiction among these findings. When, in 1977, President Carter appointed a Senate Commerce Committee aide (Michael Pertschuk) to chair the Federal Trade Commission (FTC) and a House Commerce Committee aide (Charles Curtis) to head the Federal Power Commission (FPC), he was not yielding to congressional pressure but serving a constituency he shared with the congressional Democrats who dominated the commerce committees in the mid-1970s: northern urban areas where working and middle class residents supported a strong consumer orientation in antitrust and energy policy. When there is a prevailing party consensus that yokes the White House and Congress, overlapping electoral constituencies allow the president to delegate (or at least tolerate) considerable congressional initiative in recruitment and oversight without sacrificing his own programmatic interest. This is as true for activist agencies, like the FTC in the early Carter years, as for agencies undergoing lethargic "capture" or serving as "patronage dumps." For example, the FTC's quiescence in the 1960s reflected the Democratic party's consensus to attempt no vigorous antitrust policy. Similarly, neither Democratic presidents nor Democratic committee leaders have attempted to interrupt the stable nurturing of its merchant marine carrier and union clientele by the Maritime Commission, because these geographical and sectoral interests, which easily dominate maritime policy in the absence of organized opposition, were important to both presidential and congressional constituencies.

The degree to which constituency overlap produces policy consensus between president and Congress is shaped by what Stephen Skowronek calls "political time." [56] When there is a clearly dominant political regime and public philosophy, we may expect little conflict over bureaucratic behavior between the two branches. However, a "preemptive" president who does not represent the majority party (Andrew Johnson or Richard Nixon, for example), or one presiding at a time of incipient realignment in which the once-prevailing consensus is disintegrating (Franklin Pierce, Jimmy Carter), will be plagued by disloyal subordinates in the cabinet and bureaucracy and a struggle for control with one or more congressional factions. In such times, the president faces a Herculean task of control and must be ever inventive.

Nixon's attempts to restructure the bureaucracy and impound appropriated funds exemplify the desperation of a determined leader in a
situation that made his brand of leadership almost impossible.[57] Agency
leaders may exhibit seemingly schizophrenic behavior in response to
conflicting signals from Congress and the president.[58] At such political
junctures, the roughly equal endowment of bureaucracy-shaping powers in the presidency and Congress is sharply accentuated.

In what Skowronek calls "continuing consensus" regimes, policy
congruence in the party's constituency and the tendency of the
congressional party to grant its president broad discretion in administration minimize conflict in ways that, as noted above, may give the appearance of congressional or even interest-group dominance. Political
realignment, however, offers the president, as victorious leder of a new
policy-centered coalition, unique opportunities to reorient the bureaucracy. Through active use of appointment, budgetary, and central
clearance powers, as well as long-term judicial strategies,[59] the president's efforts on behalf of his party coalition will appear as unambigu-
ous examples of presidential leadership.

Reagan's mastery of the commonplace administrative powers of
the presidency is of the kind observed only in realignment periods.
However, the electoral indicators associated with past realignments
were incompletely manifested in the 1980 and 1984 elections, and
scholarly opinion is divided not just on whether the current period
merits the label, but also on whether the sweeping realignments of the
past are even possible in this era of weak party organizations and
allegiances.[60] As Skowronek observes, the essence of realignment
leadership is a thorough repudiation of the political order of the recent
past. The Reagan administration clearly articulated such a repudiation,
and, perhaps because this realignment—if such it is—festered for a
longer period than most,[61] its program for a new regime had been
prepared in considerably greater detail than that of the last realignment
leader, Franklin Roosevelt. Its Achilles' heel is the failure to persuade a
majority of the public to declare a Republican affiliation and to elect a
Republican Congress. That failure leaves the Democratic party a major
forum for attacking Reagan's policy initiatives and preparing a return
to power. House committee leaders, for example, have challenged
Reagan's central clearance system in federal court, pigeonholed a
sweeping regulatory reform bill passed by the Republican Senate in
1982,[62] and spearheaded efforts to block or modify the administration's
civil service reforms.

The administration in its final years was caught in the throes of an
incomplete realignment. Without control of Congress, it was unable to
codify its revolution in statutes, and without statutory legitimation even

the most powerful administrative strategy will yield only transient changes in the relationship between government and society. The window of opportunity opened by an electoral repudiation of the previous regime does not remain open forever, as Roosevelt's difficulties in the late 1930s attest. New legislation is needed to reorient the bureaucracy permanently and to change expectations in the larger society. The Roosevelt administration had accomplished a statutory revolution by the time its momentum stalled, but the Reagan administration has not buttressed its administrative strategy with new legal authority. Reagan's Federal Energy Regulatory Commission, for example, has been very creative in attempting to deregulate the natural gas industry administratively, but as the courts have reminded the agency, it is bound to work within the confines of the 1938 and 1978 natural gas acts. Similarly, in absence of a new clean air act, mere personnel and enforcement strategies will achieve only limited environmental policy changes and the courts will compel enforcement of other policies, such as the "prevention of significant deterioration" (PSD) that the Reagan coalition finds objectionable. Without statutory legitimation, the regulatory clearance process itself is vulnerable to judicial repudiation.

The United States is a legalistic, litigious country. The written law develops deep roots: it shapes markets, creates powerful expectations, and confers rights and legitimacy. President Reagan made his greatest legislative investments in changing the budget and the tax code, but his failure to secure (or, for the most part, even seek) changes in the law to encode other substantive preferences of his coalition could make the Reagan legacy a modest one indeed.

Notes

1. Richard E. Neustadt, *Presidential Power* (New York: John Wiley & Sons, 1980), 9.
2. President's Committee on Administrative Management, *Administrative Management in the Government of the United States* (1937; reprint, Chicago: Public Administration Service, 1947), 29-30.
3. Charles G. Dawes, cited in Kermit Gordon, "Reflections on Spending," *Public Policy* 15 (1966): 1-22.
4. Allen Schick, "The Budget as an Instrument of Presidential Policy," in *The Reagan Presidency and the Governing of America,* ed. Lester N. Salamon and Michael S. Lund (Washington, D.C.: Urban Institute Press, 1985), 115.
5. Gregory B. Mills, "The Budget," in *The Reagan Record,* ed. John L. Sawhill and Isabel V. Sawhill (Cambridge, Mass.: Ballinger, 1985), 112-113; Isabel V. Sawhill and Charles F. Stone, "The Economy," in ibid., 183.

6. Calculated from tables in the *Economic Report of the President, February 1986* (Washington, D.C.: Government Printing Office, 1986), 240-241 and 276.

7. Ibid., 319, 322.

8. U.S. Congress, Congressional Budget Office, *The Economic and Budget Outlook: Fiscal Year 1986-1990* (Washington, D.C., 1985), 68, 162.

9. See, for example, Peri E. Arnold, *Making the Managerial Presidency* (Princeton: Princeton University Press, 1986); Guy Alcon, *The Invisible Hand of Planning* (Princeton: Princeton University Press, 1985); Richard Polenberg, *Reorganizing Roosevelt's Government* (Cambridge, Mass.: Harvard University Press, 1966); Barry E. Karl, *Charles E. Merriam and the Study of Politics* (Chicago: University of Chicago Press, 1974).

10. James M. Landis, *The Administrative Process* (New Haven: Yale University Press, 1938), is a classic statement of the argument.

11. Larry Berman, *The Office of Management and Budget and the Presidency 1921-1979* (Princeton: Princeton University Press, 1979).

12. *Humphreys Executor v. United States*, 295 U.S. 602 (1935). In a subsequent decision, *Wiener v. United States*, 357 U.S. 349 (1958), the president's power to remove members of the independent commissions was further restricted. For a discussion and criticism of these decisions, see Harold Seidman and Robert Gilmour, *Politics, Position and Power*, 4th ed. (New York: Oxford University Press, 1986), 269-281.

13. On reorganization attempts from Roosevelt to Nixon, see Polenberg, *Reorganizing Roosevelt's Government;* William E. Pemberton, *Bureaucratic Politics* (Columbia: University of Missouri Press, 1979); Arnold, *Making the Managerial Presidency;* Seidman and Gilmour, *Politics, Position and Power;* and Congressional Quarterly Inc., *Congressional Quarterly Almanac* (Washington, D.C.), 1949, 554-566; 1950, 362-374; 1961, 353-366.

14. This accords with the judgment of Louis Fisher and Ronald C. Moe, "Presidential Reorganization Authority: Is It Worth the Cost?" *Political Science Quarterly* 96 (Spring 1981): 301-318. For a more positive assessment of presidential reorganization efforts, see Arnold, *Making the Managerial Presidency.*

15. Congress has, by law, from time to time exempted particular agencies from OMB budgetary and legislative clearance. See Morton Rosenberg, "Presidential Control of Agency Rulemaking," a report prepared for the Committee on Energy and Commerce, U.S. House of Representatives, 97th Congress, 1st sess. (Committee Print 97-0, 1981), 24.

16. The following review of central clearance in the 1970s relies on Rosenberg, "Presidential Control of Agency Rulemaking"; Congressional Quarterly Inc., *Federal Regulatory Directory,* 5th ed. (Washington, D.C., 1986), 60-74; Lester M. Salamon, "Federal Regulations: A New Arena for Presidential Power?" in *The Illusion of Presidential Government*, ed. Hugh Heclo and Lester M. Salamon (Boulder, Colo.: Westview Press, 1981), 149-167.

17. See, for example, Bruce A. Ackerman and William T. Hassler, *Clean Coal, Dirty Air* (New Haven: Yale University Press, 1981), 91-97; and Lawrence J. White, *Reforming Regulation* (Englewood Cliffs, N.J.: Prentice-Hall, 1981). RARG included representatives of all departments except State and Defense, as well as EPA and major units of the Executive Office of the President.

18. In June 1985, House Commerce and Energy Committee chair John Dingell and four other committee chairs filed an amicus curiae brief in the District of Columbia Court of Appeals in an OSHA case *(Public Citizen Health Research Group et al. v. Rowland)*, arguing that the Reagan central clearance process constitutes a

violation of Congress's legislative power and the authority it has delegated to OSHA. The Court ruled that, as long as the agency offered reasonable justification for its reversal of a rule or standard, OMB initiative was not in itself objectionable. 796 F. 2d, 1479 (D.C. Cir. 1986).

19. Carter's directive stated that "agencies shall periodically review their existing regulations to determine whether they are achieving the policy goals of this order." Reagan's order no. 12291 requires agencies to "initiate reviews of currently effective orders . . . and perform Regulatory Impact Analyses" of major existing rules. The OMB is authorized to set up schedules for such analyses and to designate existing regulations for review.

20. In 1981 the NHTSA rescinded its previous requirement that all automobiles built after 1982 be equipped with passive restraints—either automatically fastening seat belts or airbags. In 1983, the Supreme Court ruled that "NHTSA's recission . . . was arbitrary and capricious." *Vehicle Mfrs. Assn. v. State Farm Mut.,* 463 U.S. 30, 31 (1983). Subsequently, the agency issued a new rule to phase in the passive-restraint requirement by 1989, unless, by April 1, 1989, states containing two-thirds of the nation's population had enacted seat belt use laws that met certain federal requirements (*New York Times,* September 19, 1986, A20). The Presidential Task Force on Regulatory Relief counted delay of the passive restraint rule as a major regulatory cost saving in its final report. Murray L. Weidenbaum, "Regulatory Reform under the Reagan Administration," in *The Reagan Regulatory Strategy: An Assessment,* ed. George C. Eads and Michael Fix (Washington, D.C.: Urban Institute, 1984), Table 1, 27.

21. Congressional Quarterly, *Federal Regulatory Directory,* 65, 73; Christopher C. DeMuth, "A Strategy for Regulatory Reform," *Regulation* (March-April 1984): 25-30; Weidenbaum, "Regulatory Reform," 25-29. Critics have pointed out that Weidenbaum's calculations ignore the costs consumers and businesses incur at lower levels of regulation, such as the repair costs of weaker automobile bumpers, personal injury costs from driving cars without passive restraints, and long-term damage to health and property from air and water pollution.

22. Fifty-four percent of the agencies that reported employment increases had missions related to national defense or international relations. In contrast, ACTION, the Civil Rights Commission, Consumer Product Safety Commission, Federal Trade Commission, Environmental Protection Agency, and the Departments of Education, Energy, Interior, and Labor lost 14 to 59 percent of their positions between 1980 and 1983. U.S. House of Representatives, Committee on Education and Labor, "The State of Affirmative Action in the Federal Government," 98th Congress, 2d sess. (Committee Print, 1984). Employment in the Environmental Protection Agency rebounded in 1985, as widespread public and congressional disapproval of the administration's heavy-handed attempts to undo environmental regulation produced an apparent retreat.

23. Paul Van Riper, *History of the U.S. Civil Service* (Evanston, Ill.: Row, Peterson, 1958), 315-347.

24. G. Calvin MacKenzie, *The Politics of Presidential Appointments* (New York: Free Press, 1981), 11-40. See also John W. Macy, Bruce Adams, and J. Jackson Walker, *America's Unelected Government* (Cambridge, Mass.: Ballinger, 1983), 23-42.

25. Macy, Adams, and Walker, *America's Unelected Government,* 38-40; MacKenzie, *The Politics of Presidential Appointments,* 63-69; Richard P. Nathan, *The Administrative Presidency* (New York: John Wiley & Sons, 1983), 38-39.

26. U.S. Senate, Committee on Governmental Operations, *Study on Federal Regulation,* vol. 1, 95th Congress, 1st sess. (Senate Doc. no. 25, 1977), 153-54.

27. Polenberg, *Reorganizing Roosevelt's Government,* 21, 128-129, 167.

28. The Administrative Procedure Act, which was vetoed by Roosevelt but repassed, in milder form, in 1946, sets out detailed procedures that agencies must follow in their rule-making and judicial functions, including timely notice to interested parties of proposed rule issuance and hearings; opportunities for those parties to present testimony; and a requirement that agency decisions be based on "substantial evidence." Widely accepted today as a check on arbitrary or unfair administration, the APA was perceived at the time of its passage as a serious setback for both the president and the newly expanded bureaucracy.

29. Carter and the northern urban wing of the Democratic party tried but failed to amend the Hatch Act in 1977. Carter did score a victory for the presidency against the Administrative Procedure Act, although too late to benefit his own administration. His intervention in the RARG process had led to several challenge by groups claiming that off-the-record presidential intervention in agency rule making violated the APA. Vindication of the president's role in the review-and-clearance process came in 1981 when the Court of Appeals for the District of Columbia recognized "the basic need of the President and his White House staff to monitor the consistency of executive agency regulations with Administration policy" (*Sierra Club v. Costle,* 1981). For a discussion of the significance of this decision, and its particular relevance ot Reagan's central clearance procedure, see Rosenberg, "Presidential Control of Agency Rulemaking," 23, 26.

30. On the 1978 law, see *Congressional Quarterly Almanac,* 1978, 818-835.

31. From House debate on the Civil Service Reform Act, *Congressional Record,* 95th Congress, 2d sess. (Washington, D.C.: Government Printing Office, 1978), 25716-17, 25722-23. See also U.S. Senate, Committee on Governmental Affairs, *Report on the Civil Service Reform Act of 1978,* 95th Congress, 2d sess. (Senate Report no. 969, 1978).

32. In 1983 there were 562 cabinet and independent agency and commission appointments for which Senate confirmation was required. These were cabinet secretaries; deputy secretaries, under secretaries, and assistant secretaries who head major divisions, bureaus and offices; and some counsellors in the departments and agencies, along with independent agency heads and commission members. In the White House Office, there were about fifteen counsellors and special assistants appointed without Senate confirmation. Twenty appointees in other executive office agencies were considered important enough that Congress imposed a Senate confirmation requirement. Below these positions are about 1,300 "schedule C" political appointees who occupy positions "of a confidential or policy determining character" that are exempted from the competitive civil service by the OPM. These appointees typically serve in positions below those of the SES, which includes numerous directors and deputy directors of offices. Macy, Adams, and Walker, *America's Unelected Government,* 6; and U.S. Senate, Committee on Governmental Affairs, *Policy and Supporting Positions,* 98th Congress, 2d sess. (Committee Print, 1984—a publication commonly known as the Plum Book.

33. Such was the situation confronted by President Nixon. A 1970 survey of higher grade career civil servants in eighteen domestic agencies revealed a career bureaucracy comprised of almost three times as many Democrats as Republicans, and strongly inclined against social program cutbacks. Joel D. Aberbach and Bert A. Rockman, "Clashing Beliefs within the Executive Branch: The Nixon

Administration Bureaucracy," *American Political Science Review* 70 (June 1976): 456-468.

34. U.S. House of Representatives, Committee on Post Office and Civil Service, Subcommittee on Civil Service, "Senior Executive Service," Hearings, 98th Congress, 1st and 2d sess. (November 1983-April 1984), 1-4; and *Congressional Quarterly Almanac,* 1984, 201.

35. Edie N. Goldenberg, "The Permanent Government in an Era of Retrenchment and Redirection," in *The Reagan Presidency,* 381-404. Although the number of outside (noncareer) SES positions allocated under the 1978 law was lower in 1983 than in Carter's last year, the number actually filled increased by 134, and the ratio of political appointees to career civil servants was significantly higher in the domestic agencies targeted for programmatic reorientation. U.S. House of Representatives, Committee on Post Office and Civil Service (HRPOCS), Subcommittee on Civil Service, "Civil Service Oversight," Hearings, 98th Congress, 1st sess. (March 1983); and Bernard Rosen, "Effective Continuity of U.S. Government Operations in Jeopardy," *Public Administration Review* 43 (September/October 1983): 383-392.

36. About 60 percent of federal employees belong to unions, which have statutorily guaranteed (since 1978) representational rights, but no recognized right to strike (a point the administration underlined in 1981 by firing striking air traffic controllers). Minority employees comprise about 25 percent of all nondefense civilian employees; women, about 40 percent. Both categories expanded in the 1970s but have declined slightly during the Reagan administration. Blacks and women have been disproportionately affected by RIFs, primarily because of rules favoring veterans and more senior employees. A study undertaken by the General Accounting Office in 1983 at the request of the House Post Office and Civil Service Committee could document no significant political abuse of SES law. HRPOCS, "Civil Service Oversight," 137; and HRPOCS, Subcommittee on Human Resources, "Federal Reduction in Force Procedures," Hearings, 99th Congress, 1st sess. (September 1985), 110-112; "Senior Executive Service" hearings, 5-9, 159.

37. On the new RIF rules, see "Federal Reduction in Force Procedures." On the Devine renomination and Senate (and federal employee) objections, see U.S. Senate, Committee on Governmental Affairs, "Renomination of Donald J. Devine," Hearings, 99th Congress, 1st sess. (April-June 1985).

38. The prime example here is the reorientation of airline regulatory policy from anticompetitive to procompetitive under Ford and Carter appointees to the CAB— particularly John Robson and Professors Elizabeth Bailey and Alfred Kahn. A similar shift toward deregulation of railroads and trucking was effected through appointments to the ICC in the mid-1970s. Interestingly, Reagan has done little to speed deregulation of transportation because important parts of his political constituency—the rural South, Great Plains, and West, and labor and management in the trucking industry—are unenthusiastic about deregulation. On the politics of transportation policy in the 1970s, see Martha Derthick and Paul J. Quirk, *The Politics of Deregulation* (Washington, D.C.: Brookings Institution, 1985); and Elizabeth Sanders, "The Regulatory Surge of the 1970s in Historical Perspective," in *Public Regulation: New Perspectives and Processes,* ed. Elizabeth Bailey (Cambridge, Mass.: MIT Press, 1987).

39. Michael Wines, "Auchter's Record at OSHA Leaves Labor Outraged, Business Satisfied," *National Journal,* October 1, 1983, 2008-2013.

40. Laurence E. Lynn, Jr., "The Reagan Administration and the Renitent Bureaucracy," in *The Reagan Presidency,* 339-370; and Richard Corrigan, "Industry

Pleased, Mine Unions Fuming over Mine Safety Enforcement Shift," *National Journal,* September 3, 1983, 1773-1775.

41. Fred I. Greenstein, *The Hidden Hand Presidency* (New York: Basic Books, 1982), 80-92, 113-124.

42. Arthur M. Schlesinger, Jr., *A Thousand Days* (Boston: Houghton Mifflin, 1965), 408-421, 686-689; Theodore C. Sorensen, *Kennedy* (New York: Harper & Row, 1965), 281-285; and Berman, *The Office of Management and Budget and the Presidency,* 68.

43. For an insider's view of the Nixon operation, see John Ehrlichman, *Witness to Power* (New York: Simon & Schuster, 1982), chap. 6 and 7.

44. Berman, *The Office of Management and Budget and the Presidency,* 112-124; and Nathan, *The Administrative Presidency,* 33-42.

45. Of the accomplishments of Reagan's cabinet council system, Chester A. Newland observes that, among other things: "(1) key departmental and White House officials and staffers are brought together in work on important issues, minimizing (but not eliminating) we/they White House/agency divisions which plagued most recent administrations; [and] (2) the Cabinet Councils, together with other network organizations, take initiatives and facilitate actions on vital second-level policy issues without compelling personal presidential attention to details, thus minimizing two problems of some recent administrations while compensating, in part, for President Reagan's orientation to generalization. "The Reagan Presidency: Limited Government and Political Administration," *Public Administration Review* 43 (January/February 1985): 10.

46. D. Lee Bawden and John L. Palmer, "Social Policy," and George E. Peterson, "Federalism and the States," in *The Reagan Record,* 209-210, 217-237. See also "Officials Say Budget Hits States, Cities Hardest," *Congressional Quarterly Weekly Report,* January 11, 1986, 309-311.

47. See, on the concept of vertically organized functional interests, Harold Seidman, *Politics, Position and Power,* 2d ed. (New York: Oxford University Press, 1975), chap. 6; and Terry Sanford, *Storm Over the States* (New York: McGraw-Hill), 80-81.

48. Michael Fix, "Transferring Regulatory Authority to the States," in *The Reagan Regulatory Strategy,* 153-179.

49. Congressional Quarterly, *Federal Regulatory Directory,* 691, 421; Fix, "Transferring Regulatory Authority to the States."

50. HRPOCS, Subcommittee on Human Resources, "Implementation of Circular A-76," Hearings, 98th Congress, 2d sess. (September 20 and 25, 1984), 24-46, 92-93, 124-128, 260-261. Circular A-76 suggests, as activities most amenable to contracting out, audiovisual products and services; automatic data processing (including program and systems analysis); maintenance and testing of equipment and instruments; office and administrative services (including word processing, messengers, and auditing); and laundry and dry cleaning, among others. Office of Management and Budget, Circular no. A-76 (revised), August 4, 1983, Attachment A. See also OMB, *Enhancing Government Productivity through Competition* (Washington, D.C., 1984).

51. See, for example, Eric L. Davis, "Legislative Reform and the Decline of Presidential Influence on Capitol Hill," *British Journal of Political Science* 9 (October 1979): 465-479.

52. I have elaborated on these ideas in "The Social and Geographic Roots of American Bureaucracy" (Occasional paper of the Center for Studies of Social Change, New School for Social Research, New York).

53. See, for example, Barry R. Weingast and Mark J. Moran, "Bureaucratic Discretion or Congressional Control: Regulatory Policymaking by the Federal Trade Commission," *Journal of Political Economy* 91 (1983): 765-800; and Terry M. Moe, "Regulatory Performance and Presidential Administration," *American Journal of Political Science* 26 (May 1982): 197-224.

54. *Study on Federal Regulation,* vol. 1, 153-154.

55. Richard F. Bensel, "Creating the Statutory state: The Implications of a Rule of Law Standard in American Politics," *American Political Science Review* 74 (September 1980): 739-744.

56. Stephen Skowronek, "Notes on the Presidency in the Political Order," in *Studies in American Political Development,* vol. 1, ed. Karen Orren and Stephen Skowronek (New Haven: Yale University Press, 1986), 289-302; and "Presidential Leadership in Political Time," this volume.

57. Aspects of Nixon's bureaucratic strategy are described in Ronald Randall, "Presidential Power versus Bureaucratic Intransigence: The Influence of the Nixon Administration on Welfare Policy," *American Political Science Review* 73 (September 1979): 795-810; and Nathan, *The Administrative Presidency.*

58. The Federal Power Commission under Nixon and the Federal Trade Commission under Carter provide examples of bureaucracies caught in unstable political environments (in Skowronek's terms, "preemptive" and "disjunctive" administrations). See Elizabeth Sanders, *The Regulation of Natural Gas: Policy and Politics, 1938-1978* (Philadelphia: Temple University Press, 1981); and Weingast and Moran, "Bureaucratic Discretion or Congressional Control?"

59. "Preemptive" presidents may experience control problems as a result of judicial intervention. In the early 1970s, for example, the federal courts took environmental policy much farther than the Nixon administration was willing to go, with landmark decisions interpreting the Clean Air Act. In realigning eras, Court composition lags behind changes in electoral coalitions. Roosevelt confronted a Supreme Court staffed with appointees of the old regime whose conceptions of the commerce clause and administrative discretion could not support major pieces of his legislative program. For this reason, realignment presidents are especially sensitive to the ideological composition not only of the Supreme Court, but also the District of Columbia appellate court, which hears appeals from regulatory agency decisions.

60. For divergent views on the prospects for a Reagan-led realignment, see Morris P. Fiorina and John A. Ferejohn, "Incumbency and Realignment in Congressional Elections," in *The New Direction in American Politics,* ed. John E. Chubb and Paul E. Peterson (Washington, D.C.: Brookings Institution, 1985), 91-115; and Benjamin Ginsberg and Martin Shefter, "A Critical Realignment? The New Politics, the Reconstituted Right and the Election of 1984," in *The Elections of 1984,* ed. Michael Nelson (Washington, D.C.: CQ Press, 1985), 1-26.

61. Kevin Phillips, *The Emerging Republican Majority* (Garden City, N.Y.: Anchor Books, 1970).

62. The 1982 regulatory reform bill passed by the Senate (S 1080) would have institutionalized most of the administration's central clearance system and extended it to the independent regulatory agencies. House committee leaders raised strong objections to even a weaker version of the bill, and it never came to the floor there. *Congressional Quarterly Weekly Report,* April 3, 1982, 740-742; and *Congressional Quarterly Almanac,* 1982, 523. The Supreme Court in 1983 struck down the legislative veto, denying Congress a potent measure of legislative control over the federal bureaucracy. Without the veto provision, of course, the 1982 regulatory reform package would be much less desirable from the congressional standpoint.

18. THE PRESIDENCY AND CONGRESS: AN ELECTORAL CONNECTION?

Morris P. Fiorina

This essay discusses the implications of the structure and operation of the American electoral system for the contemporary presidency. In particular, it emphasizes how the recent evolution of the electoral system exacerbates the political difficulties faced by modern presidents and how those heightened difficulties have in turn contributed to the decline of responsible government in the United States.[1] For responsible government to exist, citizens must be able to determine whom to credit or blame for the state of the nation, and they must vote on the basis of their determinations. By doing so they provide public officials with a compelling personal incentive to concern themselves about national conditions. But as the tendency of American voters to hold members of Congress responsible for national conditions has lessened, so the incentive for representatives and senators to act in the national interest has lessened. This decline of responsible government lies at the core of the difficulties confronting the contemporary presidency. These difficulties are systemic and not the transient echoes of a singularly inept Jimmy Carter that can be dispelled by an especially skilled Ronald Reagan or some future president. For in fact, and despite much popular commentary to the contrary, the politics of the 1980s fits comfortably with themes developed in writings of the 1970s.

A Question of Incentives

To a greater degree than behavioral political scientists have acknowledged, institutional arrangements shape individual incentives, which in turn affect behavior. Both formal institutions and informal ones, such as custom or practice, are important, and while in most stable democracies the former are more fundamental, their constancy means that their specific effects are more likely to be overlooked. In the United States two aspects of our formal institutions warrant discussion: the independent executive and the electoral law laid down by the Constitution.

Americans take for granted the opportunity to indicate a prefer-

ence among presidential candidates who are explicitly listed on the
ballot. In the 1983 British general election, however, electors had the
opportunity to cast a vote specifically for Margaret Thatcher in only
one of 650 constituencies. Similarly, in only one constituency (not the
same one) did voters have an opportunity to vote for Michael Foot. In
the elections in the Netherlands *no* voter had an opportunity to cast a
vote for the current prime minister, Ruud Lubbers; the Dutch ballot
lists only parties, not personal names. The same is true in Israel.
German voters in one constituency had the opportunity to vote for
Helmut Kohl for chancellor in 1980. As a result of the election and
subsequent maneuvering, however, Helmut Schmidt of the Social
Democratic party assumed the office; but in the fall of 1982, with no
new elections having taken place, Kohl replaced Schmidt.

Most of the advanced democracies do not elect their chief
executives independently from the members of their legislature. Rather,
the executives are the leaders of parties that control blocs of legislative
seats (not necessarily a majority). And once selected, these chief
executives have no *legal* hold on the office; their tenure depends on
maintaining the support of the parties that selected them. As Anthony
King observes, the American system is unusual in permitting the
accession to office of presidents who have little national political
experience and little acquaintance with, let alone preexisting support
among, members of the legislature.[2] Although the typical European
parliamentarian has some direct responsibility for choosing an executive whom he or she knows firsthand, the typical American representative or senator has neither direct responsibility for, nor firsthand
knowledge of, the elected president.

The formal separation of executive and legislative offices in the
United States is reinforced further by the differences in the electoral
systems that determine the officeholders. Representatives are elected
from geographically distinct single-member districts in which the high
vote getter, majority or not, wins the seat. Only half of all House
elections and two-thirds of all senatorial elections coincide with
presidential elections. Formally, the electoral coalitions of legislative
and executive officeholders are completely independent. All voters in a
district or state conceivably could cast a vote for a legislative candidate
of one party and a presidential candidate of another. A substantial and
increasing segment of the citizenry does choose to avail itself of this
opportunity.

Again, contrast the American situation with that in the majority of
other democracies. In Great Britain, for example, electors who wished
to see Margaret Thatcher win office in 1983 had only one means of
registering their choice—by casting a vote for the Conservative candi-

date for member of Parliament (MP) in the constituency, regardless of the personal characteristics, achievements, and beliefs of that individual. In some of the continental democracies such considerations cannot even arise; the choice is that of voting for a particular party, not for any particular candidate.

In sum, in the United States no two representatives have a common constituency (only pairs of senators do), and while the president's geographical constituency necessarily overlaps those of representatives and senators, his electoral support within any particular constituency might have little overlap with that of the relevant representative or senator. Besides, all these officeholders never stand for election simultaneously.

Informal institutional arrangements also play a critical role in any political system. After all, British MPs represent constituencies different from that of the prime minister, but if anything, the unity and cohesion of British government traditionally has been viewed as even higher than in the more formally centralized governments of most continental democracies. Evidently, informal practices can unify what formal institutions put asunder, and perhaps vice versa. The informal institutions of major importance here are practices that are associated with political parties, especially the nomination of candidates for office.

Throughout U.S. history, political parties have helped to overcome the formal separation of offices that was established by the Constitution. Whenever voters and elites can be induced to think and act in partisan terms, a degree of cohesion is overlaid on the political system. If a party's officeholders do not differ on the policies they can be expected to support, voters have little reason to differentiate among individual candidates and great reason to support or oppose the entire party. And if voters think more in terms of parties than individuals, candidates will have greater reason to concern themselves with the performance and prospects of the party as a whole. These behavior patterns are mutually reinforcing.[3]

In the modern period, however, various factors have brought the capacity of parties to stimulate such unifying forces to a low ebb. For one thing, today's parties do not have as much control of tangible resources, such as jobs and contracts, as the parties did in the pre-Progressive era. Thus, their ability to motivate activists now must rest largely on other grounds, and one tool for fostering cohesion among officeholders is no longer available. Probably of much greater importance is the decline in the parties' ability to control nominations. The spread of the direct primary has expanded the arena in which nominations are won, and in this expanded arena, party endorsement—if it is permitted—may count for little or nothing. The increased importance of money and the new campaign technologies it can purchase, which also can be provided outside the party, have further contributed to the decline in party influence over nominations. What is the result of such changes? Parties that do not nominate candidates and elect their nominees hardly can be expected to enforce cohesion on those who are elected. And voters react in natural fashion: when candidates differentiate themselves, sensible voters take account of the differences and do not vote blindly for party labels.

Again, such behavior is mutually reinforcing. And again, we might contrast this situation with that in the other Western democracies. Only in the United States are candidates chosen directly through mass participation. Only in the United States do elected legislators have so little influence in the choice of candidates for chief executive. Only in the United States do the formal party organizations have so little control over the campaigns for legislative or executive office.

In sum, the formal institutional structure and informal institutions that are associated with political parties in most Western democracies provide relatively stronger incentives for cohesive behavior in the political realm than do American institutions. This is certainly true in the abstract, but what about the reality? Are the incentive patterns implicit in institutional structure discernible in the actual behavior of politicians and voters?

Voting Behavior in Contemporary American Elections

Presidential Elections

So much is known about voting behavior in presidential elections that any attempt to provide a concise summary inevitably oversimplifies a rich and constantly growing body of knowledge. Nevertheless, most analysts would accept the following general portrait.[4]

Americans cast their presidential votes on the basis of four general factors: longstanding party affiliations, attitudes toward individual candidates, general conditions in the country which are taken as a reflection on the performance of the incumbent administration, and the policies advocated by the candidates. The relationship of party affiliation to voting has declined somewhat in the past fifteen years, although it remains a major correlate of the vote, as Table 18-1 indicates. The other three factors have waxed and waned somewhat more. In 1956, 1964, and 1972, the characteristics of one or both of the candidates appear to have made an especially large difference. In 1968, 1980, and 1984 reactions to the performance of the incumbent administration were particularly important. In 1964 and 1972, the ideologies of certain

Table 18-1 Decline of Party-Line Voting in U.S. National Elections, 1956-1984

Year	Presidential		House		Senate	
	Party-line[a]	Defector[a]	Party-line[a]	Defector[a]	Party-line	Defector[a]
1956	76%	15%	82%	9%	79%	12%
1958	—	—	84	11	85	9
1960	79	13	80	12	77	15
1962	—	—	83	12	b	b
1964	79	15	79	15	78	16
1966	—	—	76	16	b	b
1968	69	23	74	19	74	19
1970	—	—	76	16	78	12
1972	67	25	75	17	69	22
1974	—	—	74	18	73	19
1976	74	15	72	19	70	19
1978	—	—	69	22	71	20
1980	70	22	69	23	71	21
1982	—	—	77	14	77	17
1984	80	12	74	22	75	20

[a] Party-line + Defector + Independent = 100%
[b] Data not available.

SOURCE: Gary Jacobson, *The Politics of Congressional Elections,* 2d ed. (Boston: Little, Brown, 1987), 107; and Thomas Mann and Raymond Wolfinger, "Candidates and Parties in Congressional Elections," *American Political Science Review* 74 (September 1980): 617-632.

candidates and the policies associated with those ideologies were especially significant.

Of course, the four factors are not so distinct either logically or in reality as casual commentary sometimes presumes. For example, reactions to the performance of past administrations underpin the party affiliations that exist among the citizenry—hardly a revolutionary idea.[5] Moreover, voter attitudes toward candidates surely are related to the policies they advocate and, at least for incumbents, their performance in office. Certainly, too, the perceived policy positions of the candidates depend somewhat on the party affiliations they carry and on the record of their past actions. The close connections among these influences on presidential voting make it imprudent to rank them in terms of relative importance. Each must be considered if an analysis of any presidential election is to be complete.

Congressional Elections

While the study of presidential elections flourished during the
1950s and 1960s, the study of congressional elections languished.
Several early analyses suggested that congressional elections were low-
information party-line affairs and by implication less interesting than
the more complex presidential elections.[6] Of late, however, congressional elections have attracted a major share of academic attention.[7]

Party affiliation remains the single most influential correlate of the
vote in congressional elections, although as Table 18-1 indicates, party-
line voting has declined considerably since 1956. Nevertheless, in both
American executive and legislative elections party affiliation continues
to be important and provides the major point of commonality in these
election returns. We cannot say the same for other factors, however.
The issue basis of congressional elections remains very thin; congressional voters are more informed and aware than scholars previously
believed, but—especially in House elections—only a small minority has
any knowledge of the incumbent's voting record and issue stands, let
alone the stands of the much less well known challenger.[8]

During the period in which scant attention was paid to congressional elections, prevailing scholarly opinion held that deviations from
the basic partisan vote division stemmed largely from the influence of
national conditions and presidential level forces, such as presidential
coattails and referenda voting on the president's handling of the
economy. Surprisingly, recent congressional elections research has
found little support for this traditional conception of congressional
elections. There is virtually no evidence that evaluations of Jimmy
Carter's performance played any direct role in the 1978 congressional
elections; one relevant analysis is entitled "The Fiction of Congressional Elections as Presidential Events." [9] The elections of 1974 and
1980 were similar, although effects of presidential performance evaluations were discernible in 1976.[10] Some effects of economic conditions (as
opposed to the president's perceived success in dealing with them) are
evident in recent elections, but again, these effects are smaller than
anticipated, inconsistent across studies, and the issue of how they affect
individual voting is controversial.[11]

If the importance of party affiliations is declining, and issues,
national conditions, and national performance have only weak effects
on congressional elections, what then underlies voter choice? In
particular, what accounts for the election-to-election changes that are
overlaid on the basic partisan division?

The answer lies in the fourth general factor—the candidates. But
if, as mentioned, the issue stands of the candidates are not so important,

what then is? The principal reason for the reawakening of interest in congressional elections in the late 1970s was the discovery that a significant incumbency effect had developed. Scholars such as Robert Erikson and David Mayhew called attention to important changes in the patterns of election outcomes, changes that seemed most pronounced in the mid- to late 1960s.[12] At the same time that the relationship between party affiliation and the vote showed signs of loosening, the relationship between incumbency and the vote increased from a marginal one to a significant one. Erikson estimated that the electoral advantage stemming from incumbency status increased from less than 2 percent in the 1950s to approximately 5 percent in the 1960s, and 8 percent in the 1970s.[13]

Figure 18-1 illustrates the increased importance of incumbency in the congressional vote. In the early postwar period the outcomes in most congressional districts were clustered around the point representing a 50-50 split between the parties. As one looked at more lopsided margins, one found fewer and fewer districts, except at the extremes where uncontested southern Democratic districts and a few rock-ribbed Republican districts fell. As the years went by, however, the distribution gradually became more bimodal. The marginal, or closely contested, districts became fewer, and the safe, lopsided outcome districts became more numerous. This shift in the shape of the distribution was complete by 1972 and has persisted to the present. The 5 to 10 percent increase in the vote going to incumbents accounts for the shift in the distribution, but what accounts for that increase?

Recent studies suggest that various factors underlie the increased advantage of congressional incumbency. Incumbents have voted themselves ever more "perks"—staff, offices, trips home, access to mass communications—which can be used to form a taxpayer-financed political organization. Observers have estimated that the campaign resources that are provided free to incumbents would cost as much as a million dollars per term on the open market. To a great extent, the information constituents receive *about* their incumbent is provided *by* their incumbent, and one would certainly expect such information to be highly favorable.[14]

Among other things, today's incumbents emphasize their efforts to aid constituents in dealing with the federal bureaucracies. As government has grown, both the number of individuals and groups receiving (or trying to receive) government benefits and the number encountering regulatory constraints has increased accordingly. Traditionally, members of Congress have played the role of ombudsman for their constituents and have tried to broker federal dollars into their districts. Thus, as the supply of government services, money, and regulation has grown, the demand for congressional assistance has increased. And, like most entrepreneurs, members probably have done what they could to stimulate demand.[15] Some appreciative constituents appear to support attentive incumbents regardless of either their party ties or ideological considerations. Constituency service is both nonpartisan and nonideological; it is highly individualistic; and it is not an important source of votes for presidents. In short, increased voting for congressional incumbents that is based on constituency service inevitably weakens the electoral links between presidents and members of their party in Congress.

The preceding characterizations describe House elections more accurately than Senate elections, which have received much less academic scrutiny, in part because of technical problems in using national surveys to study them, and in part because their smaller number and highly variable nature makes them more difficult to generalize about. In one important respect, contemporary Senate elections clearly differ from House elections: constituency service—and thus the advantage of incumbency—plays a smaller role. On the other hand, Senate and House elections are similar in several ways. Party affiliation is important, although less so than in earlier times (see Table 18-1). The same studies that were cited in connection with House elections show that national conditions and presidential performance also have little effect on Senate voting in recent elections. These studies indicate that the particular candidates running make a major difference in the voting, although the qualities that voters care about in candidates appear to differ across the two arenas—issue stands and ideology are more important in Senate elections. Specific differences notwithstanding, contemporary Senate elections are as idiosyncratic as House elections; thus, the gap between Senate and presidential voting also has widened in recent years.

Finally, the decline in the importance of party affiliations among voters enhances or even creates the situation in which individual candidate behavior matters. Candidates emphasize the personal and particularistic because they believe they can win votes that way, and they can win votes that way only if citizens ignore such impersonal factors as party and ideology and vote on personal and particularistic grounds. Once the dynamic starts, it is self-reinforcing: increased emphasis on the particular further weakens the relevance of the general, which further enhances the importance of the particular.

Have Congressional Elections Always Been That Way?

Although recent congressional election studies provide a convincing portrait of the past few congressional elections, it would be a

Figure 18-1 Patterns of Competitiveness in Congressional Elections, by Percentage of Two-party Vote Received by Democratic Candidates, Selected Years, 1948-1984

Percent of races

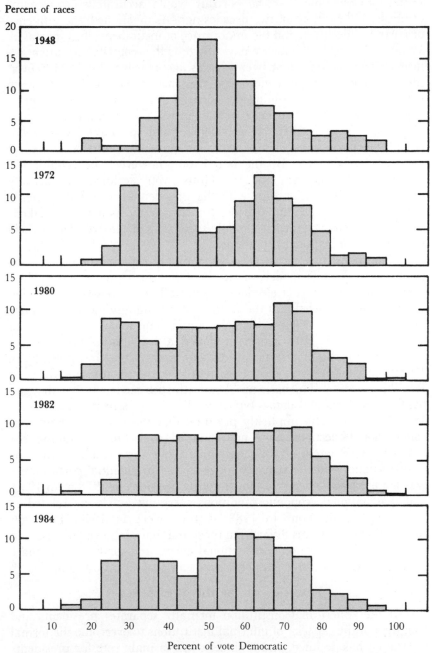

Percent of vote Democratic

SOURCE: Morris P. Fiorina and John A. Ferejohn, "Incumbency and Realignment in Congressional Elections," in John E. Chubb and Paul E. Peterson, eds. *The New Direction in American Politics* (Washington, D.C.: Brookings Institution, 1985), 97.

mistake to presume that the portrait would accurately describe the congressional elections of two decades ago. As mentioned, the influence of party has declined, and the importance of incumbency has increased. What little historical data we have suggests that constituency attentiveness was not so important twenty years ago as it is today.[16] Moreover, there is good reason to believe that the anemic relationships between national conditions, including presidential performance, and congressional voting were far stronger in past times. For example, in the late 1950s one could predict the presidential and the House vote about equally well on the basis of party identification and measures of national performance. By the late 1960s, however, the relationship between such measures and the House vote declined considerably relative to their relationships with the presidential vote.[17] Apparently the constituency-oriented behavior of new incumbents led to a weakening of some voters' tendencies to hold legislators of the president's party responsible for national conditions.

This helps to explain why some highly sophisticated and well-publicized statistical models of expected seat losses have missed their mark so widely in recent elections. Edward Tufte's well-known model, for example, predicted that the Democrats would lose more than thirty House seats in the 1978 midterm elections.[18] The actual loss was fifteen seats. Douglas Hibbs's model predicted a Republican loss of forty House seats in 1982. The actual loss was twenty-six. Most recently, in 1986, old and new models consistently overpredicted the five-seat Republican loss.[19] The basic problem with such models is that they are based on longitudinal data—typically all midterms in the post-World War II period—and implicitly presume that the essential features of congressional elections have not changed over time, including the importance to voters of their opinions about the president. But the cross-sectional evidence strongly suggests that presidential performance was not as closely related to House voting decisions in 1978 as in 1950, and that national economic conditions were not as closely related to House voting decisions in 1982 as they were in 1958. Pre-1966 congressional midterms differ from those that have followed precisely in their stronger association with national events and conditions. As more elections take place, this temporal shift can be built into the models.[20]

Implications for the Presidency

If the American Constitution formally separates presidents and Congress, if the capacity of informal institutions to overcome the formal separation has declined, and if citizens increasingly vote for presidents and members of Congress for somewhat different reasons, what results follow? Walter Dean Burnham and others have argued that the presidential and congressional electoral arenas are becoming increasingly separate as individual career incentives reinforce the formal separation of offices.[21] The increased importance of incumbency and decreased importance of national effects in congressional elections are central components of this argument.

Since the post-Civil War era, when careerist ambitions became widespread among both senators and representatives, a president could count on a degree of self-interested support from the members of his congressional party. When voters supported parties rather than individual candidates, and national conditions and presidential performance became major factors in determining party support, the party in government faced Ben Franklin's classic choice of hanging together lest they all hang separately. Individual members of Congress had a compelling personal incentive to do all that they could do to see to it that a national administration of their party was perceived as effective.

Consider that the Democrats lost 116 seats in the midterm elections of 1894, the Republicans 75 seats in the midterm elections of 1922, the Democrats 56 seats in 1946, and the Republicans 49 seats in 1958. In contrast to 1946, a Democratic president who was widely believed to be in over his head lost a mere 15 seats in 1978; in contrast to 1958, a Republican president presiding over the most serious recession since the Depression lost only 26 seats in 1982. If, as in earlier elections, a quarter to a half of the congressional party faced a real threat of defeat from an unsatisfactory presidential performance, one can be rather confident that members of that party would be more concerned about their president's standing and performance than Jimmy Carter's congressional compatriots were in 1978.[22]

Similarly, when presidential coattails were longer than they are today, members of the congressional party did not wish to run on the same ticket with an unattractive presidential candidate. In 1920 James Cox helped make his party's House delegation 59 seats poorer, and in 1932 Herbert Hoover presided over a Republican loss of 101 seats. By comparison, the Democrats lost only 12 seats in the George McGovern debacle in 1972, and in 1980 Carter helped drag down only 33. If members of the president's party in Congress do not believe that his coattails helped them win office, they naturally will be less inclined to bear any burdens for the sake of his success in office. As Gary Jacobson observes:

> Members of Congress who believe that they got elected with the help of the president are more likely to cooperate with him, if not from simple gratitude than from a sense of shared fate; they will prosper

politically as the administration prospers. Those convinced that they were elected on their own, or despite the top of the ticket, have much less incentive to cooperate.[23]

Presidential coattails and performance have declined as factors in congressional elections. For any given swing in the national vote for a party's House candidates, fewer seats will change hands than in the 1940s, when more seats were near the tipping point (see Figure 18-1). Tufte precisely characterized this effect of the incrased incumbency advantage in a 1973 article on "swing ratios," which measure the responsiveness of the legislative seat division to the national vote division in legislative elections. A ratio of approximately 3 percent of the seats to each 1 percent gain for a party in the national vote in the early postwar period declined to one of approximately 2 percent of the seats to each 1 percent vote gain by the 1970s.[24] Thus, members of the president's party in Congress need to be less fearful of any given swing against their president today than a generation ago simply because fewer of their districts fall in the range where the swing will exceed their normal vote margin.

Recent research also suggests that any given swing in presidential voting is less likely to carry over into the congressional vote today than was the case a generation ago. Studies by Randall Calvert and John Ferejohn show that effects of presidential level factors in general have declined as an influence in congressional elections.[25]

As Table 18-2 indicates, the connection between aggregate presidential and House voting has dropped 75 percent since the New Deal

Table 18-2   Responsiveness of House Party Division to Presidential Voting, 1868-1976

Historical period	Responsiveness of congressional vote to presidential vote[a]	Swing ratio[a]	Overall responsiveness[b]
1868-1896	.95	4.40	4.18
1900-1928	.57	1.95	1.11
1932-1944	.81	3.20	2.51
1948-1964	.37	2.40	.89
1968-1976	.19	2.02	.38

SOURCE: John Ferejohn and Randall Calvert, "Presidential Coattails in Historical Perspective," *American Journal of Political Science* 28 (February 1984): 127-146.

[a] Numerical entries are regression coefficients.
[b] Numerical entries are the product of the two preceding columns. The interpretation is the percentage gain in House seats associated with a 1 percent gain in the *presidential* vote.

period. The table also shows the 33 percent decline in the swing ratio. Calvert and Ferejohn observe that "the remaining responsiveness of the composition of the House to the presidential vote is a pale reflection of its previous levels." [26]

The decline in party voting and coattail voting and the lessened influence of national conditions on the congressional vote lead each individual officeholder to see a different mandate in the election returns. Perhaps the most graphic single demonstration of that assertion appears in Table 18-3. At the turn of the century, fewer than fifteen congressional districts gave majorities of their votes to a congressional candidate of one party and a presidential candidate of the other. The number of such districts remained relatively small until after 1940, when ticket splitting began to increase dramatically. In 1984, 44 percent of congressional districts were carried by congressional and presidential candidates of different parties. One can hardly blame members today for seeing mixed signals in the returns. They run on their personal records and attribute their reelections to their personal records. Republican or Democrat, members of Congress belong to the "Reelect Me" party.[27]

The implications of this electoral disintegration for the contemporary presidency are clear and disturbing. Generations of American

Table 18-3   Districts Carried by Congressional and Presidential Candidates of Different Parties, 1900-1984

Year	Percentage
1900	3%
1908	7
1916	11
1924	12
1932	14
1940	15
1948	21
1952	19
1956	30
1960	26
1964	33
1968	32
1972	44
1976	29
1980	34
1984	44

SOURCE: Gary Jacobson, *The Politics of Congressional Elections*, 2d ed. (Boston: Little, Brown, 1987), 151.

political commentators have argued that the president is the only elected official with a *direct* political interest in the state of the entire nation. Members of Congress may agree with the president that a problem, say inflation, has become a pressing national concern. They also may agree that no easy solution exists, that any effective action to address the problem will impose significant costs on some elements of the nation. But here the agreement ends. The president's national constituency bears the burdens of public policies but also enjoys the benefits. Therefore, the president will bite the bullet and push policies that impose costs, as long as the corresponding benefits are significantly greater.

Congressional districts and states, however, are not microcosms of the country. The United States has never seen a national inflation so severe that a representative would accept 25 percent unemployment in his district in order to halt it. Even in the 1890s, one of the heydays of party government in the United States, such extreme local effects split presidents and their fellow partisans in Congress. Today's members refuse to accept even modest costs in their districts in order to provide significant national benefits. In Sen. Howard H. Baker, Jr.'s, colorful words, they walk up to the bullet and gum it a little bit. Carter's embarrassing struggles with the inflation and energy problems in the late 1970s provide the best illustration. Each proposal his administration put forth was taken apart by members who were disturbed by differential effects, especially geographical ones. Their refusal to back the president is perfectly comprehensible in an era of weak party ties, weaker coattails, weak effects of national conditions, and "every man for himself" politics.

Thus, the situation of the contemporary presidency is not a happy one. The occupant of that office must expect to be judged on his success in maintaining peace, high employment, low inflation, adequate and inexpensive energy, harmonious racial relations, an acceptable moral climate, and a generally contented nation. Meanwhile, his co-partisans on the Hill are relatively insulated from such concerns. No longer expecting to gain much from the president's successes or suffer much from his failures, they have little incentive to bear any risk on his behalf. Former Speaker Thomas P. O'Neill, Jr., lamented that the Democratic congressional party had become little more than an organizational convenience: "Members are more home-oriented. They no longer have to follow the national philosophy of the party. They can get reelected on their newsletter, or on how they serve their constituents." [28] By holding the president responsible for national conditions, the electorate has removed the critical incentives that have brought some cohesion to an institutionally fragmented national government. By holding only the presidency responsible, the citizenry allows the Congress to profit electorally from irresponsibility.

The 1980s: A New Era?

The themes that are developed in the preceding sections emerge from research conducted during the 1970s, based primarily on data gathered in the 1960s and 1970s. How well do those themes apply to the elections of the 1980s and the presidency shaped by them? At first glance, the elections of the 1980s appear to constitute a break with those of the past decade and a half, but a closer view reveals a picture more impressive for its familiarity than for its freshness.

In 1980 the Republicans won an impressive victory. Added to Ronald Reagan's personal triumph was evidence of a seemingly strong coattail effect—thirty-three seats gained in the House and twelve seats in the Senate, which gave the Republicans control of a chamber for the first time since the Eighty-third Congress (1953-55). Such gains also gave surface credence to the argument that the nation had turned to the right, and numerous commentators of a conservative stripe lost little time in advancing such interpretations. Many Democratic politicians accepted that view or at least considered it plausible enough to justify lying low for a decent interval. The legislative successes of the first year of Reagan's presidency certainly were aided by the seeming clarity of the election returns.

Yet the Republican victory was not so sweeping as it first appeared. In the House, when all was tallied up, 90 percent of the unindicted Democratic incumbents who ran, won—a slightly smaller percentage than in 1976. In 1964, however, only 75 percent of the Republican House incumbents managed to reach safe harbor against the Democratic tide. Even if the value of incumbency relative to national forces dropped marginally between 1976 and 1980, it still appears quite impressive in comparison with the pre-1966 period. Calvert and Ferejohn thus assess coattail effects for recent elections:

> Although the 1972 and 1980 elections exhibited a partial return to the higher levels of efficiency [responsiveness of congressional vote to presidential vote] characteristic of the 1956-1964 period, the efficiency levels after 1968 are on the order of two-thirds of their earlier levels.[29]

Whatever interpretation of the 1980 House elections is the most appropriate, the subsequent elections of the 1980s unequivocally support the twin theses of insulation and incumbency. In the major recession year of 1982, twenty-two Republican incumbents went down to defeat, a figure that compares favorably to the thirty-five defeated in the recession year of 1958. In the landslide reelection of Ronald Reagan in 1984, only thirteen Democratic incumbents were defeated, and the net gain for the Republicans was only fourteen seats. Finally, in 1986 House incumbents set an all-time record with a reelection rate of 98 percent; only six (five of them Republicans) suffered rejection at the polls. In House elections incumbency is alive and thriving, and incumbents are as insulated as ever.

But what of the Senate? Have not Senate elections registered the political sea changes of the 1980s, first heralding the rise of the Reagan era with a twelve-seat Republican gain in 1980, then signaling its demise with an eight-seat loss in 1986? Despite the large shifts, here, too, there is much less than meets the eye. Consider 1980. After the initial shouts of jubilation and lamentation had subsided, disinterested analysts noticed a significant feature of the voting. Nationally, Democratic senatorial candidates had actually outpolled Republican candidates by about three million votes; the aggregate national vote was 52.3 percent to 47.7 percent. The Republican victory was fashioned largely from close wins in small states.

A brief examination of the twelve seats the Democrats lost provides additional perspective. In three states (Alabama, Alaska, and Florida), the Democratic incumbent suffered a primary defeat, and the divided party was unable to hold the seat in the ensuing general election. Two other incumbents had problems distinct from any resurgence of Republicanism. Herman Talmadge of Georgia was mired in personal and financial scandals. Considering that Carter carried Georgia, Talmadge can hardly be counted as a casualty of the Reagan landslide. Warren Magnuson of Washington was attacked by his opponent as old and tired, a tactic that very nearly upset his comparably aged colleague on the other side of the political spectrum— Barry Goldwater, who had the Reagan revolution working *for* him!

The remaining seven incumbents, particularly the six liberals, are more often viewed as central to the significance of the 1980 returns. When one looks closely (Table 18-4), however, one sees a group of extremely weak candidates. With the exception of Gaylord Nelson, these liberal senators were living on borrowed time. In all probability, only the Watergate-induced Democratic tide of 1974 gave them the opportunity to run in 1980. Reagan's coattails might have done them in, the National Conservative Political Action Committee (NCPAC) might have done them in, almost anything might have done them in. It did not take much. If this group had lost in a more normal 1974 election, the Republicans still might have taken control of the Senate in 1980. But they would have done so with about half the number of Democratic defeats, not including the most widely publicized liberal

Table 18-4 Democratic Senate Incumbents Defeated in 1980

	Percentage of the total vote	
	1974	*1980*
Birch Bayh (Ind.)	50.7%	46.2%
Frank Church (Idaho)	56.1	46.8
John C. Culver (Iowa)	52.0	45.5
John A. Durkin (N.H.)	53.6[a]	47.8
George McGovern (S.D.)	53.0	39.4
Warren G. Magnuson (Wash.)	60.7	45.8
Robert B. Morgan (N.C.)	62.1	49.4
Gaylord Nelson (Wis.)	61.8	48.3
Herman E. Talmadge (Ga.)	71.7	49.1

SOURCE: *America Votes 14: A Handbook of Contemporary American Election Statistics, 1980,* compiled and edited by Richard M. Scammon and Alice McGillivray (Washington, D.C.: Congressional Quarterly Inc., 1981).

[a] Special 1975 election called after 1974 general election resulted in a virtual tie.

ones, and there would have been less talk of a shift to the right or a new era in American politics.

The 1986 Senate elections produced a mirror image of the 1980 results. The dramatic Democratic gain of eight seats and the accompanying regain of control of the Senate was heralded by many commentators as evidence that the Reagan era had ended. But such interpretations founder on precisely the same grounds as those of 1980. Preliminary returns indicate that Democratic senatorial candidates outpolled Republican candidates nationally by less than half a million votes; the aggregate vote was 50.3 percent Democratic to 49.7 percent Republican. The Democratic victory was largely fashioned on very close wins in smaller states. Consider Table 18-5. Of the six Republican incumbents defeated only one, Mark Andrews, had achieved an impressive victory in 1980, when everything supposedly was working in a Republican direction. Again, the point is not that the farm economy, disenchantment with Reagan, and so forth did not matter; rather, the point is that *everything* matters for incumbents with thin margins. But it is unwise to base interpretations of an election on a factor that shifts an outcome from 51 percent Republican to 49 percent Republican, when that factor would scarcely be noticed if the shift had been from 61 percent Republican to 59 percent Republican.

In sum, Senate elections are probably the least useful guides to trends in national politics. With 47 percent of the national vote the Republicans purportedly dealt a historic defeat to the Democrats in

Table 18-5 Republican Senate Seats Lost in 1986

	Percentage of total vote Republican	
	1980	*1986*
Incumbents defeated		
Denton (Ala.)	50%	49%
Hawkins (Fla.)	52	45
Mattingly (Ga.)	51	49
Andrews (N.D.)	70	49
Abdnor (S.D.)	58	48
Gorton (Wash.)	54	49
Incumbents retired		
Mathias (Md.)	66	39
Laxalt (Nev.)	59	45
East (N.C.)	50	48

SOURCE: *Congressional Quarterly's Guide to U.S. Elections* (Washington, D.C.: Congressional Quarterly Inc., 1985); and *Congressional Quarterly Weekly Report*, November 8, 1986, 2864-2871.

1980. Despite a higher national vote of 49 percent, the Republicans supposedly suffered a historic loss in 1986. These peculiar results occur because state electorates differ widely in size, from seven million in California to a quarter-million in Nevada (in off-year elections). Moreover, each seat alternates between presidential year and midterm in its timing. The individual candidates are more visible and the media more widely used than in any elections other than presidential. Idiosyncracy, or at least individualism, is at a maximum in Senate elections. They certainly are not the principal means by which voters send a message to the incumbent president.

Of course, perceptions of reality can be almost as important as reality itself. After the 1980 election, Democrats appeared to lie low, and some actually may have feared continued Republican electoral gains. For their part, the Republicans maintained near-perfect party cohesion on the principal elements of Reagan's economic program.[30] Thus, even if one can discount the inherent significance of the 1980 returns, what about their perceived significance? Did not Reagan's leadership performance in 1981 and 1982 recall the glory days of Lyndon B. Johnson and Franklin D. Roosevelt? Did it not mark a return to an earlier era when presidents and their congressional parties were more apt to govern together and then electioneer together?

To be sure, Reagan won some impressive early legislative victories, but even Carter won a few. What about the overall pattern of executive-legislative relations in the early years of the Reagan administration? Richard Fleisher and Jon Bond report a fascinating analysis of congressional support for Presidents Carter and Reagan.[31] Using data from 1959 to 1974, they developed a model of presidential support in Congress based on party membership, popular support in the Gallup poll, and ideological similarity, as measured by conservative coalition support scores. The model predicts legislative support for presidents in their first year, given the characteristics of the Congresses they faced. Fleisher and Bond conclude that, overall, Reagan's support was not strikingly high; rather, Carter's was abnormally low. Reagan's support was actually 1 percent *lower* than their model predicted, while Carter's was 7 percent lower. Only 26 representatives (including 21 southern Democrats) supported Reagan at a level 10 percent or more higher than predicted, while 167 representatives (including 166 Democrats) supported Carter at a level 10 percent or more lower than expected.

Table 18-6 contains additional data on presidential leadership. Evidently Reagan did enjoy unprecedented first-year support among senators of his own party. In the House, however, he fared less well. Although Reagan's first-year support among his House co-partisans was higher than Carter's, and noticeably higher than Richard M. Nixon's, it was lower than that of Dwight Eisenhower and other presidents elected prior to the mid-1960s' growth in the congressional incumbency advantage. In the short term, Reagan's early record was impressive. When viewed from a more historical perspective, however, it appears less remarkable.

Table 18-6   First-Year Presidential Support among In-Party Members of the House and Senate, 1953-1981

Year	President	House	Senate
1953	Eisenhower	74%	68%
1961	Kennedy	73	65
1965	Johnson	74	64
1969	Nixon	57	66
1977	Carter	63	70
1981	Reagan	68	80

SOURCE: *Congressional Quarterly Almanac* for the years 1953, 1961, 1965, 1969, 1977, 1981; pages 78, 620, 1099, 1040, 23-B, 20-C, respectively.

NOTE: These presidential support scores are a rough measure of the comity between the president and members of his own party in the House and Senate. The scores represent the percentage of votes on which the House and Senate voted "yea" or "nay" *in agreement* with the president's recorded position.

To discount the historic significance of the 1980 and 1984 elections and the political success of the Reagan presidency is not to disparage the recent achievements of the Republican party. That judgment holds even taking into account the losses of 1986. To their credit, the Republicans of the 1980s have behaved more like a serious political party than has anyone for at least two decades. In 1980, for example, Reagan appealed not just for personal support but also for the election of Republicans to the House and Senate. In 1982 he explicitly appealed for continued support of his policies rather than distance himself from his party's candidates. And in 1984 Reagan did not seek only a personal victory as had Nixon in 1972.

In contrast to these earlier elections much has been made of the "themelessness" of 1986. Perhaps 1986 was especially themeless, but one wonders how much of a theme any congressional election, particularly a midterm election, has. In the midst of a severe recession in 1982 Democratic candidates attacked Reaganomics, while Republican candidates urged a steady hand. Does that constitute a theme? One tries in vain to recollect the theme of the 1978 elections. The Watergate theme, in 1974, is probably the exception rather than the rule. In 1986 Reagan did appeal strenuously for voters to support Republican senators as part of his effort to change the course of American government. His appeal didn't work, of course, but probably most themes don't. In an era when "all politics is local," recognized themes are the post hoc consensus of the media elites.

Over and above the efforts of Ronald Reagan, the work of the Republican National Committee (RNC) deserves special notice.[32] RNC efforts transcend the commitment of a single party leader. The RNC is leading the way to a resurgence of party interest in candidate recruitment and the conduct of campaigns. Given the importance of good candidates in American elections, the RNC has begun to build a solid base by actively recruiting and helping train candidates for local offices and state legislatures. These candidates also have received financial support for their campaigns. At the federal level the party has targeted Democratic House and Senate seats where Republican prospects look favorable and has intervened actively to recruit and help nominate strong challengers. These challengers have been sent to "campaign schools" and have received financial assistance through the party's congressional campaign committees. In these and other ways the Republicans are reviving a collective party spirit not often seen in recent years. Their performance is particularly refreshing because it comes on the heels of the Democratic party's disheartening performance between 1976 and 1980. Current Democratic efforts and accomplishments still pale by comparison to the Republicans', but they too are on the upswing.

Such indications of party resurgence, especially on the Republican side, offer one of the few possibilities for containing and reversing the fissiparous tendencies discussed in this chapter. If members of Congress can be made more dependent on their party, and if the party apparatus is under firm presidential control, greater cohesion can be enforced. The first "if" obviously is the bigger of the two. Simple gratitude for their selection and training does not suffice; candidates must *need* their party. One possibility is continued change in the pattern of campaign financing so that congressional candidates increasingly would rely on party rather than individual and PAC contributions. This would entail statutory change, of course, and we should not expect members to submit happily to presidential and party control. But campaign financing reforms are probably the best means of strengthening party cohesion and national party leadership. "Follow the money" applies quite generally to human activity, not just to Watergate coverups.

Summary

The contemporary presidency constitutes one electoral system and the Congress 535 others. Although these systems overlap, their intersection now has less in common than in much of our earlier history. As a result of the increased separation of the electoral systems, the contemporary presidency occupies a lonely position. The citizenry attaches high expectations to the occupant of the office and expresses its disappointment at the polls when those expectations are not met. But no president can accomplish much without the help of Congress, and the contemporary Congress is not the focus of the same expectations as the presidency. Each individual member emphasizes his or her personal qualities and record, each is expected to work for the interests of the district or state; electoral success is largely dependent on meeting these expectations. Unfortunately, members often profit by protecting short-term particular interests, which hinders efforts to advance longer-term national interests. As modern social science theory has demonstrated, adding up the preferences of the parts need not result in a good thing for the whole.[33] Thus, until members of Congress believe that their personal fates coincide with that of the president, and that both depend on doing well by the country, the political failure that has become familiar in recent decades will continue.

Notes

This essay was originally prepared while the author was a Fellow at the Center for Advanced Study in the Behavioral Sciences. He gratefully acknowledges the financial support provided by the Guggenheim Foundation and the National Science Foundation (BNS8206304).

1. The argument that follows is synthetic. Among the scholars who have most stimulated my thinking are Walter Dean Burnham, Robert Erikson, John Ferejohn, David Mayhew, and Edward Tufte. Numerous useful studies by these and other scholars are cited below. Parts of the argument are developed more fully in my article "The Decline of Collective Responsibility in American Politics," *Daedalus* (Summer 1980): 25-45.

2. Anthony King, "How Not to Select Presidential Candidates: A View from Europe," in *The American Elections of 1980,* ed. Austin Raney (Washington, D.C.: American Enterprise Institute, 1981), 303-328.

3. Fiorina, "Decline of Collective Responsibility."

4. For excellent treatments of recent elections, see Paul Abramson, John Aldrich, and David Rohde, *Change and Continuity in the 1980 Elections,* rev. ed. (Washington, D.C.: CQ Press, 1983), and the same authors' *Change and Continuity in the 1984 Elections,* rev. ed. (Washington, D.C.: CQ Press, 1987).

5. Morris Fiorina, *Retrospective Voting in American National Elections* (New Haven: Yale University Press, 1981).

6. The *locus classicus* is Donald Stokes and Warren Miller, "Party Government and the Saliency of Congress," *Public Opinion Quarterly* 26 (1962): 531-546.

7. For a good overview, see Gary Jacobson, *The Politics of Congressional Elections* (Boston: Little, Brown, 1983).

8. Jacobson, *The Politics of Congressional Elections*, 121. He writes, "Alert readers will have noticed that issues were hardly a prominent item in the discussion of voting behavior. The reason is that they show up so infrequently as having any measurable impact on individual voting in these election studies once other variables have been taken into account."

9. Lyn Ragsdale, "The Fiction of Congressional Elections as Presidential Events," *American Politics Quarterly* 8 (1980): 375-379.

10. On the effects of presidential performance in the 1974 and 1976 congressional elections, see Fiorina, *Retrospective Voting,* chap. 8. On 1980 and 1984, see Abramson, Aldrich, and Rohde, *Change and Continuity in the 1980 Elections,* 220-221, and *Change and Continuity in the 1984 Elections,* 270-272.

11. The failure to find a direct effect of economic conditions or presidential performance on the congressional vote does not preclude those factors' influencing the voting in other less direct ways. Jacobson and Kernell, for example, argue that national conditions and presidential performance affect the voting indirectly by influencing the calculations of potential candidates and contributors. The latter lie low in bad years for their party and ante up in good years (bad and good being defined in terms of national conditions). This behavior leads to self-fulfilling expectations as poorly funded bad candidates go down to defeat in bad years and adequately funded good candidates drive to victory in good ones. The argument undoubtedly has considerable merit (not to mention empirical support), but it is doubtful that candidates and contributors would continue to delude themselves were there not some basis in reality for their expectations. See Gary Jacobson and Samuel Kernell, *Strategy and Choice in Congressional Elections* (New Haven: Yale University Press, 1981).

12. Robert Erikson, "Malapportionment, Gerrymandering and Party Fortunes in Congressional Elections," *American Political Science Review* 66 (1972): 1234-1245; and David Mayhew, "Congressional Elections: The Case of the Vanishing Marginals," *Polity* 6 (1974): 195-317.
13. Erikson, "Party Fortunes" and personal communication.
14. Glenn Parker, "The Advantage of Incumbency in House Elections," *American Politics Quarterly* 4 (1980): 449-464.
15. Morris P. Fiorina, *Congress—Keystone of the Washington Establishment* (New Haven: Yale University Press, 1977); and Bruce Cain, John Ferejohn, and Morris Fiorina, *The Personal Vote: Constituency Service and Electoral Independence* (Cambridge, Mass.: Harvard University Press, 1987), chap. 2.
16. Morris P. Fiorina, "Congressmen and their Constituent: 1958 and 1978," in *Proceedings of the Thomas P. O'Neill, Jr., Symposium on the U.S. Congress,* ed. Dennis Hale (Boston: Eusey Press, 1982), 33-64.
17. Fiorina, *Retrospective Voting,* 42-43. This decline is consistent with Richard Born's pinpointing of the mid-1960s as the period in which the value of incumbency grew fastest. See Richard Born, "Generational Replacement and the Growth of Incumbent Reflection Margins in the U.S. House," *American Political Science Review* 73 (1979): 811-817.
18. Edward Tufte, "Determinants of the Outcomes of Midterm Congressional Elections," *American Political Science Review* 69 (1975): 812-826. The model incorporates three variables: the "benchmark," or standing division of party support, presidential performance ratings, and election-year variation in real per capita income.
19. Douglas A. Hibbs, "President Reagan's Mandate from the 1980 Election: A Shift to the Right?" *American Politics Quarterly* 10 (1982): 387-420; and James E. Campbell, "Evaluating the 1986 Congressional Election Forecasts," *PS* (Winter 1987): 37-42.
20. Alternatively, different research designs can illuminate the changing relationship between economic conditions and congressional voting. Using state-level data Benjamin Radcliff finds a strong relationship before 1960 and no relationship thereafter. See his "Solving a Puzzle: Aggregate Analysis and Economic Voting Revisited" (Paper presented at the annual meeting of the Midwet Political Science Association, Chicago, 1986).
21. Walter Dean Burnham, "Insulation and Responsiveness in Congressional Elections," *Political Science Quarterly* 90 (1975): 411-435.
22. The objection might be raised that as recently as 1974 an incumbent congressional party paid dearly for the sins of the national administration: the Republicans lost forty-nine seats in the House. As Burnham points out, however, 1974 was noteworthy in that Republican losses were relatively small by historical standards: "In all probability, considerably more than a dozen Republican incumbents survived the 1974 tide who would have lost under pre-1960 conditions." Burnham, "Insulation and Responsiveness," 426.
23. Jacobson, *The Politics of Congressional Elections,* 132.
24. Edward Tufte, "The Relationship between Seats and Votes in Two-Party Systems," *American Political Science Review* 67 (1973): 540-554.
25. Randall Calvert and John Ferejohn, "Coattail Voting in Recent Presidential Elections," *American Political Science Review* 77 (June 1983), and "Presidential Coattails in Historical Perspective," *American Journal of Political Science* 28 (February 1984): 127-146.
26. Calvert and Ferejohn, "Coattail Voting."

27. "The Thoughts of Chairman Scammon," *Regulation* (August/September 1982), 9.
28. *Congressional Quarterly Weekly Report,* September 13, 1980, 2696.
29. Calvert and Ferejohn, "Coattail Voting," 27-28.
30. Similarly, even after a modest twenty-six-seat gain in the 1982 elections, the Democrats appeared confident that the electorate had demanded a tempering of Reaganomics. Many Republicans appeared to share that view.
31. Richard Fleisher and John Bond, "Assessing Presidential Support in the House: Lessons from Reagan and Carter," *Journal of Politics* 45 (August 1983): 745-758.
32. On the activities of the RNC, see Gary Jacobson, "Congressional Campaign Finance and the Revival of the Republican Party," in *Proceedings of the O'Neill Symposium,* 313-330; and James Reichley, "The Rise of National Parties," in *The New Direction in American Politics,* ed. John Chubb and Paul Peterson (Washington, D.C.: Brookings Institution, 1985), 175-200.
33. Several theoretical propositions underlie this claim. See Kenneth Arrow, *Social Choice and Individual Values,* 2d ed. (New Haven: Yale University Press, 1970). Arrow has shown that any method of aggregation that is responsive to unrestricted individual preferences (e.g., majority rule) will fail in certain specified ways. In addition, game theory has studied the now well-known idea of the "Prisoner's Dilemma": rational individual behavior may lead inexorably to poor collective outcomes. For a comprehensive discussion see Russel Hardin, *Collective Action* (Washington, D.C.: Resources for the Future, 1982).

19. THE PRESIDENCY AND THE JUDICIARY

Robert Scigliano

The presidency and the judiciary share a common power under different names and perform similar tasks although in different ways. The framers of the Constitution arranged matters so that the two branches might act from a common interest in restraining Congress, but some of their sharpest differences have been with each other.

The Common Power

The executive and judicial branches are part of a system of separated powers that has its origin more in a theory of government than in its practice, especially in the works of the English philosopher John Locke and the French philosopher Baron de Montesquieu. Writing in the late seventeenth century, Locke seems to have been the first person to speak of executive power as something different from legislative power. The person who holds this power, he says, executes laws made by the legislative authority or, put another way, employs the common force as directed by the legislature. Before civil society or government existed, each man was in a state of nature, executing the law of nature for himself. There is no separate judicial power in Locke's scheme: judging is considered to be part of executive power. For example, Locke refers to "the administration of justice" as an element of the execution of the laws. However, he does consider judging to be a distinct activity, and he insists on the need for "indifferent [impartial] and upright" judges.[1]

Montesquieu is the bridge between Locke and the American framers. Writing in the first part of the eighteenth century, about a half century after Locke, he was "the oracle who is always consulted and cited" on the subject of separation of powers, according to *The Federalist*. Adopting Locke's view that the power of judging is executive in nature, Montesquieu at first called this power executive power relating to domestic matters, and then simply executive power. We do not know why he did this, but perhaps he wanted to emphasize that, in his opinion, the courts typically executed the laws.[2]

Apparently influenced by Locke and Montesquieu, many Americans at the time of the founding thought of judges as engaged in the execution of the laws. In the Constitutional Convention, for example, Gouverneur Morris observed that "the judiciary ... was part of the executive." Madison saw "an analogy between the executive and judicial departments [branches] in several respects" and mentioned that both the executive and judges executed, interpreted, and applied the laws.[3]

Madison was right. Executive officials necessarily interpret and apply laws when enforcing them, and judges enforce laws when they interpret and apply them. Consider the industrial foremen during World War II who wanted to invoke the National Labor Relations Act to protect their efforts to organize a labor union. The executive agency charged with enforcing the act had to decide that foremen were "employees" before it could extend the act's protections to them; and the courts agreed with the designation, thereby supporting enforcement of the act. Unfortunately for the unionizing foremen, Congress then legislated them out of the law.[4]

Many framers thought that judges could be associated rather closely with the president. A presidential cabinet containing the chief justice and the heads of the executive departments was proposed by several delegates at the Constitutional Convention. In one version, called a council of state, the president could 'submit any matter to the discussion" of his council and could "require the written opinions" of its members. The chief justice, who would preside over the body in the president's absence, had the specific duty to "recommend such alterations of and additions to the laws of the U.S. as may in his opinion be necessary to the due administration of justice, and such as may promote useful learning and inculcate sound morality throughout the nation." These proposals failed because most of the framers were opposed to saddling the president with a cabinet, not because they were opposed to a Supreme Court justice's membership on it. Indeed, in the final version of the Constitution, they did not prohibit judges from also serving in the executive branch, even though they did not allow members of Congress or the executive to serve in each other's ranks, or members of Congress to be judges. Thus a Supreme Court justice could be an ambassador and a secretary of state could be a member of the Supreme Court although neither official could be a senator or representative.[5]

President George Washington, who was fastidious in observing constitutional proprieties, saw nothing amiss in sending Chief Justice John Jay his circulars to department secretaries asking for legislation to be recommended by Congress. On numerous occasions Washington and his secretary of the treasury, Alexander Hamilton, consulted the chief justice on matters of foreign policy and national security, including the constitutionality of Washington's Neutrality and Whiskey Rebellion proclamations. The president asked the Supreme Court as a whole for its written opinion on questions related to American neutrality in the war that broke out in Europe at the end of 1792, and he asked Chief Justice Oliver Ellsworth, Jay's successor, for his written opinion concerning a demand by the House of Representatives for papers connected with the Jay Treaty. When Jay, as Washington's special ambassador to Great Britain, negotiated that treaty, he was a member of the Supreme Court; a few years later, Ellsworth, in a similar appointment by John Adams, negotiated a settlement of differences between the United States and France while serving on the Court. Jay served for about six months in 1789 as chief justice and Washington's secretary of foreign affairs, until Thomas Jefferson was able to assume the latter office; and when John Marshall was appointed to succeed Ellsworth as chief justice in 1801, he continued as secretary of state for several weeks until replaced by James Madison.[6]

Congress evidently saw nothing wrong with using judges to assist the executive. When it enacted Hamilton's plan for funding the public debt in 1790, it accepted the treasury secretary's recommendation that the chief justice be a member of the commission to manage the fund for paying off the debt. A pension law that was passed in 1791 to handle the claims of Revolutionary War veterans made federal judges, in effect, aides to the secretary of war, for they were to examine pension claims and submit their reports to the secretary, who would approve or correct the reports and forward them to Congress. Supreme Court justices were included in the task, for in those days they "rode circuit," that is, periodically conducted court with district judges in the territorial circuits to which they were assigned.[7]

Thus, in the earliest years of the Republic, presidents and Congress alike engaged judges in the business of the executive branch with hardly a thought that they might be violating the principle of separation of powers. Because Washington, most members of Congress, and the justices of the Supreme Court, including Jay, Ellsworth, and Marshall, had been delegates to the national or state ratifying conventions, we can assume that they acted with some notion of what the Constitution allowed.

Yet a stricter notion of separation of powers, one that placed the judiciary at a greater distance from the presidency, was emerging in the 1790s. No serious objections were made to the departmental caretaker duties performed by Chief Justices Jay and Marshall, but the appointments of Jay and Ellsworth as ambassadors did draw criticism, especially within the Senate, when those nominations were approved. The Supreme Court itself decided that formal advice giving to the president was improper, and in 1793 it politely declined Washington's request for answers to questions. "Your judgment will discern what is right," the president was told. By this time, the chief justice's name had been dropped from circulars that the president sent to his department secretaries. Not long after, the practice of informal advice giving by individual members of the Court declined sharply.[8]

All members of the Supreme Court balked when Congress assigned them the task of deciding the pension claims of veterans in their circuit courts. "Neither the legislative nor the executive branch can constitutionally assign to the judicial any duties but such as are properly judicial, and to be performed in a judicial manner," declared Chief Justice Jay and Justice William Cushing in the New York circuit court; "[T]he business is not of a judicial nature," decided Justices John Blair and James Wilson in the Pennsylvania circuit; and, argued Justice James Iredell in the North Carolina circuit, "[T]he legislative, executive, and judicial departments are each formed in a separate and independent manner." Jay and Cushing said they were willing to "execute the act in the capacity of commissioners," that is, apparently, to consider themselves to be acting as executive officers and not as judges; but Blair, Wilson, and Iredell refused any cooperation. The Supreme Court acting in its own right never decided the question because Congress amended the law to relieve the judiciary of any responsibility for enforcing it.[9]

The presidency and the judiciary further adjusted their relations after the 1790s, moving toward clearer institutional separation and a clearer differentiation of the common power they exercised. Jefferson's eight years in the presidency hastened the separation, for little common ground existed between the judiciary and a president who regarded it as "the stronghold" of his defeated Federalist enemy: "There the remains of federalism are to be preserved and fed from the treasury, and from that battery all the works of republicanism are to be beaten down and erased."[10]

In the view of separation of powers that has prevailed since the 1790s, Supreme Court justices are supposed to have little to do with the executive branch—or the legislative branch, for that matter. For a justice to enter into executive service, as Jay, Ellsworth, and, in a small way, Marshall, did, would be considered improper. In fact, only Justice Robert H. Jackson has done it since then, acting as the chief American prosecutor at the trials of the defeated Nazi leaders at Nuremberg, Germany. Many persons today would probably disapprove of a justice's serving even in a quasi-judicial capacity off the Court, as Chief

Justice Earl Warren did in chairing the commission that investigated the assassination of President John F. Kennedy, and as a number of justices had done previously, usually without a murmur of criticism. It still seems acceptable for justices to speak out, in a nonpartisan way, on matters that directly affect the court system, as Chief Justice Warren E. Burger made it a practice to do, in giving the president and Congress his views on judicial workloads, the need for more judges, and reforms in the Court's jurisdiction. Perhaps most Americans would not object to the longstanding though intermittent practice of justices giving the president their views on appointments to the Supreme Court or lower federal courts, although it is interesting that this kind of advice giving has always taken place privately.

Public sentiment is strongly opposed to judges acting as informal presidential advisers or helpers. Such activities have not been an issue until recently, partly because they were not generally known until long after they had occurred but mostly beause they seem not to have taken place very often. Apart from Chief Justice Jay's assistance to the Washington administration, which was rendered before the protocol between justices and the executive had been established, not many justices have been involved in significant ways with the executive branch. Such involvement appears to be mainly a phenomenon of this century (or perhaps judicial secrets have been harder to keep in modern America) and seems to have occurred mostly between justices and the presidents who appoint them. In each instance, the parties were continuing a previous political relationship. The issue came to a head in 1968, when President Lyndon B. Johnson nominated Justice Abe Fortas, an old friend whom he had appointed to the Court three years earlier, to succeed Earl Warren as chief justice. Fortas's activities as a presidential adviser already had been widely reported in the press, and his nomination as chief justice led to further inquiry into his ties to Johnson. One account called him "a close and confidential adviser on everything from race riots to Vietnam." These reports were offered in the Senate as a major reason why Fortas's appointment should not be approved (it was not), and the justice's supporters as well as his critics expressed concern about judicial politicking at the White House.[11]

No executive position has been held by a Supreme Court justice since Jackson in 1946; no justice has performed judicial functions outside the Court since Warren in 1964; and none seems to have lent his services as a White House adviser since Fortas. Practice more than constitutional requirements has brought about this situation, so effectively that today we hardly ever think of judges and executive officers as sharing the common task of executing the laws.

The Two Executives

In their execution of the laws, the president and the judiciary play complementary parts. As a federal court described the relationship in an 1837 decision, "[T]he judicial and executive powers are closely allied; they are necessary to each other in the discharge of the duties of both departments." [12] The differences between the two branches are important, to be sure. The president is an active agent in law enforcement with an energy—sometimes referred to as "force" by the framers—that pervades the entire government. He is an Argus with hundreds of thousands of eyes; his subordinates in the executive branch ceaselessly watch over the laws and those to whom they apply. He can do many things, as the framers wished, do them quickly and with decision, and, when necessary, do them secretly. Those who are slow in yielding to him are prodded, those who might think of violating his orders are admonished. And when prods and threats fail, the president's minions take the recalcitrant and disobedient to court to be coerced into compliance, punished for their disobedience, or, if they are fortunate, told that they have not offended the law after all.

Judges, on the other hand, are (or were intended to be) passive in their enforcement of the laws. They "can take no active resolution whatever," according to *The Federalist*. Theirs is the power of judgment, really not a power at all. To overcome their "natural feebleness," the Constitution gave them their offices during good behavior (practically speaking, for life) and prohibited legislative reductions in their salaries. Yet, although judges act only upon the specific parties in cases brought to them, they, too, serve law enforcement generally, for many persons take note of what happens in court and govern themselves accordingly.[13]

Like the president, the Supreme Court primarily supervises the work of others. Several hundred judges in the federal district (trial) courts and, above them, in the federal courts of appeals handle nearly all judicial business before it gets to the Supreme Court, which relatively few cases do. The thousands of state court judges also act under the Court's supervision when their business involves "federal questions," which under today's expanded notion of federal authority covers a great deal of their litigation. The Supreme Court alone decides about 250 to 300 cases a year on their merits nowadays, less than a handful of which come into the Court without having first passed through other tribunals.

The executive assists the judiciary in several ways. It assigns marshals to the judges to serve their writs and other orders, to make arrests, to guard prisoners, and to transport the convicted to prisons it maintains. Moreover, it brings the judges much of their business. The executive arm of government institutes all criminal cases and a large portion of the civil cases that are tried in courts. (The government is often the defendant in other civil suits.) In the twelve months ending on June 30, 1986, the government was a party, one way or another, in more than two-fifths of the cases that were filed in federal district courts and courts of appeals (which take their appeals laterally from decisions of administrative agencies as well as vertically from the district courts); it was also a party in nearly all of the minor matters tried before United States magistrates (who are appointed by federal district judges). In the 1984 term of the Supreme Court, which extended from October of that year to the summer of 1985, the executive participated, in some way, in more than one-third of the appeals from lower federal and state courts that the Court considered accepting for decision and in about two-thirds of the cases that it accepted and decided on their merits after having heard argument on them.[14]

These figures only partially tell the story of the relationship between the executive and the judiciary. Consider the Supreme Court's caseload of 4,097 appeals in its 1984 term. The Court itself decides in nearly all appeals whether to accept cases, but it needs help in managing its agenda. The executive, through the solicitor general and his staff, who are located in the Justice Department but exercise considerable autonomy, provide a good measure of this help. The solicitor general almost always decides whether the government will appeal its defeats in lower courts to the Supreme Court, and the Court relies on him to appeal only the most deserving cases. In the 1984 term, the government appealed just 43 of its 637 lower court defeats, whereas its adversaries appealed 1,430 defeats.[15]

The solicitor general helps out in other ways. He sometimes tells the Court which appeals by the government's adversaries are worth hearing and, increasingly over the past few decades, he has entered into other people's litigation in his capacity as amicus curiae, or friend of the court. In the 1984 term, the solicitor general suggested cases for review to the justices thirty times and gave the government's support to other parties in forty-three cases that were being considered on their merits. Quite often, the Court will invite him to enter other people's fights, as it did in *Brown v. Board of Education* (1954), the case that ruled segregation in public education to be unconstitutional, and in *Baker v. Carr* (1962), which set the stage for the Court's "one person, one vote" doctrine in legislative apportionments. What seems still more remarkable, the solicitor general will on rare occasion come into Court to say that the government did not deserve to win a case in district court or the court of appeals.[16]

What does the executive ask of the Supreme Court justices in return? Only that they do their jobs in administering justice. Of course, the executive has its own idea of what justice requires: it would not have gone to trial, appealed its defeats, defended its victories in appellate court, or offered its friendly advice to the Court if it did not believe it was in the right. So in wishing that the Supreme Court should do what is right, the executive wants the Court to decide its way. And the Court usually does. In its 1984 term, it accepted for decision three-fourths of the government's appeals and 90 percent of the appeals supported by the government as amicus curiae. In comparison, the Court accepted about 2 percent of the appeals of the executive's defeated opponents. The executive branch does very well, too, in cases decided on their merits. It was on the winning side as party and amicus in four-fifths of the decisions in which victory could be declared. Clearly, the executive branch is very active and persuasive in the Supreme Court, whether in getting into Court and keeping its adversaries out or in winning cases for itself and its friends.[17]

What we have been describing is "tough" and "soft" law enforcement. The president is a tough executive and judges are soft executives. Unlike the president, whose hand grasps a sword in his capacity as commander of the armed forces, or Congress, whose collective hand clutches a purse, the judiciary, exercising judgment, holds the scales of justice. And judgment, *The Federalist* observes, is "easily overpowered, awed, or influenced" by the strength of the executive or the willfulness of the legislature.[18]

The tough executive, keeping his sword in scabbard and out of view, sometimes presents himself as softer than he is. What he executes, he or his defenders sometimes say, are laws passed by Congress—neglecting to mention that these laws in all likelihood were approved or even recommended by him. The Constitution, a president might add, imposes law enforcement as a duty, yet he and his subordinates seem to enjoy their work. He certainly resents interference with it, for he not only threatens and arrests but also calls out the military power of the nation to overcome resistance. Moreover, he cites his duty to execute the laws to justify some unusual actions: Washington's issuance of the Neutrality Proclamation in a time of foreign war, Lincoln's proclamation of a blockade of southern ports during the Civil War, and Truman's seizure of the steel industry during the Korean War, for example. And when the tough executive really has his spirits aroused, he speaks of the duty imposed by his constitutional oath "to execute the Office of President," not simply the laws of Congress, and "to preserve, protect, and defend the Constitution of the United States," not simply support it. Whatever the tough executive may say about his power, ordinary citizens recognize it in the vast array of law enforcers, administrators, investigators, prosecutors, and jailers—all of them backed by the military might of the commander in chief.[19]

The exercise of judicial power looks quite different from the exercise of executive power. Wearing robes, sitting singly or collegially, judges seem to be onlookers above the fray, usually saying little and almost never in harsh tones. Tocqueville put the matter well:

> The judicial power is by its nature devoid of action; it must be put in motion in order to produce a result. When it is called upon to repress a crime, it punishes the criminal; when a wrong is to be redressed, it is ready to redress it; when an act requires interpretation, it is prepared to interpret it; but it does not pursue criminals, hunt out wrongs, or examine evidence of its own accord.[20]

Thus it is not the judges who are to be blamed for a defendant's presence in court, but the tough executive's prosecutor or the civil plaintiff's attorney. If it is a trial court, the judge will carefully explain to the criminal defendant his rights against the government or assure the plaintiff and the defendant in a civil trial of his neutrality in their contest. Occasionally, he will dismiss a case or find a statute unconstitutional. It is true that most persons accused of crime are convicted and nearly all civil suits end in a victory for one side or the other, but it is, as the trial judge may inform the parties, not his hand that has come down harshly but that of the law or the Constitution itself. Don't blame me, his tone implies, if things have gone badly with you or, if you must find fault with somebody, blame the jury—for they rendered the verdict. With this, the soft executive moves to the next case, turning over the criminally convicted to agents of the tough executive, and usually leaving one—or both—of the parties in a civil proceeding the poorer for having pursued their rights in court. The loser may appeal his case to a higher court, where again he will be treated with courtesy and perhaps sympathy—but probably will obtain no better result.

In this view of things, it is hard to think of judges as being in law enforcement, or even as being part of government; indeed they sometimes speak as though they were not. This is the secret of their power, for the work of judges is best done when they are thought to be different from busy administrators and busybody legislators. Perhaps this is what Montesquieu had in mind when he said that "the power of judging is, in a certain respect, nothing"—that it is also, in another respect, quite something. It is most effective when kept out of sight, when its actions are supported by judgment and the source of judgment is seen to be the will of the lawmaker. Judges forget the advantage that comes from being regarded as "the living oracles" of the law when they exercise "raw judicial power," that is, when they move into the domains of lawmaking and tough, exposed execution of the laws.[21]

The Limited Alliance

The framers believed that the powers of government had to be separated to secure the liberty of citizens and that the legislative power had to be restrained to preserve separation of powers. In the words of *The Federalist,* "The legislative department is everywhere extending the sphere of its activity and drawing all power into its impetuous vortex." The framers sought to restrain Congress by dividing it and by strengthening its rivals, the presidency and the judiciary, through an array of checks and balances directed against it. To be precise, they considered the House of Representatives, with its numerous members elected directly by the people for brief terms, to be the main embodiment of the legislative power.[22]

The Constitution established two limited "alliances" against the "enterprising ambition" of the legislative power. One, between the president and the Senate against the House of Representatives, was to lead the Senate "to support the constitutional rights of the [executive], without being too much detached" from its own branch of government, in return for which the Senate received a share in presidential appointments and treaty making. The other alliance, which is of present interest, was between the president and the judiciary against Congress as a whole, but, above all, against the House. The hope was that these two "weaker branches" of government would support each other against congressional encroachments on themselves and against legislative oppressions originating in the people. The "alliance" would be based on a shared interest in self-defense and, secondarily, in a common concern with protecting rights, especially those of property, against popular majorities. Only the self-interested basis for alliance will be examined.[23]

As we have pointed out, many of the framers wanted there to be a link between judges and the executive branch in some of its activities. Their method for choosing judges and the president not only brought these officials somewhat close to each other but placed them some distance from both Congress and the people. Special electors, selected either by popular vote or by the state legislatures, would elect the president, and the president would appoint judges with the Senate's consent. Second, the terms of the president and judges were lengthened beyond those of the House of Representatives: the presidential term to four years and indefinite reeligibility and judicial terms to life—if the judges behaved themselves. The executive's major share in appointing judges meant that the judiciary would tend to reflect the constitutional and general political views of the presidency, although generally not the views of any single president.

The president and the judges were granted powers to resist congressional encroachments (or perhaps the judges had simply assumed theirs since the earliest days). The president's power, the veto, was considered a legislative power, and the courts' power came to be called judicial review. Although it extended to review of actions by the president as well as by Congress, judicial review almost always was referred to as the power to review the constitutionality of legislative actions. Some framers would have gone further in drawing the executive and judicial branches together. They made several attempts in the convention to establish a "council of revision" within which the president and members of the Supreme Court would exercise veto power over national and state legislation. The council would strengthen the president's confidence when dealing with the legislative branch, Madison and other leading members of the Convention argued. But its opponents said that such a body would form an *"improper coalition"* between the president and the Supreme Court, perhaps leading the justices to "embark *too far* in the political views" of the executive branch. Each time the proposal came up, it was rejected.[24]

How has this intended alliance worked out? Have presidents and judges generally supported each other against challenges by Congress to their constitutional authority?

As a rule, presidents have had reason to be satisfied with the judicial support they have received against Congress. Prominent among legislative restraints on executive power that have reached the judiciary have been those placed on the president's power to remove executive officers whose appointment required the Senate's consent. In *Shurtleff v. United States* (1903) the Supreme Court upheld the use of the power when legislation had not restrained its exercise, but it stated that Congress could restrain the president if it chose. Then, in the famous case of *Myers v. United States* (1926), the Court struck down, on the broadest grounds, a legislative provision that allowed the president to remove postmasters only for certain stipulated causes. The president, the Court said, could remove all executive officers—not just postmasters—for any reason whatsoever. In a later case, *United States v. Lovett* (1946), the Court again protected the president against an attempt by Congress to control removals, declaring void an appropriation rider that forbade the payment of salaries to three named executive officers unless the president renewed, and the Senate reconfirmed, their appointments. It is true that the Court qualified its *Myers* holding both in *Hum-*

phrey's Executor (Rathbun) v. United States (1935)—ruling that congressional limits were permissible if the officers were members of agencies (here the Federal Trade Commission), that exercised "quasi-legislative" or "quasi-judicial" functions—and in *Wiener v. United States* (1958), in which it ruled that limits existed on the removal of officers of such agencies (here the War Claims Commission) whether Congress imposed them or not. But these qualifications have left presidents with the power to remove, and hence to control, the vast majority of executive officers who require the Senate's consent for appointment.[25]

The Supreme Court also has prevented Congress from interfering unduly with the president's power of appointment. In *Buckley v. Valeo* (1946), it struck down a provision of the Federal Elections act that empowered the leaders of the House of Representatives and the Senate to appoint four of the voting members of the Federal Elections Commission and the president to appoint the other two voting members, with all appointments to be confirmed by both houses of Congress. The Commission, according to the Court, exercised executive powers, in addition to rule-making (quasi-legislative) and adjudicative (quasi-judicial) ones; thus its members had to receive their appointments from the president and the Senate.[26]

Related to the dispute between the president and Congress over removals has been that over the "legislative veto." This dispute goes back to the early 1930s, when Congress began to make its delegations of authority to the executive conditional, reserving the right to cancel executive actions taken pursuant to that authority or, sometimes, to repeal entire laws. Here, too, the Supreme Court sided with the president. In 1983 it ruled the legislative veto to be unconstitutional however it was employed. In this instance, *Immigration and Naturalization Service v. Chadha,* the attorney general had allowed a Kenyan national who sought to avoid deportation to his country to remain in the United States, and the House of Representatives, exercising the veto permitted by law, had overruled him. All such actions, the Court ruled, were legislative in character and must be submitted to the president to be constitutional. In one swoop, veto provisions in about two hundred laws were rendered useless.[27]

The *Chadha* case was implicated in a subsequent Supreme Court decision, *Bowsher v. Synar* (1986), in which the Court ruled that Congress could not empower the comptroller general, who heads the General Accounting Office, to direct presidential action. The Balanced Budget and Emergency Control Act of 1985 (the Gramm-Rudman-Hollings Act) had authorized this official to report to the president each year his estimates of the expected budget deficit and the spending cuts (program by program) that would be needed to keep the deficit within the limits set by the law. If Congress then failed to take appropriate action, the president was required to do so. The Court found this provision to be unconstitutional. The comptroller general was, it said, a legislative officer: although appointed by the president (from among three candidates nominated by leaders of Congress) and confirmed by the Senate, he could be removed from office only by the joint effort of the two branches. Yet the Balanced Budget Act invested him with executive power—reporting to and ultimately directing the president—in the exercise of which, moreover, he was to use discretion in handling the data furnished him. "To permit an officer controlled by Congress to execute the laws," the Court declared, "would be, in effect, to permit a legislative veto." [28]

The *Myers* case was also implicated in *Bowsher,* although not in a way that the Supreme Court was willing to acknowledge. The Court discerned the comptroller general to be a legislative officer because Congress controlled his removal, not because of his functions or those of his agency, which seem to be generally of an executive nature. The Court could have followed the suggestion made by the comptroller general's counsel and, by eliminating Congress's restrictions on his removal, removed any conflict between his status and the duty assigned him by the Balanced Budget Act.[29]

Most of the constitutional conflicts reviewed so far arose in a traditional manner. Courts were asked by specific litigants to protect rights they claimed had been violated by government actions, in the course of which judges were required to determine the constitutionality of those actions. In some of these conflicts other government institutions—for example, the Senate in *Myers v. United States*—participated indirectly as amicus curiae, through briefs and sometimes arguments before the Supreme Court. The main litigant, at least, in *Buckley v. Valeo* may be called a traditional one, for James Buckley, although a U.S. senator, was pursuing a personal claim denied by the law, his right to spend his own money freely in his election. (The array of defendants in the case—the Senate secretary, the House clerk, the Elections Commission, the attorney general, and the comptroller general—was, however, unusual by the practice of the past.) Chadha's case started in the traditional manner: an appeal by Chadha to the court of appeals for the District of Columbia from the Immigration and Naturalization Service's deportation order, following the House's veto of the attorney general's decision allowing him to remain in the country. But the case was transformed into a direct confrontation between the presidency and Congress. The INS—really the solicitor general, acting, probably, at the initiative of the White House—

abandoned its opposition to Chadha and joined with him to attack the veto's constitutionality, and the House of Representatives and Senate became parties in defense of the veto and Chadha's deportation. In *Bowsher* a U.S. representative (Mike Synar) was allowed to carry into court his opposition to the authority to order presidential spending cuts that the Balanced Budget Act gave to the comptroller general (Charles Bowsher), without having to show that the provision affected him in any specific way (at least by traditional rules for obtaining standing in court). As in *Buckley,* a cluster of amici and parties became attached to the original litigants.

If members of Congress may challenge congressional legislation in court and if Congress may defend legislation there, may not one or the other use judicial proceedings to challenge executive actions as well? This is in fact what the courts now allow, although they have proceeded with some caution. Only one congressional litigant thus far has won his suit, and that case, *Kennedy v. Sampson* (1974), ended in the District of Columbia court of appeals. The court upheld a senator's contention that a pocket veto by President Nixon during an intrasessional adjournment of Congress was unconstitutional. When the same court later extended its ruling to cover intersessional pocket vetoes in a case brought by a representative, an appeal was carried to the Supreme Court. The Court dismissed the case, *Burke v. Barnes* (1987), for mootness, on the ground that the vetoed bill had expired of its own terms before it reached the president.[30]

The courts have apparently dismissed all other congressional suits against presidential actions, in form or effect. When a district judge enjoined the Nixon administration from conducting air operations over Cambodia, in *Holtzman v. Schlesinger* (1973), the second circuit court of appeals stayed the injunction and Supreme Court Justice Thurgood Marshall, acting in chambers, upheld the stay. (The operations were due to end in a few days anyway, when a congressional prohibition of them took effect.) In *Senate Select Committee v. Nixon* (1974), the District of Columbia court of appeals refused to support a congressional subpoena against Nixon for delivery of tape recordings related to the break-in at the Watergate hotel. In *Edwards v. Carter* (1978), the same court refused to require President Carter to obtain House consent to implement treaties conveying U.S. property—the Panama Canal—to Panama; and in *Goldwater v. Carter* (1979), the Supreme Court itself refused to require Carter to obtain Senate consent in order to terminate a defense treaty with Taiwan. Finally, two decisions of the District of Columbia court of appeals concerning military actions of the president may be noted. In *Crockett v. Reagan* (1982) and *Conyers v. Reagan* (1984), respectively, that court dismissed challenges to President

Reagan's right to send military personnel to El Salvador to help train its armed forces, and to send an invading force into Grenada to protect Americans there after a *coup d'état* and to restore the island to noncommunist hands.[31]

Most of these judicial abstentions in favor of the president are not as firm as they may appear. In *Conyers* the court of appeals dismissed the congressional suit because the case was moot, inasmuch as the invasion of Grenada had ended, and not because the issue of presidential warmaking was beyond judicial scrutiny. As Justice Marshall noted in *Holtzman*, "a respectable and growing body of lower court opinion" accepts the propriety of such scrutiny. The court of appeals dismissed *Edwards* because it found that the nation's property could be conveyed to another nation by treaty, not because the subject could not be examined by a court, and only four of the six justices who voted to dismiss in *Goldwater* did so because they thought the issue of terminating a treaty was beyond judicial challenge. To take a final example, the Senate was denied access to the Watergate tapes in *Senate Select Committee* because the Senate committee had failed to show that the documents were "critical" to the performance of its duties, not because executive privilege gave the president absolute control over them. And besides, what the court of appeals denied to the Senate in that case the Supreme Court gave to the Watergate special prosecutor in *United States v. Nixon* (1974), for use in the trial of persons accused of being involved in the break-in; and thus did the Senate get what it wanted from the president.[32]

Unless the Supreme Court reverses the present trend of decisions, Congress and its members will have gained significant influence in their relations with the president, in being allowed to challenge his actions in court. And the courts will have gained influence over both of the other branches. In becoming the arbiter of disputes between the presidency and Congress, they set themselves above those branches.

Let us turn to the other side of the question we have been considering. How much support has the presidency given to the judiciary in rebuffing attempts by Congress to diminish its constitutional authority? Threats against the courts have often come from Congress—for example, to impeach judges, take away appellate jurisdiction from the Supreme Court, or give the Senate appellate review over judicial decisions that invalidate federal and state laws. Most threats, moreover, have not been seriously pursued, for Congress has been more often irritated by the judiciary than resolved to take action against it. Nor have most threats raised constitutional issues. The Constitution, after all, allows Congress to impeach and remove judges for "high crimes and misdemeanors," to change the size of the Supreme

Court, to make exceptions to the Court's appellate jurisdiction, and to overrule the Court's decisions by constitutional amendments.[33]

The roster of serious efforts by Congress against the judiciary's constitutional authority comes to no more than four. In only one instance did the legislative branch seem clearly to act beyond its powers—and Jefferson, who was involved in the business, denied that it did so then.

It was Jefferson's opinion that Congress could impeach judges for political reasons: to bring them into line with the other branches of government by threatening them with removal. The experiment was tried in 1803 upon a federal district judge, John Pickering, who had committed no crime or misdemeanor in the ordinary sense, but who was insane and an alcoholic. The House of Representatives impeached and the Senate removed Pickering. Then the House, at Jefferson's instigation, turned to Samuel Chase, a member of the Supreme Court. Chase was able but intemperate: he had offended the Jeffersonians by the political views he expressed before a grand jury when performing circuit duty and still others by his conduct of trials under the sedition and revenue laws. The Senate's refusal to convict Chase, in 1805, probably saved other justices of the Supreme Court from the impeachment blade as well.

Jefferson was also behind Congress's repeal of the Judiciary Act of 1801. The act had relieved Supreme Court justices of the duty to conduct trials in their circuits by establishing a system of circuit courts, and the repeal, enacted the following year, abolished the new judgeships and returned the justices to circuit duty. Had the president and Congress acted unconstitutionally in the repeal? The Federalists thought so, but not Jefferson or a majority of Congress. And the Supreme Court itself accepted the repeal, in *Stuart v. Laird* (1803) (although some of its members had private doubts as to its constitutionality).[34]

Congress's next important attempt to restrain the judiciary in a constitutionally dubious manner occurred in 1868 when it repealed the Supreme Court's habeas corpus jurisdiction in cases arising under its post-Civil War reconstruction policy in the South. Congress had undoubted powers to take away appellate jurisdiction from the Court, and the question of constitutionality arose only because of the means it chose: its repealing legislation removed from the Court a case then before it. In this—the only one of the four instances—the president, Andrew Johnson, regarded the repeal to be unconstitutional and vetoed it, thereby adding to his own troubles with Congress without helping the Court, for the veto was overridden. But the Supreme Court itself accepted the repeal of its jurisdiction, in *Ex parte McCardle* (1869), and relinquished the case.[35]

At this point, we might rephrase our earlier question: Have presidents generally supported the judiciary in serious attempts by Congress *constitutionally* to curb it? To pose the issue in this way is also to change it, for the framers did not expect the presidency, in its alliance with the judiciary, to support judges in all actions by Congress against them. Why might not presidents support congressional actions they consider to be constitutional and justified, especially when taken in reaction to decisions that affect the presidency itself? Perhaps most of the congressional retaliations discussed above should be considered in this category, for the reasons we gave in discussing them. (The Pickering impeachment seems to be the clearest exception.)

The most celebrated action ever taken against the Supreme Court was the court reform bill of 1937. The legislation was inspired and pressed by President Franklin D. Roosevelt, who wanted Congress to allow him to appoint an additional Supreme Court justice for every sitting member over the age of seventy, up to a total of six justices. (Six of the justices were over that age.) The constitutionality of the measure, strictly speaking, was clear, for the Constitution does not fix the size of the Supreme Court, which had been changed several times in the past. Only once before, however, had the Court's size been changed for a clearly political reason: in 1866, Congress provided, for the limited purpose of preventing Andrew Johnson from making any Supreme Court appointments, that no appointments were to be made to the Court until its membership fell to six justices. (When Johnson left office, Congress set the Court's size at nine justices.)[36]

There have been recurrent efforts in Congress since the 1950s to undo various decisions of the Supreme Court. Whatever their private views of these decisions, all presidents before Ronald Reagan stood aside from the contests (although Richard M. Nixon did consider recommending a constitutional amendment to prohibit forced integration in education and housing). President Reagan has publicly supported amendments against abortion and for school prayer, but he has not placed the strength of his office behind his endorsements. Congressional support alone has thus far not been enough to secure favorable action on them.[37]

Presidency versus Judiciary

Presidents and judges occasionally have regarded each other, rather than Congress, as the encroacher upon their constitutional rights. On a few occasions, presidents have pressed attacks on the courts through Congress, notably Jefferson in the repeal of the 1801 Judiciary Act and Roosevelt in the attempt to increase the size of the Supreme

Court. But only twice have they unilaterally breached what the Supreme Court has held to be the boundary between the executive and the judiciary. In each instance, the president substituted for the regular courts of law special courts staffed by military officers. President James K. Polk authorized such courts in U.S.-occupied territory during the Mexican War to condemn ships seized for trade with the enemy, and President Abraham Lincoln authorized them during the Civil War in states where the regular courts were open, to try civilians accused of disloyal activities. War had ended before the court handed down its decisions in these cases and with it the reason for the special courts. Neither president was still in office at the time, and there was little reaction from the executive branch to what the Supreme Court had done.[38]

Much more often than judges, presidents have had reason to think that their constitutional powers have been encroached upon. Sometimes judges have earned this disfavor by telling presidents that the Constitution required them to perform acts that they thought they had a right not to perform. In *Marbury v. Madison* (1803), the Supreme Court informed Jefferson that he was obligated to deliver to William Marbury his commission to a minor judicial office (although it did not order the commission to be delivered). Jefferson also was involved in the trial of Aaron Burr for treason, when John Marshall, holding circuit court in Richmond, summoned him to appear as a witness and to bring along certain documents, unless he could satisfy the court that he should be excused. Sometimes the unwelcome news from judges has been that presidents must stop doing something they thought they had a right to do. Several federal and state judges told Lincoln during the Civil War that he had no right to suspend the writ of habeas corpus and keep under military arrest persons suspected of disloyalty or draft evasion. In *Youngstown Sheet and Tube Company v. Sawyer* (1952), the Supreme Court told President Harry S Truman that he lacked constitutional authority to seize most of the nation's steel mills when a strike threatened that industry during the Korean War. In *New York Times v. United States* (1971), it rejected the Nixon administration's argument that the executive had a constitutional right "to protect the nation against publication of information whose disclosure would endanger the national security." This decision led to the release of a purloined documentary history of the Vietnam War, the Pentagon Papers, which had been prepared within the Defense Department. And in *United States v. District Court* (1972), it ruled that the executive needed search warrants to eavesdrop by electronic means on domestic organizations suspected of subversion and violence.[39]

Our catalog of judicial restraints on the executive would be more lengthy if we included decisions that have held presidential actions to be invalid on statutory grounds. The *Youngstown* decision was based on an interpretation of statutory as well as constitutional authority. An early case, *Gilchrist v. Collector of Charleston* (1808), decided by Justice William Johnson on circuit, hampered Jefferson's ability to enforce the Embargo Act of 1807 by declaring that the act did not authorize certain of his treasury secretary's instructions to customs collectors. In *Cole v. Young* (1956), the Warren Court struck at President Eisenhower's loyalty-security program by ruling that Congress had not intended to allow the summary dismissal of government officials in non-security sensitive positions. And in a rash of lawsuits culminating in *Train v. New York* (1975), the courts told President Nixon that he could not impound monies appropriated by Congress. In the last two cases, the Supreme Court appeared hesitant to challenge the president on the constitutionality of his actions.[40]

Taking American history as a whole, the courts have not been very hard on the office of president. According to the foremost study of the subject, Glendon Schubert's *The Presidency in the Courts*, the Supreme Court held presidential orders to be invalid in only fourteen cases between 1789 and 1956—"an infinitesimal fragment" of the total number of such orders. Eight more orders, according to another study, were voided between 1956 and 1975, indicating a quickening in the tempo of judicial disapproval. But it has been unusual for the Court to strike at important actions of the president. We considered some of these actions when we reviewed judicial umpiring of constitutional disputes between the president and Congress. A few others are worth noting. The Supreme Court upheld Lincoln's engaging the country in civil war, including the blockading of southern ports, without prior congressional authorization. It declared that President Franklin Roosevelt, in settling differences with the Soviet Union, could use executive agreements for a purpose similar to treaties without the need of Senate consent. Finally, the Court refused to entertain suits that challenged the constitutionality of the Vietnam War.[41]

Our catalog of judicial restraints would be even more lengthy if we went beyond decisions that ruled on the president's constitutional powers to include those that invalidated congressional statutes that presidents have initiated or endorsed. But that endeavor would lead us too far afield. Suffice it to say that the courts can strike at the president through the legislative branch, just as he can work through Congress to strike at them, and it is often the case that the president is at least as affronted as Congress when courts declare laws unconstitutional.

The weapon of judicial defense against executive intrusions is judicial review. But what weapon can the president wield when he thinks the courts have invaded his domain? Must he obey the commands of judges when he thinks they infringe upon his rights under the Constitution? Must he obey commands that he thinks invade Congress's authority? Most Americans probably think "yes" is the only possible reply. They might say that the essence of the judicial administration of justice is in deciding cases and controversies, and that this function is undermined when anyone, including the president, stands "above the law" by refusing to accept the outcome of judicial cases. But *The Federalist* seems to indicate that the president may decide whether to enforce court judgments against others and that both he and Congress may decide whether to obey judgments they think are unwarranted. "The judiciary must ultimately depend upon the aid of the executive arm even for the efficacy of its judgments," it says in one place; elsewhere it refers to the judiciary's "total incapacity to support its usurpations [of authority] by force." [42]

In a few circumstances, presidents have refused to do as the courts have ordered. Jefferson refused to show up at Burr's trial, furnish the requested documents to the court, or even answer the court's subpoena. (He did send some papers to the government's attorney with permission to make them available as he saw fit.) Similarly, Jefferson had his attorney general tell customs collectors to ignore Justice Johnson's decision that executive instructions to them violated the Embargo Act (but then asked Congress to give him the authority he claimed he already had to issue them). Lincoln refused to acknowledge several judicial decisions ordering him or his commanders to release persons from military custody, the most famous of which concerned the case of *Ex parte Merryman* (1861).[43]

Presidents also have threatened that they would disregard judicial commands, anticipating confrontations that never happened. Jefferson would not have delivered William Marbury's commission for a judicial office if the Supreme Court had ordered it in the case of *Marbury v. Madison*—or so he said privately several years later. Lincoln informed Congress in 1863 that he would not "return to slavery any person who is free by the terms of [the Emancipation] Proclamation or by any of the acts of Congress," and he confided, in a rather enigmatic note to himself, that "[if] such return shall be held to be a legal duty by the proper court of final resort . . . I will promptly act as may then appear to be my personal duty." Franklin Roosevelt twice threatened—also privately—to disobey the Supreme Court. The first time was when it was considering cases that challenged Roosevelt's authority to take the country off the gold standard. (As it happened, the Court's decision in *Norman v. Baltimore Railroad Company* [1935] left his action intact.)

The second instance occurred when the Court, to Roosevelt's annoyance, agreed to decide whether he could appoint a special military tribunal to try Nazi saboteurs landed from submarines on the American coast. The Court affirmed his authority in *Ex parte Quirin* (1942).[44]

Most recently, in the Watergate tapes case, President Nixon hinted that he might not give over the tapes, whatever the Supreme Court ordered. As his counsel said in oral arguments before the justices, "This matter is being submitted to this Court for its guidance and judgment with respect to the law. The president, on the other hand, has his obligations under the Constitution." Because Nixon realized, as he has stated in his *Memoirs,* that defiance of a clear ruling against him would have brought about his impeachment, he considered "abiding" by an unfavorable ruling without actually "complying" with it, that is, providing only excerpts of the tapes in his possession. Nixon required at least a month to carry off his plan, and, to stall that long, he needed a division of opinion on the Court—perhaps, he thought, only a single dissent. But the Court ruled against him unanimously.[45]

No president, so far as we know, has continued to enforce a law after the courts have definitively ruled it to be unconstitutional, nor has any president urged that he had such a right. However, Jefferson implied that he did in commenting on his duty toward the Sedition Act, and so did Martin Van Buren, whose views were influenced by Jefferson's. In Jefferson's case, federal judges, including justices of the Supreme Court on circuit duty, had upheld the validity of the Sedition Act in prosecutions by the Adams administration of newspaper editors and others. When he came into office, Jefferson, in his own words, "discharged every person under punishment under the Sedition law because I considered, and now consider [in 1804], that law to be a nullity." Van Buren's stand was even stronger. A president, he declared, would violate his oath of office and open himself to impeachment if he executed an unconstitutional law. If a president has a right—or duty—to refuse to support laws he thinks are void, even when the courts have said otherwise, is he not free—or required—to continue enforcing them when he disagrees with judicial decisions that have ruled them void? [46]

Jefferson and Lincoln sought to justify noncompliance with judicial decisions that were aimed directly at them, in contrast to those that affected them through invalidations of congressional laws. Neither addressed his remarks to the courts, however. When he was informed that Chief Justice Marshall wanted papers for the Burr trial, Jefferson wrote to the government attorney in the case that it was "the necessary right of the president of the United States to decide, independently of all other authority, what papers coming to him as president the public interest permits to be communicated." As to Marshall's power to require his appearance in court as a witness: "Would the executive be independent of the judiciary, if he were subject to the *commands* of the latter, and to imprisonment for disobedience; if the several courts could bandy him from pillar to post, keep him constantly trudging from north to south and east to west, and withdraw him entirely from his constitutional duties?" Lincoln explained to Congress, with Chief Justice Roger B. Taney's *Merryman* decision obviously in mind, that if he had exercised legislative power in suspending the writ of habeas corpus (which he thought he had not), his action was justified by public necessity and supported by his oath of office, to "preserve, protect, and defend the Constitution." Lincoln left it to his attorney general to answer Taney, which he did by asserting executive independence of judicial commands. "No court or judge," the attorney general declared, "can take cognizance of the political acts of the president or undertake to revise and reverse his political decisions." The president, he added, was "eminently and exclusively political in all his principal decisions." [47]

Aside from the plea of public necessity, how can presidential assertions of independence from judicial control be justified? The justification, it seems, derives from the principle of separation of powers. The Constitution makes the three branches of government equal and independent of each other; checks and balances serve to keep them that way. Judges need not accept actions by Congress or the president that they consider to be unconstitutional. Why should the president not have a similar right when he believes that judicial actions regarding his authority, or Congress's for that matter, lack constitutional support? Do not equality and independence imply reciprocity among the branches of government? At the very least, should not the president be able to require the courts to reaffirm their opinions of his powers one or more times before he accepts their decisions as conclusive? [48]

The president has a case against judicial determination of his powers and control of his actions. But to accept it is to raise other questions. Would not it tend to make him superior to law or to the judges whom the Constitution makes guardians of the law? Is there not a danger in this, as President Truman expressed when asked if he would accept what the Supreme Court might decide in the steel seizure case? "Certainly," Truman replied, he had "no ambition to be a dictator." [49] But again, the judicial case against the president tends to make judges superior to him in violation of the principle of separation of powers upon which a government of law rests.

The claims of the two branches cannot be resolved on the level of principle because they are incompatible. Nor can one of the claims be chosen as preferable in principle to the other because both are essential to the constitutional system. What statesmen must try to do is to compromise when conflicts arise from these claims and, when it is necessary to act on a choice, to say as little publicly as possible.

Conclusion

As we have seen, the powers of the presidency and the judiciary have a common origin in the doctrines of Locke and Montesquieu. These powers interact in law enforcement. The framers assumed that presidents and judges would be the weaker parts of American government. To enhance their shared interest in supporting each other against the excesses of Congress, they drew these officials toward each other. We then examined the presidency and judiciary in their relations with Congress and each other.

The reader will have noticed that executive-judicial relationships have experienced conflict as well as harmony and that conflict has occupied a larger place in recent years. The framers did not expect the presidency and the courts to stand by each other in all their disputes, but only in those in which Congress was the aggressor. If they thought that separation of powers usually would be imperiled by the legislature, they did not believe this would always be the case. Indeed, it is hard to say whether Congress was constitutionally at fault in some of its conflicts with the presidency or judiciary. Moreover, those framers who foresaw connections between the two branches did not calculate on the connections' weakening as they have. Nor, it seems, did anyone foresee the impressive growth of presidential and judicial power that has taken place over the years, especially in this century.

It is interesting to compare relations between the presidency and the judiciary a generation ago and today. Schubert's study of those relations assesses them in the following terms: "In every major constitutional crisis between the executive and the judiciary, the president emerged the victor." The courts "normally do not attempt to second-guess the president on fundamental issues of public policy." The judiciary "can neither force him [the president] to do anything, nor prevent him from doing anything he may decide to do." [50] Prior to the 1950s, the courts probably were not quite so weak; since then they certainly have been much stronger. Indeed, they have in fact told the president what to do and kept him from doing things he wanted to do, willingly second-guessing him on matters of major importance. He has been informed that he cannot pocket veto legislation during short congressional recesses, that he cannot refuse to spend appropriated funds, that he cannot conduct electronic surveillance of subversives without search warrants, that he cannot prevent the printing by newspapers of classified documents, and that he must turn over documents for use in criminal trials. The courts also have ordered his subordinates about more frequently in cases in which presidential authority has been less obviously at stake. Federal officials, including cabinet secretaries—but not prosecutors, members of Congress, or judges—recently have lost their absolute immunity from private suits when engaged in their official responsibilities; and in a case decided in 1982, the president came within one vote on the Supreme Court of losing some of his immunity as well.[51] Finally, although the judiciary formerly excluded many executive actions from their scrutiny by stating that they raised political and not judicial questions, the Supreme Court has discarded large parts of the doctrine of "political questions" since the 1950s.

This surge of judicial power, which has been directed not just at the presidency, seems to originate in more than the willfulness of judges or any strength given them by the Constitution. Once the foot-draggers in our governmental system, the courts have become an advance guard urging on the president, Congress, and the state governments. It is as if the Supreme Court, the leader in this movement, had decided after its showdowns with the New Deal in 1937 that never again would it be exposed to serious attack on its weaker, left flank. In any event, the judiciary, the least democratic and, in constitutional intent, the weakest of the branches of the national government, has become the instrument of powerful democratic forces in our society.

Notes

The author wishes to acknowledge the research opportunity provided him by the White Burkett Miller Center of Public Affairs of the University of Virginia.

1. John Locke, *Two Treatises of Government,* ed. Peter Laslett (New York: New American Library, 1965), "Second Treatise," para. 87-88, 125, 131, 219.
2. Alexander Hamilton, James Madison, and John Jay, *The Federalist,* ed. Jacob E. Cooke (Middletown, Conn.: Wesleyan University Press, 1961), no. 47, 324; and Baron de Montesquieu, *The Spririt of Laws,* trans. Thomas Nugent (New York: Hafner, 1949), book 11, chap. 6, 151-156.
3. See *The Records of the Federal Convention of 1987,* ed. Max Farrand (New Haven: Yale University Press, 1937), vol. 2, 299 (Morris), 34 (Madison); see also Robert Scigliano, *The Supreme Court and the Presidency* (New York: Free Press, 1971), 4-5.
4. Robert Scigliano, "Trade-Unionism and the Industrial Foreman," *Journal of Business,* 57 (October 1954): 293-300.
5. Proposal of G. Morris and C. Pinckney, *Records of Federal Convention,* 342; see

also Ellsworth's proposal, ibid., 328. Constitution of the United States, Art. I, sec. 6(2).

6. *Diaries of George Washington, 1748-1799,* ed. John C. Fitzpatrick (Boston: Houghton Mifflin, 1925), vol. 4, 139, 143; Frank Monaghan, *John Jay: Defender of Liberty* (Indianapolis: Bobbs-Merrill, 1935); and Samuel B. Crandall, *Treaties: Their Making and Enforcement,* Studies in History, Economics and Public Law, vol. 21 (New York: Columbia University Press, 1904), 115-116, 120. See also Russell Wheeler, "Extrajudicial Activities of the Early Supreme Court," in *Supreme Court Review, 1973,* ed. Phillip B. Kurland (Chicago: University of Chicago Press, 1974), 123-158.

7. See Alexander Hamilton, "Report Relative to a Provision for the Support of Public Credit," January 9, 1790, in *Papers,* ed. Harold C. Syrett and Jacob E. Cooke (New York: Columbia University Press, 1962), vol. 6, 107. Act of March 23, 1791, in Hayburn's Case, 1 Law. Ed. 436 (1792), 437-438n.

8. Scigliano, *Supreme Court and Presidency,* 83; and Charles Warren, *The Supreme Court in United States History,* rev. ed. (Boston: Little, Brown, 1926), vol. 1, 111.

9. Hayburn's Case, 407, 436-438.

10. Letter to John Dickinson, December 19, 1801, in Thomas Jefferson, *Writings,* ed. Andrew A. Lipscomb and Albert E. Bergh (Washington: Thomas Jefferson Memorial Association, 1903), vol. 10, 302.

11. See the discussion of extrajudicial activity in Scigliano, *Supreme Court and Presidency,* chap. 3. For additional information on Justice Fortas, see Bob Woodward and Scott Armstrong, *The Brethren Inside the Supreme Court* (New York: Simon & Schuster, 1979), 127.

12. *U.S. v. Kendall,* 26 F. Cas. 702 (1837), 749-750, C. C. (No. 15, 517).

13. *The Federalist,* no. 70, 472; no. 78, 522-523.

14. In the period July 1, 1985-June 30, 1986, 296,318 cases were filed in federal district courts, of which the government was involved in 41,490 criminal cases and 91,830 civil cases (as plaintiff in 60,779 cases and as defendant in 31,051 cases); 33,589 appeals were filed in federal courts of appeals, of which the government was involved in 5,134 criminal cases and (apparently) in 9,602 civil cases; and 96,501 cases were disposed of by magistrates, of which the government was involved in 91,570 petty offenses and an undetermined number of minor civil matters. Computed from data provided in *Annual Report of the Director of the Administrative Office of the United States Courts, 1986* (Washington, D.C.: n.d.), appendix, tables C-1 and D-1, 56, 60 (district courts); ibid., appendix, table B-1, 54 (courts of appeals); ibid., Table 13, 10 (magistrates). "Annual Report of the Solicitor General for the Supreme Court Term Ended July 7, 1985," mimeographed draft, 1986; to be incorporated in the *Annual Report of the Attorney General of the United States, 1985* (Washington, D.C.: in press), tables II-A; II-B, II-C, D, E (cases considered) and Table III (cases decided on merits.

In its 1984 term, the Supreme Court considered 4,097 cases for review, of which the government was petitioner or appellant in 43 cases and respondent or appellee in 1,430 cases. The Court decided 175 cases on their merits, after argument, of which the government participated in 114. In addition, the government participated in 4 of the 10 cases that the Court decided on its original docket in the term.

15. Computed from data provided in "Annual Report of Solicitor General," 3, and tables II-A and II-B.

16. Ibid., tables II-A, II-B, and III. *Brown v. Board of Education,* 347 U.S. 483 (1954); *Baker v. Carr,* 369 U.S. 186 (1962). See Wade H. McCree, Jr., "The So-

licitor General and His Client," *Washington University Law Quarterly* 59 (1981): 337-347.

17. The Court accepted for review thirty-three of the government's forty-three appeals as petitioner and appellant and twenty-five of twenty-eight other appeals that the government supported as amicus curiae.

It is not possible to say how the government did in three cases in which it was appellant and in two cases in which it was amicus curiae, for here the solicitor general's report informs us only that the Court summarily "dismissed, affirmed, or reversed." Computed from "Annual Report of Solicitor General," tables II-A and II-B.

The Court accepted for review 29 of 1,430 appeals by the government's opponents. For the reason indicated above, it is not possible to say how opponents did in 4 cases. Ibid., tables 11-A 11-B.

The government won 113 of the 143 cases decided on the merits with or without argument in the 1984 term, with 3 decisions not possible to classify. Ibid., Table III.

18. *The Federalist*, no. 78, 522-523.

19. Constitution, Art. II, sec. 1(9). See Abraham Lincoln, Message to Congress in Special Session, July 4, 1861, in Lincoln, *Collected Works,* ed. Roy P. Basler et al. (New Brunswick, N.J.: Rutgers University Press, 1953), vol. 4, 430.

20. Alexis de Tocqueville, *Democracy in America,* ed. Phillips Bradley (New York: Vintage Books, 1954), vol. 1, 103-104.

21. *The Federalist*, no. 78, 523n, has Montesquieu say that the judicial power "is next to nothing," but Montesquieu's words are "en quelque façon nulle." Blackstone, *Commentaries on the Laws of England,* facsimile 1st ed. (Chicago: University of Chicago Press, 1979), vol. 1, 69; *Doe v. Bolton,* 410 U.S. 179 (1973), White dissenting, 222.

22. *The Federalist*, no. 48, 333-334; and see ibid., no. 51, 350.

23. Ibid., no. 48, 334; no. 51, 350; no. 49, 338.

24. See, e.g., ibid., no. 78, 524. *Records of Federal Convention,* vol. 1, 21, 97-98, 138; vol. 2, 73-80 (the first quotation is on page 75); also, an attempt was made to allow the president and Supreme Court separately to disapprove legislation, ibid., vol. 2, 298-302. *The Federalist*, no. 73, 499.

25. *Shurtleff v. U.S.,* 189 U.S. 311 (1903); *Myers v. U.S.,* 222 U.S. 52 (1926); *U.S. v. Lovett,* 328 U.S. 303 (1946); *Humphrey's Executor (Rathbun) v. U.S.,* 295 U.S. 602 (1935); and *Wiener v. U.S.,* 357 U.S. 349 (1958).

26. *Buckley v. Valeo,* 424 U.S. 1 (1975).

27. *Immigration and Naturalization Service v. Chadha,* 462 U.S. 919 (1983).

28. *Bowsher v. Synar,* 106 S.Ct. 3181 (1986); and ibid., at 3189.

29. *U.S. Law Week,* April 29, 1986, 3709; *New York Times,* April 24, 1986, D-19.

30. *Kennedy v. Sampson,* 511 F.2d 430 (D.C. Cir. 1974); *Barnes v. Kline,* 759 F.2d 21 (D.C. Cir. 1985), renamed *Burke v. Barnes* in the Supreme Court (106 S.Ct. 1258 [1986]). *Congressional Quarterly Weekly Report,* January 17, 1987, 125.

31. *Holtzman v. Schlesinger,* 361 F. Supp. 553 (1973); 414 U.S. 1304 (1973). *Senate Select Committee v. Nixon,* 498 F.2d 725 (D.C. Cir. 1974). *Edwards v. Carter,* 580 F.2d 1055 (D.C. Cir. 1978); *Goldwater v. Carter,* 444 U.S. 996 (1979). See also *Dole v. Carter,* 569 F.2d 1109 (10th Cir. 1977). *Crockett v. Reagan,* 558 F. Supp. 893 (D.D.C. 1982), affirmed 720 F.2d 1365 (D.C. Cir. 1983), cert. denied 468 U.S. 1251 (1984); *Conyers v. Reagan,* 578 F. Supp. 324 (D.D.C. 1984), appeal dismissed 765 F.2d 1124 (D.C. Cir. 1985).

32. *U.S. v. Nixon,* 418 U.S. 683 (1974), 706, 708, and 712 *n,* 19.

33. See Warren, *Supreme Court in U.S. History,* vol. 1, chap. 16; and Walter F. Murphy, *Congress and the Court* (Chicago: University of Chicago Press, 1962), 8-14, 20-24, 31-32, 35-41. Constitution, Art. I, secs. 2(5) and 3(6); Art. III, secs. 1 and 2(2); Art. V.

34. *Stuart v. Laird,* 1 Cr. 299 (1803).

35. James D. Richardson, ed., *The Messages and Papers of the Presidents of the United States, 1789-1897* (Washington, D.C.: Government Printing Office, 1896), vol. 6, Veto Message to the Senate, March 25, 1868, 647. *Ex parte McCardle,* 7 Wall. 506 (1869).

36. See Joseph Alsop and Turner Catledge, *The 168 Days* (Garden City, N.Y.: Doubleday, Doran, 1938).

37. See Murphy, *Congress and the Court,* 161, 167, 170, 182, 213, 226. Richard Nixon, *Memoirs* (New York: Grosset & Dunlap, 1978). 444.

38. *Jecker v. Montgomery,* 13 How. 498 (1851); *Ex parte Milligan,* 4 Wall. 2 (1866); *Ex parte Quirin,* 317 U.S. 1 (1942); and *In re Yamashita,* 327 U.S. 1 (1946).

39. *Marbury v. Madison,* 1 Cr. 137 (1803); *Youngstown Sheet and Tube Co. v. Sawyer,* 343 U.S. 579 (1952); *New York Times v. U.S.,* 403 U.S. 713 (1971); and *U.S. v. District Court,* 407 U.S. 297 (1972).

40. *Gilchrist v. Collector of Charleston,* 10 F. Cas. 355 (1808), Circ. Ct., S. Car., No. 5420; *Cole v. Young,* 351 U.S. 536 (1956); see also *Peters v. Hobby,* 349 U.S. 331 (1955). *Train v. N.Y.,* 420 U.S. 35 (1975).

41. Glendon A. Schubert, Jr., *The Presidency in the Courts* (Minneapolis: University of Minnesota Press, 1957), 355 and appendix A, 303-320; Michael A. Genovese, *The Supreme Court, the Constitution, and Presidential Power* (Lanham, Md.: University Press of America, 1980), appendix, 303-320. The Prize Cases, 2 Black 635 (1863); *U.S. v. Belmont,* 301 U.S. 324 (1937) and *U.S. v. Pink,* 315 U.S. 203 (1942); *Mora v. McNamara,* 389 U.S. 934 (1967) and *Mass. v. Laird,* 400 U.S. 886 (1970).

42. *The Federalist,* nos. 78 and 81, 523, 545. The framers mainly thought of judicial review in terms of legislation, as these two numbers testify, because Congress was considered to be the main source of constitutional encroachments. See also J. Skelly Wright, "The Role of the Supreme Court in a Democratic Society—Judicial Activism or Restraint," *Cornell Law Review* 54 (November 1968): 11.

43. *Ex parte Merryman,* 17 F. Cas. 144 (1861), Cir. Ct. Md., No. 9487.

44. Jefferson, Letter to George Hay, June 2, 1807, *Writings,* vol. 11, 215; Lincoln, Annual Message to Congress, December 8, 1863, *Collected Works,* vol. 7, 51; ibid., fragment [c. Aug. 26, 1863?], vol. 6, 41. *Norman v. Baltimore & Ohio Railroad,* 294 U.S. 240 (1935); *Ex parte Quirin,* 317 U.S. 1 (1942). For Roosevelt's threats, see Scigliano, *Supreme Court and Presidency,* 48-49.

45. James D. St. Clair, *U.S. Law Week,* July 16, 1974, 3012; Nixon, *Memoirs,* 1043, 1052. One justice did not participate in the case.

46. Jefferson, Letter to Mrs. John Adams, July 22, 1804, in *Writings,* vol. 2, 43; Martin Van Buren, *Inquiry into the Origin and Course of Political Parties in the United States* (New York: Hurd & Houghton, 1867), 342-343.

47. Jefferson, Letter to John Hay, June 12, 1807, in *Writings,* vol. 2, 228; ibid., June 20, 1807, 241 (emphasis in original). Scigliano, *Supreme Court and Presidency,* 41, 43.

48. See Tocqueville, *Democracy in America,* vol. 1, 106.

49. Truman, quoted in *New York Times,* May 2, 1952, 1.

50. Schubert, *Presidency in the Courts,* 4, 347-348, 354.

51. *Butz v. Economou,* 438 U.S. 478 (1978); *Fitzgerald v. Nixon,* 457 U.S. 731 (1982).

20. A NEW VICE PRESIDENCY?

Joseph Pika

Although the 1970s were difficult years for the American presidency, they may ultimately represent a period of renaissance for the vice presidency. Opposition to U.S. involvement in Southeast Asia, the Watergate investigation, heightened congressional assertiveness, and the intense frustrations occasioned by energy shortages and terrorism took a heavy toll on presidents Richard M. Nixon, Gerald R. Ford, and Jimmy Carter. Vice presidents also experienced rough sledding: Spiro Agnew resigned in 1973, pleading nolo contendere to a Justice Department charge of accepting bribes; Ford and Nelson Rockefeller became the nation's first unelected vice presidents under provisions of the Constitution's recently added Twenty-fifth Amendment; and Rockefeller, who had long been the target of criticism by conservative Republicans and whose congressional confirmation hearings produced a number of embarrassing revelations, was dropped from the Republican ticket in 1976. But from 1973 to 1980, the vice presidency also may have undergone fundamental changes that transformed the office into an integral part of the modern presidency. Serving presidents who were receptive to their activism, Rockefeller and Walter Mondale may have enlarged the possibilities and influence of an office sometimes ridiculed even by its occupants.

The emergence of a new vice presidency would have two especially important implications. Such a transformation would provide additional evidence for the study of how political institutions evolve, a process often associated with the presidency. Moreover, if vice presidents really have become part of the day-to-day workings of the presidency, we may have ended a recurrent nightmare of the political system—a vice president thrust into the presidency but largely unprepared to assume the office's duties. The "Truman syndrome" may be a good name for this phenomenon, since it describes the situation that confronted Vice President Harry S Truman when he succeeded Franklin D. Roosevelt in April 1945. Roosevelt had served as president since March 1933, guiding the country during a period of economic depression and international danger; Truman had been vice president less than three months, and had met with the president only ten times before being called upon to replace him. Since then, concern over instability at the top of the government has been heightened by the proliferation of nuclear weapons, continuing conflict with the Soviet Union, and frequent reminders of presidential frailty.

The Vice President as Policy Adviser

What is new about the vice presidency? Both journalists and academics have drawn attention to the expanded policy role that was played by Rockefeller and Mondale, a new set of responsibilities that supplemented the job's traditional ceremonial and political activities.[1] Before agreeing to serve as vice president, Rockefeller sought an explicit mandate from Ford to direct the Domestic Council, an important center of White House decision making in domestic policy since its inception in the Nixon administration. From this vantage point, Rockefeller expected to direct the nation's domestic policy agenda much as Henry Kissinger had dominated foreign policy from his position as head of the National Security Council staff. Mondale, whose role in the Carter White House expanded considerably after 1977, became a senior presidential adviser on a wide range of topics and oversaw the annual effort to set the administration's legislative agenda.

Both vice presidents benefited from having an expanded staff, ready access to the Oval Office, and presidents who were receptive to their advice and involvement. As Paul Light demonstrates, the vice president's staff grew from twenty aides in 1960 to more than seventy in the Carter presidency. This expansion made it possible for vice presidents to develop an independent staff structure that largely paralleled the president's, including policy specialists as well as scheduling, speech writing, and press aides. Thus, when Rockefeller and Mondale participated in group meetings or met with the president privately, as they both did weekly, they benefited from a substantial amount of analytic support. Mondale enjoyed additional advantages: he was only the second vice president to have an office in the West Wing of the White House amidst the president's closest advisers (Agnew had briefly occupied a White House office) and he had an open invitation to attend any meeting on the president's schedule. The result for both Rockefeller and Mondale was an enlarged, more challenging position that went well beyond the job's traditional responsibilities to lobby Congress, serve as an administration spokesman to the general public and important interest groups, attend ceremonial functions in the president's stead, and assist the party's candidates for office.

Previous vice presidents had only limited policy responsibilities. These were exercised through service on study commissions and interdepartmental committees that often were more symbolic gestures than genuine policy assignments. In the long history of the office, only Henry Wallace, Franklin Roosevelt's vice president from 1941 to 1945, wielded substantial authority, as head of the Economic Defense Board and its successor, the Board of Economic Warfare. Rockefeller and Mondale seemed to usher in a new era. To be sure, conflict with the White House staff and Ford's turn to budget austerity prevented Rockefeller from dominating the domestic agenda as he had hoped. (A major review of domestic priorities that was conducted under his direction produced nineteen policy initiatives for the 1976 State of the Union address, but only six were included in modified form.) [2] But Rockefeller met with greater success in other areas: he overcame extensive opposition to win presidential support for an innovative approach to the energy crisis (Congress, however, never approved creation of the Energy Independence Authority), worked to establish the White House Office of Science and Technology Policy, and used his personal meetings with the president to push other priorities, albeit unsuccessfully. Mondale parlayed his extensive Washington experience, contacts with the Democratic party's liberal wing, and interpersonal skills into a White House presence as a senior adviser. Overseeing the agenda-setting process was a routine assignment of limited duration that freed Mondale to become a generalist who moved into and out of issues as he chose.

Even the most enthusiastic observers of the enhanced vice presidency of the 1970s recognized its contingent nature. "If the next President does not want an active Vice-President and does not want to spend time in conference with his running mate, there is no law or constitutional provision that can compel him to do so," Light observed.[3] Nonetheless, the more presidents adhere to the Rockefeller-Mondale precedents, the more firmly such practices become part of White House lore. Although subject to reversal by any president at any time, informal norms may begin to channel or even constrain presidential use of the vice presidency.

In fact, an impressive array of precedents has begun to accumulate and a mechanism has developed to transmit them from one vice president to the next. Like his predecessor, George Bush enjoys a West Wing office, has a weekly slot on the president's schedule, receives the President's Daily Briefing on foreign policy, and can attend any meetings he wishes.[4] Bush learned about the job from Mondale, just as Mondale did from Rockefeller and from Hubert H. Humphrey, Lyndon B. Johnson's vice president and one of Mondale's long-time

mentors. Rockefeller met with Mondale on several occasions and
provided him with an extensive review of staff operations.[5] Even if
Mondale consciously sought to avoid several aspects of Rockefeller's
experience, he could not help but draw lessons from his predecessor.[6]
Bush met with Mondale during the transition period and seems to have
incorporated far more of Mondale's practices.[7] Ford received advice
from a variety of sources during his confirmation hearings, including a
private letter of advice from Humphrey.[8] Ford's experience as vice
president and that of his staff in working with the Nixon White House
produced several new approaches that were designed to foster "broader
incorporation into [White House] staff operations of the Vice President." [9] Thus, an ill-defined but cumulative set of "lessons" has begun
to develop, which are further reinforced by academic and journalistic
accounts.

Presidential and Vice-Presidential Roles

Students of the presidency customarily examine the major roles
associated with the office. A similar approach to the vice presidency
reveals how meager its responsibilities are and how recent is their
vintage.

An untold number of roles have been ascribed to the president.[10]
Their origins, however, are circumscribed: the Constitution, statutes
passed by Congress, or practice and precedent established by predecessors. Lists of the president's constitutional roles typically include chief
diplomat, commander-in-chief, chief legislator, chief magistrate, and
chief administrator. Roles such as economic manager and party leader
can be traced to nonconstitutional sources: in these cases, the 1946
Employment Act and informal precedents, respectively. Although the
modern era has seen a proliferation of new presidential tasks, the
executive's constitutional roles have been the basis for a substantial
expansion of presidential power. This is especially true of the formulation of foreign and domestic policy, in which presidents have come to
take the lead in shaping the national agenda. Vice-presidential roles
offer a sharp contrast both in significance and origin.

Constitutional Roles

Under the Constitution, vice presidents serve as heir designate in
the event of a vacancy in the presidency. They also preside over the
Senate, casting a vote only in the event of a tie. Far from serving as the
basis for expanded influence, as in the case of the presidency, these
constitutional roles have seriously inhibited the job's development.

Many obstacles have prevented a close working relationship from
developing between the president and vice president. Part of the

explanation seems to lie in the constitutional design of the office: vice presidents, by their mere presence, serve to remind presidents of their own mortality. Thus, it is not surprising to find that presidents are reluctant to work closely with their designated successors. Other political leaders and the public also seem to resent vice presidents for the same reason. Following William Henry Harrison's death, John Tyler became the first vice president to succeed to the presidency; he had to overcome congressional resistance to his assuming the title of president rather than "acting president." Presidents who came to the office by vice-presidential succession, as a group, have been held in lesser regard than their predecessors by the public and historians alike.[11] Serving as vice president during a period of presidential illness has been an even more difficult experience; cabinet members and White House aides often actively communicate their resentment of the person who is most likely to prosper at their mentor's expense. Such jealousy emerged, somewhat surprisingly, in June 1985, when Ronald Reagan underwent surgery for cancer of the colon. Although Reagan had worked out an arrangement with Vice President Bush to cover the eight-hour period when he would be under general anesthetic, considerable infighting reportedly emerged between the presidential and vice-presidential staffs, so much so that Bush was forced to make a public denial of such difficulties.[12] Thus, the heir designate role has not been an easy one.

Presiding over the Senate, a position that would seem to provide extensive opportunities for vice-presidential influence, has actually been a source of weakness by making the office a "constitutional hybrid," lacking a home in either branch of government.[13] Historically, the result was that vice presidents were excluded not only from executive branch activities[14] but also from a meaningful legislative role, as Senate norms emerged to minimize the presiding officer's discretion in controlling business and debate. Even the vice president's power to cast tie-breaking votes has declined. John Adams cast twenty-nine tie-breakers and John C. Calhoun twenty-eight, but recent vice presidents have been less fortunate: Johnson cast none, Agnew two, Mondale one, and Bush five. Vice presidents have "dwelt in a constitutional limbo somewhere between the legislative and executive branches," functioning as a full-time member of neither.[15]

Two constitutional amendments have had a bearing on the vice presidency. The Twenty-fifth Amendment, ratified in 1967, established procedures for dealing with presidential disabilities and for filling vice-presidential vacancies, a timely change that provided guidelines to select Ford and Rockefeller.[16] The Twelfth Amendment (1804) had a more profound effect on the office. It provided for separate Electoral College balloting for president and vice president in order to avoid a repeat of the tie vote between Thomas Jefferson and his party's vice-presidential nominee, Aaron Burr, that occurred in the presidential election of 1800, throwing the election into the House of Representatives. (Under the original Constitution, all electoral votes were cast for president, with the runner-up candidate becoming vice president.) Most academics, however, regard the Twelfth Amendment as having reduced "the Vice-Presidency to an insignificant office sought only by insignificant men," an outcome that was correctly anticipated by some members of Congress at the time of its passage.[17] The revised selection process, together with popularly based political parties, ensured that vice-presidential nominations would be used "to add balance to the ticket, to placate a faction of the party, or to curry a swing state."[18] Vice presidents literally became also-rans, party tag-alongs of mediocre qualifications and accomplishments rather than the presumably second most qualified candidate for president, which seemed to have been the case with Adams and Jefferson, the nation's first two vice presidents. Thus, the vice president's constitutional roles have inhibited rather than encouraged the office's institutional development.

Statutory Roles

Vice presidents, unlike presidents, have not been given numerous responsibilities—or the influence that goes with them—by law. The greatest potential for influence lies in the vice president's statutory membership on the National Security Council (NSC). But even here, the vice president's actual involvement hinges on the president's preferred style of foreign policy making. Although the NSC is available to help presidents coordinate many facets of foreign policy, its use is optional rather than mandatory. John F. Kennedy, for example, created an ad hoc group of advisers to help him resolve the Cuban missile crisis. It included some NSC members but not Vice President Johnson. Nixon sidestepped the NSC altogether (as well as Vice President Agnew) when deciding to invade Cambodia (1970), reestablish ties with mainland China (1972), and sign the SALT I agreement with the Soviet Union (1972). And, although Reagan used the NSC staff to conduct secret negotiations with Iran in 1985-86, he did not work through the full council. Thus, membership in the NSC does not ensure vice-presidential access to decision making.

Practice and Precedent

Practice and precedent have by far been the most important determinants of vice-presidential roles. The development of these roles is a twentieth-century phenomenon. Some roles of the modern president can be traced to precedents established by nineteenth-century and turn-of-the-century predecessors, such as Jefferson's active leadership of Congress, James K. Polk's and Abraham Lincoln's expansion of war and emergency powers, and Theodore Roosevelt's effective use of the press to shape a national agenda. In contrast, early harbingers of vice-presidential power are few and far between, making the office a distinctly recent product.

The inclusion of vice presidents in meetings of the cabinet was not actively considered until the last years of the nineteenth century. Adams was the last vice president to participate in cabinet meetings until Woodrow Wilson asked Vice President Thomas Marshall to preside over these sessions during the president's trip abroad to negotiate a peace treaty at Versailles. Although a few presidents relied on their vice presidents for policy advice (notably Polk, Lincoln, and William McKinley), Jefferson started the tradition of emphasizing the vice president's legislative role, a convenient arrangement since President Adams, a political opponent, excluded him from cabinet meetings anyway. In 1896, Theodore Roosevelt, then a vice-presidential candidate, suggested that vice presidents be given a seat in the cabinet (although as president he never followed the practice himself) and the idea was endorsed by both tickets in the 1920 presidential election. Calvin Coolidge, Harding's vice president, regularly attended cabinet meetings. New practices, however, are often fragile. Charles Dawes, who was elected on the Republican ticket with Coolidge in 1924, announced even before the inauguration that he would not become part of the cabinet because to do so would limit the freedom of future presidents in selecting advisers. After being reinstituted under Herbert C. Hoover, however, the practice of including vice presidents in meetings of the cabinet has been routinely followed.[19]

It is not clear when vice presidents began to serve as representatives of the administration to domestic and foreign audiences. Jefferson set the original pattern when he refused Adams's request to visit France as a diplomatic representative. John Nance Garner, who was Franklin Roosevelt's vice president from 1933 to 1940, was the first to travel abroad in an official capacity, and his successor, Henry Wallace, was dispatched on several wartime missions. Thomas Marshall, a popular speaker during his term in office, was heavily involved in Liberty Loan campaigns during World War I but does not appear to have served as a spokesman for the administration. Alben Barkley, Truman's vice president, is credited with expanding these largely ceremonial activities, which have been regularly performed by more recent occupants of the office.

In addition to ceremonial appearances, today's vice presidents are called upon to carry explicit political messages to Congress and to important interest groups, but the origin of these activities is quite recent. Given the vice president's constitutional duty to preside over the Senate, it is surprising to discover that historically few vice presidents lobbied actively for congressional passage of administration proposals; even more surprisingly, several actively conspired with administration opponents to defeat such proposals.[20] Franklin Roosevelt suggested in 1920, while running as the Democrats' vice-presidential nominee, that liaison with Congress was an area of potentially greater vice-presidential activity.[21] He later used Garner in this way. Garner, a former congressional party leader himself, is credited with devising the system of weekly White House conferences with congressional leaders that have become a mainstay of legislative-executive relations. Garner also functioned as an effective New Deal lobbyist until 1937, when he asserted his independence by opposing Roosevelt's proposal to expand the Supreme Court. His relationship with Roosevelt broke down completely when the president decided to violate the precedent of serving only two terms. Garner's successors have varied widely in their role as congressional lobbyists, but it is instructive to note that of the ten men who have served as vice president since Garner, seven brought congressional experience to the job.

Most of the vice presidency's activities are relatively recent developments that have been firmly translated into public expectations. Today it is practically inconceivable that a vice president would publicly oppose a president's nominee for an appointive post or openly question administration policy, steps that were not uncommon as late as the first third of this century. A critical change in the office occurred in 1940, when Roosevelt became the first presidential candidate to demand the right to select his own running mate. Party bosses, who traditionally controlled nominating conventions, had shown no concern for compatibility between the presidential and vice-presidential nominees in selecting the national ticket. As a consequence, it was the exception rather than the rule to find the members of a victorious ticket serving as a team after their election. Since 1940, however, presidential nominees have gradually won the right to stress compatibility as a criterion for vice-presidential nominations, thereby making it possible for the candidate to select someone who is expected to be an administration "lieutenant."[22] In this way, recent vice presidents are more likely to become trusted advisers although traditional concerns for balancing the ticket may still be weighed more heavily in the nomination process.

An Expanded Political Role

Since World War II, succession crises and presidential electoral politics have thrust the vice presidency more frequently into the national spotlight. These events account for the office's new-found political prominence.

Between 1945 and 1976, the presidency was occupied nearly half the time by three men who originally were chosen to serve as vice president. Death, assassination, and resignation played havoc with the customary obscurity of the vice presidency. Roosevelt and Kennedy died in office, and their successors, Truman and Johnson, achieved reelection to full terms of their own. Nixon's resignation from the presidency led to Ford's brief tenure. The frailty of presidents was further underscored by the medical problems of Presidents Eisenhower, Johnson, and Reagan. In addition unsuccessful assassination attempts were made upon Truman, Ford, and Reagan. In the postwar era, only Mondale, Carter's vice president, did not enter national consciousness because of concern about the president's health.

During the same period, vice presidents have become more prominent figures in presidential elections. Partly because of the recent spate of unexpected transfers of power, the vice presidency has emerged as an important springboard to a party's presidential nomination. Winning the presidency, however, has not proved as easy. Not since Martin Van Buren has an incumbent vice president been elected president, but the job has become an important source of candidates. Among recent vice presidents, Nixon, Humphrey, and Mondale have received their party's presidential nomination and Bush, from the start, was regarded as a strong contender to follow suit. Of the eight men who won the Democratic presidential nomination between 1948 and 1984, half had once served as vice president, as had two of the six Republican nominees. Vice-presidential candidates are also receiving more attention during the general election campaign. Repeating the precedent set in 1976, a televised vice-presidential debate was held in 1984.

Bush as Vice President

Seldom has the vice president's heir designate role been so prominent as during the Reagan era. The oldest person ever to be sworn in as president, Reagan is also the oldest ever to serve in that office. Blessed with robust health, the president survived an assassination attempt and a major operation for colon cancer. Confusion about succession and disability surfaced at the time of John Hinckley's attempt on Reagan's life in March 1981. Secretary of State Alexander Haig issued a statement from the White House implying that he stood behind the vice president in the line of succession; at the George Washington University Hospital, Reagan's White House aides hastily convened in a supply closet to discuss how they would deal with the Twenty-fifth Amendment's provisions for presidential disability.[23] Four years later, when Reagan was put under general anesthesia during his cancer operation, Bush became the first vice president since the amendment was ratified to assume the duties of acting president.

Bush's term as vice president, however, has consisted of far more than a few dramatic moments. From the outset, Bush sought to emulate practices that Mondale had found helpful in making himself a vital part of the Carter administration. Like his predecessor, Bush actively sought and received a White House office and a regular slot on the president's weekly schedule (lunch on Thursdays). Again adopting Mondale's strategy, Bush sought a generalist assignment rather than having his time and energy absorbed in dealing with smaller, more specific responsibilities.[24]

Bush carefully cultivated a style that reflected the inherent limits of the vice presidency. As he told one interviewer, "It just doesn't work if you try to grab a lot of turf and do a lot of things." In other words, Bush was "Keeping His Profile Low So He Can Keep His Influence High," as the title of a *National Journal* article put it.[25] In essence, Bush pursued the sort of self-effacing strategy vice presidents must master if they are to gain admission to an administration's inner councils. Avoiding trouble, maintaining absolute loyalty, and doing the dirty work are essential parts of the script. One must also be highly conscious of appearances. Thus, when he returned to Washington after Reagan had been wounded, Bush directed his helicopter not to land on the White House lawn, the usual site of the president's arrivals and departures. Instead, he landed elsewhere and traveled to the White House by motorcade, thereby avoiding any appearance of usurping presidential prerogatives.

In many respects, Bush had a more difficult time becoming a trusted adviser than did Carter's vice president. Unlike Mondale, Bush was the president's prime opponent for the party's 1980 nomination, a competition that was bound to have produced a certain amount of ill-will, especially from Bush's description of Reagan's tax and spending proposals as "voodoo economics." Bush's support within the Republican party came from its minority eastern and moderate wing; Mondale, in contrast, was far more firmly planted in the Democratic mainstream than Carter. Carter's and Reagan's markedly different styles of managing the White House also may have made life tougher for Bush. By most accounts, Carter was personally engaged in White House details and delegated few matters to others. Reagan's much vaunted chairman of the board style rested on substantial delegations to a small group of senior aides—the first-term troika of James A. Baker III (a Bush ally), Edwin Meese, and Michael K. Deaver (later joined by William Clark). Donald Regan, Baker's replacement as chief of staff, felt it less desirable and necessary to share power within the White House after Reagan's first-term advisers left the administration or moved to other jobs. In all, Bush faced more obstacles than Mondale in establishing a role in administration decision making.

Bush did share several advantages with Mondale. In sharp contrast to the outsider presidents they served, both Mondale and Bush were experienced Washington insiders. Mondale's ties to Congress and Democratic interest groups provided the basis for his critical role in legislative agenda setting, while Bush's foreign policy expertise ultimately proved his greatest resource for wielding influence. Both also benefited from cooperative staffwork. Bush's 1980 campaign manager, Baker, served as Reagan's first-term chief of staff; in 1985, Craig Fuller, a former aide to the president, became Bush's chief of staff. Mondale's staff, which like Bush's worked closely with its presidential counterpart during the election campaign, was even more thoroughly integrated into the Carter White House.

Bush's Influence

Bush gradually assumed a prominent role in the first Reagan administration because of his willingness to perform the kinds of thankless tasks traditionally relegated to vice presidents and his acknowledged expertise in foreign policy, an area of weakness and disorder during much of Reagan's presidency.

Chairing task forces, attending state funerals, giving commencement addresses, receiving visitors, raising campaign funds, and lobbying Congress are duties that all vice presidents can expect to be asked to perform. Bush seems to have done so with greater enthusiasm than most. During his first nine months in office he chaired task forces to reduce federal regulations and to coordinate federal assistance to Atlanta in its effort to solve a series of apparently race related murders. (Two more task force chairships were added later.) He attended two funerals, one inauguration, and one Independence Day ceremony and delivered five commencement addresses. Bush met with 122 foreign leaders, delivered several speeches in support of the administration's economic program, and did some lobbying to win Senate support for the sale of the AWACS to Saudi Arabia. He became an important administration liaison to labor, black, and Hispanic leaders, a difficult job in view of the administration's sometimes rocky relations with these groups. He campaigned with 129 Republican candidates and helped raise more than $20 million during the 1982 midterm elections; he tried to exceed those figures in 1986.[26]

Bush's mark in the Reagan administration, however, was made through his foreign policy assignments. As a former ambassador to the United Nations, chief of the American liaison office in Peking, and director of the Central Intelligence Agency, Bush's foreign policy experience was conspicuous in the White House. Richard Allen, the only other White House figure with a claim to international expertise, was hampered by an explicit decision to deemphasize his role as the president's national security adviser in order to avoid the kinds of clashes with the Department of State that had typified earlier administrations. Despite these precautions, however, Bush became a center of controversy early in 1981 when Haig proposed a blueprint for managing crises that placed himself, as secretary of state, in control. Reagan's staff opposed this arrangement and proposed instead to give Bush ongoing responsibility to head the Special Situation Group (SSG) for handling international crises. Haig voiced his displeasure at this decison during a House subcommittee hearing, which drew public attention to the issue. Despite the conflict and its apparent significance, Bush's assignment did not prove to be an important one in the administration's foreign policy apparatus. The SSG did not meet during the first nine months, and no organizational machinery was established for an even longer time.

Bush as Public Relations Diplomat

Bush's influence grew out of his world travels and his role as a personal adviser to the president. As shown in Table 20-1, during his first four years in office Bush traveled abroad more extensively than any of his predecessors. Many of these trips involved relatively

Table 20-1   Foreign Trips by Recent Vice Presidents

Vice President	*Number of foreign trips*
Richard M. Nixon	7
Lyndon B. Johnson	10
Hubert H. Humphrey	12
Spiro Agnew	7
Gerald R. Ford	1
Nelson Rockefeller	6
Walter Mondale	14
George Bush (first term)	20

SOURCES: Nixon through Mondale: Joel K. Goldstein, *The Modern American Vice Presidency,* 159. Bush data compiled from indexes of the *New York Times* and *Washington Post.*

unimportant ceremonial duties—traditional goodwill missions, funeral delegations, and the like. But several trips may have been considerably more important, and, collectively, they constitute a potentially significant role.

Five trips by Bush seem to have had more than ordinary significance: mainland China and the Soviet Union in 1982, Western Europe in 1983, and the Soviet Union again in 1984 and 1985. China was added to the vice president's Asia-Pacific itinerary in spring 1982. The administration's plans to sell arms to Taiwan had resulted in steadily deteriorating relations with the mainland government. After talking with the deputy prime minister and foreign minister of China, Bush reportedly returned to Washington with ideas for the president on how to resolve the diplomatic wrangle. As head of the American delegations to the funerals of three Soviet leaders—Leonid Brezhnev, Yuri Andropov, and Constantin Chernenko—Bush became one of the first American officials to hold serious discussions with their successors. Andropov was especially a mystery to the West, despite his having been part of the Kremlin leadership for fifteen years. Bush later joked that they had talked "spook to spook"; Andropov had served as head of the KGB, Soviet counterpart to the director of the CIA. Thus, Bush drew upon his experience in China and his opportunity to speak with the new Soviet leaders to carve out a special administration role.

By far the most sustained foreign policy role that Bush has played flowed from his visits to West European capitals in 1983 to engage in what Hedrick Smith of the *New York Times* termed "public relations diplomacy." Appealing to West European public opinion, U.S. and Soviet leaders had jousted for some time through a round of press releases and announced initiatives on the Geneva arms talks. One issue was whether NATO would continue to deploy intermediate range missiles in Europe; another was what type of strategy the United States should adopt in its ongoing disarmament talks with the Soviets. Bush served as both public and private point man in the administration offensive. In West Germany, Bush publicly read Reagan's invitation to Andropov to discuss a ban on all intermediate range missiles in Europe, the "zero option." His visits drummed up publicity to blunt the Soviets' public relations efforts and the nascent European nuclear freeze movement; he also was able to deliver the president's message privately to European leaders and convey their responses to Washington.[27] West Germany, the Netherlands, Belgium, Italy, France, Britain, and the Scandinavian nations were stops on Bush's two trips.

Equally important to the administration, of course, was the growing significance of the arms control issue in domestic politics. Around the time of Bush's first trip, Democrats Alan Cranston and

Walter Mondale declared their presidential candidacies, stressing the issues of arms control strategies and the freeze. Thus, Bush's European trips were undertaken with an eye to domestic politics as well as foreign policy. A similar tour of the Western allied nations to discuss the American positions on the Strategic Defense Initiative ("Star Wars") and SALT II was undertaken during the summer of 1985.

It is difficult to estimate the importance of Bush's private advice to the president on foreign policy. In this respect, Richard Viguerie, a conservative Republican critic of Bush, has suggested that the vice president is "the dog that doesn't bark," a reference to one of the more famous Sherlock Holmes stories.[28] Bush has been credited with strongly advocating the AWACS sale in 1981, cautioning the president on the implications of selling weapons to Taiwan, and urging a Middle East peace initiative. He headed an SSG evaluation of U.S. policy toward Lebanon in August 1983 after American casualties were sustained, and he was dispatched to visit U.S. forces after the Marine barracks were bombed in October. In December 1983, he hand delivered a letter from Reagan to the president of El Salvador, warning of policy consequences unless death squads were halted. Yet, Bush's effectiveness has relied on his keeping his advice to the president in total confidence. He attends the president's national security briefing each morning, but the extent to which he speaks as well as listens is not known.

Bush and the New Vice Presidency

Has the Bush experience, taken as a whole, continued the development of a new vice presidency? The short answer is that any evaluation based purely on the public record is premature. The same can be said of the Rockefeller and Mondale vice presidencies, which so far have been assessed largely on the basis of observers' and co-workers' estimates rather than a thorough evaluation of the documentary record. Nonetheless, a limited analysis can be made.

We can be fairly certain of a few things. Unlike his immediate predecessors, Bush has not been deeply involved in routine White House policy making; he has not overseen an important staff unit like Rockefeller or coordinated a vital stage of the policy process like Mondale. For a time, crisis management promised to provide Bush with this kind of institutional prominence, but that never fully materialized. Instead, Bush has fashioned what appears from the outside to be an important policy role based on extensive foreign travels and access to the president. Perhaps it is only fitting that a White House known for its capacity to project favorable images of the president would spawn a vice president skilled in public relations diplomacy. His effectiveness in performing this role no doubt boosted his importance within the Reagan White House even more than it would have in other recent administrations.

Bush's experience also illustrates how the performance of what many have regarded as mundane ceremonial duties can have policy significance. Many of his tasks, of course, clearly were not important. For example, on his trip to attend the inauguration of a new Honduran president in early 1985, Bush was accompanied by baseball stars Gary Carter of the New York Mets and Nolan Ryan of the Houston Astros. Their visit, including a meeting with the president of El Salvador and other foreign leaders, was reported in the sports section of the *New York Times*.[29] Nonetheless, Bush seems to have benefited from his ceremonial assignments. When visiting foreign nations and meeting dignitaries, vice presidents share in the performance of a president's unifying role as chief of state. More concretely, such travels build a valuable network of contacts that form the basis for offering advice to the president. Firsthand knowledge of problems and personalities can enhance the vice president's role as adviser. A proper evaluation of Bush's contributions in this area is especially dependent on future documentary research and on Reagan's memoirs.

Bush's Oil Blooper

In view of Bush's experience in foreign policy and his careful cultivation of the loyalist style, it is ironic that one of his major missteps involved an apparent departure from administration policy on oil prices and relations with OPEC. The incident illustrates certain enduring weaknesses of the vice presidency.

On March 31, 1986, the eve of his departure for an eight-day tour of the Middle East to discuss regional security issues, Bush held a news conference in which he noted the importance of stabilizing oil prices, which just the day before had reached their lowest level in eight years. Bush said that although the major purpose of his trip to Saudi Arabia was not to set oil prices, "I think it is essential that we talk about stability and that we not just have a continued free fall, like a parachutist jumping out without a parachute." The three-month decline in oil prices, from twenty-seven dollars a barrel to less than ten dollars, had occurred largely because the Saudis had more than doubled their daily oil production in an effort to force other oil producers to accept production quotas. One result had been rising unemployment and bank and business failures in Texas, Louisiana, Oklahoma, and Alaska; on the other hand, American consumers and the economy as a whole were benfitting from the price decline.[30]

Bush's comments attracted unusual attention, in part because they echoed views that Energy Secretary John S. Herrington had voiced the day before. Many observers viewed the two statements as signaling a change in administration policy, which had been resolutely committed to the market as a means to set prices and opposed to a possible oil import tax. Such speculation was front-page news; it triggered repercussions in the stock and bond markets and temporarily halted the slide in oil prices. King Fahd of Saudi Arabia called in the American ambassador to ask for an explanation of administration policy. The next day, the White House was forced to deny publicly that administration policy was changing.

Bush and his staff issued a number of clarifications to minimize his apparent differences with official policy and to limit the political damage. The president, who reportedly felt that Bush's comments had been " 'misinterpreted' by the news media," ultimately denied a reporter's suggestion during a nationally televised news conference that Bush had "gone off the reservation," straying from administration policy.[31] The political fallout, however, was less readily contained as Bush's opponents for the 1988 Republican presidential nomination, the press, and a number of Democrats speculated about the motives behind the vice president's statement and its probable effect on his campaign. Critics stressed Bush's background in the oil industry, his two terms in the House of Representatives as a member of the Texas delegation, and his need for oil-state support in the presidential election. Everyone was quick to note that his statement would hardly prove popular in New Hampshire, Iowa, and Michigan, three oil-consuming states that were likely to play an important role in the 1988 delegate selection process.[32] Some observers speculated that this was the "real" George Bush in action ("It was as if his whole resumé was talking");[33] others suspected it was Bush's first effort to put some distance between himself and the administration on a sensitive issue; and still others attributed it largely to poor communications between the presidential and vice-presidential staffs.[34]

Out of the Loop and Above the Fray

Beyond the immediate reaction, the oil blooper illustrates the conflicting pressures and delicate balance of forces that surround modern vice presidents. As junior members of the successful election tickets, vice presidents are automatically regarded as major contenders for their party's presidential nomination. The electoral implications of all their activities receive careful scrutiny, especially if, like Bush, they are serving with a lame duck president. Yet for as long as they remain in office, vice presidents must resist the urge to strike an independent pose because their effectiveness and influence within the administration hinge heavily on their being viewed as a team player by the president's aides. Open conflict with administration policy or even advocacy of new policy can result in the vice president's exclusion from White House decision making.

The tensions inherent in the vice presidency are obvious. For the sake of his political future, the vice president must at some point become more assertive, project a distinctive image, and establish an identity that will carry him through the campaign. Early in 1986, Bush was confronted with increased demands to present his own message. He hesitated for fear of upstaging President Reagan. As Craig Fuller, Bush's chief of staff explained it:

> I don't think that he is unwilling to let people know where he stands. But he doesn't want to do it in a way that will ever cause the President to question their relationship. He is very comfortable with an operating style that maximizes his effectiveness as a Vice President, even if, at times, it might not work to his long-term political advantage.[35]

It is precisely the tendency toward servility and self-effacement that could be the bane of the vice presidency. If these traits become deeply ingrained in the office's incumbents during their service, they may spend four or eight years just a heartbeat away from the presidency and actually emerge "less qualified for the presidency than before becoming vice-president." [36] Writing on the eve of the Rockefeller and Mondale era, Allan P. Sindler and Arthur M. Schlesinger, Jr., expressed the fear that this had become the fate of modern vice presidents. In the desire to be accepted in their administrations, vice presidents endorse policies with which they disagree and perform tasks that many regard as demeaning. Over time, a succession of vice presidents has exchanged the office's independent status for a taste of power; the price has been a subordinate role.

Such a portrait can be overdrawn. The working relationship that is developed by any executive pair may well overcome such pressures; vice presidents may be totally confident of their position within the president's circle of advisers and feel no pressure to comply supinely with any and all presidential demands. To say this of course, is to introduce a challenging counterweight to the thesis of a new vice presidency. It emphasizes an inescapable feature of the office: a vice president's role within the administration depends on what the president wishes. And the price of inclusion may be inordinately high. In an ironic twist, the Rockefeller and Mondale experiences, if they become the yardstick against which future vice presidents will be evaluated, may increase the pressure on vice presidents to sacrifice their independence or be regarded as failures.

Thus, the new vice presidency, if it exists, may be a mixed blessing for the political system. Improved access to the president does ensure greater vice-presidential exposure to the sorts of problems a successor would confront in the event of the president's death or disability; it may thereby help avoid a recurrence of the Truman syndrome. But the rules of access remain unchanged: vice presidents become an integral part of the modern presidency at presidential sufferance. Thus, they are subject to the whims of individual presidents as well as the jealousies of the court politics that encircle the chief executive. It remains an open question whether the public would be better served if vice presidents were less influential and, therefore, less constrained—out of the loop and above the fray.

Notes

1. Joel K. Goldstein, *The Modern American Vice Presidency: The Transformation of a Political Institution* (Princeton: Princeton University Press, 1982), draws a distinction between *institutional* and *political* duties performed by vice presidents (134-135). Paul Light, *Vice-Presidential Power: Advice and Influence in the White House* (Baltimore: Johns Hopkins University Press, 1984), divides the job into ceremonial, political, and policy activities (28ff). For other general discussions of the vice presidency, see Thomas Cronin, "Rethinking the Vice-Presidency," in *Rethinking the Presidency*, ed. Thomas E. Cronin (Boston: Little, Brown, 1982) for a twelve-part job description (326-327); and Michael Turner, *The Vice President as Policy Maker: Rockefeller in the Ford White House* (Westport, Conn.: Greenwood, 1982).
2. Turner, *Vice-President as Policy Maker,* 85 and 210/*n.* 91.
3. Light, *Vice-Presidential Power,* 1-2.
4. Ibid., 265.
5. Letter, Rockefeller to Mondale, December 10, 1976, Cannon Papers, Box 22, "Transition—Rockefeller (4)," Gerald R. Ford Library, Ann Arbor, Mich.
6. Mondale rejected both Rockefeller's practice and Humphrey's advice by stoutly avoiding line assignments.
7. Light, *Vice-Presidential Power,* 248-249.
8. Humphrey had good cause to alert Ford to the tentative nature of authority delegated by the president. As he wrote to Ford, "The President can give you assignments and trust you with authority—grant you some power as he sees fit. Likewise he can remove the authority and power at his will. I used to call this Humphrey's law—'He who giveth can taketh away and often does.'" Letter, Humphrey to Ford, October 30, 1973, Ford Vice-Presidential Papers, Box 242, Ford Library.
9. Memorandum, John Marsh to President, December 20, 1974, Marsh Files, Box 87, "President 12/74-2/75," Ford Library.
10. For a discussion and critique of this approach, see David L. Paletz, "Perspectives on the Presidency," in *The Institutionalized Presidency,* ed. Norman Thomas and Hans Baade (Dobbs Ferry, N.Y.: Oceana, 1972).

11. Steven J. Jarding, "Historical Assessments of Succession Presidents," *Extensions* (Fall 1985): 14-15. Jarding found that "succession presidents cannot overcome the martyred image of their predecessors" (15) and that this judgment endures among historians.
12. *New York Times*, July 24, 1985; August 16, 1985; and September 26, 1985.
13. The term is used by John D. Feerick, *From Falling Hands: The Story of Presidential Succession* (New York: Fordham University Press, 1965), ix; and by Cronin, "Rethinking the Vice-Presidency," 329.
14. Lyndon B. Johnson was the first vice president to have an office in the presidential compound, in this case in the Old Executive Office Building. With the provision of additional office space in the West Wing, Vice Presidents Mondale and Bush actually enjoyed three prestigious office locations since they also retained quarters in the Capitol.
15. Donald Young, *American Roulette: The History and Dilemma of the Vice Presidency* (New York: Viking, 1979), 3-4.
16. The Twenty-fifth Amendment provides that the vice president shall serve as acting president when a presidential disability is declared either by the president or the vice president and a majority of the cabinet. It also provides that a vacancy in the vice presidency can be filled by presidential appointment, with the consent of both houses of Congress.
17. Quote from Young, *American Roulette*, 21. Congressional reaction is reported by Feerick, *From Falling Hands*, 73-74.
18. Goldstein, *Modern Vice Presidency*, 48. See also Danny M. Adkison, "The Electoral Significance of the Vice Presidency," *Presidential Studies Quarterly* 12 (Summer 1982): 330-336.
19. Young, *American Roulette*, 123, 156-157.
20. This was especially true of vice presidents Burr, Calhoun, and Fairbanks.
21. The suggestion appeared in an article published in the *Saturday Evening Post* during October 1920; see the discussion in Feerick, *From Falling Hands*, 182.
22. Vice-presidential nominees were selected by the conventions of both parties in 1948 and by the Democrats in 1952 and 1956.
23. Laurence I. Barrett, *Gambling with History: Reagan in the White House* (New York: Penguin, 1984), 114-115; and *New York Times*, June 12, 1983.
24. *New York Times*, January 21, 1981.
25. Quote from *New York Times*, October 28, 1981. Title from article written by Dick Kirschten, *National Journal*, June 20, 1981, 1096.
26. *New York Times*, October 28, 1981; January 30, 1983; *New York Times Magazine*, February 23, 1986.
27. *New York Times*, February 25, 1983.
28. Ibid., June 23, 1983.
29. Ibid., February 5, 1986.
30. *Washington Post*, April 1 and 2, 1986; see also *Wall Street Journal*, April 3, 1986, for a discussion of the financial and diplomatic implications of the statement.
31. *Washington Post*, April 9, 1986.
32. *New York Times*, April 9, 1986; *Washington Post*, April 9, 1986.
33. *Washington Post*, April 9, 1986.
34. On these interpretations, see the following: *New York Times*, April 5 and 6, 1986; April 9, 1986; *Washington Post*, April 9, 1986; and the column of Evans and Novak, *Washington Post*, April 9, 1986.
35. *New York Times Magazine*, February 23, 1986.
36. Allan P. Sindler, *Unchosen Presidents: The Vice President and Other Frustrations*

of Presidential Succession (Berkeley: University of California Press, 1976), 36. See also Arthur M. Schlesinger, Jr., "On the Presidential Succession," *Political Science Quarterly* 89 (Fall 1974): 475-505.

CONTRIBUTORS

John H. Aldrich teaches political science at Duke University. He is the author of *Before the Convention* (1980); coauthor of *Change and Continuity in the 1980 Elections* (1982) and *Change and Continuity in the 1984 Elections* (1987), among other books; and coeditor of the *American Journal of Political Science*. His current projects focus on political parties and on public opinion and electoral behavior.

John P. Burke teaches political science at the University of Vermont. He is the author of *Bureaucratic Responsibility* (1986). He is currently writing a book on the institutional presidency and is coauthor of a forthcoming study of presidential decision making concerning America's involvement in Vietnam.

George C. Edwards III is visiting professor of social sciences at the U.S. Military Academy and professor of political science at Texas A & M University. He is the author of *At the Margins* (1988), *The Public Presidency* (1983), *Presidential Influence in Congress* (1980), and *Implementing Public Policy* (1980); coauthor of *Presidential Leadership* (1985) and *The Policy Predicament* (1978); editor of *Public Policy Implementation* (1984); and coeditor of *National Security and the U.S. Constitution* (1988), *The Presidency and Public Policy Making* (1985), *Studying the Presidency* (1983), and *Public Policy-Making* (1976). His forthcoming book is on presidential public approval.

James Fallows, the former chief speech writer for President Jimmy Carter, is Washington editor of *The Atlantic*. He is coauthor of *Who Runs Congress?* (1972), *The System* (1976), and *Inside the System* (1976); and author of *The Water Lords* (1971) and *National Defense* (1981), winner of the American Book Award. He has written extensively for magazines and is the former editor of *The Washington Monthly*.

Morris P. Fiorina is a professor of government at Harvard University. He is the author of *Representatives, Roll Calls, and Constituencies*

(1974), *Congress: Keystone of the Washington Establishment* (1977), *Retrospective Voting in American National Elections* (1981); and coauthor of *The Personal Vote: Constituency Service and Electoral Independence* (1987). His current research focuses on the relationships between electoral and legislative politics.

Benjamin Ginsberg teaches government at Cornell University. He is the author of *The Consequences of Consent* (1982) and *The Captive Public* (1986), coauthor of *Poliscide* (1976), and coeditor of *Do Elections Matter?* (1986). He has written many articles for the *American Political Science Review,* the *Political Science Quarterly,* and the *Washington Post,* among others. He is currently writing a book on the politics and policies of the Reagan administration.

Michael B. Grossman teaches political science at Towson State University. He is the author of *The City and the Council: Views from the Inside and the Outside* (1974) and of articles in the *Political Science Quarterly* and the *Washington Journalism Review,* among others. He is coauthor with Martha Kumar of *Portraying the President: The White House and the News Media* (1981) and of the forthcoming *The Pessimist and the Persuader: Carter, Reagan, and the Media.*

Martha Joynt Kumar teaches political science at Towson State University and is an associate editor of *Presidential Studies Quarterly.* She is a contributor to *The Judiciary Committees* (1975) and to *Studying the Presidency* (1983). She is coauthor with Michael Grossman of *Portraying the President: The White House and the News Media* (1981) and of the forthcoming *The Pessimist and the Persuader: Carter, Reagan, and the Media.*

Sidney M. Milkis teaches politics and is a research associate with the Gordon Public Policy Center at Brandeis University. His articles on the presidency and political parties have appeared in the *Political Science Quarterly* and *Administration and Society,* as well as several edited volumes. He is coauthor with Richard A. Harris of two forthcoming works, *Deregulating the Public Lobby Regime: A Tale of Two Agencies* and *Remaking American Politics.* He is completing a book on the modern presidency and the American party system.

Bruce Miroff teaches political science at the State University of New York at Albany. He is the author of *Pragmatic Illusions: The Presidential Politics of John F. Kennedy* (1975) and of numerous articles on the presidency and political leadership. He is currently working on a new book, *The Tribe of the Eagle: American Images of Political Leadership.*

Michael Nelson is associate professor of political science at Vanderbilt University. A former editor of *The Washington Monthly,* his articles have appeared in the *Journal of Politics,* the *Political Science Quarterly, The Public Interest, Saturday Review, The Virginia Quarterly Review, Harvard Business Review, Newsweek, Presidential Studies Quarterly,* and *Congress and the Presidency,* among others. He has won writing awards for his articles on classical music and baseball, including the ASCAP-Deems Taylor Award. He is coauthor of *Presidents, Politics, and Policy* (1984), coeditor of *The Culture of Bureaucracy* (1979) and *Presidential Selection* (1987), and editor of *The Elections of 1984* (1985). He edits the series "Interpreting American Politics" for Johns Hopkins University Press and is compiling *Guide to the Presidency* for Congressional Quarterly.

Mark A. Peterson teaches government at Harvard University. He is the author or coauthor of several articles and papers on the presidency and Congress, and on the interest group system. He is currently preparing a book on domestic policy making by the president and Congress, and initiating a project on the origins of American health care policy.

Joseph Pika teaches political science at the University of Delaware. His articles on presidential relations with Congress and interest groups have appeared in the *Political Science Quarterly, Presidential Studies Quarterly,* and *Administration and Society.* His current research traces presidential relations with interest groups from Roosevelt through Reagan.

Paul J. Quirk teaches at the University of Illinois at Chicago and has a research appointment in the Institute of Government and Public Affairs, University of Illinois. He is the author of *Industry Influence in Federal Regulatory Agencies* (1981) and coauthor of *The Politics of Deregulation* (1985), winner of the Louis Brownlow Book Award of the National Academy of Public Administration. He has written articles and essays on agenda-setting, prescription-drug regulations, and presidential leadership. His current projects include research on cooperation in public policy making and a book on policy formation.

Bert A. Rockman teaches political science at the University of Pittsburgh where he is research professor in the University Center for International Studies. He is the author of *The Leadership Question: The Presidency and the American System* (1984), coauthor of *Bureaucrats and Politicians in Western Democracies* (1981), and coeditor of

Elite Studies and Communist Politics (1985). He is the author or coauthor of articles in the *American Political Science Review,* the *British Journal of Political Science,* and the *American Journal of Political Science,* among others. His present research is focused on executive and political change in Washington.

Francis E. Rourke teaches political science at Johns Hopkins University. He is the author of several books about executive branch politics, including *Secrecy and Publicity: Dilemmas of Democracy* (1961), *Bureaucracy and Foreign Policy* (1972), and *Bureaucracy, Politics, and Public Policy* (1978). He is currently engaged in a study supported by the Russell Sage Foundation on the presidency and the bureaucracy.

Elizabeth Sanders teaches political science at the Graduate Faculty of the New School for Social Research. She is the author of *The Regulation of Natural Gas* (1981) and articles on the New Deal, regulation and welfare policies, and voting behavior. She is currently writing a book on the rise of the interventionist state from 1880 to 1980.

Robert Scigliano teaches political science at Boston College. He is the author of *South Vietnam: Nation Under Stress* (1963) and *The Supreme Court and the Presidency* (1971), and coauthor of a monograph, *Representation* (1978). He is currently engaged in a study of warmaking and foreign relations under the Constitution.

Martin Shefter teaches political science at Cornell University. He is the author of *Political Crisis/Fiscal Crisis* (1985) and of numerous articles on American political development and urban politics. He is currently writing a book with Benjamin Ginsberg on cleavages and coalitions in contemporary American politics.

Stephen Skowronek is professor of political science at Yale University. He is the author of *Building a New American State: The Expansion of National Administrative Capacities, 1877-1920* (1982) and managing editor of *Studies in American Political Development.* He is currently writing a book on the politics of presidential leadership.

Jeffrey K. Tulis teaches political science at Princeton University. He is the author of *The Rhetorical Presidency* (1987), coauthor of *The Presidency in the Constitutional Order* (1981), and coeditor of a new book series on constitutional theory. He is currently writing a book on institutional deference.

Jack L. Walker is chairman of the Department of Political Science at the University of Michigan and is the former director of its Institute for Public Policy Studies. He is the author of *Race and the City* (1973) and of numerous articles in the *American Political Science Review*. He is coauthor of *Dynamics of the American Presidency* (1964). He is currently working on a study of the origins and maintenance of interest groups in America.

Thomas Weko is a Ph.D. candidate in political science at the University of Minnesota. He is currently a research fellow at the Brookings Institution, where he is completing a study on presidential management of the federal bureaucracy.

INDEX